ADO.NET Cookbook

Bill Hamilton

Beijing · Cambridge · Farnham · Köln · Paris · Sebastopol · Taipei · Tokyo

ADO.NET Cookbook
by Bill Hamilton

Copyright © 2003 O'Reilly Media, Inc. All rights reserved.
Printed in the United States of America.

Published by O'Reilly Media, Inc., 1005 Gravenstein Highway North, Sebastopol, CA 95472.

O'Reilly Media, Inc. books may be purchased for educational, business, or sales promotional use. Online editions are also available for most titles (*safari.oreilly.com*). For more information, contact our corporate/institutional sales department: (800) 998-9938 or *corporate@oreilly.com*.

Editor:	Brian Jepson
Production Editor:	Matt Hutchinson
Production Services:	Argosy Publishing, Inc.
Cover Designer:	Emma Colby
Interior Designer:	David Futato

Printing History:

September 2003:   First Edition.

 This book uses RepKover™, a durable and flexible lay-flat binding.

ISBN: 0-596-00439-7
[C]

Table of Contents

Preface

Microsoft ADO.NET is the latest data access technology from Microsoft. ADO.NET is a collection of classes that are part of the .NET Framework, and is designed to provide consistent access to data in loosely coupled n-tier application architectures such as web services. ADO.NET can be used to access a variety of data sources including databases such as Microsoft SQL Server, Oracle, and Microsoft Access, as well as XML, OLE DB, and ODBC data sources.

ADO.NET separates data access from manipulation. Connected classes available in .NET data providers connect to a data source, execute commands, and retrieve results. Disconnected classes let you access and manipulate data offline and later synchronize changes with the underlying data source. XML support is tightly integrated with ADO.NET, allowing you to load, access, and manipulate data using XML as well as the disconnected classes simultaneously.

ADO.NET is very different from its predecessor ADO. With the increasing popularity of .NET and ADO.NET, there are many questions from developers about how to solve specific problems and how to implement solutions most efficiently. This book is a reference containing solutions and techniques that make using ADO.NET easier and more productive. You may have already encountered some of these problems; others you may never see. Some of the solutions are responses to problems that have been posted in various discussion groups, while others are real problems encountered while building applications.

This book is organized into chapters, with each chapter containing solutions (stated as recipes) to a specific problem category. Each recipe consists of a single question and its solution followed by a discussion. The question-answer format provides complete solutions to problems, making it easy to read and use. Nearly every recipe contains a complete, documented code sample showing you how to solve the specific problem, as well as a discussion of how the underlying technology works and a discussion of alternatives, limitations, and other considerations when appropriate. All of the code—both C# and VB.NET—is available from the web site (*http://www.oreilly.com/catalog/adonetckbk*).

Who This Book Is For

You don't have to be an experienced .NET developer to use this book; it is designed for users of all levels. This book provides solutions to problems that developers face every day. Reference or tutorial books can teach general concepts but do not usually provide help solving real-world problems. This book teaches by example; the natural way for most people to learn.

While some of the samples in this book use advanced techniques, these problems are frequently faced by developers with all levels of experience. The code samples are all complete, well commented, and thoroughly explained to help you apply them and solve your own problems quickly, easily, and efficiently. At the same time, you will understand exactly how and why the solution works, the requirements, trade-offs, and drawbacks. This book is designed to move you up the learning curve quickly. The solutions show good programming discipline and techniques to further help less experienced developers.

You don't need to retype the code in this book since it is available on the O'Reilly web site (*http://www.oreilly.com/catalog/adonetckbk*). Only code important to the solution is listed in this book. Enough code is presented so that the book can be used without loading the actual code. The book does not list user interface code, its background code, or code generated automatically by Visual Studio .NET.

What You Need to Use This Book

To run the samples in this book, you will need a computer running Windows 2000 or later. The Web Forms solutions require Microsoft Internet Information Server (IIS) Version 5 or later.

To open and compile the samples in this book, you will need Visual Studio .NET 2003. Most of the samples require Microsoft SQL Server 2000. Oracle solutions require Oracle 8*i* Version 3 (release 8.1.7) or later.

Some of the solutions require classes that are not installed with either Visual Studio .NET or SQL Server. These classes are mentioned in the solutions and in the installation notes bundled with the example code.

How This Book Is Organized

This book is organized into 10 chapters, each of which focus on a particular topic in creating ADO.NET solutions. Each recipe consists of a specific problem, stated as a question, followed by a solution and discussion. To give you an overview of this book's contents, the following paragraphs summarize each chapter:

Chapter 1, *Connecting to Data*

The solutions in this chapter show how to connect to a variety of data sources from ADO.NET. Connecting to data sources involves connections strings, security-related issues including storing connection strings and how to use them, and the different authentication methods available. Solutions show how to set up, monitor, and optimize connection pooling.

Chapter 2, *Retrieving and Managing Data*

The DataSet is a data source-independent, disconnected, in-memory relational database that provides sophisticated navigational capabilities. The solutions in this chapter show how to retrieve data using SQL statements, parameterized SQL statements, stored procedures, and batched queries, into both untyped and strongly typed DataSet objects. Solutions show how to understand the data that is returned. You'll learn how to use messaging and web services to retrieve data.

Chapter 3, *Searching and Analyzing Data*

The solutions in this chapter focus on searching for records in views and tables, calculating values based on values in the same or other tables, and navigating data relations between tables. You'll understand how to use globalization and localization to create applications for multiple cultures. Solutions show alternate techniques to retrieve hierarchical data, including the COMPUTE BY and SHAPE clauses.

Chapter 4, *Adding and Modifying Data*

This chapter focuses on issues related to inserting and updating data, and using web services, remoting, and messaging to update data. You'll learn how to manage auto-increment columns with SQL Server and sequences with Oracle. Solutions show how to change primary keys and how to use GUID primary keys, as well as how to work with master-detail data.

Chapter 5, *Copying and Transferring Data*

This chapter focuses on copying data between ADO.NET classes and between ADO and ADO.NET classes, serializing and deserializing data, merging data, encrypting data, and securing login credentials.

Chapter 6, *Maintaining Database Integrity*

The solutions in this chapter show how to use manual and automatic transactions and DBMS transactions from ADO.NET. You'll learn how to identify and handle concurrency errors, how to set isolation levels, how to simulate pessimistic concurrency, how to use SQL Server pessimistic concurrency with locking hints, and how to update master-detail data without concurrency errors.

Chapter 7, *Binding Data to .NET User Interfaces*

This chapter focuses on binding simple and complex data to Web Forms and Windows Forms. You'll learn how to manage master-detail data in Web Forms, how to update complex data, how to data-bind images, and how to use Crystal

Reports dynamically at runtime. Solutions show how to control user editing of data with data views. For applications without a user interface, you'll learn how to use design-time features in classes without a user interface.

Chapter 8, *Working with XML*

The solutions in this chapter show how to use XML with ADO.NET. You'll learn how to load schema and data from XML into a DataSet, about the DiffGram format and how to use it to determine what changes were made to a DataSet. You'll also learn how to read XML data directly from a SQL Server using FOR XML. Solutions show how to use XPath queries, how to control the format of XML output, and how to use XML template queries to fill a DataSet. Optimizing update performance by batching data updates with OpenXML is shown.

Chapter 9, *Optimizing .NET Data Access*

This chapter shows how to improve application performance and responsiveness with asynchronous processing as well as how to cancel those processes, how to cache data to improve performance while retrieving data, and how to use custom paging to improve performance over automatic paging. Solutions show how to work with BLOB data in SQL Server and Oracle. You'll learn how to optimize loading data into a SQL Server using bulk loading with SQL XML and how to optimize updating data with batch updates by handling DataAdapter events. You'll also learn how to effectively debug stored procedures using Visual Studio .NET.

Chapter 10, *Enumerating and Maintaining Database Objects*

This chapter shows how to get schema information and metadata from databases, manage database objects, and enumerate installed OLE DB providers and ODBC drivers using DDL, SQL-DMO, information schema views, and system stored procedures. You'll learn how to use JRO to manage a Microsoft Access database. A solution shows how to get a query execution plan using the SQL Server SET statement.

In some cases, recipes are related. Where appropriate, recipes reference other solutions.

An Appendix contains a brief tutorial, *Converting from C# to VB Syntax*.

What Was Left Out

This book is not a reference or a primer about ADO.NET. A good primer and reference to ADO.NET is *ADO.NET in a Nutshell* by Bill Hamilton and Matthew Mac-Donald (O'Reilly). The MSDN Library is also invaluable. It is included with Visual Studio .NET and available online at *http://msdn.microsoft.com/library/default.asp*. SQL Server Books Online, installed with Microsoft SQL Server and available in MSDN Library Online, is an excellent reference to SQL Server.

This is not a book about how to use Visual Studio .NET to build, compile, and deploy applications. See *Mastering Visual Studio .NET* by Ian Griffiths, Jon Flanders, and Chris Sells (O'Reilly) for excellent coverage of these topics.

Conventions Used in This Book

This book uses the following typographic conventions:

Constant width

> Used for program listings. Also used within paragraphs to refer to program elements such as namespaces, classes, and method names.

Bold constant width

> Used in program listings, to highlight an important part of the code.

//...

> Ellipses in C# code indicate text that has been omitted for clarity.

<!-- ... -->

> Ellipses in XML schemas and documents indicate text that has been omitted for clarity.

Italic

> Used for URLs, names of directories and files, options, and occasionally for emphasis.

 This icon indicates a tip, suggestion, or general note.

 This icon indicates a warning or caution.

About the Code

Nearly every recipe in this book contains a code sample. The sample is not just a fragment, but rather a complete solution that takes the form of either a Windows Forms or a Web Forms application.

In many cases, the solution code contains additional code that lets you explore alternatives, test performance, and see information that will help you understand key concepts. Multiple solutions are sometimes presented. Where appropriate, one alternative will be recommended; in other cases, alternatives are equivalent and selection should be based on your specific application requirements.

Complete error handling is not included for each solution. Omitting error handling makes the solution easier to understand by focusing on the key concepts.

Error handling that is a key part of the solution is included and explained thoroughly. These principles can also be applied to other solutions in this book.

All of the code examples in the book use C# as a programming language. Listing VB.NET solutions would have made the book less readable, added hundreds of pages to its length, and increased both cover price and weight. VB.NET code for all solutions in addition to C# code is available on the book's web site, *http://www.oreilly.com/catalog/adonetckbk*. There are also release notes explaining installation and configuration.

.NET introduced the C# programming language as well as VB.NET. Both languages compile to the same intermediate language (IL) used by .NET and are more similar than different; differences are mainly syntactic. They can also be mixed within the same solution. Most VB.NET programmers have little trouble converting C# samples. The book *C# and VB.NET Conversion Pocket Reference* by Jose Mojica (O'Reilly) provides a concise (139-page) reference with all the details about converting between C# and VB.NET. The Appendix covers this as well.

The solutions using SQL Server use the Northwind sample database. Some solutions require additional tables and stored procedures; these can be installed using the installation script from the example code from the web site. The Oracle solutions use either the SCOTT sample database installed with Oracle, or, in some cases where SCOTT is inadequate, a version of Northwind that has been ported to Oracle. Instructions for creating this database are also available in the example code.

Some solutions require stored procedures. Most are written for Microsoft SQL Server; however, in some cases Oracle is used because the recipe solves a problem specific to Oracle—identity columns in SQL Server versus sequences in Oracle, for example. SQL Server's T-SQL is somewhat similar to Oracle's PL/SQL; Oracle users, or users familiar with other procedural extensions to SQL, should have little difficulty understanding or adapting these stored procedures. The disconnected parts of the ADO.NET are database independent and are, for the most part, portable without modification regardless of the underlying data source.

Configuration Files

Configuration files are XML-based files that can be used to store application settings so that they can be changed as needed without recompiling the application. The Windows Forms and Web Forms solutions each use a configuration file to store all configuration settings.

The configuration file for all Web Forms solutions contains the following elements.

Web.config

```
<appSettings>
  <add key="DataConnectString"
```

```
                  value="Data Source=(local);user id=sa;password=;Initial Catalog=Northwind;" />
    </appSettings>
```

The configuration file for all Windows Forms solutions follows.

App.config

```
    <?xml version="1.0" encoding="utf-8" ?>
    <configuration>
      <appSettings>
        <add key="Project_Directory" value="c:\\AdoDotNetCookbook\\CS\\" />
        <add key="Temp_Directory" value="c:\\temp\\" />

        <add key="Sql_ConnectString" value=
          "Data Source=(local);user id=sa;password=;Initial Catalog=Northwind;" />
        <add key="Sql_SqlAuth_ConnectString" value=
          "Data Source=(local);Initial Catalog=Northwind;User ID=sa;password=;" />
        <add key="Sql_Master_ConnectString" value=
          "Data Source=(local);Integrated security=SSPI;Initial Catalog=master;" />
        <add key="Sql_Msde_ConnectString" value="Data Source=(local)\vsdotnet;
          Integrated security=SSPI;Initial Catalog=Northwind;" />

        <add key="OleDb_ConnectString" value="Provider=SQLOLEDB;
          Data Source=(local);Integrated Security=SSPI;Initial Catalog=Northwind;" />
        <add key="OleDb_SqlAuth_ConnectString" value="Provider=SQLOLEDB;
          Data Source=(local);Initial Catalog=Northwind;User ID=sa;password=;" />
        <add key="OleDb_Oracle_ConnectString" value=
          "Provider=MSDAORA;Data Source=ORCL;User Id=scott;Password=tiger;" />
        <add key="OleDb_Shape_ConnectString" value="Provider=MSDataShape;
          Data Provider=SQLOLEDB;Data Source=(local);
          Initial Catalog=Northwind;Integrated Security=SSPI;" />
        <add key="OleDb_Msde_ConnectString" value="Provider=SQLOLEDB;
          Data Source=(local)\vsdotnet;Integrated security=SSPI;
          Initial Catalog=Northwind;" />

        <add key="Oracle_ConnectString" value=
          "Data Source=ORCL;User Id=ADODOTNETCOOKBOOK;Password=password;" />
        <add key="Oracle_Scott_ConnectString" value=
          "Data Source=ORCL;User Id=scott;Password=tiger;" />

        <add key="Odbc_ConnectString" value=
          "DRIVER={SQL Server};SERVER=(local);UID=sa;PWD=;DATABASE=Northwind;" />

        <add key="MsAccess_ConnectString" value="Provider=Microsoft.Jet.OLEDB.4.0;
          Data Source=c:\\AdoDotNetCookbook\\DB\\MsAccess\\Northwind.mdb;" />
        <add key="MsAccess_Secure_ConnectString"
          value="Provider=Microsoft.Jet.OLEDB.4.0;
          Data Source=c:\\AdoDotNetCookbook\\DB\\MsAccess\\NorthwindPassword.mdb;" />
        <add key="MsAccess_Database_Filename"
          value="c:\\AdoDotNetCookbook\\DB\\MsAccess\\Northwind.mdb" />
        <add key="MsAccess_SecureMdw_Filename"
          value="c:\\AdoDotNetCookbook\\DB\\MsAccess\\Northwind.mdw" />

        <add key="Excel_0115_ConnectString" value='Provider=Microsoft.Jet.OLEDB.4.0;
```

```
    Data Source=c:\AdoDotNetCookbook\CS\Chapter01\Categories.xls;
    Extended Properties="Excel 8.0;HDR=YES";' />

  <add key="TextFile_0119_ConnectString"
    value='Provider=Microsoft.Jet.OLEDB.4.0;
    Data Source=c:\AdoDotNetCookbook\CS\Chapter 01\;
    Extended Properties="text;HDR=yes;FMT=Delimited";' />
  </appSettings>
</configuration>
```

Platform Notes

The solutions in this book were developed using Visual Studio .NET version 1.1. The differences between Version 1.1 and Version 1.0 of the .NET Framework are significant overall, but do not affect ADO.NET much. A complete list of differences between Version 1.1 and Version 1.0 of the .NET Framework can be found at *http://www.gotdotnet.com/team/upgrade/apiChanges.aspx*.

Comments and Questions

We at O'Reilly have tested and verified the information in this book to the best of our ability, but mistakes and oversights do occur. Please let us know about errors you may find, as well as your suggestions for future editions, by writing to:

O'Reilly & Associates
1005 Gravenstein Highway North
Sebastopol, CA 95472
(800) 998-9938 (in the U.S. or Canada)
(707) 829-0515 (international or local)
(707) 829-0104 (fax)

To ask technical questions or comment on the book, send email to:

bookquestions@oreilly.com

We have a web site for this book where examples, errata, and any plans for future editions are listed. You can access this site at:

http://www.oreilly.com/catalog/adonetckbk/

For more information about this book and others, see the O'Reilly web site:

http://www.oreilly.com

Acknowledgments

This book was originally conceived in March 2002. It's been a long effort that wouldn't have been possible without the help and support of many people.

Brian Jepson, editor, provided valuable advice about content, structure, and writing. His suggestions about grammar, voice, and style made this book better in ways that nobody will ever know about. Brian also pushed me to get this book done by setting aggressive timelines that kept me up nights—for this I'm also grateful. I've truly enjoyed working with him on this project.

John Osborn, executive editor, conceived the original idea for this book and believed in and supported this project. John is representative of O'Reilly and its employees. Together they make the difficult, often (very) tedious, task of writing a book much easier with their fairness, directness, professionalism, and honesty. I write for O'Reilly because I believe this publisher is truly dedicated to creating a high-quality book that provides great value for the reader. A big plus is that they have a low-bureaucracy environment—contracts, for example, are short and written in plain English, allowing me to understand them without legal advice.

Technical reviewer Shawn Wildermuth provided valuable feedback about the technical content. He pointed out where my explanations needed clarification and where they needed more detail. Shawn also suggested some great, new recipe ideas that I have included in this book.

The ADO.NET programming community gladly shared what they know. I began working with .NET in Beta 1 and, together with this community, learned how to be productive with ADO.NET. With the help of these people, most of whom I don't know and am unlikely to meet, I was able understand ADO.NET well enough to write this book. I hope that this book makes it easier for you to get through the tough times that I remember well.

Thanks also to my friends and family for their encouragement and support. They are always there when I need to take my mind off work.

Finally, thanks to Molly for her support, understanding, patience, and encouragement. I know that in my time off I don't want to think about technology. Molly is an artist and I can't imagine or understand how she put up with me talking about this book when I was struggling with a topic or with motivation. And she did this without complaining or yawning. I love you Molly—you make me laugh and smile.

CHAPTER 1

Connecting to Data

1.0   Introduction

This chapter describes how to connect to a variety of data sources from ADO.NET; how to handle security-related issues including storing connection strings and using different authentication methods; and how to set up, monitor, and optimize connection pooling.

ADO.NET Overview

ADO.NET is designed to support data access requirements of loosely coupled n-tier application architectures including web services. ADO.NET can access a variety of different data sources, including relational databases such as Microsoft SQL Server, Oracle, and Microsoft Access, as well as other data sources such as Microsoft Excel, Outlook, and text files.

A .NET data provider is used to connect to a data source, execute commands, and retrieve results. The .NET Framework ships with four .NET-managed data providers: Microsoft SQL Server, Oracle, OLE DB, and ODBC.

Other providers are also available—for example, Oracle has developed its own .NET data provider for Oracle. Data providers also exist for databases such as Sybase and MySQL. Database-specific providers usually access the underlying data store directly and offer the best performance, broadest functionality, and support for database-specific features. Since a data provider needs only to implement a set of standard interfaces, the capabilities and performance of data providers for the same data source can differ significantly.

In addition to database-specific providers, the OLE DB .NET data provider allows access to most OLE DB data sources through OLE DB providers. Similarly, the ODBC .NET data provider uses the ODBC drivers to access most ODBC data sources. You can also develop your own data provider to access proprietary data sources or to meet special requirements.

ADO.NET is fundamentally different from ADO despite sharing a similar name. ADO.NET is based on a disconnected architecture and has both connected and disconnected classes. Each data provider is responsible for providing the connected classes:

Connection

A unique session with the data source.

Command

Executes SQL statements and stored procedures against the data source.

DataReader

Forward-only, read-only access to a query result set stream.

DataAdapter

Bridges the connected classes with the disconnected classes; also used to fill a disconnected DataSet and update the data source with changes made to a disconnected DataSet.

The disconnected classes are part of the ADO.NET classes in the .NET Framework. They provide a consistent programming model regardless of the data source or data provider. The disconnected classes include:

DataSet

An in-memory relational database.

DataTable

A single table of memory-resident data.

DataColumn

The schema of a column in a DataTable.

DataRow

A row of data in the DataTable.

DataView

A data-bindable view of a DataTable used for custom sorting, filtering, searching, editing, and navigation.

DataRelation

A parent/child relationship between two DataTable objects in a DataSet.

Constraint

A constraint on one or more columns in a DataTable used to maintain data integrity.

The DataSet retains no information about the source of the data used to fill it with data. It maintains both current and original versions of data allowing the data source to be updated with changes at some future time. Disconnected data classes facilitate transport-independent marshaling vertically between application tiers and horizontally across a distributed application, and persisting data.

ADO.NET and XML converge in .NET. You can save the DataSet as an XML document, or fill it from an XML document. You can access and modify data simultaneously using both the DataSet classes and XML classes.

Connections, Connection Strings, and Connection Pooling

Database connections are a critical and limited resource. Connections must be managed to ensure that an application performs well and is scalable. SQL Server and Oracle data providers provide connection pooling while the OLE DB and ODBC providers use the pooling provided by OLE DB or ODBC respectively.

Connections should be opened as late as possible and closed as soon as possible using either the Close( ) or Dispose( ) method. The connection should be used as briefly as possible, meaning that connections should not last longer than a method call. Connections should not be passed between methods—in addition to creating performance problems and limiting scalability, this can lead to security vulnerabilities.

Data providers use a connection string containing a collection of attribute/value pairs to establish the connection with the database. Recipes 1.1 through 1.11 show how to connect to different data sources.

Connection strings need to be stored securely while still being configurable. Recipe 1.12 shows how to use different techniques to store connection strings and compare them. Recipe 1.13 shows how to use the Data Links Properties dialog box to allow the user to build connection strings at runtime.

SQL Server supports both SQL Server authentication and integrated authentication. SQL Server authentication is easier to program, but not as secure or manageable as integrated security, which uses Windows authentication to authenticate and authorize data access. Integrated security can be used from ASP.NET applications, but because the ASPNET account that is used by most ASP.NET applications has limited permissions, it needs to be configured to allow integrated security to be used from an ASP.NET application. Recipe 1.8 demonstrates this.

Connection pooling allows an application to reuse connections from a pool instead of repeatedly creating and destroying them. This can significantly improve the performance and scalability of applications by reusing connections and eliminating the overhead of establishing new connections. Recipes 1.15, 1.16, and 1.17 show how to take advantage of connection pooling, how to configure connection pooling with different .NET data providers, and how to use connection pooling together with transactions.

You can use the SQL Server Profiler to monitor SQL Server connections. You can also use the Windows Performance Monitor. .NET also adds Common Language Runtime (CLR) Data counters to the Window Performance Monitor that you can use to monitor, optimize, and troubleshoot connections in SQL Server. Recipe 1.14 shows how to monitor connections in ADO.NET applications.

.NET data providers implement common interfaces in their classes. You write database-independent code by operating on these interfaces rather than on the actual classes. Code becomes more portable but the database-specific functionality available in the provider is usually lost. Recipe 1.11 shows how to develop database-independent code by using common interfaces.

See "About the Code" in the Preface for information about the code shown in the solutions.

1.1   Connecting to an ODBC Data Source

Problem

You want to access your data source using an ODBC provider from your .NET application.

Solution

Use the ODBC .NET data provider to access data exposed through an ODBC driver.

The sample code contains a single event handler:

Connect Button.Click
> Creates an OdbcDataAdapter and uses it to fill a DataTable with the Category table from the Northwind sample database. The default view of the table is bound to a data grid on the form.

The C# code is shown in Example 1-1.

Example 1-1. File: OdbcConnectForm.cs

```
// Namespaces, variables, and constants
using System;
using System.Configuration;
using System.Data;
using System.Data.Odbc;

// ...

private void connectButton_Click(object sender, System.EventArgs e)
{
    // Create the DataAdapter.
    String sqlSelect = "SELECT CategoryID, CategoryName, Description " +
        "FROM Categories";
    OdbcDataAdapter da = new OdbcDataAdapter(sqlSelect,
        ConfigurationSettings.AppSettings["Odbc_ConnectString"]);

    // Create the table, fill it, and bind the default view to the grid.
    DataTable dt = new DataTable( );
```

Example 1-1. File: OdbcConnectForm.cs (continued)

```
    da.Fill(dt);
    dataGrid.DataSource = dt.DefaultView;
}
```

Discussion

The ODBC .NET data provider communicates with native ODBC drivers through COM interop (.NET's interoperability layer for COM). The following ODBC providers are guaranteed to be compatible with the ODBC.NET data provider:

- Microsoft SQL Server ODBC Driver
- Microsoft ODBC Driver for Oracle
- Microsoft Access (Jet) ODBC Driver

The .NET data provider for ODBC connects to ODBC data sources through the OdbcConnection object. The ODBC driver connection string is specified using the ConnectionString property. It includes settings needed to establish the connection to the data source. The connection string format closely matches the ODBC connection string format. Additionally, you can specify an ODBC data source name (DSN) or file DSN by setting the ConnectionString attribute to *"DSN=myDSN"* or *"FileDSN=myFileDSN"*. For more information about specifying ODBC connection strings, see the topic "SQLDriverConnect" in the *ODBC Programmer's Reference* within MSDN Library.

Visual Studio also supports creating ODBC data source connections visually:

- Create a data connection in Server Explorer and drag it onto a form or design surface. Configure the OdbcConnection object that appears in the component tray.
- Drag an OdbcConnection from the Data tab of the Toolbox onto a form or design surface. Configure the ConnectionString property in the Properties window of the OdbcConnection object that appears.

The .NET ODBC data provider requires a reference to the System.Data.Odbc namespace in .NET Framework Version 1.1. In Version 1.0, the namespace is Microsoft.Data.Odbc. Add a .NET Reference to Microsoft.Data.Odbc.dll for a .NET Framework Version 1.0 project.

The .NET ODBC .NET data provider ships with .NET Framework Version 1.1. The data provider can be downloaded from *http://msdn.microsoft.com/downloads* for .NET Framework Version 1.0.

1.2   Connecting to a Microsoft Excel Workbook

Problem

You want to access data stored in a Microsoft Excel workbook.

Solution

Use the OLE DB Jet provider to create, access, and modify data stored in an Excel workbook.

The sample code contains two event handlers:

Form.Load

> Creates an OleDbDataAdapter that uses the Jet OLE DB provider to access an Excel workbook. Custom insert and update logic is created for the DataAdapter. A DataTable is filled from the first worksheet, Sheet1, in the Excel workbook and the default view of the table is bound to a data grid on the form.

Update Button.Click

> Uses the DataAdapter created in the Form.Load event handler to update the Excel workbook with the programmatic changes.

The C# code is shown in Example 1-2.

Example 1-2. File: ExcelForm.cs

```
// Namespaces, Variables, and Constants
using System;
using System.Configuration;
using System.Data;

private OleDbDataAdapter da;
private DataTable dt;

// ...

private void ExcelForm_Load(object sender, System.EventArgs e)
{
    // Create the DataAdapter.
    da = new OleDbDataAdapter("SELECT * FROM [Sheet1$]",
        ConfigurationSettings.AppSettings["Excel_0115_ConnectString"]);

    // Create the insert command.
    String insertSql = "INSERT INTO [Sheet1$] " +
        "(CategoryID, CategoryName, Description) " +
        "VALUES (?, ?, ?)";
    da.InsertCommand =
        new OleDbCommand(insertSql, da.SelectCommand.Connection);
    da.InsertCommand.Parameters.Add("@CategoryID", OleDbType.Integer, 0,
        "CategoryID");
```

Example 1-2. File: ExcelForm.cs (continued)

```csharp
        da.InsertCommand.Parameters.Add("@CategoryName", OleDbType.Char, 15,
            "CategoryName");
        da.InsertCommand.Parameters.Add("@Description", OleDbType.VarChar, 100,
            "Description");

        // Create the update command.
        String updateSql = "UPDATE [Sheet1$] " +
            "SET CategoryName=?, Description=? " +
            "WHERE CategoryID=?";
        da.UpdateCommand =
            new OleDbCommand(updateSql, da.SelectCommand.Connection);
        da.UpdateCommand.Parameters.Add("@CategoryName", OleDbType.Char, 15,
            "CategoryName");
        da.UpdateCommand.Parameters.Add("@Description", OleDbType.VarChar, 100,
            "Description");
        da.UpdateCommand.Parameters.Add("@CategoryID", OleDbType.Integer, 0,
            "CategoryID");

        // Fill the table from the Excel spreadsheet.
        dt = new DataTable( );
        da.Fill(dt);
        // Define the primary key.
        dt.PrimaryKey = new DataColumn[] {dt.Columns[0]};

        // Records can only be inserted using this technique.
        dt.DefaultView.AllowDelete = false;
        dt.DefaultView.AllowEdit = true;
        dt.DefaultView.AllowNew = true;
        // Bind the default view of the table to the grid.
        dataGrid.DataSource = dt.DefaultView;
    }
    private void updateButton_Click(object sender, System.EventArgs e)
    {
        da.Update(dt);
    }
```

Discussion

You can use the Jet OLE DB provider to access Microsoft Excel as a data source. The Jet database engine can access other database file formats through Indexed Sequential Access Method (ISAM) drivers specified in the Extended Properties attribute of the connection. Excel 2000 and 2002 are supported with the Excel 8.0 source database type as shown in the following example:

```
Provider=Microsoft.Jet.OLEDB.4.0;Data Source=myBook.xls;
    Extended Properties="Excel 8.0;HDR=YES";
```

The Extended Properties attribute can, in addition to the ISAM version property, specify whether or not tables include headers as field names in the first row of a range using an HDR attribute.

There are three ways in which you can reference Excel workbook data within a SQL statement:

- Specify the worksheet name followed by a dollar sign to access the entire range used in the worksheet:

  ```
  SELECT * FROM [MySheet$]
  ```
- Specify a range explicitly using cells:

  ```
  SELECT * FROM [MySheet$A1:E5]
  ```
- Specify a range with a defined name, as shown in the solution:

  ```
  SELECT * FROM MyRange
  ```

The following subsections discuss how to use Excel as an ADO.NET data source.

Create table

The CREATE TABLE command will create a table in an Excel workbook. The workbook for the connection will be created if it does not exist. For example:

```
CREATE TABLE MySheet (Field1 char(10), Field2 float, Field3 date)
```

Create data

You can use the INSERT command, either static or parameterized, to insert data into a worksheet or range:

```
INSERT INTO [MySheet$]  (Field1, Field2, Field3)
VALUES ('testdata', 1.234, '09/28/1979');
```

Retrieve data

Use either a DataAdapter or a DataReader to retrieve data from an Excel workbook. Create a SQL SELECT statement referencing a worksheet or a range in an Excel workbook and execute the statement to fill a DataSet using a DataAdapter or to create a DataReader. For example:

```
SELECT * FROM [MySheet$]
```

Update data

The UPDATE command, either static or parameterized, can update data in a worksheet or range. For example:

```
UPDATE [MySheet$]
SET Field2 = '2.345',
    Field3 = '10/18/1964'
WHERE
    Field1 = 'testdata'
```

Delete data

The Jet OLE DB provider does not allow DELETE operations. An error will be raised if an attempt is made to execute a DELETE statement affecting one or more records.

1.3   Connecting to a Password-Protected Access Database

Problem

You want to connect to a Microsoft Access database that has a database password.

Solution

Use the Jet OLEDB:Database Password attribute in the connection string to specify the password.

The sample code contains a single event handler:

Connect Button.Click

> Creates and opens a connection to a password-secured Microsoft Access database using the OLE DB .NET data provider. Information about the database is displayed from the properties of the OleDbConnection object.

The C# code is shown in Example 1-3.

Example 1-3. File: AccessPasswordForm.cs

```
// Namespaces, variables, and constants
using System;
using System.Configuration;
using System.Text;
using System.Data;
using System.Data.OleDb;

// ...

private void connectButton_Click(object sender, System.EventArgs e)
{
    StringBuilder result = new StringBuilder();

    // Build the connections string incorporating the password.
    String connectionString =
        ConfigurationSettings.AppSettings["MsAccess_Secure_ConnectString"]+
        "Jet OLEDB:Database Password=" + passwordTextBox.Text + ";";

    result.Append("ConnectionString: " + Environment.NewLine +
        connectionString + Environment.NewLine + Environment.NewLine);
```

Example 1-3. File: AccessPasswordForm.cs (continued)

```
OleDbConnection conn = new OleDbConnection(connectionString);
try
{
    conn.Open( );

    // Retrieve some database information.
    result.Append(
        "Connection State: " + conn.State + Environment.NewLine +
        "OLE DB Provider: " + conn.Provider +
        Environment.NewLine +
        "Server Version: " + conn.ServerVersion +
        Environment.NewLine);

    conn.Close( );
    result.Append("Connection State: " + conn.State);
}
catch(System.Data.OleDb.OleDbException ex)
{
    conn.Close( );
    result.Append("ERROR: " + ex.Message);
}

resultTextBox.Text = result.ToString( );
}
```

Discussion

A Microsoft Access database password requires that users enter a password to obtain access to the database and database objects. This is also known as share-level security. A password does not allow groups or users to have distinct levels of access or permissions. Anyone with the password has unrestricted access to the database.

The Set Database command from the Tools → Security menu is used to set up a database password.

The OLE DB provider for Microsoft Jet has several provider-specific connection string attributes in addition to those defined by ADO.NET. To open a database secured by a Microsoft Access database password, use the Jet OLEDB:Database Password attribute in the connection string to specify the password. This corresponds to the OLE DB property DBPROP_JETOLEDB_DATABASEPASSWORD.

A Microsoft Access database password does not provide strong security and should only be used as a simple deterrent.

1.4   Connecting to a Secured Access Database

Problem

You want to connect to a Microsoft Access database that has been secured with user-level security and a workgroup file.

Solution

Use the Jet OLEDB:System Database attribute in the connection string to specify the path and filename of the workgroup information file or system database.

The sample code contains a single event handler:

Connect Button.Click

Creates and opens a connection to a Microsoft Access database secured with user-level security and a workgroup file using the OLE DB .NET data provider. Information about the database is displayed from the properties of the OleDbConnection object.

The C# code is shown in Example 1-4.

Example 1-4. File: AccessSecureForm.cs

```
// Namespaces, variables, and constants
using System;
using System.Configuration;
using System.Text;
using System.Data.OleDb;

// ...

private void connectButton_Click(object sender, System.EventArgs e)
{
    StringBuilder result = new StringBuilder();

    // Build the connection string with security information.
    String connectionString =
        ConfigurationSettings.AppSettings["MsAccess_ConnectString"] +
        @"Jet OLEDB:System database=" +
        ConfigurationSettings.AppSettings["MsAccess_SecureMdw_Filename"] +
        ";" + "User ID=" + userIdTextBox.Text + ";" +
        "Password=" + passwordTextBox.Text + ";" +
        Environment.NewLine + Environment.NewLine;

    result.Append(connectionString);
```

Example 1-4. File: AccessSecureForm.cs (continued)

```csharp
    // Create the connection.
    OleDbConnection conn = new OleDbConnection(connectionString);

    try
    {
        // Attempt to open the connection.
        conn.Open( );

        result.Append(
            "Connection State: " + conn.State + Environment.NewLine +
            "OLE DB Provider: " + conn.Provider +
            Environment.NewLine +
            "Server Version: " + conn.ServerVersion +
            Environment.NewLine);

        conn.Close( );

        result.Append("Connection State: " + conn.State +
            Environment.NewLine);
    }
    catch(System.Data.OleDb.OleDbException ex)
    {
        result.Append("ERROR: " + ex.Message);
    }

    resultTextBox.Text = result.ToString( );
}
```

Discussion

Microsoft Access user-level security requires an additional file—the workgroup information or *MDW* file—in addition to the database or *MDB* file. This file contains the user and group information for the secured database while the actual permissions are stored in the database file.

When you connect to a secured Jet database, the user ID and password are validated against the values in the *MDW* file. The permissions are obtained from the *MDB* file. To connect, the location of both the database file and the workgroup file must be supplied.

The OLE DB provider for Microsoft Jet has several provider-specific connection string attributes in addition to those defined by ADO.NET. To open a database secured by Microsoft Access user-level security, use the Jet OLEDB:System Database attribute in the connection string to specify the path and filename of the workgroup information file or system database. This corresponds to the OLE DB property DBPROP_JETOLEDB_SYSDBPATH.

1.5   Connecting to an Access Database from ASP.NET

Problem

You know your connection string is correct, but still can't connect to your Microsoft Access database from your ASP.NET application. What are the differences between connecting from a Windows Forms .NET application and an ASP.NET application?

Solution

You must grant the necessary file permissions for accessing a Jet database (Microsoft's transparent data access engine) to the default user account used by ASP.NET.

Discussion

When a user retrieves a page from an ASP.NET web site, code runs on the server to generate and deliver the page. By default, IIS (Internet Information Server) uses the system account to provide the security context for all processes. This account can access the IIS computer, but is not allowed to access network shares on other computers.

To allow an ASP.NET application to connect to a Microsoft Access database, IIS must be configured to use an account other than the system account. The new account must be configured to have permission to access all files and folders needed to use the Access database. If the Access database is on a remote computer, the account also requires access to that computer.

The following sections describe how to configure the IIS Server and the Access computer to allow ASP.NET to connect to an Access database.

Configure IIS

The system account cannot authenticate across a network. Enable impersonation in the web.config file for a given ASP.NET application so that ASP.NET impersonates an account on the Microsoft Access computer with the required access permissions to the Access database. For example:

```
<identity impersonate="true" userName="domain\username"
    password="myPassword" />
```

This method stores the username and password in clear text on the server. Ensure that IIS is configured to prevent users of the web site from viewing the contents of the *web.config* file—this is the default configuration. Other ways to impersonate a user from an ASP page are described in the Microsoft Knowledge Base article Q248187.

The Microsoft Jet engine uses the *TEMP* folder on the IIS computer that is accessing the Access database. The user identity requires NTFS (Windows NT File System) full-control permissions on the *TEMP* folder. Ensure that the TEMP and TMP environment variables are properly configured.

Configure the Access server

On the Access computer, the user account that is used to access the database requires Read, Write, Execute, and Change permissions on the database file. The user identity needs Read, Write, Execute, Delete, and Change permissions on the folder containing the database files. The user account requires permissions to access the share that contains the database file and folders.

The user account must be recognized by the Access computer. For a domain user account, add it to the permissions list on both computers. For a user account local to the IIS computer, create a duplicate account on the Access computer with the same name and password.

Grant the user account Log on Locally and Access this Computer from the Network permission to access the computer in the local security policy. These permissions are assigned within the Security Settings\Local Policies\User Rights Assignment node in the Local Security Policy tool.

1.6 Using an IP Address to Connect to SQL Server

Problem

You want to connect to a SQL Server using its IP address instead of its server name.

Solution

Use the Network Address and Network Library attributes of the connection string.

The sample code contains a single event handler:

Connect Button.Click
Creates and opens a connection to a SQL Server using its IP address. Information about the SQL Server is displayed from the properties of the SqlConnection object.

The C# code is shown in Example 1-5.

Example 1-5. File: ConnectSqlServerIpAddressForm.cs

```
// Namespaces, variables, and constants
using System;
using System.Data.SqlClient;

// ...

private void connectButton_Click(object sender, System.EventArgs e)
{
    String connString =
        "Network Library=dbmssocn;Network Address=127.0.0.1;" +
        "Integrated security=SSPI;Initial Catalog=Northwind";

    SqlConnection conn = new SqlConnection(connString);
    conn.Open();

    // Return some information about the server.
    resultTextBox.Text =
        "ConnectionState = " + conn.State + Environment.NewLine +
        "DataSource = " + conn.DataSource + Environment.NewLine +
        "ServerVersion = " + conn.ServerVersion + Environment.NewLine;

    conn.Close();

    resultTextBox.Text += "ConnectionState = " + conn.State;
}
```

Discussion

SQL Server network libraries are dynamic-link libraries (DLLs) that perform network operations required for client computers and SQL Server computers to communicate. A server can monitor multiple libraries simultaneously; the only requirement is that each network library to be monitored is installed and configured.

Available network libraries for SQL Server 2000 include:

AppleTalk ADSP
> Allows Apple Macintosh to communicate with SQL Server using native Apple-Talk protocol.

Banyan VINES
> Supports Banyan VINES Sequenced Packet Protocol (SPP) across Banyan VINES IP network protocol.

Multiprotocol
> Automatically chooses the first available network protocol to establish a connection generally with performance comparable to using a native network library. TCP/IP Sockets, NWLink IPX/SPX, and Named Pipes are supported.

Named Pipes
    Interprocess communication (IPC) mechanism provided by SQL Server for communication between clients and servers.

NWLink IPX/SPX
    The native protocol of Novell Netware networks.

TCP/IP Sockets
    Uses standard Windows sockets to communicate across the TCP/IP protocol.

Clustered installations of SQL Server support only Named Pipes and TCP/IP protocols. AppleTalk, Banyan Vines, and Multiprotocol protocols are unavailable if named instances are installed on the server.

For more information about network libraries and configuring network libraries, see Microsoft SQL Server Books Online.

The use of the SQL Server TCP/IP Sockets improves performance and scalability with high volumes of data. It avoids some security issues associated with named pipes. As with any protocol, the client and the server must be configured to use TCP/IP.

To connect to SQL Server using an IP address, the TCP/IP network library must be used to connect to the SQL Server. This is done by specifying the library in the connection string as either the attribute `Net` or `Network Library` with a value of *dbmssocn*. Specify the IP address using the `Data Source`, `Server`, `Address`, `Addr`, or `Network Address` parameter. The following connection string demonstrates using an IP address to specify the data source:

```
Network Library=dbmssocn;Network Address=127.0.0.1;
    Integrated security=SSPI;Initial Catalog=Northwind
```

In the example, the IP address is the local machine. This could also be specified as (`local`). To specify a SQL Server other than a local instance, specify the IP address of the computer on which SQL Server is installed.

Default instances of SQL Server listen on port 1433. Named instances of SQL Server dynamically assign a port number when they are first started. The example above does not specify the port number and therefore uses the default port 1433 of the SQL Server. If the SQL Server is configured to listen on another port, specify the port number following the IP address specified by the `Network Address` attribute separated by a comma as shown in the following snippet, which connects to a local SQL Server listening on port 1450:

```
Network Address=(local),1450
```

1.7 Connecting to a Named Instance of SQL Server or Microsoft Data Engine (MSDE)

Problem

You want to connect to a named instance of a SQL Server or Microsoft Data Engine (MSDE).

Solution

You need to understand what a SQL Server or MSDE named instance is and how to connect to one. The sample code contains a single event handler:

Connect Button.Click

> Creates and opens a connection to a named instance of a SQL Server. Information about the SQL Server is displayed from the properties of the SqlConnection object.

The C# code is shown in Example 1-6.

Example 1-6. File: ConnectNamedInstanceForm.cs

```
// Namespaces, variables, and constants
using System;
using System.Configuration;
using System.Windows.Forms;
using System.Text;
using System.Data.SqlClient;

// ...

private void connectButton_Click(object sender, System.EventArgs e)
{
    StringBuilder result = new StringBuilder();

    SqlConnection conn = new SqlConnection(
        ConfigurationSettings.AppSettings["Sql_Msde_ConnectString"]);

    try
    {
        conn.Open();

        // Return some information about the server.
        result.Append(
            "ConnectionState = " + conn.State + Environment.NewLine +
            "DataSource = " + conn.DataSource + Environment.NewLine +
            "ConnectionState = " + conn.State + Environment.NewLine +
            "ServerVersion=" + conn.ServerVersion +
            Environment.NewLine);
    }
```

Example 1-6. File: ConnectNamedInstanceForm.cs (continued)

```
catch(Exception ex)
{
    MessageBox.Show(ex.Message);
}
finally
{
    conn.Close( );
}

result.Append("ConnectionState = " + conn.State);

resultTextBox.Text = result.ToString( );
}
```

Discussion

SQL Server 2000 introduced the ability to install multiple copies of SQL Server on a single computer. Only one copy can function as the default instance at any time; it is identified by the network name of the computer on which it is running. All other copies are named instances and are identified by the network name of the computer plus an instance name. The format is <computerName>\<instanceName>. This format is used in the connection string to specify the Data Source attribute for a named instance.

Each instance operates independently of the other instances installed on the same computer. Each instance has its own set of system and user databases that are not shared between instances and it runs within its own security context. The maximum number of instances supported on SQL Server 2000 is 16. The Microsoft Distributed Transaction Coordinator (DTC) and the Microsoft Search services are installed and used simultaneously by every installed instance of SQL Server. Client tools such as Enterprise Manager and Query Analyzer are also shared.

The System.Data.SqlClient class cannot automatically discover the port number of a named instance of SQL Server listening on a port other than the default 1433. To connect to a named instance of SQL Server listening on a custom port, specify the port number following the instance name in the connection string separated by a comma. For, if the named instance *msde01* was set up to listen on port 1450, the following connection string might be used:

```
Data Source=(local)\msde01,1450;Integrated security=SSPI;
    Initial Catalog=Northwind
```

1.8 Connecting to SQL Server Using Integrated Security from ASP.NET

Problem

You want to coordinate Windows security accounts between an ASP.NET application and SQL Server.

Solution

Connect to SQL Server from ASP.NET using Windows Authentication in SQL Server.

Discussion

Connecting to a SQL Server database provides two different authentication modes:

Windows Authentication
> Uses the current security identity from the Windows NT or Windows 2000 user account to provide authentication information. It does not expose the user ID and password and is the recommended method for authenticating a connection.

SQL Server Authentication
> Uses a SQL Server login account providing a user ID and password.

Integrated security requires that the SQL Server is running on the same computer as IIS and that all application users are on the same domain so that their credentials are available to IIS. The following areas of the application need to be configured:

- Configure the ASP.NET application so that Integrated Windows Authentication is enabled and Anonymous Access is disabled.

- The *web.config* file establishes the authentication mode that the application uses and that the application will run as or impersonate the user. Add the following elements to the *web.config* file:

    ```
    <authentication mode="Windows" />
    <identity impersonate="true" />
    ```

- The connection string must contain attributes that tell the SQL Server that integrated security is used. Use the Integrated Security=SSPI attribute-and-value pair instead of the User ID and Password attributes in the connection string. The older attribute-and-value pair Trusted_Connection=Yes is also supported.

- Add users and groups from the domain and set their access permissions as required.

By default, ASP.NET applications run in the context of a local user ASPNET on IIS. The account has limited permissions and is local to the IIS computer and therefore not recognized as a user on remote computers. To overcome this limitation when SQL Server is not on the same computer as IIS, run the web application in the context of a domain user recognized on both IIS and SQL Server computers.

In addition to the areas identified where IIS and SQL Server are on the same computer, the following additional items must be configured if the SQL Server is on a different computer:

- Ensure that the mapped domain user has required privileges to run the web application.
- Configure the web application to impersonate the domain user. Add the following elements to the *web.config* file for the web application:

```
<authentication mode="Windows" />
<identity impersonate="true" userName="domain\username"
        password="myPassword" />
```

1.9   Connecting to an Oracle Database

Problem

You want to connect to an Oracle database.

Solution

You can connect to an Oracle database using either the Oracle .NET data provider or the OLE DB .NET data provider.

The sample code contains two event handlers:

Oracle Button.Click
> Creates and opens a connection to an Oracle database using the Oracle .NET data provider. Information about the database is displayed from the properties of the OracleConnection object.

OLE DB Button.Click
> Creates and opens a connection to an Oracle database using the OLE DB .NET data provider. Information about the database is displayed from the properties of the OleDbConnection object.

The C# code is shown in Example 1-7.

Example 1-7. File: ConnectOracleForm.cs

```
// Namespaces, variables, and constants
using System;
using System.Configuration;
using System.Data.OleDb;
using System.Data.OracleClient;
```

Example 1-7. File: ConnectOracleForm.cs (continued)

```csharp
// ...

private void oracleProviderButton_Click(object sender, System.EventArgs e)
{
    // Connect to Oracle using Microsoft Oracle .NET data provider.
    OracleConnection conn = new OracleConnection(
        ConfigurationSettings.AppSettings["Oracle_Scott_ConnectString"]);

    resultTextBox.Text = "Connection with ORACLE Provider" +
        Environment.NewLine;
    try
    {
        conn.Open( );

        resultTextBox.Text += "ConnectionState = " + conn.State +
            Environment.NewLine +
            "DataSource = " + conn.DataSource +
            Environment.NewLine +
            "ServerVersion = " + conn.ServerVersion +
            Environment.NewLine;
    }
    catch(OracleException ex)
    {
        resultTextBox.Text += "ERROR: " + ex.Message;
    }
    finally
    {
        conn.Close( );
        resultTextBox.Text += "ConnectionState = " + conn.State;
    }
}

private void oleDbButton_Click(object sender, System.EventArgs e)
{
    // Connect to Oracle using OLE DB .NET data provider.
    OleDbConnection conn = new OleDbConnection(
        ConfigurationSettings.AppSettings["OleDb_Oracle_ConnectString"]);

    resultTextBox.Text = "Connection with OLE DB Provider" +
        Environment.NewLine;
    try
    {
        conn.Open( );

        resultTextBox.Text += "ConnectionState = " + conn.State +
            Environment.NewLine +
            "DataSource = " + conn.DataSource +
            Environment.NewLine +
            "ServerVersion = " + conn.ServerVersion +
            Environment.NewLine;
    }
    catch(OleDbException ex)
```

Example 1-7. File: ConnectOracleForm.cs (continued)

```
    {
        resultTextBox.Text += "ERROR: " + ex.Message;
    }
    finally
    {
        conn.Close( );
        resultTextBox.Text += "ConnectionState = " + conn.State +
            Environment.NewLine;
    }
}
```

Discussion

You can access an Oracle database using three different provider types: native Oracle, OLE DB, and ODBC. These alternatives are discussed in the following subsections.

Native Oracle

The Microsoft Oracle .NET data provider accesses an Oracle database using the Oracle Call Interface (OCI) through Oracle client connectivity software. The provider can access Oracle 7.3.4 or later and requires Oracle 8i Release 3 (8.1.7) or later client software. The classes are located in the System.Data.OracleClient namespace. An example of a connection string using integrated security is shown in the following snippet:

```
    Data Source=myOracleDb;Integrated Security=yes;
```

Without integrated security, the connection string is:

```
    Data Source=myOracleDb;User Id=scott;Password=tiger;
```

The Microsoft Oracle .NET data provider is included with .NET Framework Version 1.1. It is not included with the .NET Framework Version 1.0, but you can download it from *http://msdn.microsoft.com/downloads*. The Oracle .NET data provider can access Oracle8 Release 8.0 or later and requires the Oracle9i Client Release 2 (9.2) or later.

Here are desciptions of available managed providers:

* Oracle has released a .NET data provider. It is available for free download from *http://otn.oracle.com/software/tech/windows/odpnet/content.html*.
* Data Direct Technologies licenses a fully managed provider that does not require client libraries for Oracle8i Release 2 (8.1.6) or later databases. More information is available at *http://www.datadirect-technologies.com/products/dotnet/dotnetindex.asp*.

Native providers generally perform better than OLE DB or ODBC providers because they are built specifically for the database and because they remove a layer of indirection from the application to the database.

OLE DB

You can use the OLE DB .NET data provider with the Oracle OLE DB provider (MSDAORA) to access Oracle data not supported by a .NET Oracle provider. An example of the connection string is shown here:

```
Provider=MSDAORA;Data Source=myOracleDb;User Id=scott;Password=tiger;
```

The OLE DB provider should be used primarily as a bridge from applications that already use OLE DB. Use a native Oracle .NET data provider where practical.

ODBC

Finally, the ODBC .NET data provider can connect to an Oracle database. An example of the connection string is shown here:

```
Driver={Microsoft ODBC for Oracle};Server=myOracleDb;
    Trusted_Connection=yes;
```

The ODBC .NET data provider should be used primarily as a bridge from applications that already use ODBC. Use a native Oracle .NET data provider where practical.

TNSNAMES.ORA

Oracle uses a configuration file named *TNSNAMES.ORA* to locate the Oracle database and determine how to connect to it based on the Data Source or Database attribute in the connection string.

An example of an entry in the *TNSNAMES.ORA* file for the alias MYORCLDB follows:

```
MYORCLDB =
  (DESCRIPTION =
    (ADDRESS_LIST =
      (ADDRESS = (PROTOCOL = TCP)
        (HOST = myserver)(PORT = 1521))
    )
    (CONNECT_DATA =
      (SERVER = DEDICATED)
      (SERVICE_NAME = orcl.myurl.com)
    )
  )
```

In this simple example, the connection to the alias MYORLCDB uses TCP/IP on port 1521 (the default) and is running on the computer called myserver. The name of the Oracle service is ORCL.MYURL.COM.

1.10 Connecting to Exchange or Outlook

Problem

You want to use ADO.NET to extract data from Microsoft Outlook or Microsoft Exchange.

Solution

Use the OLE DB Jet provider to access Exchange and Outlook data.

The sample code contains two event handlers:

Form.Load

> Displays a form that allows the user to specify the mailbox name and mail profile to connect to.

Connect Button.Click

> Creates and opens a connection to Outlook or Exchange data using the OLE DB .NET data provider. A DataAdapter is used to fill a table with the *Subject* and *Content* of each message in the *Inbox*. The default view of the table is bound to a data grid on the form.

The C# code is shown in Example 1-8.

Example 1-8. File: ConnectExchangeDataForm.cs

```
// Namespaces, variables, and constants
using System;
using System.Windows.Forms;
using System.Data;
using System.Data.OleDb;

// ...

private void ConnectExchangeDataForm_Load(object sender,
    System.EventArgs e)
{
    mailboxNameTextBox.Text = "Personal Folders";
    profileTextBox.Text = "Outlook";
}

private void connectButton_Click(object sender, System.EventArgs e)
{
    String sqlText = "SELECT Subject, Contents FROM Inbox";

    // Build the connection string.
    String connectionString="Provider=Microsoft.Jet.OLEDB.4.0;" +
        "Outlook 9.0;" +
        "MAPILEVEL=" + mailboxNameTextBox.Text + "|;" +
        "PROFILE=" + profileTextBox.Text + ";" +
```

Example 1-8. File: ConnectExchangeDataForm.cs (continued)

```
    "TABLETYPE=0;" +
    "DATABASE=" + System.IO.Path.GetTempPath( );

// Create the DataAdapter.
OleDbDataAdapter da = new OleDbDataAdapter(sqlText, connectionString);

// Create and fill the table.
DataTable dt = new DataTable("Inbox");
try
{
    da.Fill(dt);
    dataGrid.DataSource = dt.DefaultView;
}
catch(Exception ex)
{
    MessageBox.Show("ERROR: " + ex.Message);
    return;
}
}
```

Discussion

The .NET data provider for OLE DB does not support OLE DB Version 2.5 interfaces including the Microsoft OLE DB Provider for Exchange. The Jet OLE DB provider can access an Outlook or Exchange store. An example of the connection string:

```
Microsoft.Jet.OLEDB.4.0;Outlook 9.0;MAPILEVEL=Personal Folders|;
    PROFILE=Outlook;TABLETYPE=0;DATABASE=c:\temp;
```

The connection string attributes-and-value pairs are described in Table 1-1.

Table 1-1. Outlook or Exchange connection string attributes

Element	Description
Database name	DATABASE=path
	With an Identifier of Outlook 9.0, the path to store temporary system tables.
	With an Identifier of Exchange 4.0, the path and filename to a Microsoft Access database in which to store temporary system tables.
Identifier	Outlook 9.0 to connect to Outlook 2000 and later.
	Exchange 4.0 to connect to Exchange 4.x and 5.x.
Password	PASSWORD=password
	Outlook or Exchange password. This parameter is not required if your network logon password is passed to the Outlook or Exchange server. This parameter is optional.
Profile name	PROFILE=profile
	The name of the Outlook or Exchange profile to use. If this not specified, the default profile is used.

Table 1-1. Outlook or Exchange connection string attributes (continued)

Element	Description
Table path	MAPILEVEL=<storage>|<folderPath>
	<storage> is the exact mailbox name on the server, a personal folder, or public folder as it appears in the *Outlook Folder* list.
	<folderPath> is the path to the folder immediately above the folder to access using the SQL statement. The folder path is required only when accessing folders below the top level of folders within the store; the pipe (|) character is always required. When listing nested folders, separate each folder name with a backslash (\).
Table type	TABLETYPE=0 for folders (default value).
	TABLETYPE=1 for address books.

1.11 Writing Database-Independent Code

Problem

You need to develop an application that can be used with different data providers, but does not lose functionality that is specific to the different providers. You want to create provider-independent code and use it with the provider-specific code that you might need.

Solution

The solution shows how to use interfaces that are inherited by .NET connected classes (such as Connection and DataReader) to create provider-independent code that can be used with provider-specific code to access unique functionality.

The sample code contains a method and two event handlers:

GetData( )

> This method is a .NET data provider-independent method that accepts .NET data provider-specific Connection and DataAdapter arguments as generic IDbConnection and IDbDataAdapter interface types. The interfaces are used to fill a DataSet from the Customers table in Northwind. The default view of the Customers DataTable is bound to the data grid on the form.
>
> Finally, the provider-specific Connection for the IDbConnection is identified and provider-specific logic executed.

SQL Button.Click

> This event handler is provider-specific code that creates a SqlConnection and a SqlDataAdapter object and passes them as arguments into the provider-independent GetData( ) method.

OLE DB Button.Click

This event handler is provider-specific code that creates an OleDbConnection and an OleDbDataAdapter object and passes them as arguments into the provider-independent GetData( ) method.

The C# code is shown in Example 1-9.

Example 1-9. File: DatabaseIndependentCodeForm.cs

```csharp
// Namespaces, variables, and constants
using System;
using System.Configuration;
using System.Windows.Forms;
using System.Data;
using System.Data.Common;
using System.Data.SqlClient;
using System.Data.OleDb;

// ...

private void GetData(IDbConnection conn, IDbDataAdapter da)
{
    // Create the command and assign it to the IDbDataAdapter interface.
    IDbCommand cmd = conn.CreateCommand( );
    cmd.CommandText = "SELECT * FROM Customers";
    da.SelectCommand = cmd;
    // Add a table mapping.
    da.TableMappings.Add("Table", "Customers");

    dataGrid.DataSource = null;

    // Fill the DataSet.
    DataSet ds = new DataSet( );
    da.Fill(ds);

    // Bind the default view for the Customer table to the grid.
    dataGrid.DataSource = ds.Tables["Customers"].DefaultView;

    // Identify provider-specific connection type and process appropriately.
    if (conn is SqlConnection)
    {
        MessageBox.Show("Specific processing for SQL data provider.");
    }
    else if(conn is OleDbConnection)
    {
        MessageBox.Show("Specific processing for OLE DB data provider.");
    }
}

private void sqlButton_Click(object sender, System.EventArgs e)
{
```

Example 1-9. File: DatabaseIndependentCodeForm.cs (continued)

```
    // Create a SQL Connection and DataAdapter.
    SqlConnection conn = new SqlConnection(
        ConfigurationSettings.AppSettings["Sql_ConnectString"]);
    SqlDataAdapter da = new SqlDataAdapter();

    dataGrid.CaptionText = "SQL .NET Provider";

    // Call provider-independent function to retrieve data.
    GetData(conn, da);
}

private void oleDbButton_Click(object sender, System.EventArgs e)
{
    // Create a OLE DB Connection and DataAdapter.
    OleDbConnection conn = new OleDbConnection(
        ConfigurationSettings.AppSettings["OleDb_ConnectString"]);
    OleDbDataAdapter da = new OleDbDataAdapter();

    dataGrid.CaptionText = "OLE DB .NET Provider";

    // Call provider-independent function to retrieve data.
    GetData(conn, da);
}
```

Discussion

The IDbConnection, IDbCommand, IDataAdapter, and IDataReader interfaces are implemented by Connection, Command, DataAdapter, and DataReader classes in .NET data providers. You can pass these provider-independent base classes as interface arguments instead of the provider-specific inherited classes. This allows applications that support multiple data providers to reuse common provider-independent code.

The provider-specific functionality of the classes is not available when the base interfaces are used. The is operator is used to identify the provider-specific class of the provider-independent interface. Branching logic is then used execute code specific to that class.

1.12   Storing Connection Strings

Problem

You need to choose the best place to store connection strings that you need in your application to increase maintainability, simplify future modifications, and eliminate the need to recompile the application when it is modified.

Solution

There are several alternatives for storing connection strings, including hard-coding the connection string in your application, storing it in an application configuration file or the Windows Registry, representing it using a Universal Data Link (UDL) file, or in a custom file.

Discussion

A connection string is made up of a semi-colon delimited collection of attribute/value pairs that define how to connect a data source. Although connection strings tend to look similar, the available and required attributes are different depending on the data provider and on the underlying data source. There are a variety of options providing differing degrees of flexibility and security.

Persist Security Info

The Persist Security Info connection string attribute specifies whether the data source can hang on to, or persist, sensitive information such as user authentication credentials. Its value should be kept at the default false. If its value is true, the connection information—including the password—can be obtained by querying the connection, allowing an untrusted party to have access to sensitive information when a Connection is passed or persisted to a disk. This is an issue only when passing connected objects such as Connection or DataAdapter; disconnected objects such as DataSet and DataTable do not store information about the original source of their data.

Before a data source object is initialized for the first time, sensitive information can be retrieved from it regardless of the setting of the Persist Security Info property. Avoid passing uninitialized data source objects.

The Persist Security Info connection string attribute is supported by the SQL Server, OLE DB, and Oracle .NET Framework data providers. Although not supported by the ODBC .NET Framework data provider, its behavior is as if Persist Security Info is false and cannot be changed. Check the documentation for other data providers to determine specific implementation details.

Connecting to a database server requires passing credentials—username and password—to the server in a connection string. These credentials, together with the data source name, need to be kept private to protect unauthorized access to the data source. There are two approaches for obtaining these credentials:

- Prompting for connection credentials at runtime.
- Storing predetermined connection credentials on the server and using them at runtime to connect to the database server.

Integrated Security

Integrated security is the most secure way to connect to a SQL Server and should be used unless it is impractical to do so. Integrated security uses the identity of the current active user rather than an explicit user ID and password in the connection string to authorize access to the database. Integrated security avoids storing usernames and passwords in connection strings and its use is recommended where possible instead of SQL Server Authentication.

To use integrated security in the connection string, specify the value SSPI for the Integrated Security attribute and do not specify User ID and Password connection string attributes:

```
Integrated Security=SSPI
```

See Recipe 1.8 for information about connecting to SQL Server using integrated security from ASP.NET.

Often, it is not practical to prompt for connection credentials because of disadvantages including:

Security

Transferring connection information from the browser to the server can expose connection credentials if they are not encrypted.

Connection pooling

Each user must be recognized separately by the server. This does not allow effective connection pooling and can limit the scalability of the application. For more on connection pooling, see Recipe 1.15.

Single sign-on

It is difficult to integrate with single sign-on strategies, which are becoming increasingly important in enterprise environments (for example, where numerous applications are aggregated into portals).

Server applications

Cannot be used by applications that otherwise have no user interface, such as an XML web service.

There are a number of techniques that you can use to store predetermined connection credentials. These, together with their advantages and drawbacks, are discussed in the following subsections.

Always configure predetermined accounts with the minimum permissions required.

Never use sa or any other administrative account.

Never use blank passwords.

Hardcode in the application

An obvious technique for storing connection strings is hardcoding them into the application. Although this approach results in the best performance, it has poor flexibility; the application needs to be recompiled if the connection string needs to be changed for any reason. Security is poor. The code can be disassembled to expose connection string information. Caching techniques together with external storage techniques eliminate nearly all performance benefits of hardcoding over external storage techniques.

Hardcoding connection string information is not advised; external server-side storage is preferred in nearly all cases because of the increased flexibility, security, and configuration ease. A discussion of available external storage options follows.

Application configuration file

An application configuration file is an XML-based text file that is used to store application-specific settings used at runtime by the application. The naming convention for and deployment location of the file depend on the type of application:

Executable application
> The name of the configuration file is the name of the application executable with a *.config* extension—for example, *myApplication.exe.config*. It is located in the same directory as the executable file.

ASP.NET application
> A web application can have multiple configuration files all named *web.config*. Each configuration file supplies configuration settings for its directory and all of its child directories; it also overrides any configuration settings inherited from parent directories.

> The machine configuration file—*machine.config*, located in the *CONFIG* subdirectory of the .NET runtime installation—contains configuration information that applies to the computer. The *machine.config* file is checked for configuration settings defined in an <appSettings> element before the application configuration file is checked.
>
> It is best to put application settings in the application configuration file both to facilitate deployment and to keep the machine configuration file manageable and secure.

The <appSettings> element of the application file is used to store custom application settings as a collection of key-value pairs. You can store a connection string as shown:

```
<configuration>
    <appSettings>
        <add key="ConnectionString"
```

```
    value="Data Source=(local);Initial Catalog=Northwind;User ID=sa;password=;"
        />
    </appSettings>
</configuration>
```

The AppSettings property of the System.Configuration.ConfigurationSettings class is used to retrieve the value for a specific key within the appSettings element; the ConfigurationSettings class cannot be used to write settings to a configuration file.

Application configuration files facilitate deployment because the files are simply installed alongside other application files. One drawback is that application configuration files are not inherently secure since they store information as clear text in a file that is accessible through the file system. Encrypt the connection and other sensitive information within the configuration file and ensure that NTFS file permissions are set to restrict access to the file. Recipe 5.7 shows techniques to encrypt data.

Make sure you name the application configuration file for a Windows Forms application *App.config*—this is the default. At build time, this file is automatically copied into the startup directory by Visual Studio .NET with the name *applicationName.exe.config*.

If you name the application configuration file *applicationName.exe.config* within your solution, you will have to copy it to the startup directory each time you modify it and each time you build the solution; the build process deletes it from the startup directory.

Universal data link (UDL) file

The OLE DB .NET data providers supports UDL filenames in its connection string. The UDL file is a resource external to the application that encapsulates connection properties in a separate file. It must be protected using NTFS security to prevent connection information from being exposed or altered. The SQL Server .NET data provider does not support UDL files in its connection string. UDL files are not encrypted; cryptography cannot be used to increase security. NTFS directory and file encryption can secure a UDL file so that even if unauthorized access is gained to the file or the physical disk is stolen, the user ID and password of the user who encrypted the file would still be required to access its contents.

Windows registry

You can store connection strings in the Windows registry as a subkey of HKEY_LOCAL_MACHINE\SOFTWARE. You can encrypt these settings within the registry subkey and restrict access to the subkey to increase the security of this technique. This technique is easy to use because of programmatic support for registry access in .NET classes Registry and RegistryKey in the Microsoft.Win32 namespace.

Storing connection strings in the registry is usually discouraged because of deployment issues; the registry settings must be deployed with the application, defeating

> **NTFS Encryption**
>
> NTFS was enhanced in Windows 2000 with the Encrypted File System (EFS) that provides file- and directory-level encryption. Actually, EFS encrypts only files—directories are simply marked so that new files in the directory are encrypted. Encryption and decryption of files is both automatic and transparent for the user who set the encryption.
>
> Encrypted files are visible to any user who can access the system but the *contents* of the encrypted files can only be viewed by the user who set the encryption. If necessary, standard NT security methods can hide directories and files from view of specific users and user groups.
>
> EFS is a separate mechanism that is used together with the standard security subsystem.

benefits of *xcopy* deployment. Application code can also be restricted in its access to the registry, further complicating deployment.

Custom file

A custom file is any file that is used to for proprietary storage of application settings that are typically used at runtime. There is generally no particular advantage to using a custom file to store connection information so the technique is not recommended. The approach requires extra coding and forces concurrency and other issues to be explicitly addressed.

1.13 Using the Data Link Properties Dialog Box

Problem

You want to display the Data Link Properties dialog box from an application so that users can create their own database connections just as they can from the Server Explorer window in the Visual Studio .NET IDE.

Solution

Use COM interop with the OLE DB Service Component to display the Data Link Properties dialog box.

You'll need a reference to the Primary Interop Assembly (PIA) for ADO provided in the file *ADODB.DLL*; select adodb from the .NET tab in Visual Studio .NET's Add Reference Dialog. You'll also need a reference to the Microsoft OLE DB Service Component 1.0 Type Library from the COM tab in Visual Studio .NET's Add Reference Dialog.

The sample code contains a single event handler:

Data Link Dialog Button.Click
Creates and displays a Data Link Properties dialog box using the Microsoft OLE DB Service Component through COM interop.

The C# code is shown in Example 1-10.

Example 1-10. File: DataLinkDialogForm.cs

```
// Namespaces, variables, and constants
using System;

// ...

private void dataLinkDialogButton_Click(object sender, System.EventArgs e)
{
    ADODB.Connection conn = new ADODB.Connection( );
    object oConn = (object) conn;

    MSDASC.DataLinks dlg = new MSDASC.DataLinks( );
    dlg.PromptEdit(ref oConn);

    connectionStringTextBox.Text = conn.ConnectionString;
}
```

Discussion

COM interop can open a Data Link Properties dialog box allowing a user to select an OLE DB provider and set its properties. You can use the results programmatically to construct the connection string for an ADO.NET connection object at runtime with a GUI (graphical user interface).

1.14   Monitoring Connections

Problem

You want to monitor the opening and closing of connections and the number of connections in the connection pool while an application is running.

Solution

Use the Windows Performance Monitor and the SQL Profiler to monitor connections and connection pooling. See Recipe 1.15 for more information on connection pooling.

Discussion

The following subsections discuss monitoring connection pooling for SQL Server and ODBC .NET Framework data providers.

SQL Server

You can monitor SQL Server connections and connection pooling using the SQL Server Profiler or the Windows Performance Monitor as described in the following subsections.

SQL Server Profiler. To use the SQL Server Profiler to monitor connection pooling:

1. Start the Profiler using one of the following methods
   - From Windows desktop: Start → All Programs → Microsoft SQL Server → Profiler.
   - From SQL Enterprise Manager: Tools → SQL Profiler.
2. When the SQL Server Profiler appears, select File → New → Trace.
3. Supply connection details and click OK. The Trace Properties dialog box will appear.
4. Select the Events tab of the Trace Properties dialog box.
5. In the Selected Events list box, ensure that the Audit Login and Audit Logout events appear beneath the Security Audit node. Remove all other events from the list. Click the Run button to start the trace.
6. The new Profiler window will display a table containing Audit Login events when connections are established and Audit Logout events when connections are closed.

Windows Performance Monitor. To use the Windows Performance Monitor to monitor connection pooling:

1. Start Performance Monitor by selecting Start → All Programs → Administrative Tools → Performance.
2. Add performance counters to monitor connection pooling with one of the following methods:
   - Right-click the graph and select Add Counters from the popup menu.
   - Click the add button above the graph.
3. In the Performance object drop down list, select ".NET CLR Data."

   The SQL Server .NET data provider adds performance counters that can tune connection pooling and troubleshoot pooling problems. Table 1-2 describes the counters.

Table 1-2. SQL Server .NET provider performance counters

Counter	Description
SqlClient: Current # of pooled and non-pooled connections	Current number of connections, both pooled and non-pooled
SqlClient: Current # pooled connections	Current number of pooled connections
SqlClient: Current # connection pools	Current number of connection pools
SqlClient: Peak # pooled connections	The largest number of connections in all pools since the process started
SqlClient: Total # failed connects	The total number of attempts to open a connection that have failed for any reason

4. Select the counters to monitor from the list box and click the Add button. Click the Close button.

ODBC

To enable ODBC performance monitoring:

1. Open the ODBC Data Source Administrator in Control Panel → Administrative Tools.
2. Select the Connection Pooling tab.
3. Ensure that the PerfMon Enable checkbox is checked.
4. Start Performance Monitor by selecting Start → All Programs → Administrative Tools → Performance.
5. Add performance counters to monitor connection pooling with one of the following methods:
   - Right-click the graph and select Add Counters from the popup menu.
   - Click the add button above the graph.
6. In the Performance object drop down list, select ODBC Connection Pooling. Table 1-3 describes the ODBC Connection Pooling counters.

Table 1-3. ODBC connection pooling counters

Counter	Description
Connections Currently Active	Number of connections currently used by applications
Connections Currently Free	Number of connections in the pool available for requests
Connections/Sec Hard	Number of real connections per second
Connections/Sec Soft	Number of connections server from the pool per second
Disconnections/Sec Hard	Number of real disconnects per second
Disconnections/Sec Soft	Number of disconnects from the pool per second

1.15   Taking Advantage of Connection Pooling

Problem

You need to understand connecting pooling and make sure that your applications use it.

Solution

To effectively use connection pooling, you need to understand the concepts underlying connection pooling, how connection pooling is implemented by the major .NET data providers, and how to ensure that connection pooling is used by an application.

Discussion

Connection pooling allows an application to reuse connections from a pool instead of repeatedly creating and destroying new connections. Connection pooling can significantly improve the performance and scalability of applications by allowing a smaller number of connections to service the connection requirements of an application and because the overhead of establishing a new connection is eliminated.

A connection pool is created for each unique connection string. An algorithm associates items in the pool based on an exact match with the connection string; this includes capitalization, order of name value pairs, and even spaces between name/value pairs. Dynamically generated connection strings must be identical so that connection pooling is used. If delegation is used, there will be one pool per delegate user. When transactions are used, one pool is created per transaction context. (For more information, see Recipe 1.17.) When the connection pool is created, connection objects are created and added to the pool to satisfy the minimum pool size specified.

When a connection is requested by an application and the maximum pool size has been reached, the request is queued. The request is satisfied by reallocating a connection that is released back to the pool when the Connection is closed or disposed. The connection pool manager removes expired connections and connections that have had their connection with the server severed from the pool.

The Connection object should be closed as soon as it is no longer needed so that it is added to or returned to the connection pool. This is done by calling either the Close( ) or Dispose( ) method of the Connection. Connections that are not explicitly closed might not be added to or returned to the connection pool.

> The DataAdapter automatically opens and closes a Connection as required if it is not already open when a method such as Fill( ), FillSchema( ), or Update( ) is called. The Connection must be explicitly closed if it is already open prior to the DataAdapter operation.

The following subsections detail connection pooling for specific .NET Framework data providers.

SQL Server and Oracle

The .NET data providers for SQL Server and Oracle provide efficient, transaction-aware support for connection pooling. Pools are created for each process and not destroyed until the process ends. Connection pooling is enabled by default.

Controlling SQL Server and Oracle .NET data provider connection pooling with connection string attribute/value pairs is discussed in Recipe 1.16.

OLE DB

The OLE DB .NET data provider pools connections by using resource pooling provided by the OLE DB core components.

The default OLE DB services that are enabled for a provider are specified by the value for the registry `HKEY_CLASSES_ROOT\CLSID\<Provider's CLSID>\OLE_DBSERVICES` DWORD value. Table 1-4 describes the alternatives.

Table 1-4. OLE DB services enabled values

OLE_DBSERVICES value	Description
0xffffffff	All services (default).
0xfffffffe	All services except Pooling and AutoEnlistment.
0xfffffffb	All services except Client Cursor.
0xfffffff0	All services except Pooling, AutoEnlistment, and Client Cursor.
0x00000000	No services.
missing value	No aggregation. All services are disabled.

You can override the default OLE DB provider services by specifying a value for the OLE DB Services attribute in the connection string. Table 1-5 describes possible values.

Table 1-5. OLE DB services connection string values

OLE DB Services attribute value	Default services enabled
-1	All services (default)
-2	All services except Pooling and AutoEnlistment
-5	All services except Client Cursor
-7	All services except Pooling, AutoEnlistment, and Client Cursor
0	No services

The following three configurable settings control OLE DB connection pooling:

SPTimeout
> The length of time in seconds that an unused connection remains in the pool before it is released. This can be configured for each provider and defaults to 60 seconds.

Retry Wait
> The length of time in seconds before an attempt to acquire a connection is reattempted when the server is not responding. This is global to all providers and defaults to 64 seconds.

ExpBackOff
> The factor by which the retry wait time is increased when a connection attempt fails before reattempting the connection. This is global to all providers and defaults to a factor of 2.

OLE DB connection pooling is enabled by default; you can control it in three different ways:

- Specify a value for the OLE DB Services attribute in the connection string.
- Edit the registry to enable or disable pooling for an individual provider or globally by changing registry values. For more information, see Recipe 1.16.
- Use the OLE DB API (Application Programming Interface) from an application to enable or disable connection pooling. The SPTimeout and Retry Wait can be configured programmatically only by manipulating the registry entries. For more information about the OLE DB API, see the *OLE DB Programmer's Reference* in MSDN Library.

ODBC

The ODBC .NET data provider pools connections by using the connection pooling provided by the ODBC Driver Manager (DM). Pooling parameters for an ODBC driver affect all applications that use that driver, unless changed from within a native ODBC application.

The following two configurable settings control ODBC connection pooling:

CPTimeout
> The length of time in seconds that an unused connection remains in the pool before it is released.

Wait Retry
> The length of time before an attempt to acquire a connection is reattempted when the server is not responding.

Connection pooling is enabled by default. You can enable, disable, and configure it in three ways:

- Use the ODBC Data Source Administrator, introduced with ODBC 3.5 (MDAC 1.5), to enable or disable pooling for the entire driver and to control the CPTimeout and Wait Retry settings.
- Edit the registry. For more information, see Recipe 1.16.
- Use the ODBC API from an ODBC application to limit the scope of pooling to the environment handler or to the driver, and to configure other pooling options. For more information about the ODBC API, see the *ODBC Programmer's Reference* in the MSDN Library.

1.16   Setting Connection Pooling Options

Problem

You need to know the different connection pooling options and how you can control them.

Solution

Use the connection string to control connection pooling for the SQL Server, OLE DB .NET, Oracle, or ODBC.NET data provider.

The sample code contains a method and four event handlers:

Form.Load
> Creates a Connection, attaches an event handler to its StateChange event, and sets default properties for controls on the form that are used to specify connection properties. The UpdateConnection( ) method is called to dynamically construct a connection string from the specified properties.

UpdateConnectionString( )
> This method dynamically constructs a connection string from the connection string properties specified by the user in text boxes on the form. This method is called to update the connection string when the user changes the value of any of the controls used to specify connection string properties.

Open Button.Click
> Opens the Connection that is based on the connection string constructed in the UpdateConnectionString( ) method.

Close Button.Click
> Closes the connection string.

Connection.StateChange
> Displays original and current state information about the connection when its state changes.

The C# code is shown in Example 1-11.

Example 1-11. File: ConnectionPoolingOptionsForm.cs

```csharp
// Namespaces, variables, and constants
using System;
using System.Configuration;
using System.Windows.Forms;
using System.Data;
using System.Data.SqlClient;

private SqlConnection conn;

// ...

private void ConnectionPoolingOptionsForm_Load(object sender,
    System.EventArgs e)
{
    conn = new SqlConnection( );
    conn.StateChange += new StateChangeEventHandler(conn_StateChange);

    connectionStringTextBox.Text =
        ConfigurationSettings.AppSettings["Sql_ConnectString"];
    connectTimeoutTextBox.Text = "15";
    connectLifetimeTextBox.Text = "0";
    minPoolSizeTextBox.Text = "0";
    maxPoolSizeTextBox.Text = "100";
    poolCheckBox.Checked = true;

    UpdateConnectionString( );
}

private void UpdateConnectionString( )
{
    connectionStringTextBox.Text =
        ConfigurationSettings.AppSettings["Sql_ConnectString"] +
        "Connection Timeout = " + connectTimeoutTextBox.Text + ";" +
        "Connection Lifetime = " + connectLifetimeTextBox.Text + ";" +
        "Min Pool Size = " + minPoolSizeTextBox.Text + ";" +
        "Max Pool Size = " + maxPoolSizeTextBox.Text + ";" +
        "Pooling = " + poolCheckBox.Checked.ToString( );
}

private void openButton_Click(object sender, System.EventArgs e)
{
    try
    {
        conn.ConnectionString = connectionStringTextBox.Text;
        conn.Open( );
    }
    catch(SqlException ex)
    {
        MessageBox.Show("ERROR: " + ex.ToString( ), "Open Connection",
            MessageBoxButtons.OK, MessageBoxIcon.Error);
    }
```

Example 1-11. File: ConnectionPoolingOptionsForm.cs (continued)

```
    catch(InvalidOperationException ex)
    {
        MessageBox.Show("ERROR: " + ex.ToString(), "Open Connection",
            MessageBoxButtons.OK, MessageBoxIcon.Error);
    }
}

private void closeButton_Click(object sender, System.EventArgs e)
{
    conn.Close();
}

private void conn_StateChange(object sender, StateChangeEventArgs e)
{
    connectionStateTextBox.Text =
        "Connection.StateChange event occurred" +
        Environment.NewLine +
        "OriginalState = " + e.OriginalState.ToString() +
        Environment.NewLine +
        "CurrentState = " + e.CurrentState.ToString();
}
```

Discussion

The following subsections describe how to control connection pooling for SQL Server, Oracle, OLE DB, and ODBC .NET data providers.

SQL Server

The connection string attributes that control connection pooling for the SQL Server .NET data provider are described in Table 1-6.

Table 1-6. SQL Server connection string pooling attributes

Attribute	Description
Connection Lifetime	Length of time in seconds after creation after which a connection is destroyed. The default is 0 indicating that connection will have the maximum time-out.
Connection Reset	Specifies whether the connection is reset when removed from the pool. The default is true.
Enlist	Specifies whether the connection is automatically enlisted in the current transaction context of the creation thread if that transaction context exists. The default is true.
Max Pool Size	Maximum number of connections allowed in the pool. The default is 100.
Min Pool Size	Minimum number of connections maintained in the pool. The default is 0.
Pooling	Specifies whether the connection is drawn from a pool or when necessary created and added to a pool. The default is true.

Oracle

The connection string attributes that control connection pooling for the Oracle .NET data provider are described in Table 1-7.

Table 1-7. Oracle connection string pooling attributes

Attribute	Description
Connection Lifetime	Length of time in seconds after creation after which a connection is destroyed. The default is 0 indicating that connection will have the maximum time-out.
Enlist	Specifies whether the connection is automatically enlisted in the current transaction context of the creation thread if that transaction context exists. The default is true.
Max Pool Size	Maximum number of connections allowed in the pool. The default is 100.
Min Pool Size	Minimum number of connections maintained in the pool. The default is 0.
Pooling	Specifies whether the connection is drawn from a pool or when necessary created and added to a pool. The default is true.

OLE DB

The OLE DB .NET data provider uses resource pooling support provided by the OLE DB Service component. You can override the default OLE DB provider services by specifying a value for the OLE DB Services attribute in the connection string. For more information, see Recipe 1.15.

OLE DB Resource pooling configuration is controlled using registry entries. There is no user interface to configure these entries—the registry must be edited directly. The registry entries are identified by the *<Provider's CLSID>*. CLSID values for some Microsoft OLE DB providers are:

- SQLOLEDB (SQL Server):

      HKEY_CLASSES_ROOT\CLSID\{0C7FF16C-38E3-11d0-97AB-00C04FC2AD98}

- Microsoft.Jet.OLEDB.4.0 (Jet):

      HKEY_CLASSES_ROOT\CLSID\{dee35070-506b-11cf-b1aa-00aa00b8de95}

- MSDAORA (Oracle):

      HKEY_CLASSES_ROOT\CLSID\{e8cc4cbe-fdff-11d0-b865-00a0c9081c1d}

- MSDASQL (OLE DB Provider for ODBC):

      HKEY_CLASSES_ROOT\CLSID\{c8b522cb-5cf3-11ce-ade5-00aa0044773d}

Some OLE DB provider configuration options set by registry entries are:

    HKEY_CLASSES_ROOT\CLSID\<Provider's CLSID>\SPTimeout

The session pooling timeout is the number of seconds that an unused session remains in the pool before timing out and being closed. This is a DWORD value with a default of *60* if the registry entry is not specified.

The following registry entries are global to all providers:

`HKEY_LOCAL_MACHINE\SOFTWARE\Microsoft\DataAccess\Session Pooling\Retry Wait`
> The amount of time that the service component will wait until attempting to contact the server again in the event of a failed connection attempt. This is a `DWORD` value with a default of *64* if no registry value is present.

`HKEY_LOCAL_MACHINE\SOFTWARE\Microsoft\DataAccess\Session Pooling\ExpBackOff`
> Determines the factor by which the service components will wait between reconnect attempts in the event of a failed connection attempt. This is a `DWORD` value with a default of *2* if no registry value is present.

`HKEY_CLASSES_ROOT\CLSID\{2206CDB0-19C1-11D1-89E0-00C04FD7A829}`
> A `DWORD` value that specifies the maximum lifetime in seconds of a pooled connection. The default is *600*. The CLSID is for the MSDAINITIALIZE component, which is the OLE DB service component manager that is used to parse OLE DB connection strings and initialize the appropriate provider.

ODBC

The ODBC .NET data provider uses the connection pooling support provided by the ODBC Driver Manager (DM). Connection pooling is supported by Version 3.0 or later of the ODBC DM; the version of the ODBC driver does not matter.

The following two registry settings control ODBC connection pooling:

`Wait Retry`
> The time in seconds that that the pool is blocked when the server is not responding. This setting affects all applications using the ODBC driver. The registry key specifies a REG_SZ value:
>
> `HKEY_LOCAL_MACHINE\SOFTWARE\ODBC\ODBCINST.INI\<Driver_Name>\CPTimeout`

`CPTimeout`
> The time in seconds that unused connections remain in the pool. This setting affects all ODBC drivers on the system. The registry key specifies a REG_SZ value:
>
> `HKEY_LOCAL_MACHINE\SOFTWARE\ODBC\ODBCINST.INI\ODBC Connection Pooling`

You can control ODBC connection pooling in three ways:

- Using the `ODBC Data Source Administrator` to enable or disable pooling for the entire driver, and to control the `CPTimeout` and `Wait Retry` settings
- Editing the registry settings described above.
- Using the ODBC API to control pooling options from an ODBC application. For more information about the ODBC API, see the *ODBC Programmer's Reference* in the MSDN Library.

1.17 Using Transactions with Pooled Connections

Problem

You want to use connection pooling with transactions in your .NET application to maximize performance.

Solution

The discussion explains how to use connection pooling with transactions.

Discussion

Connections participating in transactions are drawn from the connection pool and assigned based on an exact match with the transaction context of the requesting thread and with the connection string.

Each connection pool is divided into a subdivision for connections without a transaction context and zero or more subdivisions for connections associated with a particular transaction context. Each of these subdivisions, whether associated with a transaction context or not, uses connection pooling based on exact matching of the connection string as described in Recipe 1.15.

When a thread associated with a particular transaction context requests a connection, one from the appropriate pool enlisted with that transaction is automatically returned.

When a connection is closed it is returned to the appropriate subdivision in the connection pool based on the transaction context. This allows a connection to be closed without generating an error even if a distributed transaction is still pending. The transaction can committed or aborted later.

1.18 Changing the Database for an Open Connection

Problem

You want to change the database that a connection uses without recreating the connection.

Solution

Use the ChangeDatabase( ) method to change the database for a connection.

The sample code creates a Connection to the Northwind database using the SQL Server .NET data provider. The connection is changed to use the pubs database. Finally the connection is closed. The Database property of the SqlConnection object is displayed throughout the sample for the different connection states.

The C# code is shown in Example 1-12.

Example 1-12. File: ChangeDatabaseForm.cs

```
// Namespaces, variables, and constants
using System;
using System.Configuration;
using System.Text;
using System.Data;
using System.Data.SqlClient;

// ...

StringBuilder result = new StringBuilder( );

// Create the connection accessing Northwind database.
SqlConnection conn = new SqlConnection(
    ConfigurationSettings.AppSettings["Sql_ConnectString"]);
result.Append("Connection String:" + Environment.NewLine);
result.Append(conn.ConnectionString + Environment.NewLine + Environment.NewLine);

// Open the connection.
conn.Open( );
result.Append("Connection.State: " + conn.State + Environment.NewLine);
result.Append("Database: " + conn.Database + Environment.NewLine);

// Change the database to pubs.
conn.ChangeDatabase("pubs");
result.Append("Database: " + conn.Database + Environment.NewLine);

// Close the connection.
conn.Close( );
result.Append("Connection.State: " + conn.State + Environment.NewLine);
result.Append("Database: " + conn.Database);

resultTextBox.Text = result.ToString( );
```

Discussion

The ChangeDatabase( ) method is defined in the IDbConnection interface that represents a connection to a data source and is implemented by .NET data providers for relational databases including those for SQL Server, Oracle, and OLE DB. The ChangeDatabase( ) method is used to change the current database for an open connection. It takes a single parameter that specifies the name of the database to use in place of the current database. The name of the database must be valid or an ArgumentException will be raised. If the connection is not open when the method is called, an InvalidOperationException is raised. A provider-specific exception is raised if the database cannot be changed for any reason.

The Database property of the Connection object is updated dynamically and returns the current database for an open connection or the name of a database that will be used by a closed connection when it is opened.

When the Connection is closed after ChangeDatabase( ) is called, the database is reset to that specified in the original connection string.

1.19   Connecting to a Text File

Problem

You want to use ADO.NET to access data stored in a text file.

Solution

Use the OLE DB Jet provider to access data in a text file.

The sample code creates an OleDbDataAdapter that uses the Jet OLE DB provider to load the contents of the text file *Categories.txt*, shown in Example 1-13, into a DataTable and displays the contents in a data grid on the form.

Example 1-13. File: Categories.txt

```
"CategoryID","CategoryName","Description"
1,"Beverages","Soft drinks, coffees, teas, beers, and ales"
2,"Condiments","Sweet and savory sauces, relishes, spreads, and seasonings"
3,"Confections","Desserts, candies, and sweet breads"
4,"Dairy Products","Cheeses"
5,"Grains/Cereals","Breads, crackers, pasta, and cereal"
6,"Meat/Poultry","Prepared meats"
7,"Produce","Dried fruit and bean curd"
8,"Seafood","Seaweed and fish"
```

The C# code is shown in Example 1-14.

Example 1-14. File: ConnectTextFileForm.cs

```
// Namespaces, variables, and constants
using System;
using System.Configuration;
using System.Windows.Forms;
using System.Data;
using System.Data.OleDb;

// ...

// Create the data adapter to retrieve all rows from text file.
OleDbDataAdapter da =
```

Example 1-14. File: ConnectTextFileForm.cs (continued)

```
    new OleDbDataAdapter("SELECT * FROM [Categories.txt]",
    ConfigurationSettings.AppSettings["TextFile_0119_ConnectString"]);

// Create and fill the table.
DataTable dt = new DataTable("Categories");
da.Fill(dt);

// Bind the default view of the table to the grid.
categoriesDataGrid.DataSource = dt.DefaultView;
```

Discussion

The Jet OLE DB provider can read records from and insert records into a text file data source. The Jet database engine can access other database file formats through Indexed Sequential Access Method (ISAM) drivers specified in the `Extended Properties` attribute of the connection. Text files are supported with the text source database type as shown in the following example:

```
Provider=Microsoft.Jet.OLEDB.4.0;Data Source=c:\MyTextFileDirectory;
    Extended Properties="text;HDR=yes;FMT=Delimited";
```

The `Extended Properties` attribute can, in addition to the ISAM version property, specify whether or not tables include headers as field names in the first row of a range using an `HDR` attribute.

It is not possible to define all characteristics of a text file through the connection string. You can access files that use non-standard text delimiters and fixed-width text files by creating a *schema.ini* file in the same directory as the text file. As an example, a possible *schema.ini* file for the *Categories.txt* file used in this solution is:

```
[Categories.txt]
Format=CSVDelimited
ColNameHeader=True
MaxScanRows=0
Character=OEM
Col1=CategoryID Long Width 4
Col2=CategoryName Text Width 15
Col3=Description Text Width 100
```

The *schema.ini* file provides the following schema information about the data in the text file:

- Filename
- File format
- Field names, widths, and data types
- Character set
- Special data type conversions

The first entry in the *schema.ini* file is the text filename enclosed in square brackets. For example:

```
[Categories.txt]
```

The `Format` option specifies the text file format. Table 1-8 describes the different options.

Table 1-8. Schema.ini format options

Format	Description
CSV Delimited	Fields are delimited with commas: `Format=CSVDelimited` This is the default value.
Custom Delimited	Fields are delimited with a custom character. You can use any single character except the double quotation mark (") as a delimiter: `Format=Delimited(customCharacter)`
Fixed Length	Fields are fixed length: `Format=FixedLength` If the `ColumnNameHeader` option is `True`, the first line containing the column names must be comma-delimited.
Tab Delimited	Fields are delimited with tabs: `Format=TabDelimited`

You can specify the fields in the text file in two ways:

- Include the field names in the first row of the text file and set the `ColNameHeader` option to `True`.
- Identify each column using the format `ColN` (where *N* is the one-based column number) and specify the name, width, and data type for each column.

The `MaxScanRows` option indicates how many rows should be scanned to automatically determine column type. A value of 0 indicates that all rows should be scanned.

The `ColN` entries specify the name, width, and data type for each column. This entry is required for fixed-length formats and optional for character-delimited formats. The syntax of the `ColN` entry is:

```
ColN=columnName dataType [Width n]
```

The parameters in the entry are:

columnName
> The name of the column. If the column name contains spaces, it must be enclosed in double quotation marks.

dataType
> The data type of the column. This value can be `Bit`, `Byte`, `Currency`, `DateTime`, `Double`, `Long`, `Memo`, `Short`, `Single`, or `Text`.

DateTime values must be in one of the following formats: dd-mmm-yy, mm-dd-yy, mmm-dd-yy, yyyy-mm-dd, or yyyy-mmm-dd, where mm is the month number and mmm are the characters specifying the month.

Width *n*

The literal value Width followed by the integer value specifying the column width.

The Character option specifies the character set; you can set it to either ANSI or OEM.

CHAPTER 2

Retrieving and Managing Data

2.0   Introduction

The DataSet is a disconnected, in-memory relational database that provides sophisti-cated navigational capabilities. It acts as a container for other objects including DataTable, DataColumn, DataRow, and DataRelation. The DataAdapter works with the DataSet to update the data source with changes made offline to the DataSet. You can also data bind a DataSet to a variety of Windows Forms and Web Forms controls, in particular, any control that supports the IList interface. The DataSet maintains both current and original versions of its data. Although data appears to be changed, it is not permanently changed until the AcceptChanges( ) method is called either explic-itly or implicitly to commit the changes. Recipe 2.6 shows how to access rows marked for deletion.

The DataReader provides forward-only, read-only access to a result set. The DataReader offers the best performance for accessing data by avoiding the overhead associated with the DataSet. The Connection object underlying a DataReader remains open and cannot be used for any other purpose while data is being accessed. This makes the DataReader unsuitable for communicating data remotely between application tiers, or interacting with the data dynamically. If you want to discard a result set in a DataReader before the entire result set has been read, call the Cancel( ) method of the DataReader before calling the Close( ) method. This discards the results on the server so they are not transmitted to the client. Simply calling Close( ) causes the remain-ing results to be pulled to the client to empty the stream. Since the DataReader reads a result set stream directly from a connection, there is no way to know the number of records in a DataReader. Recipe 2.7 demonstrates techniques that simulate a record count for a DataReader and discusses limitations of the techniques.

You can define DataSet and DataReader object schemas programmatically or infer them from a database schema. Retrieving schema information from the database has its limitations. For example, data relations cannot be created in a DataSet from the database schema.

The DataSet is data source independent and uses .NET Framework data types to define column schema in tables. These data types are not the same as .NET data provider types; the provider data types are mapped to .NET Framework data types. Recipe 2.8 shows the mappings for SQL Server, Oracle, OLE DB, and ODBC .NET data providers to .NET Framework data types as well as the DataReader type accessors for each.

The DataAdapter can map table and column names in the database to tables and columns with different names in a DataTable. This allows the application to use different column and table names than are used by the database. The DataAdapter automatically maps names when retrieving and updating data. Recipe 2.16 demonstrates table and column mapping.

A variety of error information is available when a DataAdapter fails while updating data. Recipe 2.15 shows what error information is available and how to work with it.

In addition to recipes for working with the DataSet, DataReader, and DataAdapter classes, this chapter covers the following:

Strongly typed DataSets
> A strongly typed DataSet is a collection of classes that inherit from and extend the DataSet, DataTable, and DataRow classes, providing additional properties, methods, and events, and making them easier to use. Because they are typed, you'll get type mismatch and other errors at compilation rather than at runtime (also, strongly typed DataSets work with Visual Studio .NET's IntelliSense). They are, however, slightly slower than untyped DataSet objects because of extra overhead. Because they are typed, they can make maintaining interfaces in distributed applications more complicated and difficult to administer. Recipe 2.3 discusses the different ways to create and use a strongly typed DataSet. Recipes 2.18 and 2.19 show how to override the default naming used by and behavior of a strongly typed DataSet.

Stored procedures
> Stored procedure output parameters are generally used to return results from a single row and are slightly faster than a DataReader for this purpose with connection pooling enabled; without connection pooling, the opposite is true. Additionally, the DataReader is capable of returning metadata for the row. Accessing output parameters is straightforward with disconnected classes and a data adapter, but not when using the DataReader. Recipe 2.9 shows how. Stored procedures can also return a *return value* parameter, which usually returns status or error information. Recipe 2.12 shows how get a stored procedure return value.

> Passing input arguments to a stored procedure is straightforward. Recipe 2.14 shows how to pass null values.

SQL has a RAISERROR function that lets you generate custom errors from the stored procedure and return them to the caller. Recipe 2.10 shows how to raise and handle stored procedure errors.

In addition to stored procedures, Oracle has *packages* that serve as containers for stored procedures and functions. Recipe 2.20 shows how to use Oracle packages from ADO.NET.

Scalar functions are routines that take one or more parameters and return a single value. Recipe 2.13 shows how to execute a scalar function and get the return value.

In addition to using parameters with stored procedures, ADO.NET allows you to execute parameterized SQL statements. Recipe 2.21 shows how to create and execute these statements.

Queries

SQL Server supports *batch queries* that return multiple result sets from a single request to the server. Recipe 2.4 shows how to process the result sets using both a DataSet and a DataReader.

Sometimes it's useful to know whether a query returned any records; therefore, Recipe 2.11 shows you how to find out when using both a DataTable and a DataReader.

Web services and messaging

Web services allow distributed applications running on disparate platforms to communicate using open standards and protocols. Recipe 2.5 shows how to create a web service that processes a query request, and how to call the web service from a .NET application.

Messaging allows applications running on disparate platforms to communicate whether they are connected or disconnected. Recipe 2.22 shows how to use messaging to query a database.

2.1   Retrieving Hierarchical Data into a DataSet

Problem

You want to fill a DataSet with parent and related child data, even if the DataSet already has a schema that includes the relationship.

Solution

There are several techniques you can use to load parent and child data into a DataSet.

The sample code contains three event handlers:

Form.Load

Sets up the sample by creating a DataSet with table schemas for both the Orders table and the Order Details table from Northwind and a DataRelation object relating these two tables. The default view of the parent table, Orders, is bound to a data grid on the form.

Load DataSet Button.Click

Starts by clearing the data from the DataSet and refreshing the data grid. DataAdapter objects are created for both the parent and the child table. The Orders and Order Details are then filled using data adapters in the sequence specified and enforcing constraints during the load as specified by the user.

The C# code is shown in Example 2-1.

Example 2-1. File: HierarchicalDataSetForm.cs

```
// Namespaces, variables, and constants
using System;
using System.Configuration;
using System.Windows.Forms;
using System.Data;
using System.Data.SqlClient;

private DataSet ds;

// ...

private void HierarchicalDataSetForm_Load(object sender,
    System.EventArgs e)
{
    ds = new DataSet( );

    // Get the schema for the Orders table.
    DataTable parentTable = new DataTable("Orders");
    SqlDataAdapter da = new SqlDataAdapter("SELECT * FROM Orders",
        ConfigurationSettings.AppSettings["Sql_ConnectString"]);
    da.FillSchema(parentTable, SchemaType.Source);
    ds.Tables.Add(parentTable);

    // Get the schema for the Order Details table.
    DataTable childTable = new DataTable("Order Details");
    da = new SqlDataAdapter("SELECT * FROM [Order Details]",
        ConfigurationSettings.AppSettings["Sql_ConnectString"]);
    da.FillSchema(childTable, SchemaType.Source);
    ds.Tables.Add(childTable);

    // Add the relation between the tables.
    DataRelation dr = new DataRelation("Order_OrderDetails_Relation",
        parentTable.Columns["OrderID"], childTable.Columns["OrderID"]);
    ds.Relations.Add(dr);
```

Example 2-1. File: HierarchicalDataSetForm.cs (continued)

```
    // Bind the default view of the Orders table with the grid.
    dataGrid.DataSource = parentTable.DefaultView;
}

private void loadDataSetButton_Click(object sender, System.EventArgs e)
{
    // Remove all data from the DataSet and refresh the grid.
    ds.Clear( );
    dataGrid.Refresh( );

    // Create parent and child data adapters.
    SqlDataAdapter daParent = new SqlDataAdapter("SELECT * FROM Orders",
        ConfigurationSettings.AppSettings["Sql_ConnectString"]);
    SqlDataAdapter daChild = new SqlDataAdapter(
        "SELECT * FROM [Order Details]",
        ConfigurationSettings.AppSettings["Sql_ConnectString"]);

    // Enforce constraints as specified by user.
    ds.EnforceConstraints = (enforceConstraintsCheckBox.Checked);

    try
    {
        if (loadParentFirstRadioButton.Checked)
        {
            // Load parent data first.
            daParent.Fill(ds, "Orders");
            daChild.Fill(ds, "Order Details");
        }
        else
        {
            // Load child data first.
            daChild.Fill(ds, "Order Details");
            daParent.Fill(ds, "Orders");
        }
    }
    catch (Exception ex)
    {
        MessageBox.Show(ex.Message);
        return;
    }

    ds.EnforceConstraints = true;
}
```

Discussion

By default, a DataRelation is created with constraints as in the example; however, an
overloaded constructor can override this behavior if necessary. If constraints are created, it is important that each record in the child table refers to a valid parent record,
otherwise a ConstraintException is raised. Two techniques can be used to load parent

and related child data without error into a DataSet with a schema that includes data relations defined:

- Load data from the parent tables before loading data from the child table. This ensures that each record in the child table refers to a valid parent record.
- The EnforceConstraints property of the DataSet indicates whether constraint rules are followed when data is added to or modified in the DataSet. Turn constraints off by setting the EnforceConstraints property to false prior to loading the data and back to true once the data is loaded. With this approach the order in which the data is loaded is not important. If one or more constraints cannot be enforced when EnforceConstraints is set back to true, a ConstraintException will be raised and EnforceConstraints stay set to false.

2.2   Building a DataSet Programmatically

Problem

You want to build a DataSet programmatically—including adding tables, columns, primary keys, and relations—from a schema that you have designed.

Solution

The following example shows how to build a complex DataSet programmatically, including how to build and add tables, columns, primary key constraints, relations, and column mappings. Use this as a template for building your own DataSet.

The sample code creates a DataSet. A DataTable object is created representing the Orders table in Northwind. Columns are added, including the auto-increment primary key, to the table. The table is added to the DataSet. The process is repeated for a DataTable representing the Order Details table in Northwind. A DataRelation is created relating the two tables. Finally, the tables are filled with data from Northwind.

The C# code is shown in Example 2-2.

Example 2-2. File: BuildDataSetProgramaticallyForm.cs

```
// Namespaces, variables, and constants
using System;
using System.Configuration;
using System.Data;
using System.Data.SqlClient;

// ...

// Create the DataSet.
DataSet ds = new DataSet("MyDataSet");
```

Example 2-2. File: BuildDataSetProgramaticallyForm.cs (continued)

```csharp
// Build the Orders (parent) table.
DataTable parentTable = new DataTable("Orders");

DataColumnCollection cols = parentTable.Columns;
// Add the identity field.
DataColumn column = cols.Add("OrderID", typeof(System.Int32));
column.AutoIncrement = true;
column.AutoIncrementSeed = -1;
column.AutoIncrementStep = -1;
// Add the other fields.
cols.Add("CustomerID", typeof(System.String)).MaxLength = 5;
cols.Add("EmployeeID", typeof(System.Int32));
cols.Add("OrderDate", typeof(System.DateTime));
cols.Add("RequiredDate", typeof(System.DateTime));
cols.Add("ShippedDate", typeof(System.DateTime));
cols.Add("ShipVia", typeof(System.Int32));
cols.Add("Freight", typeof(System.Decimal));
cols.Add("ShipName", typeof(System.String)).MaxLength = 40;
cols.Add("ShipAddress", typeof(System.String)).MaxLength = 60;
cols.Add("ShipCity", typeof(System.String)).MaxLength = 15;
cols.Add("ShipRegion", typeof(System.String)).MaxLength = 15;
cols.Add("ShipPostalCode", typeof(System.String)).MaxLength = 10;
cols.Add("ShipCountry", typeof(System.String)).MaxLength = 15;
// Set the primary key.
parentTable.PrimaryKey = new DataColumn[] {cols["OrderID"]};
// Add the Orders table to the DataSet.
ds.Tables.Add(parentTable);

// Build the Order Details (child) table.
DataTable childTable = new DataTable("Order Details");

cols = childTable.Columns;
// Add the PK fields.
cols.Add("OrderID", typeof(System.Int32)).AllowDBNull = false;
cols.Add("ProductID", typeof(System.Int32)).AllowDBNull = false;
// Add the other fields.
cols.Add("UnitPrice", typeof(System.Decimal)).AllowDBNull = false;
cols.Add("Quantity", typeof(System.Int16)).AllowDBNull = false;
cols.Add("Discount", typeof(System.Single)).AllowDBNull = false;
// Set the primary key.
childTable.PrimaryKey = new DataColumn[]
    {
        cols["OrderID"],
        cols["ProductID"]
    };
// Add the Order Details table to the DataSet.
ds.Tables.Add(childTable);

// Add the relationship between parent and child tables.
ds.Relations.Add("Order_OrderDetails_Relation",
    parentTable.Columns["OrderID"], childTable.Columns["OrderID"], true);
```

Example 2-2. File: BuildDataSetProgramaticallyForm.cs (continued)

```
// Fill the tables from the data source.
SqlDataAdapter da;
String sqlText;

sqlText = "SELECT OrderID, CustomerID, EmployeeID, OrderDate, " +
    "RequiredDate, ShippedDate, ShipVia, Freight, ShipName, " +
    "ShipAddress, ShipCity, ShipRegion, ShipPostalCode, ShipCountry " +
    "FROM Orders";
da = new SqlDataAdapter(sqlText,
    ConfigurationSettings.AppSettings["Sql_ConnectString"]);
da.Fill(parentTable);

sqlText = "SELECT OrderID, ProductID, UnitPrice, Quantity, Discount " +
    "FROM [Order Details]";
da = new SqlDataAdapter(sqlText,
    ConfigurationSettings.AppSettings["Sql_ConnectString"]);
da.Fill(childTable);
```

Discussion

The steps to build a complex DataSet programmatically, as shown in the code for the solution, are:

1. Design the DataSet identifying the tables, columns, indexes, constraints, and data relations that need to be created.

2. Create a new DataSet, naming it in the constructor.

3. Create a new DataTable, naming it in the constructor.

4. Add a column to the ColumnCollection of the table using the Add( ) method exposed by the Columns property of the DataTable specifying the name and data type of the column. If the column is a character-type column, define its maximum length. If the column is an auto-increment column, set the AutoIncrement property to true and set both the AutoIncrementSeed and AutoIncrementStep properties of the column to -1. (For more information about using auto-increment columns, see Recipe 4.1). Repeat step 4 for each column in the table.

5. Define the primary key for the table by setting the PrimaryKey property of the DataTable to the array of primary key DataColumn objects.

6. Add the new table to the DataSet using the Add( ) method of the DataTableCollection exposed by the Tables property of the DataSet.

7. Repeat steps 3–6 for each table in the DataSet.

8. Create a data relationship between two related tables in the DataSet by using the Add( ) method of the DataRelationCollection exposed by the Relations property of the DataSet. Specify the relationship name, the related columns, and whether constraints are to be created when calling the Add( ) method. Repeat step 8 for each data relationship in the DataSet.

The steps continue, demonstrating how to fill the new DataSet:

9. To fill the DataSet with data from the data source, create a DataAdapter defining the SQL select statement and the connection string in the constructor.

10. Use the Fill( ) method of the DataSet to fill the table. Specify the table name to be filled in the second argument of the Fill( ) method.

11. Repeat steps 9 and 10 for each table to be filled. See Recipe 2.1 for information about how to fill related tables from the data source without raising constraint violation errors.

2.3   Creating a Strongly Typed DataSet

Problem

You want to create a strongly typed object wrapper around a DataSet.

Solution

Use one of the three techniques shown in the discussion to create a strongly typed DataSet using either the Visual Studio .NET IDE or a command line approach.

Discussion

A strongly typed DataSet is a collection of classes that inherit from and extend the DataSet, DataTable, and DataRow classes, and provide additional properties, methods, and events based on the DataSet schema. You can use all of the functionality in classes from which the strongly typed classes inherit in the same way as with untyped classes.

A strongly typed DataSet class contains, in addition to a single class extending the DataSet class, three classes for each table in the DataSet extending each of the DataTable, DataRow, and DataRowChangeEvent classes. This recipe describes these classes and discusses their commonly used methods and properties.

There is a class named *TableName*DataTable for each table in the strongly typed DataSet. It has the base class DataTable. Table 2-1 lists commonly used methods of this class specific to the strongly typed DataSet.

Table 2-1. TableNameDataTable methods

Method	Description
Add*TableName*Row( )	Adds a row to the table. The method has two overloads: one takes a *TableName*Row object as the argument, while the other takes a set of arguments containing the column values.
FindBy*PrimaryKeyField1* ... *PrimaryKeyFieldN*( )	Takes *N* arguments which are the values of the primary key fields of the row to find. Returns a *TableName*Row object, if found.
New*TableName*Row( )	Takes no arguments and returns a new *TableName*Row object with the same schema as the table to be used for adding new rows to the table in the strongly typed DataSet.

There is a class named *TableName*Row for each table in the strongly typed DataSet. It has the base class DataRow and represents a row of data in the table. Table 2-2 lists commonly used properties and methods of this class specific to the strongly typed DataSet.

Table 2-2. TableNameRow class properties and methods

Property/method	Description
Typed Accessor	Sets and get the value of a column. The typed accessor is exposed as a property having the same name as the underlying data column.
Is*ColumnName*Null( )	Returns a Boolean value indicating whether the field contains a null value.
Set*ColumnName*Null( )	Sets the value of the underlying field to a null value.
Get*ChildTableName*Rows( )	Returns the rows for the table as an array of *ChildTableName*Row objects.
*Parent*TableNameRow( )	Returns the parent row as an object of type *ParentTableName*Row.

There is a class named *TableName*RowChangeEvent for each table in the strongly typed DataSet. It has the base class EventArgs. Table 2-3 describes the properties of this class.

Table 2-3. TableNameRowChangeEvent properties

Property	Description
Action	A value from the System.Data.DataRowAction enumeration that describes the action performed on a row that caused the event to be raised.
Row	The *TableName*Row object for which the event was raised.

A strongly typed DataSet has some advantages over using an untyped DataSet:

- The schema information is contained within the strongly typed DataSet resulting in a performance over retrieving schema information at runtime. The schema of an untyped DataSet can also be defined programmatically, as discussed in Recipe 2.1, resulting in similar performance.

- Programming is more intuitive and code is easier to maintain. Table, column, and other object names are accessed through properties having names based on the underlying data source object names rather than by using index or delimited string arguments. The Visual Studio .NET IDE provides autocomplete functionality for strongly typed DataSet names.

- Type mismatch errors and errors resulting from misspelled or out of bounds arguments used with DataSet objects can be detected during compilation, rather than at runtime.

The disadvantages of a strongly typed DataSet object include:

- Additional overhead when executing. If strongly typed functionality is not required, performance is better with an untyped DataSet rather than with a typed DataSet.

- A strongly typed DataSet must be regenerated when the structure of the underlying data source changes. Applications using these strongly typed DataSet objects will need to be rebuilt with a reference to the new strongly typed DataSet. With an untyped DataSet, as long as the new schema is a superset of the old schema, existing clients can simply ignore any new data and do not need to be recompiled.

Four ways to generate a typed DataSet class are described in the following subsections.

Using the Visual Studio .NET IDE to generate a typed DataSet

The first and easiest method uses Visual Studio .NET following these steps:

1. Drop a DataAdapter object from the Data tab in the Visual Studio .NET Toolbox onto a design surface such as a form or a component. The Data Adapter Configuration Wizard will appear.
2. Press Next to continue to the Choose Your Data Connection dialog.
3. Select an existing connection or create a new one as required. Press Next to continue to the Choose a Query Type dialog.
4. Select the Use SQL statements radio button and press Next to continue to the Generate the SQL Statements dialog.
5. Press the Advanced Options... button.
6. Uncheck all three check boxes on the Advanced SQL Generation Options dialog and press OK.
7. Press the Query Builder... button.
8. Select only one table on the Add Table dialog and press Add. Press Close.
9. Check the columns from the table to include or (All Columns) and press OK.
10. Press Next to continue to the View Wizard Results dialog.
11. Press Finish to complete the wizard.
12. Repeat steps 1–11 for the other tables that you want to have included in the strongly typed DataSet.

13. Right-click on the design surface and select Generate DataSet.

14. Provide a name for the strongly typed DataSet, select the tables to be included, and press OK to generate the new strongly typed DataSet.

15. To relate tables in the new strongly typed DataSet, open the XSD file for the new DataSet in the Solution Explorer window.

16. Right-click on the child table in XSD schema designer, select Add → New Relation… from the shortcut menu, and complete the dialog. Repeat this step to create all required relationships.

17. Instances of the strongly typed DataSet can now be created programmatically either by using the new keyword in C# or the New keyword in Visual Basic .NET or by dragging the DataSet object from the Data tab in the Visual Studio .NET Toolbox onto a design surface such as a component or form.

Using the TypedDataSetGenerator class to generate a typed DataSet

The second technique is to derive a class from the TypedDataSetGenerator class. The static Generate( ) method of the TypedDataSetGenerator class is used to create a strongly typed DataSet. The prototype of the method is:

```
public static void Generate(DataSet dataSet, CodeNamespace codeNamespace,
    ICodeGenerator codeGenerator);
```

The arguments of the method are:

DataSet
> The DataSet used to specify the schema for the typed DataSet.

codeNamespace
> The target namespace for the typed DataSet.

codeGenerator
> A class capable of dynamically rendering source code in a specific language and used to create the typed DataSet.

Using an XSD schema file to generate a typed DataSet

The other two methods require an XSD schema file. You can generate this file in a number of ways: using the Visual Studio .NET tools, third-party tools, or the DataSet WriteXmlSchema( ) method. You can create a strongly typed DataSet from the *XSD* schema file using Visual Studio .NET or using the XML Schema Definition Tool.

To create a strongly typed DataSet from the *XSD* schema using Visual Studio .NET, follow these steps:

1. Right-click on the project in the Solution Explorer window, choose Add/Existing Item... from the shortcut menu, and select the *XSD* file to add it to the project.

2. Select the XSD schema file from the Solution Explorer window and open it in the designer window.

---

3. Right-click on the designer window and select Generate DataSet.

4. Instances of the strongly typed DataSet can now be created programmatically by using the new keyword in C# or the New keyword in Visual Basic .NET or by dragging the DataSet object from the Data tab in the Visual Studio .NET Toolbox onto a design surface such as a component or form.

The second way to create a strongly typed DataSet from an XSD schema is to use the XML Schema Definition Tool (*XSD.EXE*) found in the .NET Framework SDK *bin* directory. Follow these steps:

Generate the strongly typed DataSet class file from the *XSD* schema file by issuing the following command from the command prompt:

```
xsd mySchemaFile.xsd /d /l:CS
```

The /d switch specifies that source code for a strongly typed DataSet should be created.

The /l:CS switch specifies that the utility should use the C# language, which is the default if not specified. For VB.NET, use the switch /l:VB.

The XML Schema Definition Tool offers other options. For more information, see the .NET Framework SDK documentation or the MSDN Library.

The class file that is generated for the strongly typed DataSet is named using the DataSet name in the XSD schema and has an extension corresponding to the programming language: *.cs* for C# and *.vb* for VB.NET. The strongly typed DataSet class can now be added to a project.

 If the strongly typed DataSet file is not visible as a child node of the XSD Schema in the Solution Explorer window, select Show All Files from the Project menu.

2.4   Processing a Batch SQL Statement

Problem

You have a batch SQL query that returns multiple result sets and you need to work with the result sets in ADO.NET.

Solution

Use the NextResult( ) method to iterate through and process SQL queries that return multiple result sets.

The sample code contains three event handlers:

Go Button.Click

> Defines a SQL batch query statement that selects all Orders and Order Details records from Northwind. Depending on the radio button checked by the user, either a DataAdapter is used to fill a DataSet with multiple tables or a Command object is used to create a DataReader containing multiple result sets. In either case the results are displayed in a data grid for the DataSet and in a text box for the DataReader.

DataSet RadioButton.CheckedChanged

> Displays a data grid to show the results of a batch query when loaded into a DataSet. Hides the text box for the DataReader results.

DataReader RadioButton.CheckedChanged

> Displays a text box to show the results of a batch query when loaded into a DataReader. Hides the data grid for the DataSet results.

The C# code is shown in Example 2-3.

Example 2-3. File: BatchSqlStatementForm.cs

```csharp
// Namespaces, variables, and constants
using System;
using System.Configuration;
using System.Text;
using System.Data;
using System.Data.SqlClient;

// Table name constants
private const String ORDERS_TABLE        = "Orders";
private const String ORDERDETAILS_TABLE  = "OrderDetails";

// Field name constants
private const String ORDERID_FIELD       = "OrderID";

// Relation name constants
private const String ORDERS_ORDERDETAILS_RELATION =
    "Orders_OrderDetails_Relation";

// ...

private void goButton_Click(object sender, System.EventArgs e)
{
    // Batch SQL query returning two result sets
    String sqlText = "select OrderID, CustomerID, EmployeeID, OrderDate," +
        "RequiredDate, ShippedDate, ShipVia, Freight, ShipName, " +
        "ShipAddress, ShipCity, ShipRegion, ShipPostalCode, " +
        "ShipCountry " +
        "FROM Orders;" +
        "SELECT OrderID, ProductID, UnitPrice, Quantity, Discount " +
        "FROM [Order Details];";
```

Example 2-3. File: BatchSqlStatementForm.cs (continued)

```
if (dataSetRadioButton.Checked)
{
    SqlDataAdapter da = new SqlDataAdapter(sqlText,
        ConfigurationSettings.AppSettings["Sql_ConnectString"]);

    // Map the automatically generated table names Table and Table1.
    da.TableMappings.Add("Table", ORDERS_TABLE);
    da.TableMappings.Add("Table1", ORDERDETAILS_TABLE);

    // Fill the DataSet with the results of the batch query.
    DataSet ds = new DataSet();
    da.Fill(ds);

    // Add a relation between the Order and Order Details tables.
    ds.Relations.Add(new DataRelation(ORDERS_ORDERDETAILS_RELATION,
        ds.Tables[ORDERS_TABLE].Columns[ORDERID_FIELD],
        ds.Tables[ORDERDETAILS_TABLE].Columns[ORDERID_FIELD],
        true));

    // Bind the default view of the Orders table to the grid.
    resultDataGrid.DataSource = ds.Tables[ORDERS_TABLE];
}
else
{
    StringBuilder sb = new StringBuilder();

    // Create a new connection and command to fill the DataReader.
    SqlConnection conn = new SqlConnection(
        ConfigurationSettings.AppSettings["Sql_ConnectString"]);
    SqlCommand cmd = new SqlCommand(sqlText, conn);
    conn.Open();

    // Execute the batch query.
    SqlDataReader dr = cmd.ExecuteReader();

    // Process each result set in the DataReader.
    int nResultSet = 0;
    do
    {
        sb.Append("RESULT SET: " + (++nResultSet) +
            Environment.NewLine);

        // Iterate over the rows in the DataReader.
        while(dr.Read())
        {
            // Output each field in the DataReader row.
            for(int i = 0; i < dr.FieldCount; i++)
                sb.Append(dr[i] + "; ");

            sb.Append(Environment.NewLine);
        }
```

Example 2-3. File: BatchSqlStatementForm.cs (continued)

```
            sb.Append(Environment.NewLine);
        } while(dr.NextResult( ));
        dr.Close( );
        conn.Close( );

        // Display the results.
        resultTextBox.Text = sb.ToString( );
    }
}

private void dataSetRadioButton_CheckedChanged(object sender,
    System.EventArgs e)
{
    // Display the data grid for DataSet results.
    resultDataGrid.Visible = true;
    resultTextBox.Visible = false;
}

private void dataReaderRadioButton_CheckedChanged(object sender,
    System.EventArgs e)
{
    // Display the text box for DataReader results.
    resultDataGrid.Visible = false;
    resultTextBox.Visible = true;
}
```

Discussion

A batch command is defined as a collection of SQL statements separated by semico-lons. The batch command can fill a DataSet or build a DataReader. Working with the results is different for each of these scenarios as described in the following sections.

The batch statement can also be contained in a stored procedure. Everything is the same as for the example where the SQL batch command is defined in the code once the Command is executed.

 The Oracle .NET data provider does not support batch SQL statements. To execute a batch query against an Oracle database it is necessary to use an Oracle package that returns multiple REF CURSOR output parameters. For more information, see the solution in Recipe 2.20.

DataSet

The Fill( ) method of the DataAdapter adds multiple result sets from a batch query to a DataSet. One table is created in the DataSet for each result set. By default, these tables will be named *Table*, *Table1*, *Table2*, and so on. You can make these names more meaningful by specifying table mappings in the TableMappings collection of the DataAdapter. For more information about using table mappings, see Recipe 2.16.

Data relationships between the tables added with a batch query must be created programmatically. As with non-batch queries, you can define the relations and foreign key constraints for the tables prior to filling them with the results of the batch query.

When using the Fill( ) method of the DataAdapter with a batch fill operation, if one of the result sets contains an error, all subsequent processing is skipped and result sets are not added to the DataSet.

When using the FillSchema( ) method of the DataAdapter with a batch query and the OLE DB data provider, the schema is returned for only the first query. To retrieve the schema for all result sets, use the Fill( ) method with the MissingSchemaAction argument set to AddWithKey.

DataReader

As with a single statement command, a batch command is used to build a DataReader by calling the ExecuteReader( ) method of the Command object. The NextResult( ) method of the DataReader is used to advance to the next result set where the method returns true if there is another result set. Iterating over the DataReader is demonstrated in the sample code using the following technique:

```
do {

    ... process the result set

} while(dr.NextResult( ));
```

Initially, the DataReader is positioned on the first result set. Once NextResult( ) is called there is no way to return to the previous result set.

2.5   Using a Web Service as a Data Source

Problem

You want to use a web service as the data source for a client application.

Solution

Create a web service that returns a DataSet to a client, and then invoke the web service from the client to retrieve the DataSet.

The XML web service code contains one method:

LoadOrders( )
> Creates a DataSet containing all Orders and Order Details data from Northwind. A DataRelation is created relating the tables. The DataSet is returned by the method.

The client-side code instantiates the web service class and calls the `LoadOrders( )` method to create a `DataSet` containing the Orders and Order Details data from Northwind. The default view of the Orders table is bound to a data grid on the form.

The C# code for the XML web service is shown in Example 2-4.

Example 2-4. File: NorthwindServiceCS.asmx.cs

```
// Namespaces, variables, and constants
using System;
using System.ComponentModel;
using System.Web.Services;
using System.Configuration;
using System.Data;
using System.Data.SqlClient;

public const String ORDERS_TABLE = "Orders";
public const String ORDERDETAILS_TABLE = "OrderDetails";

public const String ORDERID_FIELD = "OrderID";

public const String ORDERS_ORDERDETAILS_RELATION =
    "Order_OrderDetails_Relation";

// ...

[WebMethod]
public DataSet LoadOrders( )
{
    DataSet ds = new DataSet( );

    SqlDataAdapter da;

    // Fill the Order table and add it to the DataSet.
    da = new SqlDataAdapter("SELECT * FROM Orders",
        ConfigurationSettings.AppSettings["DataConnectString"]);
    DataTable orderTable = new DataTable(ORDERS_TABLE);
    da.FillSchema(orderTable, SchemaType.Source);
    da.Fill(orderTable);
    ds.Tables.Add(orderTable);

    // Fill the OrderDetails table and add it to the DataSet.
    da = new SqlDataAdapter("SELECT * FROM [Order Details]",
        ConfigurationSettings.AppSettings["DataConnectString"]);
    DataTable orderDetailTable = new DataTable(ORDERDETAILS_TABLE);
    da.FillSchema(orderDetailTable, SchemaType.Source);
    da.Fill(orderDetailTable);
    ds.Tables.Add(orderDetailTable);

    // Create a relation between the tables.
    ds.Relations.Add(ORDERS_ORDERDETAILS_RELATION,
        ds.Tables[ORDERS_TABLE].Columns[ORDERID_FIELD],
```

Example 2-4. File: NorthwindServiceCS.asmx.cs (continued)

```
    ds.Tables[ORDERDETAILS_TABLE].Columns[ORDERID_FIELD],
    true);

  return ds;
}
```

The C# web services client-side code is shown in Example 2-5.

Example 2-5. File: WebServiceDataSourceForm.cs

```
// Namespaces, variables, and constants
using System;
using System.Windows.Forms;
using System.Data;

// Table name constants
private const String ORDERS_TABLE= "Orders";

// ...

// Create the Web Service object.
NorthwindServiceCS nws = new NorthwindServiceCS();
// Load the DataSet containing orders and order details.
DataSet ds = nws.LoadOrders();

// Bind the default view of the orders table to the grid.
dataGrid.DataSource = ds.Tables[ORDERS_TABLE].DefaultView;
```

Discussion

An XML web service is software that is accessible using Internet standards such as XML and HTTP. Because it is accessible through open-standard interfaces, web services make it easy to allow heterogeneous systems to work together.

.NET makes it very easy to build XML web services. In .NET, web services are implemented as *.ASMX* files beginning with a @WebService directive. For example, the solution code contains the following directive:

```
<%@ WebService Language="c#" Codebehind="NorthwindServiceCS.asmx.cs"
    Class="NorthwindServiceCS" %>
```

Methods in the web service class that are exposed over the Web are tagged with the WebMethod attribute; untagged methods can be used only internally by the web service. To deploy the web service, copy it to a virtual directory that has script execute permissions on an IIS web server that has ASP.NET support.

To use the web service class, use *wsdl.exe* to create the client-side proxy class. For the solution, the command is:

```
wsdl.exe http://localhost/NorthwindWebServiceCS/NorthwindServiceCS.asmx
```

Then, as with a local class, the client is able to instantiate the web service class using the new operator.

For more information about creating and consuming XML web services, see the MSDN Library.

The solution shows that there is very little difference between implementing the LoadOrders( )methods to retrieve a DataSet containing the Orders and Order Details data from Northwind as a local class or as a web services class.

2.6   Accessing Deleted Rows in a DataTable

Problem

When you delete rows from a DataSet they are really marked for deletion until changes are committed by calling AcceptChanges( ) either directly or indirectly. You want to access the rows that you have deleted from a DataTable.

Solution

Use either a DataView or the Select( ) method of the DataTable to access deleted rows.

The sample code contains three event handlers:

Form.Load
> Sets up the sample by creating a DataTable containing Orders data from Northwind. A view containing the Current rows is bound to a data grid on the form.

Current Rows RadioButton.CheckedChanged
> Sets the view of the Orders data to display only Current rows. The text box displaying information about deleted rows is cleared.

Deleted Rows RadioButton.CheckedChanged
> Sets the view of the Orders data to display only Deleted rows. The DataTable for the DataView is retrieved and the Select( ) method is used to get the Deleted rows. The overloaded indexer in C#, or Item( ) property in VB.NET, is used to retrieve the OrderID from the Original version of these deleted rows. This information is displayed in the text box on the form.

The C# code is shown in Example 2-6.

Example 2-6. File: AccessDeletedRowsForm.cs

```
// Namespaces, variables, and constants
using System;
using System.Configuration;
using System.Text;
using System.Data;
using System.Data.SqlClient;
```

Example 2-6. File: AccessDeletedRowsForm.cs (continued)

```csharp
private DataView dv;

// ...

private void AccessDataSetDeletedRowsForm_Load(object sender,
    System.EventArgs e)
{
    // Fill the Orders table.
    SqlDataAdapter da = new SqlDataAdapter("SELECT * FROM Orders",
        ConfigurationSettings.AppSettings["Sql_ConnectString"]);
    DataTable dt = new DataTable("Orders");
    da.Fill(dt);

    // Define a view of just the Current rows.
    dv = new DataView(dt, null, null, DataViewRowState.CurrentRows);
    dataGrid.DataSource = dv;

    currentRadioButton.Checked = true;
}

private void currentRadioButton_CheckedChanged(object sender,
    System.EventArgs e)
{
    // Filter to include only current rows.
    dv.RowStateFilter = DataViewRowState.CurrentRows;
    dataGrid.ReadOnly = false;

    deletedTextBox.Clear( );
}

private void deletedRadioButton_CheckedChanged(object sender,
    System.EventArgs e)
{
    // Filter the view to include only deleted rows.
    dv.RowStateFilter = DataViewRowState.Deleted;
    dataGrid.ReadOnly = true;

    // Get the DataTable from the DataView.
    DataTable dt = dv.Table;
    // Filter using the DataTable RowState.
    DataRow[] delRows = dt.Select(null, null, DataViewRowState.Deleted);

    StringBuilder sb = new StringBuilder("Deleted Records:" +
        Environment.NewLine);
    // Iterate over the collection of deleted rows.
    foreach(DataRow row in delRows)
        sb.Append("Order ID: " + row["OrderID",
        DataRowVersion.Original] + Environment.NewLine);

    deletedTextBox.Text = sb.ToString( );
}
```

Discussion

ADO.NET manages the state of the rows while they are being modified. Rows are assigned a state from the DataRowState enumeration described in Table 2-4.

Table 2-4. DataRowState enumeration

Value	Description
Added	The row has been added to the collection of rows in the table but AcceptChanges( ) has not been called.
Deleted	The row has been deleted from the collection of rows in the table but AcceptChanges( ) has not been called.
Detached	The row does not belong to the collection of rows in a DataTable.
Modified	The data in the row has been changed but AcceptChanges( ) has not been called.
Unchanged	The data in the row has not been changed since it was loaded or since AcceptChanges( ) was last called.

When AcceptChanges( ) is called on the DataSet, DataTable, or DataRow, either explicitly or implicitly by calling the Update( ) method of the DataAdapter, the following occurs:

- All rows with a row state of Deleted are removed.
- All other rows are assigned a row state of Unchanged and the Original row version values are overwritten with the Current version values.

When RejectChanges( ) is called on the DataSet, DataTable, or DataRow, the following occurs:

- All rows with a row state of Added are removed.
- All other rows are assigned a row state of Unchanged and the Current row version values are overwritten with the Original row version values.

Each DataRow has a RowState property that returns the current state of the row.

ADO.NET maintains several versions of the data in each row while it is being modified to allow the disconnected to be later reconciled with the data source. Table 2-5 describes the DataRowVersion enumeration values.

Table 2-5. DataRowVersion enumeration

Value	Description
Current	Current value. This version does not exist for rows with a state of Deleted.
Default	Default value as determined by the DataRowState:
	• The Current version for rows with Added, Modified, or Unchanged state
	• The Original version for rows with Deleted state
	• The Proposed value for rows with Detached state

Table 2-5. DataRowVersion enumeration (continued)

Value	Description
Original	Original value. This version does not exist for rows with a state of Added.
Proposed	Proposed value. This value exists during a row edit operation started either implicitly or explicitly with the BeginEdit( ) method and for Detached rows.

The HasVersion( ) method of the DataRow object checks whether a particular row version exists.

The DataViewRowState enumeration is used to retrieve a particular version of data or to determine whether a version exists. It is used for this purpose by both the Select( ) method of the DataTable and by the RowStateFilter property of the DataView. You can retrieve more than one version by using a Boolean OR of DataViewRowState values. Table 2-6 describes the DataViewRowState enumeration values.

Table 2-6. DataViewRowState enumeration

Value	Description
Added	The Current version of all Added rows.
CurrentRows	The Current version of all Unchanged, Added, and Modified rows. This is the default value.
Deleted	The Original version of all Deleted rows.
ModifiedCurrent	The Current version of all Modified rows.
ModifiedOriginal	The Original version of all Modified rows.
None	No rows.
OriginalRows	The Original version of Unchanged, Modified, and Deleted rows.
Unchanged	The Current version of all Unchanged rows.

The Current version of each row is retrieved by default when accessing rows in a DataTable or in a DataView. The solution demonstrates an approach for getting Deleted rows from both a DataTable and a DataView. Deleted rows include only those marked for deletion using the Delete( ) method of the DataRow or the DataView, not the Remove( ) or RemoveAt( ) method of the DataRowCollection, which instead immediately removes the specified DataRow from the collection.

The solution demonstrates two techniques for retrieving the deleted rows:

To get the Deleted rows from the DataTable, use an overload of the Select( ) method of the DataTable to return an array of deleted DataRow objects. The overload accepts an argument having a DataViewRowState enumeration value. To retrieve deleted rows, pass a value of Deleted as the argument.

To get the Deleted rows from the DataView, set the RowStateFilter property of the DataView to Deleted. Deleted rows are also visible, along with other rows, when you set the RowStateFilter property to ModifiedOriginal and OriginalRows.

2.7   Counting Records in a DataReader

Problem

You want to determine how many records there are in a DataReader.

Solution

Use one of the following three techniques:

- Iterate over the rows in the DataReader.

- Issue a COUNT(*) query as part of a batch query. Note that not all data sources support batch queries. If not, execute the statements separately one after the other for a similar result.

- Use the @@ROWCOUNT function to return the number or rows in a DataReader after the DataReader has been closed. This technique is SQL Server specific.

The sample code uses a single stored procedure:

SP0207_GetOrders

Returns a result set containing all records in the Orders table in Northwind. Also, the stored procedure returns the @@ROWCOUNT value for the query in an output parameter. The stored procedure is shown in Example 2-7.

Example 2-7. Stored procedure: SP0207_GetOrders

```
ALTER PROCEDURE SP0207_GetOrders
    @RowCount int output
AS
    set nocount on

    select * from Orders

    set @RowCount = @@ROWCOUNT

    RETURN
```

The C# code is shown in Example 2-8.

Example 2-8. File: DataReaderRowCountForm.cs

```
// Namespaces, variables, and constants
using System;
using System.Configuration;
using System.Data;
using System.Data.SqlClient;

// ...
```

Example 2-8. File: DataReaderRowCountForm.cs (continued)

```csharp
// Batch query to retrieve the COUNT of records and
// all of the records in the Orders table as two result sets.
String sqlText = "SELECT COUNT(*) FROM Orders; " +
    "SELECT * FROM Orders;";

// Create the connection.
SqlConnection conn = new SqlConnection(
    ConfigurationSettings.AppSettings["Sql_ConnectString"]);
SqlCommand cmd = new SqlCommand(sqlText, conn);
conn.Open( );

// Create a DataReader on the first result set.
SqlDataReader dr = cmd.ExecuteReader( );
// Get the count of records from the select count(*) statement.
dr.Read( );
resultTextBox.Text = "Orders table record count, using COUNT(*)= " +
    dr.GetInt32(0) + Environment.NewLine;

// Move to the data result set.
dr.NextResult( );
int count = 0;
// Iterate over the records in the DataReader.
while(dr.Read( ))
{
    count++;

    // ... Do something interesting with the data here.
}

// Close the DataReader and the connection.
dr.Close( );

resultTextBox.Text += "Orders table record count, " +
    "iterating over result set = " + count +
    Environment.NewLine;

// Create the stored procedure to use in the DataReader.
cmd = new SqlCommand("SP0207_GetOrders", conn);
cmd.CommandType = CommandType.StoredProcedure;
// Create the output paramter to return @@ROWCOUNT.
cmd.Parameters.Add("@RowCount", SqlDbType.Int).Direction =
    ParameterDirection.Output;

// Create a DataReader for the result set returned by
// the stored procedure.
dr = cmd.ExecuteReader( );

// ... Process the data in the DataReader.

// Close the DataReader.
dr.Close( );
// The output parameter containing the row count is now available.
```

Example 2-8. File: DataReaderRowCountForm.cs (continued)

```
resultTextBox.Text += "Orders table record count, " +
    "returning @@ROWCOUNT from stored procedure = " + cmd.Parameters["@RowCount"].Value;

conn.Close( );
```

Discussion

The DataReader provides forward-only, read-only access to a stream of rows from a data source. It is optimized for performance by reading data directly from a connection to a data source. As a result, there is no way to determine the number of records in the result set for the DataReader without iterating through all of the records. Additionally, because the DataReader is forward-only, you cannot move backwards in DataReader so when iterating, you must process data at the same time. This technique provides the only accurate count of records in the DataReader.

A second technique demonstrated in the solution counts the records using the COUNT aggregate function for the command text used to build the DataReader. This technique can have discrepancies with the number of records actually in the DataReader because of the timing lag between issuing the COUNT function and creating the DataReader.

The solution also demonstrates using the SQL Server @@ROWCOUNT variable, which returns the number of rows affected by the previous statement, to return the number of records in the result set used to create the DataReader. The count is returned as an output parameter and is therefore not available until the DataReader is closed. Although this does not improve the availability of the record count, centralizing the count in the stored procedure is less prone to coding errors than the counting approach. For more information about output parameters, see Recipe 2.9.

The HasRows( ) method of the DataReader was introduced in Version 1.1 of the .NET Framework. It returns a Boolean value indicating whether the DataReader contains at least one row.

There is also no way to determine the number of result sets in a DataReader built using a batch query without iterating over the result sets using the NextResult( ) method.

2.8   Mapping .NET Data Provider Data Types to .NET Framework Data Types

Problem

You want to convert between .NET provider data types and .NET Framework data types.

Solution

You need to understand the .NET Framework data types; their mappings to SQL Server, OLE DB, ODBC, and Oracle data types; and how to properly cast them. The .NET Framework typed accessors and .NET Framework provider-specific typed accessors for use with the DataReader class are also important.

Discussion

The ADO.NET DataSet and contained objects are data source independent. The DataAdapter is used to retrieve data into the DataSet and to reconcile modifications made to the data to the data source at some later time. The implication is that data in the DataTable objects contained in the DataSet are .NET Framework data types rather than data types specific to the underlying data source or the .NET data provider used to connect to that data source.

While the DataReader object for a data source is specific to the .NET data provider used to retrieve the data, the values in the DataReader are stored in variables with .NET Framework data types.

The .NET Framework data type is inferred from the .NET data provider used to fill the DataSet or build the DataReader. The DataReader has typed accessor methods that improve performance by returning a value as a specific .NET Framework data type when the data type is known, thereby eliminating the need for additional type conversion. For more information about using typed accessors with a DataReader, see Recipe 9.6.

Some DataReader classes expose data source specific accessor methods as well. For example, the SqlDataReader exposes accessor methods that return SQL Server data types as objects of System.Data.SqlType.

The following example shows how to cast a value from a DataReader to a .NET Framework data type and how to use the .NET Framework typed accessor and the SQL Server-specific typed accessor:

```
// Create the connection and the command.
SqlConnection conn = new SqlConnection(
    ConfigurationSettings.AppSettings["Sql_ConnectString"]);
SqlCommand cmd = new SqlCommand(
    "SELECT CategoryID, CategoryName FROM Categories", conn);

// Open the connection and build the DataReader.
conn.Open();
SqlDataReader dr = cmd.ExecuteReader();

// Get the CategoryID from the DataReader and cast to int.
int categoryId = Convert.ToInt32(dr[0]);

// Get the CategoryID using typed accessor.
int taCategoryId = dr.GetInt32(0);
```

```
// Get the CategoryID using the SQL Server-specific accessor.
System.Data.SqlTypes.SqlInt32 sqlCategoryId = dr.GetSqlInt32(0);
```

In all cases, a null value for a .NET Framework data type is represented by System.DBNull.Value.

Table 2-7 lists the inferred .NET Framework data type, the .NET Framework typed accessor for the DataReader, and the SQL Server–specific typed accessor for each SQL Server data type.

Table 2-7. Data types and accessors for SQL Server .NET data provider

SQL Server data type	.NET Framework data type	.NET Framework typed accessor	SQLType typed accessor
bigint	Int64	GetInt64( )	GetSqlInt64( )
binary	Byte[]	GetBytes( )	GetSqlBinary( )
bit	Boolean	GetBoolean( )	GetSqlBit( )
char	String Char[]	GetString( ) GetChars( )	GetSqlString( )
datetime	DateTime	GetDateTime( )	GetSqlDateTime( )
decimal	Decimal	GetDecimal( )	GetSqlDecimal( )
float	Double	GetDouble( )	GetSqlDouble( )
image	Byte[]	GetBytes( )	GetSqlBinary( )
int	Int32	GetInt32( )	GetSqlInt32( )
money	Decimal	GetDecimal( )	GetSqlMoney( )
nchar	String Char[]	GetString( ) GetChars( )	GetSqlString( )
ntext	String Char[]	GetString( ) GetChars( )	GetSqlString( )
numeric	Decimal	GetDecimal( )	GetSqlDecimal( )
nvarchar	String Char[]	GetString( ) GetChars( )	GetSqlString( )
real	Single	GetFloat( )	GetSqlSingle( )
smalldatetime	DateTime	GetDateTime( )	GetSqlDateTime( )
smallint	Int16	GetInt16( )	GetSqlInt16( )
smallmoney	Decimal	GetDecimal( )	GetSqlDecimal( )
sql_variant	Object	GetValue( )	GetSqlValue( )
text	String Char[]	GetString( ) GetChars( )	GetSqlString( )
timestamp	Byte[]	GetBytes( )	GetSqlBinary( )
tinyint	Byte	GetByte( )	GetSqlByte( )
uniqueidentifier	Guid	GetGuid( )	GetSqlGuid( )
varbinary	Byte[]	GetBytes( )	GetSqlBinary( )
varchar	String Char[]	GetString( ) GetChars( )	GetSqlString( )

Table 2-8 lists the inferred .NET Framework data type, the .NET Framework typed accessor for the `DataReader` for each OLE DB type, and the corresponding ADO type.

Table 2-8. Data types and accessors for OLE DB .NET data provider

OLE DB data type	ADO type	.NET Framework data type	.NET Framework typed accessor
DBTYPE_BOOL	adBoolean	Boolean	GetBoolean( )
DBTYPE_BSTR	adBSTR	String	GetString( )
DBTYPE_BYTES	adBinary	Byte[]	GetBytes( )
DBTYPE_CY	adCurrency	Decimal	GetDecimal( )
DBTYPE_DATE	adDate	DateTime	GetDateTime( )
DBTYPE_DBDATE	adDBDate	DateTime	GetDateTime( )
DBTYPE_DBTIME	adDBTime	DateTime	GetDateTime( )
DBTYPE_DBTIMESTAMP	adDBTimeStamp	DateTime	GetDateTime( )
DBTYPE_DECIMAL	adDecimal	Decimal	GetDecimal( )
DBTYPE_ERROR	adError	ExternalException	GetValue( )
DBTYPE_FILETIME	adFileTime	DateTime	GetDateTime( )
DBTYPE_GUID	adGUID	Guid	GetGuid( )
DBTYPE_HCHAPTER	adChapter	See footnote 1	GetValue( )
DBTYPE_I1	adTinyInt	Byte	GetByte( )
DBTYPE_I2	adSmallInt	Int16	GetInt16( )
DBTYPE_I4	adInteger	Int32	GetInt32( )
DBTYPE_I8	adBigInt	Int64	GetInt64( )
DBTYPE_IDISPATCH[2]	adIDispatch	Object	GetValue( )
DBTYPE_IUNKNOWN[2]	adIUnknown	Object	GetValue( )
DBTYPE_NUMERIC	adNumeric	Decimal	GetDecimal( )
DBTYPE_PROPVARIANT	adPropVariant	Object	GetValue( )
DBTYPE_R4	adSingle	Single	GetFloat( )
DBTYPE_R8	adDouble	Double	GetDouble( )
DBTYPE_STR	adChar	String	GetString( )
DBTYPE_UI1	adUnsignedTinyInt	Byte	GetByte( )
DBTYPE_UI2	adUnsignedSmallInt	UInt16	GetValue( )
DBTYPE_UI4	adUnsignedInt	UInt32	GetValue( )
DBTYPE_UI8	adUnsignedBigInt	UInt64	GetValue( )
DBTYPE_UDT	adUserDefined	Not supported	Not supported
DBTYPE_VARIANT	adVariant	Object	GetValue( )

Table 2-8. Data types and accessors for OLE DB .NET data provider (continued)

OLE DB data type	ADO type	.NET Framework data type	.NET Framework typed accessor
DBTYPE_VARNUMERIC	adVarNumeric	Not supported	Not supported
DBTYPE_WSTR	adWChar	String	GetString( )

[1] Supported using the DataReader. For more information, see Recipe 2.20.
[2] The object reference is a marshaled representation of the pointer.

Table 2-9 lists the inferred .NET Framework data type and the .NET Framework typed accessor for the DataReader for each ODBC data type.

Table 2-9. Data types and accessors for ODBC .NET data provider

ODBC data type	.NET Framework data type	.NET Framework typed accessor
SQL_BIGINT	Int64	GetInt64( )
SQL_BINARY	Byte[]	GetBytes( )
SQL_BIT	Boolean	GetBoolean( )
SQL_CHAR	String Char[]	GetString( ) GetChars( )
SQL_DECIMAL	Decimal	GetDecimal( )
SQL_DOUBLE	Double	GetDouble( )
SQL_GUID	Guid	GetGuid( )
SQL_INTEGER	Int32	GetInt32( )
SQL_LONG_VARCHAR	String Char[]	GetString( ) GetChars( )
SQL_LONGVARBINARY	Byte[]	GetBytes( )
SQL_NUMERIC	Decimal	GetDecimal( )
SQL_REAL	Single	GetFloat( )
SQL_SMALLINT	Int16	GetInt16( )
SQL_TINYINT	Byte	GetByte( )
SQL_TYPE_TIMES	DateTime	GetDateTime( )
SQL_TYPE_TIMESTAMP	DateTime	GetDateTime( )
SQL_VARBINARY	Byte[]	GetBytes( )
SQL_WCHAR	String Char[]	GetString( ) GetChars( )
SQL_WLONGVARCHAR	String Char[]	GetString( ) GetChars( )
SQL_WVARCHAR	String Char[]	GetString( ) GetChars( )

Table 2-10 lists the inferred .NET Framework data type, the .NET Framework typed accessor for the DataReader, and the Oracle-specific typed accessor for each Oracle data type.

Table 2-10. Data types and accessors for Oracle .NET data provider

Oracle data type	.NET Framework data type	.NET Framework typed accessor	OracleType typed accessor
BFILE	Byte[]	GetBytes( )	GetOracleBFile( )
BLOB	Byte[]	GetBytes( )	GetOracleLob( )
CHAR	String Char[]	GetString( ) GetChars( )	GetOracleString( )
CLOB	String Char[]	GetString( ) GetChars( )	GetOracleLob( )
DATE	DateTime	GetDateTime( )	GetOracleDateTime( )
FLOAT	Decimal	GetDecimal( )	GetOracleNumber( )[2]
INTEGER	Decimal	GetDecimal( )	GetOracleNumber( )[2]
INTERVAL YEAR TO MONTH[1]	Int32	GetInt32( )	GetOracleMonthSpan( )
INTERVAL DAY TO SECOND[1]	TimeSpan	GetTimeSpan( )	GetOracleTimeSpan( )
LONG	String Char[]	GetString( ) GetChars( )	GetOracleString( )
LONG RAW	Byte[]	GetBytes( )	GetOracleBinary( )
NCHAR	String Char[]	GetString( ) GetChars( )	GetOracleString( )
NCLOB	String Char[]	GetString( ) GetChars( )	GetOracleLob( )
NUMBER	Decimal	GetDecimal( )	GetOracleNumber( )[2]
NVARCHAR2	String Char[]	GetString( ) GetChars( )	GetOracleString( )
RAW	Byte[]	GetBytes( )	GetOracleBinary( )
REF CURSOR	n/a	n/a	n/a
ROWID	String Char[]	GetString( ) GetChars( )	GetOracleString( )
TIMESTAMP[1]	DateTime	GetDateTime( )	GetOracleDateTime( )
TIMESTAMP WITH LOCAL TIME ZONE[1]	DateTime	GetDateTime( )	GetOracleDateTime( )
TIMESTAMP WITH TIME ZONE[1]	DateTime	GetDateTime( )	GetOracleDateTime( )
UNSIGNED INTEGER	Decimal	GetDecimal( )	GetOracleNumber( )[2]
VARCHAR2	String Char[]	GetString( ) GetChars( )	GetOracleString( )

[1] Available only when using both Oracle 9i client and server software.

[2] The Oracle NUMBER type has a maximum of 38 significant digits while the .NET Framework decimal type has a maximum of 28. An OverflowException will be raised if the Oracle NUMBER type has more than 28 significant digits.

For details about inferred .NET Framework data types, .NET Framework typed accessors for the DataReader, and provider-specific typed accessors for other .NET data providers, consult the documentation for the specific .NET data provider.

2.9   Returning an Output Parameter Using a DataReader

Problem

You want to access an output parameter returned by a stored procedure that you have used to create a DataReader.

Solution

Add a parameter to a Command's ParameterCollection and specify the ParameterDirection as either Output or InputOutput.

The sample code uses a single stored procedure:

SP0209_OutputValueWithDataReader
> Returns a result set containing all records from the Orders table in Northwind. The stored procedure takes one input and one output parameter and sets the value of the output parameter to the value of the input parameter.

The sample code creates a DataReader from a stored procedure command as shown in Example 2-9. The stored procedure returns a single output parameter, and then the stored procedure sets this value to the value of the input parameter specified by the user. The code displays the value of the output parameter at four different stages of working with the result set in the DataReader:

- Before the DataReader is created
- Immediately after the DataReader is created
- After all rows in the DataReader have been read
- After the DataReader is closed

Example 2-9. Stored procedure: SP0209_OutputValueWithDataReader

```
CREATE PROCEDURE SP0209_OutputValueWithDataReader
    @ValueIn int,
    @ValueOut int output
AS
    set nocount on

    set @ValueOut = @ValueIn
```

Example 2-9. Stored procedure: SP0209_OutputValueWithDataReader

```
select * from Orders

RETURN
```

The C# code is shown in Example 2-10.

Example 2-10. File: SpOutputValueDataReaderForm.cs

```csharp
// Namespaces, variables, and constants
using System;
using System.Configuration;
using System.Text;
using System.Data;
using System.Data.SqlClient;

// ...

StringBuilder result = new StringBuilder( );

// Create the connection.
SqlConnection conn = new SqlConnection(
    ConfigurationSettings.AppSettings["Sql_ConnectString"]);

// Create the command.
SqlCommand cmd = new SqlCommand("SP0209_OutputValueWithDataReader", conn);
cmd.CommandType = CommandType.StoredProcedure;

// Define the input parameter for the command.
cmd.Parameters.Add("@ValueIn", SqlDbType.Int);
// Set the input parameter value.
cmd.Parameters[0].Value = Convert.ToInt32(outputValueTextBox.Text);

// Define the output parameter for the command.
SqlParameter outParam = cmd.Parameters.Add("@ValueOut", SqlDbType.Int);
outParam.Direction = ParameterDirection.Output;

result.Append("Before execution, output value = " + outParam.Value +
    Environment.NewLine);

// Open the connection and create the DataReader.
conn.Open( );
SqlDataReader dr = cmd.ExecuteReader( );

result.Append("After execution, output value = " + outParam.Value +
    Environment.NewLine);

// Iterate over the records for the DataReader.
int rowCount = 0;
while (dr.Read( ))
{
    rowCount++;
```

Example 2-10. File: SpOutputValueDataReaderForm.cs (continued)

```
    // ... Code to process result set in DataReader
}

result.Append("After reading all " + rowCount + " rows, output value = " +
    outParam.Value + Environment.NewLine);

// Close the DataReader.
dr.Close( );
result.Append("After DataReader.Close( ), output value = " +
    outParam.Value + Environment.NewLine);

// Close the connection.
conn.Close( );

resultTextBox.Text = result.ToString( );
```

Discussion

Output parameters allow a stored procedure to pass a data value or cursor variable back to the caller. To use an output parameter with a DataReader, add the output parameter to the ParameterCollection for the Command object used to create the DataReader. Specify the ParameterDirection property of the Parameter as Output or InputOutput. Table 2-11 describes all values in the ParameterDirection enumeration. Once all parameters are defined, build the DataReader using the ExecuteReader( ) method of the Command object.

Table 2-11. ParameterDirection enumeration

Value	Description
Input	The parameter is an input parameter allowing the caller to pass a data value to the stored procedure.
InputOutput	The parameter is both an input and output parameter, allowing the caller to pass a data value to the stored procedure and the stored procedure to pass a data value back to the caller.
Output	The parameter is an output parameter allowing the stored procedure to pass a data value back to the caller.
ReturnValue	The parameter represents the value returned from the stored procedure.

Output parameters from the stored procedure used to build a DataReader are not available until the DataReader is closed by calling the Close( ) method or until Dispose( ) is called on the DataReader. You do not have to read any of records in the DataReader to obtain an output value.

2.10   Raising and Handling Stored Procedure Errors

Problem

You want to catch and handle an error raised from a stored procedure.

Solution

Use a try...catch block to catch serious errors. Use the SqlConnection.InfoMessage event handler to catch informational and warning messages.

The sample code, as shown in Example 2-11, uses a single stored procedure and two event handlers:

SP0210_Raiserror

> Accepts two input parameters specifying the severity and the state of an error and raises an error with the specified severity and state.

Raise Error Button.Click

> Creates a connection and attaches a handler for warning and information messages from the SQL Server. A Command is created for the *SP0210_Raiserror* stored procedure and the input parameters are defined. The user-specified severity and state are assigned to the input parameters and the stored procedure command is executed within a try statement.

SqlConnection.InfoMessage

> Called when a warning or informational message is raised by the SQL Server.

Example 2-11. Stored procedure: SP0210_Raiserror

```
CREATE PROCEDURE SP0210_Raiserror
    @Severity int,
    @State int = 1
AS
    if @Severity>=0 and @Severity <=18
        RAISERROR ('Error of severity %d raised from SP 0210_Raiserror.', @Severity,
            @State, @Severity)

    if @Severity>=19 and @Severity<=25
        RAISERROR ('Fatal error of severity %d raised from SP 0210_Raiserror.',
            @Severity, @State, @Severity) WITH LOG

    RETURN
```

The C# code is shown in Example 2-12.

Example 2-12. File: RaiserrorForm.cs

```csharp
// Namespaces, variables, and constants
using System;
using System.Configuration;
using System.Data;
using System.Data.SqlClient;

// ...

private void raiseErrorButton_Click(object sender, System.EventArgs e)
{
    resultTextBox.Text =
        "Severity: " + severityTextBox.Text + Environment.NewLine +
        "State: " + stateTextBox.Text + Environment.NewLine +
        Environment.NewLine;

    // Create the connection.
    SqlConnection conn = new SqlConnection(
        ConfigurationSettings.AppSettings["Sql_ConnectString"]);
    // Attach handler for SqlInfoMessage events.
    conn.InfoMessage += new SqlInfoMessageEventHandler(conn_InfoMessage);

    // Define a stored procedure command and the parameters.
    SqlCommand cmd = new SqlCommand("SP0210_Raiserror", conn);
    cmd.CommandType = CommandType.StoredProcedure;
    cmd.Parameters.Add("@Severity", SqlDbType.Int);
    cmd.Parameters.Add("@State", SqlDbType.Int);
    // Set the value for the stored procedure parameters.
    cmd.Parameters["@Severity"].Value = severityTextBox.Text;
    cmd.Parameters["@State"].Value = stateTextBox.Text;

    // Open the connection.
    conn.Open();
    try
    {
        // Try to execute the stored procedure.
        cmd.ExecuteNonQuery();
    }
    catch(System.Data.SqlClient.SqlException ex)
    {
        // Catch SqlException errors.
        resultTextBox.Text += "ERROR: " + ex.Message;
    }
    catch(Exception ex)
    {
        // Catch other errors.
        resultTextBox.Text += "OTHER ERROR: " + ex.Message;
    }
    finally
    {
        // Close the connection.
        conn.Close();
    }
}
```

Example 2-12. File: RaiserrorForm.cs (continued)

```csharp
private void conn_InfoMessage(object sender, SqlInfoMessageEventArgs e)
{
    resultTextBox.Text += "MESSAGE: " + e.Message;
}
```

Discussion

Errors and messages are returned from a SQL Server stored procedure to a calling application using the RAISERROR (note the spelling) function. The error message severity levels are listed in Table 2-12.

Table 2-12. RAISERROR error message severity levels

Severity level	Description
0–10	Informational
11–16	Error which can be corrected by the user
17–19	Resource or system error
20–25	Fatal error indicating a system problem

Severity levels greater than 20 result in the connection being closed.

Since severity levels 10 or less are considered to be informational, they raise a SqlInfoMessageEvent rather than an error. This is handled by subscribing a SqlInfoMessageEventHandler to the InfoMessage event of the SqlConnection object.

If the error has severity level 11 or greater, a SqlException is thrown by the SQL Server .NET data provider.

For more information about the RAISERROR function, look up RAISERROR in SQL Server Books Online.

2.11   Testing for No Records

Problem

You need to determine whether any records were returned from a query that you just executed.

Solution

Use the DataRowCollection.Count property, the DataReader.HasRows property, or the DataReader.Read( ) method.

The sample code creates and fills a DataTable and uses the Count property of the DataRowCollection to determine if the query used to create the table returned any rows. Next, a DataReader is created and both the HasRows property and the Read( ) method are used to determine whether the query used to create the DataReader returned any rows.

The C# code is shown in Example 2-13.

Example 2-13. File: NoRecordTestForm.cs

```csharp
// Namespaces, variables, and constants
using System;
using System.Configuration;
using System.Text;
using System.Data;
using System.Data.SqlClient;

// Table name constants
private const String ORDERS_TABLE = "Orders";

// ...

StringBuilder result = new StringBuilder( );

// Fill the Orders DataTable.
SqlDataAdapter da = new SqlDataAdapter("SELECT * FROM Orders",
    ConfigurationSettings.AppSettings["Sql_ConnectString"]);
DataTable orderTable = new DataTable(ORDERS_TABLE);
da.Fill(orderTable);

// Test Orders DataTable for records.
bool tableHasRecords = orderTable.Rows.Count > 0;
result.Append("DataTable " + ORDERS_TABLE + ": Has records = " +
    tableHasRecords + Environment.NewLine);

// Create the Orders DataReader.
SqlConnection conn = new SqlConnection(
    ConfigurationSettings.AppSettings["Sql_ConnectString"]);
SqlCommand cmd = new SqlCommand("SELECT * FROM ORDERS", conn);
conn.Open( );
SqlDataReader orderReader = cmd.ExecuteReader( );

// Test Orders DataReader for records.
result.Append("DataReader " + ORDERS_TABLE + ": Has records = " +
    orderReader.HasRows + Environment.NewLine);

// Test Orders DataReader for records.
bool readerHasRecords = orderReader.Read( );
result.Append("DataReader " + ORDERS_TABLE + ": Has records = " +
    readerHasRecords + Environment.NewLine);

orderReader.Close( );
conn.Close( );

resultTextBox.Text = result.ToString( );
```

Discussion

The DataTable contains a DataRowCollection object that contains all DataRow objects in the table. The DataRowCollection has a Count property that returns the number of rows in the table. The Count property for an empty table has a value of 0.

The HasRows property of the DataReader returns a Boolean value indicating whether the DataReader has any records.

Another way is to use the Read( ) method to advance the DataReader to the next record. This returns a value of true if a record is available and false otherwise. The first call to the Read( ) method will indicate whether any records were returned by the DataReader. This was the only way to determine whether the DataReader contained any records prior to the introduction of the HasRows property in .NET Framework 1.1.

2.12 Retrieving Stored Procedure Return Values Using a DataReader

Problem

You are using a stored procedure to create a DataReader and need to get the return value. When you try to access the value, it is null. How can you access the return value?

Solution

Use a parameter defined with a ParameterDirection property of ReturnValue.

The sample code uses a single stored procedure, as shown in Example 2-14:

SP0212_ReturnValueWithDataReader
> Returns a result set containing all records from the Orders table in Northwind. The stored procedure takes a single input parameter which it simply returns.

Example 2-14. Stored procedure: SP0212_ReturnValueWithDataReader

```
CREATE PROCEDURE SP0212_ReturnValueWithDataReader
    @ValueIn int=0
AS
    set nocount on

    select * from Orders

    RETURN @ValueIn
```

The sample code creates a DataReader from a stored procedure command. The stored procedure returns the value of the single input parameter specified by the user. The code displays the value of the return parameter at five different stages of working with the result set in the DataReader:

- Before the DataReader is created
- Immediately after the DataReader is created
- After all rows in the DataReader have been read
- After the DataReader is closed
- After the Connection is closed

The C# code is shown in Example 2-15.

Example 2-15. File: SpReturnValueDataReaderForm.cs

```csharp
// Namespaces, variables, and constants
using System;
using System.Configuration;
using System.Text;
using System.Data;
using System.Data.SqlClient;

// ...

StringBuilder result = new StringBuilder( );

// Create the connection.
SqlConnection conn = new SqlConnection(
    ConfigurationSettings.AppSettings["Sql_ConnectString"]);

// Create the command.
SqlCommand cmd = new SqlCommand("SP0212_ReturnValueWithDataReader", conn);
cmd.CommandType = CommandType.StoredProcedure;

// Define the input parameter for the command.
cmd.Parameters.Add("@ValueIn", SqlDbType.Int);
// Set the input parameter value.
cmd.Parameters["@ValueIn"].Value = Convert.ToInt32(returnValueTextBox.Text);

// Define the return parameter for the command.
SqlParameter retParam = cmd.Parameters.Add("@ReturnValue", SqlDbType.Int);
retParam.Direction = ParameterDirection.ReturnValue;

result.Append("Before execution, return value = " + retParam.Value +
    Environment.NewLine);

// Open the connection and create the DataReader.
conn.Open( );
SqlDataReader reader = cmd.ExecuteReader( );

result.Append("After execution, return value = " + retParam.Value +
    Environment.NewLine);
```

Example 2-15. File: SpReturnValueDataReaderForm.cs (continued)

```
// Iterate over the records for the DataReader.
int rowCount = 0;
while (reader.Read( ))
{
    rowCount++;

    // Code to process result set in DataReader.
}

result.Append("After reading all " + rowCount + " rows, return value = " +
    retParam.Value + Environment.NewLine);

// Close the DataReader.
reader.Close( );
result.Append("After DataReader.Close( ), return value = " +
    retParam.Value + Environment.NewLine);

// Close the connection.
conn.Close( );
result.Append("After Connection.Close( ), return value = " +
    retParam.Value);

resultTextBox.Text = result.ToString( );
```

Discussion

Every stored procedure returns an integer value to the caller. If the value for the return code is not explicitly set, it defaults to 0. The return value is accessed from ADO.NET through a parameter that represents it. The parameter is defined with a ParameterDirection property of ReturnValue (Table 2-13 describes all values in the ParameterDirection enumeration). The data type of the ReturnValue parameter must be set to Integer. Once all parameters are defined, build the DataReader using the ExecuteReader( ) method of the Command object.

Table 2-13. ParameterDirection enumeration

Value	Description
Input	The parameter is an input parameter allowing the caller to pass a data value to the stored procedure.
InputOutput	The parameter is both an input and output parameter, allowing the caller to pass a data value to the stored procedure and the stored procedure to pass a data value back to the caller.
Output	The parameter is an output parameter allowing the stored procedure to pass a data value back to the caller.
ReturnValue	The parameter represents the value returned from the stored procedure.

Return parameters from the stored procedure used to build a DataReader are not available until the DataReader is closed by calling the Close( ) method or until

Dispose( ) is called on the DataReader. You do not have to read any of records in the DataReader to obtain a return value.

2.13 Executing SQL Server User-Defined Scalar Functions

Problem

Your SQL Server 2000 database includes a user-defined function that returns a scalar value. You want to retrieve the value from this function using ADO.NET.

Solution

Invoke the function as you would a query or stored procedure.

The sample code, as shown in Example 2-16, uses a single SQL Server function:

ExtendedPrice

> Calculates and returns the extended price for an order line item based on the unit price, quantity, and discount.

Example 2-16. SQL Server function: ExtendedPrice

```
CREATE FUNCTION dbo.ExtendedPrice
(
    @UnitPrice money,
    @Quantity smallint,
    @Discount real
)
RETURNS money
AS

BEGIN
    RETURN ((@UnitPrice * @Quantity) * (1 - @Discount))
END
```

The sample code defines a SQL statement that uses the ExtendedPrice user-defined function. The statement is used by a DataAdapter to fill a DataTable with all records from the Order Details table in Northwind together with the extended price calculation for each record. The default view of the table is bound to a data grid on the form.

The C# code is shown in Example 2-17.

Example 2-17. File: ScalarFunctionForm.cs

```
// Namespaces, variables, and constants
using System;
using System.Configuration;
```

Example 2-17. File: ScalarFunctionForm.cs (continued)

```
using System.Data;
using System.Data.SqlClient;

// ...

String sqlText = "SELECT *, " +
    "dbo.ExtendedPrice(UnitPrice, Quantity, Discount) ExtendedPrice " +
    "FROM [Order Details]";

// Create DataAdapter and fill the table.
SqlDataAdapter da = new SqlDataAdapter(sqlText,
    ConfigurationSettings.AppSettings["Sql_ConnectString"]);
DataTable dt = new DataTable( );
da.Fill(dt);

// Bind the default view for the table to the grid.
resultDataGrid.DataSource = dt;
```

Discussion

A user-defined scalar function is a SQL routine that accepts one or more scalar input parameters and returns a single value. A user-defined scalar function is invoked from a query or executed like a stored procedure using an EXECUTE statement.

You can invoke scalar functions where scalar expressions can be used. To invoke a scalar function, use the following syntax:

```
[databaseName.]ownerName.functionName([argument1][, ...])
```

In the solution code, the ExtendedPrice function is called as shown by:

```
dbo.ExtendedPrice(UnitPrice, Quantity, Discount)
```

This calculates the extended price for each row in the Order Details table based on the UnitPrice, Quantity, and Discount values. The result is returned as a result set column named ExtendedPrice.

2.14   Passing Null Values to Parameters

Problem

You need to pass a null value to a parameter.

Solution

Use the System.DbNull.Value static value.

The sample code, as shown in Example 2-18, uses a single stored procedure:

SP0214_NullParameter
> Accepts a single parameter and a returns one-row result set containing a single value indicating whether that input parameter was null.

Example 2-18. Stored procedure: SP0214_NullParameter

```
CREATE PROCEDURE SP0214_NullParameter
    @ValueIn int
AS
    if @ValueIn is null
        select 1 as IsParameterNull
    else
        select 0 as IsParameterNull

    return 0
```

The sample code contains two event handlers:

Go Button.Click
> Creates a stored procedure command for *SP0214_NullParameter* and defines its single input parameter. The input parameter is set to System.DbNull.Value if the user has checked the Null Parameter check box on the form; otherwise it is set to the value that the user has entered in the Parameter text box. The stored procedure is executed using the ExecuteScalar( ) method and the value returned indicates whether the input parameter for the stored procedure is null.

Null Parameter CheckBox.CheckedChange
> Clears the value of the Parameter text box if checked and enables the Parameter text box if not checked.

The C# code is shown in Example 2-19.

Example 2-19. File: NullParameterForm.cs

```
// Namespaces, variables, and constants
using System;
using System.Configuration;
using System.Data;
using System.Data.SqlClient;

// ...

private void goButton_Click(object sender, System.EventArgs e)
{
    // Create the connection.
    SqlConnection conn = new SqlConnection(
        ConfigurationSettings.AppSettings["Sql_ConnectString"]);

    // Create the stored procedure command.
    SqlCommand cmd = new SqlCommand("SP0214_NullParameter", conn);
    cmd.CommandType = CommandType.StoredProcedure;
```

Example 2-19. File: NullParameterForm.cs (continued)

```
    // Define the parameter.
    cmd.Parameters.Add("@ValueIn", SqlDbType.Int);
    // Set the value of the paramter.
    if (isNullCheckBox.Checked)
        cmd.Parameters[0].Value = System.DBNull.Value;
    else
        cmd.Parameters[0].Value = parameterTextBox.Text;

    // Retrieve whether parameter null from stored procedure.
    try
    {
        conn.Open();
        bool isNullParm = Convert.ToBoolean(cmd.ExecuteScalar());
        resultTextBox.Text = "Null Parameter = " + isNullParm;
    }
    catch (Exception ex)
    {
        resultTextBox.Text = ex.Message;
    }
    finally
    {
        conn.Close();
    }
}

private void isNullCheckBox_CheckedChanged(object sender,
    System.EventArgs e)
{
    if(isNullCheckBox.Checked)
        parameterTextBox.Text = "";

    parameterTextBox.Enabled = !isNullCheckBox.Checked;
}
```

Discussion

System.DBNull is not the same as null in C# or Nothing in VB.NET. System.DBNull indicates that the object represents missing or nonexistent data, typically in a database, while null and Nothing indicate that an object or variable has not yet been initialized.

Passing a null parameter value into a stored procedure is not very different than passing any other parameter value. Construct the parameter using either the Parameter constructor or the Add( ) method of the ParameterCollection for the Command object. The value is set by passing System.DBNull.Value for the value argument when constructing the parameter or by setting the Value property of the Parameter object to System.DBNull.Value.

To test for a null value, the IsDBNull( ) method returns a Boolean value that indicates whether an object expression evaluates to System.DBNull. This is the same as comparing an object to the System.DBNull.Value using an equality operator.

If the stored procedure accepts optional parameters—parameters for which a default value is specified—you can set these parameters to null in C# or Nothing in VB.NET. This is not the same as setting the parameter value to System.DBNull.Value. The parameter value is set to the default value specified for the parameter.

2.15   Retrieving Update Errors

Problem

You want to access all of the error information available after an update fails.

Solution

Use one of the available properties (such as HasErrors) and methods (such as GetErrors()) to obtain the error information.

The schema of table TBL0215 used in this solution is shown in Table 2-14.

Table 2-14. TBL0215 schema

Column name	Data type	Length	Allow nulls?
UniqueId	int	4	No
NumericField	int	4	No
StringNoNullsField	nvarchar	50	No
ConstrainedNegativeField	int	4	No

The sample code contains two event handlers:

Form.Load

> Sets up the sample by creating a table to demonstrate error information retrieval, using a DataAdapter to fill it with sample data, and adding it to a DataSet. The ContinueUpdateOnError property of the DataAdapter is set to true so that an exception is not raised if an error is encountered during an update. Finally, the default view of the table is bound to the data grid on the form.

Update Button.Click

> Sets an error description for the first column of the first row using the SetColumnError() method if the user has checked the Test Column Error check box. The Update() method of the DataAdapter is called to update changes that the user has made to the data back to the database. After the update, the HasErrors property of the DataSet is tested to determine if the DataSet has any errors. The collection of DataTable objects in the DataSet (in this case there is only one) is iterated again and the HasErrors property for each table is checked to see if the table has any errors. The collection of DataRow objects having errors in the table are accessed using the GetErrors() method on the table. For each

row in error, the HasErrors property is checked to determine if the row has any errors and the RowError property of a row having errors is accessed to get the text describing the error. The collection of DataColumn objects having errors in the row are accessed using the row's GetColumnsInError( ) method. For each column having an error, the row's GetColumnError( ) method is used to get the error description for the column.

The C# code is shown in Example 2-20.

Example 2-20. File: RetrieveProviderErrorsForm.cs

```csharp
// Namespaces, variables, and constants
using System;
using System.Configuration;
using System.Text;
using System.Data;
using System.Data.SqlClient;

private const String TABLENAME = "TBL0215";
private DataSet ds;
private SqlDataAdapter da;

// ...

private void RetrieveProviderErrorsForm_Load(object sender,
    System.EventArgs e)
{
    String sqlText = "SELECT * FROM " + TABLENAME;

    // Create the DataAdapter and its CommandBuilder.
    da = new SqlDataAdapter(sqlText,
        ConfigurationSettings.AppSettings["Sql_ConnectString"]);
    da.ContinueUpdateOnError = true;
    SqlCommandBuilder cb = new SqlCommandBuilder(da);

    // Create a table and fill it.
    DataTable dt = new DataTable(TABLENAME);
    dt.Columns.Add("UniqueId", typeof(Int32));
    dt.Columns.Add("NumericField");      // Data type not specified
    dt.Columns.Add("StringNoNullsField", typeof(String));
    dt.Columns.Add("ConstrainedNegativeField", typeof(Int32));
    da.Fill(dt);

    // Create the DataSet and add the table.
    ds = new DataSet();
    ds.Tables.Add(dt);

    // Bind the default view for the table to the grid.
    dataGrid.DataSource = dt.DefaultView;
}

private void updateButton_Click(object sender, System.EventArgs e)
{
    StringBuilder result = new StringBuilder();
```

Example 2-20. File: RetrieveProviderErrorsForm.cs (continued)

```
    if (testColumnErrorCheckBox.Checked)
        // Set a column error on to demonstrate.
        ds.Tables[0].Rows[0].SetColumnError(0, "test error");
    else
        // Clear the demonstration column error.
        ds.Tables[0].Rows[0].SetColumnError(0, "");

    da.Update(ds, TABLENAME);

    result.Append("Dataset.HasErrors = " + ds.HasErrors +
        Environment.NewLine);

    // Iterate over the collection of tables in the DataSet.
    foreach(DataTable dt in ds.Tables)
    {
        // Display whether the table has errors.
        result.Append("\tTable [" + dt.TableName + "] HasErrors = " +
            dt.HasErrors + Environment.NewLine);

        int rowCount = 0;
        // Iterate over the rows in the table having errors.
        foreach(DataRow row in dt.GetErrors())
        {
            // Display whether error information for the row.
            result.Append("\t\tRow [" + (++rowCount) +
                "] HasErrors = " + row.HasErrors +
                Environment.NewLine);
            if(row.RowError != "")
                result.Append("\t\t" + row.RowError +
                    Environment.NewLine);

            // Iterate over the column errors for the row.
            foreach(DataColumn col in row.GetColumnsInError())
            {
                // Display error information for the column.
                result.Append("\t\t\tColumn [" + col.ColumnName +
                    "]: " + row.GetColumnError(col) +
                    Environment.NewLine);
            }
        }
    }

    resultTextBox.Text = result.ToString();
}
```

Discussion

The Update( ) method of the DataAdapter is used to reconcile changes made to a
DataSet back to the underlying data source. If errors occur during the reconciliation,

the `ContinueUpdateOnError` property of the `DataAdapter` specifies whether the update continues with remaining rows or stops processing:

- If `ContinueUpdateOnError` is `true` and an error is encountered during the update, the `RowError` property of the `DataRow` causing the error is set to the error message that would have been raised, the update of the row is skipped, and updating continues with subsequent rows. No exception is raised.

- If `ContinueUpdateOnError` is `false`, the `DataAdapter` raises a `DBConcurrencyException` when a row update attempt fails.

Once the update has completed, there are a number of properties and methods you can use to investigate errors in the `DataSet`, `DataTable`, `DataRow`, and `DataColumn` objects:

`HasErrors`
> This property exists for the `DataSet`, `DataTable`, and `DataRow` objects. It returns a Boolean value indicating whether there are any errors within the object. Checking the `HasErrors` property for an object before calling specific error retrieval methods can improve performance by eliminating unnecessary calls to the more time consuming error retrieval methods.

`GetErrors( )`
> This method of the `DataTable` returns an array of `DataRow` objects having errors.

`RowError`
> This property of the `DataRow` returns the custom error description for the row.

`GetColumnsInError( )`
> This method of the `DataRow` returns an array of columns containing errors. Rather than iterating over the collection of columns in a row and checking each for an error, this method reduces error processing by returning only those columns having an error.

`GetColumnError( )`
> This method of the `DataRow` returns the error description for a column. Column errors are set using the `SetColumnError( )` method of the `DataRow`; errors for individual columns are not set by the `DataAdapter`.

`ClearErrors( )`
> This method of the `DataRow` clears all errors for a row including both the `RowError` and errors set using the `SetColumnError( )` method.

The solution code demonstrates how to use these error checking methods and properties when updates are made with user-specified data.

2.16   Mapping Table and Column Names Between the Data Source and DataSet

Problem

You want to control the names assigned to tables and columns when you fill a DataSet using a DataAdapter.

Solution

Use DataTableMapping and DataColumnMapping objects to map the names of database tables and columns in the data source to different names in a DataSet when using a DataAdapter.

The sample code defines a SQL statement to retrieve the CategoryID, CategoryName, and Description columns from the Categories table in Northwind. A DataAdapter is created with a DataTableMapping object to map the database table name Categories to the name tblmapCategories in the DataSet. Three DataColumnMapping objects are created to map the database column names to different names in the table in the DataSet. The DataAdapter is used to fill a new DataSet. Finally, the default view of the mapped Categories table is bound to the data grid on the form.

The C# code is shown in Example 2-21.

Example 2-21. File: MappingsForm.cs

```
// Namespaces, variables, and constants
using System;
using System.Configuration;
using System.Data;
using System.Data.Common;
using System.Data.SqlClient;

// ...

// Create the DataAdapter.
String sqlText = "SELECT CategoryID, CategoryName, Description " +
    "FROM Categories";
SqlDataAdapter da = new SqlDataAdapter(sqlText,
    ConfigurationSettings.AppSettings["Sql_ConnectString"]);

// Create the table mapping to map the default table name 'Table'.
DataTableMapping dtm = da.TableMappings.Add("Table", "tblmapCategories");
// Create the column mappings for the Categories table.
dtm.ColumnMappings.Add("CategoryID", "colmapCategoryID");
dtm.ColumnMappings.Add("CategoryName", "colmapCategoryName");
dtm.ColumnMappings.Add("Description", "colmapDescription");
```

Example 2-21. File: MappingsForm.cs (continued)

```
// Create the DataSet and fill.
DataSet ds = new DataSet( );
da.Fill(ds);

// Retrieve and display the mapped name of the table as grid caption.
dataGrid.CaptionText = "TableName: " + ds.Tables[0].ToString( );

// Bind the default view of the Categories table to the grid.
dataGrid.DataSource = ds.Tables["tblmapCategories"].DefaultView;
```

Discussion

When the Fill( ) method of the DataAdapter is used to fill a DataSet, the column names used in the DataSet default to the column names defined in the data source.

A DataAdapter has a collection of DataTableMapping objects in its DataTableMappingCollection accessed through its TableMappings property. These objects map the name of a table in the data source to a DataTable with different name in the DataSet. When a batch query is used to fill multiple tables within a DataSet, the table names default to *Table*, *Table1*, *Table2*, and so on. You can use table mapping to rename tables created within the DataSet to match the table names in the data source or to map the tables returned from a batch query to DataTable objects that already exist within the DataSet.

Each table mapping object has a collection of DataColumnMapping objects in its DataColumnMappingCollection that are accessed through its ColumnMappings property. These objects map the name of a column in the data source to a column with a different name in the DataSet for the table associated with the containing table mapping object.

The Fill( ) method of the DataAdapter always uses mapping information (if present) to retrieve data from a data source. The FillSchema( ) method accepts an argument specifying whether to use mapping information when retrieving schema information from a data source. Like the Fill( ) method, the Update( ) method always uses mapping information (if present) when submitting DataSet changes back to the data source.

In the solution, the Categories table retrieved by the query is mapped to a table in the DataSet called tblmapCategories with the following code:

```
    DataTableMapping dtm = da.TableMappings.Add("Table", "tblmapCategories");
```

Without the table mapping, a table named Table will be created when the Fill( ) method is called. For a query returning a single table, the table mapping can also be specified by using an overload of the Fill( ) method as shown:

```
    da.Fill(ds, "tblmapCategories");
```

The solution also maps the three column names returned by the query, `CategoryID`, `CategoryName`, and `Description` using the following code:

```
dtm.ColumnMappings.Add("CategoryID", "colmapCategoryID");
dtm.ColumnMappings.Add("CategoryName", "colmapCategoryName");
dtm.ColumnMappings.Add("Description", "colmapDescription");
```

The column mapping objects are added to the table mapping object for the table containing the columns to be mapped.

2.17 Displaying Columns from a Related DataTable

Problem

You want to add a column to a `DataTable` that displays a value from a row in a related table in the `DataSet`.

Solution

Use expression columns to retrieve lookup values based on `DataRelation` objects.

The sample code creates a new `DataSet` containing the Orders table and the Order Details table from Northwind. A `DataRelation` is created between the tables. A column is added to the Order Details table that gets the *CustomerID* from the parent Order using the relation created between the tables. Finally, the default view of the Orders table is bound to the data grid on the form.

The C# code is shown in Example 2-22.

Example 2-22. File: LookupColumnsForm.cs

```
// Namespaces, variables, and constants
using System;
using System.Configuration;
using System.Data;
using System.Data.SqlClient;

// Table name constants
private const String ORDERS_TABLE        = "Orders";
private const String ORDERDETAILS_TABLE  = "OrderDetails";

// Relation name constants
private const String ORDERS_ORDERDETAILS_RELATION =
    "Orders_OrderDetails_Relation";

// Field name constants
private const String ORDERID_FIELD       = "OrderID";
private const String CUSTOMERID_FIELD    = "CustomerID";
private const String QUANTITY_FIELD      = "Quantity";
```

Example 2-22. File: LookupColumnsForm.cs (continued)

```
// ...

DataSet ds = new DataSet( );

// Fill the Orders table and add it to the DataSet.
SqlDataAdapter da = new SqlDataAdapter("SELECT * FROM Orders",
    ConfigurationSettings.AppSettings["Sql_ConnectString"]);
DataTable ordersTable = new DataTable(ORDERS_TABLE);
da.Fill(ordersTable);
ds.Tables.Add(ordersTable);

// Fill the OrderDetails table and add it to the DataSet.
da = new SqlDataAdapter("SELECT * FROM [Order Details]",
    ConfigurationSettings.AppSettings["Sql_ConnectString"]);
DataTable orderDetailsTable = new DataTable(ORDERDETAILS_TABLE);
da.Fill(orderDetailsTable);
ds.Tables.Add(orderDetailsTable);

// Create a relation between the tables.
ds.Relations.Add(ORDERS_ORDERDETAILS_RELATION,
    ordersTable.Columns[ORDERID_FIELD],
    orderDetailsTable.Columns[ORDERID_FIELD],
    true);

// Add a column to Orders for the total items in all Order Detail rows.
ordersTable.Columns.Add("TotalQuantity", typeof(int),
    "Sum(Child." + QUANTITY_FIELD + ")");

// Add a column to Order Details getting CustomerID from Order parent.
orderDetailsTable.Columns.Add(CUSTOMERID_FIELD, typeof(string),
    "Parent(" + ORDERS_ORDERDETAILS_RELATION + ")." + CUSTOMERID_FIELD);

// Bind the default view of the Order table to the grid.
resultDataGrid.DataSource = ordersTable.DefaultView;
```

Discussion

An expression column creates a calculated column that displays information from a related record. You can refer to a column in a parent record by affixing Parent. to the beginning of the name of the column in the parent table. If there are multiple parent records because of multiple data relations, the name of the DataRelation is specified within parentheses and Parent(*DataRelationName*). is affixed to the name of the column in the parent table.

The sample code creates a calculated column in the Order Details table retrieving the *CustomerID* from the parent *Orders* record for each Order Details record:

```
orderDetailsTable.Columns.Add(CUSTOMERID_FIELD, typeof(string),
    "Parent(" + ORDERS_ORDERDETAILS_RELATION + ")." + CUSTOMERID_FIELD);
```

When the constants are replaced with their values, this code is equivalent to:

```
orderDetailsTable.Columns.Add("CustomerID", typeof(string),
    "Parent(Orders_OrderDetails_Relation).CustomerID");
```

Similarly, you can refer to child records within an expression by affixing the beginning of the column name in the child table with Child. or Child(*DataRelationName*). depending on whether the row has child records from multiple tables. Additionally, since multiple child records can exist for a parent record, the reference to the child column must be used within an aggregate function. Supported aggregates are listed in Table 2-15.

Table 2-15. Aggregate functions supported in DataColumn expressions

Aggregate	Description
Avg	Average of all values
Count	Number of values
Max	Largest value
Min	Smallest value
StDev	Statistical standard deviation of all values
Sum	Sum of all values
Var	Statistical variance of all values

The sample code creates a calculated column in the Orders table for the total quantity of all order detail items for an order with the following code:

```
ordersTable.Columns.Add("TotalQuantity", typeof(int),
    "Sum(Child." + QUANTITY_FIELD + ")");
```

When the constants are replaced with their values, the code is:

```
ordersTable.Columns.Add("TotalQuantity", typeof(int),
    "Sum(Child.Quantity)");
```

Unlike the sample code referencing a parent row, the DataRelation name is omitted because only one DataRelation exists and it is unnecessary in this case.

If the parent record has no child records, the aggregate function returns a null reference in C# or Nothing in VB.NET.

2.18   Controlling the Names Used in a Strongly Typed DataSet

Problem

You want to assign your own names to the classes and properties for strongly typed DataSet classes.

Solution

Use annotations in the XML schema to control the names of classes and properties in strongly typed DataSet classes.

The sample uses one *XSD* file:

CategoriesDS_AnnotatedName.xsd

The schema used to generate the strongly typed DataSet. The schema is annotated so that you can access the collection of rows in the table by using the Categorys property of the DataSet rather than categories, each row by using the Category property of the row collection rather than CategoriesRow, and the CategoryName field by using the Name property of the row rather than CategoryName. The annotations are marked in bold in the Example 2-23.

Example 2-23. File: TypedDataSets\CategoriesDS_AnnotatedName.xsd

```
<?xml version="1.0" standalone="yes" ?>
<xs:schema id="CategoriesDS_AnnotatedName"
    targetNamespace=
    "http://www.tempuri.org/CategoriesDS_AnnotatedName.xsd"
    xmlns:mstns="http://www.tempuri.org/CategoriesDS_AnnotatedName.xsd"
    xmlns="http://www.tempuri.org/CategoriesDS_AnnotatedName.xsd"
    xmlns:xs="http://www.w3.org/2001/XMLSchema"
    xmlns:msdata="urn:schemas-microsoft-com:xml-msdata"
    xmlns:codegen="urn:schemas-microsoft-com:xml-msprop"
    attributeFormDefault="qualified" elementFormDefault="qualified">
    <xs:element name="CategoriesDS_AnnotatedName" msdata:IsDataSet="true">
        <xs:complexType>
            <xs:choice maxOccurs="unbounded">
                <xs:element name="Categories"
                    codegen:typedName="Category"
                    codegen:typedPlural="Categorys">
                    <xs:complexType>
                        <xs:sequence>
                            <xs:element
                            name="CategoryID"
                            msdata:ReadOnly="true"
                            msdata:AutoIncrement="true"
                            type="xs:int" />
                            <xs:element
                            name="CategoryName"
                            type="xs:string"
                            codegen:typedName="Name" />
                            <xs:element
                            name="Description"
                            type="xs:string"
                            minOccurs="0" />
                        </xs:sequence>
                    </xs:complexType>
                </xs:element>
            </xs:choice>
```

```
            </xs:complexType>
            <xs:unique name="Constraint1" msdata:PrimaryKey="true">
                <xs:selector xpath=".//mstns:Categories" />
                <xs:field xpath="mstns:CategoryID" />
            </xs:unique>
        </xs:element>
    </xs:schema>
```

The sample code creates a strongly typed DataSet based on the Categories table in Northwind. The user specifies whether the one based on the default or annotated schema file is used. In either case, data is loaded into the DataSet and the collections of rows and columns in the DataSet are iterated over to display the data and to demonstrate the effect of the schema annotations.

The C# code is shown in Example 2-24.

Example 2-24. File: TypedDataSetNamesForm.cs

```csharp
// Namespaces, variables, and constants
using System;
using System.Configuration;
using System.Text;
using System.Data;
using System.Data.SqlClient;

// Table name constants
private const String CATEGORIES_TABLE = "Categories";

// ...

StringBuilder result = new StringBuilder( );

// Create the DataAdapter.
SqlDataAdapter da = new SqlDataAdapter("SELECT * FROM Categories",
    ConfigurationSettings.AppSettings["Sql_ConnectString"]);

if (annotatedRadioButton.Checked)
{
    // Create the typed DataSet with name annotations.
    CategoriesDS_AnnotatedName ds = new CategoriesDS_AnnotatedName( );
    // Fill the Categories table within DataSet.
    da.Fill(ds, CATEGORIES_TABLE);

    result.Append("Annotated Names" + Environment.NewLine +
        Environment.NewLine);
    // Iterate over the rows collection and display columns.
    // Note that the row collection is Categorys
    // and that each row is Category.
    foreach(CategoriesDS_AnnotatedName.Category row in ds.Categorys)
    {
        // Note that the CategoryName field is referred to simply as Name.
        result.Append(row.CategoryID + "\t" + row.Name + "\t" +
```

Example 2-24. File: TypedDataSetNamesForm.cs (continued)

```
            row.Description + Environment.NewLine);
    }
}
else
{
    // Create the typed DataSet without name annotations.
    CategoriesDS ds = new CategoriesDS( );
    da.Fill(ds, CATEGORIES_TABLE);

    result.Append("Default" + Environment.NewLine + Environment.NewLine);
    // Iterate over the rows collection and display columns.
    foreach(CategoriesDS.CategoriesRow row in ds.Categories)
    {
        result.Append(row.CategoryID + "\t" + row.CategoryName + "\t" +
            row.Description + Environment.NewLine);
    }
}

resultTextBox.Text = result.ToString( );
```

Discussion

Annotations are modifications to the XSD schema used to generate a strongly typed DataSet that allows the names of elements in the strongly typed DataSet to be customized without changing the underlying schema. This allows more meaningful element names to be used resulting in code that is easier to read, use, and maintain. Table 2-16 lists available annotations.

Table 2-16. Available annotations

Annotation	Description
typedChildren	Name of the method that returns objects from a child data relation.
typedName	Name of the object.
typedParent	Name of the method that returns an object from a parent data relation.
typedPlural	Name of the collection of objects.
nullValue	Value or behavior if the underlying value is DBNull. Table 2-17 lists possible values for this annotation. The default value is _throw.

Table 2-17 describes possible values for the nullValue annotation.

Table 2-17. Values for nullValue annotation

nullValue	Description
Replacement Value	A value having the same type as the element to be returned
_empty	Return String.Empty for a String Return an object created from an empty constructor for other objects Throw an exception for primitive types

Table 2-17. Values for nullValue annotation (continued)

nullValue	Description
_null	Return a null reference for objects Throw an exception for primitive types
_throw	Raise an exception

Table 2-18 lists the different objects in a strongly typed DataSet and the default names and available annotations for each.

Table 2-18. Default values and available annotations for elements of strongly typed DataSet objects

Element	Default name	Annotation
DataTable	*TableName*DataTable	typedPlural
DataTable methods	New*TableName*Row Add*TableName*Row Delete*TableName*Row	typedName
DataRowCollection	*TableName*	typedPlural
DataRow	*TableName*Row	typedName
DataColumn	DataTable.*ColumnName*Column DataRow.*ColumnName*	typedName
Property	*PropertyName*	typedName
Child accessor	Get*ChildTableName*Rows	typedChildren
Parent accessor	*TableName*Row	typedParent
DataSet events	*TableName*RowChangeEvent *TableName*RowChangeEventHandler	typedName

The use annotations, a reference to the codegen namespace, must be included in the XSD schema, as shown:

```
xmlns:codegen="urn:schemas-microsoft-com:xml-msprop"
```

The codegen namespace allows the names of methods, properties, relations, constraints, and events in the strongly typed DataSet to be customized.

2.19   Replacing Null Values in a Strongly Typed DataSet

Problem

When a column in a database has a null value, you want the value in the DataSet to be a string indicating that no value is available.

Solution

Use annotations in the XML schema to control the handling of null values.

The sample uses one *XSD* file:

CategoriesDS_AnnotatedNull.xsd

> The schema used to generate the strongly typed DataSet. The schema is annotated so the null Description values are replaced with the string "- no description available -". The annotations are marked in bold in Example 2-25.

Example 2-25. File: TypedDataSets\CategoriesDS_AnnotatedNull.xsd

```
<?xml version="1.0" standalone="yes" ?>
<xs:schema id="CategoriesDS_AnnotatedNull"
    targetNamespace=
    "http://www.tempuri.org/CategoriesDS_AnnotatedNull.xsd"
    xmlns:mstns="http://www.tempuri.org/CategoriesDS_AnnotatedNull.xsd"
    xmlns="http://www.tempuri.org/CategoriesDS_AnnotatedNull.xsd"
    xmlns:xs="http://www.w3.org/2001/XMLSchema"
    xmlns:msdata="urn:schemas-microsoft-com:xml-msdata"
    xmlns:codegen="urn:schemas-microsoft-com:xml-msprop"
    attributeFormDefault="qualified" elementFormDefault="qualified">
    <xs:element name="CategoriesDS_AnnotatedNull" msdata:IsDataSet="true">
        <xs:complexType>
            <xs:choice maxOccurs="unbounded">
                <xs:element name="Categories">
                    <xs:complexType>
                        <xs:sequence>
                        <xs:element
                        name="CategoryID"
                        msdata:ReadOnly="true"
                        msdata:AutoIncrement="true"
                        type="xs:int" />
                        <xs:element
                        name="CategoryName"
                        type="xs:string" />
                        <xs:element
                        name="Description"
                        type="xs:string"
                        minOccurs="0"
                        codegen:nullValue=
                        "- no description available -" />
                        </xs:sequence>
                    </xs:complexType>
                </xs:element>
            </xs:choice>
        </xs:complexType>
        <xs:unique name="Constraint1" msdata:PrimaryKey="true">
            <xs:selector xpath=".//mstns:Categories" />
            <xs:field xpath="mstns:CategoryID" />
        </xs:unique>
    </xs:element>
</xs:schema>
```

The sample code creates a strongly typed DataSet based on the Categories table in Northwind. The user specifies whether the one based on the default or annotated schema file is used. In either case, data is loaded into the DataSet. A row is added to the Categories table with a Description value of null. The data in the table is written to the text box on the form to demonstrate the effect of the schema annotation on null column values.

The C# code is shown in Example 2-26.

Example 2-26. File: TypedDataSetNullsForm.cs

```csharp
// Namespaces, variables, and constants
using System;
using System.Configuration;
using System.Text;
using System.Data;
using System.Data.SqlClient;

// Table name constants
private const String CATEGORIES_TABLE = "Categories";

// ...

StringBuilder result = new StringBuilder( );

// Create the DataAdapter.
SqlDataAdapter da = new SqlDataAdapter("SELECT * FROM Categories",
    ConfigurationSettings.AppSettings["Sql_ConnectString"]);

if (annotatedRadioButton.Checked)
{
    // Create the typed DataSet without null annotation.
    CategoriesDS_AnnotatedNull ds = new CategoriesDS_AnnotatedNull( );
    // Fill the Categories table within DataSet.
    da.Fill(ds, CATEGORIES_TABLE);

    // Add a row with a null Description.
    ds.Categories.AddCategoriesRow("New Category", null);

    result.Append("Annotated Nulls" + Environment.NewLine +
        Environment.NewLine);
    // Iterate over the rows collection and display columns.
    foreach(CategoriesDS_AnnotatedNull.CategoriesRow row in ds.Categories)
    {
        // Get the Description.
        String description = row.Description;

        // Note that the null Description is replaced.
        result.Append(row.CategoryID + "\t" + row.CategoryName + "\t" +
            description + Environment.NewLine);
    }
}
else
```

Example 2-26. File: TypedDataSetNullsForm.cs (continued)

```
{
    // Create the typed DataSet annotated for nulls.
    CategoriesDS ds = new CategoriesDS( );
    da.Fill(ds, CATEGORIES_TABLE);

    // Add a row with a null Description.
    ds.Categories.AddCategoriesRow("New Category", null);

    result.Append("Default" + Environment.NewLine + Environment.NewLine);
    // Iterate over the rows collection and display columns.
    foreach(CategoriesDS.CategoriesRow row in ds.Categories)
    {
        // Use Is<field>Null method or StrongTypingException will
        // result when null row.Description is accessed.
        String description = row.IsDescriptionNull( ) ?
            "NULL" : row.Description;

        // Note that the null Description is not replaced.
        result.Append(row.CategoryID + "\t" + row.CategoryName + "\t" +
            description + Environment.NewLine);
    }
}

resultTextBox.Text = result.ToString( );
```

Discussion

Annotations to XSD schemas used to generate strongly typed DataSet objects are discussed in detail in Recipe 2.18.

2.20   Retrieving Data from an Oracle Package

Problem

Given an Oracle package that returns multiple result sets for related tables as REF CURSOR data types, you want to access this data using a DataReader and load the data into a DataSet.

Solution

Use the data type OracleType.Cursor.

The sample code creates a Command for an Oracle package *CURSPKG* that takes a Customer ID input parameter. The package calls a stored procedure that returns two result sets—Orders and Order Details data from Northwind for the specified customer—as Oracle REF CURSOR output parameters.

A DataAdapter is created from the Command, retrieves the Orders and Order Details result sets, and loads them into a DataSet. A relation is created between the tables and the default view for the Orders table is bound to the data grid on the form.

Next, a DataReader is created from the Command. The Orders and Order Details result sets are displayed in a text box.

The Oracle package is shown in Example 2-27, and the package body is shown in Example 2-28.

Example 2-27. File: Packages\CURSPKG

```
CREATE OR REPLACE PACKAGE CURSPKG
AS
  TYPE T_CURSOR IS REF CURSOR;
  PROCEDURE GetCustomerOrdersWithDetails (
    pCustomerID IN CHAR,
    curOrders OUT T_CURSOR,
    curOrderDetails OUT T_CURSOR);
END CURSPKG;
```

Example 2-28. File: Package Bodies\CURSPKG

```
CREATE OR REPLACE PACKAGE BODY CURSPKG
AS
  PROCEDURE GetCustomerOrdersWithDetails
  (
    pCustomerID IN CHAR,
    curOrders OUT T_CURSOR,
    curOrderDetails OUT T_CURSOR
  )
  IS
    V_CURSOR1 T_CURSOR;
    V_CURSOR2 T_CURSOR;
  BEGIN
    OPEN V_CURSOR1 FOR
    SELECT * FROM ORDERS
    WHERE CustomerID = pCustomerID;

    OPEN V_CURSOR2 FOR
    SELECT * FROM ORDERDETAILS
    WHERE OrderID IN
      (SELECT OrderID FROM ORDERS WHERE
      CustomerID = pCustomerID);

    curOrders := V_CURSOR1;
    curOrderDetails := V_CURSOR2;
  END GetCustomerOrdersWithDetails;
END CURSPKG;
```

The C# code is shown in Example 2-29.

Example 2-29. File: OracleRefCursorsForm.cs

```csharp
// Namespaces, variables, and constants
using System;
using System.Text;
using System.Data;
using System.Data.OracleClient;

// ...

// Create the connection.
OracleConnection conn = new OracleConnection(
    ConfigurationSettings.AppSettings["Oracle_ConnectString"]);

// Create the command for the Oracle package.
OracleCommand cmd = new OracleCommand();
cmd.Connection = conn;
cmd.CommandType = CommandType.StoredProcedure;
cmd.CommandText = "CURSPKG.GetCustomerOrdersWithDetails";
// Add the parameters.
cmd.Parameters.Add("pCustomerID", OracleType.Char, 5);
cmd.Parameters.Add("curOrders", OracleType.Cursor).Direction = ParameterDirection.Output;
cmd.Parameters.Add("curOrderDetails", OracleType.Cursor).Direction =
    ParameterDirection.Output;
// Set the Customer ID parameter value to user entry.
customerIdTextBox.Text = customerIdTextBox.Text.ToUpper();
cmd.Parameters["pCustomerID"].Value = customerIdTextBox.Text;

// Create the DataAdapter and table mappings.
OracleDataAdapter da = new OracleDataAdapter(cmd);
da.TableMappings.Add("Table", "ORDERS");
da.TableMappings.Add("Table1", "ORDERDETAILS");


// Fill the DataSet from the Oracle package.
DataSet ds = new DataSet();
da.Fill(ds);

// Create a relation.
ds.Relations.Add("ORDERS_ORDERDETAILS_RELATION",
    ds.Tables["ORDERS"].Columns["ORDERID"],
    ds.Tables["ORDERDETAILS"].Columns["ORDERID"]);

// Bind the default view for the Orders table to the grid.
dataGrid.DataSource = ds.Tables["ORDERS"].DefaultView;


// Create the DataReader from the Oracle package.
conn.Open();
OracleDataReader dr = cmd.ExecuteReader();

// Output the Orders table for the customer.
StringBuilder result = new StringBuilder("ORDERS" + Environment.NewLine);
while(dr.Read())
```

Example 2-29. File: OracleRefCursorsForm.cs (continued)

```
{
    for(int i = 0; i < dr.FieldCount; i++)
        result.Append(dr[i].ToString( ) + "; ");

    result.Append(Environment.NewLine);
}

// Move to the REF CURSOR for the next result set.
dr.NextResult( );

// Output the Order Details for the customer.
result.Append(Environment.NewLine + "ORDER DETAILS" + Environment.NewLine);
while(dr.Read( ))
{
    for(int i = 0; i < dr.FieldCount; i++)
        result.Append(dr[i].ToString( ) + "; ");

    result.Append(Environment.NewLine);
}

conn.Close( );

// Output the result.
resultTextBox.Text = result.ToString( );
```

Discussion

You cannot use a collection of SQL statements as a batch query within an Oracle stored procedure. Instead, you must use an Oracle package, that is, a container that groups stored procedures and functions. An Oracle package consists of a header and a body. The package header defines the name of the package and provides method signatures for each procedure or function in the package. The package body contains the code for the stored procedures and functions defined in the package header.

 A REF CURSOR is an Oracle data type that points into a result set returned by a query. A REF CURSOR differs from a normal cursor in that while a cursor points to a specific result set, a REF CURSOR is a variable that can point to different result sets—a reference to a cursor—and can be assigned at execution time.

A REF CURSOR is typically used to pass result sets from a stored procedure to a client.

You can access a result using an output parameter that references an Oracle REF CURSOR. The parameter name must match the name of the REF CURSOR and it must have the data type OracleType.Cursor.

If the package returns more than one REF CURSOR parameter, an OracleDataReader accesses them in the order they were added to the parameters collection. The NextResult( ) method of the DataReader advances to the next REF CURSOR.

2.21   Using Parameterized SQL Statements

Problem

You want to create and execute a SQL statement having parameters that are set dynamically.

Solution

Add parameters to the Command object's Parameters collection.

The sample code contains two event handlers and one method:

Form.Load

Sets up the sample by creating a DataTable containing all Customers data from Northwind. The default view of the table is bound to a Customers data grid on the form. The handler for the CurrentCellChanged event of the data grid is called to initialize the grid containing Orders with the data for the row selected by default in the Customers data grid.

DataGrid.CurrentCellChanged

Gets the CustomerID from the data grid when the rows selected in the data grid changes and calls the LoadOrderGrid( ) method to update the Orders displayed to match the selected Customer.

LoadOrderGrid( )

This method defines a parameterized SQL statement. A Command is built from the statement and the single parameter, @CustomerID is created and set to the customerId argument passed into the method. The Command is used by a DataAdapter to fill a DataTable with the Orders for the specified Customer. The default view of the table is bound to the Customers data grid on the form.

The C# code is shown in Example 2-30.

Example 2-30. File: UsingParameterizedQueriesForm.cs

```
// Namespaces, variables, and constants
using System;
using System.Configuration;
using System.Data;
using System.Data.SqlClient;

// Table name constants
private const String CUSTOMERS_TABLE = "Customers";
private const String ORDERS_TABLE    = "Orders";
```

Example 2-30. File: UsingParameterizedQueriesForm.cs (continued)

```
// ...

private void UsingParameterizedQueriesForm_Load(object sender,
    System.EventArgs e)
{
    String sqlText = "SELECT * FROM Customers";

    // Retrieve table with all customers.
    SqlDataAdapter da = new SqlDataAdapter(sqlText,
        ConfigurationSettings.AppSettings["Sql_ConnectString"]);
    DataTable dt = new DataTable(CUSTOMERS_TABLE);
    da.Fill(dt);

    // Bind the default view of the Customers table to the customers grid.
    customerDataGrid.DataSource = dt.DefaultView;
    // Fire the CurrentCellChanged event to refresh the orders grid.
    customerDataGrid_CurrentCellChanged(null, null);
}

private void customerDataGrid_CurrentCellChanged(object sender,
    System.EventArgs e)
{
    // Get the current row in the customers grid.
    int row = customerDataGrid.CurrentRowIndex;
    // Get the customer ID from the view.
    String customerId =
        ((DataView)customerDataGrid.DataSource).
        Table.Rows[row][0].ToString( );
    // Retrieve the orders for the customer.
    LoadOrderGrid(customerId);
}

private void LoadOrderGrid(String customerId)
{
    String sqlText = "SELECT * FROM Orders " +
        "WHERE CustomerID = @CustomerID";

    // Create a connection and parameterized command.
    SqlConnection conn = new SqlConnection(
        ConfigurationSettings.AppSettings["Sql_ConnectString"]);
    SqlCommand cmd = new SqlCommand(sqlText, conn);
    // Add the CustomerID parameter and set its value.
    cmd.Parameters.Add("@CustomerID", SqlDbType.NChar, 5);
    cmd.Parameters["@CustomerID"].Value = customerId;

    // Get the Orders result set for the Customer.
    SqlDataAdapter da = new SqlDataAdapter(cmd);
    DataTable dt = new DataTable(ORDERS_TABLE);
    da.Fill(dt);

    // Bind the default view of the orders table to the orders grid.
    orderDataGrid.DataSource = dt.DefaultView;
```

Example 2-30. File: UsingParameterizedQueriesForm.cs (continued)

```
    // Set the caption of the orders grid.
    orderDataGrid.CaptionText = "Orders [CustomerID: " + customerId + "]";
}
```

Discussion

Parameterized queries allow one or more parameters to be replaced at runtime using `Parameter` objects in the `ParameterCollection` class of the `Command` object. These can also be the `Command` classes exposed by the `DataAdapter`. Using parameters is both easier than and less prone to errors than dynamically building queries. You're not responsible for creating delimeters such as single quotes around strings and pound signs around dates. Code is reusable and not specific to the data provider.

The SQL Server data provider uses the parameter names in the query and order is not important. The OLE DB data provider uses positional parameter markers, the question mark (?), and order is important. Consult the documentation for other .NET data providers for information about using parameters in queries.

2.22 Querying Data Asynchronously with Message Queuing

Problem

You want to asynchronously retrieve data from a system that is not always connected.

Solution

You must:

- Use message queuing to construct and send a data request from the client.
- Access and process the requesting message at the server.
- Compose and send a response message containing the result set to the client.
- Retrieve the response at the client and deserialize it into a `DataSet`.

The sample code contains three event handlers:

Send `Button.Click`
> Checks if the query message queue exists and creates it if necessary. A `MessageQueue` object is created to access the queue. A message is sent to the queue containing the `CustomerID` which the user wants information about.

Process Query `Button.Click`
> Checks if the query message queue exists and creates it if necessary. A `MessageQueue` object is created to access the queue. An attempt is made to receive

a message from the queue, waiting one second before giving up. If a message is received, the CustomerID is extracted from the message and the message queue is closed. A DataSet is created and a DataAdapter is used to return the record for the requested CustomerID into a Customer DataTable in the DataSet. A result queue is created if necessary and a message labeled with the CustomerID and containing the DataSet with the asynchronous query results is sent to the queue.

Process Result Button.Click

Checks if the result message queue exists and creates it if necessary. A MessageQueue object is created to access the queue and the formatter set to deserialize the DataSet in the message bodies. An attempt is made to receive a message from the queue, waiting for one second before giving up. If a message is received, the DataSet in the body is deserialized and the contents are displayed.

The C# code is shown in Example 2-31.

Example 2-31. File: MessageQueueQueryForm.cs

```csharp
// Namespaces, variables, and constants
using System;
using System.Configuration;
using System.IO;
using System.Text;
using System.Messaging;
using System.Data;
using System.Data.SqlClient;

private const String QUEUENAMEQUERY  = @".\Private$\adodotnetcb0222query";
private const String QUEUENAMERESULT = @".\Private$\adodotnetcb0222result";

private System.Messaging.MessageQueue messageQueue;

// ...

private void sendButton_Click(object sender, System.EventArgs e)
{
    // Create the query queue if it does not exist.
    if(!MessageQueue.Exists(QUEUENAMEQUERY))
        MessageQueue.Create(QUEUENAMEQUERY);

    // Create an object to access the query queue.
    MessageQueue mq = new MessageQueue(QUEUENAMEQUERY);

    // Send a message containing the user-enetered customer ID.
    String msg = "CustomerId=" + customerIdTextBox.Text;
    mq.Send(msg);

    resultTextBox.Text = "Query sent.";
}

private void processQueryButton_Click(object sender, System.EventArgs e)
{
```

Example 2-31. File: MessageQueueQueryForm.cs (continued)

```csharp
    // Create the query queue if it does not exist.
    if(!MessageQueue.Exists(QUEUENAMEQUERY))
        MessageQueue.Create(QUEUENAMEQUERY);

    // Create an object to access the query queue.
    MessageQueue mq = new MessageQueue(QUEUENAMEQUERY);
    // Set the formatter for (de)serialization of message bodies.
    mq.Formatter = new XmlMessageFormatter(new Type[] {typeof(String)});

    // Receive a message from the query queue.
    System.Messaging.Message msg;
    try
    {
        msg = mq.Receive(new TimeSpan(0, 0, 1));
        resultTextBox.Text = "Query " + msg.Id + " received." +
            Environment.NewLine;
    }
    catch(MessageQueueException ex)
    {
        resultTextBox.Text = ex.Message;
        return;
    }

    // Get the customer ID from the message body.
    String customerId = ((String)msg.Body).Substring(11);
    // Close the queue.
    mq.Close();

    // Create a DataAdapter to retrieve data for the specified customer.
    String sqlText = "SELECT * FROM Customers WHERE CustomerID='" +
        customerId + "'";
    SqlDataAdapter da = new SqlDataAdapter(sqlText,
        ConfigurationSettings.AppSettings["Sql_ConnectString"]);
    // Fill the Customer table in the DataSet with customer data.
    DataSet ds = new DataSet();
    da.Fill(ds, "Customers");

    // Create the result queue if it does not exist.
    if(!MessageQueue.Exists(QUEUENAMERESULT))
        MessageQueue.Create(QUEUENAMERESULT);

    // Create an object to access the result queue.
    mq = new MessageQueue(QUEUENAMERESULT);

    // Send a message with the customer DataSet to the queue.
    mq.Send(ds, customerId);

    resultTextBox.Text = "Response sent.";
}

private void processResultButton_Click(object sender, System.EventArgs e)
{
    StringBuilder result = new StringBuilder();
```

Example 2-31. File: MessageQueueQueryForm.cs (continued)

```
    // Create the result queue if it does not exist.
    if(!MessageQueue.Exists(QUEUENAMERESULT))
        MessageQueue.Create(QUEUENAMERESULT);

    // Create an object to access the result queue.
    MessageQueue mq = new MessageQueue(QUEUENAMERESULT);
    // Set the formatter for (de)serialization of message bodies.
    mq.Formatter = new XmlMessageFormatter(new Type[] {typeof(DataSet)});

    // Receive a message from the result queue.
    System.Messaging.Message msg;
    try
    {
        msg = mq.Receive(new TimeSpan(0, 0, 1));
    }
    catch(MessageQueueException ex)
    {
        resultTextBox.Text = ex.Message;
        return;
    }

    // Create the customer DataSet from the message body.
    DataSet ds = (DataSet)msg.Body;

    // Display the results of the query.
    result.Append("QUERY RESULTS:" + Environment.NewLine);
    if (ds.Tables["Customers"].Rows.Count == 0)
        result.Append("Customer not found for ID = '" +
            msg.Label + "'.");
    else
        for(int i = 0; i < ds.Tables[0].Columns.Count; i++)
        {
            result.Append(ds.Tables[0].Columns[i].ColumnName +
                " = " + ds.Tables[0].Rows[0][i] +
                Environment.NewLine);
        }

    resultTextBox.Text = result.ToString();
}
```

Discussion

Message Queuing (MSMQ) provides an inter-application messaging infrastructure that allows messages to be sent between disconnected applications. MSMQ provides for message transport, queuing, transactional message support, error handling and auditing, and makes available a variety of Application Programming Interfaces to interact with MSMQ programmatically. The System.Messaging namespace contains the .NET classes that support MSMQ.

To send a message using MSMQ, perform the following actions:

- Create a connection to the message queue to which you want to send the message.
- Specify a formatter—an object that controls the type of data that can be sent in the message body and how it is persisted—for the data that you want to send. Table 2-19 describes the different formatters available.

Table 2-19. .NET predefined formatters

Formatter	Description
ActiveXMessageFormatter	Serializes or deserializes primitive data types and other objects using a format compatible with MSMQ ActiveX Component to allow interoperability with previous versions of MSMQ. It is fast and produces a compact serialization.
BinaryMessageFormatter	Serializes or deserializes an object or an object graph using a binary format. It is fast and produces a compact serialization.
XMLMessageFormatter	Serializes or deserializes objects and primitive data types into XML based on an XSD schema. This is the default formatter for MessageQueue components.

- Call the Send( ) method of the MessageQueue to write the Message to the queue. The object to be sent is passed as an argument to the method.

When the Send( ) method of the MessageQueue is called, the body of the message is serialized using the XMLMessageFormatter if the Formatter property is not specified.

To read a message and recreate the serialized body, formatter properties must be set before reading the message. The properties that must be set are specific to the formatter:

ActiveXMessageFormatter
> No properties must be set.

BinaryMessageFormatter
> Specify the format of the root object and the type descriptions either in the constructor or by explicitly setting the TopObjectFormat and TypeFormat properties.

XmlMessageFormatter
> Specify the target types or target type names either in the constructor or by explicitly setting the TargetTypes or TargetTypeNames property.

The message can now be read by using the Receive( ) method of the MessageQueue. You can retrieve the serialized object from the Body property of the Message returned by the Receive( ) method.

For more information about Microsoft Message Queue (MSMQ), see the MSDN Library.

CHAPTER 3

Searching and Analyzing Data

3.0   Introduction

This chapter focuses on searching for records in views and tables, calculating values based on values in the same or other tables, and navigating data relations between tables.

The DataView is a data-bindable view of a DataTable that presents data with different sort orders and filters. You can create multiple views for each table; every table has a default data view. The DataViewManager class helps to manage the default data views for tables in a DataSet. Recipe 3.1 demonstrates how to use the DataView and DataViewManager class to filter and sort data in a DataSet. Recipe 3.12 shows how to filter a data view for rows that have null values.

The DataRelation class creates a parent/child relation between two tables in a DataSet. The DataRelation maintains referential integrity and you can use it to cascade updates and deletes. It can also be used to navigate between the tables. Recipe 3.4 shows how to use the data relation to get the parent row and the child rows for any row.

The DataTable and DataView classes both provide several ways to locate records from specified criteria. Searching an existing table or view saves a roundtrip to the database server. Although the DataView is created from a DataTable, searching is done differently in each. Recipe 3.8 shows how to find rows in a DataTable while Recipe 3.9 shows how to find rows in a DataView. You can create a DataView from a typed DataSet to search or filter. Recipe 3.11 shows how to convert untyped rows from the DataView to typed DataRow objects.

ADO.NET does not provide a way to compare two DataSet objects with identical schemas to determine the data differences between the two. Recipe 3.3 creates a method GetDataSetDifference( ) that returns the differences as a DiffGram, which is an XML format that identifies original and current versions of data and is used by .NET to serialize and persist the DataSet.

In addition to recipes about the `DataRelation`, `DataSet`, `DataTable`, and `DataView` classes, this chapter covers:

Expression columns

> Expression columns are calculated from column values in the same row or from an aggregation of values from rows in the table or in a related table. The expression column is not stored but calculated whenever its value is requested and can be used like any other columns. For example, you can sort and filter tables and views on an expression column. Recipe 3.2 shows how to add an expression column to a table to calculate a value that is calculated from other values in the same row. Recipe 3.7 shows how to create an expression column to get a value from a parent table and an expression column that will aggregate values from a child table.

Globalization and localization

> *Globalizing* is creating applications that support multiple cultures. *Localizing* is customizing an application to support a specific culture primarily by translating the user interface. The `System.Globalization` namespace contains classes that control the display of culture-specific values such as currencies and dates. Recipe 3.5 shows how to display data formatted based on a user's culture settings.

Advanced queries

> ADO.NET does not provide a way to get the `TOP N` rows from a `DataTable` based on the value of a column in the table. Recipe 3.10 shows how to build a filter on the `DataView` at runtime to return the `TOP N` rows.

> Queries sometimes need to be based on data from more than one data source. Recipe 3.6 shows how to return a result set from a query based on more than one table using *ad-hoc connector names* that allow data from heterogeneous data sources to be accessed by providing the connection information in the SQL statement.

> The `COMPUTE BY` clause returns both summary and detail data in a single result set from a single `SELECT` statement. Recipe 3.13 shows how to execute a `COMPUTE BY` statement and how to navigate the result set.

> The Shape language uses Data Shaping Services for OLE DB as an alternative to `JOIN` and `GROUP BY` syntax to generate hierarchical result sets. Recipe 3.14 shows how to use the Shape language to get a hierarchical result set from SQL Server using the OLE DB .NET data provider, and how to navigate the result set.

3.1   Filtering and Sorting Data

Problem

You have a `DataSet` filled with data, but you need to work with only a subset of the records and also to sort them. You need a way to both filter and sort the records in your `DataSet` without requerying the data source.

Solution

Use DataViewManager and DataView objects to filter and sort a DataSet.

The sample code contains two event handlers:

Form.Load
> Sets up the sample by creating a DataSet containing the Customers and Orders tables from the Northwind sample database and a relation between them. The default view for the Customers table is bound to the data grid on the form.

Refresh Button.Click
> Applies the filters and sort order specified by the user to the data views for the tables accessed through the DataViewManager object.

The C# code is shown in Example 3-1.

Example 3-1. File: FilterSortForm.cs

```
// Namespaces, variables, and constants
using System;
using System.Configuration;
using System.Data;
using System.Data.SqlClient;

// Table name constants
private const String CUSTOMERS_TABLE      = "Customers";
private const String ORDERS_TABLE         = "Orders";

// Relation name constants
private const String CUSTOMERS_ORDERS_RELATION =
    "Customers_Orders_Relation";

// Field name constants
private const String CUSTOMERID_FIELD     = "CustomerID";
private const String ORDERID_FIELD        = "OrderID";
private const String CONTACTNAME_FIELD    = "ContactName";

private DataSet ds;

// ...

private void FilterSortForm_Load(object sender, System.EventArgs e)
{
    ds = new DataSet();

    SqlDataAdapter da;

    // Fill the Customers table and add it to the DataSet.
    da = new SqlDataAdapter("SELECT * FROM Customers",
        ConfigurationSettings.AppSettings["Sql_ConnectString"]);
    DataTable customersTable = new DataTable(CUSTOMERS_TABLE);
    da.Fill(customersTable);
    ds.Tables.Add(customersTable);
```

Example 3-1. File: FilterSortForm.cs (continued)

```
    // Fill the Order table and add it to the DataSet.
    da = new SqlDataAdapter("SELECT * FROM Orders",
        ConfigurationSettings.AppSettings["Sql_ConnectString"]);
    DataTable orderTable = new DataTable(ORDERS_TABLE);
    da.Fill(orderTable);
    ds.Tables.Add(orderTable);

    // Create a relation between the tables.
    ds.Relations.Add(CUSTOMERS_ORDERS_RELATION,
        ds.Tables[CUSTOMERS_TABLE].Columns[CUSTOMERID_FIELD],
        ds.Tables[ORDERS_TABLE].Columns[CUSTOMERID_FIELD],
        true);

    // Bind the DataViewManager to the grid.
    dataGrid.SetDataBinding(ds.DefaultViewManager, CUSTOMERS_TABLE);
}

private void refreshButton_Click(object sender, System.EventArgs e)
{
    DataViewManager dvm = new DataViewManager(ds);

    String countryFilter = "";
    if (customerCountryTextBox.Text != "")
        countryFilter = "Country = '" +
            customerCountryTextBox.Text + "'";

    // Sort on the contact name, as appropriate.
    if(contactSortCheckBox.Checked)
        dvm.DataViewSettings[CUSTOMERS_TABLE].Sort =
            CONTACTNAME_FIELD;

    // Filter the Customers view for the country.
    dvm.DataViewSettings[CUSTOMERS_TABLE].RowFilter = countryFilter;

    // Filter to Orders view for the employee.
    String employeeIdFilter = "";
    if (orderEmployeeIdTextBox.Text != "")
    {
        try
        {
            employeeIdFilter = "EmployeeId = " +
                Int32.Parse(orderEmployeeIdTextBox.Text);
        }
        catch (FormatException)
        {
            orderEmployeeIdTextBox.Text = "";
        }
    }
    dvm.DataViewSettings[ORDERS_TABLE].RowFilter = employeeIdFilter;

    // Bind the DataViewManager to the grid.
    dataGrid.SetDataBinding(dvm, CUSTOMERS_TABLE);
}
```

Discussion

The DataView filters and sorts the data in DataTable objects in the DataSet. The DataViewManager can simplify working with multiple views within a DataSet, but is not required. The DataViewManager object exposes a DataViewSettingCollection object through the DataViewSettings property. The collection contains a single DataViewSetting object for each table in the DataSet. The object is accessed using the name or ordinal of the table by using an indexer in C# or by using the Item( ) property in VB.NET. The DataViewSetting object allows access to the ApplyDefaultSort, RowFilter, RowStateFilter, and Sort properties of a DataView created from the DataViewManager for the table. Accessing these properties is identical to accessing the same properties directly through the DataView.

The RowFilter property of the DataView accesses the expression that filters the view. The Sort property of the DataView sorts the view on a single or multiple columns in either ascending or descending order.

In the sample, a filter field is provided on both the Orders and Order Details table (the Country and EmployeeID fields, respectively). Additionally, the sample allows the data grid to be optionally sorted on the ContactName column. The filter and sort properties are controlled by setting the RowFilter and Sort properties of the DataViewSetting for the appropriate table.

3.2   Using Expression Columns to Display Calculated Values

Problem

You need to display a calculated value for each row in a DataTable and to filter and sort the table on this value.

Solution

Add an expression column to the table and display it. Sort and filter on the expression column from the default DataView for the table.

The sample code contains two event handlers:

Form.Load

> Sets up the sample by creating a DataTable containing the Order Details table from the Northwind sample database. An expression column calculating the extended price for each detail line is created and added to the table. Finally, the default view for the table is bound to the data grid on the form.

Apply Button.Click

> Applies the filter and sort order entered by the user to the Extended Price expression column in the data view.

The C# code is shown in Example 3-2.

Example 3-2. File: ExpressionColumnForm.cs

```csharp
// Namespaces, variables, and constants
using System;
using System.Configuration;
using System.Windows.Forms;
using System.Data;
using System.Data.SqlClient;

// ...

private void ExpressionColumnForm_Load(object sender, System.EventArgs e)
{
    // Define the table and fill it with data.
    DataTable dt = new DataTable("OrderDetails");
    String selectText = "SELECT * FROM [Order Details]";
    SqlDataAdapter da = new SqlDataAdapter(selectText,
        ConfigurationSettings.AppSettings["Sql_ConnectString"]);
    da.Fill(dt);

    // Add an expression column to the table.
    dt.Columns.Add(new DataColumn("ExtendedPrice", typeof(Decimal),
        "(Quantity * UnitPrice) * (1 - Discount)"));
    // Define the DataView object.
    dv = dt.DefaultView;

    // Bind the DataView to the DataGrid.
    resultDataGrid.DataSource = dv;
}

private void applyButton_Click(object sender, System.EventArgs e)
{
    bool isLowerBound = false;
    bool isUpperBound = false;

    Decimal lowerBound = 0;
    Decimal upperBound = 0;

    if(filterLowerBound.Text.Trim( ).Length > 0)
    {
        isLowerBound = true;
        try
        {
            lowerBound = Decimal.Parse(filterLowerBound.Text);
        }
        catch(System.FormatException)
        {
            MessageBox.Show("Invalid entry for lower bound.",
                "Error", MessageBoxButtons.OK,
                MessageBoxIcon.Error);
            return;
        }
    }
```

Example 3-2. File: ExpressionColumnForm.cs (continued)

```csharp
if(filterUpperBound.Text.Trim( ).Length>0)
{
    isUpperBound = true;
    try
    {
        upperBound = Decimal.Parse(filterUpperBound.Text);
    }
    catch(System.FormatException)
    {
        MessageBox.Show("Invalid entry for upper bound.",
            "Error", MessageBoxButtons.OK,
            MessageBoxIcon.Error);
        return;
    }
}

String filter = "";
if(isLowerBound)
    filter = "ExtendedPrice >= " + lowerBound;

if(isUpperBound)
    filter += ((isLowerBound)?" AND " : "") +
        "ExtendedPrice <= " + upperBound;

// Set the filter.
dv.RowFilter=filter;

// Set the sort.
if(sortNoneRadioButton.Checked)
    dv.Sort = "";
else if(sortAscRadioButton.Checked)
    dv.Sort = "ExtendedPrice";
else if(sortDescRadioButton.Checked)
    dv.Sort = "ExtendedPrice DESC";
}
```

Discussion

An expression column contains a value that is calculated from other column values
in the same row, or from an aggregate of rows in the table or in a related table. The
DataType of the column must be compatible with the return value of the expression.
For information about expression syntax, see the "DataColumn.Expression Property" topic in the MSDN Library.

An expression column is added to a table either through one of the DataColumn constructors that take the expression for the column as the third argument (the technique used in the sample code) or by setting the Expression property of the column
to the expression.

In the sample, an expression column named ExtendedPrice is created with a data type of Decimal. The column calculates the extended price for the column using the expression (Quantity * UnitPrice) * (1 - Discount).

After the column is added to the table, the RowFilter and Sort properties of a DataView bound to the table with the expression column can sort or filter data in the same way as they can on any other column. This is shown in the sample code and discussed in more detail in Recipe 3.1.

3.3 Determining the Differences in Data Between Two DataSet Objects

Problem

You have two DataSet objects with the same schema but containing different data and need to determine the difference between the data in the two.

Solution

Compare the two DataSet objects with the GetDataSetDifference( ) method shown in this solution and return the differences between the data as a DiffGram.

The sample code contains two event handlers and a single method:

Form.Load
> Sets up the sample by creating two DataSet objects each containing a different subset of records from the Categories table from the Northwind sample database. The default view for each table is bound to a data grid on the form.

Get Difference Button.Click
> Simply calls GetDataSetDifference( ) when the user clicks the button.

GetDataSetDifference( )
> This method takes two DataSet objects with identical schemas as arguments and returns a DiffGram of the differences between the data in the two.

The C# code is shown in Example 3-3.

Example 3-3. File: DataSetDifferenceForm.cs

```
// Namespaces, variables, and constants
using System;
using System.Configuration;
using System.IO;
using System.Data;
using System.Data.SqlClient;

// Field name constants
private const String CATEGORYID_FIELD = "CategoryID";
```

Example 3-3. File: DataSetDifferenceForm.cs (continued)

```csharp
DataSet dsA, dsB;

// ...

private void DataSetDifferenceForm_Load(object sender, System.EventArgs e)
{
    SqlDataAdapter da;
    String sqlText;

    // Fill table A with Category schema and subset of data.
    sqlText = "SELECT CategoryID, CategoryName, Description " +
        "FROM Categories WHERE CategoryID BETWEEN 1 AND 5";
    DataTable dtA = new DataTable("TableA");
    da = new SqlDataAdapter(sqlText,
        ConfigurationSettings.AppSettings["Sql_ConnectString"]);
    da.Fill(dtA);
    da.FillSchema(dtA, SchemaType.Source);
    // Set up the identity column CategoryID.
    dtA.Columns[0].AutoIncrement = true;
    dtA.Columns[0].AutoIncrementSeed = -1;
    dtA.Columns[0].AutoIncrementStep = -1;
    // Create DataSet A and add table A.
    dsA = new DataSet();
    dsA.Tables.Add(dtA);

    // Fill table B with Category schema and subset of data.
    sqlText = "SELECT CategoryID, CategoryName, Description "
        "FROM Categories WHERE CategoryID BETWEEN 4 AND 8";
    DataTable dtB = new DataTable("TableB");
    da = new SqlDataAdapter(sqlText,
        ConfigurationSettings.AppSettings["Sql_ConnectString"]);
    da.Fill(dtB);
    da.FillSchema(dtB, SchemaType.Source);
    // Set up the identity column CategoryID.
    dtB.Columns[0].AutoIncrement = true;
    dtB.Columns[0].AutoIncrementSeed = -1;
    dtB.Columns[0].AutoIncrementStep = -1;
    // Create DataSet B and add table B.
    dsB = new DataSet();
    dsB.Tables.Add(dtB);

    // Bind the default views for table A and table B to DataGrids
    // on the form.
    aDataGrid.DataSource = dtA.DefaultView;
    bDataGrid.DataSource = dtB.DefaultView;
}

private void getDifferenceButton_Click(object sender, System.EventArgs e)
{
    resultTextBox.Text = GetDataSetDifference(dsA, dsB);
}
```

Example 3-3. File: DataSetDifferenceForm.cs (continued)

```csharp
private String GetDataSetDifference(DataSet ds1, DataSet ds2)
{
    // Accept any edits within the DataSet objects.
    ds1.AcceptChanges( );
    ds2.AcceptChanges( );

    // Create a DataSet to store the differences.
    DataSet ds = new DataSet( );

    DataTable dt1Copy = null;
    // Iterate over the collection of tables in the first DataSet.
    for (int i = 0; i < ds1.Tables.Count; i++)
    {
        DataTable dt1 = ds1.Tables[i];
        DataTable dt2 = ds2.Tables[i];

        // Create a copy of the table in the first DataSet.
        dt1Copy = dt1.Copy( );

        // Iterate over the collection of rows in the
        // copy of the table from the first DataSet.
        foreach(DataRow row1 in dt1Copy.Rows)
        {
            DataRow row2 = dt2.Rows.Find(row1[CATEGORYID_FIELD]);
            if(row2 == null)
            {
                // Delete rows not in table 2 from table 1.
                row1.Delete( );
            }
            else
            {
                // Modify table 1 rows that are different from
                // table 2 rows.
                for(int j = 0; j < dt1Copy.Columns.Count; j++)
                {
                    if(row2[j] == DBNull.Value)
                    {
                        // Column in table 2 is null,
                        // but not null in table 1
                        if(row1[j] != DBNull.Value)
                            row1[j] = DBNull.Value;
                    }
                    else if (row1[j] == DBNull.Value)
                    {
                        // Column in table 1 is null,
                        // but not null in table 2
                        row1[j] = row2[j];
                    }
                    else if(row1[j].ToString( ) !=
                        row2[j].ToString( ))
                    {
```

Example 3-3. File: DataSetDifferenceForm.cs (continued)

```
                    // Neither column in table 1 nor
                    // table 2 is null, and the
                    // values in the columns are
                    // different.
                    row1[j] = row2[j];
                }
            }
        }
    }

    foreach(DataRow row2 in dt2.Rows)
    {
        DataRow row1 =
            dt1Copy.Rows.Find(row2[CATEGORYID_FIELD]);
        if(row1 == null)
        {
            // Insert rows into table 1 that are in table 2
            // but not in table 1.
            dt1Copy.LoadDataRow(row2.ItemArray, false);
        }
    }

    // Add the table to the difference DataSet.
    ds.Tables.Add(dt1Copy);
}

// Write a XML DiffGram with containing the differences between tables.
StringWriter sw = new StringWriter();
ds.WriteXml(sw, XmlWriteMode.DiffGram);

return sw.ToString();
}
```

Discussion

A DiffGram is an XML format used to specify original and current values for the data elements in a DataSet. It does not include any schema information. The DiffGram is used by .NET Framework applications as the serialization format for the contents of a DataSet including changes made to the Dataset.

A DiffGram is XML-based, which makes it platform and application independent. It is not, however, widely used or understood outside of Microsoft .NET applications.

The DiffGram format is divided into three sections: current, original, and errors. The original and current data in the DiffGram can also be used to report the differences between data in two DataSet objects. For more information about the DiffGram XML format, see Recipe 8.8.

The sample code contains a method GetDataSetDifference( ) that takes two DataSet objects with the same schema as arguments and returns a DiffGram containing the differences in data when the second DataSet is compared to the first. Table 3-1 describes how the differences between the DataSet objects appear in the DiffGram.

Table 3-1. DiffGram representation of DataSet differences

Condition	DiffGram representation
Row is the same in both DataSet 1 and DataSet 2	Row data appears only in the current data section of the DiffGram.
Row is in both DataSet 1 and DataSet 2 but the rows do not contain the same data	Row data appears in the current data section of the DiffGram. The row element contains the attribute diffgr:hasChanges with a value of *"modified"*. The data in the current section is the updated data. The original data appears in the original <diffgr:before> block of the DiffGram.
Row is in DataSet 2 but not in DataSet 1	Row data appears in the current data section of the DiffGram. The row element contains the attribute diffgr:hasChanges with a value of *"inserted"*.
Row is DataSet 1 but not in DataSet 2	Row data appears only in the original <diffgr:before> block of the DiffGram.

The sample begins by loading different subsets of data from the Categories table and displaying it in two grids on the form. This data is editable within the grids to allow DataSet differences as reported in the DiffGram to be investigated. In this example, the DataSet objects both contain just a single table. To determine the difference between the DataSet objects, the tables within the DataSet objects are compared as described next and changes are applied to the data in a copy of the first DataSet until it matches the second DataSet. Once all differences in all tables are processed, the DiffGram of the copy of the first DataSet contains the difference in the second DataSet when compared to the first DataSet.

More specifically, as each table is processed, a copy is made of it. The data in the copy of the first table is modified to make it consistent with the data in the second table. The modified copy of the first table is then added to the DataSet containing the differences between the two DataSet objects.

The process of modifying the data in the copy of the first table to match the data in second table involves several steps:

- Rows that are in the copy of the first table but not in the second table (based on the primary key value) are deleted from the copy of the first table.
- If the row is found in the second table, the columns are compared and any differences in the columns in the second table are changed in the column in the first table.
- Rows that are in the second table but not in the copy of the first table are inserted into the copy of the first table without accepting changes.

3.4 Navigating Between Parent and Child Records Using a DataRelation

Problem

You want to navigate between the parent and child records in a hierarchical DataSet.

Solution

Use a DataRelation to find the child rows for a parent row in a related table, or to find the parent row for a child row in a related table.

The sample code starts by creating a DataSet containing the Orders and Order Details tables from the Northwind sample database and a relation between them. The code then iterates over the Orders and uses the relation to return all Order Detail rows for each order. Finally, the sample code retrieves the CustomerID field from the parent row and displays it for each child.

The C# code is shown in Example 3-4.

Example 3-4. File: NavigateDataRelationForm.cs

```csharp
// Namespaces, variables, and constants
using System;
using System.Configuration;
using System.Text;
using System.Data;
using System.Data.SqlClient;

// Table name constants
private const String ORDERS_TABLE          = "Orders";
private const String ORDERDETAILS_TABLE    = "OrderDetails";

// Relation name constants
private const String ORDERS_ORDERDETAILS_RELATION =
    "Orders_OrderDetails_Relation";

// Field name constants
private const String ORDERID_FIELD         = "OrderID";
private const String PRODUCTID_FIELD       = "ProductID";
private const String QUANTITY_FIELD        = "Quantity";
private const String CUSTOMERID_FIELD      = "CustomerID";

// ...

DataSet ds = new DataSet();

SqlDataAdapter da;
```

Example 3-4. File: NavigateDataRelationForm.cs (continued)

```csharp
// Fill the Order table and add it to the DataSet.
da = new SqlDataAdapter("SELECT * FROM Orders",
    ConfigurationSettings.AppSettings["Sql_ConnectString"]);
DataTable orderTable = new DataTable(ORDERS_TABLE);
da.Fill(orderTable);
ds.Tables.Add(orderTable);

// Fill the OrderDetails table and add it to the DataSet.
da = new SqlDataAdapter("SELECT * FROM [Order Details]",
    ConfigurationSettings.AppSettings["Sql_ConnectString"]);
DataTable orderDetailTable = new DataTable(ORDERDETAILS_TABLE);
da.Fill(orderDetailTable);
ds.Tables.Add(orderDetailTable);

// Create a relation between the tables.
ds.Relations.Add(ORDERS_ORDERDETAILS_RELATION,
    ds.Tables[ORDERS_TABLE].Columns[ORDERID_FIELD],
    ds.Tables[ORDERDETAILS_TABLE].Columns[ORDERID_FIELD],
    true);

StringBuilder result = new StringBuilder( );

// Iterate over the first 10 order records.
for (int i = 0; i < 10; i++)
{
    // Display data from the Order record.
    result.Append("Order ID:" + orderTable.Rows[i][ORDERID_FIELD] +
        Environment.NewLine);

    // Iterate over the OrderDetails records for the Order.
    foreach(DataRow row in
        orderTable.Rows[i].GetChildRows(ORDERS_ORDERDETAILS_RELATION))
    {
        // Display data for the OrderDetails record.
        result.Append("\tProduct: " + row[PRODUCTID_FIELD] +
            "; Quantity: " + row[QUANTITY_FIELD] +
            // Retrieve CustomerID from the parent Orders record.
            "; Customer ID: " + row.GetParentRow
            (ORDERS_ORDERDETAILS_RELATION)[CUSTOMERID_FIELD] +
            Environment.NewLine);
    }

    result.Append(Environment.NewLine);
}

resultTextBox.Text = result.ToString( );
```

Discussion

The GetChildRows( ) method of a row in the parent table returns the child rows as an array of DataRow objects for a specified DataRelation. The method takes an optional second argument that you can use to specify the version of the data to retrieve as one of the `DataRowVersion` enumeration values: `Current`, `Default`, `Original`, or `Proposed`.

Similarly, the `GetParentRow( )` method of a row in the child table returns the parent row as a `DataRow` object for a specified `DataRelation`. Again, an optional second argument allows a specific version of the data to be returned.

The `GetParentRows( )` method can also be called on a row in the child table to return parent rows in situations where the child row can have multiple parents. This method returns an array of `DataRow` objects. Few commercial database products support many-to-many relationships between parent and child records. Many-to-many relationships are decomposed into two one-to-many relationships through an intermediate table in relational database management systems (RDBMS).

3.5 Localizing Client-Side Data in a Web Forms Application

Problem

You need to format dates and currency values according to the culture of the client rather than the server.

Solution

Use client culture and encoding to return data to the client formatted according to the client's localization settings rather than the server's settings.

The sample code-behind for the Web Forms page contains one event handler and a single method:

`Form.Load`
> Creates the `CultureInformation` object based on the user's settings.

`RefreshData( )`
> This method sets the `CurrentCulture` for the current thread and demonstrates the effect on output of different data types.

The C# code for the code-behind is shown in Example 3-5.

Example 3-5. File: ADOCookbookCS0305.aspx.cs

```
// Namespaces, variables, and constants
using System;
using System.Threading;
using System.Globalization;
using System.Data;
using System.Data.SqlClient;
```

Example 3-5. File: ADOCookbookCS0305.aspx.cs (continued)

```csharp
// This value would normally be retrieved from a user profile.
private String DEFAULTUSERCULTURE = "en-US";

private CultureInfo ci;

// ...

private void Page_Load(object sender, System.EventArgs e)
{
    if(!IsPostBack)
        ci = new CultureInfo(DEFAULTUSERCULTURE);
    else
    {
        // Create the CultureInfo object as specified by the user.
        if(enUsRadioButton.Checked)
            ci = new CultureInfo("en-US");
        else if(enCaRadioButton.Checked)
            ci = new CultureInfo("en-CA");
        else if(jaJpRadioButton.Checked)
            ci = new CultureInfo("ja-JP");
        else if(frFrRadioButton.Checked)
            ci = new CultureInfo("fr-FR");
    }

    RefreshData();
}

private void RefreshData()
{
    if(ci != null)
    {
        // Set the culture for the current thread.
        Thread.CurrentThread.CurrentCulture = ci;

        // Retrieve details about the culture.
        cultureNameLabel.Text = CultureInfo.CurrentCulture.Name +
            " (" + Thread.CurrentThread.CurrentCulture.Name + ")";
        cultureEnglishNameLabel.Text =
            CultureInfo.CurrentCulture.EnglishName;
        cultureNativeNameLabel.Text =
            CultureInfo.CurrentCulture.NativeName;
    }

    // Sample data that might come from a database
    // displayed according to culture set by user.
    dateLabel.Text = DateTime.Now.ToString("D");
    shortDateLabel.Text = DateTime.Now.ToString("d");

    Double d = 12345.678;
    numberLabel.Text = d.ToString();

    currencyLabel.Text = d.ToString("c");
}
```

Discussion

In a globalized application, a server can be processing requests for users around the world. Culture information for each user must be stored and made available to the server when it is processing each request from the user so that culture-specific operations are performed properly.

There are many ways to store the culture information for a user. You can store it persistently on the client in a cookie. Or you can store it in a database on the server and store it to a session variable when the client logs in or on an ad-hoc basis. No matter how the culture information is stored, it needs to be made available to the server as the client navigates through the site. For example, you can do this using session variables, the URL, or hidden fields. Once the server knows the culture of the user, it can use this information in culture-specific operations. Fortunately, .NET provides a collection of classes which makes this relatively easy.

The System.Globalization namespace contains classes that specify culture-related information. These classes are useful in writing globalized applications. Within this namespace, the CultureInfo class represents information about a specific culture and is used in culture-specific operations such as formatting numbers, currencies, and dates. The CultureInfo class has four constructor overloads, each allowing the culture to be specified differently. The sample code uses the constructor that takes the culture name in the format *{languagecode2}-{country | regioncode2}*, in which:

languagecode2
> Is the lowercase two-letter code derived from ISO 639-1.

country
> Is the uppercase two-letter code derived from ISO 3166. If *country* is not available, the *regioncode2* is used.

regioncode2
> Is the three-letter code derived from ISO-639-2. *regioncode2* is used when *country* is not available.

For example, the culture name for U.S. English is *en-US*.

Once the CultureInfo object is instantiated, you can assign it to the CurrentCulture property of the current thread by code with a SecurityPermission having the ControlThread flag set. Setting the CurrentCulture property affects subsequent culture-specific operations; setting it to the culture of the current user results in output specific to the user's culture.

3.6   Combining Data in Tables from Heterogeneous Data Sources

Problem

You want to create a report that is based on data from tables in more than one data source.

Solution

Use ad-hoc connector names in SQL statements.

The sample code retrieves data from both a SQL Server table and a Microsoft Access table to create a single result set. Specifically, Northwind Order data is retrieved from SQL Server and Northwind Order Details data is retrieved from Access and joined to the Order information.

The C# code is shown in Example 3-6.

Example 3-6. File: CombiningDataFromMultipleDatabasesForm.cs

```
// Namespaces, variables, and constants
using System;
using System.Configuration;
using System.Data;
using System.Data.SqlClient;

// ...

// Fill the table with data from SQL Server and MS Access.
String sqlSelect = "SELECT o.OrderID, o.CustomerID, o.OrderDate, " +
    "od.ProductId, od.UnitPrice, od.Quantity, od.Discount " +
    "FROM Orders o INNER JOIN " +
    "OPENROWSET('Microsoft.Jet.OLEDB.4.0','" +
    ConfigurationSettings.AppSettings["MsAccess_Database_Filename"] +
    "';'admin';'',[Order Details]) " +
    "AS od ON o.OrderID = od.OrderID " +
    "ORDER BY o.OrderID, od.ProductID";
SqlDataAdapter da = new SqlDataAdapter(sqlSelect,
    ConfigurationSettings.AppSettings["Sql_ConnectString"]);
DataTable dt = new DataTable( );
da.Fill(dt);

// Set up and bind a view with data from both tables.
DataView dv = dt.DefaultView;
dv.AllowDelete = false;
dv.AllowEdit = false;
dv.AllowNew = false;
dataGrid.DataSource = dv;
```

Discussion

Microsoft SQL Server 2000 and later supports two methods to access data from heterogeneous data sources through OLE DB: linked servers and ad hoc connector names.

You can refer to linked servers in SQL statements using a four-part name comprised of the names of the linked server, the catalog, the schema within the catalog, and data object. These names are separated with periods. If the data sources are going to be accessed frequently, defining them as linked servers rather than through ad hoc connector names as shown in the sample will improve performance. For more information about using linked servers, see Microsoft SQL Server Books Online.

Ad-hoc connector names allow data from heterogeneous data sources to be accessed without setting up linked servers by providing the information required to connect to each data source in the SQL statement. This is done using either the OPENROWSET or the OPENDATASOURCE function to open the row set from the OLE DB data source. Both functions take arguments containing all connection information required to access the data source. The functions allow the row sets to be subsequently referenced like any other table in SQL statements.

For more information about OPENROWSET and OPENDATASOURCE functions, see Microsoft SQL Server Books Online.

3.7   Using Expression Columns to Display Aggregate Values

Problem

You want to add summary information such as averages, sums, and counts to a table based on related child rows.

Solution

Use expression columns to perform aggregate calculations based on child rows.

The sample code starts by creating a DataSet containing the Orders and Order Details tables from Northwind sample database and a relation between them. An expression is added to the Order Details table to calculate the extended price for each row. Aggregate values for the total extended price of the order and the number of Order Detail rows are added to the Orders table. Finally, the default view of the Orders table is bound to the data grid to display the results.

The C# code is shown in Example 3-7.

Example 3-7. File: ChildAggregateForm.cs

```
// Namespaces, variables, and constants
using System;
using System.Configuration;
using System.Data;
using System.Data.SqlClient;

// Table name constants
private const String ORDERS_TABLE        = "Orders";
private const String ORDERDETAILS_TABLE = "OrderDetails";

// Relation name constants
private const String ORDERS_ORDERDETAILS_RELATION =
    "Orders_OrderDetails_Relation";

// Field name constants
private const String ORDERID_FIELD       = "OrderID";

// ...

DataSet ds = new DataSet();

SqlDataAdapter da;

// Fill the Order table and add it to the DataSet.
da = new SqlDataAdapter("SELECT * FROM Orders",
    ConfigurationSettings.AppSettings["Sql_ConnectString"]);
DataTable orderTable = new DataTable(ORDERS_TABLE);
da.Fill(orderTable);
ds.Tables.Add(orderTable);

// Fill the OrderDetails table and add it to the DataSet.
da = new SqlDataAdapter("SELECT * FROM [Order Details]",
    ConfigurationSettings.AppSettings["Sql_ConnectString"]);
DataTable orderDetailTable = new DataTable(ORDERDETAILS_TABLE);
da.Fill(orderDetailTable);
ds.Tables.Add(orderDetailTable);

// Create a relation between the tables.
ds.Relations.Add(ORDERS_ORDERDETAILS_RELATION,
    ds.Tables[ORDERS_TABLE].Columns[ORDERID_FIELD],
    ds.Tables[ORDERDETAILS_TABLE].Columns[ORDERID_FIELD],
    true);

// Create the expression column for the line total.
orderDetailTable.Columns.Add("OrderDetailTotal", typeof(Decimal),
    "(Quantity * UnitPrice) * (1-Discount)");
// Create the OrderDetails aggregate values in the Order table.
orderTable.Columns.Add("OrderDetailCount", typeof(int),
    "COUNT(Child.ProductId)");
orderTable.Columns.Add("OrderTotal", typeof(Decimal),
    "SUM(Child.OrderDetailTotal)");
```

Example 3-7. File: ChildAggregateForm.cs (continued)

```
// Bind the DataSet to the grid.
childAggregateDataGrid.DataSource = ds.DefaultViewManager;
childAggregateDataGrid.DataMember = ORDERS_TABLE;
```

Discussion

You can create aggregate columns within a table to display summary information for related child records. When a DataRelation exists between a parent and child table in a DataSet, you can refer to a child record by adding the prefix Child. to the column name in the child table. In the sample code, COUNT(Child.ProductID) returns the number of Order Details child records for the parent Order record. Expression columns support aggregate functions as shown in Table 3-2.

Table 3-2. Aggregate functions supported by expression columns

Function	Description
AVG	Average of all values
COUNT	Number of values
MAX	Largest value
MIN	Smallest value
STDEV	Statistical standard deviation of all values
SUM	Sum of all values
VAR	Statistical variance of all values

If the parent table has more than one child table, the relationship must be specified in the aggregate function. The fully qualified syntax to access the count of child Order Details records would be:

```
COUNT(Child("Orders_OrderDetails_Relation").ProductId)
```

You can refer to the parent table for a child in a similar manner by adding the prefix Parent. to the column name. In the previous example, for a row in the Order Details table, Parent.CustomerID refers to the CustomerID for the parent Orders row.

3.8   Finding Rows in a DataTable

Problem

You need to find a row or group of rows in a DataTable meeting certain criteria.

Solution

Choose from the three techniques shown in the sample code to locate data in the table meeting user-specified criteria.

The sample code contains two event handlers:

Form.Load
> Sets up the sample by creating a DataTable containing the Orders table from the Northwind sample database. The default view of the table is bound to the data grid on the form.

Find Button.Click
> Uses three different techniques—the DataTable.Select( ) method, the DataTable.Rows.Find( ) method, and the DataView.RowFilter property—to find rows in the Orders table matching the user-specified Country.

The C# code is shown in Example 3-8.

Example 3-8. File: FindDataTableRowsForm.cs

```
// Namespaces, variables, and constants
using System;
using System.Configuration;
using System.Data;
using System.Data.SqlClient;

// Table name constants
private const String ORDERS_TABLE      = "Orders";

// Field name constants
private const String ORDERID_FIELD      = "OrderID";
private const String SHIPCOUNTRY_FIELD = "ShipCountry";

// ...

private void FindDataTableRowsForm_Load(object sender, System.EventArgs e)
{
    // Fill the Orders table.
    SqlDataAdapter da = new SqlDataAdapter("SELECT * FROM Orders",
        ConfigurationSettings.AppSettings["Sql_ConnectString"]);
    DataTable dt = new DataTable(ORDERS_TABLE);
    da.Fill(dt);
    da.FillSchema(dt, SchemaType.Source);

    // Bind the table to the grid.
    dataGrid.DataSource = dt.DefaultView;
}

private void findButton_Click(object sender, System.EventArgs e)
{
    // Get the table bound to the grid.
    DataTable dt = ((DataView)dataGrid.DataSource).Table;
```

Example 3-8. File: FindDataTableRowsForm.cs (continued)

```
// Build the filter using contents of the text box.
String filter = SHIPCOUNTRY_FIELD + " = '" +
    shipCountryTextBox.Text + "'";

// Locate the records using the Select( ) method of the DataTable.
DataRow[] drc = dt.Select(filter);
resultTextBox.Text = "DataTable.Select returned " + drc.Length +
    " record(s)." + Environment.NewLine;

// Iterate over the collection of rows filtered in the previous step
// and find them in the table using the Find( ) method of the
// DataRowCollection for the DataTable.
int findCount = 0;
foreach(DataRow row in drc)
{
    DataRow foundRow = dt.Rows.Find(row[ORDERID_FIELD]);
    if (foundRow != null)
        findCount++;
}
resultTextBox.Text += "DataTable.Rows.Find returned " + findCount +
    " record(s)." + Environment.NewLine;

// Locate records using the RowFilter property of the DataView.
DataView dv = new DataView(dt);
dv.RowFilter = filter;
resultTextBox.Text += "DataView.RowFilter returned " + dv.Count +
    " record(s).";
}
```

Discussion

There are three ways to locate one or more rows in a table:

- Use the Select( ) method of the DataTable to return an array of DataRow objects matching the specified filter criteria. By default, the rows in the array are ordered by the primary key or, lacking a primary key, by the order in which the rows were added to the table. A sort order can be specified in an optional argument. The Select( ) method also takes an optional argument that can also be used to select records matching a specified row state from the DataViewRowState enumeration.

- Use the Find( ) method of the DataRowCollection of the table to return a row matching the primary key value or values passed as an object argument or an array of object arguments, respectively. To use the Find( ) method, the DataTable to which the DataRowCollection belongs must have a primary key defined, otherwise a MissingPrimaryKeyException is raised. If the primary key does not exist in the DataRowCollection, the method returns null.

- Use a DataView based on the DataTable to locate records in one of the following ways:
  - Use the RowFilter property of the DataView. Create a DataView based on the DataTable and set the RowFilter property to a filter expression.
  - Use the Find() method of the DataView to return the index of the row matching the sort key value or values passed as an object argument or an array of object arguments, respectively. If the sort key value does not exist in the DataView, null is returned.
  - Use the FindRows() method of the DataView to return an array of DataRowView objects whose columns match the specified sort key value. If the sort key value does not exist, an empty DataRowView array is returned.

For more information about the Find() and FindRows() methods of the DataView, see Recipe 3.9.

3.9   Finding Rows in a DataView

Problem

You need to find a row or group of rows in a DataView meeting certain criteria.

Solution

Use a sorted DataView to find rows using columns that are not part of the primary key.

The sample code contains two event handlers:

Form.Load
> Sets up the sample by creating a DataTable containing the Orders table from the Northwind database. A DataView of the table sorted by the CustomerID and EmployeeID is created.

Find Button.Click
> Uses the FindRows() method of the DataView to retrieve the array of DataRowView objects matching the *CustomerID* and *OrderID* specified. The code iterates over the collection to return the results.

The C# code is shown in Example 3-9.

Example 3-9. File: DataViewSearchPerformanceForm.cs

```
// Namespaces, variables, and constants
using System;
using System.Configuration;
using System.Text;
using System.Data;
using System.Data.SqlClient;
```

Example 3-9. File: DataViewSearchPerformanceForm.cs (continued)

```
private DataView dv;

// ...

private void DataViewSearchPerformanceForm_Load(object sender,
    System.EventArgs e)
{
    // Fill the source table with schema and data.
    SqlDataAdapter da = new SqlDataAdapter("SELECT * FROM Orders",
        ConfigurationSettings.AppSettings["Sql_ConnectString"]);
    DataTable dt = new DataTable("Orders");
    da.FillSchema(dt, SchemaType.Source);
    da.Fill(dt);

    // Create the data view for the Orders table and sort.
    dv = new DataView(dt);
    dv.Sort = "CustomerID, EmployeeID";
}

private void findButton_Click(object sender, System.EventArgs e)
{
    StringBuilder result = new StringBuilder();
    DataRowView[] foundRows;

    // Find the rows by the sort key value ProductID.
    try
    {
        foundRows = dv.FindRows(new object[] {customerIdTextBox.Text,
            employeeIdTextBox.Text});
    }
    catch (FormatException ex)
    {
        resultTextBox.Text = ex.Message;
        return;
    }

    // Display the results.
    if(foundRows.Length == 0)
    {
        result.Append("No rows found.");
    }
    else
    {
        result.Append("ORDER\tREQUIRED DATE" + Environment.NewLine);

        // Iterate over the collection of found rows.
        foreach(DataRowView row in foundRows)
        {
            result.Append(row["OrderID"] + "\t" +
                row["RequiredDate"] +
                Environment.NewLine);
        }
```

Example 3-9. File: DataViewSearchPerformanceForm.cs (continued)

```
        result.Append("COUNT\t" + foundRows.Length +
            Environment.NewLine);
    }

    resultTextBox.Text = result.ToString( );
}
```

Discussion

The Find( ) and FindRows( ) methods of the DataView search for rows in a DataView using its sort key values. The search values must match the sort key values exactly to return a result; wild card matches are not possible.

The primary difference between the Find( ) and FindRows( ) methods is that Find( ) returns the zero-based index of the first row that matches the search criteria (or –1 if no match is found) while FindRows( ) returns a DataRowView array of all matching rows (or an empty array if no match is found). The DataRow for a DataRowView can be accessed using the DataRow property of the DataRowView.

Before either method can be used, a sort order must be specified or an exception will be raised. You can do this in two ways:

- Set the ApplyDefaultSort property of the DataView to true. This automatically creates an ascending sort order based on the primary column or columns of the table. The default sort can be applied only when the Sort property of the DataView is a null reference or an empty string and when the underlying DataTable has a primary key defined. By default, the AutoDefaultSort property is set to false, so it must be explicitly set.

- Setting the Sort property of the DataView to a string containing one or more column names followed by nothing, or ASC for an ascending sort, or by DESC for a descending sort. Use commas to separate multiple sort column names.

Both the Find( ) and FindRows( ) methods take a single input argument. This is an object value if the DataView is sorted on a single column or an array of objects containing values for all of the columns defined by the Sort property in the same order as specified by the Sort property.

The Find( ) and FindRows( ) methods perform better than the RowFilter property when a result set from the DataView matching specific criteria is required rather than a dynamic view on the subset of data. This is because setting the RowFilter property of the DataView causes the index for the DataView to be rebuilt, while the Find( ) and FindRows( ) methods use the existing index.

3.10   Selecting the Top n Rows in a DataTable

Problem

You want to create a grid that shows the top five rows in a DataTable, based on the values in one of the columns.

Solution

Use an appropriate sort order with a DataView filter.

The sample code contains two event handlers:

Form.Load

> Sets up the sample by creating a DataTable containing the Orders table from the Northwind sample database. The default view of the table is bound to the data grid on the form.

Select Button.Click

> Builds a filter on the DataView to limit the number of rows to the user-specified count with the largest Freight values.

The C# code is shown in Example 3-10.

Example 3-10. File: DataViewTopNSelectForm.cs

```
// Namespaces, variables, and constants
using System;
using System.Configuration;
using System.Windows.Forms;
using System.Text;
using System.Data;
using System.Data.SqlClient;

private DataView dv;

// Table name constants
private const String ORDERS_TABLE  = "Orders";

// Field name constants
private const String ORDERID_FIELD = "OrderID";
private const String FREIGHT_FIELD = "Freight";

// ...

private void DataViewTopNSelectForm_Load(object sender,
    System.EventArgs e)
{
    // Fill the Orders table.
    SqlDataAdapter da = new SqlDataAdapter("SELECT * FROM Orders",
        ConfigurationSettings.AppSettings["Sql_ConnectString"]);
    DataTable dt = new DataTable(ORDERS_TABLE);
```

Example 3-10. File: DataViewTopNSelectForm.cs (continued)

```csharp
    da.Fill(dt);
    da.FillSchema(dt, SchemaType.Source);

    // Get the default view for the table and bind it to the grid.
    dv = dt.DefaultView;
    dataGrid.DataSource = dv;
}

private void selectButton_Click(object sender, System.EventArgs e)
{
    // This example will select the top n freight values.
    // Set the field name variable.
    String topNFieldName = FREIGHT_FIELD;

    int topN = 0;
    try
    {
        topN = Convert.ToInt32(topNTextBox.Text);

        if(topN <= 0)
        {
            MessageBox.Show("Enter an Integer greater than 0.", "",
                MessageBoxButtons.OK, MessageBoxIcon.Stop);
            return;
        }
    }
    catch(System.FormatException)
    {
        MessageBox.Show("Enter an Integer greater than 0.", "",
            MessageBoxButtons.OK, MessageBoxIcon.Stop);
        return;
    }

    // Clear the filter on the view.
    dv.RowFilter = "";
    // Sort the view descending on the top n field.
    dv.Sort = topNFieldName + " DESC";

    // Create a filter for all records with a value greater than the nth.
    StringBuilder rowFilter = new StringBuilder(topNFieldName + ">=" +
        dv[topN-1][topNFieldName]);
    // Apply the filter to the view.
    dv.RowFilter = rowFilter.ToString( );

    // Handle where there is more than one record with the nth value.
    // Eliminate enough rows from the bottom of the dv using a filter on
    // the primary key to return the correct number (top n) of values.
    bool refilter = false;
    // Iterate over all records in the view after the nth.
    for(int i = dv.Count; i > topN; i--)
    {
```

Example 3-10. File: DataViewTopNSelectForm.cs (continued)

```
        // Exclude the record using a filter on the primary key.
        rowFilter.Append(" AND " + ORDERID_FIELD + "<>" +
            dv[i-1][ORDERID_FIELD]);
        refilter = true;
    }

    // Reapply the view filter if necessary.
    if (refilter)
        dv.RowFilter = rowFilter.ToString( );

    // Bind the view to the grid.
    dataGrid.DataSource = dv;
    dataGrid.CaptionText = ORDERS_TABLE + " table: Top " + topN +
        " records for " + FREIGHT_FIELD + " value.";
}
```

Discussion

While it is possible to locate, sort, and filter records in a DataTable or DataView, there is no method in either class to select the top *n* rows.

The procedure to get the user-specified top *n* rows with the largest Freight value involves several steps. First, sort the DataView on the Freight field in descending order; this places the top *n* records at the top of the view. Next, get the Freight value for the *n*th record and set the DataView filter to contain only rows with a Freight value greater than or equal to that value. Add the appropriate delimiters when making non-numeric comparisons in the filter expression.

At this point, we are done unless there can be more than one instance of the value in the *n*th record, as is the case with Freight. In this case, iterate over the records following the *n*th record and add criteria to a copy of the data view filter to exclude them from the view. Use either the primary key or a unique column or combination of columns to identify the row to be excluded in each case. Apply the new filter to the view. If the view is ordered on the primary key or unique columns in addition to the top *n* columns, this can be used in the initial data view filter to limit returned records in cases where there might be duplicate values in the *n*th record. This would be used instead of the technique just outlined. However, the technique shown requires no sort other than on the top *n* column.

The solution can be extended with little change to handle multiple column top *n* criteria as well as ascending sorts.

Finally, the T-SQL TOP clause limits the number of rows returned by an SQL statement from the data source. This might be a more appropriate solution in some cases, especially when the disconnected table does not already exist. For more information, look up "TOP clause" in Microsoft SQL Server Books Online.

3.11 Getting Typed DataRows from DataViews

Problem

When using a DataView to find rows in a typed DataSet, you want to convert the rows you find to typed DataRow objects having all the properties and methods defined in your typed DataSet.

Solution

Cast the DataRow object returned by the Row property of a DataRowView to a typed DataRow.

The sample code contains two event handlers:

Form.Load
> Sets up the sample by creating a typed DataSet containing the Categories table from the Northwind sample database. The default view of the typed Categories table sorted by the CategoryID is bound to the data grid on the form.

Find Button.Click
> Finds the row in the view matching the user specified CategoryID, gets the underlying table row, and casts that to the typed row.

The C# code is shown in Example 3-11.

Example 3-11. File: TypedDataRowFromDataViewForm.cs

```
// Namespaces, variables, and constants
using System;
using System.Configuration;
using System.Windows.Forms;
using System.Text;
using System.Data;
using System.Data.SqlClient;

private DataView dv;

// Table name constants
private const String CATEGORIES_TABLE = "Categories";

// ...

private void TypedDataRowFromDataViewForm_Load(object sender,
    System.EventArgs e)
{
    // Create the typed DataSet.
    CategoriesDS dsTyped = new CategoriesDS( );

    // Create and fill the Categories table.
    String sqlText =
```

Example 3-11. File: TypedDataRowFromDataViewForm.cs (continued)

```csharp
        "SELECT CategoryID, CategoryName, Description FROM Categories";
    SqlDataAdapter da = new SqlDataAdapter(sqlText,
        ConfigurationSettings.AppSettings["Sql_ConnectString"]);
    da.Fill(dsTyped.Categories);

    // Get the default view and set the sort key.
    dv = dsTyped.Categories.DefaultView;
    dv.Sort = "CategoryID";
    // Bind the default view of the Categories table to the grid.
    dataGrid.DataSource = dv;
}

private void findButton_Click(object sender, System.EventArgs e)
{
    int categoryId = 0;
    try
    {
        categoryId = Convert.ToInt32(categoryIdTextBox.Text);
        // Get the index of the find row in the view.
        int viewRowIndex = dv.Find(categoryId);
        if (viewRowIndex == -1)
            MessageBox.Show("Row not found for Category ID = " +
                categoryId);
        else
        {
            // Cast the underlying row in the view to a typed row.
            CategoriesDS.CategoriesRow typedRow =
                (CategoriesDS.CategoriesRow)dv[viewRowIndex].Row;

            // Display the located typed row.
            MessageBox.Show(typedRow.CategoryID + " - " +
                typedRow.CategoryName);
        }
    }
    catch (Exception ex)
    {
        MessageBox.Show(ex.Message);
    }
}
```

Discussion

The DataView indexer in C# or Item property in VB.NET allows access to the DataRowView objects, or Windows Form control views of a DataRow, contained in the DataView. The DataRowView object in turn exposes a Row property that is a reference to the underlying DataRow object. Just as DataTable objects contain DataRow objects, DataView objects contain DataRowView objects.

The Find( ) method of the DataView returns the index of the row matching the specified search criteria. You can use the index to get a single DataRowView from the

DataView. The Row property of this DataRowView object is used to return the underlying DataRow object. The typed DataSet classes—including the DataTable, DataColumn, and DataRow objects—inherit from the ADO.NET disconnected classes allowing you to cast the DataRow to the strongly typed row.

3.12 Filtering for Null Values

Problem

You want to filter a DataView for rows that have null values.

Solutions

Use the IS NULL clause with the RowFilters property of the DataView.

The sample code contains two event handlers:

Form.Load
> Sets up the sample by creating a DataTable containing the Orders table from the Northwind sample database. The default view of the table is bound to the data grid on the form.

Filter Button.Click
> Toggles on and off the filter on the data view that selects only rows with a null ShipRegion.

The C# code is shown in Example 3-12.

Example 3-12. File: FilterNullValuesForm.cs

```
// Namespaces, variables, and constants
using System;
using System.Configuration;
using System.Data;
using System.Data.SqlClient;

// Table name constants
private const String ORDERS_TABLE     = "Orders";

// Field name constants
private const String SHIPREGION_FIELD = "ShipRegion";

// ...

private void FilterNullValuesForm_Load(object sender, System.EventArgs e)
{
    // Create and fill the Orders table.
    DataTable dt = new DataTable(ORDERS_TABLE);
    SqlDataAdapter da = new SqlDataAdapter("SELECT * FROM Orders",
        ConfigurationSettings.AppSettings["Sql_ConnectString"]);
    da.Fill(dt);
```

Example 3-12. File: FilterNullValuesForm.cs (continued)

```
    // Bind the default view to the grid.
    dataGrid.DataSource = dt.DefaultView;
}


private void filterButton_Click(object sender, System.EventArgs e)
{
    String filter = SHIPREGION_FIELD + " IS NULL";

    DataView dv = (DataView)dataGrid.DataSource;

    if(filterButton.Text == "Apply Filter")
    {
        // Apply the filter.
        dv.RowFilter = filter;
        dataGrid.CaptionText =
            "Orders table: filtered for null ShipRegion field.";
        filterButton.Text = "Remove Filter";
    }
    else
    {
        // Remove the filter.
        dv.RowFilter = "";
        dataGrid.CaptionText = "Orders table: no filter.";
        filterButton.Text = "Apply Filter";
    }
}
```

Discussion

Every DataTable has a default DataView associated with it that can filter a table for records meeting specific criteria. In the solution, the RowFilter property of the DefaultView is filtered for rows containing a null ShipRegion field. The result of applying the filter is immediately reflected in any controls bound to the DataView object in addition to the any operations performed on the records within the DataView.

Alternatively, you can use the Select( ) method on the DataTable underlying the DataView to retrieve an array of DataRow objects containing only rows with the null ShipRegion using the same filter expression.

3.13   Executing Queries That Use COMPUTE BY

Problem

The SQL Server .NET data provider does not support the COMPUTE BY clause but you want to execute a COMPUTE BY statement using ADO.NET.

Solution

Use the COMPUTE BY statement from the Command object of the OLE DB .NET data provider.

The sample code defines a COMPUTE BY statement and executes it using the ExecuteReader( ) method of the OleDbCommand object. Multiple result sets are returned by the DataReader and then these are displayed.

The C# code is shown in Example 3-13.

Example 3-13. File: ComputeForm.cs

```csharp
// Namespaces, variables, and constants
using System;
using System.Text;
using System.Data;
using System.Data.OleDb;

// ...

StringBuilder result = new StringBuilder( );

String sqlSelect = "select OrderID, ProductID, Quantity " +
    "FROM [Order Details] " +
    "ORDER BY ProductID " +
    "COMPUTE SUM(quantity) by ProductID";

OleDbConnection conn = new OleDbConnection(
  ConfigurationSettings.AppSettings["OleDb_Shape_ConnectString"]);
OleDbCommand cmd = new OleDbCommand(sqlSelect, conn);
conn.Open( );

OleDbDataReader dr = cmd.ExecuteReader( );

do
{
    result.Append("Order\tProduct\tQuantity" + Environment.NewLine);
    while(dr.Read( ))
    {
        result.Append(dr.GetInt32(0) + "\t" + dr.GetInt32(1) + "\t" +
            dr.GetInt16(2) + Environment.NewLine);
    }

    // Get the sum.
    dr.NextResult( );
    dr.Read( );
    result.Append("SUM\t\t" + dr.GetInt32(0) + Environment.NewLine);
    result.Append(Environment.NewLine);
} while(dr.NextResult( ));

dr.Close( );
conn.Close( );

resultTextBox.Text = result.ToString( );
```

Discussion

The SQL Server .NET data provider does not support the COMPUTE BY clause, but the OLE DB .NET data provider does. The results are returned as multiple pairs of result sets, the first of which contains the selected details and the second containing the results of the aggregate functions specified (the sum of the quantity ordered for the product in this example) in the COMPUTE BY clause. This pattern is repeated for the remaining pairs of result sets.

Microsoft states that the COMPUTE and COMPUTE BY clauses are provided in SQL Server 7.0 and later versions for backward compatibility. The ROLLUP operator provides similar functionality and is recommended instead. The main difference is that ROLLUP returns a single result set instead of multiple result sets. For more information about the ROLLUP operator, see Microsoft SQL Server Books Online.

3.14   Using the Shape Language to Retrieve Hierarchical Data

Problem

You want to use the Shape language with ADO.NET to retrieve hierarchical data from a SQL Server.

Solution

Execute the SHAPE command as shown in the following example using the OLE DB provider.

The sample code defines a SHAPE query to retrieve the TOP 5 Orders from Northwind and the Order Details for each of the Orders. A DataReader based on the query is created. The code iterates over the rows in the DataReader displaying the data for each Order row. If the value for the column can be cast to the IDataReader interface, it is a DataReader containing the Order Details for the Order row. The value for the column is cast to a DataReader and the collection of records is iterated over and displayed.

The C# code is shown in Example 3-14.

Example 3-14. File: ShapeForm.cs

```
// Namespaces, variables, and constants
using System;
using System.Configuration;
using System.Text;
using System.Data;
using System.Data.OleDb;
```

Example 3-14. File: ShapeForm.cs (continued)

```
// ...

StringBuilder result = new StringBuilder( );

// SHAPE SQL to retrieve TOP five Orders and associated Order Detail records.
String shapeText = "SHAPE {select TOP 5 * from Orders} AS Orders " +
    "APPEND ({select * from [Order Details]} AS 'Order Details' " +
    "RELATE OrderID TO OrderID)";

// Create the connection.
OleDbConnection conn = new OleDbConnection(
    ConfigurationSettings.AppSettings["OleDb_Shape_ConnectString"]);

// Create a command and fill a DataReader with the
// SHAPE result set.
OleDbCommand cmd = new OleDbCommand(shapeText, conn);
conn.Open( );
OleDbDataReader orderDR = cmd.ExecuteReader( );

// Iterate over the collection of rows in the DataReader.
while(orderDR.Read( ))
{
    result.Append("ORDER" + Environment.NewLine);
    // Iterate over the collection of Order columns in the DataReader.
    for(int colOrder = 0; colOrder < orderDR.FieldCount; colOrder++)
    {
        if (orderDR[colOrder] is IDataReader)
        {
            // The column is an IDataReader interface.
            result.Append(Environment.NewLine);
            result.Append(orderDR.GetName(colOrder).ToUpper( ) +
                Environment.NewLine);

            // Create a DataReader for the Order Detail from the
            // IDataReader interface column.
            OleDbDataReader orderDetailDR =
                (OleDbDataReader)orderDR.GetValue(colOrder);
            // Iterate over records in the Order Detail DataReader.
            while(orderDetailDR.Read( ))
            {
                // Iterate over the Order Detail columns
                // in the Data Reader.
                for(int colOrderDetail = 0;
                    colOrderDetail < orderDetailDR.FieldCount;
                    colOrderDetail++)
                {
                    result.Append("    " +
                    orderDetailDR.GetName(colOrderDetail) +
                    ": " + orderDetailDR[colOrderDetail] +
                    Environment.NewLine);
                }
                result.Append(Environment.NewLine);
```

Example 3-14. File: ShapeForm.cs (continued)

```
                }
            }
            else
            {
                result.Append(orderDR.GetName(colOrder)+ ": " +
                    orderDR[colOrder] + Environment.NewLine);
            }
        }
        result.Append(Environment.NewLine);
    }

    orderDR.Close( );
    conn.Close( );

    resultTextBox.Text = result.ToString( );
```

Discussion

You can retrieve hierarchical result sets or *chapters* (OLE DB type DBTYPE_HCHAPTER) from SQL Server using the OLE DB .NET data provider. The chapter is returned as a field in the data reader with a data type of Object that is a DataReader.

Hierarchical result sets combine the results for multiple queries into a single structure. They are generated using the Data Shaping Service for OLE DB first introduced in ADO 2.0. This provider supports the Shape language allowing the result set hierarchies to be constructed. Shaping is an alternative to JOIN and GROUP BY syntax that you can use to access parent/child data and associated summary data.

The connection string using data shaping is shown here:

```
Provider=MSDataShape;Data Provider=SQLOLEDB;Data Source=(local);
    Initial Catalog=Northwind;Integrated Security=SSPI;
```

For more information about data shaping or the MSDataShape provider, see the MSDN library.

CHAPTER 4

Adding and Modifying Data

4.0 Introduction

This chapter focuses on issues related to inserting and updating data as well as using web services, remoting, and messaging to update data.

Web services allow distributed applications running on disparate platforms to communicate using open standards and ubiquitous protocols. Recipe 4.11 shows how to create a web service that lets a client update a database, and how to call the web service from a .NET application. Similarly, Recipe 4.12 shows how to create a.NET remoting component that lets a client update a database, and how to call the remote objects from a .NET application.

Messaging allows applications running on disparate platforms to communicate whether they are connected or disconnected. Recipe 4.13 shows how to use messaging to update a database.

In addition to these topics, this chapter also covers:

Identity and auto-increment columns

> ADO.NET provides an auto-incrementing column type that generates a unique value for each new row. There is no mechanism to ensure that the values are unique from the values produced by other users. Recipe 4.1 shows how to use auto-incrementing columns to ensure that the values generated by different users do not conflict.

> SQL Server has an identity column that is also an auto-incrementing column type. This value is used rather than the ADO.NET auto-increment column type when adding new records; there is no automatic way to keep these values synchronized after new rows in a DataTable have been inserted into a SQL Server table. Recipe 4.2 shows you how to synchronize the DataTable to the values in the database. Recipe 4.3 shows you how to synchronize these values with a Microsoft Access database.

> Oracle does not support auto-increment columns but rather uses a *sequence*, that is, a procedure that generates a series of unique values. Recipe 4.4 shows

how to synchronize auto-incrementing columns in a DataTable with Oracle sequence values after a row has been inserted into an Oracle database.

Primary keys and relationships

Recipe 4.5 shows how to add master-detail records to a DataSet where the primary key of the parent table is an auto-incrementing column.

A Globally Unique Identifier (GUID) is a 128-bit integer that is statistically unique. Recipe 4.6 shows how to add records to a DataSet containing master-detail records with both parent and child tables having a GUID primary key.

Changing the primary key value in a database is a little more complicated than changing it in a DataTable and updating it to the database. When the primary key is changed in the DataTable, the default behavior is for the update to look for a row matching the modified value for the primary key rather than the original. Recipe 4.8 demonstrates how to change the primary key in a database.

In a relational database, many-to-many relationships use a junction table to join two other tables. Recipe 4.10 shows how to update changes made to the tables and relationships between the rows without causing referential integrity errors.

DataSet twiddling

A DataSet keeps no connection or data source information about its data source. This allows a DataSet to be loaded with data from one data source and updated back to another data source, perhaps for auditing or logging purposes. Recipe 4.7 shows how this is done.

CommandBuilder

A CommandBuilder can quickly and easily generate *update logic* for a DataAdapter in small or test applications. A CommandBuilder cannot generate valid update logic if the table or column names contain special characters or spaces. Recipe 4.14 shows how to make the CommandBuilder delimit table and column names to overcome this problem.

Stored procedure parameters

Although of questionable usefulness in a production environment, ADO.NET allows you to retrieve stored procedure parameters information at runtime. SQL Server also lets you do the same thing using a system stored procedure. Recipe 4.9 shows you both techniques.

4.1   Using Auto-Incrementing Columns Without Causing Conflicts

Problem

You want to use an AutoIncrement column in a table without producing values that may be duplicated in records added by other users.

Solution

Use the `AutoIncrementSeed` and `AutoIncrementStep` properties of the `AutoIncrement` column.

The sample code contains two event handlers:

Form.Load

> Sets up the sample by creating a `DataTable` and programmatically defining the schema to match the Categories table in Northwind. The `AutoIncrementSeed` and `AutoIncrementStep` property values are both set to –1 for the `AutoIncrement` primary key column, the CategoryID. A `DataAdapter` is created and used to fill the `DataTable`. The default view of the table is bound to the data grid on the form.

Add Button.Click

> Creates a new row in the Categories `DataTable` using the entered CategoryName and Description values and the automatically generated CategoryID field.

The C# code is shown in Example 4-1.

Example 4-1. File: AutoIncrementWithoutConflictForm.cs

```csharp
// Namespaces, variables, and constants
using System;
using System.Configuration;
using System.Data;
using System.Data.SqlClient;

// Table name constants
private const String CATEGORIES_TABLE    = "Categories";

// Field name constants
private const String CATEGORYID_FIELD    = "CategoryID";
private const String CATEGORYNAME_FIELD  = "CategoryName";
private const String DESCRIPTION_FIELD   = "Description";

private DataTable dt;

// ...

private void AutoIncrementWithoutConflictForm_Load(object sender,
    System.EventArgs e)
{
    // Create the Categories table.
    dt = new DataTable(CATEGORIES_TABLE);

    // Add the identity column.
    DataColumn col = dt.Columns.Add(CATEGORYID_FIELD,
        typeof(System.Int32));
    col.AllowDBNull = false;
    col.AutoIncrement = true;
    col.AutoIncrementSeed = -1;
    col.AutoIncrementStep = -1;
```

Example 4-1. File: AutoIncrementWithoutConflictForm.cs (continued)

```
    // Set the primary key.
    dt.PrimaryKey = new DataColumn[] {col};

    // Add the other columns.
    col = dt.Columns.Add(CATEGORYNAME_FIELD, typeof(System.String));
    col.AllowDBNull = false;
    col.MaxLength = 15;
    dt.Columns.Add(DESCRIPTION_FIELD, typeof(System.String));

    // Fill the table.
    SqlDataAdapter da = new SqlDataAdapter("SELECT * FROM Categories",
        ConfigurationSettings.AppSettings["Sql_ConnectString"]);
    da.Fill(dt);

    // Bind the default view for the table to the grid.
    categoryDataGrid.DataSource = dt.DefaultView;
}

private void addButton_Click(object sender, System.EventArgs e)
{
    // Add a new row.
    DataRow row = dt.NewRow( );
    row[CATEGORYNAME_FIELD] = categoryNameTextBox.Text;
    row[DESCRIPTION_FIELD] = descriptionTextBox.Text;
    dt.Rows.Add(row);
}
```

Discussion

An `AutoIncrement` column generates a series of values beginning with the `AutoIncrementSeed` value and is incremented by the `AutoIncrementStep` value with each new value. This easily allows you to generate unique values for an integer-type column. A potential problem occurs when new rows are being inserted into an existing table for an identity field (in SQL Server) where the generated values conflict with existing values in the table because of, perhaps, new records added to the data source by other users. In this case, instead of being interpreted as new records by the data source, these records are incorrectly interpreted as updates of existing records.

The problem can be avoided by setting the `AutoIncrementSeed` value to −1 and the `AutoIncrementStep` value to −1 thereby generating a sequence of negative values that does not conflict with the values generated by the data source, as long as the data source does not generate negative values. When the disconnected data is reconciled with the underlying data (see Recipe 4.2), the data source correctly identifies the records that have negative `AutoIncrement` field values as new records, adds them to the data source, and in the process generates new values for the `AutoIncrement` field. Recipe 4.2 discusses synchronizing these data source-generated values with the disconnected data.

4.2 Getting an Identity Column Value from SQL Server

Problem

When you add a row into a SQL Server table that has an identity column, the value assigned to the column in the DataTable is replaced by a value generated by the database. You need to retrieve the new value to keep the DataTable synchronized with the database.

Solution

There are two ways to synchronize identity values generated by the data source: use either the first returned record or the output parameters of a stored procedure.

The sample uses a single stored procedure:

InsertCategories

> Used to add a new Categories record to the Northwind database. The stored procedure returns the CategoryId value generated by the data source as both an output parameter and in the first returned record.

The sample code contains two event handlers:

Form.Load

> Sets up the sample by creating a DataTable and programmatically defining the schema to match the Categories table in Northwind. The AutoIncrementSeed and AutoIncrementStep property values are both set to –1 for the AutoIncrement primary key column, the CategoryID. A DataAdapter is created and used to fill the DataTable. The insert command and its parameters are defined for the DataAdapter so that new rows can be added to the data source and the CategoryID value generated by the data source can be retrieved using either the output parameter values or first returned record from the InsertCategories stored procedure. The default view of the table is bound to the data grid on the form.

Add Button.Click

> Creates a new row in the Categories DataTable using the entered CategoryName and Description values and the automatically generated CategoryID field. The Update( ) method of the DataAdapter is used to insert the row into the data source and synchronize the identity value generated by the data source to the AutoIncrement column value—its value, both before and after is displayed.

The C# code is shown in Example 4-2.

Example 4-2. Stored procedure: InsertCategories

```sql
CREATE PROCEDURE InsertCategories
    @CategoryId int output,
    @CategoryName nvarchar(15),
    @Description ntext
AS
    SET NOCOUNT ON

    insert Categories(
        CategoryName,
        Description)
    values (
        @CategoryName,
        @Description)

    if @@rowcount=0
        return 1

    set @CategoryID = Scope_Identity()

    select Scope_Identity() CategoryId

    return 0
```

The C# code is shown in Example 4-3.

Example 4-3. File: IdentityValueForm.cs

```csharp
// Namespaces, variables, and constants
using System;
using System.Configuration;
using System.Data;
using System.Data.SqlClient;

// Table name constants
private const String CATEGORIES_TABLE        = "Categories";

// Field name constants
private const String CATEGORYID_FIELD        = "CategoryID";
private const String CATEGORYNAME_FIELD      = "CategoryName";
private const String DESCRIPTION_FIELD       = "Description";

// Stored procedure name constants
public const String GETCATEGORIES_SP         = "GetCategories";
public const String INSERTCATEGORIES_SP      = "InsertCategories";

// Stored procedure parameter name constants for Categories table
public const String CATEGORYID_PARM          = "@CategoryID";
public const String CATEGORYNAME_PARM        = "@CategoryName";
public const String DESCRIPTION_PARM         = "@Description";

private DataTable dt;
private SqlDataAdapter da;
```

Example 4-3. File: IdentityValueForm.cs (continued)

```
// ...

private void IdentityValueForm_Load(object sender, System.EventArgs e)
{
    // Create the Categories table.
    dt = new DataTable(CATEGORIES_TABLE);

    // Add the identity column.
    DataColumn col = dt.Columns.Add(CATEGORYID_FIELD,
        typeof(System.Int32));
    col.AllowDBNull = false;
    col.AutoIncrement = true;
    col.AutoIncrementSeed = -1;
    col.AutoIncrementStep = -1;
    // Set the primary key.
    dt.PrimaryKey = new DataColumn[] {col};

    // Add the other columns.
    col = dt.Columns.Add(CATEGORYNAME_FIELD, typeof(System.String));
    col.AllowDBNull = false;
    col.MaxLength = 15;
    dt.Columns.Add(DESCRIPTION_FIELD, typeof(System.String));

    // Create the DataAdapter.
    da = new SqlDataAdapter(GETCATEGORIES_SP,
        ConfigurationSettings.AppSettings["Sql_ConnectString"]);
    da.SelectCommand.CommandType = CommandType.StoredProcedure;

    // Create the insert command for the DataAdapter.
    da.InsertCommand = new SqlCommand(INSERTCATEGORIES_SP,
        da.SelectCommand.Connection);
    da.InsertCommand.CommandType = CommandType.StoredProcedure;
    // Add the output parameter.
    SqlParameter param = da.InsertCommand.Parameters.Add(CATEGORYID_PARM,
        SqlDbType.Int, 0, CATEGORYID_FIELD);
    param.Direction = ParameterDirection.Output;
    // Add the other parameters.
    da.InsertCommand.Parameters.Add(CATEGORYNAME_PARM, SqlDbType.NVarChar,
        15, CATEGORYNAME_FIELD);
    da.InsertCommand.Parameters.Add(DESCRIPTION_PARM, SqlDbType.NText,
        0, DESCRIPTION_FIELD);

    // Fill the table with data.
    da.Fill(dt);

    // Bind the default table view to the grid.
    dataGrid.DataSource = dt.DefaultView;
}

private void addButton_Click(object sender, System.EventArgs e)
{
```

Example 4-3. File: IdentityValueForm.cs (continued)

```
    // Add the row to the Category table.
    DataRow row = dt.NewRow( );
    row[CATEGORYNAME_FIELD] = categoryNameTextBox.Text;
    row[DESCRIPTION_FIELD] = descriptionTextBox.Text;
    dt.Rows.Add(row);

    resultTextBox.Text = "Identity value before update = " +
        row[CATEGORYID_FIELD] + Environment.NewLine;

    // Set the method used to return the data source identity value.
    if(outputParametersCheckBox.Checked &&
        firstReturnedRecordCheckBox.Checked)
        da.InsertCommand.UpdatedRowSource = UpdateRowSource.Both;
    else if(outputParametersCheckBox.Checked)
        da.InsertCommand.UpdatedRowSource =
            UpdateRowSource.OutputParameters;
    else if(firstReturnedRecordCheckBox.Checked)
        da.InsertCommand.UpdatedRowSource =
            UpdateRowSource.FirstReturnedRecord;
    else
        da.InsertCommand.UpdatedRowSource = UpdateRowSource.None;

    // Update the data source.
    da.Update(dt);

    resultTextBox.Text += "Identity value after update = " +
        row[CATEGORYID_FIELD];
}
```

Discussion

As discussed in Recipe 4.1, the AutoIncrementSeed and AutoIncrementStep property values for the AutoIncrement column should both be set to –1 to prevent conflict with the positive identity values generated by the data source.

The values created for an AutoIncrement column will have new identity values generated by the data source when they are updated back to the data source. There are two ways in which the data source generated value can be retrieved and this solution demonstrates both. The UpdatedRowSource property of the Command object specifies how results from calling the Update( ) method of the DataAdapter are applied to the DataRow. Table 4-1 lists possible values.

Table 4-1. Values for the UpdateRowSource enumeration

Value	Description
Both	Both the data in the first returned row and the output parameters are mapped to the DataSet row that has been inserted or updated. This is the default value unless the command is generated by a CommandBuilder.
FirstReturnedRecord	The data in the first returned row is mapped to the DataSet row that has been inserted or updated.

Table 4-1. Values for the UpdateRowSource enumeration (continued)

Value	Description
None	Return values and parameters are ignored. This is the default value if the command is generated by a `CommandBuilder`.
OutputParameters	Output parameters are mapped to the `DataSet` row that has been inserted or updated.

The stored procedure `InsertCategories` has a single output parameter `@CategoryId` that is used to return the value of the data source generated identity value. The value is set to the new identity value by the stored procedure statement:

```
set @CategoryID = Scope_Identity( )
```

The column to be updated in the row is identified by the source column of the `Parameter` object, in this case, the fourth argument in the constructor.

The stored procedure also returns a result set containing a single row with a single value—CategoryId—containing the new identity value generated by the data source. The result set is returned by the stored procedure statement:

```
select Scope_Identity( ) CategoryId
```

The columns are updated from the data source to the row matching column names, taking into account any column mappings that might be in place.

You can also apply the `FirstReturnedRecord` when using a batch SQL statement. Replace the `InsertCommand` command constructor for the `DataAdapter` with the following code:

```
// Create the insert command for the DataAdapter.
String sqlText="INSERT Categories(CategoryName, Description) VALUES" +
    "(@CategoryName, @Description);" +
    "SELECT Scope_Identity( ) CategoryId";
da.InsertCommand = new SqlCommand(sqlText, da.SelectCommand.Connection);
da.InsertCommand.CommandType = CommandType.Text;
```

Batch SQL commands do not support output parameters, so only the `FirstReturnedRecord` method will work with a batch SQL command.

> The `SCOPE_IDENTITY( )` function was introduced in SQL Server 2000 to make it easier to work with identity values. While `SCOPE_IDENTITY( )` and `@@IDENTITY` both return the last identity value generated in any column in the current session, `SCOPE_IDENTITY( )` returns values inserted within the current scope while `@@IDENTITY` is not limited to the current scope. For more information, see Microsoft SQL Server Books Online.

4.3   Getting an AutoNumber Value
         from Microsoft Access

Problem

If you add a row into a Microsoft Access table that has an AutoNumber column, the value assigned to the column in the DataTable is replaced by a value generated by the database. You need to retrieve the new value to keep the DataTable synchronized with the database.

Solution

Use the RowUpdated event handler to retrieve the new AutoNumber value generated by Microsoft Access.

The sample code contains three event handlers:

Form.Load

Sets up the sample by creating a DataTable and programmatically defining the schema to match the Categories table in Northwind. The AutoIncrementSeed and AutoIncrementStep property values are both set to −1 for the AutoIncrement primary key column, the CategoryID. A DataAdapter is created and used to fill the DataTable. The insert command and its parameters are defined for the DataAdapter so that new rows can be added to the data source. An event handler is defined for the RowUpdated event of the DataAdapter to retrieve the AutoNumber value generated for the CategoryID by Access. The default view of the table is bound to the data grid on the form.

Add Button.Click

Creates a new row in the Categories DataTable using the entered CategoryName and Description values and the automatically generated CategoryID field. The Update( ) method of the DataAdapter is used to insert the row into the data source and the DataAdapter RowUpdated event handler synchronizes the AutoNumber value generated by Access to the AutoIncrement column value; its value, both before and after is displayed.

DataAdapter.RowUpdated

Retrieves the AutoNumber CategoryID value generated by Access for inserted rows and updates the DataRow with that value synchronizing it with the Access database.

The C# code is shown in Example 4-4.

Example 4-4. File: MsAccessAutonumberValueForm.cs

```
// Namespaces, variables, and constants
using System;
```

Example 4-4. File: MsAccessAutonumberValueForm.cs (continued)

```csharp
using System.Configuration;
using System.Windows.Forms;
using System.Data;
using System.Data.OleDb;

// DataTable name constants
private const String CATEGORIES_TABLE          = "Categories";

// Field name constants
private const String CATEGORYID_FIELD          = "CategoryID";
private const String CATEGORYNAME_FIELD         = "CategoryName";
private const String DESCRIPTION_FIELD          = "Description";

// Stored procedure name constants
public const String GETCATEGORIES_SP           = "GetCategories";
public const String INSERTCATEGORIES_SP        = "InsertCategories";

// Stored procedure parameter name constants for Categories dt
public const String CATEGORYID_PARM            = "@CategoryID";
public const String CATEGORYNAME_PARM          = "@CategoryName";
public const String DESCRIPTION_PARM           = "@Description";

private DataTable dt;
private OleDbDataAdapter da;

// ...

private void MsAccessAutonumberValueForm_Load(object sender,
    System.EventArgs e)
{
    // Create the Categories dt.
    dt = new DataTable(CATEGORIES_TABLE);

    // Add the identity column.
    DataColumn col = dt.Columns.Add(CATEGORYID_FIELD,
        typeof(System.Int32));
    col.AllowDBNull = false;
    col.AutoIncrement = true;
    col.AutoIncrementSeed = -1;
    col.AutoIncrementStep = -1;
    // Set the primary key.
    dt.PrimaryKey = new DataColumn[] {col};

    // Add the other columns.
    col = dt.Columns.Add(CATEGORYNAME_FIELD, typeof(System.String));
    col.AllowDBNull = false;
    col.MaxLength = 15;
    dt.Columns.Add(DESCRIPTION_FIELD, typeof(System.String));

    // Create the DataAdapter.
    String sqlSelect = "SELECT CategoryID, CategoryName, Description " +
        "FROM Categories";
```

Example 4-4. File: MsAccessAutonumberValueForm.cs (continued)

```
da = new OleDbDataAdapter(sqlSelect,
    ConfigurationSettings.AppSettings["MsAccess_ConnectString"]);

// Create the insert command for the DataAdapter.
String sqlInsert = "INSERT INTO Categories " +
    "(CategoryName, Description) VALUES (?, ?)";
da.InsertCommand = new OleDbCommand(sqlInsert,
    da.SelectCommand.Connection);
da.InsertCommand.Parameters.Add(CATEGORYNAME_PARM, OleDbType.Char,
    15, CATEGORYNAME_FIELD);
da.InsertCommand.Parameters.Add(DESCRIPTION_PARM, OleDbType.VarChar,
    100, DESCRIPTION_FIELD);

// Handle this event to retrieve the autonumber value.
da.RowUpdated += new OleDbRowUpdatedEventHandler(OnRowUpdated);

// Fill the table with data.
try
{
    da.Fill(dt);
}
catch (OleDbException ex)
{
    MessageBox.Show(ex.Message);
}

// Bind the default dt view to the grid.
dataGrid.DataSource = dt.DefaultView;
}

private void addButton_Click(object sender, System.EventArgs e)
{
    // Add the row to the Category table.
    DataRow row = dt.NewRow( );
    row[CATEGORYNAME_FIELD] = categoryNameTextBox.Text;
    row[DESCRIPTION_FIELD] = descriptionTextBox.Text;
    dt.Rows.Add(row);

    resultTextBox.Text = "Identity value before update = " +
        row[CATEGORYID_FIELD] + Environment.NewLine;

    // Update the table with the new row.
    try
    {
        da.Update(dt);
        resultTextBox.Text += "Identity value after update = " +
            row[CATEGORYID_FIELD] + Environment.NewLine +
            Environment.NewLine;
    }
    catch(OleDbException ex)
    {
```

Example 4-4. File: MsAccessAutonumberValueForm.cs (continued)

```
        MessageBox.Show(ex.Message);
    }
}

private void OnRowUpdated(object Sender, OleDbRowUpdatedEventArgs args)
{
    // Retrieve autonumber value for inserts only.
    if(args.StatementType == StatementType.Insert)
    {
        // SQL command to retrieve the identity value created
        OleDbCommand cmd = new OleDbCommand("SELECT @@IDENTITY",
            da.SelectCommand.Connection);

        // Store the new identity value to the CategoryID in the table.
        args.Row[CATEGORYID_FIELD] = (int)cmd.ExecuteScalar();
    }
}
```

Discussion

Microsoft Access does not support stored procedures or batch command processing. It is therefore not possible to map returned stored procedure output parameters, or a result set, back to the row being inserted or updated, as is possible for Microsoft SQL server (see Recipe 4.2). Microsoft Access 2000 and later does support @@IDENTITY, which allows the last AutoNumber value generated to be retrieved.

To use @@IDENTITY, attach a handler to the OnRowUpdated event of the DataAdapter. The OnRowUpdated event will be called after any update to the row is made in the data source. The AutoNumber is only generated for rows that are inserted, so check that the update type of the event has a StatementType of Insert. Next, retrieve the new AutoNumber value by executing the following command:

```
SELECT @@IDENTITY
```

Finally, store this value, that is the AutoNumber value generated by Microsoft Access, to the AutoIncrement column in the DataRow.

This solution will only work using the Jet 4.0 OLE DB provider or later.

4.4   Getting a Sequence Value from Oracle

Problem

When you add a row into an Oracle table that uses a sequence to generate the value for a primary key column, the value assigned to the column in the DataTable is replaced by a value generated by the database. You need to retrieve the new value to keep the DataTable synchronized with the database.

Solution

Use Oracle's CURRVAL and NEXTVAL keywords.

The sample code executes a stored procedure to insert a record into an Oracle table and uses the output parameter of the stored procedure to return the sequence value generated for the primary key column. The sequence value for the new record is displayed.

The sample uses a single stored procedure:

SP0404_INSERT

> Used to add a new record into table TBL0404. The primary key field value is generated by the Oracle sequence TBL0404_SEQUENCE and is returned in the output parameter pID.

The sample uses one sequence:

TBL0404_SEQUENCE

> Called by the stored procedure SP0404_INSERT to generate unique, sequential values for the primary key field ID in the table TBL0404.

The Oracle stored procedure is shown here in Example 4-5.

Example 4-5. Stored procedure: SP0404_Insert

```
CREATE PROCEDURE SP0404_INSERT
(
  pID out number,
  pFIELD1 nvarchar2,
  pFIELD2 nvarchar2
)
as

begin
  INSERT INTO TBL0404 (
    ID,
    FIELD1,
    FIELD2)
  VALUES (
    TBL0404_SEQUENCE.NEXTVAL,
    pFIELD1,
    pFIELD2
  );

  SELECT TBL0404_SEQUENCE.CURRVAL INTO pID FROM DUAL;
end;
```

The Oracle sequence is shown here in Example 4-6.

Example 4-6. Sequence: TBL0404_Sequence

```
CREATE SEQUENCE TBL0404_SEQUENCE
  INCREMENT BY 1
  START WITH 1
  MAXVALUE 1.0E28
  MINVALUE 1
  NOCYCLE
  CACHE 20
  NOORDER
```

The C# code is shown in Example 4-7.

Example 4-7. File: OracleSequenceValuesForm.cs

```csharp
// Namespaces, variables, and constants
using System;
using System.Configuration;
using System.Windows.Forms;
using System.Data;
using System.Data.OracleClient;

private const String STOREDPROCEDURENAME = "SP0404_INSERT";

// Stored procedure parameter name constants for table
private const String ID_PARM        = "pID";
private const String FIELD1_PARM    = "pField1";
private const String FIELD2_PARM    = "pField2";

// ...

// Create the connection.
OracleConnection conn = new OracleConnection(
    ConfigurationSettings.AppSettings["Oracle_ConnectString"]);

// Create the command for the insert stored procedure.
OracleCommand cmd = new OracleCommand( );
cmd.Connection = conn;
cmd.CommandText = STOREDPROCEDURENAME;
cmd.CommandType = CommandType.StoredProcedure;
// Add the parameters and set values for them.
cmd.Parameters.Add(ID_PARM, OracleType.Int32).Direction =
    ParameterDirection.Output;
cmd.Parameters.Add(FIELD1_PARM, OracleType.NVarChar, 50);
cmd.Parameters.Add(FIELD2_PARM, OracleType.NVarChar, 50);
cmd.Parameters[FIELD1_PARM].Value = field1TextBox.Text;
cmd.Parameters[FIELD2_PARM].Value = field2TextBox.Text;

// Execute the insert query.
conn.Open( );
try
{
    cmd.ExecuteNonQuery( );
}
```

Example 4-7. File: OracleSequenceValuesForm.cs (continued)

```
catch(Exception ex)
{
    MessageBox.Show(ex.Message, "Retrieving Oracle Sequence Values",
        MessageBoxButtons.OK, MessageBoxIcon.Error);
    return;
}
finally
{
    conn.Close( );
}

// Retrieve and display the sequence value.
int sequenceValue = (int)cmd.Parameters[ID_PARM].Value;
MessageBox.Show("Inserted record with ID = " + sequenceValue,
    "Retrieving Oracle Sequence Values", MessageBoxButtons.OK,
    MessageBoxIcon.Information);
```

Discussion

Oracle does not support auto-increment fields in the same way that SQL Server does. Instead, Oracle uses a sequence generator, which is a database object that is used to generate a sequence of unique values for a primary key column, but is not related to the table containing the column. As a result, a sequence generator can generate unique values for more than one table.

The SQL command CREATE SEQUENCE is used to create a new sequence as shown in the previous sample. The increment, start value, maximum value, cycling, and caching can be specified when creating the sequence.

Oracle stores the definition of sequences for a database in a single data dictionary table in the SYSTEM table namespace. As a result, all sequence definitions are always available.

A sequence is referenced in SQL statements using the NEXTVAL and CURRVAL keywords. NEXTVAL generates and returns the next sequence number while CURRVAL can be used to refer to that value as needed.

Oracle does not support batch queries to return data as SQL Server does. You can, however, return the sequence value by setting the return value of a stored procedure. The sample demonstrates using the NEXTVAL and CURRVAL keywords to generate the new sequence value when inserting a row using a stored procedure and subsequently setting the stored procedure's return value.

4.5   Adding Parent/Child Rows with Auto-Incrementing Keys

Problem

You want to insert related parent/child rows into a DataSet where the primary key of the parent table is an automatically incrementing value.

Solution

Use the DataColumn object's AutoIncrementSeed and AutoIncrementStep properties.

The sample code contains two event handlers:

Form.Load

Sets up the example by creating a DataSet containing a parent and child table. Each table has an AutoIncrement column that is the primary key and has both a seed and step value of −1. A relation is created between the parent and child table. The default view of the parent table is bound to the data grid on the form.

Add Record Button.Click

Adds a new row to the parent table along with a random number of rows to the child table.

The C# code is shown in Example 4-8.

Example 4-8. File: AddParentChildAutoIncrementForm.cs

```csharp
// Namespaces, variables, and constants
using System;
using System.Data;
using System.Data.SqlClient;

// Table name constants
private const String PARENTTABLENAME    = "ParentTable";
private const String CHILDTABLENAME     = "ChildTable";

// Table column name constants for Parent table
private const String PARENTID_FIELD     = "ParentId";
private const String FIELD1_FIELD       = "Field1";
private const String FIELD2_FIELD       = "Field2";

// Table column parameter name constants for Parent table
private const String CHILDID_FIELD      = "ChildId";
private const String FIELD3_FIELD       = "Field3";
private const String FIELD4_FIELD       = "Field4";

private DataSet ds;

// ...
```

Example 4-8. File: AddParentChildAutoIncrementForm.cs (continued)

```csharp
private void AddParentChildAutoIncrementForm_Load(object sender,
    System.EventArgs e)
{
    DataColumnCollection cols;
    DataColumn col;

    // Build the parent table.
    DataTable parentTable = new DataTable(PARENTTABLENAME);
    cols = parentTable.Columns;
    col = cols.Add(PARENTID_FIELD, typeof(Int32));
    col.AutoIncrement = true;
    col.AutoIncrementSeed = -1;
    col.AutoIncrementStep = -1;
    cols.Add(FIELD1_FIELD, typeof(String)).MaxLength = 50;
    cols.Add(FIELD2_FIELD, typeof(String)).MaxLength = 50;

    // Build the child table.
    DataTable childTable = new DataTable(CHILDTABLENAME);
    cols = childTable.Columns;
    col = cols.Add(CHILDID_FIELD, typeof(Int32));
    col.AutoIncrement = true;
    col.AutoIncrementSeed = -1;
    col.AutoIncrementStep = -1;
    cols.Add(PARENTID_FIELD, typeof(Int32)).AllowDBNull = false;
    cols.Add(FIELD3_FIELD, typeof(String)).MaxLength = 50;
    cols.Add(FIELD4_FIELD, typeof(String)).MaxLength = 50;

    // Add the tables to the DataSet and create the relationship.
    ds = new DataSet();
    ds.Tables.Add(parentTable);
    ds.Tables.Add(childTable);
    ds.Relations.Add(new DataRelation("Parent_Child_Relation",
        parentTable.Columns[PARENTID_FIELD],
        childTable.Columns[PARENTID_FIELD], true));

    // Bind the parent table default view to the grid.
    dataGrid.DataSource = parentTable.DefaultView;
}

private void addRecordButton_Click(object sender, System.EventArgs e)
{
    // Add a record to the parent table.
    DataRow parentRow = ds.Tables[PARENTTABLENAME].NewRow();
    parentRow[FIELD1_FIELD] = Guid.NewGuid().ToString();
    parentRow[FIELD2_FIELD] = Guid.NewGuid().ToString();
    ds.Tables[PARENTTABLENAME].Rows.Add(parentRow);

    // Add some child records for the parent.
    for(int i = 0; i <= new Random((int)DateTime.Now.Ticks).Next(5); i++)
    {
        ds.Tables[CHILDTABLENAME].Rows.Add(new object[]
```

Example 4-8. File: AddParentChildAutoIncrementForm.cs (continued)

```
        {null, (int)parentRow[PARENTID_FIELD],
        Guid.NewGuid().ToString(), Guid.NewGuid().ToString()});
    }
}
```

Discussion

The example adds a single row to the parent table and a random number of rows—from one to five—to the child table. The auto-increment primary key of the parent table is used as the foreign key value when constructing the records added to the child table.

When a record is added to the parent table or the child table, a new primary key value is generated starting in the sequence –1, –2, –3, and so on, because of the auto-increment properties of the column. The `AutoIncrementSeed` and `AutoIncrementStep` properties are both set to –1 to ensure that when the `DataSet` is ultimately resolved to the data source, the values do not conflict with values within the data source (this assumes that the data source uses positive integers for the primary key values). For more information about avoiding conflicts when using `AutoIncrement` columns, see Recipe 4.1.

4.6   Adding Records with a GUID Primary Key

Problem

You want to add records to a `DataTable` that uses a GUID as its primary key and has related child records.

Solution

Use the `DataTable.RowChanging` event handler.

The sample code contains three event handlers:

`Form.Load`
> Sets up the sample by creating a `DataSet` containing two tables, a parent and child, both having a GUID primary key column with the `DefaultValue` set to a new GUID. A relation based on the parent table GUID and a foreign key GUID in the child table is added to the `DataSet`. The default view of the parent table is bound to the data grid on the form. Event handlers are added for the `RowChanging` event in both the parent and child `DataTable` objects.

Parent `DataTable.RowChanging`
> Sets the default value of the primary key column in the parent table to a new GUID value when a new row has been added to the parent table.

Child DataTable.RowChanging

Sets the default value of the primary key column in the child table to a new
GUID value when a new row has been added to the child table.

The C# code is shown in Example 4-9.

Example 4-9. File: AddGuidPKRecordForm.cs

```csharp
// Namespaces, variables, and constants
using System;
using System.Data;
using System.Data.SqlClient;

// Table name constants
private const String PARENTTABLENAME      = "ParentTable";
private const String CHILDTABLENAME       = "ChildTable";

// Table column name constants for Parent table
private const String PARENTID_FIELD       = "ParentId";
private const String FIELD1_FIELD         = "Field1";
private const String FIELD2_FIELD         = "Field2";

// Table column parameter name constants for Parent table
private const String CHILDID_FIELD        = "ChildId";
private const String FIELD3_FIELD         = "Field3";
private const String FIELD4_FIELD         = "Field4";

private DataSet ds;

// ...

private void AddGuidPKRecordForm_Load(object sender, System.EventArgs e)
{
    DataColumnCollection cols;
    DataColumn col;

    // Build the parent table.
    DataTable parentTable = new DataTable(PARENTTABLENAME);
    cols = parentTable.Columns;
    col = cols.Add(PARENTID_FIELD, typeof(Guid));
    col.DefaultValue = Guid.NewGuid( );
    parentTable.PrimaryKey = new DataColumn[] {col};
    cols.Add(FIELD1_FIELD, typeof(String)).MaxLength = 50;
    cols.Add(FIELD2_FIELD, typeof(String)).MaxLength = 50;

    // Build the child table.
    DataTable childTable = new DataTable(CHILDTABLENAME);
    cols = childTable.Columns;
    col = cols.Add(CHILDID_FIELD, typeof(Guid));
    col.DefaultValue = Guid.NewGuid( );
    childTable.PrimaryKey = new DataColumn[] {col};
    cols.Add(PARENTID_FIELD, typeof(Guid)).AllowDBNull = false;
    cols.Add(FIELD3_FIELD, typeof(String)).MaxLength = 50;
    cols.Add(FIELD4_FIELD, typeof(String)).MaxLength = 50;
```

Example 4-9. File: AddGuidPKRecordForm.cs (continued)

```
    // Add the tables to the DataSet and create the relationship.
    ds = new DataSet( );
    ds.Tables.Add(parentTable);
    ds.Tables.Add(childTable);
    ds.Relations.Add(new DataRelation("Parent_Child_Relation",
        parentTable.Columns[PARENTID_FIELD],
        childTable.Columns[PARENTID_FIELD], true));

    // Bind the parent table default view to the grid.
    dataGrid.DataSource = parentTable.DefaultView;

    // Event handlers to generate new GUIDs for primary keys
    parentTable.RowChanging +=
        new DataRowChangeEventHandler(parentTable_RowChanging);
    childTable.RowChanging +=
        new DataRowChangeEventHandler(childTable_RowChanging);
}

private void parentTable_RowChanging(object sender,
    DataRowChangeEventArgs e)
{
    if(e.Action == DataRowAction.Add)
        ds.Tables[PARENTTABLENAME].Columns[
            PARENTID_FIELD].DefaultValue = Guid.NewGuid( );
}

private void childTable_RowChanging(object sender,
    DataRowChangeEventArgs e)
{
    if(e.Action == DataRowAction.Add)
        ds.Tables[CHILDTABLENAME].Columns[
            CHILDID_FIELD].DefaultValue = Guid.NewGuid( );
}
```

Discussion

A Globally Unique Identifier (GUID) is a 128-bit integer that is statistically unique; you can use it wherever a unique identifier is needed. The System.Guid type is a .NET structure that contains members to facilitate working with GUIDs.

The RowChanging event of the DataTable is raised when a DataRow is changing. The action that occurred on the row can be determined by the Action property of the DataRowChangingEventArgs argument of the event handler. The Action property is set to one of the DataRowAction values detailed in Table 4-2.

Table 4-2. DataRowAction enumeration

Value	Description
Add	The row has been added to the table.
Change	The row has been changed.

Table 4-2. DataRowAction enumeration (continued)

Value	Description
Commit	The changes made to the row have been committed.
Delete	The row has been deleted from the table.
Nothing	The row has not been changed.
Rollback	The changes made to the row have been rolled back.

The DefaultValue of the GUID primary key column in both parent and child tables is set to a new GUID using the NewGuid( ) method of the Guid structure when the tables are defined. This causes a new GUID value to be assigned to the primary key when the first row is added. Because the DefaultValue for the column is calculated once when the property is set rather than as each new row is added, it must be changed after each row is added to the table so that each row has a different GUID primary key value. This is done by handling the RowChanging event for each table. When a row has been added, that is, the Action property of the DataRowChangingEventArgs argument is Add, the DefaultValue for the primary key column is set to a new GUID.

4.7 Updating a Data Source with Data from a Different Data Source

Problem

You want to update a data source using changes made to another data source for data replication or auditing purposes.

Solution

Use the GetChanges( ) method of the DataSet to identify changes made to a DataSet and replicate these changes into a different data source.

The sample code contains two event handlers:

Form.Load

Sets up the example by setting up two DataSet objects each containing a single table. The first table is filled with the Customers table from Northwind stored in SQL Server; the second is filled with the Customers table from Northwind stored in a MSDE instance. The default view of each table is bound to a data grid on the form.

Update Destination Button.Click

Creates a new DataSet containing only the records that have changed in the original data source. This DataSet is then used to apply the changes to a second data source using its DataAdapter; the DataSet for the second data source is reloaded. Finally, the first data source is updated with the changes.

The C# code is shown in Example 4-10.

Example 4-10. File: UpdateDataFromDifferentDataSourceForm.cs

```
// Namespaces, variables, and constants
using System;
using System.Configuration;
using System.Windows.Forms;
using System.Data;
using System.Data.SqlClient;

private DataSet dsSource, dsDest;
private SqlDataAdapter daSource, daDest;

// ...

private void UpdateDataFromDifferentDataSourceForm_Load(object sender,
    System.EventArgs e)
{
    // Create the DataAdapter for the source records.
    daSource = new SqlDataAdapter("SELECT * FROM Customers",
        ConfigurationSettings.AppSettings["Sql_ConnectString"]);
    SqlCommandBuilder cbSource = new SqlCommandBuilder(daSource);
    dsSource = new DataSet();
    // Get the schema and data for the source.
    daSource.FillSchema(dsSource, SchemaType.Source, "Customers");
    daSource.Fill(dsSource, "Customers");
    // Bind the default view of the customers table to the grid.
    dataGridSource.DataSource = dsSource.Tables["Customers"].DefaultView;

    // Create the DataAdapter for the destination records.
    daDest = new SqlDataAdapter("SELECT * FROM Customers",
        ConfigurationSettings.AppSettings["Sql_Msde_ConnectString"]);
    SqlCommandBuilder cbDest = new SqlCommandBuilder(daDest);
    dsDest = new DataSet();
    // Get the schema and data for the destination.
    daDest.FillSchema(dsDest, SchemaType.Source, "Customers");
    daDest.Fill(dsDest, "Customers");
    // Bind the default view of the customers table to the grid.
    dataGridDest.DataSource = dsDest.Tables["Customers"].DefaultView;
}

private void updateDestButton_Click(object sender, System.EventArgs e)
{
    try
    {
        // Create a DataSet of the added, modified, and deleted records.
        DataSet dsDelta = dsSource.GetChanges(DataRowState.Added |
            DataRowState.Modified | DataRowState.Deleted);
        if (dsDelta != null)
            // Update the destination with the delta DataSet.
            daDest.Update(dsDelta, "Customers");
```

Example 4-10. File: UpdateDataFromDifferentDataSourceForm.cs (continued)

```
        // Reload the destination DataSet.
        dsDest.Clear( );
        daDest.Fill(dsDest, "Customers");

        // Update the source.
        daSource.Update(dsSource, "Customers");
    }
    catch(Exception ex)
    {
        MessageBox.Show("ERROR: " + ex.Message, "Fill Destination",
            MessageBoxButtons.OK, MessageBoxIcon.Error);
    }
}
```

Discussion

The ADO.NET DataSet contains data and schema information within its contained objects, but not information about the provider that was used to retrieve the data or the original source of the data. The DataSet tracks changes made to data by maintaining multiple versions of each row allowing the data to be reconciled later to a data source using a DataAdapter. The data source to which the DataSet is reconciled is usually, but does not have to be, the original data source.

The GetChanges( ) method of the DataSet creates a copy of the DataSet containing all changes that have been made to it since it was last retrieved from the data source or since AcceptChanges( ) was last called.

To replicate the changes made to the first data source into the second data source, the GetChanges( ) method of the first DataSet is called to retrieve a subset of rows that have been added, modified, or deleted. This is the subset returned if the DataRowState filter argument is not specified. Next, the Update( ) method of the destination DataAdapter is called using the DataSet containing the changes as the data object argument; this applies the changes to the destination data source. The destination DataSet is then cleared and reloaded to reflect the applied changes. Finally, the changes are applied to the first data source.

The technique demonstrated in this example relies on the changes made to a DataSet and can therefore be used only to keep a second data source synchronized to a data source that is being modified. It is called one-way replication. The destination data source server does not have to be the same as the source database server, so an Oracle table could be synchronized to reflect all changes made to a SQL Server table. In fact, the data sources do not even have to be databases. If the destination data is not identical to the source data or if the destination is updated outside of this synchronizing application, primary key violations will occur if records with the same primary key as the source are inserted into the destination. Concurrency errors will result if records are modified within or deleted from the destination source. You could use application-specific logic to handle the DataAdapter.RowUpdating to resolve these concurrency errors. For more information about the RowUpdating event, see the Discussion section in Recipe 6-7.

The technique demonstrated in this example requires only slight modification to create an audit trail of changes made to a DataSet. Instead of using the update logic generated by the CommandBuilder for the destination DataAdapter, create custom update logic to write the changes made to the source data, along with any other required audit information such as a user ID or the date and time of the change, to the data destination. One or more values from the DataRowState enumeration can be used to filter the changes returned by the GetChanges( ) method to further control the logging.

4.8   Updating a Primary Key Value

Problem

You changed a primary key value in a DataTable and updated the change back to the underlying data source, but the value in the data source remained unchanged. You need to update a primary key value in the data source underlying the DataTable.

Solution

Use the SourceVersion property of SqlParameter to update the primary key value in the data source.

The schema of table TBL0408 used in this solution is shown in Table 4-3.

Table 4-3. TBL0408 schema

Column name	Data type	Length	Allow nulls?
Id	int	4	No
Field1	nvarchar	50	Yes
Field2	nvarchar	50	Yes

The sample code contains two event handlers:

Form.Load
> Sets up the sample by creating a single DataTable containing an integer primary key called Id and two string fields called Field1 and Field2. A DataAdapter is created and the select, delete, insert, and update commands are defined for it. Finally, the table is filled using the DataAdapter and the default view of the table is bound to the data grid on the form.

Update Button.Click
> Calls the Update( ) method of the DataAdapter defined in the Form.Load event to reconcile the changes made, including those made to the primary key, with the SQL Server database.

The C# code is shown in Example 4-11.

Example 4-11. File: UpdatePrimaryKeyForm.cs

```csharp
// Namespaces, variables, and constants
using System;
using System.Configuration;
using System.Data;
using System.Data.SqlClient;

private const String TABLENAME = "TBL0408";

private DataTable dt;
private SqlDataAdapter da;

// ...

private void UpdatePrimaryKeyForm_Load(object sender, System.EventArgs e)
{
    // Define the table.
    dt = new DataTable(TABLENAME);
    DataColumnCollection cols;
    cols = dt.Columns;
    DataColumn col = cols.Add("Id", typeof(Int32));
    dt.PrimaryKey = new DataColumn[] {col};
    cols.Add("Field1", typeof(String)).MaxLength = 50;
    cols.Add("Field2", typeof(String)).MaxLength = 50;

    // Create the DataAdapter and connection.
    da = new SqlDataAdapter( );
    SqlConnection conn = new SqlConnection(
        ConfigurationSettings.AppSettings["Sql_ConnectString"]);

    // Build the select command.
    String sqlText = "SELECT Id, Field1, Field2 FROM " + TABLENAME;
    da.SelectCommand = new SqlCommand(sqlText, conn);

    // Build the delete command.
    sqlText = "DELETE FROM " + TABLENAME + " WHERE Id=@Id";
    SqlCommand deleteCommand = new SqlCommand(sqlText, conn);
    deleteCommand.Parameters.Add("@Id", SqlDbType.Int, 0, "Id");
    da.DeleteCommand = deleteCommand;

    // Build the insert command.
    sqlText = "INSERT " + TABLENAME + " (Id, Field1, Field2) VALUES " +
        "(@Id, @Field1, @Field2)";
    SqlCommand insertCommand = new SqlCommand(sqlText, conn);
    insertCommand.Parameters.Add("@Id", SqlDbType.Int, 0, "Id");
    insertCommand.Parameters.Add("@Field1", SqlDbType.NVarChar, 50,
        "Field1");
    insertCommand.Parameters.Add("@Field2", SqlDbType.NVarChar, 50,
        "Field2");
    da.InsertCommand = insertCommand;
```

Example 4-11. File: UpdatePrimaryKeyForm.cs (continued)

```
    // Build the update command.
    sqlText="UPDATE " + TABLENAME + " SET " +
        "Id=@Id, Field1=@Field1, Field2=@Field2 WHERE Id=@IdOriginal";
    SqlCommand updateCommand = new SqlCommand(sqlText, conn);
    updateCommand.Parameters.Add("@Id", SqlDbType.Int, 0, "Id");
    updateCommand.Parameters.Add("@Field1", SqlDbType.NVarChar, 50,
        "Field1");
    updateCommand.Parameters.Add("@Field2", SqlDbType.NVarChar, 50,
        "Field2");
    updateCommand.Parameters.Add("@IdOriginal", SqlDbType.Int, 0, "Id");
    updateCommand.Parameters["@IdOriginal"].SourceVersion =
        DataRowVersion.Original;
    da.UpdateCommand = updateCommand;

    // Fill the table from the data source.
    da.Fill(dt);

    // Bind the default view for the table to the grid.
    dataGrid.DataSource = dt.DefaultView;
}

private void updateButton_Click(object sender, System.EventArgs e)
{
    // Update the table to the data source.
    da.Update(dt);
}
```

Discussion

ADO.NET maintains up to three versions of each DataRow in a DataTable: the current, original, and proposed. The current version is accessed by default. All versions can be accessed using an overloaded DataRow indexer (C#) or an overload of the Item() property (VB.NET). Table 4-4 describes the different values of the DataRowVersion enumeration.

Table 4-4. DataRowVersion enumeration

Value	Description
Current	The current values in the row, representing the latest edits. This value is always available.
Default	The default row version. If the row is being edited, this is the Proposed version; otherwise it is the Current version.
Original	The original values for the row. Not available for rows that have been added since data was last retrieved from data source or since AcceptChanges() was last called.
Proposed	The proposed values for the row. Only available after BeginEdit() is called for the DataRow() until EndEdit() or CancelEdit() is called.

To change the primary key in the table in the database, the UpdateCommand of the DataAdapter needs to locate the row based on the original primary key and update the primary key value with the current value of the primary key in addition to updating the other row values with their current values. In the sample, this is done using the following SQL update command:

```
sqlText="UPDATE " + TABLENAME + " SET " +
    "Id=@Id, Field1=@Field1, Field2=@Field2 WHERE Id=@IdOriginal";
```

The primary key—Id field—is updated with the current value of the Id field, where the Id field of the row matches the original value of the Id field.

The current value for the Id field is set with the following code:

```
updateCommand.Parameters.Add("@Id", SqlDbType.Int, 0, "Id");
```

The original value for the Id field is set by the following two lines of code in the sample:

```
updateCommand.Parameters.Add("@IdOriginal", SqlDbType.Int, 0, "Id");
updateCommand.Parameters["@IdOriginal"].SourceVersion =
    DataRowVersion.Original;
```

The first line is the same as for the current version. The second line sets the SourceVersion property of the parameter so that the original value for the Id field is used when loading the value. The UpdateCommand correctly identifies the row to be updated based on the original value of the Id field and updates the row with the current Id value.

Updating the primary key in a database is not normally necessary. Some RDBMSs do not support updating the primary key. Additionally, if a data relation is based on the primary key, related foreign key fields in the child tables will have to be updated to maintain referential integrity.

4.9 Getting Stored Procedure Parameter Information at Runtime

Problem

You want to get information about the parameters used by a stored procedure at runtime.

Solution

Use DeriveParameters( ) method of the CommandBuilder. With Microsoft SQL Server, you could also use system stored procedures.

The sample code demonstrates either one of these techniques, as specified by the user. In either case, the results are stored to a DataTable and its default view is bound to a data grid on the form.

The C# code is shown in Example 4-12.

Example 4-12. File: SpParameterForm.cs

```csharp
// Namespaces, variables, and constants
using System;
using System.Configuration;
using System.Data;
using System.Data.SqlClient;
using System.Data.OleDb;

// ...

String procedureName = "Sales by Year";

// Create the table to hold the results.
DataTable dt = new DataTable();

if(commandBuilderRadioButton.Checked)
{
    // Build a command object for the 'Sales by Year' stored procedure.
    SqlConnection conn = new SqlConnection(
        ConfigurationSettings.AppSettings["Sql_ConnectString"]);
    SqlCommand cmd = new SqlCommand(procedureName, conn);
    cmd.CommandType = CommandType.StoredProcedure;

    // Get the parameters.
    conn.Open();
    SqlCommandBuilder.DeriveParameters(cmd);
    conn.Close();

    // Define table columns to hold the results.
    dt.Columns.Add("Name");
    dt.Columns.Add("Direction");
    dt.Columns.Add("SqlType");

    // Retrieve the results from the command object to the table.
    foreach (SqlParameter param in cmd.Parameters)
        dt.Rows.Add(new object[] {param.ParameterName,
            param.Direction.ToString(),
            param.SqlDbType.ToString()});

    dataGrid.CaptionText = "Stored procedure '" + procedureName +
        "' parameters using CommandBuilder.DeriveParameters";
}
else if(spRadioButton.Checked)
{
    // Build a command object to use SQL Server stored procedure
    // to retrieve parameters.
    SqlConnection conn = new SqlConnection(
        ConfigurationSettings.AppSettings["Sql_ConnectString"]);
    SqlCommand cmd = new SqlCommand("sp_sproc_columns", conn);
    cmd.CommandType = CommandType.StoredProcedure;
    SqlParameter param = cmd.Parameters.Add("@procedure_name",
        SqlDbType.NVarChar, 390);
    param.Value = procedureName;
```

Example 4-12. File: SpParameterForm.cs (continued)

```
    // Fill the results table.
    SqlDataAdapter da = new SqlDataAdapter(cmd);
    da.Fill(dt);

    dataGrid.CaptionText = "Stored procedure '" + procedureName +
        "' parameters using sp_proc_columns.";
}

// Bind the default view of the results table to the grid.
dataGrid.DataSource = dt.DefaultView;
```

Discussion

This solution demonstrates two techniques to retrieve information about parameters for a stored procedure.

DeriveParameters( ) method

The first technique uses the static DeriveParameters( ) method of the CommandBuilder object to populate the Parameters collection of the Command object with the parameter information for the stored procedure specified by the Command. Any existing information in the Parameters collection is overwritten.

The example demonstrates creating a stored procedure Command object. The name of the stored procedure and the Connection object are both specified in the Command constructor. The Connection is opened and the DeriveParameters( ) method is called to retrieve the information about the parameters for the stored procedure into a Parameters collection. The collection is iterated over to extract information about the parameters, which is subsequently displayed.

If the stored procedure specified does not exist, an InvalidOperationException is raised.

> The DeriveParameters( ) method incurs a performance penalty because it requires an extra round trip between the application and the data server to retrieve parameter metadata. It is more efficient to populate the parameters collection explicitly if the parameter information is known. As a result, the DeriveParameters( ) method is not recommended for use in production environments. The method exists primarily for design-time or ad-hoc use.

Microsoft SQL Server System stored procedure: sp_sproc_columns

The second technique is specific to Microsoft SQL Server. The system stored procedure sp_sproc_columns returns parameter information for one or more stored procedures. Unlike the DeriveParameters( ) method, you cannot use it to automatically populate a Parameters collection with parameter information. It does, however, return more information than the `DeriveParameters( )` method, and you can use it to return results for more than one stored procedure at a time. It also supports filtering options and does not require a stored procedure `Command` object. Executing this procedure returns a result set in which the rows correspond to stored procedure columns. For more information about the parameter information returned, see SQL Server Books Online.

The example demonstrates retrieving information about parameters for only a single stored procedure by specifying the name of the stored procedure in the `@procedure_name` parameter. See SQL Server Books Online for other parameters that you can use to filter the information returned.

4.10   Updating a DataSet with a Many-to-Many Relationship

Problem

You have a `DataSet` that contains two tables that have a many-to-many relationship between them using a third junction table. You get referential integrity errors when you try to update changes to the data in this `DataSet` back to the data source. You need to do this successfully.

Solution

Use the techniques described in the discussion.

The schema of table TBL0410Parent used in this solution is shown in Table 4-5.

Table 4-5. TBL0410Parent schema

Column name	Data type	Length	Allow nulls?
ParentId	int	4	No
Field1	nvarchar	50	Yes
Field2	nvarchar	50	Yes

The schema of table TBL0410Child used in this solution is shown in Table 4-6.

Table 4-6. TBL0410Child schema

Column name	Data type	Length	Allow nulls?
ChildId	int	4	No
Field3	nvarchar	50	Yes
Field4	nvarchar	50	Yes

The schema of table TBL0410ParentChild used in this solution is shown in Table 4-7.

Table 4-7. TBL0410ParentChild schema

Column name	Data type	Length	Allow nulls?
ParentId	int	4	No
ChildId	int	4	No

The solution uses eleven stored procedures described in Table 4-8.

Table 4-8. Stored procedures for solution in Recipe 4.10

Name	Description
SP0410_DeleteChild	Deletes the Child record specified by the `ChildId` input parameter.
SP0410_DeleteParent	Deletes the Parent record specified by the `ParentId` input parameter.
SP0410_DeleteParentChild	Deletes the ParentChild record specified by the `ParentId` and `ChildId` input parameters.
SP0410_GetChild	Gets the Child record corresponding to the `ChildId` specified or returns all Child records if no `ChildId` is specified.
SP0410_GetParent	Gets the Parent record corresponding to the `ParentId` specified or returns all Parent records if no `ParentId` is specified.
SP0410_GetParentChild	Gets the ParentChild records corresponding to the `ParentId` specified or returns all ParentChild records if no `ParentId` is specified.
SP0410_InsertChild	Adds a new Child record. The stored procedure returns the `ChildId` value generated by the data source as both an output parameter and in the first returned record.
SP0410_InsertParent	Adds a new Parent record. The stored procedure returns the `ParentId` value generated by the data source as both an output parameter and in the first returned record.
SP0410_InsertParentChild	Adds a new ParentChild record.
SP0410_UpdateChild	Updates the Child record matching the specified `ChildId`.
SP0410_UpdateParent	Updates the Parent record matching the specified `ParentId`.

The sample code contains five event handlers and four methods:

Form.Load

> This event handler sets up the sample by creating a DataSet containing a parent, child, and many-to-many junction table, as well as the DataRelation objects between them. A DataAdapter object is created for each table and the stored procedures to select, delete, insert, and update records in the data source are specified for each. The LoadData( ) method is called to retrieve data for each table in the DataSet. Finally, the default view for the parent and the child tables are bound to data grids on the form.

LoadData( )

> This method calls the Fill( ) method of the DataAdapter for each of the parent, child, and junction tables.

CreateData( )

> This method creates random data in both the parent and child tables and randomly creates relationships between them by adding records to the junction table.

UpdateData( )

> This method updates all changes in the DataSet back to the data source by calling in the correct order the Update( ) method of the DataAdapter object for subsets of the data in each of the parent, child, and junction tables.

Create Button.Click

> This event handler calls the CreateData( ) method to add random data to the DataSet.

Modify Button.Click

> This event handler makes random changes to the data in the DataSet:

> - Rows from the parent and child table are deleted or have values in their fields modified.
> - Parent/child relationships are eliminated by deleting records from the junction table.
> - The CreateData( ) method is called to create new data.
> - The UpdateData( ) method is called to update all of the changes made to the DataSet with the data source.

Delete Button.Click

> This event handler deletes all data from the parent, child, and junction table. The UpdateData( ) method is called to update the changes made to the DataSet with the data source.

Refresh Button.Click

> This event handler clears all data from the DataSet. LoadData( ) is then called to load all data from the data source into the parent, child, and junction tables in the DataSet.

The 11 stored procedures used in this example are shown in Examples 4-13 through 4-23.

Example 4-13. Stored procedure: SP0410_DeleteChild

```
CREATE PROCEDURE SP0410_DeleteChild
    @ChildId int
AS
    SET NOCOUNT ON

    delete
    from
```

Example 4-13. Stored procedure: SP0410_DeleteChild (continued)

```
        TBL0410Child
    where
        ChildId=@ChildId

    return 0
```

Example 4-14. Stored procedure: SP0410_DeleteParent

```
CREATE PROCEDURE SP0410_DeleteParent
    @ParentId int
AS
    SET NOCOUNT ON

    delete
    from
        TBL0410Parent
    where
        ParentId=@ParentId

    return 0
```

Example 4-15. Stored procedure: SP0410_DeleteParentChild

```
CREATE PROCEDURE SP0410_DeleteParentChild
    @ParentId int,
    @ChildId int
AS
    SET NOCOUNT ON

    delete
    from
        TBL0410ParentChild
    where
        ParentId=@ParentId and
        ChildId=@ChildId

    return 0
```

Example 4-16. Stored procedure: SP0410_GetChild

```
CREATE PROCEDURE SP0410_GetChild
    @ChildId int=null
AS
    SET NOCOUNT ON

    if @ChildId is not null
    begin
        select
            ChildID,
            Field3,
            Field4
```

Example 4-16. Stored procedure: SP0410_GetChild (continued)

```
    from
        TBL0410Child
    where
        ChildId=@ChildId

    return 0
end

select
    ChildId,
    Field3,
    Field4
from
    TBL0410Child

return 0
```

Example 4-17. Stored procedure: SP0410_GetParent

```
CREATE PROCEDURE SP0410_GetParent
    @ParentId int=null
AS
    SET NOCOUNT ON

    if @ParentId is not null
    begin
        select
            ParentId,
            Field1,
            Field2
        from
            TBL0410Parent
        where
            ParentId=@ParentId

        return 0
    end

    select
        ParentId,
        Field1,
        Field2
    from
        TBL0410Parent

    return 0
```

Example 4-18. Stored procedure: SP0410_GetParentChild

```
CREATE PROCEDURE SP0410_GetParentChild
    @ParentId int=null
```

Example 4-18. Stored procedure: SP0410_GetParentChild (continued)

```
AS
    if @ParentId is not null
    begin
        select
            ParentId,
            ChildID
        from
            TBL0410ParentChild
        where
            ParentId=@ParentId

        return 0
    end

    select
        ParentId,
        ChildID
    from
        TBL0410ParentChild

    return 0
```

Example 4-19. Stored procedure: SP0410_InsertChild

```
CREATE PROCEDURE SP0410_InsertChild
    @ChildId int output,
    @Field3 nvarchar(50)=null,
    @Field4 nvarchar(50)=null
AS
    SET NOCOUNT ON

    insert TBL0410Child(
        Field3,
        Field4)
    values (
        @Field3,
        @Field4)

    if @@rowcount=0
        return 1

    set @ChildId=Scope_Identity()

    select @ChildId ChildId

    return 0
```

Example 4-20. Stored procedure: SP0410_InsertParent

```
CREATE PROCEDURE SP0410_InsertParent
    @ParentId int output,
```

Example 4-20. Stored procedure: SP0410_InsertParent (continued)

```
    @Field1 nvarchar(50)=null,
    @Field2 nvarchar(50)=null
AS
    SET NOCOUNT ON

    insert TBL0410Parent(
        Field1,
        Field2)
    values (
        @Field1,
        @Field2)

    if @@rowcount=0
        return 1

    set @ParentId=Scope_Identity( )

    select @ParentId ParentId

    return 0
```

Example 4-21. Stored procedure: SP0410_InsertParentChild

```
CREATE PROCEDURE SP0410_InsertParentChild
    @ParentId int,
    @ChildId int
AS
    SET NOCOUNT ON

    insert TBL0410ParentChild(
        ParentId,
        ChildId)
    values (
        @ParentId,
        @ChildId)

    if @@rowcount=0
        return 1

    return 0
```

Example 4-22. Stored procedure: SP0410_UpdateChild

```
CREATE PROCEDURE SP0410_UpdateChild
    @ChildId int,
    @Field3 nvarchar(50)=null,
    @Field4 nvarchar(50)=null
AS
    SET NOCOUNT ON

    update
        TBL0410Child
```

Example 4-22. Stored procedure: SP0410_UpdateChild (continued)

```
set
    Field3=@Field3,
    Field4=@Field4
where
    ChildId=@ChildId

if @@rowcount=0
    return 1

return 0
```

Example 4-23. Stored procedure: SP0410_UpdateParent

```
CREATE PROCEDURE SP0410_UpdateParent
    @ParentId int,
    @Field1 nvarchar(50)=null,
    @Field2 nvarchar(50)=null
AS
    SET NOCOUNT ON

    update
        TBL0410Parent
    set
        Field1=@Field1,
        Field2=@Field2
    where
        ParentId=@ParentId

    if @@rowcount=0
        return 1

    return 0
```

The C# code for updating a DataSet with a many-to-one relationship is shown in Example 4-24.

Example 4-24. File: UpdateManyToManyRelationshipForm.cs

```
// Namespaces, variables, and constants
using System;
using System.Configuration;
using System.Windows.Forms;
using System.Data;
using System.Data.SqlClient;

private DataSet ds;
private SqlDataAdapter daParent, daParentChild, daChild;

private const String PARENTTABLENAME       = "TBL0410Parent";
private const String PARENTCHILDTABLENAME  = "TBL0410ParentChild";
private const String CHILDTABLENAME        = "TBL0410Child";
```

Example 4-24. File: UpdateManyToManyRelationshipForm.cs (continued)

```csharp
// Table column name constants for Parent table
private const String PARENTID_FIELD        = "ParentId";
private const String FIELD1_FIELD          = "Field1";
private const String FIELD2_FIELD          = "Field2";

// Table column parameter name constants for Child table
private const String CHILDID_FIELD         = "ChildId";
private const String FIELD3_FIELD          = "Field3";
private const String FIELD4_FIELD          = "Field4";

// Stored procedure name constants
private const String DELETEPARENT_SP       = "SP0410_DeleteParent";
private const String GETPARENT_SP          = "SP0410_GetParent";
private const String INSERTPARENT_SP       = "SP0410_InsertParent";
private const String UPDATEPARENT_SP       = "SP0410_UpdateParent";
private const String DELETEPARENTCHILD_SP  =
    "SP0410_DeleteParentChild";
private const String GETPARENTCHILD_SP     = "SP0410_GetParentChild";
private const String INSERTPARENTCHILD_SP  =
    "SP0410_InsertParentChild";
private const String DELETECHILD_SP        = "SP0410_DeleteChild";
private const String GETCHILD_SP           = "SP0410_GetChild";
private const String INSERTCHILD_SP        = "SP0410_InsertChild";
private const String UPDATECHILD_SP        = "SP0410_UpdateChild";

// stored procedure parameter name constants for Parent table
private const String PARENTID_PARM         = "@ParentId";
private const String FIELD1_PARM           = "@Field1";
private const String FIELD2_PARM           = "@Field2";

// Stored procedure parameter name constants for Child table
private const String CHILDID_PARM          = "@ChildId";
private const String FIELD3_PARM           = "@Field3";
private const String FIELD4_PARM           = "@Field4";

// ...

private void UpdateManyToManyRelationshipForm_Load(object sender,
    System.EventArgs e)
{
    DataColumnCollection cols;
    DataColumn col;

    // Build the parent table.
    DataTable parentTable = new DataTable(PARENTTABLENAME);
    cols = parentTable.Columns;
    col = cols.Add(PARENTID_FIELD, typeof(Int32));
    col.AutoIncrement = true;
    col.AutoIncrementSeed = -1;
    col.AutoIncrementStep = -1;
    cols.Add(FIELD1_FIELD, typeof(String)).MaxLength = 50;
    cols.Add(FIELD2_FIELD, typeof(String)).MaxLength = 50;
```

Example 4-24. File: UpdateManyToManyRelationshipForm.cs (continued)

```csharp
// Build the ParentChild table.
DataTable parentChildTable = new DataTable(PARENTCHILDTABLENAME);
cols = parentChildTable.Columns;
cols.Add(PARENTID_FIELD, typeof(Int32)).AllowDBNull = false;
cols.Add(CHILDID_FIELD, typeof(Int32)).AllowDBNull = false;
parentChildTable.PrimaryKey = new DataColumn[]
    {cols[PARENTID_FIELD], cols[CHILDID_FIELD]};

// Build the child table.
DataTable childTable = new DataTable(CHILDTABLENAME);
cols = childTable.Columns;
col = cols.Add(CHILDID_FIELD, typeof(Int32));
col.AutoIncrement = true;
col.AutoIncrementSeed = -1;
col.AutoIncrementStep = -1;
cols.Add(FIELD3_FIELD, typeof(String)).MaxLength = 50;
cols.Add(FIELD4_FIELD, typeof(String)).MaxLength = 50;

// Add the tables to the DataSet and create the relationship.
ds = new DataSet();
ds.Tables.Add(parentTable);
ds.Tables.Add(parentChildTable);
ds.Tables.Add(childTable);
ds.Relations.Add(new DataRelation("Parent_ParentChild",
    parentTable.Columns[PARENTID_FIELD],
    parentChildTable.Columns[PARENTID_FIELD], true));
ds.Relations.Add(new DataRelation("Child_ParentChild",
    childTable.Columns[CHILDID_FIELD],
    parentChildTable.Columns[CHILDID_FIELD], true));


// Create the Parent DataAdapter.
daParent = new SqlDataAdapter(GETPARENT_SP,
    ConfigurationSettings.AppSettings["Sql_ConnectString"]);
daParent.SelectCommand.CommandType = CommandType.StoredProcedure;

// Build the parent delete command.
SqlCommand deleteCommand = new SqlCommand(DELETEPARENT_SP,
    daParent.SelectCommand.Connection);
deleteCommand.CommandType = CommandType.StoredProcedure;
deleteCommand.Parameters.Add(PARENTID_PARM, SqlDbType.Int, 0,
    PARENTID_FIELD);
daParent.DeleteCommand = deleteCommand;

// Build the parent insert command.
SqlCommand insertCommand = new SqlCommand(INSERTPARENT_SP,
    daParent.SelectCommand.Connection);
insertCommand.CommandType = CommandType.StoredProcedure;
insertCommand.Parameters.Add(PARENTID_PARM, SqlDbType.Int, 0,
    PARENTID_FIELD);
insertCommand.Parameters.Add(FIELD1_PARM, SqlDbType.NVarChar, 50,
    FIELD1_FIELD);
```

Example 4-24. File: UpdateManyToManyRelationshipForm.cs (continued)

```csharp
insertCommand.Parameters.Add(FIELD2_PARM, SqlDbType.NVarChar, 50,
    FIELD2_FIELD);
daParent.InsertCommand = insertCommand;

// Build the parent update command.
SqlCommand updateCommand = new SqlCommand(UPDATEPARENT_SP,
    daParent.SelectCommand.Connection);
updateCommand.CommandType = CommandType.StoredProcedure;
updateCommand.Parameters.Add(PARENTID_PARM, SqlDbType.Int, 0,
    PARENTID_FIELD);
updateCommand.Parameters.Add(FIELD1_PARM, SqlDbType.NVarChar, 50,
    FIELD1_FIELD);
updateCommand.Parameters.Add(FIELD2_PARM, SqlDbType.NVarChar, 50,
    FIELD2_FIELD);
daParent.UpdateCommand = updateCommand;


// Create the Child DataAdapter.
daChild = new SqlDataAdapter(GETCHILD_SP,
    ConfigurationSettings.AppSettings["Sql_ConnectString"]);
daChild.SelectCommand.CommandType = CommandType.StoredProcedure;

// Build the child delete command.
deleteCommand = new SqlCommand(DELETECHILD_SP,
    daChild.SelectCommand.Connection);
deleteCommand.CommandType = CommandType.StoredProcedure;
deleteCommand.Parameters.Add(CHILDID_PARM, SqlDbType.Int, 0,
    CHILDID_FIELD);
daChild.DeleteCommand = deleteCommand;

// Build the child insert command.
insertCommand = new SqlCommand(INSERTCHILD_SP,
    daChild.SelectCommand.Connection);
insertCommand.CommandType = CommandType.StoredProcedure;
insertCommand.Parameters.Add(CHILDID_PARM, SqlDbType.Int, 0,
    CHILDID_FIELD);
insertCommand.Parameters.Add(FIELD3_PARM, SqlDbType.NVarChar, 50,
    FIELD3_FIELD);
insertCommand.Parameters.Add(FIELD4_PARM, SqlDbType.NVarChar, 50,
    FIELD4_FIELD);
daChild.InsertCommand = insertCommand;

// Build the child update command.
updateCommand = new SqlCommand(UPDATECHILD_SP,
    daChild.SelectCommand.Connection);
updateCommand.CommandType = CommandType.StoredProcedure;
updateCommand.Parameters.Add(CHILDID_PARM, SqlDbType.Int, 0,
    CHILDID_FIELD);
updateCommand.Parameters.Add(FIELD3_PARM, SqlDbType.NVarChar, 50,
    FIELD3_FIELD);
updateCommand.Parameters.Add(FIELD4_PARM, SqlDbType.NVarChar, 50,
    FIELD4_FIELD);
daChild.UpdateCommand = updateCommand;
```

Example 4-24. File: UpdateManyToManyRelationshipForm.cs (continued)

```
    // Create the ParentChild DataAdapter.
    daParentChild = new SqlDataAdapter(GETPARENTCHILD_SP,
        ConfigurationSettings.AppSettings["Sql_ConnectString"]);
    daParentChild.SelectCommand.CommandType = CommandType.StoredProcedure;

    // Build the ParentChild delete command.
    deleteCommand = new SqlCommand(DELETEPARENTCHILD_SP,
        daParentChild.SelectCommand.Connection);
    deleteCommand.CommandType = CommandType.StoredProcedure;
    deleteCommand.Parameters.Add(PARENTID_PARM, SqlDbType.Int, 0,
        PARENTID_FIELD);
    deleteCommand.Parameters.Add(CHILDID_PARM, SqlDbType.Int, 0,
        CHILDID_FIELD);
    daParentChild.DeleteCommand = deleteCommand;

    // Build the ParentChild insert command.
    insertCommand = new SqlCommand(INSERTPARENTCHILD_SP,
        daParentChild.SelectCommand.Connection);
    insertCommand.CommandType = CommandType.StoredProcedure;
    insertCommand.Parameters.Add(PARENTID_PARM, SqlDbType.Int, 0,
        PARENTID_FIELD);
    insertCommand.Parameters.Add(CHILDID_PARM, SqlDbType.Int, 0,
        CHILDID_FIELD);
    daParentChild.InsertCommand = insertCommand;

    LoadData();

    dataGridParent.DataSource = parentTable.DefaultView;
    dataGridChild.DataSource = childTable.DefaultView;
}

private void LoadData()
{
    // Fill the dataset.
    daParent.Fill(ds, PARENTTABLENAME);
    daChild.Fill(ds, CHILDTABLENAME);
    daParentChild.Fill(ds, PARENTCHILDTABLENAME);
}

private void CreateData(int parentRows, int childRows)
{
    // Create some data update the data source with it.
    for(int iParent = 0; iParent < parentRows; iParent++)
    {
        DataRow parentRow = ds.Tables[PARENTTABLENAME].NewRow();
        parentRow[FIELD1_FIELD] = Guid.NewGuid().ToString();
        parentRow[FIELD2_FIELD] = Guid.NewGuid().ToString();
        ds.Tables[PARENTTABLENAME].Rows.Add(parentRow);
    }

    for(int iChild = 0; iChild < childRows; iChild++)
    {
```

Example 4-24. File: UpdateManyToManyRelationshipForm.cs (continued)

```
            DataRow childRow = ds.Tables[CHILDTABLENAME].NewRow( );
            childRow[FIELD3_FIELD] = Guid.NewGuid().ToString( );
            childRow[FIELD4_FIELD] = Guid.NewGuid().ToString( );
            ds.Tables[CHILDTABLENAME].Rows.Add(childRow);
        }

        // Randomly create the parent-child relationships.
        Random r = new Random((int)DateTime.Now.Ticks);
        foreach(DataRow rowParent in ds.Tables[PARENTTABLENAME].Rows)
        {
            if(rowParent.RowState != DataRowState.Deleted)
            {
                foreach(DataRow rowChild in
                    ds.Tables[CHILDTABLENAME].Rows)
                {
                    if(rowChild.RowState != DataRowState.Deleted &&
                        r.Next(2) == 1)
                    {
                        // Check to see that row doesn't exist
                        // before adding.
                        if(ds.Tables[PARENTCHILDTABLENAME].
                            Rows.Find(new object[]
                            {rowParent[PARENTID_FIELD],
                            rowChild[CHILDID_FIELD]}) == null)
                        {
                            ds.Tables[PARENTCHILDTABLENAME].
                                Rows.Add(new object[]
                                {rowParent[PARENTID_FIELD],
                                rowChild[CHILDID_FIELD]});
                        }
                    }
                }
            }
        }
    }
}

private void UpdateData( )
{
    try
    {
        daParentChild.Update(ds.Tables[PARENTCHILDTABLENAME].Select(
            null, null, DataViewRowState.Deleted));
        daChild.Update(ds.Tables[CHILDTABLENAME].Select(
            null, null, DataViewRowState.Deleted));
        daParent.Update(ds.Tables[PARENTTABLENAME].Select(
            null, null, DataViewRowState.Deleted));
        daParent.Update(ds.Tables[PARENTTABLENAME].Select(
            null, null, DataViewRowState.ModifiedCurrent));
        daParent.Update(ds.Tables[PARENTTABLENAME].Select(
            null, null, DataViewRowState.Added));
        daChild.Update(ds.Tables[CHILDTABLENAME].Select(
            null, null, DataViewRowState.ModifiedCurrent));
```

Example 4-24. File: UpdateManyToManyRelationshipForm.cs (continued)

```csharp
            daChild.Update(ds.Tables[CHILDTABLENAME].Select(
                null, null, DataViewRowState.Added));
            daParentChild.Update(ds.Tables[PARENTCHILDTABLENAME].Select(
                null, null, DataViewRowState.Added));
    }
    catch (Exception ex)
    {
        MessageBox.Show(ex.Message);
    }
}

private void createDataButton_Click(object sender, System.EventArgs e)
{
    // Create parent and child records.
    CreateData(4,4);

    UpdateData( );
    MessageBox.Show("Data created.","Many-to-Many Relationships",
        MessageBoxButtons.OK, MessageBoxIcon.Information);
}

private void modifyButton_Click(object sender, System.EventArgs e)
{
    Random r = new Random((int)DateTime.Now.Ticks);

    // Randomly delete or modify rows from the child and parent rows.
    for(int i = ds.Tables[CHILDTABLENAME].Rows.Count; i > 0; i--)
    {
        DataRow childRow = ds.Tables[CHILDTABLENAME].Rows[i - 1];

        if(r.Next(2) == 0)
        {
            childRow[FIELD3_FIELD] = Guid.NewGuid().ToString( );
            childRow[FIELD4_FIELD] = Guid.NewGuid().ToString( );
        }
        else
            childRow.Delete( );
    }

    for(int i = ds.Tables[PARENTTABLENAME].Rows.Count; i > 0; i--)
    {
        DataRow parentRow = ds.Tables[PARENTTABLENAME].Rows[i - 1];

        if(r.Next(2) == 0)
        {
            parentRow[FIELD1_FIELD] = Guid.NewGuid().ToString( );
            parentRow[FIELD2_FIELD] = Guid.NewGuid().ToString( );
        }
        else
            parentRow.Delete( );
    }
```

Example 4-24. File: UpdateManyToManyRelationshipForm.cs (continued)

```csharp
        // Randomly delete m-n parent/child relationships.
        for(int i = ds.Tables[PARENTCHILDTABLENAME].Rows.Count; i > 0; i--)
        {
            DataRow parentChildRow =
                ds.Tables[PARENTCHILDTABLENAME].Rows[i - 1];

            if(r.Next(2) == 0)
                parentChildRow.Delete( );
        }

        // Insert two rows into Parent, Child, and random ParentChild.
        CreateData(2,2);

        UpdateData( );

        MessageBox.Show("Data randomly modified.",
            "Many-to-Many Relationships", MessageBoxButtons.OK,
            MessageBoxIcon.Information);
    }

    private void deleteButton_Click(object sender, System.EventArgs e)
    {
        // Delete the Parent records.
        for(int i = ds.Tables[PARENTTABLENAME].Rows.Count; i > 0 ;i--)
            ds.Tables[PARENTTABLENAME].Rows[i - 1].Delete( );

        // Delete the Child records.
        for(int i = ds.Tables[CHILDTABLENAME].Rows.Count; i > 0; i--)
            ds.Tables[CHILDTABLENAME].Rows[i - 1].Delete( );

        // Delete the ParentChild records.
        for(int i = ds.Tables[PARENTCHILDTABLENAME].Rows.Count; i > 0 ;i--)
            ds.Tables[PARENTCHILDTABLENAME].Rows[i - 1].Delete( );

        UpdateData( );

        MessageBox.Show("Data deleted.", "Many-to-Many Relationships",
            MessageBoxButtons.OK, MessageBoxIcon.Information);
    }

    private void refreshButton_Click(object sender, System.EventArgs e)
    {
        ds.Clear( );

        LoadData( );
    }
```

Discussion

To avoid referential integrity problems when updating a data source with changes in a DataSet having tables related with a many-to-many relationship, update the rows in the following order:

1. Deleted junction rows
2. Deleted child rows
3. Deleted parent rows
4. Updated parent rows
5. Inserted parent rows
6. Updated child rows
7. Inserted child rows
8. Inserted junction rows

Pass DataViewRowState.Deleted into the Select( ) method of the DataTable object to get the subset of deleted rows from a table. Similarly, pass DataViewRowState.Added to obtain inserted rows and DataViewRowState.ModifiedCurrent to obtain modified rows.

A few more considerations involving the primary key:

- If the primary key cannot be modified once added, the updated and inserted rows can be processed in the same statement. Pass a bitwise combination into the select method as shown here:

  ```
  daParent.Update(ds.Tables[PARENTTABLENAME].Select(null, null,
      DataViewRowState.Added | DataViewRowState.ModifiedCurrent));
  ```

- If the primary key can be modified, the database must cascade the updated primary key values to the child records; otherwise, a referential integrity violation will occur. If the foreign key is used as part of the concurrency handling process, the UpdateCommand property of child tables must accept either its Original or the Current value.

- If the primary key is an AutoIncrement value and its value is generated by the database, the InsertCommand must return the primary key value from the data source and use it to update the value in the DataSet. The DataSet will then automatically cascade this new value to the child records.

4.11   Updating Server Data Using a Web Service

Problem

You want to update a data source using an XML web service and use the web service from your client application.

Solution

Use a DataSet object.

The XML web service code contains two methods:

LoadOrders( )
>   Creates and returns a DataSet containing the Orders and Order Details tables from Northwind and a DataRelation between those tables.

UpdateOrders( )
>   Takes a DataSet argument containing the changes made to the DataSet created by the LoadOrders( ) method, creates two DataAdapter objects with CommandBuilder generated update logic for each, and uses the DataAdapter objects to update the Orders and Order Details tables in Northwind.

The client-side code contains two event handlers:

Form.Load
>   Sets up the example by calling the LoadOrders( ) method in the web service to populate a DataSet. The default view of the Orders table is bound to the data grid on the form.

Update Button.Click
>   Calls the UpdateOrders( ) method in the web service passing a DataSet containing changes made to the DataSet since the form was loaded or since the last time the UpdateOrders( ) method was called.

The C# code for the XML web service is shown in Example 4-25.

Example 4-25. File: NorthwindServiceCS.asmx.cs

```
// Namespaces, variables, and constants
using System;
using System.ComponentModel;
using System.Web.Services;
using System.Configuration;
using System.Data;
using System.Data.SqlClient;

public const String ORDERS_TABLE          = "Orders";
public const String ORDERDETAILS_TABLE  = "OrderDetails";

public const String ORDERID_FIELD         = "OrderID";

public const String ORDERS_ORDERDETAILS_RELATION =
    "Order_OrderDetails_Relation";

// ...

[WebMethod]
public DataSet LoadOrders( )
{
    DataSet ds = new DataSet( );
```

Example 4-25. File: NorthwindServiceCS.asmx.cs (continued)

```
    SqlDataAdapter da;

    // Fill the Order table and add it to the DataSet.
    da = new SqlDataAdapter("SELECT * FROM Orders",
        ConfigurationSettings.AppSettings["DataConnectString"]);
    DataTable orderTable = new DataTable(ORDERS_TABLE);
    da.FillSchema(orderTable, SchemaType.Source);
    da.Fill(orderTable);
    ds.Tables.Add(orderTable);

    // Fill the OrderDetails table and add it to the DataSet.
    da = new SqlDataAdapter("SELECT * FROM [Order Details]",
        ConfigurationSettings.AppSettings["DataConnectString"]);
    DataTable orderDetailTable = new DataTable(ORDERDETAILS_TABLE);
    da.FillSchema(orderDetailTable, SchemaType.Source);
    da.Fill(orderDetailTable);
    ds.Tables.Add(orderDetailTable);

    // Create a relation between the tables.
    ds.Relations.Add(ORDERS_ORDERDETAILS_RELATION,
        ds.Tables[ORDERS_TABLE].Columns[ORDERID_FIELD],
        ds.Tables[ORDERDETAILS_TABLE].Columns[ORDERID_FIELD],
        true);

    return ds;
}

[WebMethod]
public bool UpdateOrders(DataSet ds)
{
    // Create the DataAdapters for order and order details tables.
    SqlDataAdapter daOrders =
        new SqlDataAdapter("SELECT * FROM Orders",
        ConfigurationSettings.AppSettings["DataConnectString"]);
    SqlDataAdapter daOrderDetails =
        new SqlDataAdapter("SELECT * FROM [Order Details]",
        ConfigurationSettings.AppSettings["DataConnectString"]);

    // Use CommandBuilder to generate update logic.
    SqlCommandBuilder cbOrders = new SqlCommandBuilder(daOrders);
    SqlCommandBuilder cbOrderDetails =
        new SqlCommandBuilder(daOrderDetails);

    // Update parent and child records.
    daOrderDetails.Update(ds.Tables[ORDERDETAILS_TABLE].Select(null, null,
        DataViewRowState.Deleted));
    daOrders.Update(ds.Tables[ORDERS_TABLE].Select(null, null,
        DataViewRowState.Deleted));
    daOrders.Update(ds.Tables[ORDERS_TABLE].Select(null, null,
        DataViewRowState.ModifiedCurrent));
    daOrders.Update(ds.Tables[ORDERS_TABLE].Select(null, null,
        DataViewRowState.Added));
```

Example 4-25. File: NorthwindServiceCS.asmx.cs (continued)

```
    daOrderDetails.Update(ds.Tables[ORDERDETAILS_TABLE].Select(null, null,
        DataViewRowState.ModifiedCurrent));
    daOrderDetails.Update(ds.Tables[ORDERDETAILS_TABLE].Select(null, null,
        DataViewRowState.Added));

    return true;
}
```

The C# web services client-side code is shown in Example 4-26.

Example 4-26. File: UpdateServerThroughWebServiceForm.cs

```
// Namespaces, variables, and constants
using System;
using System.Windows.Forms;
using System.Data;

// Table name constants
private const String ORDERS_TABLE       = "Orders";
private const String ORDERDETAILS_TABLE = "OrderDetails";

private DataSet ds;

// ...

private void UpdateServerThroughWebServiceForm_Load(object sender,
    System.EventArgs e)
{
    Cursor.Current = Cursors.WaitCursor;

    // Create the Web Service object.
    NorthwindServiceCS nws = new NorthwindServiceCS( );
    // Load the DataSet containing orders and order details.
    ds = nws.LoadOrders( );

    // Bind the default view of the orders table to the grid.
    dataGrid.DataSource = ds.Tables[ORDERS_TABLE].DefaultView;

    Cursor.Current = Cursors.Default;
}

private void updateButton_Click(object sender, System.EventArgs e)
{
    Cursor.Current = Cursors.WaitCursor;

    // Get the changes to the data.
    DataSet dsChanges = ds.GetChanges( );

    if (dsChanges!=null)
    {
        // Create the Web Service object.
        NorthwindServiceCS nws = new NorthwindServiceCS( );
```

Example 4-26. File: UpdateServerThroughWebServiceForm.cs (continued)

```
        // Update the changes to the order and order detail
        // informatation.
        bool retVal = nws.UpdateOrders(dsChanges);
    }
    Cursor.Current = Cursors.Default;
}
```

Discussion

An XML web service is software that is accessible using Internet standards such as XML and HTTP. Because they are accessible through open-standard interfaces, web services make it easy to allow heterogeneous systems to work together.

.NET makes it very easy to build XML web services. In .NET, web services are implemented as *.ASMX* files beginning with a @WebService directive. For example, the solution code contains the following directive:

```
<%@ WebService Language="c#" Codebehind="NorthwindServiceCS.asmx.cs"
    Class="NorthwindServiceCS" %>
```

Methods in the web service class that are exposed over the Web are tagged with the WebMethod attribute. Untagged methods can only be used internally by the web service. To deploy the web service, copy it to a directory on a web server that can be addressed by a URL.

To use the web service class, use *wsdl.exe* to create the client-side proxy class. For the solution, the command is:

```
wsdl.exe http://localhost/NorthwindWebServiceCS/NorthwindServiceCS.asmx
```

Then, as with a local class, the client is able to instantiate the web service class using the new operator.

For more information about creating and consuming XML web services, see the MSDN Library.

In the solution, the GetChanges() method is called on the client-side DataSet to create a copy of the DataSet containing only the changes. This DataSet is passed to the web service instead of the entire DataSet to minimize the bandwidth required to transmit data to the web service across a potentially slow link.

The UpdateOrders() method in the web service updates the database with the changes using method calls with different subsets of the DataSet as arguments. This technique, used to avoid referential integrity problems, is discussed in more detail in Recipe 4.10.

If this web service is intended for use by clients other than .NET clients—J2EE, for example—the DataSet should be marshaled as XML instead of the DataSet class, which is specific to .NET. This can easily be done using the WriteXml() and ReadXml() methods of the DataSet class.

The solution shows that there is very little difference between implementing the LoadOrders( ) and UpdateOrders( ) methods as a local class or web services class.

4.12   Updating Server Data Using .NET Remoting

Problem

You want to update a data source using .NET remoting and use the remote application from your client application.

Solution

Use System.MarshalByRefObject to create a remoteable class.

The server-side code that registers the remoteable class for remote activation contains one event handler and one configuration file:

Start Server Button.Click
>   Registers the remoteable class RemoteClass for remote activation.

Server-side configuration file
>   Contains parameters used to register the class and the channel on the server so that the class can be activated from another application domain.

The remoteable class code contains two methods:

LoadOrders( )
>   Creates and returns a DataSet containing the Orders and Order Details tables from Northwind and a DataRelation between those tables.

UpdateOrders( )
>   Takes a DataSet argument containing the changes made to the DataSet created by the LoadOrders( ) method, creates two DataAdapter objects with CommandBuilder-generated update logic for each, and uses the DataAdapter objects to update the Orders and Order Details tables in Northwind.

The client-side code contains two event handlers and one configuration file:

Form.Load
>   Sets up the example by calling the LoadOrders( ) method in the remote object to populate a DataSet. The default view of the Orders table is bound to the data grid on the form.

Update Button.Click
>   Calls the UpdateOrders( ) method in the remote object passing a DataSet containing changes made to the DataSet since the form was loaded or since the last time the UpdateOrders( ) method was called.

Client-side configuration file

Contains parameters used to register the remote class and channel on the client so that the remote class can be instantiated by the client.

The C# server-side code that registers the remoteable class for activation is shown in Example 4-27.

Example 4-27. File: NorthwindServerCS\MainForm.cs

```csharp
// Namespaces, variables, and constants
using System;
using System.Configuration;
using System.Windows.Forms;
using System.Runtime.Remoting;
using System.Runtime.Remoting.Channels;
using System.Runtime.Remoting.Channels.Tcp;

using ADOCookbookCS.NorthwindRemoteCS;

private bool isStarted = false;

// ...

private void startServerButton_Click(object sender, System.EventArgs e)
{
    if (!isStarted)
    {
        // config file
        RemotingConfiguration.Configure(
            "NorthwindServerCS.exe.config");

        serverResultTextBox.Text += "Remote server started." +
            Environment.NewLine +
            "  ApplicationName = " +
            RemotingConfiguration.ApplicationName +
            Environment.NewLine +
            "  ApplicationId = " +
            RemotingConfiguration.ApplicationId +
            Environment.NewLine +
            "  ProcessId = " +
            RemotingConfiguration.ProcessId;

        isStarted = true;
    }
    else
    {
        serverResultTextBox.Text +=
            "Remote Server already started." + Environment.NewLine;
    }
}
```

The server-side configuration file is shown in Example 4-28.

Example 4-28. File: NorthwindServerCS\NorthwindServerCS.exe.config

```xml
<configuration>
    <system.runtime.remoting>
        <application name="RemoteClass (WellKnownServiceType)">
            <service>
                <wellknown
                    mode="SingleCall"
                    type="ADOCookbookCS.NorthwindRemoteCS.RemoteClass, NorthwindRemoteCS"
                    objectUri="RemoteClass">
                </wellknown>
            </service>
            <channels>
                <channel ref="tcp server" port="1234" />
            </channels>
        </application>
    </system.runtime.remoting>
</configuration>
```

The C# remoteable class code is shown in Example 4-29.

Example 4-29. File: NorthwindRemoteCS\NorthwindRemoteCS.cs

```csharp
// Namespaces, variables, and constants
using System;
using System.Data;
using System.Data.SqlClient;

// ...

namespace ADOCookbookCS.NorthwindRemoteCS
{
    /// <summary>
    /// Summary description for NorthwindRemote
    /// </summary>
    public class RemoteClass : MarshalByRefObject
    {
        public const String SQL_CONNECTIONSTRING =
            "Data Source=(local);Integrated security=SSPI;" +
            "Initial Catalog=Northwind;";

        // Table name constants
        private const String ORDERS_TABLE        = "Orders";
        private const String ORDERDETAILS_TABLE  = "OrderDetails";

        // Relation name constants
        private const String ORDERS_ORDERDETAILS_RELATION =
            "Orders_OrderDetails_Relation";

        // Field name constants
        private const String ORDERID_FIELD       = "OrderID";

        public DataSet LoadOrders()
        {
            DataSet ds = new DataSet();
```

Example 4-29. File: NorthwindRemoteCS\NorthwindRemoteCS.cs (continued)

```csharp
    SqlDataAdapter da;

    // Fill the Order table and add it to the DataSet.
    da = new SqlDataAdapter("SELECT * FROM Orders",
        SQL_CONNECTIONSTRING);
    DataTable orderTable = new DataTable(ORDERS_TABLE);
    da.FillSchema(orderTable, SchemaType.Source);
    da.Fill(orderTable);
    ds.Tables.Add(orderTable);

    // Fill the OrderDetails table and add it to the DataSet.
    da = new SqlDataAdapter("SELECT * FROM [Order Details]",
        SQL_CONNECTIONSTRING);
    DataTable orderDetailTable =
        new DataTable(ORDERDETAILS_TABLE);
    da.FillSchema(orderDetailTable, SchemaType.Source);
    da.Fill(orderDetailTable);
    ds.Tables.Add(orderDetailTable);

    // Create a relation between the tables.
    ds.Relations.Add(ORDERS_ORDERDETAILS_RELATION,
        ds.Tables[ORDERS_TABLE].Columns[ORDERID_FIELD],
        ds.Tables[ORDERDETAILS_TABLE].
        Columns[ORDERID_FIELD], true);

    return ds;
}

public bool UpdateOrders(DataSet ds)
{
    // Create the DataAdapters for order and order details
    // tables.
    SqlDataAdapter daOrders =
        new SqlDataAdapter("SELECT * FROM Orders",
        SQL_CONNECTIONSTRING);
    SqlDataAdapter daOrderDetails = new
        SqlDataAdapter("SELECT * FROM [Order Details]",
        SQL_CONNECTIONSTRING);

    // Use CommandBuilder to generate update logic.
    SqlCommandBuilder cbOrders =
        new SqlCommandBuilder(daOrders);
    SqlCommandBuilder cbOrderDetails =
        new SqlCommandBuilder(daOrderDetails);

    // Update parent and child records.
    daOrderDetails.Update(
        ds.Tables[ORDERDETAILS_TABLE].Select(null, null,
        DataViewRowState.Deleted));
    daOrders.Update(ds.Tables[ORDERS_TABLE].Select(
        null, null, DataViewRowState.Deleted));
    daOrders.Update(ds.Tables[ORDERS_TABLE].Select(null,
```

Example 4-29. File: NorthwindRemoteCS\NorthwindRemoteCS.cs (continued)

```
                null, DataViewRowState.ModifiedCurrent));
            daOrders.Update(ds.Tables[ORDERS_TABLE].Select(null,
                null, DataViewRowState.Added));
            daOrderDetails.Update(
                ds.Tables[ORDERDETAILS_TABLE].Select(null, null,
                DataViewRowState.ModifiedCurrent));
            daOrderDetails.Update(
                ds.Tables[ORDERDETAILS_TABLE].Select(null, null,
                DataViewRowState.Added));

            return true;
        }
    }
}
```

The C# client-side code that activates the remoteable class remotely is shown in Examples 4-30 and 4-31.

Example 4-30. File: RemotingForm.cs

```
// Namespaces, variables, and constants
using System;
using System.Windows.Forms;
using System.Runtime.Remoting;
using System.Runtime.Remoting.Channels;
using System.Runtime.Remoting.Channels.Tcp;
using System.Data;
using ADOCookbookCS.NorthwindRemoteCS;

// Table name constants
private const String ORDERS_TABLE = "Orders";

private RemoteClass rs;

private DataSet ds;

// ...

private void RemotingForm_Load(object sender, System.EventArgs e)
{

    Cursor.Current = Cursors.WaitCursor;

    RemotingConfiguration.Configure("RemotingForm.exe.config");
    rs = new RemoteClass();

    // Load the DataSet containing orders and order details.
    ds = new DataSet();
    ds = rs.LoadOrders();

    // Bind the default view of the orders table to the grid.
    dataGrid.DataSource = ds.Tables[ORDERS_TABLE].DefaultView;
```

Example 4-30. File: RemotingForm.cs (continued)

```
    Cursor.Current = Cursors.Default;
}

private void updateButton_Click(object sender, System.EventArgs e)
{
    Cursor.Current = Cursors.WaitCursor;

    // Get the changes to the data.
    DataSet dsChanges = ds.GetChanges();

    // Update the changes to the order and order detail informtation.
    if (dsChanges != null)
        rs.UpdateOrders(dsChanges);

    Cursor.Current = Cursors.Default;
}
```

Example 4-31. File: RemotingForm.exe.config

```xml
<configuration>
    <system.runtime.remoting>
        <application>
            <client url="tcp://localhost:1234">
                <wellknown
                type="ADOCookbookCS.NorthwindRemoteCS.RemoteClass, NorthwindRemoteCS"
                    url="tcp://localhost:1234/RemoteClass">
                </wellknown>
            </client>
            <channels>
                <channel ref="tcp client" />
            </channels>
        </application>
    </system.runtime.remoting>
</configuration>
```

Discussion

A remoteable class, unlike a conventional class, can be used by clients running outside of application domain of the remoteable class. All that is required to make a class remoteable is to derive it from System.MarshalByRefObject.

When a client creates an instance of a remote class, a proxy is created in the client's application domain instead of an actual object. The proxy acts exactly like the object, but is actually a reference to the object. This proxy communicates with the remote class through a channel connecting the two application domains.

There are two different activation types for remote servers:

well known
> The server must activate the remote object.

activated
> The client can request to activate the remote object.

This solution uses a well known remote class. Therefore, the remote server must be started prior to running the solution. This is done by running the application *NorthwindServerCS.exe* and pressing the Start Server button.

Before the class can be instantiated remotely, a server process must register it so that it can be activated from another application domain. This can be done either by calling the `RegisterActivatedServiceType()` or `RegisterWellKnownServiceType()` of the `RemotingConfiguration` class with the appropriate parameters or by calling the `Configure()` method of the `RemotingConfiguration` class with the name of the configuration file as an argument. The solution uses the `Configure()` method with the code:

```
RemotingConfiguration.Configure("NorthwindServerCS.exe.config");
```

For a well known (server-activated) class, the server registration code would be:

```
RemotingConfiguration.RegisterWellKnownServiceType(
    typeof(ADOCookbookCS.NorthwindRemoteCS.RemoteClass),
    "RemoteClass", WellKnownObjectMode.SingleCall);
```

For an activated (client-activated) class, the server registration code would be:

```
RemotingConfiguration.RegisterActivatedServiceType(typeof(RemoteClass));
```

A server channel also must be created and registered when one of the two methods, for a well known or an activated class, is used. When a configuration file is used, the channel information is specified within the file. The server channel can be either one that accepts TCP connections from the client or one that accepts HTTP connections from the client. The code to register a TCP channel that listens on port 1234 is:

```
TcpServerChannel channel = new TcpServerChannel(1234);
ChannelServices.RegisterChannel(channel);
```

The code to register a HTTP channel that listens on port 1234 is:

```
HttpServerChannel channel = new HttpServerChannel (1234);
ChannelServices.RegisterChannel(channel);
```

To create an instance of the remote class, the client must first register either a TCP or HTTP client channel by creating an instance of either the `TcpClientChannel` or `HttpClientChannel` class and using the `RegisterChannel()` method of the `ChannelServices` class to register the channel. The code is similar to the code for registering a server channel.

Next, if the client wants to be able to instantiate the remote object using the new operator, the client must register the remote class in the local application domain using the RegisterWellKnownClientType() or the RegisterActivatedClientType() method of the RemotingConfiguration class with the appropriate parameters or by calling the Configure() method of the RemotingConfiguration class. The solution uses the Configure() method with the code:

```
RemotingConfiguration.Configure("RemotingForm.exe.config");
```

For a well known class, the client registration code would be:

```
RemotingConfiguration.RegisterWellKnownClientType(
    typeof(RemoteClass), "tcp://localhost:1234/RemoteClass");
```

For an activated class, the client registration code would be:

```
RemotingConfiguration.RegisterActivatedClientType(
    typeof(RemoteClass), "tcp://localhost:1234");
```

Once the client and server have performed the necessary registration, the remote class can be instantiated by the client using the new operator as shown here:

```
rs = new RemoteClass();
```

As mentioned earlier, this creates a proxy for the remote object on client that you can use in exactly the same way as if the object were local.

In the solution, the GetChanges() method is called on the client-side DataSet to create a copy of the DataSet containing only the changes. This DataSet is passed to the UpdateOrders() method of the remote object instead of to the entire DataSet to minimize the required bandwidth across a potentially slow connection.

The UpdateOrders() method updates the database with the changes using method calls with different subsets of the DataSet as arguments. This technique, used to avoid referential integrity problems, is discussed in more detail in Recipe 4.10.

The solution shows that there is very little difference between implementing the LoadOrders() and UpdateOrders() methods as a local class or a remoteable class.

4.13 Updating Data Asynchronously Using Message Queuing

Problem

You need to asynchronously update data on a database on system that is not always connected.

Solution

You must use message queuing and an XML DiffGram to:

- Construct and send an MSMQ message containing a DiffGram to the server.
- Extract the DiffGram from the message and use it to update the data source at the server.
- Construct and send a message containing the latest DataSet to the client.
- Retrieve the response at the client and deserialize it into a DataSet.

The sample code contains four event handlers:

Form.Load
> Sets up the sample by loading a DataSet with the Customers table from the Northwind database. The default view of the table is bound to a data grid on the form.

Send Update Button.Click
> Checks if the update message queue exists and creates it if necessary. A MessageQueue object is created to access the queue. A message is created containing a DiffGram of the changes made to the DataSet containing the Customers table. This message is sent to the update queue.

Process Update Button.Click
> Checks if the update message queue exists and creates it if necessary. A MessageQueue object is created to access the queue. An attempt is made to receive a message from the queue, waiting one second before giving up. If a message is received, a DataAdapter that uses a CommandBuilder to generate updating logic is created and used to update the database with the changes in the DataSet contained in the body of the message. The latest version of the Customers table is retrieved into a new DataSet. A *result* queue is created if necessary and a message containing the latest DataSet is sent to the queue.

Receive Update Button.Click
> Checks if the result message queue exists and creates it if necessary. A MessageQueue object is created to access the queue and the formatter set to deserialize the DataSet in the message bodies. An attempt is made to receive a message from the queue, waiting one second before giving up. If a message is received, the DataSet in the body is deserialized and the default view of the Categories DataTable is bound to the data grid on the form.

The C# code is shown in Example 4-32.

Example 4-32. File: MessageQueueUpdateForm.cs

```
// Namespaces, variables, and constants
using System;
using System.Configuration;
using System.Windows.Forms;
```

Example 4-32. File: MessageQueueUpdateForm.cs (continued)

```csharp
using System.Messaging;
using System.Data;
using System.Data.SqlClient;

private const String CUSTOMERS_TABLE = "Customers";

private const String QUEUENAMEUPDATE = @".\Private$\adodotnetcb0413update";
private const String QUEUENAMERESULT = @".\Private$\adodotnetcb0413result";

private DataSet ds;

// ...

private void MessageQueueUpdateForm_Load(object sender, System.EventArgs e)
{
    // As a starting point, load the data directly.
    // Create the DataAdapter to load customers data.
    SqlDataAdapter da = new SqlDataAdapter("SELECT * FROM Customers",
        ConfigurationSettings.AppSettings["Sql_ConnectString"]);
    // Get the schema and data for the customers table.
    ds = new DataSet( );
    da.FillSchema(ds, SchemaType.Source, CUSTOMERS_TABLE);
    da.Fill(ds, CUSTOMERS_TABLE);

    // Bind the default view of the customers table to the grid.
    dataGrid.DataSource = ds.Tables[CUSTOMERS_TABLE].DefaultView;
}

private void sendUpdateButton_Click(object sender, System.EventArgs e)
{
    // Create the result queue if it does not exist.
    if(!MessageQueue.Exists(QUEUENAMEUPDATE))
        MessageQueue.Create(QUEUENAMEUPDATE);

    // Create an object to access the result queue.
    MessageQueue mq = new MessageQueue(QUEUENAMEUPDATE);
    // Set the formatter for serialization of message bodies.
    mq.Formatter = new XmlMessageFormatter(new Type[] {typeof(DataSet)});

    // Create a message containing the changes.
    mq.Send(ds.GetChanges( ));

    MessageBox.Show("Update message sent.","MessageQueue Update",
        MessageBoxButtons.OK, MessageBoxIcon.Information);
}

private void processUpdateButton_Click(object sender, System.EventArgs e)
{
    // Create the result queue if it does not exist.
    if(!MessageQueue.Exists(QUEUENAMEUPDATE))
        MessageQueue.Create(QUEUENAMEUPDATE);
```

Example 4-32. File: MessageQueueUpdateForm.cs (continued)

```csharp
    // Create an object to access the result queue.
    MessageQueue mq = new MessageQueue(QUEUENAMEUPDATE);
    // Set the formatter for deserialization of message bodies.
    mq.Formatter = new XmlMessageFormatter(new Type[] {typeof(DataSet)});

    // Receive a message from the query queue.
    System.Messaging.Message msg;
    try
    {
        msg = mq.Receive(new TimeSpan(0,0,1));
    }
    catch(MessageQueueException ex)
    {
        MessageBox.Show(ex.Message, "MessageQueue Receive Error",
            MessageBoxButtons.OK, MessageBoxIcon.Error);
        return;
    }

    // Create the DataAdapter and CommandBuilder to update.
    SqlDataAdapter da =
        new SqlDataAdapter("SELECT * FROM " + CUSTOMERS_TABLE,
        ConfigurationSettings.AppSettings["Sql_ConnectString"]);
    SqlCommandBuilder cb = new SqlCommandBuilder(da);

    if (msg.BodyStream.Length > 0)
    {
        // Get the DataSet of changes from the message body.
        DataSet dsChanges = (DataSet)msg.Body;

        // Process the updates.
        da.Update(dsChanges, CUSTOMERS_TABLE);
    }

    // Get the updated DataSet.
    DataSet dsUpdate = new DataSet();
    da.Fill(dsUpdate, CUSTOMERS_TABLE);

    // Create the result queue if it does not exist.
    if(!MessageQueue.Exists(QUEUENAMERESULT))
        MessageQueue.Create(QUEUENAMERESULT);

    // Create an object to access the result queue.
    mq = new MessageQueue(QUEUENAMERESULT);
    // Send a message with the update DataSet to the queue.
    mq.Send(dsUpdate);

    MessageBox.Show("Update processed. Refreshed DataSet sent.",
        "MessageQueue Process", MessageBoxButtons.OK,
        MessageBoxIcon.Information);
}

private void receiveUpdateButton_Click(object sender, System.EventArgs e)
{
```

Example 4-32. File: MessageQueueUpdateForm.cs (continued)

```
    // Create the result queue if it does not exist.
    if(!MessageQueue.Exists(QUEUENAMERESULT))
        MessageQueue.Create(QUEUENAMERESULT);

    // Create an object to access the result queue.
    MessageQueue mq = new MessageQueue(QUEUENAMERESULT);
    // Set the formatter for deserialization of message bodies.
    mq.Formatter = new XmlMessageFormatter(new Type[] {typeof(DataSet)});

    // Receive a message from the result queue.
    System.Messaging.Message msg;
    try
    {
        msg = mq.Receive(new TimeSpan(0,0,1));
    }
    catch(MessageQueueException ex)
    {
        MessageBox.Show("ERROR: " + ex.Message, "MessageQueue Receive",
            MessageBoxButtons.OK, MessageBoxIcon.Error);
        return;
    }

    // Refresh the DataSet underlying the DataGrid.
    ds = (DataSet)msg.Body;
    dataGrid.DataSource = ds.Tables[CUSTOMERS_TABLE].DefaultView;

    MessageBox.Show("Retrieved and loaded refreshed data.",
        "MessageQueue Receive", MessageBoxButtons.OK,
        MessageBoxIcon.Information);
}
```

Discussion

The discussion in Recipe 2.22 provides an overview of Message Queuing (MSMQ).

For more information about DiffGrams, see Recipe 8.8.

4.14   Overcoming Keyword Conflicts When Using CommandBuilders

Problem

Your data includes table and column names that conflict with SQL keywords. You can overcome this with brackets or quotes in SELECT statements that you write, but the CommandBuilder creates illegal update statements. You need to know how to use the CommandBuilder with your data.

Solution

Use the QuotePrefix and QuoteSuffix properties of the CommandBuilder object to delimit database server object names containing spaces or other illegal characters.

The sample code contains two event handlers:

Preview Button.Click
> Displays the delete, insert, and update commands using the delimiters specified by the user for the QuotePrefix and QuoteSuffix properties, and either the OLE DB or SQL Server data provider as specified by the user.

Retrieve OLE DB Button.Click
> Uses the GetOleDbSchemaTable( ) method of the OleDbConnection object to retrieve the default prefix and suffix delimiters for the data source.

The C# code is shown in Example 4-33.

Example 4-33. File: CommandBuilderKeywordConflictForm.cs

```csharp
// Namespaces, variables, and constants
using System;
using System.Configuration;
using System.Data;
using System.Data.SqlClient;
using System.Data.OleDb;

// ...

private void previewButton_Click(object sender, System.EventArgs e)
{
    String sqlText = "SELECT OrderID, ProductID, Quantity, " +
        "UnitPrice, Discount FROM [Order Details]";

    if (oleDbRadioButton.Checked)
    {
        // Build the DataAdapter and the CommandBuilder.
        OleDbDataAdapter da = new OleDbDataAdapter(sqlText,
            ConfigurationSettings.AppSettings["OleDb_ConnectString"]);
        OleDbCommandBuilder cb = new OleDbCommandBuilder(da);

        // Set the prefix and suffix.
        cb.QuotePrefix = quotePrefixTextBox.Text;
        cb.QuoteSuffix = quoteSuffixTextBox.Text;

        // Display CommandBuilder commands with the prefix and suffix.
        resultTextBox.Text =
            "DeleteCommand: " + cb.GetDeleteCommand( ).CommandText +
            Environment.NewLine + Environment.NewLine +
            "InsertCommand: " + cb.GetInsertCommand( ).CommandText +
            Environment.NewLine + Environment.NewLine +
            "UpdateCommand: " + cb.GetUpdateCommand( ).CommandText;
    }
```

Example 4-33. File: CommandBuilderKeywordConflictForm.cs (continued)

```
            else
            {
                // Build the DataAdapter and the CommandBuilder.
                SqlDataAdapter da = new SqlDataAdapter(sqlText,
                    ConfigurationSettings.AppSettings["Sql_ConnectString"]);
                SqlCommandBuilder cb = new SqlCommandBuilder(da);

                // Set the prefix and suffix.
                cb.QuotePrefix = quotePrefixTextBox.Text;
                cb.QuoteSuffix = quoteSuffixTextBox.Text;

                // Display CommandBuilder commands with the prefix and suffix.
                resultTextBox.Text =
                    "DeleteCommand: " + cb.GetDeleteCommand( ).CommandText +
                    Environment.NewLine + Environment.NewLine +
                    "InsertCommand: " + cb.GetInsertCommand( ).CommandText +
                    Environment.NewLine + Environment.NewLine +
                    "UpdateCommand: " + cb.GetUpdateCommand( ).CommandText;
            }
        }

        private void retrieveOleDbButton_Click(object sender, System.EventArgs e)
        {
            // Retrieve the quote prefix and suffix for the server.
            OleDbConnection conn = new OleDbConnection(
                ConfigurationSettings.AppSettings["OleDb_ConnectString"]);
            conn.Open( );
            DataTable tableSchema =
                conn.GetOleDbSchemaTable(OleDbSchemaGuid.DbInfoLiterals,
                new object[] {});
            conn.Close( );

            // Set the primary key to enable find on LiteralName column.
            tableSchema.PrimaryKey =
                new DataColumn[] {tableSchema.Columns["LiteralName"]};

            // Get the prefix and suffix from the OleDbLiteral enumeration.
            DataRow row;
            row = tableSchema.Rows.Find("Quote_Prefix");
            quotePrefixTextBox.Text =
                ((row == null) ? "" : row["LiteralValue"].ToString( ));
            row = tableSchema.Rows.Find("Quote_Suffix");
            quoteSuffixTextBox.Text =
                ((row == null) ? "" : row["LiteralValue"].ToString( ));
        }
```

Discussion

The QuotePrefix and QuoteSuffix properties of the CommandBuilder object specify the beginning and ending characters used to delimit database server object names, such as tables and columns in the updating commands generated by the CommandBuilder.

This is necessary when the object names contain special characters or reserved tokens; otherwise, the commands will fail when executed.

For example, in SQL Server 2000 and later, database object names can contain any valid Microsoft Windows NT/2000/XP character including spaces and punctuation marks. T-SQL is more restrictive with identifiers that can be used without delimiters. You can use QuotePrefix and QuoteSuffix to delimit the SQL Server object names when required by T-SQL.

The QuotePrefix and QuoteSuffix values have no effect on the CommandText of SelectCommand. These delimiters must be specified as part of the SelectCommand that the CommandBuilder is based on.

The default values for QuotePrefix and QuoteSuffix are empty strings.

The example demonstrates using QuotePrefix and QuoteSuffix with both the OLE DB and SQL Server CommandBuilder objects. As you can see, they function nearly identically.

> The CommandBuilder makes it easy to update the data source with changes made to the DataSet. Update logic is created automatically so no understanding is required of how to code the actual delete, insert, and update SQL statements. The CommandBuilder drawbacks include slower performance because of the time that it takes to request metadata and construct the updating logic, updates that are limited to simple single-table scenarios, and a lack of support for stored procedures. Because of these drawbacks, the CommandBuilder is seldom used in enterprise application development.

The example also demonstrates retrieving the default quote prefix and suffix from the database server. The GetOleDbSchemaTable( ) method of the OleDbConnection object returns schema information from a data source based on a GUID argument indicating one of the OleDbSchemaGuid values. The value DbInfoLiterals returns a list of provider-specific literals used in text commands. The literals are returned as a table of rows. Within this table, there is a column named LiteralName. The rows containing the default values for the quote prefix and suffix are identified by a LiteralName value of Quote_Prefix and Quote_Suffix, respectively. The actual values are stored in the LiteralValue column.

CHAPTER 5

Copying and Transferring Data

5.0   Introduction

This chapter focuses on copying data between ADO.NET classes and between ADO and ADO.NET classes, serializing and deserializing data, and encrypting data and login credentials to build secure applications.

Copying rows from one DataTable to another and copying tables from one DataSet to another are operations performed frequently in data-centric applications. Recipes 5.1 and 5.2 show different ways to copy data and discuss the advantages, limitations, and disadvantages of the different approaches.

The DataReader provides connected forward-only, read-only access to a data stream while the DataSet provides disconnected access to data stored as an in-memory relational database. There is no built-in method to convert a DataReader to a DataSet, so Recipe 5.3 shows how it's done.

In addition, this chapter covers:

Serializing and deserializing data

> Serialization allows data conversion to a format that can be persisted or transported. The .NET framework supports serialization and deserialization with the System.Runtime.Serialization namespace. Support for binary, XML, and SOAP formats is built in and serialization can easily be customized if required. Recipes 5.4 and 5.5 show how to serialize and deserialize data.

> As well as copying data, ADO.NET supports merging disconnected data in DataTable or DataSet objects into each other. Recipe 5.6 shows how merging works and how to use the arguments that control the merge operation.

Security and encryption

> The .NET Framework provides extensive support for encryption in the System.Security.Cryptography namespace. The classes in the namespace are both easy and intuitive to use. You can use the cryptography classes to encrypt a disconnected data class such as a DataSet prior to transmission in a

remoting or web services call. Encrypting the data allows it to be transmitted securely using HTTP as a transmission protocol. An encrypted protocol such as HTTPS is not required. Recipe 5.7 explores cryptographic algorithms, public keys, private keys, and demonstrates encryption solutions using symmetric and asymmetric keys.

ASP.NET uses the classes in the System.Web.Security namespace to implement security in web service applications. Securing authentication credentials—usually a username and password—during transmission and storage in a database is critical to building secure distributed applications. Recipe 5.8 demonstrates how to protect credentials using a hash algorithm with password salt.

ADO

The OLE DB DataAdapter supports importing ADO Recordset or Record objects into a DataTable or DataSet. This is a one-way operation: changes made to the DataTable or DataSet can't be updated back to ADO using the data adapter. ADO.NET does not, however, provide a way to convert a DataTable or DataSet to an ADO Recordset; therefore, Recipe 5.10 shows how to do this.

With evolution of ADO to ADO.NET, a few functions got lost along the way. Recipes 5.11 and 5.12 recreate the ADO Recordset GetString( ) and GetRows( ) methods in ADO.NET.

5.1   Copying Rows from One DataTable to Another

Problem

You have records in a DataTable that you need to copy to another DataTable.

Solution

Use the ImportRow( ) method of the DataTable to copy DataRow objects from one DataTable to another. Three techniques for selecting records to copy are demonstrated in the following example:

- Use the Rows property to access rows in the DataRowCollection of the DataTable using the row index.
- Use the Select( ) method of the DataTable.
- Use the RowFilter property of a DataView for the DataTable.

The sample code creates a source DataTable containing the Orders table from Northwind. A second empty target DataTable is created with the same schema. One of the three techniques, as specified by the user, is used to copy records from the source table to the target table.

The C# code is shown in Example 5-1.

Example 5-1. File: CopyRowsBetweenTablesForm.cs

```
// Namespaces, variables, and constants
using System;
using System.Configuration;
using System.Data;
using System.Data.SqlClient;

// Table name constants
private const String ORDERS_TABLE        = "Orders";

// Field name constants
private const String ORDERID_FIELD       = "OrderID";

// ...

// Fill the source table with schema and data.
SqlDataAdapter da = new SqlDataAdapter("SELECT * FROM Orders",
    ConfigurationSettings.AppSettings["Sql_ConnectString"]);
DataTable dt = new DataTable(ORDERS_TABLE);
da.FillSchema(dt, SchemaType.Source);
da.Fill(dt);

// Clone the schema to the copy table.
DataTable dtCopy = dt.Clone();

if(rowRadioButton.Checked)
{
    // Use ImportRow method to import the first three rows.
    for (int i = 0; i < 3; i++)
    {
        dtCopy.ImportRow(dt.Rows[i]);
    }
}
else if (selectRadioButton.Checked)
{
    // Copy using result of Select() method.
    foreach(DataRow row in dt.Select(ORDERID_FIELD + " <= 10300"))
    {
        dtCopy.ImportRow(row);
    }
}
else if (filteredDataViewRadioButton.Checked)
{
    // Copy using result of filtered DataView.
    DataView categoryView = dt.DefaultView;
    categoryView.RowFilter = ORDERID_FIELD + " >= 10300 AND " +
        ORDERID_FIELD + " < 10400";
    for (int i = 0; i < categoryView.Count; i++)
    {
        dtCopy.ImportRow(categoryView[i].Row);
    }
}
```

Example 5-1. File: CopyRowsBetweenTablesForm.cs (continued)

```
// Bind the default view of the copy table to the grid.
dataGrid.DataSource = dtCopy.DefaultView;
```

Discussion

Rows can be copied between tables using the ImportRow( ) methods of the DataTable object. The ImportRow( ) method requires that both the source and destination table have the same structure. In this example, the Clone( ) method of the DataTable creates a table with identical structure, but any technique that creates a table with an identical structure can be used.

Additionally, the Copy( ) method of the DataTable object can create a new DataTable having the same structure and data as the original as shown in the following code sample:

```
// Create the source table.
DataTable dtSource = new DataTable("Source");

// ... Fill the source table with data.

// Create the destination table and copy the source table.
DataTable dtDest = new DataTable("Dest");
dtDest = dtSource.Copy( );
```

5.2   Copying Tables from One DataSet to Another

Problem

You need to copy an existing schema and data from one DataSet to another.

Solution

Use one of the following techniques:

- Use the Copy( ) method of the DataTable when all of the data for a table needs to be copied.

- Use the Clone( ) method of the DataTable to create the schema for each table in the destination DataSet when only a subset of the data needs to be copied. You can use the ImportRows( ) method of the DataTable to copy the subset of rows from the source to the destination table.

Once the destination tables are created and the data is copied into them, the example shows how to create the DataRelation objects from the source DataSet in the destination DataSet.

The sample code contains two event handlers:

Form.Load

Sets up the sample by creating a DataSet containing the Orders and Order Details tables from Northwind and a relation between the two tables. The default view for the Orders table is bound to a data grid on the form.

Copy Button.Click

Creates a destination DataSet and copies the schema and specified data into it from the source DataSet created in the Form.Load event handler.

The C# code is shown in Example 5-2.

Example 5-2. File: CopyTablesBetweenDataSetsForm.cs

```csharp
// Namespaces, variables, and constants
using System;
using System.Configuration;
using System.Windows.Forms;
using System.Data;
using System.Data.SqlClient;

// Table name constants
private const String ORDERS_TABLE        = "Orders";
private const String ORDERDETAILS_TABLE  = "OrderDetails";

// Relation name constants
private const String ORDERS_ORDERDETAILS_RELATION =
    "Orders_OrderDetails_Relation";

// Field name constants
private const String ORDERID_FIELD       = "OrderID";
private const String ORDERDATE_FIELD      = "OrderDate";
private const String EMPLOYEEID_FIELD    = "EmployeeID";

private DataSet dsSource;

// ...

private void CopyTablesBetweenDataSetsForm_Load(object sender,
    System.EventArgs e)
{
    dsSource = new DataSet("Source");

    SqlDataAdapter da;

    // Fill the Order table and add it to the DataSet.
    da = new SqlDataAdapter("SELECT * FROM Orders",
        ConfigurationSettings.AppSettings["Sql_ConnectString"]);
    DataTable orderTable = new DataTable(ORDERS_TABLE);
    da.FillSchema(orderTable, SchemaType.Source);
    da.Fill(orderTable);
    dsSource.Tables.Add(orderTable);
```

Example 5-2. File: CopyTablesBetweenDataSetsForm.cs (continued)

```csharp
        // Fill the OrderDetails table and add it to the DataSet.
        da = new SqlDataAdapter("SELECT * FROM [Order Details]",
            ConfigurationSettings.AppSettings["Sql_ConnectString"]);
        DataTable orderDetailTable = new DataTable(ORDERDETAILS_TABLE);
        da.FillSchema(orderDetailTable, SchemaType.Source);
        da.Fill(orderDetailTable);
        dsSource.Tables.Add(orderDetailTable);

        // Create a relation between the tables.
        dsSource.Relations.Add(ORDERS_ORDERDETAILS_RELATION,
            dsSource.Tables[ORDERS_TABLE].Columns[ORDERID_FIELD],
            dsSource.Tables[ORDERDETAILS_TABLE].Columns[ORDERID_FIELD],
            true);

        // Bind the source and destination DataSet to the grids.
        sourceDataGrid.DataSource = dsSource.Tables[ORDERS_TABLE].DefaultView;
    }

    private void copyButton_Click(object sender, System.EventArgs e)
    {
        // Create the destination DataSet into which to copy tables
        DataSet dsDest = new DataSet("Destination");

        if (copyAllRadioButton.Checked)
        {
            foreach(DataTable sourceTable in dsSource.Tables)
            {
                // First technique: when all rows need to be copied
                dsDest.Tables.Add(sourceTable.Copy());
            }
        }
        else if (copySubsetRadioButton.Checked)
        {

            int employeeId = 0;
            try
            {
                employeeId = Convert.ToInt32(employeeIdTextBox.Text);
            }
            catch (Exception ex)
            {
                MessageBox.Show(ex.Message);
                return;
            }

            // Second technique: can be used to import subset
            foreach(DataTable dtSource in dsSource.Tables)
            {
                // Add logic to selectively copy tables.

                dsDest.Tables.Add(dtSource.Clone());
            }
```

Example 5-2. File: CopyTablesBetweenDataSetsForm.cs (continued)

```csharp
        // Copy rows for selected employee from the Orders table.
        foreach(DataRow parentRow in
            dsSource.Tables[ORDERS_TABLE].Select(
            EMPLOYEEID_FIELD + "=" + employeeId))
        {
            dsDest.Tables[ORDERS_TABLE].ImportRow(parentRow);

            // Copy the Order Details for the Order.
            foreach(DataRow childRow in
                parentRow.GetChildRows(
                ORDERS_ORDERDETAILS_RELATION))
            {
                dsDest.Tables[
                    ORDERDETAILS_TABLE].ImportRow(childRow);
            }
        }
    }

    // Create the relations in the destination DataSet.
    // Iterate over the collection of relations in the source.
    foreach(DataRelation sourceRelation in dsSource.Relations)
    {
        // Get the name of the parent and child table for the relation.
        String parentTableName = sourceRelation.ParentTable.TableName;
        String childTableName = sourceRelation.ChildTable.TableName;

        // Get the number of parent columns for the source relation.
        int nCol = sourceRelation.ParentColumns.Length;

        // Create an array of parent columns in the destination.
        DataColumn[] parentCols = new DataColumn[nCol];
        for(int i = 0; i < nCol; i++)
            parentCols[i] = dsDest.Tables[parentTableName].Columns[
                sourceRelation.ParentColumns[i].Ordinal];

        // Create an array of child columns in the destination.
        DataColumn[] childCols = new DataColumn[nCol];
        for(int i = 0; i < nCol; i++)
            childCols[i] = dsDest.Tables[childTableName].Columns[
                sourceRelation.ChildColumns[i].Ordinal];

        // Create the relation in the destination DataSet.
        dsDest.Relations.Add(
            new DataRelation(sourceRelation.RelationName,
            parentCols, childCols, false));
    }

    // Set the enforce constraints flag to match the source DataSet.
    dsDest.EnforceConstraints = dsSource.EnforceConstraints;

    // Bind the default view of the Orders table to the grid.
    destDataGrid.DataSource = dsDest.Tables[ORDERS_TABLE].DefaultView;
}
```

Discussion

This sample demonstrates two scenarios for copying tables from one DataSet to another.

In the first scenario, all of the data and tables in the source DataSet are copied to the destination. This is accomplished by iterating over the collection of tables in the source DataSet and using the Copy( ) method of each DataTable object to copy both the schema and data for each table into the destination DataSet.

In the second scenario, only a subset of the data in the source DataSet is copied to the destination. Since there is a relation in place between the Orders and Order Details tables in this case, only the child records related to the selected parent records are copied to the destination.

Once the data has been copied, the DataRelation objects are copied by iterating over the collection of DataRelation objects in the source DataSet, and adding them to the destination DataSet. This involves creating an array of parent and source columns for the destination DataRelation from the parent and child column ordinals in the source DataRelation. This information, together with the name of the source DataRelation is used to create the DataRelation in the destination DataSet. Finally, the EnforceConstraints property in the destination DataRelation is set to match the source.

5.3   Converting a DataReader to a DataSet

Problem

You need to transfer data from a DataReader to a DataSet.

Solution

Create a DataTable schema in the destination DataSet using the schema information returned by the GetSchemaTable( ) method of the DataReader. Then, use the GetData( ) method of the DataReader to load each row of data into an array of objects, and add it to the DataTable using the Add( ) method of the contained DataRowCollection.

The C# code is shown in Example 5-3.

Example 5-3. File: ConvertDataReaderToDataSetForm.cs

```
// Namespaces, variables, and constants
using System;
using System.Configuration;
using System.Collections;
using System.Data;
using System.Data.SqlClient;
```

Example 5-3. File: ConvertDataReaderToDataSetForm.cs (continued)

```csharp
// Table name constants
private const String ORDERS_TABLE         = "Orders";
private const String ORDERDETAILS_TABLE   = "OrderDetails";

// Relation name constants
private const String ORDERS_ORDERDETAILS_RELATION =
    "Orders_OrderDetails_Relation";

// Field name constants
private const String ORDERID_FIELD        = "OrderID";

// ...

DataSet ds = new DataSet( );

// SQL for batch query
String sqlText = "SELECT * FROM Orders; " +
    "SELECT * FROM [Order Details];";

// Create connection and command.
SqlConnection conn = new SqlConnection(
    ConfigurationSettings.AppSettings["Sql_ConnectString"]);
SqlCommand cmd = new SqlCommand(sqlText, conn);

// Open DataReader with KeyInfo.
conn.Open( );
SqlDataReader dr = cmd.ExecuteReader(CommandBehavior.KeyInfo);

// Loop over the result sets of the DataReader.
do
{
    DataTable schemaTable = dr.GetSchemaTable( );
    if (schemaTable != null)
    {
        ArrayList pkCols = new ArrayList( );

        DataTable dataTable = new DataTable( );
        foreach(DataRow schemaRow in schemaTable.Rows)
        {
            DataColumn col = new DataColumn( );
            col.ColumnName = schemaRow["ColumnName"].ToString( );
            col.DataType = (Type)schemaRow["DataType"];
            // set the length of the field for string types only
            if (schemaRow["DataType"].ToString( ) == "System.String")
                col.MaxLength = (Int32)schemaRow["ColumnSize"];
            col.Unique = (bool)schemaRow["IsUnique"];
            col.AllowDBNull = (bool)schemaRow["AllowDBNull"];
            col.AutoIncrement = (bool)schemaRow["IsAutoIncrement"];
            // If part of the key, add the column name to the
            // array of columns comprising the primary key.
            if ((bool)schemaRow["IsKey"])
                pkCols.Add(col);
```

Example 5-3. File: ConvertDataReaderToDataSetForm.cs (continued)

```
                dataTable.Columns.Add(col);
            }

            // Add the primary key to the table.
            dataTable.PrimaryKey =
                (DataColumn[])pkCols.ToArray(typeof(DataColumn));
            // Add the table to the DataSet.
            ds.Tables.Add(dataTable);

            object[] aData = new object[dataTable.Columns.Count];
            // Read all rows from the DataReader.
            while(dr.Read())
            {
                // Read the row from the DataReader into an array.
                dr.GetValues(aData);
                // Add the row from the array to the DataTable.
                dataTable.Rows.Add(aData);
            }
        }
    }
    while (dr.NextResult());

    conn.Close();

    // Name the tables added to the DataSet.
    ds.Tables[0].TableName = ORDERS_TABLE;
    ds.Tables[1].TableName = ORDERDETAILS_TABLE;

    // Manually add a relation between the tables.
    ds.Relations.Add(ORDERS_ORDERDETAILS_RELATION,
        ds.Tables[ORDERS_TABLE].Columns[ORDERID_FIELD],
        ds.Tables[ORDERDETAILS_TABLE].Columns[ORDERID_FIELD],
        true);

    // Bind the Order table default view to the grid.
    dataGrid.DataSource = ds.Tables[ORDERS_TABLE].DefaultView;
```

Discussion

While the DbDataAdapter class—from which DataAdapter classes in .NET providers for relational databases inherit—defines an overload of the Fill() method that converts a DataReader to a DataSet, this method is declared protected and cannot be accessed (unless you write a custom DataAdapter). There is no built-in mechanism for converting the connected DataReader object to a disconnected DataTable. Internally, ADO.NET uses the DataReader through the DataAdapter to populate the DataTable object. This sample demonstrates how this can be done programmatically.

Both the SQL Server and OLE DB DataReader expose a GetSchemaTable() method that returns a table containing the column metadata of the DataReader. You can use this table in turn to define the DataTable object, into which the DataReader data will be copied.

The GetSchemaTable( ) method returns the metadata described in Table 5-1 for each column.

Table 5-1. DataReader GetSchemaTable() metadata

Column name	Description
ColumnName	The name of the column.
ColumnOrdinal	The zero-based ordinal of the column.
ColumnSize	The maximum length of a column value. This is the data size of fixed-length data types.
NumericPrecision	The maximum precision of numeric data type columns. Null for non-numeric data type columns.
NumericScale	The number of digits to the right of the decimal for DBTYPE_DECIMAL or DBTYPE_NUMERIC data type columns. Otherwise, null.
IsUnique	Indicates whether the value in the column must be unique within all records.
IsKey	Indicates whether the column is part of the primary key or a unique key uniquely identifying the record.
BaseServerName	The instance name of the data server used by the DataReader.
BaseCatalogName	The name of the catalog in the data store.
BaseColumnName	The name of the column in the data store.
BaseSchemaName	The name of the schema in the data store.
BaseTableName	The name of the table in the data store.
DataType	The .NET Framework data type of the column.
AllowDBNull	Indicates whether null values are allowed in the column.
ProviderType	The .NET data provider data type of the column.
IsAliased	Indicates whether the column name is an alias.
IsExpression	Indicates whether the column is an expression.
IsIdentity	Indicates whether the column is an identity column.
IsAutoIncrement	Indicates whether values for the columns are automatically in fixed increments for each new row.
IsRowVersion	Indicates whether the column is a read-only persistent row identifier.
IsHidden	Indicates whether the column is hidden.
IsLong	Indicates whether the column contains a Binary Long Object (BLOB).
IsReadOnly	Indicates whether the column value cannot be modified.

The DataReader can contain multiple result sets. In the solution, each of these is loaded into a separate DataTable within the DataSet.

The conversion process uses the GetSchemaData( ) method to retrieve metadata about the columns in the result set of the DataReader and inserts it into a DataTable, where each row in the table corresponds to a column in the result set. A target DataTable is created to hold the result set in the DataReader. The solution iterates over the rows in the schema DataTable and constructs a DataColumn for each record in the DataReader using the metadata that is stored in the columns as described in Table 5-1. This process is repeated for each result set in the DataReader.

If the DataReader returns multiple result sets, it does not contain enough information, nor is it possible to add information, to create relations between the tables. These have to be created programmatically within the DataSet if they are needed.

5.4 Serializing Data

Problem

You need to serialize the contents of a DataSet so that you can store the data on a disk or transfer it across a network.

Solution

You can serialize a DataSet into XML, binary, or SOAP formats and save the serialized DataSet to a stream (such as a file or network stream).

The sample code creates a DataSet containing the Orders and Order Details tables from Northwind and a relation between the two tables. A file stream is created and the DataSet is serialized to the stream using a specified format.

The C# code is shown in Example 5-4.

Example 5-4. File: SerializeForm.cs

```
// Namespaces, variables, and constants
using System;
using System.Configuration;
using System.Windows.Forms;
using System.IO;
using System.Data;
using System.Data.SqlClient;
using System.Runtime.Serialization;
using System.Runtime.Serialization.Formatters.Binary;
using System.Runtime.Serialization.Formatters.Soap;
using System.Xml.Serialization;

// Table name constants
private const String ORDERS_TABLE        = "Orders";
private const String ORDERDETAILS_TABLE  = "OrderDetails";

// Relation name constants
private const String ORDERS_ORDERDETAILS_RELATION =
    "Orders_OrderDetails_Relation";
```

Example 5-4. File: SerializeForm.cs (continued)

```
// Field name constants
private const String ORDERID_FIELD        = "OrderID";

private SaveFileDialog sfd;

// ...

private void goButton_Click(object sender, System.EventArgs e)
{
    DataSet ds = new DataSet( );

    SqlDataAdapter da;

    // Fill the Order table and add it to the DataSet.
    da = new SqlDataAdapter("SELECT * FROM Orders",
        ConfigurationSettings.AppSettings["Sql_ConnectString"]);
    DataTable orderTable = new DataTable(ORDERS_TABLE);
    da.FillSchema(orderTable, SchemaType.Source);
    da.Fill(orderTable);
    ds.Tables.Add(orderTable);

    // Fill the OrderDetails table and add it to the DataSet.
    da = new SqlDataAdapter("SELECT * FROM [Order Details]",
        ConfigurationSettings.AppSettings["Sql_ConnectString"]);
    DataTable orderDetailTable = new DataTable(ORDERDETAILS_TABLE);
    da.FillSchema(orderDetailTable, SchemaType.Source);
    da.Fill(orderDetailTable);
    ds.Tables.Add(orderDetailTable);

    // Create a relation between the tables.
    ds.Relations.Add(ORDERS_ORDERDETAILS_RELATION,
        ds.Tables[ORDERS_TABLE].Columns[ORDERID_FIELD],
        ds.Tables[ORDERDETAILS_TABLE].Columns[ORDERID_FIELD],
        true);

    // Create and open the stream for serializing.
    Stream stream = null;
    try
    {
        stream = File.Open(fileNameTextBox.Text, FileMode.Create,
            FileAccess.Write);
    }
    catch(Exception ex)
    {
        MessageBox.Show(ex.Message, "Serializing Data",
            MessageBoxButtons.OK, MessageBoxIcon.Error);
        return;
    }

    // Serialize.
    if (xmlWriteRadioButton.Checked)
    {
```

Example 5-4. File: SerializeForm.cs (continued)

```
            ds.WriteXml(stream, XmlWriteMode.WriteSchema);
        }
        else if (xmlSerializerRadioButton.Checked)
        {
            XmlSerializer xs = new XmlSerializer(typeof(DataSet));
            xs.Serialize(stream, ds);
        }
        else if(soapRadioButton.Checked)
        {
            SoapFormatter sf = new SoapFormatter( );
            sf.Serialize(stream, ds);
        }
        else if(binaryRadioButton.Checked)
        {
            BinaryFormatter bf = new BinaryFormatter( );
            bf.Serialize(stream, ds);
        }

        stream.Close( );

        MessageBox.Show("Serialization complete.", "Serializing Data",
            MessageBoxButtons.OK, MessageBoxIcon.Information);
}

private void fileDialogButton_Click(object sender, System.EventArgs e)
{
    // File dialog to save file
    if(xmlWriteRadioButton.Checked || xmlSerializerRadioButton.Checked)
        sfd.Filter = "XML files (*.xml)|*.xml";
    else if(soapRadioButton.Checked)
        sfd.Filter = "SOAP files (*.soap)|*.soap";
    else if(binaryRadioButton.Checked)
        sfd.Filter = "Binary files (*.bin)|*.bin";

    sfd.Filter += "|All files (*.*)|*.*";
    sfd.FilterIndex = 0;

    if (sfd.ShowDialog( ) == DialogResult.OK)
        fileNameTextBox.Text = sfd.FileName;
}
```

Discussion

Serialization converts an object into a stream of data that can be transported or saved as a file. Deserialization reconstructs the original object from the file.

The most basic data serialization is done by writing the contents of the DataSet object to XML using the WriteXml( ) or GetXml( ) method. The contents are then deserialized with the ReadXml( ) method. These methods, unlike the others shown in this solution, are limited to serializing and deserializing DataSet objects and provide little control over serialization format.

The XmlSerializer class serializes and deserializes objects into XML classes. It performs *shallow* serialization: only the read-write property values of the class are serialized, not the underlying data. The XML stream generated by the XmlSerializer class is compliant with the World Wide Web Consortium (*http://www.w3.org*) XML Schema Definition (XSD) language 1.0 recommendations. The XmlSerializer object can serialize to any object that inherits from System.IO.Stream. When constructing the XmlSerializer object, you must specify the type of object that can be serialized by the instance.

You can also use the XmlSerializer class to serialize an object into a SOAP XML stream that conforms to Section 5 of the World Wide Web Consortium document "Simple Object Access Protocol (SOAP) 1.1." To do this, use the overloaded constructor that accepts the XmlTypeMapping argument. For more information, see the topic "*XmlSerializer Constructor*" in the MSDN library.

The IFormatter interface provides functionality for formatting serialized objects. The class to be serialized must be marked with the SerializableAttribute attribute; otherwise, a SerializationException will be raised. A class can implement the ISerializable interface to override the default serialization behavior.

The System.Runtime.Serialization.Formatter class provides base functionality for the serialization formatters:

System.Runtime.Serialization.Formatters.Binary
> This namespace contains the BinaryFormatter class that can serialize and deserialize objects in binary format.

System.Runtime.Serialization.Formatters.Soap
> This namespace contains the SoapFormatter classes that can serialize and deserialize objects in SOAP format.

The BinaryFormatter and SoapFormatter both perform *deep* serialization: the values in the object's variables are serialized. If the object holds references to other objects, they will be serialized as well. The NonSerializedAttribute attribute can exclude a variable from the serialization process.

Both the BinaryFormatter and SoapFormatter implement the IFormatter and IRemotingFormatter interfaces, which provide functionality for formatting serialized objects and for sending and receiving remote procedure calls (RPC), respectively. The methods for serialization and deserialization in both interfaces are called Serialize( ) and Deserialize( ). Overloaded versions determine whether the call is a remote call.

The Serialize( ) method of the IFormatter interface serializes the object to a Stream object. This includes all classes that have the base class System.IO.Stream, such as:

- System.IO.BufferedStream
- System.IO.FileStream
- System.IO.MemoryStream
- System.Net.Sockets.NetworkStream
- System.Security.Cryptography.CryptoStream

Once the serialization object has been created, serialization is accomplished by calling the Serialize( ) method of the serializing object with arguments referencing the destination stream and the object to be serialized.

The Deserialize( ) method of the IFormatter interface deserializes the specified Stream object to recreate the object graph that was previously serialized. For more information about deserializing data, see Recipe 5.5.

5.5   Deserializing Data

Problem

You have a DataSet that has been serialized and written to a file. You want to recreate the DataSet from this file.

Solution

Use the serializer object's Deserialize( ) method and cast the result as a DataSet.

The sample code loads a file stream containing a previously serialized DataSet in a specified format and deserializes it to recreate the original DataSet.

The C# code is shown in Example 5-5.

Example 5-5. File: DeserializeForm.cs

```
// Namespaces, variables, and constants
using System;
using System.Windows.Forms;
using System.IO;
using System.Data;
using System.Runtime.Serialization;
using System.Runtime.Serialization.Formatters;
using System.Runtime.Serialization.Formatters.Binary;
using System.Runtime.Serialization.Formatters.Soap;
using System.Xml.Serialization;

private OpenFileDialog ofd;
```

Example 5-5. File: DeserializeForm.cs (continued)

```csharp
// ...

private void goButton_Click(object sender, System.EventArgs e)
{
    // Create and open the stream for deserializing.
    Stream stream = null;
    try
    {
        stream = File.Open(fileNameTextBox.Text, FileMode.Open,
            FileAccess.Read);
    }
    catch(Exception ex)
    {
        MessageBox.Show(ex.Message, "Deserializing Data",
            MessageBoxButtons.OK, MessageBoxIcon.Error);
        return;
    }

    // Deserialize the DataSet from the stream.
    DataSet ds = null;
    try
    {
        if (xmlReadRadioButton.Checked)
        {
            ds = new DataSet( );
            ds.ReadXml(stream);
        }
        else if (xmlSerializerRadioButton.Checked)
        {
            XmlSerializer xs = new XmlSerializer(typeof(DataSet));
            ds = (DataSet)xs.Deserialize(stream);
        }
        else if(soapRadioButton.Checked)
        {
            SoapFormatter sf = new SoapFormatter( );
            ds = (DataSet)sf.Deserialize(stream);
        }
        else if(binaryRadioButton.Checked)
        {
            BinaryFormatter bf = new BinaryFormatter( );
            ds = (DataSet)bf.Deserialize(stream);
        }
    }
    catch (System.Exception ex)
    {
        MessageBox.Show(ex.Message, "Deserializing Data",
            MessageBoxButtons.OK, MessageBoxIcon.Error);
        return;
    }
    finally
    {
        stream.Close( );
    }
```

Example 5-5. File: DeserializeForm.cs (continued)

```csharp
    // Bind the DataSet to the grid.
    dataGrid.DataSource = ds.DefaultViewManager;

    MessageBox.Show("Deserialization complete.", "Deserializing Data",
        MessageBoxButtons.OK, MessageBoxIcon.Information);
}

private void fileDialogButton_Click(object sender, System.EventArgs e)
{
    // File dialog to save file
    if(xmlReadRadioButton.Checked || xmlSerializerRadioButton.Checked)
        ofd.Filter = "XML files (*.xml)|*.xml";
    else if(soapRadioButton.Checked)
        ofd.Filter = "SOAP files (*.soap)|*.soap";
    else if(binaryRadioButton.Checked)
        ofd.Filter = "Binary files (*.bin)|*.bin";

    ofd.Filter += "|All files (*.*)|*.*";
    ofd.FilterIndex = 0;

    if (ofd.ShowDialog() == DialogResult.OK)
        fileNameTextBox.Text = ofd.FileName;
}
```

Discussion

This sample deserializes any of the serialized DataSet objects from Recipe 5.4.

The sample allows the user to select a file and specify a serialization type. The appropriate serializing object is created and in the case of the XmlSerializer object, its type is specified in the constructor. The Deserialize( ) method of the serializer object is then used to deserialize the file stream into an object graph. This is then cast to a DataSet to complete the deserialization.

See the discussion in Recipe 5.4 for more information about the serialization and the formatter classes that can serialize ADO.NET objects.

5.6   Merging Data

Problem

You have two DataSet objects with the same schema, but containing different data. You need to combine data from these two DataSet objects without creating duplicate rows.

Solution

Use the DataSet.Merge() method with the appropriate MissingSchemaAction enumeration values.

The sample code contains four event handlers and a single method:

Form.Load
> Sets up the sample by creating two DataSet objects each with a single DataTable containing different subset of data from the Employees table in Northwind. The default view for each table is bound to a data grid on the form.

MergeA Button.Click
> The first Button.Click calls the Merge() method to merge the first DataSet into the second.

MergeB Button.Click
> A second Button.Click calls the Merge() method to merge the second DataSet into the first.

Clear Button.Click
> A third Button.Click clears the data grid displaying the results of either merge.

Merge()
> This method takes two DataTable arguments. The first DataTable is copied to a new DataTable and the second DataTable is merged into it with the specified MissingSchemaAction. The default view of the result DataTable is bound to a data grid on the form.

The C# code is shown in Example 5-6.

Example 5-6. File: MergingDataForm.cs

```
// Namespaces, variables, and constants
using System;
using System.Configuration;
using System.Windows.Forms;
using System.Data;
using System.Data.SqlClient;

private SqlDataAdapter daA, daB;
private DataSet dsA, dsB;

// ...

private void MergingDataForm_Load(object sender, System.EventArgs e)
{
    // Fill the schema and data for table A.
    String sqlText = "SELECT EmployeeID, LastName, FirstName, Title " +
        "FROM Employees WHERE EmployeeID BETWEEN 1 AND 5";
    // Set up the DataAdapter and CommandBuilder for table A.
    SqlCommandBuilder cbA = new SqlCommandBuilder(daA);
    daA = new SqlDataAdapter(sqlText,
```

Example 5-6. File: MergingDataForm.cs (continued)

```
        ConfigurationSettings.AppSettings["Sql_SqlAuth_ConnectString"]);
    // Define DataSet A and fill its table A with schema and data.
    dsA = new DataSet("A");
    daA.FillSchema(dsA, SchemaType.Source, "Employees");
    daA.Fill(dsA, "Employees");
    // Bind the default view for table A to the grid.
    dataGridA.DataSource = dsA.Tables["Employees"].DefaultView;

    // Fill the schema and data for table B.
    sqlText = "SELECT EmployeeID, LastName, FirstName, " +
        "BirthDate, HireDate " +
        "FROM Employees WHERE EmployeeID BETWEEN 4 AND 8";
    // Set up the DataAdapter and CommandBuilder for table B.
    daB = new SqlDataAdapter(sqlText,
        ConfigurationSettings.AppSettings["Sql_SqlAuth_ConnectString"]);
    SqlCommandBuilder cbB = new SqlCommandBuilder(daB);
    // Define DataSet B and fill its table B with schema and data.
    dsB = new DataSet("B");
    daB.FillSchema(dsB, SchemaType.Source, "Employees");
    daB.Fill(dsB, "Employees");
    // Bind the default view for table B to the grid.
    dataGridB.DataSource = dsB.Tables["Employees"].DefaultView;
}

private void Merge(DataTable dtSource, DataTable dtDest)
{
    // Set the missing schema value to the default and read
    // actual value, if otherwise, from the radio buttons.
    MissingSchemaAction msa = MissingSchemaAction.Add;

    if(addWithKeyRadioButton.Checked)
        msa = MissingSchemaAction.AddWithKey;
    else if(errorRadioButton.Checked)
        msa = MissingSchemaAction.Error;
    else if(ignoreRadioButton.Checked)
        msa = MissingSchemaAction.Ignore;

    // Create the merge DataSet and copy table B into it.
    DataSet ds = new DataSet("Merge");
    ds.Tables.Add(dtDest.Copy());

    try
    {
        // Merge table A into the DataSet.
        ds.Merge(dtSource, false, msa);
    }
    catch (Exception ex)
    {
        MessageBox.Show(ex.Message);
    }
```

Example 5-6. File: MergingDataForm.cs (continued)

```
    // Bind the merge result table default view to the grid.
    dataGridMerge.DataSource = ds.Tables[0].DefaultView;
    dataGridMerge.CaptionText = "Merge Results: " +
        dtSource.DataSet.DataSetName + " into " +
        dtDest.DataSet.DataSetName;
}

private void mergeAIntoBButton_Click(object sender, System.EventArgs e)
{
    Merge(dsA.Tables["Employees"], dsB.Tables["Employees"]);
}

private void mergeBIntoAButton_Click(object sender, System.EventArgs e)
{
    Merge(dsB.Tables["Employees"], dsA.Tables["Employees"]);
}

private void clearResultsButton_Click(object sender, System.EventArgs e)
{
    dataGridMerge.DataSource = null;
    dataGridMerge.CaptionText = "";
}
```

Discussion

The Merge() method of the DataSet can merge a DataRow array, a DataTable, or a DataSet into an existing DataSet. If the existing DataSet has a primary key defined, the incoming data is matched to rows having the same primary key values. Where matches are found, the existing row is updated with the new values. Otherwise, rows are appended to the existing table.

There are two arguments that can be optionally specified in the overloaded Merge() methods.

The first, preserveChanges, is a Boolean value that indicates whether incoming values will overwrite changes made to the existing DataSet. If preserveChanges is false, the default, both the Current and Original row are overwritten with incoming values and the RowState of the row is set to the RowState of the incoming row. Exceptions are shown in Table 5-2.

Table 5-2. Exceptions to PreserveChanges argument when PreserveChanges = false.

Incoming RowState	Existing RowState	New RowState
Unchanged	Modified, Deleted, or Added	Modified
Added	Unchanged, Modified, or Deleted	Modified. Also, data in the Original version of the existing row is not overwritten because the Original version of the incoming row does not exist.

If preserveChanges is specified as true, the values in the Current version of the existing row are maintained while values in the Original version of the existing row are overwritten with the Original values for the incoming row. The RowState of the existing row is set to Modified. Exceptions are shown in Table 5-3.

Table 5-3. Exceptions to PreserveChanges argument when PreserveChanges = true

Incoming RowState	Existing RowState	New RowState
Any	Deleted	Deleted
Added	Any	Modified. Data in the Original version of the row is not overwritten because the Original version of the incoming row does not exist.

The second argument is the missingSchemaAction argument, which accepts a value from the MissingSchemaAction enumeration that specifies how the Merge( ) method will handle schema elements in the incoming data that are not part of the existing DataSet. Table 5-4 describes the values in the MissingSchemaAction enumeration.

Table 5-4. MissingSchemaAction enumeration

Value	Decription
Add	Add the new schema information and populate the new schema with incoming values. This is the default value.
AddWithKey	Add the new schema and primary key information and populate the new schema with incoming values.
Error	Throw an exception if the incoming schema does not match the schema of the existing DataSet.
Ignore	Ignore new schema information.

5.7   Transmitting a DataSet Securely

Problem

You need to securely send a DataSet over a connection that is not secure.

Solution

Encrypt and decrypt the DataSet using the .NET cryptographic services, and serialize and save the encrypted DataSet to a stream (such as a file or network stream).

The sample code contains two event handlers:

Encrypt Button.Click
> The first Button.Click creates a DataSet and encrypts it using the algorithm specified by the user and writes the encrypted DataSet to a file.

Decrypt Button.Click

The second Button.Click decrypts a file containing a DataSet previously encrypted using an algorithm specified by the user and uses the file to recreate the DataSet previously encrypted.

The C# code is shown in Example 5-7.

Example 5-7. File: SecureTransmissionForm.cs

```csharp
// Namespaces, variables, and constants
using System;
using System.Configuration;
using System.Windows.Forms;
using System.Xml;
using System.IO;
using System.Runtime.Serialization;
using System.Runtime.Serialization.Formatters.Binary;
using System.Security.Cryptography;
using System.Data;
using System.Data.SqlClient;

// Table name constants
private const String ORDERS_TABLE          = "Orders";
private const String ORDERDETAILS_TABLE    = "OrderDetails";

// Relation name constants
private const String ORDERS_ORDERDETAILS_RELATION =
    "Orders_OrderDetails_Relation";

// Field name constants
private const String ORDERID_FIELD         = "OrderID";

private RSACryptoServiceProvider rSAReceiver;

private const int keySize = 128;

// DES key and IV
private Byte[] dESKey = new Byte[]
    {0x01, 0x02, 0x03, 0x04, 0x05, 0x06, 0x07, 0x08};
private Byte[] dESIV = new Byte[]
    {0x11, 0x12, 0x13, 0x14, 0x15, 0x16, 0x17, 0x18};
// RC2 key and IV
private Byte[] rC2Key = new Byte[]
    {0x00, 0x01, 0x02, 0x03, 0x04, 0x05, 0x06, 0x07,
     0x08, 0x09, 0x0A, 0x0B, 0x0C, 0x0D, 0x0E, 0x0F};
private Byte[] rC2IV = new Byte[]
    {0x10, 0x11, 0x12, 0x13, 0x14, 0x15, 0x16, 0x17,
     0x18, 0x19, 0x1A, 0x1B, 0x1C, 0x1D, 0x1E, 0x1F};
// Rijndael key and IV
private Byte[] rijndaelKey = new Byte[]
    {0x20, 0x21, 0x22, 0x23, 0x24, 0x25, 0x26, 0x27,
     0x28, 0x29, 0x2A, 0x2B, 0x2C, 0x2D, 0x2E, 0x2F};
private Byte[] rijndaelIV = new Byte[]
```

Example 5-7. File: SecureTransmissionForm.cs (continued)

```
    {0x30, 0x31, 0x32, 0x33, 0x34, 0x35, 0x36, 0x37,
     0x38, 0x39, 0x3A, 0x3B, 0x3C, 0x3D, 0x3E, 0x3F};
// triple DES key and IV
private Byte[] tDESKey = new Byte[]
    {0x00, 0x01, 0x02, 0x03, 0x04, 0x05, 0x06, 0x07,
     0x08, 0x09, 0x0A, 0x0B, 0x0C, 0x0D, 0x0E, 0x0F,
     0x10, 0x11, 0x12, 0x13, 0x14, 0x15, 0x16, 0x17};
private Byte[] tDESIV = new Byte[]
    {0x20, 0x21, 0x22, 0x23, 0x24, 0x25, 0x26, 0x27,
     0x28, 0x29, 0x2A, 0x2B, 0x2C, 0x2D, 0x2E, 0x2F,
     0x30, 0x31, 0x32, 0x33, 0x34, 0x35, 0x36, 0x37};

// ...

[Serializable()]
internal class EncryptedMessage
{
    public byte[] Body;         // RC2 encrypted
    public byte[] Key;          // RSA encrypted RC2 key
    public byte[] IV;           // RC2 initialization vector
}


private void encryptButton_Click(object sender, System.EventArgs e)
{
    DataSet ds = new DataSet();

    SqlDataAdapter da;

    // Fill the Order table and add it to the DataSet.
    da = new SqlDataAdapter("SELECT * FROM Orders",
        ConfigurationSettings.AppSettings["Sql_ConnectString"]);
    DataTable orderTable = new DataTable(ORDERS_TABLE);
    da.FillSchema(orderTable, SchemaType.Source);
    da.Fill(orderTable);
    ds.Tables.Add(orderTable);

    // Fill the OrderDetails table and add it to the DataSet.
    da = new SqlDataAdapter("SELECT * FROM [Order Details]",
        ConfigurationSettings.AppSettings["Sql_ConnectString"]);
    DataTable orderDetailTable = new DataTable(ORDERDETAILS_TABLE);
    da.FillSchema(orderDetailTable, SchemaType.Source);
    da.Fill(orderDetailTable);
    ds.Tables.Add(orderDetailTable);

    // Create a relation between the tables.
    ds.Relations.Add(ORDERS_ORDERDETAILS_RELATION,
        ds.Tables[ORDERS_TABLE].Columns[ORDERID_FIELD],
        ds.Tables[ORDERDETAILS_TABLE].Columns[ORDERID_FIELD],
        true);
```

Example 5-7. File: SecureTransmissionForm.cs (continued)

```
// Clear the grid.
dataGrid.DataSource = null;

if(rSARadioButton.Checked)
{
    // Asymmetric algorithm
    EncryptedMessage em = new EncryptedMessage( );

    // RC2 symmetric algorithm to encode the DataSet
    RC2CryptoServiceProvider rC2 = new RC2CryptoServiceProvider( );
    rC2.KeySize = keySize;
    // Generate RC2 Key and IV.
    rC2.GenerateKey( );
    rC2.GenerateIV( );

    // Get the receiver's RSA public key.
    RSACryptoServiceProvider rSA = new RSACryptoServiceProvider( );
    rSA.ImportParameters(rSAReceiver.ExportParameters(false));
    try
    {
        // Encrypt the RC2 key and IV with the receiver's RSA
        // public key.
        em.Key = rSA.Encrypt(rC2.Key, false);
        em.IV = rSA.Encrypt(rC2.IV, false);
    }
    catch(CryptographicException ex)
    {
        MessageBox.Show(ex.Message, "Securing Transmission",
            MessageBoxButtons.OK, MessageBoxIcon.Error);
        return;
    }
    Cursor.Current = Cursors.WaitCursor;

    // Use the CryptoStream to write the encrypted DataSet to the
    // MemoryStream.
    MemoryStream ms = new MemoryStream( );
    CryptoStream cs = new CryptoStream(ms, rC2.CreateEncryptor( ),
        CryptoStreamMode.Write);
    ds.WriteXml(cs, XmlWriteMode.WriteSchema);
    cs.FlushFinalBlock( );
    em.Body = ms.ToArray( );

    cs.Close( );
    ms.Close( );

    // Serialize the encrypted message to a file.
    Stream s = File.Open(System.IO.Path.GetTempPath( ) +
        @"\rsa.dat", FileMode.Create);
    BinaryFormatter bf = new BinaryFormatter( );
    bf.Serialize(s, em);
    s.Close( );
```

Example 5-7. File: SecureTransmissionForm.cs (continued)

```
        Cursor.Current = Cursors.Default;

        MessageBox.Show("Encryption complete.",
            "Securing Transmission", MessageBoxButtons.OK,
            MessageBoxIcon.Information);
    }
    else
    {
        SaveFileDialog sfd;
        sfd = new SaveFileDialog( );
        sfd.InitialDirectory = System.IO.Path.GetTempPath( );
        sfd.Filter = "All files (*.*)|*.*";
        sfd.FilterIndex = 0;

        if (sfd.ShowDialog( ) == DialogResult.OK)
        {
            FileStream fsWrite = null;
            try
            {
                fsWrite = new FileStream(sfd.FileName,
                    FileMode.Create, FileAccess.Write);
            }
            catch (Exception ex)
            {
                MessageBox.Show(ex.Message,
                    "Securing Transmission",
                    MessageBoxButtons.OK,
                    MessageBoxIcon.Error);
                return;
            }

            Cursor.Current = Cursors.WaitCursor;

            // Symmetric algorithms
            byte[] key = null;
            byte[] iV = null;
            SymmetricAlgorithm sa = null;

            if(dESRadioButton.Checked)
            {
                sa = new DESCryptoServiceProvider( );
                key = dESKey;
                iV = dESIV;
            }
            else if(rc2RadioButton.Checked)
            {
                sa = new RC2CryptoServiceProvider( );
                sa.KeySize = 128;
                key = rC2Key;
                iV = rC2IV;
            }
            else if(rijndaelRadioButton.Checked)
```

Example 5-7. File: SecureTransmissionForm.cs (continued)

```
                {
                    sa = new RijndaelManaged( );
                    key = rijndaelKey;
                    iV = rijndaelIV;
                }
                else if(tripleDESRadioButton.Checked)
                {
                    sa = new TripleDESCryptoServiceProvider( );
                    key = tDESKey;
                    iV = tDESIV;
                }

                // Encrypt the DataSet
                CryptoStream cs = null;
                try
                {
                    cs = new CryptoStream(fsWrite,
                        sa.CreateEncryptor(key, iV),
                        CryptoStreamMode.Write);

                    ds.WriteXml(cs, XmlWriteMode.WriteSchema);
                    cs.Close( );

                    MessageBox.Show("Encryption complete.",
                        "Securing Transmission",
                        MessageBoxButtons.OK,
                        MessageBoxIcon.Information);
                }
                catch (Exception ex)
                {
                    MessageBox.Show(ex.Message,
                        "Securing Transmission",
                        MessageBoxButtons.OK,
                        MessageBoxIcon.Error);
                }
                finally
                {
                    fsWrite.Close( );
                    Cursor.Current = Cursors.Default;
                }
            }
        }
}

private void decryptButton_Click(object sender, System.EventArgs e)
{
    dataGrid.DataSource = null;
    DataSet ds = new DataSet( );

    if(rSARadioButton.Checked)
    {
        // Asymmetric algorithm
```

Example 5-7. File: SecureTransmissionForm.cs (continued)

```
    // Deserialize the encrypted message from a file.
    Stream s = null;
    try
    {
        s = File.Open(System.IO.Path.GetTempPath( ) +
            @"\rsa.dat", FileMode.Open);
    }
    catch (Exception ex)
    {
        MessageBox.Show(ex.Message, "Securing Transmission",
            MessageBoxButtons.OK, MessageBoxIcon.Error);
        return;
    }
    BinaryFormatter bf = new BinaryFormatter( );
    EncryptedMessage em = (EncryptedMessage)bf.Deserialize(s);
    s.Close( );

    // RC2 symmetric algorithm to decode the DataSet
    RC2CryptoServiceProvider rC2 = new RC2CryptoServiceProvider( );
    rC2.KeySize = keySize;

    // Decrypt the RC2 key and IV using the receiver's RSA private
    // key.
    try
    {
        rC2.Key = rSAReceiver.Decrypt(em.Key, false);
        rC2.IV = rSAReceiver.Decrypt(em.IV, false);
    }
    catch (CryptographicException ex)
    {
        MessageBox.Show(ex.Message, "Securing Transmission",
            MessageBoxButtons.OK, MessageBoxIcon.Error);
        return;
    }

    Cursor.Current = Cursors.WaitCursor;

    // Put the message body into the MemoryStream.
    MemoryStream ms = new MemoryStream(em.Body);
    // Use the CryptoStream to read the encrypted DataSet from the
    // MemoryStream.
    CryptoStream cs = new CryptoStream(ms, rC2.CreateDecryptor( ),
        CryptoStreamMode.Read);
    ds.ReadXml(cs, XmlReadMode.ReadSchema);
    cs.Close( );

    dataGrid.DataSource = ds.DefaultViewManager;

    Cursor.Current = Cursors.Default;
}
else
{
```

Example 5-7. File: SecureTransmissionForm.cs (continued)

```
// Symmetric algorithm
OpenFileDialog ofd;
ofd = new OpenFileDialog( );
ofd.InitialDirectory = System.IO.Path.GetTempPath( );
ofd.Filter = "All files (*.*)|*.*";
ofd.FilterIndex = 0;

if (ofd.ShowDialog( ) == DialogResult.OK)
{
    FileStream fsRead = null;
    try
    {
        fsRead = new FileStream(ofd.FileName,
            FileMode.Open, FileAccess.Read);
    }
    catch(Exception ex)
    {
        dataGrid.DataSource = null;
        MessageBox.Show(ex.Message,
            "Securing Transmission",
            MessageBoxButtons.OK,
            MessageBoxIcon.Error);
        return;
    }

    Cursor.Current = Cursors.WaitCursor;

    SymmetricAlgorithm sa = null;
    byte[] key = null;
    byte[] iV = null;
    if(dESRadioButton.Checked)
    {
        sa = new DESCryptoServiceProvider( );
        key = dESKey;
        iV = dESIV;
    }
    else if(rc2RadioButton.Checked)
    {
        sa = new RC2CryptoServiceProvider( );
        sa.KeySize = 128;
        key = rC2Key;
        iV = rC2IV;
    }
    else if(rijndaelRadioButton.Checked)
    {
        sa = new RijndaelManaged( );
        key = rijndaelKey;
        iV = rijndaelIV;
    }
    else if(tripleDESRadioButton.Checked)
    {
        sa = new TripleDESCryptoServiceProvider( );
```

Example 5-7. File: SecureTransmissionForm.cs (continued)

```
            key = tDESKey;
            iV = tDESIV;
        }

        // Decrypt the stream into the DataSet.
        CryptoStream cs = null;
        try
        {
            cs = new CryptoStream(fsRead,
                sa.CreateDecryptor(key, iV),
                CryptoStreamMode.Read);
            ds.ReadXml(cs, XmlReadMode.ReadSchema);
            cs.Close( );

            dataGrid.DataSource = ds.DefaultViewManager;
        }
        catch(Exception ex)
        {
            dataGrid.DataSource = null;
            MessageBox.Show(ex.Message,
                "Securing Transmission",
                MessageBoxButtons.OK,
                MessageBoxIcon.Error);
        }
        finally
        {
            fsRead.Close( );
            Cursor.Current = Cursors.Default;
        }
    }
  }
}
```

Discussion

Cryptography protects data from being viewed or modified and provides security when transmitting or serializing the data in environments that are otherwise not secure. The data can be encrypted, transmitted or serialized in its encrypted state, and later decrypted. If the data is intercepted in its encrypted state, it is much more difficult to access the data because it is necessary to first decrypt it.

Encryption algorithms are of two types: symmetric key and asymmetric key. A brief overview follows.

Symmetric key algorithms use a secret key to both encrypt and decrypt the data. Because the same key is used both to encrypt and decrypt the data, it must be kept secret. Symmetric algorithms are also known as *secret key* algorithms. Symmetric key algorithms are very fast compared to asymmetric algorithms and are therefore suitable for encrypting large amounts of data. The .NET Framework classes that implement symmetric key algorithms are:

- `DESCryptoServiceProvider`
- `RC2CryptoServiceProvider`
- `RijndaelManaged`
- `TripleDESCryptoServiceProvider`

The symmetric key algorithms provided in these classes use an initialization vector (IV) in addition to the key so that an identical plaintext message produces different ciphertext when using the same key with a different IV. Good practice is to use a different IV with each encryption.

Asymmetric key algorithms use both a private key that must be kept secret and a public key that can be made available to anyone. These key pairs are used both to encrypt data (data encrypted with the public key can only be decrypted with the private key) and sign data (data signed with the private key can only be verified with the public key). The public key is used to encrypt data that is being sent to the owner of the private key while the private key is used to digitally sign data to allow the origin of communication to be verified and to ensure that those communications have not been altered. While more secure, asymmetric key algorithms are much slower than symmetric algorithms. The .NET Framework classes that implement asymmetric key algorithms are:

- `DSACryptoServiceProvider`
- `RSACryptoServiceProvider`

To overcome the performance limitations of asymmetric key algorithms with large amounts of data and still benefit from the much stronger security they provide, only a symmetric key is encrypted, which is in turn used to encrypt the data. Here's how it works: A public key is obtained from the person to whom the data is being sent. A symmetric key is generated by the sender and subsequently encrypted using the public key received from the recipient. The data is then encrypted using the symmetric key; this is much faster than using the public key. The encrypted key and data are then sent to the owner of the public/private key pair. The recipient uses the private key to decrypt the symmetric key and can then use the symmetric key to decrypt the data.

In the sample code, both the encryption and decryption use the key and IV values defined using variable initializers only as a convenience. While the same key and IV values must be used when encrypting and decrypting data, these values will normally be set according to the specific requirements of the application.

To encrypt the data, the user can choose between four symmetric algorithms (DES, RC2, Rijndael, and Triple DES) and one asymmetric algorithm (RSA).

If one of the symmetric algorithms is chosen, the user is presented with a file dialog to specify the file to which the encrypted DataSet is written. In each case, the specified cryptographic service provider is created, the key and IV are set, and a CryptoStream object is used to encrypt the XML representation of the DataSet, which is written to the specified file. To decrypt the file, a CryptoStream object is used to decrypt the contents of the file into an XML representation of the DataSet, which is subsequently used to recreate the DataSet.

If the asymmetric (RSA) algorithm is chosen, the sample generates both an RC2 (symmetric) key and an IV. The receiver RSACryptoServiceProvider object is created in the constructor and because the default constructor is used, a new public/private key pair is generated for the receiver each time the application is run. This means that for this example, an asymmetric encryption of the DataSet can only be decrypted while the form is open. Once the form is closed, reopening it will recreate the public/private key pair for the receiver. The ExportParameters() method is used to get only the public key information as an RSAParameters object from the receiver. This is imported into a new RSACryptoServiceProvider object using the ImportParameters() method. The Encrypt() method of the RSACryptoServiceProvider is then called to encrypt both the RC2 key and the IV and store them to the appropriate variables of an EncryptedMessage object, defined as an internal class. Next, the CryptoStream object is used to write the XML representation of the DataSet, encrypted using the RC2 key and IV, to a MemoryStream object, which is then stored in the *Body* variable of the EncryptedMessage object. Finally, the EncryptedMessage is serialized to a file.

The decryption of the encrypted file is just the reverse of the encryption process. The file is deserialized to an EncryptedMessage object. The Decrypt() method of the receiver RSACryptoServiceProvider object is used to decrypt the RC2 key and IV using the receiver's private key. The CryptoStream object is then used to decrypt the XML for the DataSet stored in the *Body* variable of the EncryptedMessage object. The DataSet is recreated from the XML.

Although this example demonstrates serializing the encrypted DataSet to a file, you can use the same technique to serialize the DataSet to a stream so that it can be transmitted securely in an environment that is otherwise not secure.

5.8   Transferring Login Credentials Securely

Problem

You need to protect login credentials during transmission over the network and when they are stored within a database.

Solution

Use password *hashing* and *salting* with the .NET `FormsAuthentication` class to control user authentication and access to the application.

The schema of table TBL0508 used in this solution is shown in Table 5-5.

Table 5-5. TBL0508 schema

Column name	Data type	Length	Allow nulls?
UserName	nvarchar	50	No
PasswordHash	nvarchar	50	No
PasswordSalt	nvarchar	50	No

The sample code contains two event handlers:

Create `Button.Click`

> Creates a GUID-based salt and generates a hash of the password concatenated with the salt for a user-specified password. The username, password hash, and salt are inserted into a database.

Login `Button.Click`

> Retrieves the salt and the hash of the password and salt from the database for the specified username. The user-entered password is concatenated with the retrieved salt and the hash is generated. If the hash matches the hash retrieved from the database, the user is authenticated.

The C# code is shown in Example 5-8.

Example 5-8. File: ADOCookbookCS0508.aspx.cs

```csharp
// Namespaces, variables, and constants
using System;
using System.Configuration;
using System.Web.Security;
using System.Data;
using System.Data.SqlClient;

private const String TABLENAME = "TBL0508";

// ...

private void createButton_Click(object sender, System.EventArgs e)
{
    // Create and display the password salt.
    String passwordSalt = Guid.NewGuid().ToString();
    passwordSaltLabel.Text = passwordSalt;

    // Create and display the password hash.
    String passwordHash =
        FormsAuthentication.HashPasswordForStoringInConfigFile(
```

Example 5-8. File: ADOCookbookCS0508.aspx.cs (continued)

```
        passwordTextBox.Text + passwordSalt, "md5");
    passwordHashLabel.Text = passwordHashDBLabel.Text = passwordHash;

    // Insert UserName with the password hash and salt into the database.
    String sqlText = "INSERT " + TABLENAME +
        "(UserName, PasswordHash, PasswordSalt) " +
        "VALUES ('" + userNameTextBox.Text + "', '" + passwordHash +
        "', '" + passwordSalt + "')";
    SqlConnection conn = new SqlConnection(
        ConfigurationSettings.AppSettings["DataConnectString"]);
    SqlCommand cmd = new SqlCommand(sqlText, conn);
    conn.Open( );

    try
    {
        if(cmd.ExecuteNonQuery( ) == 1)
            statusLabel.Text = "User created.";
        else
            statusLabel.Text = "Could not create user.";
    }
    catch(SqlException)
    {
        statusLabel.Text = "Could not create user.";
    }
    finally
    {
        conn.Close( );
    }
}

private void loginButton_Click(object sender, System.EventArgs e)
{
    bool isAuthenticated = false;

    // Get the password hash and salt for the user.
    String sqlText = "SELECT PasswordHash, PasswordSalt FROM " +
        TABLENAME + " WHERE UserName = '" + userNameTextBox.Text + "'";
    SqlConnection conn = new SqlConnection(
        ConfigurationSettings.AppSettings["DataConnectString"]);
    SqlCommand cmd = new SqlCommand(sqlText, conn);

    conn.Open( );
    SqlDataReader dr = cmd.ExecuteReader( );

    // Get the DataReader first row containing user's password and salt.
    if(dr.Read( ))
    {
        // Get and display password hash and salt from the DataReader.
        String passwordHashDB = passwordHashDBLabel.Text =
            dr.GetString(0);
        String passwordSalt = passwordSaltLabel.Text = dr.GetString(1);
```

Example 5-8. File: ADOCookbookCS0508.aspx.cs (continued)

```
        // Calculate password hash based on the password entered and
        // the password salt retrieved from the database.
        String passwordHash = passwordHashLabel.Text =
            FormsAuthentication.HashPasswordForStoringInConfigFile(
            passwordTextBox.Text + passwordSalt, "md5");

        // Check whether the calculated hash matches the hash retrieved
        // from the database.
        isAuthenticated = (passwordHash == passwordHashDB);
    }
    conn.Close( );

    if(isAuthenticated)
        statusLabel.Text = "Authentication succeeded.";
    else
        statusLabel.Text = "Authentication failed.";
}
```

Discussion

Persisting a user's password can be made more secure by first hashing the password. This means that an algorithm is applied to the password to generate a one-way transformation—or *hash*—of the password making it statistically infeasible to recreate the password from the hash.

A hash algorithm creates a small binary value of fixed length from a larger binary value of an arbitrary length. The hash value is a statistically unique compact representation of the original data. A hash value can be created for and transmitted together with data. The hash can be recreated at a later time and compared to the original hash to ensure that the data has not been altered. To prevent the message from being intercepted and replaced along with a new hash, the hash is encrypted using the private key of an asymmetric key algorithm. This allows the hash to be authenticated as having come from the sender. For more information about symmetric and asymmetric key algorithms, see the discussion in Recipe 5.7. The .NET Framework classes that implement hash algorithms are:

- HMACSHA1
- MACTripleDES
- MD5CryptoServiceProvider
- SHA1Managed
- SHA256Managed
- SHA384Managed
- SHA512Managed

In the sample, the user enters his password, the password is hashed, and then the combination of user ID and password hash are compared to values stored persistently such as in a database table. If the pairs match, the user is authenticated, without comparing the actual password. Because the hash algorithm is a one-way algorithm, the user's password cannot be recreated even if unauthorized access is gained to the persistent store where the user's password hash is stored.

The .NET Framework, as part of the FormsAuthentication class, provides the method HashPasswordForStoringInConfigFile( ) that can hash a password using either SHA1 or MD5 algorithms. The method is easy to call. It takes two arguments, the password and the hash algorithm, and returns a string containing the password hash.

Security is never perfect and this technique is no exception. It can be compromised by a dictionary attack where hash values for most commonly used passwords are generated. When these values are compared with the hash of the password and a match is found, the password is then known. To thwart the dictionary attack, a random string referred to as *salt* is concatenated with the original password before generating the hash value. The salt is stored together with the hash of the password and salt. This makes a dictionary attack much more difficult to perform.

This web page should be used in conjunction with forms-based authentication. Additionally, this page should be accessed securely (i.e., https to protect the plaintext password from client to server).

The most secure technique is useless if the password policy does not prevent users from choosing easy to guess passwords, or if security is compromised by users who write passwords down on notes attached to their computer monitors, for example.

5.9   Loading an ADO Recordset into a DataSet

Problem

You want to convert an ADO Recordset generated within a legacy application to a DataSet so that you can use it in a .NET application.

Solution

Use COM interop or the Fill( ) method of the OLE DB data provider DataAdapter.

You'll need a reference to the Primary Interop Assembly (PIA) for ADO provided in the file *ADODB.DLL*. Select adodb from the .NET tab in Visual Studio .NET's Add Reference Dialog.

The sample code creates an ADO Recordset for the Orders table in Northwind. The Fill( ) method of the OleDbDataAdapter is used to load the Recordset into a DataTable.

The C# code is shown in Example 5-9.

Example 5-9. File: AdoRecordsetForm.cs

```
// Namespaces, variables, and constants
using System;
using System.Data;
using System.Data.OleDb;

// ...

// Open an ADO connection.
ADODB.Connection conn = new ADODB.Connection();
conn.Open("Provider = SQLOLEDB;Data Source = (local);" +
    "Initial Catalog = northwind","sa","",0);

// Create an ADO recordset.
ADODB.Recordset rs = new ADODB.Recordset();
rs.Open("SELECT * FROM Orders", conn,
    ADODB.CursorTypeEnum.adOpenForwardOnly,
    ADODB.LockTypeEnum.adLockReadOnly, 0);

// Create and fill a dt from the ADO recordset.
DataTable dt = new DataTable("Orders");
(new OleDbDataAdapter()).Fill(dt, rs);
conn.Close();

// Bind the default view of the dt to the grid.
dataGrid.DataSource = dt.DefaultView;
```

Discussion

One of the overloads of the OLE DB .NET DataAdapter.Fill() method accepts an ADO Recordset or Record object. The COM component that returns an ADO Recordset or Record object is consumed using COM interop.

While the data can be loaded into a DataSet in this way, there is no way to reconcile the changes made to the data in the DataSet with the data source underlying the ADO object. This must be explicitly handled.

There is no FillSchema() method which allows the schema of an ADO Recordset to be retrieved into a DataSet.

5.10   Converting a DataSet to an ADO Recordset

Problem

You need to convert a DataSet to an ADO Recordset so that you can use it in a legacy application.

Solution

You must persist the DataSet to XML, transform it to ADO Recordset schema, and load it into an ADO Recordset using COM interop.

You'll need a reference to the Primary Interop Assembly (PIA) for ADO provided in the file *ADODB.DLL*. Select adodb from the .NET tab in Visual Studio .NET's Add Reference Dialog.

The sample uses one XML file:

Orders.xslt
> The XSLT stylesheet used to transform the XML document output by the DataSet into an ADO Recordset XML document.

The sample code contains one event handler and one method:

Go Button.Click
> Converts the DataSet to an ADO Recordset using the following steps:
>
> 1. A shell XML document for the ADO Recordset is created.
>
> 2. A DataReader accesses the schema information for the data to convert using the GetSchemaTable( ) method. This information is mapped to and added to the ADO Recordset XML document.
>
> 3. The DataSet is loaded with data for a single DataTable. The XML document for the DataSet is transformed and written into the ADO Recordset XML document.
>
> 4. An ADO Recordset object is created and loaded with the ADO Recordset XML document. This completes the conversion.
>
> 5. The ADO Recordset is loaded into a DataTable using the OleDbDataAdapter. The default view for the table is bound to the data grid on the form to display the results of the conversion.

GetDataTypeInfo( )
> This method maps SQL Server specific types to data type attributes for the ds and rs namespaces used to serialize an ADO Rowset.

The XSLT file is shown in Example 5-10.

Example 5-10. File: Orders.xslt

```xml
<?xml version="1.0" ?>
<xsl:stylesheet xmlns:xsl="http://www.w3.org/1999/XSL/Transform"
    xmlns:rs="urn:schemas-microsoft-com:rowset"
    xmlns:z="#RowsetSchema"
    xmlns:msxsl="urn:schemas-microsoft-com:xslt"
    xmlns:wxh="http://element14.com/wxhnamespace"
    version="1.0">
<msxsl:script language="CSharp" implements-prefix="wxh">
    <![CDATA[
```

Example 5-10. File: Orders.xslt (continued)

```
    private String GetShortTime(String longDateTime)
    {
        return longDateTime.Substring(0,19);
    }
    ]]>
</msxsl:script>

    <xsl:output method="xml" indent="yes" />
    <xsl:template match="NewDataSet">
        <rs:data>
            <xsl:apply-templates select="Orders" />
        </rs:data>
    </xsl:template>
    <xsl:template match="Orders">
        <z:row>
            <xsl:apply-templates select="@OrderID" />
            <xsl:apply-templates select="@CustomerID" />
            <xsl:apply-templates select="@EmployeeID" />
            <xsl:apply-templates select="@OrderDate" />
            <xsl:apply-templates select="@RequiredDate" />
            <xsl:apply-templates select="@ShippedDate" />
            <xsl:apply-templates select="@ShipVia" />
            <xsl:apply-templates select="@Freight" />
            <xsl:apply-templates select="@ShipName" />
            <xsl:apply-templates select="@ShipAddress" />
            <xsl:apply-templates select="@ShipCity" />
            <xsl:apply-templates select="@ShipRegion" />
            <xsl:apply-templates select="@ShipPostalCode" />
            <xsl:apply-templates select="@ShipCountry" />
        </z:row>
    </xsl:template>
    <xsl:template match="@OrderDate">
        <xsl:attribute name="OrderDate">
            <xsl:value-of select="wxh:GetShortTime(.)" />
        </xsl:attribute>
    </xsl:template>
    <xsl:template match="@RequiredDate">
        <xsl:attribute name="RequiredDate">
            <xsl:value-of select="wxh:GetShortTime(.)" />
        </xsl:attribute>
    </xsl:template>
    <xsl:template match="@ShippedDate">
        <xsl:attribute name="ShippedDate">
            <xsl:value-of select="wxh:GetShortTime(.)" />
        </xsl:attribute>
    </xsl:template>
    <xsl:template match="@*">
        <xsl:copy-of select="." />
    </xsl:template>
</xsl:stylesheet>
```

The C# code is shown in Example 5-11.

Example 5-11. File: ConvertDataSetToAdoRecordsetForm.cs

```csharp
// Namespaces, variables, and constants
using System;
using System.Configuration;
using System.Windows.Forms;
using System.IO;
using System.Text;
using System.Xml;
using System.Xml.Xsl;
using System.Data;
using System.Data.SqlClient;
using System.Data.OleDb;

private const String ADOXMLFILE =
    ConfigurationSettings.AppSettings["Temp_Directory"] + "ADO_Orders.xml";

// ...

private void goButton_Click(object sender, System.EventArgs e)
{
    Cursor.Current = Cursors.WaitCursor;

    String sqlText = "SELECT * FROM Orders";

    // Create the connection.
    SqlConnection conn = new SqlConnection(
        ConfigurationSettings.AppSettings["Sql_ConnectString"]);
    // Create the command to load all orders records.
    SqlCommand cmd = new SqlCommand(sqlText, conn);
    conn.Open( );
    // Create a DataReader from the command.
    SqlDataReader dr = cmd.ExecuteReader(
        CommandBehavior.SchemaOnly | CommandBehavior.KeyInfo);
    // Create a table of the schema for the DataReader.
    DataTable schemaTable = dr.GetSchemaTable( );

    // Create an XML document.
    XmlDocument xmlDoc = new XmlDocument( );
    // Add ADO namespace and schema definition tags to the XML document.
    String adoXml =
        "<xml xmlns:s = 'uuid:BDC6E3F0-6DA3-11d1-A2A3-00AA00C14882' " +
        "xmlns:dt = 'uuid:C2F41010-65B3-11d1-A29F-00AA00C14882' " +
        "xmlns:rs = 'urn:schemas-microsoft-com:rowset' " +
        "xmlns:z = '#RowsetSchema'>" +
        "<s:Schema id = 'RowsetSchema'>" +
        "<s:ElementType name = 'row' content = 'eltOnly'>" +
        "</s:ElementType>" +
        "</s:Schema>" +
        "</xml>";
    xmlDoc.LoadXml(adoXml);

    // Create a namespace manager for the XML document.
    XmlNamespaceManager nm = new XmlNamespaceManager(xmlDoc.NameTable);
```

Example 5-11. File: ConvertDataSetToAdoRecordsetForm.cs (continued)

```csharp
// Add ADO prefixes.
nm.AddNamespace("s", "uuid:BDC6E3F0-6DA3-11d1-A2A3-00AA00C14882");
nm.AddNamespace("dt", "uuid:C2F41010-65B3-11d1-A29F-00AA00C14882");
nm.AddNamespace("rs", "urn:schemas-microsoft-com:rowset");
nm.AddNamespace("z", "#RowsetSchema");

// Select the s:ElementType node.
XmlNode curNode = xmlDoc.SelectSingleNode("//s:ElementType", nm);

XmlElement xe = null;
XmlAttribute xa = null;
// Iterate through the schema records for the DataReader.
foreach(DataRow sr in schemaTable.Rows)
{
    // Create an 'AttributeType' element for the schema record.
    xe = xmlDoc.CreateElement("s", "AttributeType",
        "uuid:BDC6E3F0-6DA3-11d1-A2A3-00AA00C14882");

    // Get the data type.
    SqlDbType sqlDbType = (SqlDbType)sr["ProviderType"];

    // Create the 'name' attribute.
    xa = xmlDoc.CreateAttribute("", "name", "");
    xa.Value = sr["ColumnName"].ToString();
    xe.SetAttributeNode(xa);

    // Create the 'number' attribute.
    xa = xmlDoc.CreateAttribute("rs", "number",
        "urn:schemas-microsoft-com:rowset");
    xa.Value = ((int)sr["ColumnOrdinal"] + 1).ToString();
    xe.SetAttributeNode(xa);

    // Add attribute if null values are allowed in the column.
    if((bool)sr["AllowDBNull"])
    {
        xa = xmlDoc.CreateAttribute("rs", "nullable",
            "urn:schemas-microsoft-com:rowset");
        xa.Value = sr["AllowDBNull"].ToString().ToLower();
        xe.SetAttributeNode(xa);
    }

    // Add 'writeunknown' attribute.
    xa = xmlDoc.CreateAttribute("rs", "writeunknown",
        "urn:schemas-microsoft-com:rowset");
    xa.Value = "true";
    xe.SetAttributeNode(xa);

    // Create a 'datatype' element for the column within the
    // 'AttributeType'.
    XmlElement dataele = xmlDoc.CreateElement("s", "datatype",
        "uuid:BDC6E3F0-6DA3-11d1-A2A3-00AA00C14882");
```

Example 5-11. File: ConvertDataSetToAdoRecordsetForm.cs (continued)

```csharp
String typeName, dbTypeName;
GetDataTypeInfo(sqlDbType, out typeName, out dbTypeName);

// Add a 'type' attribute specifying the data type.
xa = xmlDoc.CreateAttribute("dt", "type",
    "uuid:C2F41010-65B3-11d1-A29F-00AA00C14882");
xa.Value = typeName;
dataele.SetAttributeNode(xa);

// Add a 'dbtype' attribute, if necessary.
if (dbTypeName != "")
{
    xa = xmlDoc.CreateAttribute("rs", "dbtype",
        "urn:schemas-microsoft-com:rowset");
    xa.Value = dbTypeName;
    dataele.SetAttributeNode(xa);
}

// Add the 'maxlength' attribute.
xa = xmlDoc.CreateAttribute("dt", "maxLength",
    "uuid:C2F41010-65B3-11d1-A29F-00AA00C14882");
xa.Value = sr["ColumnSize"].ToString();
dataele.SetAttributeNode(xa);

// Add 'scale' and 'precision' attributes, if appropriate.
if(sr["DataType"].ToString() != "System.String")
{
    if(Convert.ToByte(sr["NumericScale"]) != 255)
    {
        xa = xmlDoc.CreateAttribute("rs", "scale",
            "urn:schemas-microsoft-com:rowset");
        xa.Value = sr["NumericScale"].ToString();
        dataele.SetAttributeNode(xa);
    }

    xa = xmlDoc.CreateAttribute("rs", "precision",
        "urn:schemas-microsoft-com:rowset");
    xa.Value = sr["NumericPrecision"].ToString();
    dataele.SetAttributeNode(xa);
}

// Add a 'fixedlength' attribute, if appropriate.
if (sqlDbType != SqlDbType.VarChar &&
    sqlDbType != SqlDbType.NVarChar)
{
    xa = xmlDoc.CreateAttribute("rs", "fixedlength",
        "urn:schemas-microsoft-com:rowset");
    xa.Value = "true";
    dataele.SetAttributeNode(xa);
}
```

Example 5-11. File: ConvertDataSetToAdoRecordsetForm.cs (continued)

```csharp
        // Add a 'maybe' null attribute, if appropriate.
        if(!(bool)sr["AllowDBNull"])
        {
            xa = xmlDoc.CreateAttribute("rs", "maybenull",
                "urn:schemas-microsoft-com:rowset");
            xa.Value = sr["AllowDBNull"].ToString().ToLower( );
            dataele.SetAttributeNode(xa);
        }

        // Add the 'datatype' element to the 'AttributeType'.
        xe.AppendChild(dataele);

        // Add the 'AttributeType' element to the 'ElementType'
        // attribute.
        curNode.AppendChild(xe);
    }
    // Add the 'extends' element with attribute 'type" of 'rs:rowbase'.
    xe = xmlDoc.CreateElement("s", "extends",
        "uuid:BDC6E3F0-6DA3-11d1-A2A3-00AA00C14882");
    xa = xmlDoc.CreateAttribute("", "type", "");
    xa.Value = "rs:rowbase";
    xe.SetAttributeNode(xa);
    curNode.AppendChild(xe);

    // Close the reader and connection.
    dr.Close( );
    conn.Close( );

    // Load the Orders data into a table in a DataSet.
    DataSet ds = new DataSet( );
    SqlDataAdapter da = new SqlDataAdapter(sqlText,
        ConfigurationSettings.AppSettings["Sql_ConnectString"]);
    da.Fill(ds, "Orders");

    // Write the column data as attributes.
    foreach(DataColumn dc in ds.Tables["Orders"].Columns)
        dc.ColumnMapping = MappingType.Attribute;
    // Write the DataSet to an XML document.
    XmlDataDocument ordersXml = new XmlDataDocument(ds);

    // Load the XML transformation.
    XslTransform xslt = new XslTransform( );
    xslt.Load(ConfigurationSettings.AppSettings["Project_Directory"] +
        @"Chapter 05\Orders.xslt");

    // Transform the XML document.
    XmlReader xr = xslt.Transform(ordersXml, null, (XmlResolver)null);

    // Load the transformed document into an XML document.
    XmlDocument resultXmlDoc = new XmlDocument( );
    resultXmlDoc.Load(xr);
    xr.Close( );
```

Example 5-11. File: ConvertDataSetToAdoRecordsetForm.cs (continued)

```
    StringBuilder sb = new StringBuilder(xmlDoc.OuterXml);
    // Insert the data before the closing </xml> tag.
    sb.Insert(sb.Length - 6, resultXmlDoc.InnerXml.Remove(8,
        resultXmlDoc.InnerXml.IndexOf(">") - 8));
    // Make the <z:row> elements self closing
    // (ADO import doesn't work otherwise).
    sb.Replace("></z:row>","/>");

    // Write the order data to a file as ADO XML format.
    StreamWriter sw = new StreamWriter(ADOXMLFILE);
    sw.Write(sb.ToString());
    sw.Close();

    // Create and open an ADO connection.
    ADODB.Connection adoConn = new ADODB.Connection();
    adoConn.Open("Provider = SQLOLEDB;Data Source=(local);" +
        "Initial Catalog=northwind", "sa", "", 0);

    // Create the ADO recordset.
    ADODB.Recordset rs = new ADODB.Recordset();
    try
    {
        // Load the XML into the ADO recordset.
        rs.Open(ADOXMLFILE,
            adoConn,
            ADODB.CursorTypeEnum.adOpenStatic,
            ADODB.LockTypeEnum.adLockBatchOptimistic,
            (int)ADODB.CommandTypeEnum.adCmdFile);
    }
    catch (System.Exception ex)
    {
        MessageBox.Show(ex.Message);
        adoConn.Close();

        Cursor.Current = Cursors.Default;

        return;
    }

    try
    {
        // Load the ADO recordset into a DataTable.
        OleDbDataAdapter oleDa = new OleDbDataAdapter();
        DataTable dt = new DataTable("Orders");
        oleDa.Fill(dt, rs);

        // Bind the default view of the table to the grid.
        dataGrid.DataSource = dt.DefaultView;
    }
    catch(Exception ex)
    {
        MessageBox.Show(ex.Message);
```

Example 5-11. File: ConvertDataSetToAdoRecordsetForm.cs (continued)

```
        }
        finally
        {
            adoConn.Close( );
            Cursor.Current = Cursors.Default;
        }

        dataGrid.CaptionText = "ADO Recordset Serialized as an XML document";
    }

    private void GetDataTypeInfo(SqlDbType sqlDbType, out String type,
        out String dbtype)
    {
        type = "";
        dbtype = "";

        // Convert the SqlDbType to type attributes in the dt and rs namespaces.
        switch(sqlDbType)
        {
            case SqlDbType.BigInt:
                type = "i8";
                break;
            case SqlDbType.Binary:
                type = "bin.hex";
                break;
            case SqlDbType.Bit:
                type = "Boolean";
                break;
            case SqlDbType.Char:
                type = "string";
                dbtype = "str";
                break;
            case SqlDbType.DateTime:
                type = "dateTime";
                dbtype = "variantdate";
                break;
            case SqlDbType.Decimal:
                type = "number";
                dbtype = "decimal";
                break;
            case SqlDbType.Float:
                type = "float";
                break;
            case SqlDbType.Image:
                type = "bin.hex";
                break;
            case SqlDbType.Int:
                type = "int";
                break;
            case SqlDbType.Money:
                type = "i8";
                dbtype = "currency";
```

Example 5-11. File: ConvertDataSetToAdoRecordsetForm.cs (continued)

```
            break;
        case SqlDbType.NChar:
            type = "string";
            break;
        case SqlDbType.NText:
            type = "string";
            break;
        case SqlDbType.NVarChar:
            type = "string";
            break;
        case SqlDbType.Real:
            type = "r4";
            break;
        case SqlDbType.SmallDateTime:
            type = "dateTime";
            break;
        case SqlDbType.SmallInt:
            type = "i2";
            break;
        case SqlDbType.SmallMoney:
            type = "i4";
            dbtype = "currency";
            break;
        case SqlDbType.Text:
            type = "string";
            dbtype = "str";
            break;
        case SqlDbType.Timestamp:
            type = "dateTime";
            dbtype = "timestamp";
            break;
        case SqlDbType.TinyInt:
            type = "i1";
            break;
        case SqlDbType.UniqueIdentifier:
            type = "uuid";
            break;
        case SqlDbType.VarBinary:
            type = "bin.hex";
            break;
        case SqlDbType.VarChar:
            type = "string";
            dbtype = "str";
            break;
        case SqlDbType.Variant:
            type = "string";
            break;
    }
}
```

Discussion

ADO uses UTF-8 encoding when it persists data as an XML stream. The XML persistence format used by ADO has four namespaces as described in Table 5-6.

Table 5-6. Namespaces for a serialized Rowset

Namespace URI	Prefix	Description
urn:schemas-microsoft-com: rowset	rs	OLE DB Persistence Provider Rowset, which are the elements and attributes specific to ADO Recordset properties and attributes
uuid:BDC6E3F0-6DA3-11d1-A2A3-00AA00C14882	s	XML Data Reduced, which is the XML-Data namespace that contains elements and attributes defining the schema of the current ADO Recordset
uuid:C2F41010-65B3-11d1-A29F-00AA00C14882	dt	XML Data Reduced (XDR) Datatypes, which are the data type definition specification
#RowsetSchema	z	Contains the actual data for the RecordSet using the schema defined by the s namespace

The ADO XML format has three parts: the namespace declarations, followed by the schema section and the data section. The schema section is required and contains detailed metadata about each column in the table. The data section contains an element for each row. Column data is stored as attribute-value pairs according to the schema section definitions. For an empty row set, the data section can be empty, but the <rs:data> tags must be present.

Use the dt:type attribute to specify a data type for a column. The data type can be specified directly on the column definition or on the s:datatype nested element of the column definition. ADO adopts the latter approach. If the dt:type attribute is omitted from the column definition, the column type will default to a variable length string.

The sample converts the Orders table from the Northwind sample database to an ADO Recordset. The solution begins by getting a DataTable containing the schema for the Orders table using the GetSchemaTable( ) method of the DataReader. As mentioned earlier, the ADO XML format has three sections, and this schema information will be used to define the schema section.

The sample defines the shell of the ADO XML document for the Orders table containing the namespace declarations and the nested row elements that will contain the column definition elements.

The code then iterates over the rows in the schema table and adds a child s:AttributeType column element to the s:ElementType row element. The name of the column, as well as properties shown in Table 5-7, are defined as attributes of this column, while an s: datatype nested element is created with attributes specifying the data type properties described in Table 5-8.

Table 5-7. Attributes for s:AttributeType element

Attribute	Description
Name	Column name
rs:name	Column name in the Recordset. This value defaults to the value for the name attribute. This only need to be explicitly specified if a name other than the Recordset column name is used for the value of the name attribute.
rs:number	Column ordinal.
rs:nullable	Indicates whether the column can contain a null value.
rs:writeunknown	Indicates whether a value can be written to the column.

Table 5-8. Attributes for s:datatype Element

Attribute	Description
dt:type	XML column data type
rs:dbtype	Database column data type
dt:maxLength	The maximum length of the column
rs:scale	The numeric scale of the column
rs:precision	The precision of the column
rs:fixedlength	Indicates whether the column has a fixed length
rs:maybenull	Indicates whether the column can contain a null value

Having defined the schema inline, the solution loads the Orders table into a DataSet. The MappingType is set so that the column values are written as attributes rather than nested elements. The DataSet is then serialized to an XmlDataDocument object. The XML transformation *Orders.xslt* (see Example 5-11) is then applied to the XML document and the results are output to an XmlReader. The style sheet transforms the XML format for the data in the DataSet to the format required for the ADO XML data section. The namespace declarations are removed from the <rs:data> element and the document is inserted into the ADO XML document for the Orders table, immediately before the closing </xml> tag as the data section. Finally, the </z:row> closing tags for the <z:row> elements are removed and the <z:row> elements are made self closing, since the ADO import only imports the first row, otherwise. The ADO XML document for the Orders table is saved to the file *ADO_Orders.xml* shown in Example 5-12.

Example 5-12. File: ADO_Orders.xml

```
<xml xmlns:s="uuid:BDC6E3F0-6DA3-11d1-A2A3-00AA00C14882"
    xmlns:dt="uuid:C2F41010-65B3-11d1-A29F-00AA00C14882"
    xmlns:rs="urn:schemas-microsoft-com:rowset" xmlns:z="#RowsetSchema">
    <s:Schema id="RowsetSchema">
        <s:ElementType name="row" content="eltOnly">
            <s:AttributeType name="OrderID" rs:number="1"
                rs:writeunknown="true">
                <s:datatype dt:type="int" dt:maxLength="4"
```

Example 5-12. File: ADO_Orders.xml (continued)

```
                        rs:precision="10" rs:fixedlength="true"
                        rs:maybenull="false" />
                </s:AttributeType>
            <s:AttributeType name="CustomerID" rs:number="2"
                rs:nullable="true" rs:writeunknown="true">
                <s:datatype dt:type="string" dt:maxLength="5"
                    rs:fixedlength="true" />
            </s:AttributeType>
            <s:AttributeType name="EmployeeID" rs:number="3"
                rs:nullable="true" rs:writeunknown="true">
                <s:datatype dt:type="int" dt:maxLength="4"
                    rs:precision="10" rs:fixedlength="true" />
            </s:AttributeType>

<!-- ... -->

            <s:AttributeType name="ShipCountry" rs:number="14"
                rs:nullable="true" rs:writeunknown="true">
                <s:datatype dt:type="string" dt:maxLength="15" />
            </s:AttributeType>
            <s:extends type="rs:rowbase" />
        </s:ElementType>
    </s:Schema>
    <rs:data>
        <z:row OrderID="10248" CustomerID="VINET" EmployeeID="5"
            OrderDate="1996-07-04T00:00:00"
            RequiredDate="1996-08-01T00:00:00"
            ShippedDate="1996-07-16T00:00:00" ShipVia="3"
            Freight="32.38" ShipName="Vins et alcools Chevalier"
            ShipAddress="59 rue de l'Abbaye" ShipCity="Reims"
            ShipPostalCode="51100" ShipCountry="France" />

<!-- ... -->

        <z:row OrderID="11077" CustomerID="RATTC" EmployeeID="1"
            OrderDate="1998-05-06T00:00:00"
            RequiredDate="1998-06-03T00:00:00" ShipVia="2"
            Freight="8.53" ShipName="Rattlesnake Canyon Grocery"
            ShipAddress="2817 Milton Dr." ShipCity="Albuquerque"
            ShipRegion="NM" ShipPostalCode="87110"
            ShipCountry="USA" />
    </rs:data>
</xml>
```

Finally, the XML file is loaded into an ADO Recordset object.

5.11 Exporting the Results of a Query as a String

Problem

You need to export the results of a query to a string in a manner similar to the GetString( ) method of the ADO Recordset.

Solution

Write a routine to mimic the functionality of the ADO Recordset's GetString( ) method.

The sample code contains an event handler and a method:

Go Button.Click

Sets up the sample by creating a DataTable containing the Orders table from Northwind. The GetString( ) method in this solution is called to convert the DataTable into a string similar to one that is generated by the GetString( ) method of the ADO Recordset. The string is displayed in a text box on the form.

GetString( )

This method mimics the functionality of the GetString( ) method of the ADO Recordset. The method iterates over the collection of rows and columns in the table appending the field values to a string. Null values are replaced as specified and column and row delimiters are applied.

The C# code is shown in Example 5-13.

Example 5-13. File: AdoGetStringForm.cs

```
// Namespaces, variables, and constants
using System;
using System.Configuration;
using System.Text;
using System.Data;
using System.Data.SqlClient;

// Table name constants
private const String ORDERS_TABLE = "Orders";

// ...

private void goButton_Click(object sender, System.EventArgs e)
{
    // Fill the Order table.
    SqlDataAdapter da = new SqlDataAdapter("SELECT * FROM Orders",
        ConfigurationSettings.AppSettings["Sql_ConnectString"]);
    DataTable dt = new DataTable(ORDERS_TABLE);
    da.Fill(dt);
```

Example 5-13. File: AdoGetStringForm.cs (continued)

```csharp
    // Call method to convert the DataTable to a string.
    resultTextBox.Text = GetString(dt, -1, null, null, null);
}

private String GetString(DataTable dt, int numRows,
    String columnDelimiter, String rowDelimiter, String nullExpr)
{
    if(numRows < 0)
        // Negative number of rows returns all rows
        numRows = dt.Rows.Count;
    else
        // Set number of rows to the lesser of the user entered
        // number of rows and the number of rows in the table.
        numRows = Math.Max(numRows, dt.Rows.Count);

    // Column delimiter defaults to TAB
    if(columnDelimiter == null)
        columnDelimiter = "\t";

    // Row delimiter defaults to CARRIAGE RETURN
    if(rowDelimiter == null)
        rowDelimiter = "\r";

    // Null expression defaults to empty string
    if(nullExpr == null)
        nullExpr = "";

    StringBuilder sb = new StringBuilder();

    // Iterate over the collection of rows.
    for(int i = 0; i < numRows; i++)
    {
        // Iterate over the collection of columns.
        foreach (object col in dt.Rows[i].ItemArray)
        {
            // Replace null values as they occur.
            String colString = (col == System.DBNull.Value) ?
                nullExpr : col.ToString();

            // Add the column value to the string.
            sb.Append(colString + columnDelimiter);
        }
        // Remove the column delimiter on last field.
        sb.Remove(sb.Length - columnDelimiter.Length,
            columnDelimiter.Length);
        // Append row delimiter.
        sb.Append(rowDelimiter);
    }

    return sb.ToString();
}
```

Discussion

ADO.NET does not contain a method that is equivalent to the GetString( ) method of the ADO Recordset or a method that converts the Recordset to a string.

This solution presents an ADO.NET method, which is also called GetString( ), that duplicates the functionality of the ADO GetString( ) method. The prototype for the ADO.NET method is:

```
String tableString = GetString(DataTable dt, Integer numRows, String columnDelimiter,
    String rowDelimiter, String nullExpr);
```

Parameters

tableString
> Returns a string corresponding to the rows selected from the table.

dt
> The DataTable to convert to a string.

numRows
> The number of rows in the table to convert. If this number is negative, all rows in the table are converted. If a number larger than the number of records in the table is specified, all records are converted without error.

columnDelimiter
> The character or characters that separate columns. The default value is the TAB character.

rowDelimiter
> The character or characters that separate rows. The default value is the CAR-RIAGE RETURN character.

nullExpr
> A string that is substituted for null column values in the table. The default value is an empty string.

5.12   Exporting the Results of a Query to an Array

Problem

You need to export the results of a query to an array in a manner similar to the GetRows( ) method of the ADO Recordset.

Solution

Write a routine to mimic the functionality of the ADO Recordset's GetRows( ) method.

The sample code contains an event handler and a method:

Go `Button.Click`

> Sets up the sample by creating a `DataTable` containing the Orders table from Northwind. The `GetRows()` method in this solution is called to convert the `DataTable` into an array similar to one that is generated by the `GetRows()` method of the ADO Recordset. The contents of the array are displayed to a text box on the form.

`GetRows()`

> This method mimics the functionality of the `GetRows()` method of the ADO Recordset. First, an object array is created to hold the rows and columns in the table. The number of columns in the array is set to hold either all of the columns in the table or the subset of columns defined by the optional string array of column names. The number of rows in the table is set to hold either all of the rows in the table or the subset defined by the optional start row and row count arguments. The method then iterates over the collection of rows and columns in the table and sets the values in the array to the field values.

The C# code is shown in Example 5-14.

Example 5-14. File: AdoGetRowsForm.cs

```csharp
// Namespaces, variables, and constants
using System;
using System.Configuration;
using System.Text;
using System.Data;
using System.Data.SqlClient;

// Table name constants
private const String ORDERS_TABLE = "Orders";

// ...

private void goButton_Click(object sender, System.EventArgs e)
{
    // Fill the Order table.
    SqlDataAdapter da = new SqlDataAdapter("SELECT * FROM Orders",
        ConfigurationSettings.AppSettings["Sql_ConnectString"]);
    DataTable dt = new DataTable(ORDERS_TABLE);
    da.Fill(dt);

    StringBuilder sb = new StringBuilder();

    Array a = GetRows(dt, -1, -1, null);

    // Iterate over the rows of the array.
    for(int iRow = 0; iRow < a.GetLength(0); iRow++)
    {
```

Example 5-14. File: AdoGetRowsForm.cs (continued)

```
        // Iterate over the columns of the array.
        for(int iCol = 0; iCol < a.GetLength(1); iCol++)
        {
            sb.Append(a.GetValue(iRow, iCol).ToString() + "\t");
        }
        sb.Remove(sb.Length - 2, 2);
        sb.Append(Environment.NewLine);
    }

    resultTextBox.Text = sb.ToString();
}

private Array GetRows(DataTable dt, int rowCount, int startRow,
    String[] colName)
{
    // If column names are specified, ensure that they exist in the table.
    if (colName != null)
    {
        for (int i = 0;   i < colName.Length; i++)
        {
            if (!dt.Columns.Contains(colName[i]))
                throw(new ArgumentException("The column " +
                    colName[i] +
                    " does not exist in the table."));
        }
    }

    // If no columns were specified, set the number of columns to the
    // number of columns in the table; otherwise, set the number of
    // columns to the number of items in the specified columns array.
    int nCols = (colName == null) ? dt.Columns.Count : colName.Length;

    // The table row to start exporting
    // Set to 1 if less than 1 is specified.
    startRow = (startRow < 1) ? 1 : startRow;

    // The number of rows to export calculated as the number of rows in
    // the table less the starting row number
    // If the starting row is specified as greater than the number of
    // rows in the table, set the number of rows to 0.
    int nRows = Math.Max((dt.Rows.Count - startRow) + 1, 0);
    // If the number of rows to export is specified as greater than 0,
    // set the number of rows to export as the lesser of the number
    // specified and the number of rows calculated in the table
    // starting with the specified row.
    if (rowCount >= 0)
        nRows = Math.Min(nRows, rowCount);

    // Create an object array to hold the data in the table.
    Array a = Array.CreateInstance(typeof(object), nRows, nCols);
```

Example 5-14. File: AdoGetRowsForm.cs (continued)

```
    // Iterate over the collection of rows in the table.
    for(int iRow = startRow - 1; iRow < startRow - 1 + nRows; iRow++)
    {
        if (colName == null)
        {
            // Iterate over the collection of columns in the table.
            for(int iCol = 0; iCol < dt.Columns.Count; iCol++)
            {
                // Set the cell in the array.
                a.SetValue(dt.Rows[iRow][iCol], iRow, iCol);
            }
        }
        else
        {
            for(int i = 0; i < colName.Length; i++)
            {
                // Set the cell in the array.
                a.SetValue(dt.Rows[iRow][colName[i]],
                    iRow - startRow + 1, i);
            }
        }
    }

    return a;
}
```

Discussion

There is no ADO.NET DataTable method that works like the GetRows( ) method of the ADO Recordset or method that converts the Recordset into a two-dimensional array.

This solution presents an ADO.NET method, which is also called GetRows( ), that duplicates the functionality of the ADO GetRows( ) method. The prototype for the ADO.NET method is:

```
Object[][] tableArray = GetRows(DataTable dt, Integer rowCount, Integer startRow,
    String[] colName);
```

Parameters

tableArray

Returns an array of field values corresponding to the values in the columns and rows selected from the table.

dt

The DataTable to convert to the array.

rowCount

The number of rows to export to the array.

startRow

> The row number of the first row to export.

fields

> A string array containing the names of the columns to export. If this parameter is null, all columns are exported.

Unlike the ADO method, columns cannot be specified by their ordinal values. An overloaded GetRows( ) method that accepts the column ordinals rather than names could be written to do this.

CHAPTER 6

Maintaining Database Integrity

6.0 Introduction

Transactions allow a system to maintain integrity when interacting with multiple data sources. If an update to one data source fails, all changes are rolled back to a known good state. This chapter focuses on using transactions from ADO.NET, maintaining database integrity, and resolving conflicts and concurrency problems.

.NET supports both manual and automatic transactions. Manual transactions are supported through ADO.NET classes and the transactional capabilities of the data source. The Microsoft Distributed Transaction Coordinator (DTC) manages automatic transactions.

In a manual transaction, a transaction object is associated with a connection to a data source. Multiple commands against the data source can be associated with the transaction, grouping the commands together as a single transaction. Manual transactions can also be controlled using SQL commands in a stored procedure. Manual transactions are significantly faster than automatic transactions because they do not require interprocess communication (IPC) with the DTC. Manual transactions are limited to performing transactions against a single data source.

Automatic transactions are easier to program, can span multiple data sources, and can use multiple resource managers. They are significantly slower than manual transactions.

Concurrency problems occur when multiple users attempt to modify unlocked data. Possible problems include lost updates, dirty reads, nonrepeatable reads, and phantom reads. Isolation levels specify transaction locking behavior. Locking data ensures database consistency by controlling how changes made to data within an uncommitted transaction can be used by concurrent transactions. Higher isolation levels increase data accuracy at the expense of data availability. Recipe 6.12 shows how to use transaction isolation levels. Recipe 6.13 shows how to simulate pessimistic concurrency without database locks. Recipe 6.14 shows how to use pessimistic concurrency implemented using SQL Server database locks.

Even in well designed applications, concurrency violations often occur by design. The ADO.NET DataAdapter raises events that can be handled programmatically to resolve concurrency violations as required by application requirements. Recipe 6.10 shows how to use a timestamp to check for concurrency violations, while Recipe 6.11 shows how to resolve concurrency violations with DataAdapter event handlers.

A DataSet can contain both foreign key and unique constraints as well as relationships between tables to define and maintain data and referential integrity. The order in which DataRow changes from a DataSet containing hierarchical data are updated back to the data source is important to avoid referential integrity errors during the update process. ADO.NET allows data changes of a certain type—inserts, deletes, and updates—to be identified so that they can be processed separately as required. Recipe 6.6 shows how to update a DataSet containing hierarchical data back to the data source.

6.1   Creating a Class That Participates in an Automatic Transaction

Problem

You need to create a .NET class that participates in automatic transactions.

Solution

Use the appropriate custom attributes from the System.EnterpriseServices namespace.

The sample contains a component that participates in automatic transactions. The component has a single method, TranTest( ), that instructs the transaction to succeed or fail based on an argument *success*.

The sample also contains code that instantiates the component that participates in the automatic transaction. A checkbox on the form is used to specify the *success* parameter when the TranTest( ) method is called.

The C# code is shown in Examples 6-1 and 6-2.

Example 6-1. ServicedComponentCS Project File: SC0601.cs

```
// Namespaces, variables, and constants
using System.EnterpriseServices;
using System.Runtime.CompilerServices;
using System.Reflection;
```

Example 6-1. ServicedComponentCS Project File: SC0601.cs (continued)

```
// ...

namespace AdoDotNetCookbookCS.ServicedComponentCS
{
    [Transaction(TransactionOption.Required)]
    public class SC0601 : ServicedComponent
    {
        [AutoComplete]
        public void TranTest(bool success)
        {
            // ... Do some work.

            if(success)
            {
                // don't need the next line since AutoComplete
                // ContextUtil.SetComplete( );
            }
            else
            {
                // Vote to abort.
                ContextUtil.SetAbort( );
                // Raise an exception.
                throw new System.Exception(
                    "Error in Serviced Component 0601. " +
                    "Transaction aborted.");
            }
        }
    }
}
```

Example 6-2. File: AutoTransactionForm.cs

```
// Namespaces, variables, and constants
using System;
using System.Windows.Forms;

using AdoDotNetCookbookCS.ServicedComponentCS;

// ...

SC0601 sc = new SC0601( );

try
{
    sc.TranTest(transactionSucceedCheckBox.Checked);
    MessageBox.Show("Transaction successful.", "Automatic Transactions",
        MessageBoxButtons.OK, MessageBoxIcon.Information);
}
catch(Exception ex)
```

Example 6-2. File: AutoTransactionForm.cs (continued)

```
{
    MessageBox.Show(ex.Message, "Automatic Transactions",
        MessageBoxButtons.OK, MessageBoxIcon.Error);
}
```

Discussion

The .NET Common Language Runtime (CLR) supports both manual and automatic transaction models. The automatic distributed transaction model supported by the .NET CLR is the same as that supported by Microsoft Transaction Server (MTS) and COM+. The .NET Framework provides support for transactional components through the EnterpriseServices namespace that provides .NET objects with access to COM+ services.

There are two key benefits to automatic transactions:

* They support distributed transactions that span multiple remote databases and multiple resource managers.

* Objects participating in automatic transactions do not need to anticipate how they might be used within a transaction. A client can perform different tasks with multiple objects, all in the context of a single transaction, without the participating objects being aware of the transaction.

The main drawback is:

* Additional overhead because of the interaction with the Distributed Transaction Coordinator (DTC) and the resulting reduction in performance.

During the lifetime of an automatic transaction, the objects participating in it can vote to either commit the transaction they are participating in by calling the static SetComplete( ) method of the ContextUtil class or to abort the transaction by calling the static SetAbort( ) method of the ContextUtil class. In the absence of an explicit vote, the default is to commit the transaction. The transaction is committed once it completes if none of the participating objects have voted to abort.

Alternatively, you can apply the AutoCompleteAttribute attribute to a transactional method. This attribute instructs .NET to vote to commit the transaction, provided no exceptions are encountered in the method. If an unhandled exception is thrown, the transaction is automatically rolled back.

The .NET Framework classes must be prepared before they can participate in an automatic transaction. Once an object is marked to participate in a transaction, it will automatically execute within a transaction. The object's transactional behavior is controlled by the value of the transaction attribute for the .NET class, ASP.NET page, or XML web service method using the object. This allows the instantiated object to be configured programmatically to participate automatically in an existing transaction, to start a new transaction, or to not participate in a transaction. The following steps prepare a class to participate in an automatic transaction:

1. Derive the class from the ServicedComponent class in the System.EnterprisesServices namespace.

2. Apply the declarative TransactionAttribute to the class and specify the transaction behavior, timeout, and isolation level. This is a value from the TransactionOption enumeration described in Table 6-1.

Table 6-1. TransactionOption Enumeration

Value	Description
Disabled	Automatic transactions do not control the object:
	[Transaction(TransactionOption.Disabled)]
NotSupported	The object does not run in the scope of transactions:
	[Transaction(TransactionOption.NotSupported)]
Supported	The object runs in context of an existing transaction, if one exists. The object runs without a transaction if one does not exist.
	[Transaction(TransactionOption.Supported)]
Required	The object requires a transaction and runs in context of an existing transaction, if one exists. The object starts a transaction if one does not exist.
	[Transaction(TransactionOption.Required)]
RequiresNew	The object requires a transaction. A new transaction is started for each request.
	[Transaction(TransactionOption.RequiresNew)]

3. Optionally annotate methods with the AutoComplete attribute so that the methods do not have to explicitly vote for a transaction outcome.

4. Sign the assembly with a strong name. Use the *sn.exe* utility to create a key pair using the following syntax:

```
sn -k MyApp.snk
```

Add the AssemblyKeyFileAttribute or AssemblyKeyNameAttribute assembly attribute to specify the file containing the key pair. The following code is used in the solution to sign the assembly:

```
[assembly: AssemblyDelaySign(false)]
[assembly: AssemblyKeyFile(
    @"C:\ADOCookbookCS\ServicedComponentCS\" +
"AdoDotNetCookbookCSServicedComponent.snk")]
[assembly: AssemblyKeyName("AdoDotNetCookbookCSServicedComponent")]
```

5. Register the assembly containing the class with the COM+ catalog by executing the *.NET Services Registration Tool* (*regsvcs.exe*) with the following syntax:

```
regsvcs /appname:MyApp MyAssembly.dll
```

This step isn't strictly required. If a client calling the class is managed by the CLR, the registration will be performed automatically.

6.2   Using Manual Transactions

Problem

You need to explicitly begin, control, and end a transaction within a .NET application.

Solution

Use the Connection object with structured exceptions (try...catch...finally).

The sample code contains two event handlers:

Form.Load

> Sets up the sample by filling a DataTable with the Categories table from the Northwind sample database. The default view of the table is bound to a data grid on the form.

Insert Button.Click

> Inserts user-entered data for two Categories records into the Northwind database within a manual transaction. If either record insert fails, both inserts are rolled back; otherwise, both record inserts are committed.

The C# code is shown in Example 6-3.

Example 6-3. File: ManualTransactionForm.cs

```csharp
// Namespaces, variables, and constants
using System;
using System.Configuration;
using System.Windows.Forms;
using System.Data;
using System.Data.SqlClient;

private const String CATEGORIES_TABLE = "Categories";

private DataTable dt;
private SqlDataAdapter da;

// ...

private void ManualTransactionForm_Load(object sender, System.EventArgs e)
{
    // Fill the categories table.
    String sqlText = "SELECT CategoryID, CategoryName, " +
        "Description FROM Categories";
    da = new SqlDataAdapter(sqlText,
        ConfigurationSettings.AppSettings["Sql_ConnectString"]);
    dt = new DataTable(CATEGORIES_TABLE);
    da.FillSchema(dt, SchemaType.Source);
    da.Fill(dt);
```

Example 6-3. File: ManualTransactionForm.cs (continued)

```csharp
    // Bind the default view of the table to the grid.
    dataGrid.DataSource = dt.DefaultView;
}

private void insertButton_Click(object sender, System.EventArgs e)
{
    String sqlText = "INSERT " + CATEGORIES_TABLE + " "+
        "(CategoryName, Description) VALUES " +
        "(@CategoryName, @Description)";

    // Create the connection.
    SqlConnection conn = new SqlConnection(
        ConfigurationSettings.AppSettings["Sql_ConnectString"]);
    // Create the transaction.
    conn.Open( );
    SqlTransaction tran = conn.BeginTransaction( );

    // Create command in the transaction with parameters.
    SqlCommand cmd = new SqlCommand(sqlText, conn, tran);
    cmd.Parameters.Add(new SqlParameter("@CategoryName",
        SqlDbType.NVarChar, 15));
    cmd.Parameters.Add(new SqlParameter("@Description",
        SqlDbType.NVarChar, 100));

    try
    {
        // Insert the records into the table.
        if (categoryName1TextBox.Text.Trim( ).Length == 0)
            // If CategoryName is empty, make it null (invalid).
            cmd.Parameters["@CategoryName"].Value = DBNull.Value;
        else
            cmd.Parameters["@CategoryName"].Value =
                categoryName1TextBox.Text;
        cmd.Parameters["@Description"].Value =
                description1TextBox.Text;
        cmd.ExecuteNonQuery( );

        if (categoryName2TextBox.Text.Trim( ).Length == 0)
            cmd.Parameters["@CategoryName"].Value = DBNull.Value;
        else
            cmd.Parameters["@CategoryName"].Value =
                categoryName2TextBox.Text;
        cmd.Parameters["@Description"].Value =
            description2TextBox.Text;
        cmd.ExecuteNonQuery( );

        // If okay to here, commit the transaction.
        tran.Commit( );

        MessageBox.Show("Transaction committed.");
    }
    catch (Exception ex)
```

Example 6-3. File: ManualTransactionForm.cs (continued)

```
    {
        // Exception occurred. Roll back the transaction.
        tran.Rollback( );
        MessageBox.Show(ex.Message + Environment.NewLine +
            "Transaction rollback.");
    }
    finally
    {
        conn.Close( );
    }

    // Refresh the data.
    da.Fill(dt);
}
```

Discussion

Manual transactions allow control over the transaction boundary through explicit commands to start and end the transaction. There is no built-in support for distributed transactions spanning multiple resources with manual transactions.

.NET data providers make available objects to enable manual transactions. The Connection object has a BeginTransaction( ) method that is used to start a transaction. If successful, the method returns a Transaction object that is used to perform all subsequent actions associated with the transaction, such as committing or aborting. Calling the BeginTransaction( ) method does not implicitly cause all subsequent commands to execute within the transaction. The Transaction property of the Command object must be set to a transaction that has already been started for the command to execute within the transaction.

Once started, the transaction remains in a pending state until it is explicitly committed or rolled back using the Commit( ) or Rollback( ) methods of the Transaction object. The Commit( ) method of the Transaction is used to commit the database transaction. The Rollback( ) method of the Transaction is used to roll back a database transaction from a pending state. An InvalidOperationException will be raised if Rollback( ) is called after Commit( ) has been called.

The isolation level of the transaction can be specified through an overload of the BeginTransaction( ) method and if it is not specified, the default isolation level ReadCommitted is used.

Unlike automatic transactions, manual transactions must be explicitly committed or rolled back using the Commit( ) or Rollback( ) method. If possible, use the .NET data provider transaction management exclusively; avoid using other transaction models, such as the one provided by SQL Server. If this is necessary for any reason, Recipe 6. 3 discusses using the SQL Server transaction model together with the .NET SQL Server data provider transaction management.

The IDbTransaction interface is implemented by .NET data providers that access relational databases. Applications create an instance of the class implementing the IDbTransaction interface rather than creating an instance of the interface directly. Classes that inherit IDbTransaction must implement the inherited members and typically define provider-specific functionality by adding additional members.

The SQL .NET data provider allows *savepoints* to be defined allowing a transaction to be partially rolled back to a point in the transaction other than its beginning. The OLE DB .NET data provider allows nested transactions to be started within the parent transaction; the parent transaction cannot commit until all its nested transactions have committed.

6.3 Nesting Manual Transactions with the SQL Server .NET Data Provider

Problem

You need to create a nested transaction using the SQL Server .NET data provider, but the Begin( ) command that you need is only available with the OLE DB .NET data provider. The SQL Server data provider appears to provide no built-in support for nested transactions. You want to nest transactions when using it.

Solution

Simulate nested transactions with savepoints when using the SQL Server .NET data provider, manage and control the lifetime of the SqlTransaction class, and create the required exception handling.

The sample code contains two event handlers:

Form.Load

> Sets up the sample by filling a DataTable with the Categories table from the Northwind sample database. The default view of the table is bound to a data grid on the form.

Insert Button.Click

> Inserts user-entered data for two Categories records into the Northwind database within a manual transaction. A savepoint is created if the first record insert succeeds. If the insert of the second record fails, the transaction is rolled back to the savepoint and the first record insert is committed; otherwise, both record inserts are committed.

The C# code is shown in Example 6-4.

Example 6-4. File: NestedManualTransactionForm.cs

```csharp
// Namespaces, variables, and constants
using System;
using System.Configuration;
using System.Windows.Forms;
using System.Data;
using System.Data.SqlClient;

private const String CATEGORIES_TABLE = "Categories";

private DataTable dt;
private SqlDataAdapter da;

// ...

private void NestedTransactionForm_Load(object sender, System.EventArgs e)
{
    // Fill the categories table.
    String sqlText = "SELECT CategoryID, CategoryName, " +
        "Description FROM Categories";
    da = new SqlDataAdapter(sqlText,
        ConfigurationSettings.AppSettings["Sql_ConnectString"]);
    dt = new DataTable(CATEGORIES_TABLE);
    da.FillSchema(dt, SchemaType.Source);
    da.Fill(dt);

    // Bind the default view of the table to the grid.
    dataGrid.DataSource = dt.DefaultView;
}

private void insertButton_Click(object sender, System.EventArgs e)
{
    String sqlText = "INSERT " + CATEGORIES_TABLE + " "+
        "(CategoryName, Description) VALUES " +
        "(@CategoryName, @Description)";

    // Create the connection.
    SqlConnection conn = new SqlConnection(
        ConfigurationSettings.AppSettings["Sql_ConnectString"]);
    // Create the transaction.
    conn.Open();
    SqlTransaction tran = conn.BeginTransaction();

    // Create command in the transaction with parameters.
    SqlCommand cmd = new SqlCommand(sqlText, conn, tran);
    cmd.Parameters.Add(new SqlParameter("@CategoryName",
        SqlDbType.NVarChar, 15));
    cmd.Parameters.Add(new SqlParameter("@Description",
        SqlDbType.NVarChar, 100));

    try
    {
```

Example 6-4. File: NestedManualTransactionForm.cs (continued)

```
        // Insert the records into the table.
        if (categoryName1TextBox.Text.Trim( ).Length == 0)
            // If CategoryName is empty, make it null (invalid).
            cmd.Parameters["@CategoryName"].Value = DBNull.Value;
        else
            cmd.Parameters["@CategoryName"].Value =
                categoryName1TextBox.Text;
        cmd.Parameters["@Description"].Value =
            description1TextBox.Text;
        cmd.ExecuteNonQuery( );
    }
    catch (Exception ex)
    {
        // Exception occurred. Roll back the transaction.
        tran.Rollback( );
        MessageBox.Show(ex.Message + Environment.NewLine +
            "Transaction rollback (records 1 and 2).");
        conn.Close( );
        return;
    }

    tran.Save("SavePoint1");

    try
    {
        // Insert the records into the table.
        if (categoryName2TextBox.Text.Trim( ).Length == 0)
            // If CategoryName is empty, make it null (invalid).
            cmd.Parameters["@CategoryName"].Value = DBNull.Value;
        else
            cmd.Parameters["@CategoryName"].Value =
                categoryName2TextBox.Text;
        cmd.Parameters["@Description"].Value =
            description2TextBox.Text;
        cmd.ExecuteNonQuery( );

        // If okay to here, commit the transaction.
        tran.Commit( );

        MessageBox.Show("Transaction committed (records 1 and 2).");
    }
    catch (SqlException ex)
    {
        tran.Rollback("SavePoint1");
        tran.Commit( );
        MessageBox.Show(ex.Message + Environment.NewLine +
            "Transaction commit (record 1)." + Environment.NewLine +
            "Transaction rollback (record 2).");
    }
    finally
```

Example 6-4. File: NestedManualTransactionForm.cs (continued)

```
    {
        conn.Close( );
    }

    // Refresh the data.
    da.Fill(dt);
}
```

Discussion

The OLE DB .NET data provider's transaction class OleDbTransaction has a Begin( ) method that is used to initiate a nested transaction. A nested transaction allows part of a transaction to be rolled back without rolling back the entire transaction. An InvalidOperationException is raised if the OLE DB data source does not support nested transactions.

The SQL Server .NET data provider's transaction class SqlTransaction does not have a Begin( ) method to initiate a nested transaction. Instead, it has a Save( ) method that creates a savepoint in the transaction that can later be used to roll back a portion of the transaction—to the savepoint rather than rolling back to the start of the transaction. The savepoint is named using the only argument of the Save( ) method. An overload of the Rollback( ) method of the SqlTransaction class accepts an argument that you can use to specify the name of the savepoint to roll back to.

6.4 Using ADO.NET and SQL Server DBMS Transactions Together

Problem

You need to use a DBMS transaction within a SQL Server stored procedure from an ADO.NET transaction with the SQL Server .NET data provider.

Solution

Use error-checking within a catch block as shown in Example 6-5.

The sample uses a single stored procedure:

InsertCategories_Transacted
> Used to insert a single record into the Categories table in the Northwind database within a DBMS transaction. If the record insert fails, the transaction is rolled back; otherwise, the transaction is committed.

The sample code contains two event handlers:

Form.Load

Sets up the sample by filling a DataTable with the Categories table from the Northwind sample database. The default view of the table is bound to a data grid on the form.

Insert Button.Click

Inserts user-entered data for the Categories records into the Northwind database within a manual transaction using a DBMS transacted stored procedure. The transaction is rolled back in the stored procedure if either the Force DBMS Rollback checkbox is checked or if no value is entered for the Category Name field. Otherwise, the ADO.NET manual transaction is committed.

Example 6-5. Stored procedure: InsertCategories_Transacted

```
CREATE PROCEDURE InsertCategories_Transacted
    @CategoryId int output,
    @CategoryName nvarchar(15),
    @Description ntext,
    @Rollback bit = 0
AS
    SET NOCOUNT ON

    begin tran

    insert Categories(
        CategoryName,
        Description)
    values (
        @CategoryName,
        @Description)

    if @@error<>0 or @@rowcount=0 or @Rollback=1
    begin
        rollback tran
        set @CategoryID = -1
        return 1
    end

    commit tran

    set @CategoryID = Scope_Identity( )

    select @CategoryID CategoryId

    return 0
```

The C# code is shown in Example 6-6.

Example 6-6. File: DbmsTransactionForm.cs

```csharp
// Namespaces, variables, and constants
using System;
using System.Configuration;
using System.Windows.Forms;
using System.Data;
using System.Data.SqlClient;

private SqlDataAdapter da;
private DataTable dt;

// ...

private void DbmsTransactionForm_Load(object sender, System.EventArgs e)
{
    // Fill the table.
    String sqlText = "SELECT CategoryID, CategoryName, Description " +
        "FROM Categories";
    da = new SqlDataAdapter(sqlText,
        ConfigurationSettings.AppSettings["Sql_ConnectString"]);
    dt = new DataTable("Categories");
    da.FillSchema(dt, SchemaType.Source);
    da.Fill(dt);

    // Bind the default view of the table to the grid.
    dataGrid.DataSource = dt.DefaultView;
}

private void insertButton_Click(object sender, System.EventArgs e)
{
    // Create the connection.
    SqlConnection conn = new SqlConnection(
        ConfigurationSettings.AppSettings["Sql_ConnectString"]);
    // Create the transaction.
    conn.Open( );
    SqlTransaction tran = conn.BeginTransaction( );

    // Create command in the transaction with parameters.
    SqlCommand cmd =
        new SqlCommand("InsertCategories_Transacted", conn, tran);
    cmd.CommandType = CommandType.StoredProcedure;
    cmd.Parameters.Add("@CategoryID", SqlDbType.Int).Direction =
        ParameterDirection.Output;
    cmd.Parameters.Add("@CategoryName", SqlDbType.NVarChar, 15);
    cmd.Parameters.Add("@Description", SqlDbType.NText);
    cmd.Parameters.Add("@Rollback", SqlDbType.Bit);

    try
    {
        // Set the parameters to the user-entered values.
        // Set the CategoryName to DBNull if not entered.
        if(categoryNameTextBox.Text.Trim( ).Length == 0)
            cmd.Parameters["@CategoryName"].Value = DBNull.Value;
```

Example 6-6. File: DbmsTransactionForm.cs (continued)

```
                else
                    cmd.Parameters["@CategoryName"].Value =
                        categoryNameTextBox.Text;
                cmd.Parameters["@Description"].Value = descriptionTextBox.Text;
                cmd.Parameters["@Rollback"].Value =
                    forceDbmsRollbackCheckBox.Checked ? 1 : 0;

                // Attempt to insert the record.
                cmd.ExecuteNonQuery( );

                // Success. Commit the transaction.
                tran.Commit( );
                MessageBox.Show("Transaction committed.");
            }
            catch (SqlException ex)
            {
                bool spRollback = false;
                foreach (SqlError err in ex.Errors)
                {
                    // Check if transaction rolled back in the
                    // stored procedure.
                    if(err.Number == 266)
                    {
                        MessageBox.Show(ex.Message,
                            "DBMS transaction rolled back in " +
                            "stored procedure",
                            MessageBoxButtons.OK,
                            MessageBoxIcon.Error);
                        spRollback = true;
                        break;
                    }
                }
                if (!spRollback)
                {
                    // transaction was not rolled back by the DBMS
                    // SqlException error. Roll back the transaction.
                    tran.Rollback( );
                    MessageBox.Show(ex.Message);
                }
            }
            catch (Exception ex)
            {
                // Other Exception. Roll back the transaction.
                tran.Rollback( );
                MessageBox.Show(ex.Message);
            }
            finally
            {
                conn.Close( );
            }
```

Example 6-6. File: DbmsTransactionForm.cs (continued)

```
    // Refresh the data.
    da.Fill(dt);
}
```

Discussion

SQL Server returns error 266 if a stored procedure exits with a transaction count that is not the same as when the stored procedure was entered. The count is returned by the function @@TRANCOUNT. The error simply sends a message to the client and does not affect execution of the stored procedure. It doesn't mean that the DBMS transaction in the stored procedure could not be started, completed, or terminated properly.

When calling a stored procedure from a .NET manual transaction, the transaction count entering the stored procedure is 1. Using the SQL BEGIN TRAN command in the stored procedure creates a nested transaction, increasing the transaction count to 2. If the stored procedure transaction is subsequently committed with the COMMIT TRAN command, the transaction count is decremented back to 1. Keep in mind commits of inner transactions don't free resources or make modifications permanent, and don't affect outer transactions. If ROLLBACK is called, all inner transactions to the outermost transaction are rolled back and the transaction count is decremented to 0. Error 266 is returned by the rolled back stored procedure since the transaction count entering the stored procedure is 1 while the count when exiting is 0. Attempting to commit or roll back the transaction from .NET after it has been rolled back in the stored procedure will cause an InvalidOperationException because the transaction has already been rolled back.

The solution catches exceptions raised while executing a stored procedure and checks if they correspond to SQL Server error 266, which is the mismatch between the starting and exiting stored procedure transaction count values as a result of the stored procedure rolling back the transaction. If the stored procedure has rolled back the transaction, it is not rolled back by the .NET code. All other errors raised while executing the stored procedure are rolled back by the .NET code.

6.5   Using a Transaction with a DataAdapter

Problem

You need to use a transaction when updating a data source using a DataAdapter.

Solution

Associate a Transaction with the appropriate Command object from the DataAdapter.

The sample code contains three event handlers:

Form.Load

Sets up the sample by using a DataAdapter to load a DataTable with the Orders table from the Northwind database. A CommandBuilder is used to generate the updating logic. The default view of the DataTable is bound to a data grid on the form.

Update Button.Click

Creates a new Transaction object on the Connection of the SelectCommand of the DataAdapter. The Transaction is associated with the Connection objects for the update commands generated for the DataAdapter by the CommandBuilder. The Update( ) method of the DataAdapter is called to update DataTable changes to the Orders table. If no errors are encountered, the transaction is committed; otherwise, all changes made are rolled back.

Refresh Button.Click

Clears and reloads the Orders DataTable.

The C# code is shown in Example 6-7.

Example 6-7. File: TransactionDataAdapter.cs

```
// Namespaces, variables, and constants
using System;
using System.Configuration;
using System.Windows.Forms;
using System.Data;
using System.Data.SqlClient;

private const String ORDERS_TABLE = "Orders";

private DataTable dt;
private SqlDataAdapter da;
private SqlCommandBuilder cb;

// ...

private void TransactionDataAdapterForm_Load(object sender,
    System.EventArgs e)
{
    String sqlText = "SELECT * FROM Orders";

    // Fill the Orders table for editing.
    da = new SqlDataAdapter(sqlText,
        ConfigurationSettings.AppSettings["Sql_ConnectString"]);
    // Stop updating when an error is encountered for roll back.
    da.ContinueUpdateOnError = false;
    // Create CommandBuilder and generate updating logic.
    cb = new SqlCommandBuilder(da);
    cb.GetDeleteCommand( );
    cb.GetInsertCommand( );
```

Example 6-7. File: TransactionDataAdapter.cs (continued)

```
    cb.GetUpdateCommand( );
    // Create table and fill with orders schema and data.
    dt = new DataTable(ORDERS_TABLE);
    da.FillSchema(dt, SchemaType.Source);
    da.Fill(dt);

    // Bind the default view of the table to the grid.
    dataGrid.DataSource = dt.DefaultView;
}

private void updateButton_Click(object sender, System.EventArgs e)
{
    // Create and open the connection.
    SqlConnection conn = new SqlConnection(
        ConfigurationSettings.AppSettings["Sql_ConnectString"]);
    conn.Open( );

    // Create and start the transaction.
    SqlTransaction tran = null;
    tran = conn.BeginTransaction( );

    // Associate CommandBuilder generated update commands
    // with the transaction.
    da.SelectCommand.Transaction = tran;

    // Update the data source.
    try
    {
        // Submit the changes.
        da.Update(dt);

        // Success. Commit.
        tran.Commit( );
    }
    catch (Exception ex)
    {
        // Exception. Roll back.
        tran.Rollback( );

        MessageBox.Show(ex.Message + Environment.NewLine +
            "Transaction rolled back.");
    }
    finally
    {
        conn.Close( );
    }
}

private void refreshButton_Click(object sender, System.EventArgs e)
{
```

Example 6-7. File: TransactionDataAdapter.cs (continued)

```
    // Refresh the orders data.
    dt.Clear( );
    da.Fill(dt);
}
```

Discussion

You can use a transaction with a DataAdapter to allow the roll back of updates made by the DataAdapter in the event of an error.

If, as in the solution, a CommandBuilder is used to generate the update logic for the DataAdapter, associate the Transaction with the SelectCommand of the DataAdapter as shown in the solution code:

```
    da.SelectCommand.Transaction = tran;
```

If custom update logic is used for the DataAdapter, the Transaction must be associated with the DeleteCommand, InsertCommand, and UpdateCommand of the DataAdapter, but not the SelectCommand, as shown in the following code:

```
    da.DeleteCommand.Transaction = tran;
    da.InsertCommand.Transaction = tran;
    da.UpdateCommand.Transaction = tran;
```

6.6   Avoiding Referential Integrity Problems When Updating the Data Source

Problem

You sometimes get referential integrity errors when you update a DataSet that contains related parent, child, and grandchild records back to the underlying data source, but want to perform the update without errors.

Solution

Use one DataAdapter for each DataTable to update the deleted, updated, and inserted rows as shown in the following example.

The schema of table TBL0606Parent used in this solution is shown in Table 6-2.

Table 6-2. TBL0606Parent schema

Column name	Data type	Length	Allow nulls?
ParentId	int	4	No
Field1	nvarchar	50	Yes
Field2	nvarchar	50	Yes

The schema of table TBL00606Child used in this solution is shown in Table 6-3.

Table 6-3. TBL0606Child schema

Column name	Data type	Length	Allow nulls?
ChildId	int	4	No
ParentId	int	4	No
Field3	nvarchar	50	Yes
Field4	nvarchar	50	Yes

The schema of table TBL0606Grandchild used in this solution is shown in Table 6-4.

Table 6-4. TBL0606Grandchild schema

Column name	Data type	Length	Allow nulls?
GrandchildId	int	4	No
ChildId	int	4	No
Field5	nvarchar	50	Yes
Field6	nvarchar	50	Yes

The sample uses 12 stored procedures:

SP0606_GetParent
> Used to retrieve a single record from the Parent table if the optional @ParentId parameter is specified or all Parent records if it is not

SP0606_DeleteParent
> Used to delete the record specified by the @ParentId parameter from the Parent table

SP0606_InsertParent
> Used to insert a record into the Parent table and return the *ParentId* identity value for the new record

SP0606_UpdateParent
> Used to update all field values for the record in the Parent table specified by the @ParentId input parameter

SP0606_GetChild
> Used to retrieve a single record from the Child table if the optional @ChildId parameter is specified or all Child records if it is not

SP0606_DeleteChild
> Used to delete the record specified by the @ChildId parameter from the Child table

SP0606_InsertChild
> Used to insert a record into the Child table and return the *ChildId* identity value for the new record

SP0606_UpdateChild
> Used to update all field values for the record in the Child table specified by the @ChildId input parameter

SP0606_GetGrandchild
> Used to retrieve a single record from the Grandchild table if the optional @GrandchildId parameter is specified or all Grandchild records if it is not

SP0606_DeleteGrandchild
> Used to delete the record specified by the @GrandchildId parameter from the Grandchild table

SP0606_InsertGrandchild
> Used to insert a record into the Grandchild table and return the GrandchildId identity value for the new record

SP0606_UpdateGrandchild
> Used to update all field values for the record in the Grandchild table specified by the @GrandchildId input parameter

The sample code contains four event handlers and two methods:

Form.Load
> Sets up the sample by creating a DataSet containing the Parent, Child, and Grandchild DataTable objects. DataRelation objects are created relating the tables. DataAdapter objects are created for each DataTable and the select, delete, insert, and update Command objects are specified for each using the custom logic in the twelve stored procedures used by this solution. The DataAdapter objects are used to fill the tables in the DataSet. Finally, the default view of the Parent table is bound to the data grid on the form.

CreateData( )
> This method generates a number of rows in the Parent, Child, and Grandchild DataTable objects as specified by the input parameters of the method.

UpdateData( )
> This method uses the DataAdapter for each of the Parent, Child, and Grandchild DataTable objects to update offline changes back to the database.

Create Data Button.Click
> Calls the CreateData( ) to create four Parent records, four Child records for each Parent, and four Grandchild records for each Child. Finally, the UpdateData( ) method is called to update the database with the new records.

Modify Data Button.Click
> Randomly modifies or deletes records from the Parent, Child, and Grandchild DataTable objects. The CreateData( ) method is called to create two Parent

records, two Child records for each Parent, and two Grandchild records for each Child. Finally, the UpdateData( ) method is called to update the database with the offline changes, deletions, and additions.

Delete Data Button.Click

Deletes all records from the Parent DataTable, which then cascades to delete all Child and Grandchild records clearing all data from the DataSet. Finally, the UpdateData( ) method is called to update the database with the offline deletions.

The 12 stored procedures are shown in Examples 6-8 through 6-19.

Example 6-8. Stored procedure: SP0606_GetParent

```
CREATE PROCEDURE SP0606_GetParent
    @ParentId int=null
AS
    SET NOCOUNT ON

    if @ParentId is not null
    begin
        select
            ParentId,
            Field1,
            Field2
        from
            TBL0606Parent
        where
            ParentId=@ParentId

        return 0
    end

    select
        ParentId,
        Field1,
        Field2
    from
        TBL0606Parent

    return 0
```

Example 6-9. Stored procedure: SP0606_DeleteParent

```
CREATE PROCEDURE SP0606_DeleteParent
    @ParentId int
AS
    SET NOCOUNT ON

    delete
    from
        TBL0606Parent
```

Example 6-9. Stored procedure: SP0606_DeleteParent (continued)

```
where
    ParentId=@ParentId

return 0
```

Example 6-10. Stored procedure: SP0606_InsertParent

```
CREATE PROCEDURE SP0606_InsertParent
    @ParentId int output,
    @Field1 nvarchar(50)=null,
    @Field2 nvarchar(50)=null
AS
    SET NOCOUNT ON

    insert TBL0606Parent(
        Field1,
        Field2)
    values (
        @Field1,
        @Field2)

    if @@rowcount=0
        return 1

    set @ParentId=Scope_Identity( )

    select @ParentId ParentId

    return 0
```

Example 6-11. Stored procedure: SP0606_UpdateParent

```
CREATE PROCEDURE SP0606_UpdateParent
    @ParentId int,
    @Field1 nvarchar(50)=null,
    @Field2 nvarchar(50)=null
AS
    SET NOCOUNT ON

    update
        TBL0606Parent
    set
        Field1=@Field1,
        Field2=@Field2
    where
        ParentId=@ParentId

    if @@rowcount=0
        return 1

    return 0
```

Example 6-12. Stored procedure: SP0606_GetChild

```
CREATE PROCEDURE SP0606_GetChild
    @ChildId int=null
AS
    SET NOCOUNT ON

    if @ChildId is not null
    begin
        select
            ChildID,
            ParentId,
            Field3,
            Field4
        from
            TBL0606Child
        where
            ChildId=@ChildId

        return 0
    end

    select
        ChildId,
        ParentId,
        Field3,
        Field4
    from
        TBL0606Child

    return 0
```

Example 6-13. Stored procedure: SP0606_DeleteChild

```
CREATE PROCEDURE SP0606_DeleteChild
    @ChildId int
AS
    SET NOCOUNT ON

    delete
    from
        TBL0606Child
    where
        ChildId=@ChildId

    return 0
```

Example 6-14. Stored procedure: SP0606_InsertChild

```
CREATE PROCEDURE SP0606_InsertChild
    @ChildId int output,
    @ParentId int,
    @Field3 nvarchar(50)=null,
```

Example 6-14. Stored procedure: SP0606_InsertChild (continued)

```
    @Field4 nvarchar(50)=null
AS
    SET NOCOUNT ON

    insert TBL0606Child(
        ParentId,
        Field3,
        Field4)
    values (
        @ParentId,
        @Field3,
        @Field4)

    if @@rowcount=0
        return 1

    set @ChildId=Scope_Identity( )

    select @ChildId ChildId

    return 0
```

Example 6-15. Stored procedure: SP0606_UpdateChild

```
CREATE PROCEDURE SP0606_UpdateChild
    @ChildId int,
    @ParentId int,
    @Field3 nvarchar(50)=null,
    @Field4 nvarchar(50)=null
AS
    SET NOCOUNT ON

    update
        TBL0606Child
    set
        ParentId=@ParentId,
        Field3=@Field3,
        Field4=@Field4
    where
        ChildId=@ChildId

    if @@rowcount=0
        return 1

    return 0
```

Example 6-16. Stored procedure: SP0606_GetGrandchild

```
CREATE PROCEDURE SP0606_GetGrandchild
    @GrandchildId int=null
AS
    SET NOCOUNT ON
```

Example 6-16. Stored procedure: SP0606_GetGrandchild (continued)

```
    if @GrandchildId is not null
    begin
        select
            GrandchildID,
            ChildId,
            Field5,
            Field6
        from
            TBL0606Grandchild
        where
            GrandchildId=@GrandchildId

        return 0
    end

    select
        GrandchildId,
        ChildId,
        Field5,
        Field6
    from
        TBL0606Grandchild

    return 0
```

Example 6-17. Stored procedure: SP0606_DeleteGrandchild

```
CREATE PROCEDURE SP0606_DeleteGrandchild
    @GrandchildId int
AS
    SET NOCOUNT ON

    delete
    from
        TBL0606Grandchild
    where
        GrandchildId=@GrandchildId

    return 0
```

Example 6-18. Stored procedure: SP0606_InsertGrandchild

```
CREATE PROCEDURE SP0606_InsertGrandchild
    @GrandchildId int output,
    @ChildId int,
    @Field5 nvarchar(50)=null,
    @Field6 nvarchar(50)=null
AS
    SET NOCOUNT ON
```

Example 6-18. Stored procedure: SP0606_InsertGrandchild (continued)

```
    insert TBL0606Grandchild(
        ChildId,
        Field5,
        Field6)
    values (
        @ChildId,
        @Field5,
        @Field6)

    if @@rowcount=0
        return 1

    set @GrandchildId=Scope_Identity( )

    select @GrandchildId GrandchildId

    return 0
```

Example 6-19. Stored procedure: SP0606_UpdateGrandchild

```
CREATE PROCEDURE SP0606_UpdateGrandchild
    @GrandchildId int,
    @ChildId int,
    @Field5 nvarchar(50)=null,
    @Field6 nvarchar(50)=null
AS
    SET NOCOUNT ON

    update
        TBL0606Grandchild
    set
        ChildId=@ChildId,
        Field5=@Field5,
        Field6=@Field6
    where
        GrandchildId=@GrandchildId

    if @@rowcount=0
        return 1

    return 0
```

The C# code is shown in Example 6-20.

Example 6-20. File: ReferentialIntegrityUpdateLogicForm.cs

```
// Namespaces, variables, and constants
using System;
using System.Configuration;
using System.Windows.Forms;
using System.Data;
using System.Data.SqlClient;
```

Example 6-20. File: ReferentialIntegrityUpdateLogicForm.cs (continued)

```csharp
private DataSet ds;
private SqlDataAdapter daParent, daChild, daGrandchild;

private const String PARENTTABLENAME      = "TBL00606Parent";
private const String CHILDTABLENAME       = "TBL00606Child";
private const String GRANDCHILDTABLENAME  = "TBL00606Grandchild";

// Table column name constants for Parent table
private const String PARENTID_FIELD       = "ParentId";
private const String FIELD1_FIELD         = "Field1";
private const String FIELD2_FIELD         = "Field2";

// Table column parameter name constants for Child table
private const String CHILDID_FIELD        = "ChildId";
private const String FIELD3_FIELD         = "Field3";
private const String FIELD4_FIELD         = "Field4";

// Table column parameter name constants for Grandchild table
private const String GRANDCHILDID_FIELD   = "GrandchildId";
private const String FIELD5_FIELD         = "Field5";
private const String FIELD6_FIELD         = "Field6";

// Stored procedure name constants
private const String DELETEPARENT_SP      = "SP0606_DeleteParent";
private const String GETPARENT_SP         = "SP0606_GetParent";
private const String INSERTPARENT_SP      = "SP0606_InsertParent";
private const String UPDATEPARENT_SP      = "SP0606_UpdateParent";
private const String DELETECHILD_SP       = "SP0606_DeleteChild";
private const String GETCHILD_SP          = "SP0606_GetChild";
private const String INSERTCHILD_SP       = "SP0606_InsertChild";
private const String UPDATECHILD_SP       = "SP0606_UpdateChild";
private const String DELETEGRANDCHILD_SP  = "SP0606_DeleteGrandchild";
private const String GETGRANDCHILD_SP     = "SP0606_GetGrandchild";
private const String INSERTGRANDCHILD_SP  = "SP0606_InsertGrandchild";
private const String UPDATEGRANDCHILD_SP  = "SP0606_UpdateGrandchild";

// Stored procedure parameter name constants for Parent table
private const String PARENTID_PARM        = "@ParentId";
private const String FIELD1_PARM          = "@Field1";
private const String FIELD2_PARM          = "@Field2";

// Stored procedure parameter name constants for Child table
private const String CHILDID_PARM         = "@ChildId";
private const String FIELD3_PARM          = "@Field3";
private const String FIELD4_PARM          = "@Field4";

// Stored procedure parameter name constants for Child table
private const String GRANDCHILDID_PARM    = "@GrandchildId";
private const String FIELD5_PARM          = "@Field5";
private const String FIELD6_PARM          = "@Field6";

// ...
```

Example 6-20. File: ReferentialIntegrityUpdateLogicForm.cs (continued)

```
private void ReferentialIntegrityUpdateLogicForm_Load(object sender,
    System.EventArgs e)
{
    DataColumnCollection cols;
    DataColumn col;

    // Build the parent table.
    DataTable parentTable = new DataTable(PARENTTABLENAME);
    cols = parentTable.Columns;
    col = cols.Add(PARENTID_FIELD, typeof(Int32));
    col.AutoIncrement = true;
    col.AutoIncrementSeed = -1;
    col.AutoIncrementStep = -1;
    cols.Add(FIELD1_FIELD, typeof(String)).MaxLength = 50;
    cols.Add(FIELD2_FIELD, typeof(String)).MaxLength = 50;

    // Build the child table.
    DataTable childTable = new DataTable(CHILDTABLENAME);
    cols = childTable.Columns;
    col = cols.Add(CHILDID_FIELD, typeof(Int32));
    col.AutoIncrement = true;
    col.AutoIncrementSeed = -1;
    col.AutoIncrementStep = -1;
    cols.Add(PARENTID_FIELD, typeof(Int32)).AllowDBNull = false;
    cols.Add(FIELD3_FIELD, typeof(String)).MaxLength = 50;
    cols.Add(FIELD4_FIELD, typeof(String)).MaxLength = 50;

    // Build the grandchild table.
    DataTable grandchildTable = new DataTable(GRANDCHILDTABLENAME);
    cols = grandchildTable.Columns;
    col = cols.Add(GRANDCHILDID_FIELD, typeof(Int32));
    col.AutoIncrement = true;
    col.AutoIncrementSeed = -1;
    col.AutoIncrementStep = -1;
    cols.Add(CHILDID_FIELD, typeof(Int32)).AllowDBNull = false;
    cols.Add(FIELD5_FIELD, typeof(String)).MaxLength = 50;
    cols.Add(FIELD6_FIELD, typeof(String)).MaxLength = 50;

    // Add the tables to the DataSet and create the relation between them.
    ds = new DataSet();
    ds.Tables.Add(parentTable);
    ds.Tables.Add(childTable);
    ds.Tables.Add(grandchildTable);
    ds.Relations.Add(new DataRelation("Parent_Child_Relation",
        parentTable.Columns[PARENTID_FIELD],
        childTable.Columns[PARENTID_FIELD], true));
    ds.Relations.Add(new DataRelation("Child_Grandchild_Relation",
        childTable.Columns[CHILDID_FIELD],
        grandchildTable.Columns[CHILDID_FIELD], true));

    // Create the DataAdapter objects for the tables.
    daParent = new SqlDataAdapter();
```

Example 6-20. File: ReferentialIntegrityUpdateLogicForm.cs (continued)

```
daChild = new SqlDataAdapter( );
daGrandchild = new SqlDataAdapter( );

// Build the parent select command.
SqlCommand selectCommand = new SqlCommand(GETPARENT_SP,
    new SqlConnection(
    ConfigurationSettings.AppSettings["Sql_ConnectString"]));
selectCommand.CommandType = CommandType.StoredProcedure;
daParent.SelectCommand = selectCommand;

// Build the parent delete command.
SqlCommand deleteCommand = new SqlCommand(DELETEPARENT_SP,
    daParent.SelectCommand.Connection);
deleteCommand.CommandType = CommandType.StoredProcedure;
deleteCommand.Parameters.Add(PARENTID_PARM, SqlDbType.Int, 0,
    PARENTID_FIELD);
daParent.DeleteCommand = deleteCommand;

// Build the parent insert command.
SqlCommand insertCommand = new SqlCommand(INSERTPARENT_SP,
    daParent.SelectCommand.Connection);
insertCommand.CommandType = CommandType.StoredProcedure;
insertCommand.Parameters.Add(PARENTID_PARM, SqlDbType.Int, 0,
    PARENTID_FIELD);
insertCommand.Parameters.Add(FIELD1_PARM, SqlDbType.NVarChar, 50,
    FIELD1_FIELD);
insertCommand.Parameters.Add(FIELD2_PARM, SqlDbType.NVarChar, 50,
    FIELD2_FIELD);
daParent.InsertCommand = insertCommand;

// Build the parent update command.
SqlCommand updateCommand = new SqlCommand(UPDATEPARENT_SP,
    daParent.SelectCommand.Connection);
updateCommand.CommandType = CommandType.StoredProcedure;
updateCommand.Parameters.Add(PARENTID_PARM, SqlDbType.Int, 0,
    PARENTID_FIELD);
updateCommand.Parameters.Add(FIELD1_PARM, SqlDbType.NVarChar, 50,
    FIELD1_FIELD);
updateCommand.Parameters.Add(FIELD2_PARM, SqlDbType.NVarChar, 50,
    FIELD2_FIELD);
daParent.UpdateCommand = updateCommand;

// Build the child select command.
selectCommand = new SqlCommand(GETCHILD_SP,
    new SqlConnection(
    ConfigurationSettings.AppSettings["Sql_ConnectString"]));
selectCommand.CommandType = CommandType.StoredProcedure;
daChild.SelectCommand = selectCommand;

// Build the child delete command.
deleteCommand = new SqlCommand(DELETECHILD_SP,
    daChild.SelectCommand.Connection);
```

Example 6-20. File: ReferentialIntegrityUpdateLogicForm.cs (continued)

```
deleteCommand.CommandType = CommandType.StoredProcedure;
deleteCommand.Parameters.Add(CHILDID_PARM, SqlDbType.Int, 0,
    CHILDID_FIELD);
daChild.DeleteCommand = deleteCommand;

// Build the child insert command.
insertCommand = new SqlCommand(INSERTCHILD_SP,
    daChild.SelectCommand.Connection);
insertCommand.CommandType = CommandType.StoredProcedure;
insertCommand.Parameters.Add(CHILDID_PARM, SqlDbType.Int, 0,
    CHILDID_FIELD);
insertCommand.Parameters.Add(PARENTID_PARM, SqlDbType.Int, 0,
    PARENTID_FIELD);
insertCommand.Parameters.Add(FIELD3_PARM, SqlDbType.NVarChar, 50,
    FIELD3_FIELD);
insertCommand.Parameters.Add(FIELD4_PARM, SqlDbType.NVarChar, 50,
    FIELD4_FIELD);
daChild.InsertCommand = insertCommand;

// Build the child update command.
updateCommand = new SqlCommand(UPDATECHILD_SP,
    daChild.SelectCommand.Connection);
updateCommand.CommandType = CommandType.StoredProcedure;
updateCommand.Parameters.Add(CHILDID_PARM, SqlDbType.Int, 0,
    CHILDID_FIELD);
updateCommand.Parameters.Add(PARENTID_PARM, SqlDbType.Int, 0,
    PARENTID_FIELD);
updateCommand.Parameters.Add(FIELD3_PARM, SqlDbType.NVarChar, 50,
    FIELD3_FIELD);
updateCommand.Parameters.Add(FIELD4_PARM, SqlDbType.NVarChar, 50,
    FIELD4_FIELD);
daChild.UpdateCommand = updateCommand;

// Build the grandchild select command.
selectCommand = new SqlCommand(GETGRANDCHILD_SP,
    new SqlConnection(
    ConfigurationSettings.AppSettings["Sql_ConnectString"]));
selectCommand.CommandType = CommandType.StoredProcedure;
daGrandchild.SelectCommand = selectCommand;

// Build the grandchild delete command.
deleteCommand = new SqlCommand(DELETEGRANDCHILD_SP,
    daGrandchild.SelectCommand.Connection);
deleteCommand.CommandType = CommandType.StoredProcedure;
deleteCommand.Parameters.Add(GRANDCHILDID_PARM, SqlDbType.Int, 0,
    GRANDCHILDID_FIELD);
daGrandchild.DeleteCommand = deleteCommand;

// Build the grandchild insert command.
insertCommand = new SqlCommand(INSERTGRANDCHILD_SP,
    daGrandchild.SelectCommand.Connection);
insertCommand.CommandType = CommandType.StoredProcedure;
```

Example 6-20. File: ReferentialIntegrityUpdateLogicForm.cs (continued)

```
insertCommand.Parameters.Add(GRANDCHILDID_PARM, SqlDbType.Int, 0,
    GRANDCHILDID_FIELD);
insertCommand.Parameters.Add(CHILDID_PARM, SqlDbType.Int, 0,
    CHILDID_FIELD);
insertCommand.Parameters.Add(FIELD5_PARM, SqlDbType.NVarChar, 50,
    FIELD5_FIELD);
insertCommand.Parameters.Add(FIELD6_PARM, SqlDbType.NVarChar, 50,
    FIELD6_FIELD);
daGrandchild.InsertCommand = insertCommand;

// Build the grandchild update command.
updateCommand = new SqlCommand(UPDATEGRANDCHILD_SP,
    daGrandchild.SelectCommand.Connection);
updateCommand.CommandType = CommandType.StoredProcedure;
updateCommand.Parameters.Add(GRANDCHILDID_PARM, SqlDbType.Int, 0,
    GRANDCHILDID_FIELD);
updateCommand.Parameters.Add(CHILDID_PARM, SqlDbType.Int, 0,
    CHILDID_FIELD);
updateCommand.Parameters.Add(FIELD5_PARM, SqlDbType.NVarChar, 50,
    FIELD5_FIELD);
updateCommand.Parameters.Add(FIELD6_PARM, SqlDbType.NVarChar, 50,
    FIELD6_FIELD);
daGrandchild.UpdateCommand = updateCommand;

// Fill the parent and child table.
daParent.Fill(parentTable);
daChild.Fill(childTable);
daGrandchild.Fill(grandchildTable);

// Bind the default view of the data source to the grid.
dataGrid.DataSource = parentTable.DefaultView;

}

private void CreateData(int parentRows, int childRows, int grandchildRows)
{
    // Generate some data into each of the related tables.
    for(int iParent = 0; iParent < parentRows; iParent++)
    {
        // Generate parentRows of data in the parent table.
        DataRow parentRow = ds.Tables[PARENTTABLENAME].NewRow();
        parentRow[FIELD1_FIELD] = Guid.NewGuid().ToString();
        parentRow[FIELD2_FIELD] = Guid.NewGuid().ToString();
        ds.Tables[PARENTTABLENAME].Rows.Add(parentRow);

        for(int iChild = 0; iChild < childRows; iChild++)
        {
            // Generate childRows of data in the child table.
            DataRow childRow = ds.Tables[CHILDTABLENAME].NewRow();
            childRow[PARENTID_FIELD] =
                (int)parentRow[PARENTID_FIELD];
            childRow[FIELD3_FIELD] = Guid.NewGuid().ToString();
```

Example 6-20. File: ReferentialIntegrityUpdateLogicForm.cs (continued)

```
            childRow[FIELD4_FIELD] = Guid.NewGuid().ToString();
            ds.Tables[CHILDTABLENAME].Rows.Add(childRow);

            for(int iGrandchild = 0; iGrandchild < grandchildRows;
                iGrandchild++)
            {
                // Generate grandchildRows of data in the
                // grandchild table.
                DataRow grandchildRow =
                    ds.Tables[GRANDCHILDTABLENAME].NewRow();
                grandchildRow[CHILDID_FIELD] =
                    (int)childRow[CHILDID_FIELD];
                grandchildRow[FIELD5_FIELD] =
                    Guid.NewGuid().ToString();
                grandchildRow[FIELD6_FIELD] =
                    Guid.NewGuid().ToString();
                ds.Tables[GRANDCHILDTABLENAME].Rows.Add(
                    grandchildRow);
            }
        }
    }
}

private void UpdateData()
{
    // Update the related tables.
    daGrandchild.Update(ds.Tables[GRANDCHILDTABLENAME].Select(null, null,
        DataViewRowState.Deleted));
    daChild.Update(ds.Tables[CHILDTABLENAME].Select(null, null,
        DataViewRowState.Deleted));
    daParent.Update(ds.Tables[PARENTTABLENAME].Select(null, null,
        DataViewRowState.Deleted));
    daParent.Update(ds.Tables[PARENTTABLENAME].Select(null, null,
        DataViewRowState.ModifiedCurrent));
    daParent.Update(ds.Tables[PARENTTABLENAME].Select(null, null,
        DataViewRowState.Added));
    daChild.Update(ds.Tables[CHILDTABLENAME].Select(null, null,
        DataViewRowState.ModifiedCurrent));
    daChild.Update(ds.Tables[CHILDTABLENAME].Select(null, null,
        DataViewRowState.Added));
    daGrandchild.Update(ds.Tables[GRANDCHILDTABLENAME].Select(null, null,
        DataViewRowState.ModifiedCurrent));
    daGrandchild.Update(ds.Tables[GRANDCHILDTABLENAME].Select(null, null,
        DataViewRowState.Added));
}

private void createDataButton_Click(object sender, System.EventArgs e)
{
    // Create four rows of data in each parent, child, and grandchild.
    CreateData(4, 4, 4);
    // Update the data source with the new data.
    UpdateData();
```

Example 6-20. File: ReferentialIntegrityUpdateLogicForm.cs (continued)

```csharp
    MessageBox.Show("Data created.", "Referential Integrity",
        MessageBoxButtons.OK, MessageBoxIcon.Information);
}

private void modifyButton_Click(object sender, System.EventArgs e)
{
    // Randomly delete or modify rows from the grandchild, child, and
    // parent rows.
    Random r = new Random((int)DateTime.Now.Ticks);

    // Modify grandchild rows.
    for(int i = ds.Tables[GRANDCHILDTABLENAME].Rows.Count; i > 0; i--)
    {
        DataRow grandchildRow =
            ds.Tables[GRANDCHILDTABLENAME].Rows[i - 1];

        if(r.Next(2) == 0)
        {
            grandchildRow[FIELD5_FIELD] = Guid.NewGuid().ToString();
            grandchildRow[FIELD6_FIELD] = Guid.NewGuid().ToString();
        }
        else
            grandchildRow.Delete();
    }

    // Modify or delete child rows.
    for(int i = ds.Tables[CHILDTABLENAME].Rows.Count; i > 0; i--)
    {
        DataRow childRow = ds.Tables[CHILDTABLENAME].Rows[i - 1];

        if(r.Next(2) == 0)
        {
            childRow[FIELD3_FIELD] = Guid.NewGuid().ToString();
            childRow[FIELD4_FIELD] = Guid.NewGuid().ToString();
        }
        else
            childRow.Delete();
    }

    // Modify or delete parent rows.
    for(int i = ds.Tables[PARENTTABLENAME].Rows.Count; i > 0; i--)
    {
        DataRow parentRow = ds.Tables[PARENTTABLENAME].Rows[i - 1];

        if(r.Next(2) == 0)
        {
            parentRow[FIELD1_FIELD] = Guid.NewGuid().ToString();
            parentRow[FIELD2_FIELD] = Guid.NewGuid().ToString();
        }
        else
            parentRow.Delete();
    }
```

Example 6-20. File: ReferentialIntegrityUpdateLogicForm.cs (continued)

```
    // Insert two rows into parent, child, and grandchild.
    CreateData(2 ,2, 2);

    // Update the data source with the changes.
    UpdateData( );

    MessageBox.Show("Data randomly modified.", "Referential Integrity",
        MessageBoxButtons.OK, MessageBoxIcon.Information);
}

private void deleteButton_Click(object sender, System.EventArgs e)
{
    // Delete the parent data which cascades by default
    // to child and grandchild records.
    for(int i = ds.Tables[PARENTTABLENAME].Rows.Count; i > 0; i--)
        ds.Tables[PARENTTABLENAME].Rows[i - 1].Delete( );

    // Update the data source with the changes.
    UpdateData( );

    MessageBox.Show("Data deleted.", "Referential Integrity",
        MessageBoxButtons.OK, MessageBoxIcon.Information);
}
```

Discussion

To avoid referential integrity problems when updating the data source from a DataSet containing related tables, use one DataAdapter for each DataTable to update the deleted, updated, and inserted rows in the following order:

1. Deleted grandchild rows

2. Deleted child rows

3. Deleted parent rows

4. Updated parent rows

5. Inserted parent rows

6. Updated child rows

7. Inserted child rows

8. Updated grandchild rows

9. Inserted grandchild rows

In the solution, this is done using the following code:

```
daGrandchild.Update(ds.Tables[GRANDCHILDTABLENAME].Select(null, null,
DataViewRowState.Deleted));
daChild.Update(ds.Tables[CHILDTABLENAME].Select(null, null,
    DataViewRowState.Deleted));
daParent.Update(ds.Tables[PARENTTABLENAME].Select(null, null,
    DataViewRowState.Deleted));
```

```
daParent.Update(ds.Tables[PARENTTABLENAME].Select(null, null,
    DataViewRowState.ModifiedCurrent));
daParent.Update(ds.Tables[PARENTTABLENAME].Select(null, null,
    DataViewRowState.Added));
daChild.Update(ds.Tables[CHILDTABLENAME].Select(null, null,
    DataViewRowState.ModifiedCurrent));
daChild.Update(ds.Tables[CHILDTABLENAME].Select(null, null,
    DataViewRowState.Added));
daGrandchild.Update(ds.Tables[GRANDCHILDTABLENAME].Select(null, null,
    DataViewRowState.ModifiedCurrent));
daGrandchild.Update(ds.Tables[GRANDCHILDTABLENAME].Select(null, null,
    DataViewRowState.Added));
```

There are three related tables—parent, child, and grandparent—and one DataAdapter for each table. An overload of the Select( ) method of the DataTable is used to retrieve the subset of rows identified by the state argument containing a value from the DataViewRowState enumeration:

- Added to get the subset of inserted rows
- Deleted to get the subset of deleted rows
- ModifiedCurrent to get the subset of modified rows

There are few other considerations involving the primary key:

- If the primary key cannot be modified once added, the updated and inserted rows can be processed together in the same statement.
- If the primary key can be modified after it has been added, the database must cascade the updated primary key values to the child records or else a referential integrity violation will occur. The UpdateCommand property of child tables must accept either the Original or the Current value of the foreign key if it is used in the concurrency check.
- If the primary key for the DataTable is an auto-increment value and the primary key value is generated by the data source, the InsertCommand must return the primary key value from the data source and use it to update the value in the DataSet. The DataSet can automatically cascade this new value to the foreign keys in the related child records.

6.7   Enforcing Business Rules with Column Expressions

Problem

You need to enforce a business rule based on multiple columns in a table at the user interface tier.

Solution

Use expression-based columns to enforce business rules at the user interface tier. The business rule for this solution is that the sum of *Field1* and *Field2* for a row in the table must be *10*.

The schema of table TBL0607 used in this solution is shown in Table 6-5.

Table 6-5. TBL0607 schema

Column name	Data type	Length	Allow nulls?
Id	int	4	No
Field1	nvarchar	4	No
Field2	nvarchar	4	No

The sample uses four stored procedures, which are shown in Examples 6-21 through 6-24:

SP0607_Delete
> Used to delete a record from the table TBL0607 for a specified Id

SP0607_Get
> Used to retrieve a record for a specified Id or all records from the table TBL0607

SP0607_Insert
> Used to insert a record into the table TBL0607

SP0607_Update
> Used to update a record in the table TBL0607

Example 6-21. Stored procedure: SP0607_Delete

```
CREATE PROCEDURE SP0607_Delete
    @Id int
AS
    SET NOCOUNT ON

    delete
    from
        TBL0607
    where
        Id=@Id

    return 0
```

Example 6-22. Stored procedure: SP0607_Get

```
CREATE PROCEDURE SP0607_Get
    @Id int=null
AS
    SET NOCOUNT ON
```

Example 6-22. Stored procedure: SP0607_Get (continued)

```
if @Id is not null
begin
    select
        Id,
        Field1,
        Field2
    from
        TBL0607
    where
        Id=@Id

    return 0
end

select
    Id,
    Field1,
    Field2
from
    TBL0607

return 0
```

Example 6-23. Stored procedure: SP0607_Insert

```
CREATE PROCEDURE SP0607_Insert
    @Id int,
    @Field1 int,
    @Field2 int
AS
    SET NOCOUNT ON

    insert TBL0607(
        Id,
        Field1,
        Field2)
    values (
        @Id,
        @Field1,
        @Field2)

    if @@rowcount=0
        return 1

    return 0
```

Example 6-24. Stored procedure: SP0607_Update

```
CREATE PROCEDURE SP0607_Update
    @Id int,
    @Field1 int,
```

Example 6-24. Stored procedure: SP0607_Update (continued)

```
    @Field2 int
AS
    SET NOCOUNT ON

    update
        TBL0607
    set
        Field1=@Field1,
        Field2=@Field2
    where
        Id=@Id

    if @@rowcount=0
        return 1

    return 0
```

The sample code contains three event handlers:

Form.Load

> Sets up the sample by creating a DataTable and creating a schema for it matching TBL0607 in the database. An expression column is added to the table. The calculation returns a Boolean value indicating whether the sum of Field1 and Field2 is equal to 10. A DataAdapter is created and event handler is attached to handle its RowUpdating event. Delete, insert, and update commands using the stored procedures in this solution are created for the DataAdapter. The DataAdapter is used to fill the table and its default view is bound to the data grid on the form.

DataAdapter.RowUpdating

> Checks whether a row is being updated or inserted and whether the value of the expression column is false indicating that the data is invalid according to the business rule defined by the expression in the column. If the business rule has not been met, an error is set on the row and the update for the row is skipped.

Update Button.Click

> Uses the DataAdapter to update changes made to the DataTable back to table TBL0607 in the database.

The C# code is shown in Example 6-25.

Example 6-25. File: EnforceBusinessRulesWithColumnExpressionsForm.cs

```
// Namespaces, variables, and constants
using System;
using System.Configuration;
using System.Windows.Forms;
using System.Data;
using System.Data.SqlClient;
```

```
private DataTable dt;
private SqlDataAdapter da;

private const String TABLENAME           = "TBL0607";

// Table column name constants
private const String ID_FIELD            = "Id";
private const String FIELD1_FIELD        = "Field1";
private const String FIELD2_FIELD        = "Field2";
private const String CONSTRAINT_EXPRESSION = "ConstraintExpression";

// Stored procedure name constants
private const String DELETE_SP           = "SP0607_Delete";
private const String GET_SP              = "SP0607_Get";
private const String INSERT_SP           = "SP0607_Insert";
private const String UPDATE_SP           = "SP0607_Update";

// Stored procedure parameter name constants for table
private const String ID_PARM             = "@Id";
private const String FIELD1_PARM         = "@Field1";
private const String FIELD2_PARM         = "@Field2";

// ...

private void EnforceBusinessRulesWithColumnExpressionsForm_Load(
    object sender, System.EventArgs e)
{
    DataColumnCollection cols;

    // Build the table.
    dt = new DataTable(TABLENAME);
    cols = dt.Columns;
    cols.Add(ID_FIELD, typeof(Int32));
    cols.Add(FIELD1_FIELD, typeof(Int32));
    cols.Add(FIELD2_FIELD, typeof(Int32));
    // add the primary key
    dt.PrimaryKey = new DataColumn[] {cols[ID_FIELD]};
    // Expression to evaluate whether the sum of Field1 and Field2
    // equals 10
    cols.Add(CONSTRAINT_EXPRESSION, typeof(Boolean), FIELD1_FIELD +
        "+" + FIELD2_FIELD + " = 10");

    // Create the DataAdapter, handling the RowUpdating event.
    da = new SqlDataAdapter( );
    da.RowUpdating += new SqlRowUpdatingEventHandler(da_RowUpdating);
    SqlConnection conn = new SqlConnection(
        ConfigurationSettings.AppSettings["Sql_ConnectString"]);

    // Build the select command.
    SqlCommand selectCommand = new SqlCommand(GET_SP, conn);
    selectCommand.CommandType = CommandType.StoredProcedure;
    da.SelectCommand = selectCommand;
```

```
    // Build the delete command.
    SqlCommand deleteCommand = new SqlCommand(DELETE_SP, conn);
    deleteCommand.CommandType = CommandType.StoredProcedure;
    deleteCommand.Parameters.Add(ID_PARM, SqlDbType.Int, 0, ID_FIELD);
    da.DeleteCommand = deleteCommand;

    // Build the insert command.
    SqlCommand insertCommand = new SqlCommand(INSERT_SP, conn);
    insertCommand.CommandType = CommandType.StoredProcedure;
    insertCommand.Parameters.Add(ID_PARM, SqlDbType.Int, 0, ID_FIELD);
    insertCommand.Parameters.Add(FIELD1_PARM, SqlDbType.Int, 0,
        FIELD1_FIELD);
    insertCommand.Parameters.Add(FIELD2_PARM, SqlDbType.Int, 0,
        FIELD2_FIELD);
    da.InsertCommand = insertCommand;

    // Build the update command.
    SqlCommand updateCommand = new SqlCommand(UPDATE_SP, conn);
    updateCommand.CommandType = CommandType.StoredProcedure;
    updateCommand.Parameters.Add(ID_PARM, SqlDbType.Int, 0, ID_FIELD);
    updateCommand.Parameters.Add(FIELD1_PARM, SqlDbType.Int, 0,
        FIELD1_FIELD);
    updateCommand.Parameters.Add(FIELD2_PARM, SqlDbType.Int, 0,
        FIELD2_FIELD);
    da.UpdateCommand = updateCommand;

    // Fill the table.
    da.Fill(dt);

    // Bind the default view of the table to the grid.
    dataGrid.DataSource = dt.DefaultView;
}

private void da_RowUpdating(object sender, SqlRowUpdatingEventArgs e)
{
    // For insert or update statements, check that the
    // calculated constraint column is true.
    if((e.StatementType == StatementType.Insert ||
        e.StatementType == StatementType.Update) &&
        !(bool)e.Row[CONSTRAINT_EXPRESSION])
    {
        // Constraint has not been met.
        // Set an error on the row and skip it.
        e.Row.RowError = "Constraint error.";
        e.Status = UpdateStatus.SkipCurrentRow;
    }
}

private void updateButton_Click(object sender, System.EventArgs e)
{
    try
    {
```

```
        da.Update(dt);
    }
    catch(Exception ex)
    {
        MessageBox.Show(ex.Message);
    }
}
```

Discussion

The RowUpdating event of the DataAdapter occurs during the Update( ) method before the command to update a row is executed against the data source. The event fires with each row update attempt.

The RowUpdating event handler receives an argument of type RowUpdatingEventArgs that provides information specifically related to the event as described in Table 6-6.

Table 6-6. RowUpdatingEventArgs properties

Property	Description
Command	Gets the Command to execute during the Update( ) method.
Errors	Gets errors generated by the .NET data provider when the Command was executed.
Row	Gets the DataRow to send through the Update( ) method.
StatementType	Gets the type of SQL statement to execute. This is one of the following values from the StatementType enumeration: Select, Insert, Update, or Delete.
Status	Gets or sets the action to take with the current and remaining rows during the Update( ) method. This is a value from the UpdateStatus enumeration (described in Table 6-7).
TableMapping	Gets the DataTableMapping to send through the Update( ) method.

Table 6-7 describes the values in the UpdateStatus enumeration used by the Status property of the RowUpdatingEventArgs object.

Table 6-7. UpdateStatus enumeration

Value	Description
Continue	Continue processing the rows. This is the default value.
ErrorsOccurred	The event handler reports that the update should be treated as an error.
SkipAllRemainingRows	Do not update the current row and skip updating the remaining rows.
SkipCurrentRow	Do not update the current row and continue updating with the subsequent row.

The Update( ) method of the DataAdapter raises two events for every row in the data source that is updated. The order of the events is:

1. The values in the DataRow are moved to parameter values.

2. The OnRowUpdating event is raised.

3. The update command executes against the row in the data source.

4. If the UpdatedRowSource property of the Command is set to FirstReturnedRecord or Both, the first returned result is placed in the DataRow.

5. If the UpdateRowSource property of the Command is set to OutputParameters or Both, the output parameters are placed in the DataRow.

6. The OnDataRowUpdated event is raised.

7. AcceptChanges( ) is called.

If zero rows are affected, the DBConcurrencyException is raised during the update operation on a row. This usually indicates a concurrency violation.

The solution uses the RowUpdating event of the DataAdapter to check whether the expression column in the DataTable is true, indicating that the business rule has been satisfied, before a database record is updated. If the expression if false, an error is set on the row and the Status is set to SkipCurrentRow preventing the record in the database from being updated and continuing the processing with the next row.

6.8 Creating Constraints, PrimaryKeys, Relationships Based on Multiple Columns

Problem

You need to create a constraint, primary key, or a relationship between two tables in a DataSet using more than one column.

Solution

Use the System.Data.UniqueConstraint and System.Data.ForeignKeyConstraint types.

The sample code creates a DataSet containing two tables: Parent and Child. A multi-column unique constraint and primary key are created for the Parent table. A multi-column foreign-key constraint is created on the Child table. Finally, a DataRelation between the primary key in the Parent table and the foreign key in the Child table is created.

The C# code is shown in Example 6-26.

Example 6-26. File: MultiColumnConstraintAndRelationForm.cs

```
// Namespaces, variables, and constants
using System;
using System.Text;
using System.Data;

// ...
```

Example 6-26. File: MultiColumnConstraintAndRelationForm.cs (continued)

```
StringBuilder result = new StringBuilder( );

DataSet ds = new DataSet( );

// Create the parent table.
result.Append("Creating parent table." + Environment.NewLine);
DataTable dtParent = new DataTable("Parent");
DataColumnCollection pCols = dtParent.Columns;
pCols.Add("ParentKey1", typeof(Int32));
pCols.Add("ParentKey2", typeof(Int32));
pCols.Add("ParentData1", typeof(String));
pCols.Add("ParentData2", typeof(String));

// Set the multicolumn unique constraint.
result.Append("Creating unique constraint on parent table." +
    Environment.NewLine);
dtParent.Constraints.Add(new UniqueConstraint("UConstraint",
    new DataColumn[] {pCols["ParentKey1"], pCols["ParentKey2"]}, false));

// Set the multicolumn primary key.
result.Append("Creating primary key on parent table." +
    Environment.NewLine);
dtParent.PrimaryKey = new DataColumn[] {pCols["ParentKey1"],
    pCols["ParentKey2"]};

// Add the parent table to the DataSet.
ds.Tables.Add(dtParent);

// Create the child table.
result.Append("Creating child table." + Environment.NewLine);
DataTable dtChild = new DataTable("Child");
DataColumnCollection cCols = dtChild.Columns;
cCols.Add("ChildIndex1", typeof(Int32)).Unique = true;
cCols.Add("ParentKey1", typeof(Int32));
cCols.Add("ParentKey2", typeof(Int32));
cCols.Add("ChildData1", typeof(String));
cCols.Add("ChildData2", typeof(String));
ds.Tables.Add(dtChild);

// Set the foreign-key constraint.
result.Append("Creating foreign key contraint." + Environment.NewLine);
dtChild.Constraints.Add("FKConstraint",
    new DataColumn[] {pCols["ParentKey1"], pCols["ParentKey2"]},
    new DataColumn[] {cCols["ParentKey1"], cCols["ParentKey2"]});

// Create the relation between parent and child.
result.Append("Creating relationship." + Environment.NewLine);
ds.Relations.Add("Relation",
    new DataColumn[] {dtParent.Columns["ParentKey1"], dtParent.Columns["ParentKey2"]},
    new DataColumn[] {dtChild.Columns["ParentKey1"], dtChild.Columns["ParentKey2"]},
    true);

resultTextBox.Text = result.ToString( ) + Environment.NewLine + "Done.";
```

Discussion

Unique and foreign-key constraints

The System.Data.Constraint class is an abstract class that is the base class for the two .NET Framework built-in classes:

System.Data.UniqueConstraint
> Ensures that all data in the specified column or columns in the row is unique within the table. Defining a primary key for a DataTable by setting the PrimaryKey property automatically creates a unique constraint for the specified column or columns.

System.Data.ForeignKeyConstraint
> Enforces rules about how updates of values in rows or row deletions are propagated to related tables through the DeleteRule and UpdateRule properties, which define the action to be taken.

By default, a UniqueConstraint is created on the parent table and a ForeignKeyConstraint is created on the child table when a DataRelation object is created relating the two tables. Constraints are only enforced if the EnforceConstraints property is true.

The Add( ) method of the ConstraintCollection of the DataTable, which is accessed using the Constraints property, has two overloads that you can use to add a unique constraint to a table. The prototypes are:

```
public void Add(String name, DataColumn col, Boolean isPrimaryKey);
public void Add(String name, DataColumn[] cols, Boolean isPrimaryKey);
```

The arguments are:

name
> The name of the unique constraint

col
> The unique column in the table

cols
> The array of unique data columns in the table

isPrimaryKey
> Specifies whether the columns or columns represent the primary key for the table

There are two methods that you can use to add a foreign key constraint to a table. The prototypes are:

```
public void Add(String name, DataColumn parentCol, DataColumn childCol);
public void Add(String name, DataColumn[] parentCols,
    DataColumn childCols);
```

The arguments are:

name
>   The name of the foreign key constraint

parentCol
>   The column in the parent table

childCol
>   The column in the child table

parentCols
>   The array of columns in the parent table

childCols
>   The array of columns in the child table

There is also one method that you can use to add either a unique constraint or a foreign key constraint to a table. The prototype is:

```
public void Add(Constraint constraint);
```

The argument is:

constraint
>   The unique constraint or foreign key constraint object to add to the table

PrimaryKey

The PrimaryKey property of the DataTable is used to set or get the primary key for a table. The prototypes are:

```
DataColumn[] pka = DataTable.PrimaryKey;
DataTable.PrimaryKey = pka;
```

The argument is:

pka
>   An array of columns making up the primary key

DataRelation

The Add( ) method of the DataRelationCollection of the DataSet, which is accessed using the Relations property, has seven overloads that you can use to add a relationship between two tables to the DataSet. The prototypes are:

```
public void Add(DataRelation dr);
public virtual DataRelation Add(DataColumn parentCol, DataColumn childCol);
public virtual DataRelation Add(DataColumn[] parentCols,
    DataColumn[] childCols);
public virtual DataRelation Add(String name, DataColumn parentCol,
    DataColumn childCol);
public virtual DataRelation Add(String name, DataColumn[] parentCols,
    DataColumn[] childCols);
```

```
public virtual DataRelation Add(String name, DataColumn parentCol,
    DataColumn childCol, Boolean createFKConstraint);
public virtual DataRelation Add(String name, DataColumn[] parentCols,
    DataColumn[] childCols, Boolean createFKConstraint);
```

The arguments are:

dr
> A data relationship between a parent and child table

parentCol
> A column in the parent table

childCol
> A column in the child table

parentCols
> An array of columns in the parent table

childCols
> An array of columns in the child table

name
> The name of the data relation

createFKConstraint
> Specifies whether to create a foreign key constraint

6.9   Retrieving Constraints from a SQL Server Database

Problem

You need to programmatically define constraints in a DataSet and retrieve constraint information defined in a SQL Server database.

Solution

Use the INFORMATION_SCHEMA views and SQL Server system tables to get information about primary keys, foreign keys, and check constraints.

The sample code contains one event handler:

Get Constraints Button.Click
> Uses a SQL select statement to load the specified constraint information—primary key, foreign key, or check constraint—from the INFORMATION_SCHEMA views into a DataTable.

The C# code is shown in Example 6-27.

Example 6-27. File: ConstraintForm.cs

```csharp
// Namespaces, variables, and constants
using System;
using System.Configuration;
using System.Data;
using System.Data.SqlClient;
using System.Data.OleDb;

private const String GETPRIMARYKEYCONSTRAINTS =
    "SELECT tc.CONSTRAINT_NAME, tc.TABLE_NAME, " +
    "kcu.COLUMN_NAME, kcu.ORDINAL_POSITION " +
    "FROM INFORMATION_SCHEMA.TABLE_CONSTRAINTS tc " +
    "JOIN INFORMATION_SCHEMA.KEY_COLUMN_USAGE kcu ON " +
    "tc.CONSTRAINT_NAME=kcu.CONSTRAINT_NAME " +
    "WHERE tc.CONSTRAINT_TYPE='PRIMARY KEY' " +
    "ORDER BY tc.TABLE_NAME, kcu.COLUMN_NAME, kcu.ORDINAL_POSITION";

private const String GETFOREIGNKEYCONSTRAINTS =
    "SELECT rc.CONSTRAINT_NAME, rc.UPDATE_RULE, rc.DELETE_RULE, " +
    "kcuP.TABLE_NAME ParentTable, kcuC.TABLE_NAME ChildTable, " +
    "kcuP.COLUMN_NAME ParentColumn, kcuC.COLUMN_NAME ChildColumn " +
    "FROM INFORMATION_SCHEMA.REFERENTIAL_CONSTRAINTS rc " +
    "LEFT JOIN INFORMATION_SCHEMA.KEY_COLUMN_USAGE kcuP ON " +
    "rc.UNIQUE_CONSTRAINT_NAME=kcuP.CONSTRAINT_NAME " +
    "LEFT JOIN INFORMATION_SCHEMA.KEY_COLUMN_USAGE kcuC ON " +
    "rc.CONSTRAINT_NAME=kcuC.CONSTRAINT_NAME AND " +
    "kcuP.ORDINAL_POSITION=kcuC.ORDINAL_POSITION " +
    "ORDER BY kcuP.TABLE_NAME, kcuC.TABLE_NAME, kcuP.ORDINAL_POSITION";

private const String GETCHECKCONSTRAINTS =
    "SELECT tc.TABLE_NAME, tc.CONSTRAINT_NAME, cc.CHECK_CLAUSE " +
    "FROM INFORMATION_SCHEMA.TABLE_CONSTRAINTS tc " +
    "JOIN INFORMATION_SCHEMA.CHECK_CONSTRAINTS cc ON " +
    "tc.CONSTRAINT_NAME=cc.CONSTRAINT_NAME " +
    "WHERE CONSTRAINT_TYPE='CHECK' " +
    "ORDER BY tc.TABLE_NAME, cc.CONSTRAINT_NAME";

// ...

private void getConstraintsButton_Click(object sender, System.EventArgs e)
{
    // Create the DataAdapter to retrieve schema information.
    SqlDataAdapter da = null;
    if (primaryKeyRadioButton.Checked)
        da = new SqlDataAdapter(GETPRIMARYKEYCONSTRAINTS,
            ConfigurationSettings.AppSettings["Sql_ConnectString"]);
    else if (foreignKeyRadioButton.Checked)
        da = new SqlDataAdapter(GETFOREIGNKEYCONSTRAINTS,
            ConfigurationSettings.AppSettings["Sql_ConnectString"]);
    else if (checkRadioButton.Checked)
        da = new SqlDataAdapter(GETCHECKCONSTRAINTS,
            ConfigurationSettings.AppSettings["Sql_ConnectString"]);
```

Example 6-27. File: ConstraintForm.cs (continued)

```
    // Create and fill table with schema information.
    DataTable dt = new DataTable( );
    da.Fill(dt);

    // Bind the default view of the table with the grid.
    constraintsDataGrid.DataSource = dt.DefaultView;
}
```

Discussion

Information schema views were first available in SQL Server 7.0 and later. They provide system-table independent access to SQL Server metadata. The views are based on system tables and provide a layer of abstraction that allows applications to continue to work properly if the system tables change in future releases of SQL Server. Information schema views provide an alternative to using system stored procedures that were previously and are still available. The INFORMATION_SCHEMA views conform to the SQL-92 Standard.

Information schema views are defined within each database in a schema named INFORMATION_SCHEMA. To access the views, specify the fully qualified view name. In the solution, for example, the view containing metadata about the tables in the database is accessed using the following syntax:

```
    INFORMATION_SCHEMA.TABLES
```

The metadata returned is limited to that which the user has permission to view. Like any other views, information schema views can also be joined in queries or participate in complex queries to extract specific information. For detailed information about the different views available, refer to SQL Server Books Online.

The following three subsections explain how the solution retrieves details about the primary key, the foreign key, and the check constraints in the database. The information schema views that are used in the solution are described in the subsection following those subsections.

Primary key constraints

Primary key information is obtained by querying the TABLE_CONSTRAINTS (Table 6-11) and KEY_COLUMN_USAGE (Table 6-9) information schema views. The views are joined on the CONSTRAINT_NAME field and restricted to constraints with a CONSTRAINT_TYPE of *Primary Key*. The result set is sorted on the TABLE_NAME, COLUMN_NAME, and ORDINAL_POSITION fields.

```
    SELECT
        tc.CONSTRAINT_NAME,
        tc.TABLE_NAME,
        kcu.COLUMN_NAME,
        kcu.ORDINAL_POSITION
```

```
FROM
    INFORMATION_SCHEMA.TABLE_CONSTRAINTS tc JOIN
    INFORMATION_SCHEMA.KEY_COLUMN_USAGE kcu ON
    tc.CONSTRAINT_NAME = kcu.CONSTRAINT_NAME
WHERE
    tc.CONSTRAINT_TYPE = 'PRIMARY KEY'
ORDER BY
    tc.TABLE_NAME,
    kcu.COLUMN_NAME,
    kcu.ORDINAL_POSITION
```

Foreign key constraints

Foreign key information is obtained by querying the REFERENTIAL_CONSTRAINTS (Table 6-10) and KEY_COLUMN_USAGE (Table 6-9) information schema views. The REFERENTIAL_CONSTRAINTS view is joined to the KEY_COLUMN_USAGE view on the UNIQUE_CONSTRAINT_NAME column to return information about the parent table and its columns. The REFERENTIAL_CONSTRAINTS view is joined again to the KEY_COLUMN_USAGE view on the CONSTRAINT_NAME matching the ORDINAL_POSITION of the parent column to return information about the child table and its columns. The result set is sorted in ascending order on the parent TABLE_NAME, child TABLE_NAME, and parent constraint column ORDINAL_POSITION.

```
SELECT
    rc.CONSTRAINT_NAME,
    rc.UPDATE_RULE,
    rc.DELETE_RULE,
    kcuP.TABLE_NAME ParentTable,
    kcuC.TABLE_NAME ChildTable,
    kcuP.COLUMN_NAME ParentColumn,
    kcuC.COLUMN_NAME ChildColumn
FROM
    INFORMATION_SCHEMA.REFERENTIAL_CONSTRAINTS rc LEFT JOIN
    INFORMATION_SCHEMA.KEY_COLUMN_USAGE kcuP ON
    rc.UNIQUE_CONSTRAINT_NAME = kcuP.CONSTRAINT_NAME LEFT JOIN
    INFORMATION_SCHEMA.KEY_COLUMN_USAGE kcuC ON
    rc.CONSTRAINT_NAME = kcuC.CONSTRAINT_NAME AND
    kcuP.ORDINAL_POSITION = kcuC.ORDINAL_POSITION
ORDER BY
    kcuP.TABLE_NAME,
    kcuC.TABLE_NAME,
    kcuP.ORDINAL_POSITION;
```

Check constraint

Check constraint information is obtained by querying the TABLE_CONSTRAINTS (Table 6-11) and CHECK_CONSTRAINTS (Table 6-8) information schema views. The views are joined on the CONSTRAINT_NAME field and restricted to constraints with a CONSTRAINT_TYPE of *CHECK*. The result set is sorted on the TABLE_NAME and CONSTRAINT_NAME fields.

```
SELECT
    tc.TABLE_NAME,
    tc.CONSTRAINT_NAME,
    cc.CHECK_CLAUSE
FROM
    INFORMATION_SCHEMA.TABLE_CONSTRAINTS tc JOIN
    INFORMATION_SCHEMA.CHECK_CONSTRAINTS cc ON
    tc.CONSTRAINT_NAME = cc.CONSTRAINT_NAME
WHERE
    CONSTRAINT_TYPE = 'CHECK';
ORDER BY
    tc.TABLE_NAME,
    cc.CONSTRAINT_NAME
```

Information schema views used in this solution

The four information schema views used by the solution are described in this subsection.

Table 6-8 describes the CHECK_CONSTRAINTS information schema view that is based on the sysobjects and syscomments system tables. This view contains one row for each check constraint in the database.

Table 6-8. CHECK_CONSTRAINTS information schema view

Column name	Data type	Description
CONSTRAINT_CATALOG	nvarchar(128)	Constraint qualifier
CONSTRAINT_SCHEMA	nvarchar(128)	Constraint owner name
CONSTRAINT_NAME	sysname	Constraint name
CHECK_CLAUSE	nvarchar(4000)	Transact-SQL statement

Table 6-9 describes the KEY_COLUMN_USAGE information schema view that is based on the sysobjects, syscolumns, sysreferences, spt_values, and sysindexes system tables. This view contains one row for each column in the current database that is constrained as a key.

Table 6-9. KEY_COLUMN_USAGE information schema view

Column name	Data type	Description
CONSTRAINT_CATALOG	nvarchar(128)	Constraint qualifier
CONSTRAINT_SCHEMA	nvarchar(128)	Constraint owner name
CONSTRAINT_NAME	nvarchar(128)	Constraint name
TABLE_CATALOG	nvarchar(128)	Table qualifier
TABLE_SCHEMA	nvarchar(128)	Table owner name
TABLE_NAME	nvarchar(128)	Table name
COLUMN_NAME	nvarchar(128)	Column name
ORDINAL_POSITION	int	Column ordinal

Table 6-10 describes the REFERENTIAL_CONSTRAINTS information schema view that is based on the sysobjects, sysreferences, and sysindexes system tables. This view contains one row for each foreign key constraint in the current database.

Table 6-10. REFERENTIAL_CONSTRAINTS information schema view

Column name	Data type	Description
CONSTRAINT_CATALOG	nvarchar(128)	Database name
CONSTRAINT_SCHEMA	nvarchar(128)	Constraint owner name
CONSTRAINT_NAME	sysname	Constraint name
UNIQUE_CONSTRAINT_CATALOG	nvarchar(128)	Unique database name
UNIQUE_CONSTRAINT_SCHEMA	nvarchar(128)	Unique constraint owner name
UNIQUE_CONSTRAINT_NAME	sysname	Unique constraint name
MATCH_OPTION	varchar(7)	Referential constraint-matching condition
UPDATE_RULE	varchar(9)	Action taken if the T-SQL UPDATE statement violates referential integrity defined by the constraint
DELETE_RULE	varchar(9)	Action taken if the T-SQL DELETE statement violates referential integrity defined by the constraint

Table 6-11 describes the TABLE_CONSTRAINTS information schema view that is based on the sysobjects system table. This view contains one row for each table constraint in the current database.

Table 6-11. TABLE_CONSTRAINTS information schema view

Column name	Data type	Description
CONSTRAINT_CATALOG	nvarchar(128)	Constraint name
CONSTRAINT_SCHEMA	nvarchar(128)	Constraint owner
CONSTRAINT_NAME	sysname	Constraint name
TABLE_CATALOG	nvarchar(128)	Database name
TABLE_SCHEMA	nvarchar(128)	Table owner
TABLE_NAME	sysname	Table name
CONSTRAINT_TYPE	varchar(11)	Type of constraint: CHECK, UNIQUE, PRIMARY KEY, or FOREIGN KEY
IS_DEFERRABLE	varchar(2)	Specifies whether constraint checking can be deferred; always returns the value *NO*.
INITIALLY_DEFERRED	varchar(2)	Specifies whether constraint checking is initially deferred; always returns the value *NO*

6.10   Checking for Concurrency Violations

Problem

You need to check for concurrency violations.

Solution

Use a `timestamp` column to manage data concurrency violations.

The schema of table TBL0610 used in this solution is shown in Table 6-12.

Table 6-12. TBL0610 schema

Column name	Data type	Length	Allow nulls?
Id	int	4	No
Field1	nvarchar	50	Yes
rowversion	timestamp	8	No

The sample code contains four event handlers and two methods:

Form.Load

> Sets up the sample by creating two DataTable objects: *A* and *B*. For each, a DataAdapter is created and a handler is attached to handle the RowUpdated event. The DataAdapter is used to fill the DataTable with both schema and data from table TBL0610 in the database. The update command is defined for the DataAdapter using the `timestamp` column in the WHERE clause to catch concurrency errors. The first row from both tables is displayed on the form simulating the view of two different simultaneous data users.

DataAdapter.RowUpdated

> Checks if the row was inserted or updated. For those rows, the current value of the timestamp column is retrieved from the TBL0610 in the database and used to update the row in the DataTable.

Update( )

> This method copies the specified value for Field1 from the text box into the DataTable. The DataAdapter is used to update DataTable changes to table TBL0610 in the database. If a DBConcurrencyException is encountered, the change to the row is rejected.

DisplayRow( )

> This method is used to display data from a specified row in DataTable *A* or *B* to the corresponding user display on the form.

Update Button.Click

Calls the Update( ) method to update changes made to the row in either DataTable *A* or *B*. The DisplayRow( ) method is called to update the corresponding row displayed on the form.

Refresh Button.Click

Gets the latest values for the row in DataTable *A* or *B* from table TBL0610 in the database. The DisplayRow( ) method is called to update the corresponding row displayed on the form.

The C# code is shown in Example 6-28.

Example 6-28. File: RowversionForm.cs

```csharp
// Namespaces, variables, and constants
using System;
using System.Configuration;
using System.Windows.Forms;
using System.Text;

using System.Data;
using System.Data.SqlClient;

private DataTable dtA, dtB;
private SqlDataAdapter daA, daB;

private const String TABLENAME = "TBL0610";

// ...

private void RowversionForm_Load(object sender, System.EventArgs e)
{
    // Build statements to select only the row for ID = 1
    // and to update the data for the DataAdapter.
    String selectText = "SELECT Id, Field1, rowversion FROM " +
        TABLENAME + " WHERE Id = 1";
    String updateText = "UPDATE " + TABLENAME + " " +
        "SET Field1 = @Field1 " +
        "WHERE Id = 1 AND rowversion = @rowversion";

    // Create table A and fill it with the schema.
    dtA = new DataTable("A");
    daA = new SqlDataAdapter(selectText,
        ConfigurationSettings.AppSettings["Sql_ConnectString"]);
    daA.RowUpdated += new SqlRowUpdatedEventHandler(da_RowUpdated);
    daA.FillSchema(dtA, SchemaType.Source);
    dtA.Columns["rowversion"].ReadOnly = false;
    daA.Fill(dtA);

    // Create the update command and define the parameters.
    daA.UpdateCommand = new SqlCommand(updateText,
        daA.SelectCommand.Connection);
    daA.UpdateCommand.CommandType = CommandType.Text;
```

Example 6-28. File: RowversionForm.cs (continued)

```
    daA.UpdateCommand.Parameters.Add("@Id", SqlDbType.Int, 0, "Id");
    daA.UpdateCommand.Parameters["@Id"].SourceVersion =
        DataRowVersion.Original;
    daA.UpdateCommand.Parameters.Add("@Field1", SqlDbType.NVarChar, 50,
        "Field1");
    daA.UpdateCommand.Parameters["@Field1"].SourceVersion =
        DataRowVersion.Current;
    daA.UpdateCommand.Parameters.Add("@rowversion", SqlDbType.Timestamp, 0,
        "rowversion");
    daA.UpdateCommand.Parameters["@rowversion"].SourceVersion =
        DataRowVersion.Original;

    // Create table B and fill it with the schema.
    dtB = new DataTable("B");
    daB = new SqlDataAdapter(selectText,
        ConfigurationSettings.AppSettings["Sql_ConnectString"]);
    daB.RowUpdated += new SqlRowUpdatedEventHandler(da_RowUpdated);
    daB.FillSchema(dtB, SchemaType.Source);
    dtB.Columns["rowversion"].ReadOnly = false;
    daB.Fill(dtB);

    // Create the update command and define the parameters.
    daB.UpdateCommand = new SqlCommand(updateText,
        daB.SelectCommand.Connection);
    daB.UpdateCommand.CommandType = CommandType.Text;
    daB.UpdateCommand.Parameters.Add("@Id", SqlDbType.Int, 0, "Id");
    daB.UpdateCommand.Parameters["@Id"].SourceVersion =
        DataRowVersion.Original;
    daB.UpdateCommand.Parameters.Add("@Field1", SqlDbType.NVarChar, 50,
        "Field1");
    daB.UpdateCommand.Parameters["@Field1"].SourceVersion =
        DataRowVersion.Current;
    daB.UpdateCommand.Parameters.Add("@rowversion", SqlDbType.Timestamp, 0,
        "rowversion");
    daB.UpdateCommand.Parameters["@rowversion"].SourceVersion =
        DataRowVersion.Original;

    // Display the first row (ID=1) from both tables on the form.
    DisplayRow(dtA, 0);
    DisplayRow(dtB, 0);
}

private void da_RowUpdated(object sender, SqlRowUpdatedEventArgs e)
{
    // Check if an insert or update operation is being performed.
    if(e.Status == UpdateStatus.Continue &&
        (e.StatementType == StatementType.Insert ||
        e.StatementType == StatementType.Update))
    {
        // Build a command object to retrieve the updated timestamp.
        String sqlGetRowVersion = "SELECT rowversion FROM " +
            TABLENAME + " WHERE Id = " + e.Row["Id"];
```

Example 6-28. File: RowversionForm.cs (continued)

```
        SqlConnection conn = new SqlConnection(
            ConfigurationSettings.AppSettings["Sql_ConnectString"]);
        SqlCommand cmd = new SqlCommand(sqlGetRowVersion, conn);

        // Set the timestamp to the new value in the data source and
        // call accept changes.
        conn.Open( );
        e.Row["rowversion"] = (Byte[])cmd.ExecuteScalar( );
        conn.Close( );
        e.Row.AcceptChanges( );
    }
}

private void Update(SqlDataAdapter da, DataTable dt, TextBox field1TextBox)
{
    // Move the value for the field named Field1
    // from the form to the DataTable for updating.
    dt.Rows[0]["Field1"] = field1TextBox.Text;

    // Update the row table.
    try
    {
        da.Update(dt);
    }
    catch (DBConcurrencyException ex)
    {
        // Error if timestamp does not match
        MessageBox.Show(ex.Message);
        dt.RejectChanges( );
    }
}

private void DisplayRow(DataTable dt, int index)
{
    if (dt.TableName == "A")
    {
        aIdTextBox.Text = dt.Rows[index]["Id"].ToString( );
        aField1TextBox.Text = dt.Rows[index]["Field1"].ToString( );
        aRowversionTextBox.Text = Convert.ToBase64String(
            (Byte[])dt.Rows[index]["rowversion"]);
    }
    else
    {
        bIdTextBox.Text = dt.Rows[index]["Id"].ToString( );
        bField1TextBox.Text = dt.Rows[index]["Field1"].ToString( );
        bRowversionTextBox.Text = Convert.ToBase64String(
            (Byte[])dt.Rows[index]["rowversion"]);
    }
}

private void updateButton_Click(object sender, System.EventArgs e)
{
```

Example 6-28. File: RowversionForm.cs (continued)

```
    if(((Button)sender).Tag.ToString( ) == "A")
    {
        Update(daA, dtA, aField1TextBox);
        DisplayRow(dtA, 0);
    }
    else
    {
        Update(daB, dtB, bField1TextBox);
        DisplayRow(dtB, 0);
    }
}

private void refreshButton_Click(object sender, System.EventArgs e)
{
    if(((Button)sender).Tag.ToString( ) == "A")
    {
        daA.Fill(dtA);
        DisplayRow(dtA, 0);
    }
    else
    {
        daB.Fill(dtB);
        DisplayRow(dtB, 0);
    }
}
```

Discussion

A timestamp is a data type that automatically generates an 8-byte binary value guaranteed to be unique within the database.

The T-SQL timestamp data type is not the same as the timestamp data type defined in the SQL-92 standard. The timestamp data type defined by the SQL-92 standard is equivalent to the T-SQL datetime data type.

SQL Server 2000 introduced the *data type synonym* rowversion for the timestamp data type and recommends its use wherever possible in DDL statements. One difference between the timestamp data type and its data type synonym rowversion is that the timestamp data type does not require a column name while the rowversion data type does.

A table can have only one timestamp column. The value of the timestamp field is updated with the current database timestamp value from the @@DBTS function each time a row having a timestamp column is inserted or updated. This makes it a poor choice as part of a key, especially a primary key, since the index would be rebuilt with each row inserted or updated and the performance would suffer.

The `timestamp` value is not related to the date and time that data is inserted or updated. To record the time of record inserts and updates, define a `datetime` column in the table and create update and insert triggers to set its value.

6.11   Resolving Data Conflicts

Problem

You need to effectively resolve data conflicts and prevent overwriting of existing data when attempting to update changes in a `DataSet` to a database where the underlying data has changed.

Solution

Handle the `DBConcurrencyException` within the `RowUpdated` event of the `DataAdapter`.

The schema of table TBL0611 used in this solution is shown in Table 6-13.

Table 6-13. TBL0611 schema

Column name	Data type	Length	Allow nulls?
Id	int	4	No
Field1	nvarchar	50	Yes

The sample code contains seven event handlers:

`Form.Load`
> Creates a `DataSet` *A* containing a single `DataTable` *A*, filling the schema and data for the table from TBL0611 from the database using a `DataAdapter`. The `ContinueUpdateOnError` property of the `DataAdapter` is set to true. A `CommandBuilder` object is created to generate the updating logic for the `DataAdapter`. The default view of `DataTable` *A* is bound to a data grid on the form.
>
> A conflict table is created to store the original row data for a row when a concurrency error is encountered while updating a row from `DataTable` *A* back to TBL0611 in the database. A `DataAdapter` that uses a parameterized SQL `SELECT` statement to retrieve the original row data is created. The schema for the conflict table is loaded from TBL0611 using the `DataAdapter`. The default view of the conflict table is bound to a data grid on the form.
>
> A `DataSet` *B* and a conflict table for `DataTable` *B* row update concurrency errors are created in the same way as described for `DataSet` *A*.

Refresh A `Button.Click`
> Clears the conflict table, clears the data in table *A*, and uses a `DataAdapter` to fill table *A* from TBL0611 in the database.

Refresh B `Button.Click`

Clears the conflict table, clears the data in table *B*, and uses a `DataAdapter` to fill table *B* from TBL0611 in the database.

Update A `Button.Click`

Clears the conflict table and uses a `DataAdapter` to update changes made to table *A* back to table TBL0611 in the database.

Update B `Button.Click`

Clears the conflict table and uses a `DataAdapter` to update changes made to table *B* back to table TBL0611 in the database.

`A DataAdapter.RowUpdated`

Checks to see if a concurrency error occurred when updating the row in `DataTable` *A* to table TBL0611 in the database. If an error occurred during the deletion of a row, the `RejectChanges( )` method is used to cancel the delete.

For all rows with a concurrency error, the `Id` for the row is retrieved from the row and used with the `DataAdapter` for the conflict table to try to get the original data for the row from the TBL0611 in the database. An error is set on the row in the conflict table indicating whether it was changed (the row in error was retrieved from the database) or deleted (a row in error could not be retrieved from the database).

`B DataAdapter.RowUpdated`

Checks to see if a concurrency error occurred when updating the row in `DataTable` *B* to table TBL0611 in the database. If an error occurred during the deletion of a row, the `RejectChanges( )` method is used to cancel the delete.

For all rows with a concurrency error, the `Id` for the row is retrieved from the row and used with the `DataAdapter` for the conflict table to try to get the original data for the row from the TBL0611 in the database. An error is set on the row in the conflict table indicating whether it was changed (the row in error was retrieved from the database) or deleted (a row in error could not be retrieved from the database).

The C# code is shown in Example 6-29.

Example 6-29. File: ResolveDataConflictsForm.cs

```
// Namespaces, variables, and constants
using System;
using System.Configuration;
using System.Text;
using System.Data;
using System.Data.SqlClient;

private const String TABLENAME    = "TBL0611";

private SqlDataAdapter daA, daB;
private DataSet dsA, dsB;
```

Example 6-29. File: ResolveDataConflictsForm.cs (continued)

```csharp
// ...

private void ResolveDataConflictsForm_Load(object sender,
    System.EventArgs e)
{
    // Tables A and B are filled from the same data source table.
    String sqlText = "SELECT * FROM " + TABLENAME;

    // Create the DataAdapter for table A.
    daA = new SqlDataAdapter(sqlText,
        ConfigurationSettings.AppSettings["Sql_SqlAuth_ConnectString"]);
    daA.ContinueUpdateOnError = true;
    // Handle the RowUpdated event.
    daA.RowUpdated += new SqlRowUpdatedEventHandler(daA_RowUpdated);
    // Get the schema and data for table A in the DataSet.
    dsA = new DataSet("A");
    daA.FillSchema(dsA, SchemaType.Source, TABLENAME);
    daA.Fill(dsA, TABLENAME);
    // Create the command builder.
    SqlCommandBuilder cbA = new SqlCommandBuilder(daA);
    // Bind the default view for table A to the grid.
    dataGridA.DataSource = dsA.Tables[TABLENAME].DefaultView;

    // Create a DataAdapter to retrieve original rows
    // for conflicts when updating table A.
    conflictDaA = new SqlDataAdapter(sqlText + " WHERE Id = @Id",
        ConfigurationSettings.AppSettings["Sql_ConnectString"]);
    conflictDaA.SelectCommand.Parameters.Add("@Id", SqlDbType.Int, 0);
    // Create a DataSet with the conflict table schema.
    conflictDsA = new DataSet();
    daA.FillSchema(conflictDsA, SchemaType.Source, TABLENAME);
    // Bind the default view for conflict table B to the grid.
    conflictDataGridA.DataSource =
        conflictDsA.Tables[TABLENAME].DefaultView;

    // Create the DataAdapter for table B.
    daB = new SqlDataAdapter(sqlText,
        ConfigurationSettings.AppSettings["Sql_SqlAuth_ConnectString"]);
    daB.ContinueUpdateOnError = true;
    // Handle the RowUpdated event.
    daB.RowUpdated += new SqlRowUpdatedEventHandler(daB_RowUpdated);
    // Get the schema and data for table A in the DataSet.
    dsB = new DataSet("B");
    daB.FillSchema(dsB, SchemaType.Source, TABLENAME);
    daB.Fill(dsB, TABLENAME);
    // Create the command builder.
    SqlCommandBuilder cbB = new SqlCommandBuilder(daB);
    // Bind the default view for table A to the grid.
    dataGridB.DataSource = dsB.Tables[TABLENAME].DefaultView;
```

Example 6-29. File: ResolveDataConflictsForm.cs (continued)

```csharp
    // Create a DataAdapter to retrieve original rows
    // for conflicts when updating table B.
    conflictDaB = new SqlDataAdapter(sqlText + " WHERE Id = @Id",
        ConfigurationSettings.AppSettings["Sql_ConnectString"]);
    conflictDaB.SelectCommand.Parameters.Add("@Id", SqlDbType.Int, 0);
    // Create a DataSet with the conflict table schema.
    conflictDsB = new DataSet( );
    daB.FillSchema(conflictDsB,SchemaType.Source,TABLENAME);
    // Bind the default view for conflict table B to the grid.
    conflictDataGridB.DataSource =
        conflictDsB.Tables[TABLENAME].DefaultView;
}

private void refreshAButton_Click(object sender, System.EventArgs e)
{
    // Clear the conflict table and reload the data.
    conflictDsA.Clear( );

    dsA.Clear( );
    daA.Fill(dsA, TABLENAME);
}

private void refreshBButton_Click(object sender, System.EventArgs e)
{
    // Clear the conflict table and reload the data.
    conflictDsB.Clear( );

    dsB.Clear( );
    daB.Fill(dsB, TABLENAME);
}

private void updateAButton_Click(object sender, System.EventArgs e)
{
    // Clear the conflict table and update table A to data source.
    conflictDsA.Clear( );
    daA.Update(dsA, TABLENAME);
}

private void updateBButton_Click(object sender, System.EventArgs e)
{
    // Clear the conflict table and update table B to data source.
    conflictDsB.Clear( );
    daB.Update(dsB, TABLENAME);
}

private void daA_RowUpdated(object sender, SqlRowUpdatedEventArgs e)
{
    // Check if a concurrency exception occurred.
    if (e.Status == UpdateStatus.ErrorsOccurred &&
        e.Errors.GetType( ) == typeof(DBConcurrencyException))
    {
```

Example 6-29. File: ResolveDataConflictsForm.cs (continued)

```csharp
            // If the row was deleted, reject the delete.
            if(e.Row.RowState == DataRowState.Deleted)
                e.Row.RejectChanges( );

            // Get the row ID.
            conflictDaA.SelectCommand.Parameters["@Id"].Value =
                e.Row["ID"];
            // Get the row from the data source for the conflicts table.
            if(conflictDaA.Fill(conflictDsA, TABLENAME) == 1)
                e.Row.RowError =
                    "Row has been changed in the database.";
            else
                e.Row.RowError =
                    "Row has been deleted from the database.";
        }
}

private void daB_RowUpdated(object sender, SqlRowUpdatedEventArgs e)
{
    // Bheck if a concurrency exception occurred.
    if (e.Status == UpdateStatus.ErrorsOccurred &&
        e.Errors.GetType( ) == typeof(DBConcurrencyException))
    {
        // If the row was deleted, reject the delete.
        if(e.Row.RowState == DataRowState.Deleted)
            e.Row.RejectChanges( );

        // Get the row ID.
        conflictDaB.SelectCommand.Parameters["@Id"].Value =
            e.Row["ID"];
        // Get the row from the data source for the conflicts table.
        if(conflictDaB.Fill(conflictDsB, TABLENAME) == 1)
            e.Row.RowError =
                "Row has been changed in the database.";
        else
            e.Row.RowError =
                "Row has been deleted from the database.";
    }
}
```

Discussion

The RowUpdated event of the DataAdapter occurs during the Update( ) method after the command to update a row is executed against the data source. The event fires with each row update attempt.

The RowUpdated event handler receives an argument of type RowUpdatedEventArgs that provides information specifically related to the event as described in Table 6-14.

Table 6-14. RowUpdatedEventArgs properties

Property	Description
Command	Gets or sets the Command executed when the Update( ) method is called.
Errors	Gets errors generated by the .NET data provider when the Command was executed.
RecordsAffected	Gets the number of rows changed, inserted, or deleted by the execution of the Command.
Row	Gets the DataRow sent through the Update( ) method.
StatementType	Gets the type of SQL statement executed. This is one of the following values from the StatementType enumeration: Select, Insert, Update, or Delete.
Status	Gets or sets the action to take with the current and remaining rows during the Update( ) method. This is a value from the UpdateStatus enumeration described in Table 6-15.
TableMapping	Gets the DataTableMapping sent through the Update( ) method.

Table 6-15 describes the values in the UpdateStatus enumeration used by the Status property of the RowUpdatedEventArgs object.

Table 6-15. UpdateStatus enumeration

Value	Description
Continue	Continue processing the rows. This is the default value.
ErrorsOccurred	The event handler reports that the update should be treated as an error.
SkipAllRemainingRows	Do not update the current row and skip updating the remaining rows.
SkipCurrentRow	Do not update the current row and continue updating with the subsequent row.

The Update( ) method of the DataAdapter raises two events for every row in the data source that is updated. The order of the events is:

1. The values in the DataRow are moved to parameter values.

2. The OnRowUpdating event is raised.

3. The update command executes against the row in the data source.

4. If the UpdatedRowSource property of the Command is set to FirstReturnedRecord or Both, the first returned result is placed in the DataRow.

5. If the UpdateRowSource property of the Command is set to OutputParameters or Both, the output parameters are placed in the DataRow.

6. The OnDataRowUpdated event is raised.

7. AcceptChanges( ) is called.

The DBConcurrencyException is raised during the update operation on a row if zero rows are affected. This usually indicates a concurrency violation.

6.12   Using Transaction Isolation Levels to Protect Data

Problem

You want to effectively use transaction isolation levels to ensure data consistency for a range of data rows.

Solution

Set and use isolation levels as shown in the following example.

The sample code contains three event handlers:

Start Tran `Button.Click`
> Opens a Connection and starts a transaction with the specified isolation level: Chaos, ReadCommitted, ReadUncommitted, RepeatableRead, Serializable, or Unspecified. Within the transaction, a DataTable is filled with the Orders table from the Northwind database. The default view of the table is bound to the data grid on the form.

Cancel `Button.Click`
> Rolls back the transaction, closes the connection, and clears the data grid.

`Form.Closing`
> Rolls back the transaction and closes the connection.

The C# code is shown in Example 6-30.

Example 6-30. File: TransactionIsolationLevelsForm.cs

```
// Namespaces, variables, and constants
using System;
using System.Configuration;
using System.Windows.Forms;
using System.Data;
using System.Data.SqlClient;

private SqlConnection conn;
private SqlTransaction tran;

// ...

private void startButton_Click(object sender, System.EventArgs e)
{
    startButton.Enabled = false;

    // Get the user-defined isolation level.
    IsolationLevel il = IsolationLevel.Unspecified;
    if(chaosRadioButton.Checked)
        il = IsolationLevel.Chaos;
    else if(readCommittedRadioButton.Checked)
        il = IsolationLevel.ReadCommitted;
```

Example 6-30. File: TransactionIsolationLevelsForm.cs (continued)

```
        else if(readUncommittedRadioButton.Checked)
            il = IsolationLevel.ReadUncommitted;
        else if(repeatableReadRadioButton.Checked)
            il = IsolationLevel.RepeatableRead;
        else if(serializableRadioButton.Checked)
            il = IsolationLevel.Serializable;
        else if(unspecifiedRadioButton.Checked)
            il = IsolationLevel.Unspecified;

        // Open a connection.
        conn = new SqlConnection(
            ConfigurationSettings.AppSettings["Sql_ConnectString"]);
        conn.Open();
        try
        {
            // Start a transaction.
            tran = conn.BeginTransaction(il);
        }
        catch(Exception ex)
        {
            // Could not start the transaction. Close the connection.
            conn.Close();

            MessageBox.Show(ex.Message,"Transaction Isolation Levels",
                MessageBoxButtons.OK, MessageBoxIcon.Error);
            startButton.Enabled = true;
            return;
        }

        String sqlText = "SELECT * FROM Orders";
        // Create a command using the transaction.
        SqlCommand cmd = new SqlCommand(sqlText, conn, tran);
        // Create a DataAdapter to retrieve all Orders.
        SqlDataAdapter da = new SqlDataAdapter(cmd);
        // Define a CommandBuilder for the DataAdapter.
        SqlCommandBuilder cb = new SqlCommandBuilder(da);
        // Fill table with Orders.
        DataTable dt = new DataTable();
        da.Fill(dt);

        // Bind the default view of the table to the grid.
        dataGrid.DataSource = dt.DefaultView;

        cancelButton.Enabled = true;
        dataGrid.ReadOnly = false;
    }

    private void cancelButton_Click(object sender, System.EventArgs e)
    {
        cancelButton.Enabled = false;
        dataGrid.ReadOnly = true;
```

Example 6-30. File: TransactionIsolationLevelsForm.cs (continued)

```
    // Roll back the transaction and close the connection.
    tran.Rollback();
    conn.Close();

    // Unbind the grid.
    dataGrid.DataSource = null;

    startButton.Enabled = true;
}

private void UsingLockingHintsForPessimisticLockingForm_Closing(
    object sender, System.ComponentModel.CancelEventArgs e)
{
    // Roll back the transaction and close the connection.
    tran.Rollback();
    conn.Close();
}
```

Discussion

The isolation level specifies the transaction locking behavior for a connection. It determines what changes made to data within a transaction are visible outside of the transaction while the transaction is uncommitted.

Concurrency violations occur when multiple users or processes attempt to modify the same data in a database at the same time without locking. Table 6-16 describes concurrency problems.

Table 6-16. Concurrency problems

Condition	Description
Lost Update	Two or more transactions select the same row and subsequently update that row. Data is lost because the transactions are unaware of each other and overwrite each other's updates.
Uncommitted Dependency (Dirty Read)	A second transaction selects a row that has been updated, but not committed, by another transaction. The first transaction makes more changes to the data or rolls back the changes already made resulting in the second transaction having invalid data.
Inconsistent Analysis (Nonrepeatable Read)	A second transaction reads different data each time that the same row is read. Another transaction has changed and committed the data between the reads.
Phantom Read	An insert or delete is performed for a row belonging to a range of rows being read by a transaction. The rows selected by the transaction are missing the inserted rows and still contain the deleted rows that no longer exist.

Locks ensure transactional integrity and maintain database consistency by controlling how resources can be accessed by concurrent transactions. A *lock* is an object indicating that a user has a dependency on a resource. It prevents other users from performing operations that would adversely affect the locked resources. Locks are acquired and released by user actions; they are managed internally by database software. Table 6-17 lists and describes resource lock modes used by ADO.NET.

Table 6-17. Resource lock modes

Lock mode	Description
Shared	Concurrent transactions can read the locked resource. Concurrent transactions cannot modify the locked resource while the lock is held.
Exclusive	Prevents both read and modify access to a resource by concurrent transactions.

Isolation level defines the degree to which one transaction must be isolated from other transactions. A higher isolation level increases data correctness but decreases concurrent access to data. Table 6-18 describes the different isolations levels supported by ADO.NET. The first four levels are listed in order of increasing isolation.

Table 6-18. IsolationLevel enumeration

Name	Description
ReadUncommitted	No shared locks are issued. Exclusive locks are not honored. A dirty read is possible.
ReadCommitted	Shared locks are held while data is being read by the transaction. Dirty reads are not possible. Nonrepeatable reads or phantom rows can still occur because data can be changed prior to being committed.
RepeatableRead	Shared locks are placed on all data used by the query. Other users are prevented from updating the data. Nonrepeatable reads are prevented, but phantom reads are still possible.
Serializable	A range lock—covering individual records and the ranges between them—is placed on the data preventing other users from updating or inserting rows until the transaction is complete. Phantom reads are prevented.
Chaos	Pending changes from more highly isolated transactions cannot be overwritten. This isolation level is not supported by SQL Server.
Unspecified	A different isolation level than the one specified is being used, but that level cannot be determined.

In ADO.NET, the isolation level can be set by creating the transaction using an overload of the BeginTransaction() method of the Command or by setting the IsolationLevel property of an existing Transaction object. The default isolation level is ReadCommitted.

Parallel transactions are not supported, so the isolation level applies to the entire transaction. It can be changed programmatically at any time. If the isolation level is changed within a transaction, the new level applies to all statements remaining in the transaction.

6.13   Implementing Pessimistic Concurrency Without Using Database Locks

Problem

You need the safety of pessimistic locking without the overhead of database locks.

Solution

Use extra columns and stored procedures as shown in the following examples.

The schema of table TBL0613 used in this solution is shown in Table 6-19.

Table 6-19. TBL0613 schema

Column name	Data type	Length	Allow nulls?
Id	int	4	No
Field1	nvarchar	50	Yes
Field2	nvarchar	50	Yes
LockId	uniqueidentifier	16	Yes
LockDateTime	datetime	8	Yes

The sample uses seven stored procedures, which are shown in Examples 6-31 through 6-37:

SP0613_AcquireLock
> Used to lock a record specified by an Id parameter in the table TBL0613 in the database. The lock is effected by setting the LockId field of an unlocked record, where the value of the LockId field is null, to a GUID specified by an input parameter.

SP0613_ReleaseLock
> Used to clear the lock on a record in the table TBL0613 by setting both the LockId and LockDateTime columns to null. The record is identified by an Id parameter. A LockId parameter—obtained by executing the SP0613_AcquireLock stored procedure—must be supplied to clear the lock on a record.

SP0613_Delete
> Used to delete a record specified by an Id parameter from the table TBL0613 in the database. A LockId parameter—obtained by executing the SP0613_AcquireLock stored procedure—must be supplied to delete the record.

SP0613_Get
> Used to retrieve a record specified by an Id parameter or all records from the table TBL0613 in the database. An expression column, called IsLocked, is also returned indicating whether the row is currently locked by any user.

SP0613_Insert

Used to insert a new record into the table TBL0613 in the database.

SP0613_Update

Used to update a record in the table TBL0613 in the database. A LockId parameter—obtained by executing the SP0613_AcquireLock stored procedure—must be supplied to update the record.

SP0613_PurgeExpired

Used to remove locks older than a specified number of seconds by setting the LockId and LockDateTime values for those records to null.

Example 6-31. Stored procedure: SP0613_AcquireLock

```
CREATE PROCEDURE SP0613_AcquireLock
    @Id int,
    @LockId uniqueidentifier
AS

    update TBL0613
    set
        LockID=@LockID,
        LockDateTime=GetDate( )
    where
        Id=@Id and
        LockId IS NULL

    return @@rowcount
```

Example 6-32. Stored procedure: SP0613_ReleaseLock

```
CREATE PROCEDURE SP0613_ReleaseLock
    @Id int,
    @LockID uniqueidentifier
AS
    update
        TBL0613
    set
        LockId=NULL,
        LockDateTime=NULL
    where
        Id=@Id and
        LockID=@LockID

    return @@rowcount
```

Example 6-33. Stored procedure: SP0613_Delete

```
CREATE PROCEDURE SP0613_Delete
    @Id int,
    @LockID uniqueidentifier
```

Example 6-33. Stored procedure: SP0613_Delete (continued)

```
AS
    SET NOCOUNT ON

    delete
    from
        TBL0613
    where
        Id=@Id and
        LockId=@LockId

    return @@ROWCOUNT
```

Example 6-34. Stored procedure: SP0613_Get

```
CREATE PROCEDURE SP0613_Get
    @Id int=null
AS
    SET NOCOUNT ON

    if @Id is not null
    begin
        select
            Id,
            Field1,
            Field2,
            IsLocked =
            case
                when LockId is null then 0
                else 1
            end
        from
            TBL0613
        where
            Id=@Id

        return 0
    end

    select
        Id,
        Field1,
        Field2,
        IsLocked =
        case
            when LockId is null then 0
            else 1
        end
    from
        TBL0613

    return 0
```

Example 6-35. Stored procedure: SP0613_Insert

```
CREATE PROCEDURE SP0613_Insert
    @Id int,
    @Field1 nvarchar(50),
    @Field2 nvarchar(50)
AS
    SET NOCOUNT ON

    insert TBL0613(
        Id,
        Field1,
        Field2)
    values (
        @Id,
        @Field1,
        @Field2)

    if @@rowcount=0
        return 1

    return 0
```

Example 6-36. Stored procedure: SP0613_Update

```
CREATE PROCEDURE SP0613_Update
    @Id int,
    @Field1 nvarchar(50)=null,
    @Field2 nvarchar(50)=null,
    @LockID uniqueidentifier
AS
    update
        TBL0613
    set
        Field1=@Field1,
        Field2=@Field2
    where
        Id=@Id and
        LockId=@LockId

    return @@ROWCOUNT
```

Example 6-37. Stored procedure: SP0613_PurgeExpired

```
CREATE PROCEDURE SP0613_PurgeExpired
    @timeoutSec int
AS
    SET NOCOUNT ON

    UPDATE TBL0613
    SET
        LockId = null,
        LockDateTime = null
```

Example 6-37. Stored procedure: SP0613_PurgeExpired (continued)

```
WHERE
    DATEADD(s, @timeoutSec, LockDateTime) < GETDATE();

RETURN
```

The sample code contains *seven* event handlers:

Form.Load

Sets up the sample by creating a DataTable representing the table TBL0613 in the database. A DataAdapter is created and the select, delete, insert, and update commands are built using the stored procedures for the solution. A RowUpdated event handler is attached to the DataAdapter. The schema and data for table TBL0613 is loaded into the DataTable. The ReadOnly property of the IsLocked expression field is set to false so that it can be modified programmatically as required. A LockId column is added to the DataTable to hold acquired locks because LockId values cannot be returned from TBL0613 since doing so would allow other users to retrieve locks other than their own. Finally, the default view of the table is bound to the data grid on the form.

Lock Button.Click

Used to acquire locks on all rows in the DataTable. The stored procedure SP0613_AcquireLock is executed for each row. A GUID is generated programmatically and passed as the LockId parameter into the stored procedure along with the Id for the row. A message is displayed indicating the success or failure of the locking attempt for each row.

Release Button.Click

Used to release locks on all rows in the DataTable. The stored procedure SP0613_ReleaseLock is executed for each row. The currently held LockId is passed into the stored procedure along with the Id for the row. A message is displayed indicating the success or failure of the lock release attempt for each row.

Force Release Button.Click

Executes a SQL statement that removes all locks on all rows in TBL0613 in the database. This is accomplished by setting the values of the LockId and LockDateTime fields to null.

Update Button.Click

Uses a DataAdapter to reconcile changes made to the DataTable with the table TBL0613 in the database.

Refresh Button.Click

Clears the DataTable and uses the DataAdapter to fill the table with all data from the table TBL0613 in the database.

DataAdapter.RowUpdated

Checks if a row was affected when an attempt was made to update or delete it. In both cases, the return value parameter from the stored procedure used to perform the action is 1 for success and 0 for failure. A failure results in the RowError property of the row being set.

The C# code is shown in Example 6-38.

Example 6-38. File: PessimisticUpdatesForm.cs

```csharp
// Namespaces, variables, and constants
using System;
using System.Configuration;
using System.Windows.Forms;
using System.Text;
using System.Data;
using System.Data.SqlClient;

private DataTable dt;
private SqlDataAdapter da;

private const String TABLENAME="TBL0613";

// Table column name constants
private const String ID_FIELD            = "Id";
private const String FIELD1_FIELD        = "Field1";
private const String FIELD2_FIELD        = "Field2";
private const String LOCKID_FIELD        = "LockId";
private const String LOCKDATETIME_FIELD  = "LockDateTime";
// Expression in table
private const String ISLOCKED_FIELD      = "IsLocked";

// Stored procedure name constants
private const String DELETE_SP           = "SP0613_Delete";
private const String GET_SP              = "SP0613_Get";
private const String INSERT_SP           = "SP0613_Insert";
private const String UPDATE_SP           = "SP0613_Update";

private const String ACQUIRELOCK_SP      = "SP0613_AcquireLock";
private const String RELEASELOCK_SP      = "SP0613_ReleaseLock";

// Stored procedure parameter name constants for table
private const String ID_PARM             = "@Id";
private const String FIELD1_PARM         = "@Field1";
private const String FIELD2_PARM         = "@Field2";
private const String LOCKID_PARM         = "@LockId";

private const String RETVAL_PARM         = "@RetVal";

// ...

private void PessimisticUpdatesForm_Load(object sender, System.EventArgs e)
{
    // Build the table.
    dt = new DataTable(TABLENAME);
```

Example 6-38. File: PessimisticUpdatesForm.cs (continued)

```
// Create the DataAdapter.
da = new SqlDataAdapter( );
// Add a handler for the RowUpdated event.
da.RowUpdated += new SqlRowUpdatedEventHandler(da_RowUpdated);

// Create a connection.
SqlConnection conn = new SqlConnection(
    ConfigurationSettings.AppSettings["Sql_ConnectString"]);

// Build the select command.
SqlCommand selectCommand = new SqlCommand(GET_SP, conn);
selectCommand.CommandType = CommandType.StoredProcedure;
da.SelectCommand = selectCommand;

// Build the delete command.
SqlCommand deleteCommand = new SqlCommand(DELETE_SP, conn);
deleteCommand.CommandType = CommandType.StoredProcedure;
deleteCommand.Parameters.Add(ID_PARM, SqlDbType.Int, 0, ID_FIELD);
deleteCommand.Parameters.Add(LOCKID_PARM, SqlDbType.UniqueIdentifier,
    0, LOCKID_FIELD);
deleteCommand.Parameters.Add(RETVAL_PARM, SqlDbType.Int).Direction =
    ParameterDirection.ReturnValue;
da.DeleteCommand = deleteCommand;

// Build the insert command.
SqlCommand insertCommand = new SqlCommand(INSERT_SP, conn);
insertCommand.CommandType = CommandType.StoredProcedure;
insertCommand.Parameters.Add(ID_PARM, SqlDbType.Int, 0, ID_FIELD);
insertCommand.Parameters.Add(FIELD1_PARM, SqlDbType.NVarChar, 50,
    FIELD1_FIELD);
insertCommand.Parameters.Add(FIELD2_PARM, SqlDbType.NVarChar, 50,
    FIELD2_FIELD);
da.InsertCommand = insertCommand;

// Build the update command.
SqlCommand updateCommand = new SqlCommand(UPDATE_SP, conn);
updateCommand.CommandType = CommandType.StoredProcedure;
updateCommand.Parameters.Add(ID_PARM, SqlDbType.Int, 0, ID_FIELD);
updateCommand.Parameters.Add(FIELD1_PARM, SqlDbType.NVarChar, 50,
    FIELD1_FIELD);
updateCommand.Parameters.Add(FIELD2_PARM, SqlDbType.NVarChar, 50,
    FIELD2_FIELD);
updateCommand.Parameters.Add(LOCKID_PARM, SqlDbType.UniqueIdentifier,
    0, LOCKID_FIELD);
updateCommand.Parameters.Add(RETVAL_PARM, SqlDbType.Int).Direction =
    ParameterDirection.ReturnValue;
da.UpdateCommand = updateCommand;

// Fill the table.
da.FillSchema(dt, SchemaType.Source);
da.Fill(dt);
```

Example 6-38. File: PessimisticUpdatesForm.cs (continued)

```csharp
    // Unlock the IsLocked expression column.
    dt.Columns[ISLOCKED_FIELD].ReadOnly = false;

    // Add a column to the table to control the locking.
    dt.Columns.Add("LockId", typeof(Guid));

    // Bind the default view of the table to the grid.
    dataGrid.DataSource = dt.DefaultView;
}

private void lockButton_Click(object sender, System.EventArgs e)
{
    StringBuilder sb = new StringBuilder();

    // Lock all of the rows in the table.
    SqlConnection conn = new SqlConnection(
        ConfigurationSettings.AppSettings["Sql_ConnectString"]);

    // Create a command for the lock stored procedure.
    SqlCommand cmd = new SqlCommand();
    cmd.Connection = conn;
    cmd.CommandType = CommandType.StoredProcedure;
    cmd.CommandText = ACQUIRELOCK_SP;
    cmd.Parameters.Add(ID_PARM, SqlDbType.Int);
    cmd.Parameters.Add(LOCKID_PARM, SqlDbType.UniqueIdentifier);
    cmd.Parameters.Add(RETVAL_PARM, SqlDbType.Int).Direction =
        ParameterDirection.ReturnValue;

    conn.Open();
    // Iterate over the row collection for the table.
    foreach(DataRow row in dt.Rows)
    {
        // Generate a lock ID.
        Guid lockId = Guid.NewGuid();

        // Execute the lock command to acquire a lock on the row.
        cmd.Parameters[ID_PARM].Value = row[ID_FIELD];
        cmd.Parameters[LOCKID_PARM].Value = lockId;
        cmd.ExecuteNonQuery();
        if((int)cmd.Parameters[RETVAL_PARM].Value == 0)
        {
            // Row lock could not be acquired
            sb.Append("Could not aquire lock on row [ID = " +
                row[ID_FIELD] + "]." + Environment.NewLine);
            row[LOCKID_FIELD] = DBNull.Value;
        }
        else
        {
            // Row lock acquired
            row[LOCKID_FIELD] = lockId;
            row[ISLOCKED_FIELD] = 1;
        }
    conn.Close();
```

Example 6-38. File: PessimisticUpdatesForm.cs (continued)

```csharp
    // Display an error message for locks that could not be acquired.
    if(sb.Length > 0)
        MessageBox.Show(sb.ToString( ), "Simulate Pessimistic Locking",
        MessageBoxButtons.OK, MessageBoxIcon.Error);
}

private void releaseButton_Click(object sender, System.EventArgs e)
{
    StringBuilder sb = new StringBuilder( );

    // Release lock on all of the rows in the table.
    SqlConnection conn = new SqlConnection(
        ConfigurationSettings.AppSettings["Sql_ConnectString"]);

    // Create a command for the release stored procedure.
    SqlCommand cmd = new SqlCommand( );
    cmd.Connection = conn;
    cmd.CommandType = CommandType.StoredProcedure;
    cmd.CommandText = RELEASELOCK_SP;
    cmd.Parameters.Add(ID_PARM, SqlDbType.Int);
    cmd.Parameters.Add(LOCKID_PARM, SqlDbType.UniqueIdentifier);
    cmd.Parameters.Add(RETVAL_PARM, SqlDbType.Int).Direction =
        ParameterDirection.ReturnValue;

    conn.Open( );
    // Iterate over the collection of rows in the table.
    foreach(DataRow row in dt.Rows)
    {
        // Execute the command to release the lock on the row.
        cmd.Parameters[ID_PARM].Value = row[ID_FIELD];
        cmd.Parameters[LOCKID_PARM].Value = row[LOCKID_FIELD];
        cmd.ExecuteNonQuery( );
        if((int)cmd.Parameters[RETVAL_PARM].Value == 0)
            // Row lock could not be released
            sb.Append("Could not release lock on row [ID = " +
                row[ID_FIELD] + "]." + Environment.NewLine);
        else
        {
            // Row lock released
            row[LOCKID_FIELD] = DBNull.Value;
            row[ISLOCKED_FIELD] = 0;
        }
    }
    conn.Close( );

    // Display an error message for locks which could not be released.
    if(sb.Length > 0)
        MessageBox.Show(sb.ToString( ), "Simulate Pessimistic Locking",
        MessageBoxButtons.OK, MessageBoxIcon.Error);
}
```

Example 6-38. File: PessimisticUpdatesForm.cs (continued)

```csharp
private void forceReleaseButton_Click(object sender, System.EventArgs e)
{
    // Normally, security would be used to block this statement
    // from being executed.
    // Clear all of the locks that exist on the table.

    // Create the connection.
    SqlConnection conn = new SqlConnection(
        ConfigurationSettings.AppSettings["Sql_ConnectString"]);
    String sqlText = "UPDATE " + TABLENAME + " SET " + LOCKID_FIELD + " =
        NULL, " + LOCKDATETIME_FIELD + " = NULL";
    // Create and execute the command to force release on all rows.
    SqlCommand cmd = new SqlCommand(sqlText, conn);
    conn.Open( );
    cmd.ExecuteNonQuery( );
    conn.Close( );

    // Update the lock ID.
    foreach(DataRow row in dt.Rows)
    {
        row[LOCKID_FIELD] = DBNull.Value;
        row[ISLOCKED_FIELD] = 0;
    }

    MessageBox.Show("All row locks on table released.",
        "Simulate Pessimistic Locking", MessageBoxButtons.OK,
        MessageBoxIcon.Information);
}

private void updateButton_Click(object sender, System.EventArgs e)
{
    try
    {
        // Use the DataAdapter to update the table.
        da.Update(dt);
    }
    catch(Exception ex)
    {
        // Display error message if the row is not locked for update.
        MessageBox.Show("ERROR: " + ex.Message,
            "Simulate Pessimistic Locking", MessageBoxButtons.OK,
            MessageBoxIcon.Error);
    }
}

private void refreshButton_Click(object sender, System.EventArgs e)
{
    // Refresh the data from the source.
    dt.Clear( );
    da.Fill(dt);
}
```

Example 6-38. File: PessimisticUpdatesForm.cs (continued)

```
private void da_RowUpdated(object sender, SqlRowUpdatedEventArgs e)
{
    if(e.StatementType == StatementType.Update &&
        (int)e.Command.Parameters[RETVAL_PARM].Value == 0)
    {
        // Row error if row could not be updated without lock
        e.Row.RowError = "Lock required to update this row.";
        // Continue processing the update for the other rows.
        e.Status = UpdateStatus.Continue;
    }

    if(e.StatementType == StatementType.Delete &&
        (int)e.Command.Parameters[RETVAL_PARM].Value == 0)
    {
        // Row error if row could not be deleted without lock
        e.Row.RowError = "Lock required to delete this row.";
        // Continue processing the update for the other rows.
        e.Status = UpdateStatus.Continue;
    }
}
```

Discussion

Pessimistic concurrency prevents other users from modifying data that a user is reading by locking rows of data at the data source. Other users cannot perform actions that affect the locked row until the current lock holder releases the lock. Pessimistic concurrency protects data integrity without requiring transaction rollbacks but with reduced data availability and increased resources needed to maintain server locks. A persistent connection to the database server is required, limiting scalability.

Optimistic concurrency does not lock data while it is being read. Instead, if the user wants to make a change to the data, the application determines whether another user has changed the data since it was last read. If the data has been modified, a violation is considered to have occurred. Often, the user is notified of the changes made by other users and given an opportunity to resubmit changes. Optimistic concurrency protects data integrity with transaction rollbacks and provides higher data availability without needing additional server resources for the locks. Connections to the database do not need to be persistent, making the solution more scalable. Optimistic concurrency requires a more complex programming model because violations and transactions need to be handled.

The solution simulates pessimistic locking by adding two columns to each table in which locking is simulated as shown in Table 6-20.

Table 6-20. Pessimistic locking columns

Field	Data type	Length	Allow nulls?
LockId	uniqueidentifier	16	Yes
LockDateTime	datetime	8	Yes

The LockId column is a GUID generated by the user representing a lock on a row. An unlocked row has a null value for the LockId. The LockId cannot be accessed directly by any user because doing so would allow a user to retrieve the lock issued to another user rendering the technique useless. The solution returns a Boolean IsLocked value indicating whether the field is locked by another user.

The LockDateTime field contains the date and time that a lock was issued to a user. It is used by a SQL Server Agent job that clears locks held for longer than a duration specified in seconds by periodically executing the stored procedure SP0613_PurgeExpired.

6.14   Specifying Locking Hints in a SQL Server Database

Problem

You need to pessimistically lock rows in an underlying SQL Server database.

Solution

Use SQL Server locking hints from ADO.NET.

The sample code contains three event handlers:

Start Tran Button.Click
> Creates a SQL SELECT statement to retrieve the Orders table from the Northwind database. A locking hint, either UPDLOCK or HOLDLOCK, is added to the statement as specified. A Connection is opened and a Transaction started on it with an isolation level of ReadCommitted. A DataAdapter is used on the transacted connection to fill a DataTable. A CommandBuilder is created to generate updating logic. The default view of the table is bound to the data grid on the form.

Cancel Button.Click
> Clears the data grid, rolls back the transaction, and closes the connection.

Form.Closing
> Rolls back the transaction if it exists and closes the connection.

The C# code is shown in Example 6-39.

Example 6-39. File: UsingLockingHintsForPessimisticLockingForm.cs

```
// Namespaces, variables, and constants
using System;
using System.Configuration;
using System.Data;
using System.Data.SqlClient;

private SqlConnection conn;
private SqlTransaction tran;

// ...

private void startButton_Click(object sender, System.EventArgs e)
{
    startButton.Enabled = false;

    String sqlText = "SELECT * FROM Orders WITH ";

    // Add pessimistic locking as specified by user.
    if(updLockRadioButton.Checked)
        sqlText += "(UPDLOCK)";
    else if(holdLockRadioButton.Checked)
        sqlText += "(HOLDLOCK)";

    // Create connection.
    conn = new SqlConnection(
        ConfigurationSettings.AppSettings["Sql_ConnectString"]);
    conn.Open( );
    // Start the transaction.
    tran = conn.BeginTransaction(IsolationLevel.ReadCommitted);
    // Create the command.
    SqlCommand cmd = new SqlCommand(sqlText, conn, tran);
    // Create the DataAdapter and CommandBuilder.
    SqlDataAdapter da = new SqlDataAdapter(cmd);
    SqlCommandBuilder cb = new SqlCommandBuilder(da);
    // Fill table using the DataAdapter.
    DataTable dt = new DataTable( );
    da.Fill(dt);

    // Bind the default view of the table to the grid.
    dataGrid.DataSource = dt.DefaultView;

    cancelButton.Enabled = true;
    dataGrid.ReadOnly = false;
}

private void cancelButton_Click(object sender, System.EventArgs e)
{
    cancelButton.Enabled = false;

    // Unbind the table from the grid.
    dataGrid.DataSource = null;
```

Example 6-39. File: UsingLockingHintsForPessimisticLockingForm.cs (continued)

```
    // Roll back the transaction and close the connection.
    tran.Rollback( );
    conn.Close( );

    startButton.Enabled = true;
}
```

Discussion

A lock is an object indicating that a user has a dependency on a resource. Locks ensure transactional integrity and database consistency by preventing other users from changing data being read by a user and preventing users from reading data being changed by a user. Locks are acquired and released by user actions; they are managed internally by database software.

A locking hint can be specified with SELECT, INSERT, DELETE, and UPDATE statements to instruct SQL Server as to the type of lock to use. You can use locking hints when you need control over locks acquired on objects. The SQL Server Optimizer automatically determines correct locking; hints should be used only when necessary. Locking hints override the current transaction isolation level for the session.

A locking hint is specified following the FROM clause using a WITH clause. The hint is specified within parentheses and multiple hints are separated by commas.

Tables 6-21, 6-22, and 6-23 describe the different locking hints that you can use, categorized according to their function.

Table 6-21. SQL Server locking hints for isolation level

Locking hint	Description
HOLDLOCK	Hold a shared lock until the transaction is completed instead of releasing it as soon as the required object—table, row, or data page—is no longer needed.
NOLOCK	Do not issue shared locks and do not recognize exclusive locks. Applies only to the SELECT statement.
READCOMMITTED	Use the same locking as a transaction with an isolation level of READ COMMITTED.
READUNCOMMITTED	Same as NOLOCK.
REPEATABLEREAD	Use the same locking as a transaction with an isolation level of REPEATABLE READ.
SERIALIZABLE	Use the same locking as a transaction with an isolation level of SERIALIZABLE.

Table 6-22. SQL Server locking hints for granularity

Locking hint	Description
NOLOCK	Do not issue shared locks and do not recognize exclusive locks. Applies only to the SELECT statement.
PAGLOCK	Use page locks where a single table lock would normally be used.
ROWLOCK	Use row-level locking instead of page-level and table-level locking.

Table 6-22. SQL Server locking hints for granularity (continued)

Locking hint	Description
TABLOCK	Use table-level locking instead of row-level and page-level locking. By default, the lock is held until the end of the statement.
TABLOCKX	Use an exclusive table lock preventing other users from reading or updating the table. By default, the lock is held until the end of the statement.

Table 6-23. SQL Server Locking Hints for Other Functions

Locking hint	Description
READPAST	Skip locked rows that would ordinarily appear in the result set rather than blocking the transaction by waiting for other transactions to release locks on those rows. Applies only to transactions with an isolation level of *READ COMMITTED*. Applies only to the SELECT statement.
UPDLOCK	Use update locks instead of shared locks when reading a table. This allows you to read data and later update it with a guarantee that it has not changed since you last read it while other users are not blocked from reading the data. Cannot be used with NOLOCK or XLOCK.
XLOCK	Use an exclusive lock that is held until the end of the transaction on all data processed by the statement. Can be specified with either PAGLOCK or TABLOCK granularity. Cannot be used with either NOLOCK or UPDLOCK.

There are a number ways to get information about database locks:

- The system stored procedure sp_lock returns a result set containing all active locks.

- The syslockinfo table in the master database contains information about all granted, converting, and waiting lock requests. It is a denormalized view of the data structures used internally by the lock manager.

- The SQL Server Profiler can be used to monitor and record locking information.

- The Windows Performance Monitor has a SQL Server Locks Object counter that can be used to monitor lock activity.

For more information about database locks, using locking hints, or monitoring database locks, see Microsoft SQL Server Books Online.

CHAPTER 7

Binding Data to .NET User Interfaces

7.0   Introduction

This chapter focuses on binding controls to data sources in both Web Forms and Windows Forms.

Web Forms are an ASP.NET—a web application platform—feature used to create user interfaces for web applications. You can use the ASP.NET page framework to create browser- and client device-independent Web Forms that run on a web server and are used to dynamically create web pages. In addition to traditional HTML elements, Web Forms pages acts as a container for server-side controls that implement rich web user interface (UI) functionality in reusable controls.

Windows Forms is the .NET platform for Windows application development providing classes that enable rich user interfaces to be constructed. Windows forms act as a container for reusable controls that implement rich functionality.

Windows and Web Form controls allow data to be displayed by binding to data sources. Data-binding is typically used for such purposes as displaying lookup or master-detail data, reporting, and data entry. There are two types of data binding: simple and complex. *Simple data binding* binds a control to a single data element such as the value of a field in a row of a result set. Simple binding is used by controls such as the TextBox and Label. *Complex data binding* binds the control to more than one data element—typically one or more columns from multiple rows in a result set. Controls capable of complex binding include ListBox, DataList, and DataGrid controls.

Although conceptually similar, the differences between Web Forms and Windows Forms architecture results in differences in data-binding data sources to controls between the platforms. Recipes 7.1 through 7.7 show solutions for binding data to Web Forms controls, which includes solutions for simple data binding, complex data binding with updating, binding master-detail data, and data-binding images. Recipes 7.8 through 7.13 show solutions for binding data to Windows Forms controls, which includes solutions for simple data binding, complex data binding, binding master-detail data, and data-binding images from SQL Server and Microsoft Access databases. Recipe 7.16 shows how to create a Crystal Report on a Windows Form at runtime.

Recipe 7.14 shows how to use a DataView bound to a DataGrid to control editing, deleting, and inserting data. Recipe 7.15 uses a DataView bound to a DataGrid to add search capabilities to the DataGrid.

Finally, Recipe 7.17 shows how to use ADO.NET design-time features in classes without a user interface.

7.1 Binding Simple Data to Web Forms Controls

Problem

You need to bind a field of data to a server-side control.

Solution

Use the DataBind( ) method.

The Web Forms page sample code displays the company name for the CustomerID specified by assigning the method GetCompanyName( ), which is defined in the code-behind file, to the Text property of TextBox control companyNameTextBox. The code for the Web Forms page is shown in Example 7-1.

Example 7-1. File: ADOCookbookCS0701.aspx

```
<asp:TextBox id="companyNameTextBox" style="Z-INDEX: 103; LEFT: 136px;
    POSITION: absolute; TOP: 128px" runat="server" ReadOnly="True"
    Width="280px" Text="<%# GetCompanyName(customerIdTextBox.Text) %>">
</asp:TextBox>
```

The code-behind contains one event and one method:

Page.Load
    Binds data from the source—in this case the GetCompanyName( ) method—to the companyNameTextBox server control.

GetCompanyName( )
    This method retrieves and returns the company name for a specified customer ID.

The C# code for the code-behind is shown in Example 7-2.

Example 7-2. File: ADOCookbookCS0701.aspx.cs

```
// Namespaces, variables, and constants
using System;
```

Example 7-2. File: ADOCookbookCS0701.aspx.cs (continued)

```csharp
using System.Configuration;
using System.Data;
using System.Data.SqlClient;

// ...

private void Page_Load(object sender, System.EventArgs e)
{
    companyNameTextBox.DataBind( );
}

public String GetCompanyName(String customerId)
{
    String companyName = "Not found.";

    if (customerIdTextBox.Text != "")
    {
        // Create a command to retrieve the company name for the
        // user-specified customer ID.
        String sqlText =
            "SELECT CompanyName FROM Customers WHERE CustomerID='" +
            customerIdTextBox.Text + "'";
        SqlConnection conn = new SqlConnection(
            ConfigurationSettings.AppSettings["DataConnectString"]);
        SqlCommand cmd = new SqlCommand(sqlText, conn);
        conn.Open( );

        // Execute the command.
        companyName = cmd.ExecuteScalar().ToString( );

        conn.Close( );
    }

    return companyName;
}
```

Discussion

Simple data binding binds an ASP.NET web control property to a single value in a data source. The values can be determined at runtime. Although most commonly used to set control properties to display data, any property of the control can be bound—for example, the background color or size of the control.

The Visual Studio .NET Properties window provides a tool to create data-binding expressions. It is accessed by clicking the ellipsis (...) in the (DataBindings) property.

To simple-bind a control, set the property of the control to a data-binding expression that resolves to a single value. The data-binding expression is delimited with <%# and #>. For more information about data-binding expressions, see the MSDN Library.

In the solution, the Text property of the TextBox control is bound to a CompanyName field in the data source:

```
Text="<%# GetCompanyName(customerIdTextBox.Text) %>
```

This sets the Text property to the value returned by the GetCompanyName( ) method in the code-behind page.

Instead of using an expression as previously shown, the static Eval( ) method of the DataBinder class can be used to simplify data binding when the value to bind is derived from a data source. The DataBinder class helps to extract data from a data source and makes it available to a control property. The Eval( ) method takes two arguments:

- A reference to the data source object. This is usually a DataSet, DataTable, or DataView.
- A string specifying the navigation path to the specific value in the data source. This usually references a row and a column in that row.

The syntax to retrieve the company name from the first row in a DataTable using the Eval( ) method instead of using a data-binding expression might be:

```
Text="<%# DataBinder.Eval(companyDataTable, "[0].CompanyName") %>
```

For more information about the DataBinder class and the syntax of the Eval( ) method, see the topic "Data-Binding Expressions for Web Forms Pages" in the MSDN Library.

Data-binding expressions must be resolved at runtime to provide the values to which the controls bind. This can be done explicitly by calling the DataBind( ) method of the control.

```
companyNameTextBox.DataBind( );
```

The DataBind( ) method of the Page class can be called to data-bind all controls on the form.

7.2   Binding Complex Data to Web Forms Controls

Problem

You want to bind multiple columns in multiple records to an ASP.NET control.

Solution

Set the control's advanced properties (see Table 7-1) before calling DataBind( ).

The Web Forms page sample code defines the ListBox that is populated with data by the code-behind page logic. The code for the Web Forms page is shown in Example 7-3.

Example 7-3. File: ADOCookbookCS0702.aspx

```
<asp:ListBox id="categoriesListBox" style="Z-INDEX: 102; LEFT: 88px;
    POSITION: absolute; TOP: 64px" runat="server" Width="184px"
    Height="216px">
</asp:ListBox>
```

The code-behind contains one event handler:

Page.Load
> Fills a DataTable with the CategoryID and CategoryName from the Categories table in the Northwind sample database. The ListBox server control is bound to the DataTable.

The C# code for the code-behind is shown in Example 7-4.

Example 7-4. File: ADOCookbookCS0702.aspx.cs

```csharp
// Namespaces, variables, and constants
using System;
using System.Configuration;
using System.Data;
using System.Data.SqlClient;

// ...

private void Page_Load(object sender, System.EventArgs e)
{
    // Create a DataAdapter and use it to retrieve ID and Name
    // for all categories.
    String sqlText = "SELECT CategoryID, CategoryName FROM Categories " +
        "ORDER BY CategoryName";
    SqlDataAdapter da = new SqlDataAdapter(sqlText,
        ConfigurationSettings.AppSettings["DataConnectString"]);
    DataTable table = new DataTable("Categories");
    da.Fill(table);

    // Bind the table to the list box control.
    categoriesListBox.DataSource = table.DefaultView;
    categoriesListBox.DataValueField = "CategoryID";
    categoriesListBox.DataTextField = "CategoryName";

    categoriesListBox.DataBind( );
}
```

Discussion

Complex data binding describes binding a multi-record control to multiple records in a data source. The DataGrid, DataList, and ListBox controls are examples of controls that support complex data binding.

Each control that supports complex data binding exposes a set of properties, which are slightly different for each control, that control the binding. These properties are described in Table 7-1.

Table 7-1. Complex data-binding properties

Property	Description
DataSource	Gets or sets the data source that the control is displaying data for. Valid data sources include DataTable, DataView, DataSet, DataViewManager, or any object that implements the IEnumerable interface.
DataMember	Gets or sets the table in the data source to bind to the control. You can use this property if the data source contains more than one table—a DataSet, for example.
DataKeyField	Gets or sets the key field in the data source. This allows the key field for a listing control to be stored and later accessed without displaying it in the control.
DataValueField	Gets or sets the field in the data source that provides the value for the control when an item is selected.
DataTextField	Gets or sets the field in the data source that provides the display value for the control when an item is selected.

After the properties appropriate to the control are set, call the DataBind( ) method of the control or of the Page to bind the data source to the server control.

7.3   Binding Data to a Web Forms DataList

Problem

You need to bind the result set from a query to a DataList control.

Solution

Set the DataList's advanced properties as demonstrated by this solution.

The schema of table TBL0703 that is used in the solution is shown in Table 7-2.

Table 7-2. TBL0703 schema

Column name	Data type	Length	Allow nulls?
Id	int	4	No
IntField	int	4	Yes
StringField	nvarchar	50	Yes

The Web Forms page sample code defines the DataList control and the three templates—SelectedItemTemplate, ItemTemplate, and EditItemTemplate—which control the display of data for selected items, unselected items, and items being edited. The static Eval( ) method of the DataBinder class is used to fill the field values in each template. Container.DataItem specifies the container argument for the method which when used in a list in a template resolves to DataListItem.DataItem. The code for the Web Forms page is shown Example 7-5.

Example 7-5. File: ADOCookbookCS0703.aspx

```
<asp:DataList id="dataList" style="Z-INDEX: 102; LEFT: 16px;
    POSITION: absolute; TOP: 56px" runat="server">
    <SelectedItemTemplate>
        <asp:Button id="editButton" runat="server" Text="Edit"
            CommandName="Edit">
        </asp:Button>
        <B>
        <%# DataBinder.Eval(Container.DataItem, "Id") %>;
        <%# DataBinder.Eval(Container.DataItem, "IntField") %>;
        <%# DataBinder.Eval(Container.DataItem, "StringField") %>
        </B>
    </SelectedItemTemplate>
    <ItemTemplate>
        <asp:Button id="selectButton" runat="server" Text="Select"
            CommandName="Select">
        </asp:Button>
        <%# DataBinder.Eval(Container.DataItem, "Id") %>;
        <%# DataBinder.Eval(Container.DataItem, "IntField") %>;
        <%# DataBinder.Eval(Container.DataItem, "StringField") %>
    </ItemTemplate>
    <EditItemTemplate>
        <asp:Button id="updateButton" runat="server" Text="Update"
            CommandName="Update">
        </asp:Button>
        <asp:Button id="deleteButton" runat="server" Text="Delete"
            CommandName="Delete">
        </asp:Button>
        <asp:Button id="cancelButton" runat="server" Text="Cancel"
            CommandName="Cancel">
        </asp:Button>
        <BR>
        <asp:Label id="Label1" runat="server">ID: </asp:Label>
        <asp:TextBox id="idTextBox" runat="server" Width="96px"
            ReadOnly="True"
            Text='<%# DataBinder.Eval(Container.DataItem, "Id") %>'>
        </asp:TextBox>
        <BR>
        <asp:Label id="Label2" runat="server">IntField: </asp:Label>
        <asp:TextBox id="intFieldTextBox" runat="server"
            Text='<%# DataBinder.Eval(Container.DataItem,
            "IntField") %>'>
        </asp:TextBox>
```

Example 7-5. File: ADOCookbookCS0703.aspx (continued)

```
        <BR>
        <asp:Label id="Label3" runat="server">StringField: </asp:Label>
        <asp:TextBox id="stringFieldTextBox" runat="server"
            Text='<%# DataBinder.Eval(Container.DataItem,
            "StringField") %>'>
        </asp:TextBox>
    </EditItemTemplate>
</asp:DataList>
```

The code-behind contains six event handlers and three methods:

Page.Load

Calls the CreateDataSource( ) method and binds data to the Web Forms DataList, if the page is being loaded for the first time.

CreateDataSource( )

This method fills a DataTable with the TBL0703 table and stores the DataTable to a Session variable to cache the data source for the DataList.

UpdateDataSource( )

This method creates a DataAdapter and uses it together with updating logic generated by a CommandBuilder to update the data source with changes made to the cached DataTable. The updated DataTable is stored to the Session variable, which is used to cache the data source for the DataList.

BindDataList( )

This method gets the cached data from the Session variable and binds its default view to the DataList.

DataList.CancelCommand

Sets the index of the item being edited to -1 to cancel any current editing and calls BindDataList( ) to refresh the list.

DataList.DeleteCommand

Finds and deletes the specified row from the data cached in the Session variable and calls the UpdateDataSource( ) method to persist the change back to the data source. BindDataList( ) is called to refresh the list.

DataList.EditCommand

Sets the index of the selected item to -1 to cancel its selection. The index of the item being edited is then set to the index of the row corresponding to the Edit button putting that row into edit mode. BindDataList( ) is called to refresh the list.

DataList.ItemCommand

Checks if the Select button was pressed. If it was, the index of the item being edited is set to -1 to cancel its editing. The index of the selected item is then set to the index of the row corresponding to the Select button to put that row into select mode. Finally, BindDataList( ) is called to refresh the list.

DataList.UpdateCommand

Finds and updates the specified row in the data cached in the Session variable and calls the UpdateDataSource( ) method to persist the change back to the data source. BindDataList( ) is called to refresh the list.

The C# code for the code-behind is shown in Example 7-6.

Example 7-6. File: ADOCookbookCS0703.aspx.cs

```csharp
// Namespaces, variables, and constants
using System;
using System.Configuration;
using System.Web.UI.WebControls;
using System.Data;
using System.Data.SqlClient;

private const String TABLENAME = "TBL0703";

// ...

private void Page_Load(object sender, System.EventArgs e)
{
    if(!Page.IsPostBack)
    {
        dataList.DataSource = CreateDataSource( );
        dataList.DataKeyField = "Id";
        dataList.DataBind( );
    }
}

private DataTable CreateDataSource( )
{
    DataTable dt = new DataTable(TABLENAME);

    // Create the DataAdapter and fill the table using it.
    SqlDataAdapter da = new SqlDataAdapter("SELECT * FROM " + TABLENAME +
        " ORDER BY Id",
        ConfigurationSettings.AppSettings["DataConnectString"]);
    da.Fill(dt);
    da.FillSchema(dt, SchemaType.Source);

    // Store data in session variable to store data between
    // posts to server.
    Session["DataSource"] = dt;

    return dt;
}

private DataTable UpdateDataSource(DataTable dt)
{
```

Example 7-6. File: ADOCookbookCS0703.aspx.cs (continued)

```
    // Create a DataAdapter for the update.
    SqlDataAdapter da = new SqlDataAdapter("SELECT * FROM " + TABLENAME +
        " ORDER BY Id",
        ConfigurationSettings.AppSettings["DataConnectString"]);
    // Create a CommandBuilder to generate update logic.
    SqlCommandBuilder cb = new SqlCommandBuilder(da);

    // Update the data source with changes to the table.
    da.Update(dt);

    // Store updated data in session variable to store data between
    // posts to server.
    Session["DataSource"] = dt;

    return dt;
}

private void BindDataList( )
{
    // Get the data from the session variable.
    DataView dv = ((DataTable)Session["DataSource"]).DefaultView;

    // Bind the data view to the data list.
    dataList.DataSource = dv;
    dataList.DataBind( );
}

private void dataList_CancelCommand(object source,
    System.Web.UI.WebControls.DataListCommandEventArgs e)
{
    // Set the index of the item being edited out of range.
    dataList.EditItemIndex = -1;

    BindDataList( );
}

private void dataList_DeleteCommand(object source,
    System.Web.UI.WebControls.DataListCommandEventArgs e)
{
    // Get the data from the session variable.
    DataTable dt = (DataTable)Session["DataSource"];

    // Get the ID of the row to delete.
    int id = (int)dataList.DataKeys[e.Item.ItemIndex];

    // Delete the row from the table.
    dt.Rows.Find(id).Delete( );

    // Update the data source with the changes to the table.
    UpdateDataSource(dt);
```

Example 7-6. File: ADOCookbookCS0703.aspx.cs (continued)

```
    // Set the index of the item being edited out of range.
    dataList.EditItemIndex = -1;

    BindDataList();
}

private void dataList_EditCommand(object source,
    System.Web.UI.WebControls.DataListCommandEventArgs e)
{
    // Set the index of the selected item out of range.
    dataList.SelectedIndex = -1;
    // Set the index of the item being edited to the current record.
    dataList.EditItemIndex = e.Item.ItemIndex;

    BindDataList();
}

private void dataList_ItemCommand(object source,
    System.Web.UI.WebControls.DataListCommandEventArgs e)
{
    // Check if the "select" button is pressed.
    if (e.CommandName == "Select")
    {
        // Set the index of the item being edited out of range.
        dataList.EditItemIndex = -1;
        // Set the index of the selected item to the current record.
        dataList.SelectedIndex = e.Item.ItemIndex;

        BindDataList();
    }
}

private void dataList_UpdateCommand(object source,
    System.Web.UI.WebControls.DataListCommandEventArgs e)
{
    // Get the data from the session variable.
    DataTable dt = (DataTable)Session["DataSource"];

    // Get the ID of the row to update.
    int id = (int)dataList.DataKeys[e.Item.ItemIndex];

    // Get the DataRow to update using the ID.
    DataRow dr = dt.Rows.Find(id);

    // Get the column values for the current record from the DataList.
    dr["IntField"] =
        Int32.Parse(((TextBox)e.Item.FindControl("intFieldTextBox")).Text);
    dr["StringField"] =
        ((TextBox)e.Item.FindControl("stringFieldTextBox")).Text;

    // Update the data source with the changes to the table.
    UpdateDataSource(dt);
```

Example 7-6. File: ADOCookbookCS0703.aspx.cs (continued)

```
    // Set the index of the item being edited out of range.
    dataList.EditItemIndex = -1;

    BindDataList();
}
```

Discussion

The `DataList` Web Forms control displays tabular data from a data source and controls the formatting using templates and styles. The `DataList` must be bound to a data source such as a `DataReader`, `DataSet`, `DataTable`, or `DataView`—any class that implements the `IEnumerable` interface can be bound. The easiest way to create a `DataList` control is to drag the `DataList` control onto the web page design surface.

The `DataList` Web Form control uses templates to display items, control layout, and provide functional capabilities. Table 7-3 describes the different templates for the `DataList`.

Table 7-3. DataList templates

Template	Description
AlternatingItemTemplate	Elements to render for every other row in the control. This is normally used to specify a different display style for alternating rows. This template is defined within the `<AlternatingItemTemplate>` and `</AlternatingItemTemplate>` tags.
EditItemTemplate	Elements to render when an item is put into edit mode. This template is invoked for the row specified in the `EditItemIndex` property; setting the `EditItemIndex` property to `-1` cancels the edit mode. This template is defined within the `<EditItemTemplate>` and `</EditItemTemplate>` tags.
FooterTemplate	Elements to render at the bottom of the control. The footer template cannot be data bound. This template is defined within the `<FooterTemplate>` and `</FooterTemplate>` tags.
HeaderTemplate	Elements to render at the top of the control. The header template cannot be data bound. This template is defined within the `<HeaderTemplate>` and `</HeaderTemplate>` tags.
ItemTemplate	Elements to render for each row in the data source. This template is defined within the `<ItemTemplate>` and `</ItemTemplate>` tags.
SelectedItemTemplate	Elements to render when an item in the control is selected. This template is invoked for the row specified by the `SelectedIndex` property; setting the `SelectedIndex` property to `-1` cancels the select mode. This template is defined within the `<SelectedItemTemplate>` and `</SelectedItemTemplate>` tags.
SeparatorTemplate	Elements to render between each item. The `SeparatorTemplate` cannot be data bound. This template is defined within the `<SeparatorTemplate>` and `</SeparatorTemplate>` tags.

To format the templates, right-click on the `DataList` control on the design surface and select one of the three editing submenus of the Edit Template menu. To end editing, right-click the DataList control and select End Template Editing. Templates can also be customized by editing the HTML directly. One of the item templates must contain a data bound control for the DataList control to render at runtime.

A Button, LinkButton, or ImageButton web server control can be added to the control templates. These buttons can let the user switch between the different item modes, for example. The buttons bubble their events to the containing DataList control. The events that the DataList raises in response to button clicks on the list items are described in Table 7-4.

Table 7-4. DataList Button click events

Event	Description
CancelCommand	Raised when the Cancel button is clicked for an item in the control.
DeleteCommand	Raised when the Delete button is clicked for an item in the control.
EditCommand	Raised when the Edit button is clicked for an item in the control.
ItemCommand	Raised when any button is clicked for an item in the control. The button clicked can be determined by reading the CommandName property of the DataListCommandEventArgs object in the ItemCommand event handler. This property contains the value of CommandName property of the button that was clicked.
UpdateCommand	Raised when the Update button is clicked for an item in the control.

After the properties appropriate to the control are set, call the DataBind( ) method of the control or of the page to bind the data source to the server control.

7.4   Binding Data to a Web Forms DataGrid

Problem

You want to bind the result set from a query to a DataGrid control.

Solution

Set the advanced properties of the DataGrid as demonstrated in the code for the Web Forms page as shown in Example 7-7.

Example 7-7. File: ADOCookbookCS0704.aspx

```
<asp:DataGrid id="dataGrid"
    style="Z-INDEX: 102; LEFT: 16px; POSITION: absolute; TOP: 56px"
    runat="server" AllowPaging="True" AllowSorting="True">
    <AlternatingItemStyle BackColor="#FFFF99"></AlternatingItemStyle>
</asp:DataGrid>
```

The code-behind file contains three event handlers and one method:

Page.Load

> Calls the CreateDataSource() method and binds data to the Web Forms DataGrid, if the page is being loaded for the first time.

CreateDataSource()

> This method fills a DataTable with the Orders table from the Northwind sample database and stores the DataTable to a Session variable to cache the data source for the DataGrid.

DataGrid.PageIndexChanged

> Gets the cached data from the Session variable, updates the CurrentPageIndex of the DataGrid, and binds the data to the grid.

DataGrid.SortCommand

> Gets the cached data from the Session variable, sets the sort order of the default DataView for the data, and binds that DataView to the grid.

The C# code for the code-behind is shown in Example 7-8.

Example 7-8. File: ADOCookbookCS0704.aspx.cs

```
// Namespaces, variables, and constants
using System;
using System.Configuration;
using System.Data;
using System.Data.SqlClient;

private void Page_Load(object sender, System.EventArgs e)
{
    if(!Page.IsPostBack)
    {
        dataGrid.DataSource = CreateDataSource();
        dataGrid.DataKeyField = "OrderId";
        dataGrid.DataBind();
    }
}

private DataTable CreateDataSource()
{
    DataTable dt = new DataTable();

    // Create a DataAdapter and fill the Orders table with it.
    SqlDataAdapter da = new SqlDataAdapter("SELECT * FROM Orders",
        ConfigurationSettings.AppSettings["DataConnectString"]);
    da.Fill(dt);

    // Store data in session variable to store data between
    // posts to server.
    Session["DataSource"] = dt;

    return dt;
}
```

Example 7-8. File: ADOCookbookCS0704.aspx.cs (continued)

```
private void dataGrid_PageIndexChanged(object source,
    System.Web.UI.WebControls.DataGridPageChangedEventArgs e)
{
    // Get the data from the session variable.
    DataView dv = ((DataTable)Session["DataSource"]).DefaultView;

    // Update the current page for the data grid.
    dataGrid.CurrentPageIndex = e.NewPageIndex;

    // Bind the data view to the data grid.
    dataGrid.DataSource = dv;
    dataGrid.DataBind();
}

private void dataGrid_SortCommand(object source,
    System.Web.UI.WebControls.DataGridSortCommandEventArgs e)
{
    // Get the data from the session variable.
    DataView dv = ((DataTable)Session["DataSource"]).DefaultView;

    // Set the sort of the data view.
    dv.Sort = e.SortExpression;

    // Bind the data view to the data grid.
    dataGrid.DataSource = dv;
    dataGrid.DataBind();
}
```

Discussion

The DataGrid Web Form control retrieves tabular information from a data source and renders it in a web page. The control supports functionality for selecting, editing, deleting, sorting, and navigating the data.

The DataGrid must be bound to a data source such as a DataReader, DataSet, DataTable, or DataView. Any class that implements the IEnumerable interface can be bound. The easiest way to create a DataGrid control is to drag the DataList control onto the web page design surface.

The DataGrid control uses templates to display items, control layout, and provide functional capabilities similar to the DataList as described in Recipe 7.3. The differences are:

- Item templates are created for columns in the grid rather for the entire grid.
- A DataGrid column does not have an AlternatingItemTemplate, or a SelectedItemTemplate, or a SeparatorItemTemplate.

To specify columns for and format the DataGrid, right-click on the DataList control on the design surface and select Property Builder. The DataGrid can also be customized by editing the HTML directly.

A variety of DataGrid columns can be specified, but by default, columns are automatically generated based on the fields in the data source. The DataGrid supports the column types described in Table 7-5.

Table 7-5. DataGrid column types

Column type	Description
BoundColumn	Specify the data source field to display as text.
ButtonColumn	A command button in the grid that can invoke custom logic when clicked.
EditCommandColumn	A button that supports in-place editing. These buttons raise events specific to in-place editing described in Table 7-6.
HyperlinkColumn	Displays the contents as a hyperlink.
TemplateColumn	A custom layout based on a combination of HTML and Web Server controls in a specified template.

Among the events that the DataGrid supports are those designed to help implement common data editing and manipulation functionality. These events are described in Table 7-6.

Table 7-6. Common DataGrid events for editing and navigation

Event	Description
CancelCommand( )	Raised when the in-place editing Cancel button is clicked for an item in the control.
DeleteCommand( )	Raised when the in-place editing Delete button is clicked for an item in the control.
EditCommand( )	Raised when the in-place editing Edit button is clicked for an item in the control.
ItemCommand( )	Raised when a button other than an in-place editing button is clicked.
PageIndexChanged( )	Raised when one of the page selection elements is clicked. The AllowPaging property of the control must be set to true.
SelectedIndexChanged( )	Raised when a different item is selected in the control between posts to the server.
SortCommand( )	Raised when a column header is selected for sorting.
UpdateCommand( )	Raised when the in-place editing Update button is clicked for an item in the control.

The DataGrid does not inherently support editing, paging, sorting, or updating functionality. Instead, it exposes the events listed in Table 7-6, allowing the functionality to be added using event handling code.

After the properties appropriate to the control are set, call the DataBind( ) method of the control or of the page to bind the data source to the server control.

7.5   Editing and Updating Data in a Web Forms DataGrid

Problem

You need to edit complex data using a DataGrid control and update the database with the changes made.

Solution

Bind the results of a database query to a DataGrid control and update the database with changes made in the DataGrid by configuring the appropriate properties and events.

The schema of table TBL00705 used in this solution is shown in Table 7-7.

Table 7-7. TBL0705 schema

Column name	Data type	Length	Allow nulls?
Id	int	4	No
IntField	int	4	Yes
StringField	nvarchar	50	Yes

The Web Forms page sample code defines the DataGrid control with the four columns that it contains—Edit *or* Update/Cancel button, Delete button, Id field, IntField field, StringField field—and the two templates controlling the appearance of data depending on whether the column is being edited: EditItemTemplate or ItemTemplate. The static Eval( ) method of the DataBinder class is used to fill the field values in each template. The Container.DataItem specifies the container argument for the method which, when used in a data grid, resolves to DataGridItem.DataItem. The code for the Web Forms page is shown in Example 7-9.

Example 7-9. File: ADOCookbookCS0705.aspx

```
<asp:DataGrid id="dataGrid"
    style="Z-INDEX: 102; LEFT: 16px; POSITION: absolute; TOP: 56px"
    runat="server" Width="576px" AutoGenerateColumns="False" PageSize="5"
    AllowPaging="True" AllowSorting="True">
    <AlternatingItemStyle BackColor="#FFFF99">
    </AlternatingItemStyle>
    <HeaderStyle Font-Bold="True">
    </HeaderStyle>
    <Columns>
        <asp:EditCommandColumn ButtonType="LinkButton"
            UpdateText="Update" CancelText="Cancel" EditText="Edit">
            <HeaderStyle Width="35px">
            </HeaderStyle>
```

Example 7-9. File: ADOCookbookCS0705.aspx (continued)

```
        </asp:EditCommandColumn>
        <asp:ButtonColumn Text="Delete" CommandName="Delete">
            <HeaderStyle Width="50px">
            </HeaderStyle>
        </asp:ButtonColumn>
        <asp:BoundColumn DataField="Id" ReadOnly="True"
            HeaderText="ID">
        </asp:BoundColumn>
        <asp:TemplateColumn HeaderText="Int Field">
            <ItemTemplate>
                <asp:Label runat="server"
                    Text='<%# DataBinder.Eval(Container,
                    "DataItem.IntField") %>'>
                </asp:Label>
            </ItemTemplate>
            <EditItemTemplate>
                <asp:TextBox runat="server" id="intFieldTextBox"
                    Text='<%# DataBinder.Eval(Container,
                    "DataItem.IntField") %>'>
                </asp:TextBox>
            </EditItemTemplate>
        </asp:TemplateColumn>
        <asp:TemplateColumn HeaderText="String Field">
            <ItemTemplate>
                <asp:Label runat="server"
                    Text='<%# DataBinder.Eval(Container,
                    "DataItem.StringField") %>'>
                </asp:Label>
            </ItemTemplate>
            <EditItemTemplate>
                <asp:TextBox runat="server"
                    id="stringFieldTextBox"
                    Text='<%# DataBinder.Eval(Container,
                    "DataItem.StringField") %>'>
                </asp:TextBox>
            </EditItemTemplate>
        </asp:TemplateColumn>
    </Columns>
</asp:DataGrid>
<asp:Label id="Label1"
    style="Z-INDEX: 105; LEFT: 16px; POSITION: absolute; TOP: 248px"
    runat="server" Font-Bold="True">
    New Record:
</asp:Label>
<TABLE id="Table1" style="Z-INDEX: 103; LEFT: 16px; WIDTH: 336px;
    POSITION: absolute; TOP: 272px; HEIGHT: 82px"
    cellSpacing="1" cellPadding="1" width="336" border="0">
    <TR>
        <TD style="WIDTH: 87px">ID:</TD>
        <TD>
            <INPUT id="idTextBox" style="WIDTH: 56px; HEIGHT: 22px"
                type="text" size="4" name="Text1" runat="server">
```

Example 7-9. File: ADOCookbookCS0705.aspx (continued)

```
                    </TD>
            </TR>
            <TR>
                <TD style="WIDTH: 87px">
                    Int Field:
                </TD>
                <TD>
                    <INPUT id="intFieldTextBox" style="WIDTH: 56px; HEIGHT: 22px"
                        type="text" size="4" name="Text2" runat="server">
                </TD>
            </TR>
            <TR>
                <TD style="WIDTH: 87px">
                    String Field:
                </TD>
                <TD>
                    <INPUT id="stringFieldTextBox"
                        style="WIDTH: 240px; HEIGHT: 22px" type="text" size="34"
                        name="Text3" runat="server">
                </TD>
            </TR>
        </TABLE>
        <asp:Button id="insertButton"
            style="Z-INDEX: 104; LEFT: 16px; POSITION: absolute; TOP: 360px"
            runat="server" Text="Insert">
        </asp:Button>
```

The code-behind file contains seven event handlers and three methods:

Page.Load

Calls the CreateDataSource( ) method and binds data to the Web Forms DataGrid, if the page is being loaded for the first time.

CreateDataSource( )

This method fills a DataTable with the TBL0705 table and stores the DataTable to a Session variable to cache the data source for the DataGrid.

UpdateDataSource( )

This method creates a DataAdapter and uses it with updating logic generated by a CommandBuilder to update the data source with changes made to the cached DataTable. The updated DataTable is stored to the Session variable used to cache the data source for the DataList.

BindDataGrid( )

This method gets the cached data from the Session variable and binds its default view to the DataGrid.

DataGrid.CancelCommand

Sets the index of the item being edited to −1 to cancel any current editing and calls BindDataGrid( ) to refresh the grid.

`DataGrid.DeleteCommand`

Finds and deletes the specified row from the data cached in the Session variable and calls the UpdateDataSource( ) method to persist the change back to the data source. BindDataGrid( ) is called to refresh the grid.

`DataGrid.EditCommand`

Sets the index of the item being edited to the index of the row corresponding to the Edit button. This puts that row into edit mode and calls BindDataGrid( ) to refresh the grid.

`DataGrid.UpdateCommand`

Finds and updates the specified row in the data cached in the Session variable and calls the UpdateDataSource( ) method to persist the change back to the data source. BindDataGrid( ) is called to refresh the grid.

Insert `Button.Click`

Inserts a new row into the data cached in the Session variable and calls the UpdateDataSource( ) method to persist the change back to the data source. BindDataGrid( ) is called to refresh the grid.

`DataGrid.PageIndexChanged`

Sets index of the item being edited is to −1 and calls BindDataGrid( ) to refresh the grid.

The C# code for the code-behind is shown in Example 7-10.

Example 7-10. File: ADOCookbookCS0705.aspx.cs

```
// Namespaces, variables, and constants
using System;
using System.Configuration;
using System.Web.UI.WebControls;
using System.Data;
using System.Data.SqlClient;

private const String TABLENAME = "TBL0705";

// ...

private void Page_Load(object sender, System.EventArgs e)
{
    if(!Page.IsPostBack)
    {
        dataGrid.DataSource = CreateDataSource( );
        dataGrid.DataKeyField = "Id";
        dataGrid.DataBind( );
    }
}

private DataTable CreateDataSource( )
{
    DataTable dt = new DataTable(TABLENAME);
```

Example 7-10. File: ADOCookbookCS0705.aspx.cs (continued)

```
    // Create the DataAdapter and fill the table using it.
    SqlDataAdapter da = new SqlDataAdapter("SELECT * FROM " + TABLENAME +
        " ORDER BY Id",
        ConfigurationSettings.AppSettings["DataConnectString"]);
    da.Fill(dt);
    da.FillSchema(dt, SchemaType.Source);

    // Store data in session variable to store data between
    // posts to server.
    Session["DataSource"] = dt;

    return dt;
}

private DataTable UpdateDataSource(DataTable dt)
{
    // Create a DataAdapter for the update.
    SqlDataAdapter da = new SqlDataAdapter("SELECT * FROM " + TABLENAME +
        " ORDER BY Id",
        ConfigurationSettings.AppSettings["DataConnectString"]);
    // Create a CommandBuilder to generate update logic.
    SqlCommandBuilder cb = new SqlCommandBuilder(da);

    // Update the data source with changes to the table.
    da.Update(dt);

    // Store updated data in session variable to store data between
    // posts to server.
    Session["DataSource"] = dt;

    return dt;
}

private void BindDataGrid( )
{
    // Get the data from the session variable.
    DataView dv = ((DataTable)Session["DataSource"]).DefaultView;

    // Bind the data view to the data grid.
    dataGrid.DataSource = dv;
    dataGrid.DataBind( );
}

private void dataGrid_CancelCommand(object source,
    System.Web.UI.WebControls.DataGridCommandEventArgs e)
{
    // Set the index of the item being edited out of range.
    dataGrid.EditItemIndex = -1;

    BindDataGrid( );
}
```

Example 7-10. File: ADOCookbookCS0705.aspx.cs (continued)

```csharp
private void dataGrid_DeleteCommand(object source,
    System.Web.UI.WebControls.DataGridCommandEventArgs e)
{
    // Get the data from the session variable.
    DataTable dt = (DataTable)Session["DataSource"];

    // Get the ID of the row to delete.
    int id = (int)dataGrid.DataKeys[e.Item.ItemIndex];

    // Delete the row from the table.
    dt.Rows.Find(id).Delete( );

    // Update the data source with the changes to the table.
    UpdateDataSource(dt);

    BindDataGrid( );
}

private void dataGrid_EditCommand(object source,
    System.Web.UI.WebControls.DataGridCommandEventArgs e)
{
    // Set the index of the item being edited to the selected item.
    dataGrid.EditItemIndex = e.Item.ItemIndex;

    BindDataGrid( );
}

private void dataGrid_UpdateCommand(object source,
    System.Web.UI.WebControls.DataGridCommandEventArgs e)
{
    // Get the data from the session variable.
    DataTable dt = (DataTable)Session["DataSource"];

    // Get the ID of the row to update.
    int id = (int)dataGrid.DataKeys[e.Item.ItemIndex];

    // Get the DataRow to update using the ID.
    DataRow dr = dt.Rows.Find(id);

    // Get the column values for the current record from the DataList.
    dr["IntField"] =
        Int32.Parse(((TextBox)e.Item.FindControl("intFieldTextBox")).Text);
    dr["StringField"] =
        ((TextBox)e.Item.FindControl("stringFieldTextBox")).Text;

    // Update the data source with the changes to the table.
    UpdateDataSource(dt);

    // Set the index of the item being edited out of range.
    dataGrid.EditItemIndex = -1;
```

Example 7-10. File: ADOCookbookCS0705.aspx.cs (continued)

```csharp
        BindDataGrid( );
}

private void insertButton_Click(object sender, System.EventArgs e)
{
    // Get the data from the session variable.
    DataTable dt = (DataTable)Session["DataSource"];

    // Add the new row.
    DataRow dr = dt.NewRow( );

    dr["Id"] = Int32.Parse(idTextBox.Value);
    dr["IntField"] = Int32.Parse(intFieldTextBox.Value);
    dr["StringField"] = stringFieldTextBox.Value;

    dt.Rows.Add(dr);

    // Update the data source with the changes to the table.
    UpdateDataSource(dt);

    // Clear the controls used to add the record.
    idTextBox.Value = "";
    intFieldTextBox.Value = "";
    stringFieldTextBox.Value = "";

    BindDataGrid( );
}

private void dataGrid_PageIndexChanged(object source,
    System.Web.UI.WebControls.DataGridPageChangedEventArgs e)
{
    // Update the current page for the data grid.
    dataGrid.CurrentPageIndex = e.NewPageIndex;

    BindDataGrid( );
}
```

Discussion

While Recipe 7.4 looks at the fundamentals of binding and displaying data using a Web Forms DataGrid control, this recipe shows how to delete, edit, change, and insert data into the DataGrid control and how to update the data source with the changes made.

By default, the DataGrid displays tabular data in read-only mode. With in-place editing configured, the runtime DataGrid displays two additional link button columns— Edit and Delete—for each row. When the Delete button is clicked, the row is deleted from the data source for the data grid. If the Edit button is clicked, it is replaced with Update and Cancel buttons, and the row is put into edit mode where text boxes appear in the cells allowing the values for the row to be edited. When the Cancel button is pressed, the row returns to the default appearance with an Edit button. When Update is pressed, the data source is updated with the changes made to the row and the row returns to the default appearance.

Unlike the Windows Forms DataGrid control, the Web Forms control does not automatically support in-place editing, and so a bit of code is required. Follow these steps to set up a DataGrid for in-place editing:

1. Right-click on the DataGrid and select Property Builder... from the submenu. This opens the DataGrid Properties dialog.

2. Select Columns in the left pane.

3. Select the Button Column → Edit, Update, Cancel from the Available columns list box and add them to the Selected columns list box using the greater than sign (>). Accept the defaults that are presented for the EditCommandColumn properties.

These steps prepare the DataGrid for in-place editing. Event handlers still need to be added for DataGrid events to enable in-place editing. Table 7-9 describes the events and associated generic event handling code.

Table 7-8. DataGrid event handler responses

Event	Handler response
CancelCommand	Cancel edit mode for the row being edited by setting EditItemIndex = -1
DeleteCommand	Delete the row
EditCommand	Put the row into edit mode by setting the EditItemIndex
UpdateCommand	Extract changes made from the in-place editing controls, update the data source with the changes, and cancel the edit mode for the row by setting EditItemIndex = -1

The example code for the solution shows actual implementations for these handlers.

The Web Forms DataGrid does not automatically support batch updates. To batch the updates, persist the changes to the Session variable with the following code when each change is made, rather than calling the UpdateDataSource( ) method:

```
// Store updated data in session variable to store data between
// posts to server.
Session["DataSource"] = dt;
```

Then call the UpdateDataSource( ) method when you want to update the data source with all changes made.

The Web Forms DataGrid does not support inserting records. The example shows a way to insert records outside of the DataGrid and resynchronize the DataGrid.

7.6   Synchronizing Master-Detail Web Forms DataGrids

Problem

You need to create a master-detail pair of DataGrid controls and synchronize them so that when you select a record in the master, the child grid is updated with the corresponding records.

Solution

Fill a DataSet with results from both tables, and create the necessary relations before binding the DataGrid to the DataSet.

The code for the Web Forms page is shown in Example 7-11.

Example 7-11. File: ADOCookbookCS0706.aspx

```
<form id="ADOCookbookCS0706" method="post" runat="server">
    <asp:HyperLink id="HyperLink1"
        style="Z-INDEX: 101; LEFT: 16px; POSITION: absolute; TOP: 24px"
        runat="server" NavigateUrl="default.aspx">
        Main Menu
    </asp:HyperLink>
    <br>
    <br>
    <br>
    <asp:DataGrid id="ordersDataGrid" runat="server" PageSize="5"
        AllowPaging="True">
        <SelectedItemStyle BackColor="#80FF80"></SelectedItemStyle>
        <AlternatingItemStyle BackColor="#FFFF99"></AlternatingItemStyle>
        <Columns>
            <asp:ButtonColumn Text="Detail" CommandName="Select">
            </asp:ButtonColumn>
        </Columns>
    </asp:DataGrid>
    <br>
    <br>
    <asp:DataGrid id="orderDetailsDataGrid" runat="server" PageSize="2"
        AllowPaging="True" Width="200px">
        <AlternatingItemStyle BackColor="#FFFF99"></AlternatingItemStyle>
    </asp:DataGrid>
</form>
```

The code-behind file contains four event handlers and a single method:

Page.Load
> Calls the CreateDataSource( ) method and binds the parent data to the parent Web Forms DataGrid, if the page is being loaded for the first time.

CreateDataSource( )
> This method fills a DataSet with the Orders table and the Order Details table from the Northwind sample database, creates a relation between the tables, and stores the DataSet to a Session variable to cache the data source for both parent and child DataGrid objects.

Orders DataGrid.SelectedIndexChanged
> Gets the cached data from the Session variable. If a row is selected in the Orders data grid, a DataView is created containing Order Details for the row selected in the Orders data grid and bound to the Order Details data grid; otherwise the Order Details data grid is cleared.

Orders DataGrid.PageIndexChanged
> Sets the SelectedIndex to −1 so that no Order is selected after the page is changed. The cached data is retrieved from the Session variable, the new page index for the Orders data grid is set, and the data is bound.

Order Details DataGrid.PageIndexChanged
> Gets the cached data from the Session variable, creates a DataView containing Order Details for the row selected in the Orders data grid, sets the new page index for the Order Details data grid, and binds the data.

The C# code for the code-behind is shown in Example 7-12.

Example 7-12. File: ADOCookbookCS0706.aspx.cs

```
// Namespaces, variables, and constants
using System;
using System.Configuration;
using System.Data;
using System.Data.SqlClient;

// ...

if(!Page.IsPostBack)
{
    DataSet ds = CreateDataSource( );

    // Bind the Orders data grid.
    ordersDataGrid.DataSource = ds.Tables["Orders"].DefaultView;
    ordersDataGrid.DataKeyField = "OrderID";

    Page.DataBind( );
}
```

Example 7-12. File: ADOCookbookCS0706.aspx.cs (continued)

```csharp
private DataSet CreateDataSource( )
{
    DataSet ds = new DataSet( );

    // Create a DataAdapter and fill the Orders table with it.
    SqlDataAdapter da = new SqlDataAdapter("SELECT * FROM Orders",
        ConfigurationSettings.AppSettings["DataConnectString"]);
    da.FillSchema(ds, SchemaType.Source, "Orders");
    da.Fill(ds, "Orders");

    // Create a DataAdapter and fill the Order Details table with it.
    da = new SqlDataAdapter("SELECT * FROM [Order Details]",
        ConfigurationSettings.AppSettings["DataConnectString"]);
    da.FillSchema(ds, SchemaType.Source, "OrderDetails");
    da.Fill(ds, "OrderDetails");

    // Add a relation between parent and child table.
    ds.Relations.Add("Order_OrderDetail_Relation",
        ds.Tables["Orders"].Columns["OrderID"],
        ds.Tables["OrderDetails"].Columns["OrderID"]);

    // Store data in session variable to store data between
    // posts to server.
    Session["DataSource"] = ds;

    return ds;
}

private void ordersDataGrid_SelectedIndexChanged(object sender,
    System.EventArgs e)
{
    // Get the Orders data view from the session variable.
    DataView dv =
        ((DataSet)Session["DataSource"]).Tables["Orders"].DefaultView;

    // Bind the data view to the Orders data grid.
    ordersDataGrid.DataSource = dv;

    // Bind the default view of the child table to the DataGrid.
    if(ordersDataGrid.SelectedIndex != -1)
    {
        // Get the OrderID for the selected Order row.
        int orderId =
            (int)ordersDataGrid.DataKeys[ordersDataGrid.SelectedIndex];

        // Get the selected DataRowView from the Order table.
        dv.Sort = "OrderID";
        DataRowView drv = dv[dv.Find(orderId)];

        // Bind the child view to the Order Details data grid.
        orderDetailsDataGrid.DataSource =
            drv.CreateChildView("Order_OrderDetail_Relation");
```

Example 7-12. File: ADOCookbookCS0706.aspx.cs (continued)

```
        // Position on the first page of the Order Details grid.
        orderDetailsDataGrid.CurrentPageIndex = 0;
    }
    else
        orderDetailsDataGrid.DataSource = null;

    Page.DataBind( );
}

private void ordersDataGrid_PageIndexChanged(object source,
    System.Web.UI.WebControls.DataGridPageChangedEventArgs e)
{
    // Deselect Orders row after page change.
    ordersDataGrid.SelectedIndex = -1;

    // Get the Orders data from the session variable.
    DataView dv =
        ((DataSet)Session["DataSource"]).Tables["Orders"].DefaultView;

    // Bind the data view to the data grid.
    ordersDataGrid.DataSource = dv;

    // Update the current page in data grid.
    ordersDataGrid.CurrentPageIndex = e.NewPageIndex;

    Page.DataBind( );
}

private void orderDetailsDataGrid_PageIndexChanged(object source,
    System.Web.UI.WebControls.DataGridPageChangedEventArgs e)
{
    // Get the Orders data view from the session variable.
    DataView dv =
        ((DataSet)Session["DataSource"]).Tables["Orders"].DefaultView;

    // Get the OrderID for the selected Order row.
    int orderId =
        (int)ordersDataGrid.DataKeys[ordersDataGrid.SelectedIndex];

    // Get the selected DataRowView from the Order table.
    dv.Sort = "OrderID";
    DataRowView drv = dv[dv.Find(orderId)];

    // Bind the child view to the Order Details data grid.
    orderDetailsDataGrid.DataSource =
        drv.CreateChildView("Order_OrderDetail_Relation");

    // Update the current page index.
    orderDetailsDataGrid.CurrentPageIndex = e.NewPageIndex;

    orderDetailsDataGrid.DataBind( );
}
```

Discussion

Unlike the Windows Forms DataGrid control, the Web Forms DataGrid control does not inherently support master-detail views of data. Instead, you must use two Web Forms DataGrid controls and programmatically synchronize them.

The master and child data DataGrid controls in this solution each display one DataTable from a DataSet. Displaying and paging through the data in each of the grids is fundamentally the same as shown in Recipe 7.4.

The SelectedIndexChanged event handler keeps the two data grids synchronized. When a new item is selected in the Orders DataGrid, the Order data is retrieved from the cached data in the Session variable and bound to the Order DataGrid. The OrderID is obtained from the DataKeys collection for the selected row and used to create a child DataView of the Order Details records that is bound to the Order Details DataGrid.

For information about master-detail data using the Windows Forms DataGrid, see Recipe 2.22.

7.7 Displaying an Image from a Database in a Web Forms Control

Problem

You need to display an image from a database column in an ASP.NET control.

Solution

Fill an ASP.NET Image control from a database field by pointing the ImageUrl property of an Image control to a web page that retrieves the image from the database. The solution contains three files: the Web Forms page to display the image, its code-behind file, and the code-behind page that serves the image.

The Web Forms page sample code displays the employee image in the Image control employeeImage. The code for the Web Forms page is shown in Example 7-13.

Example 7-13. File: ADOCookbookCS0707.aspx

```
<asp:Image id="employeeImage"
    style="Z-INDEX: 102; LEFT: 16px; POSITION: absolute; TOP: 56px"
    runat="server">
</asp:Image>
```

The code-behind used with the Web Forms page contains one event handler:

Form.Load

Sets the ImageUrl property of the employeeImage Image control to the web page that serves the employee image, then a parameter passed in the URL indicates the employee ID to retrieve.

The C# code for the code-behind is shown in Example 7-14.

Example 7-14. File: ADOCookbookCS0707.aspx.cs

```
using System;

// ...

private void Page_Load(object sender, System.EventArgs e)
{
    // Set the image URL to the page containing just the image.
    employeeImage.ImageUrl = "ADOCookbookCS0707b.aspx?EmployeeId=" +
        employeeIdTextBox.Text;
}
```

The code-behind that serves the image contains one event handler:

Form.Load

Retrieves the image from the database for the specified employee ID. The image is served by setting the HTTP MIME type of the output stream to *image/bmp* and writing the image to the stream.

The C# code for the code-behind is shown in Example 7-15.

Example 7-15. File: ADOCookbookCS0707b.aspx.cs

```
// Namespaces, variables, and constants
using System;
using System.Configuration;
using System.Data;
using System.Data.SqlClient;

// ...

private void Page_Load(object sender, System.EventArgs e)
{   // Create the command to retrieve employee image specified.
    SqlConnection conn = new SqlConnection(
        ConfigurationSettings.AppSettings["DataConnectString"]);
    String sqlText = "SELECT * FROM Employees WHERE EmployeeId = " +
        Request["EmployeeId"].ToString( );
    SqlCommand cmd = new SqlCommand(sqlText, conn);
    // Create a DataReader containing the record for the employee.
    conn.Open( );
    SqlDataReader dr = cmd.ExecuteReader( );
    if(dr.Read( ))
    {
```

Example 7-15. File: ADOCookbookCS0707b.aspx.cs (continued)

```
            // Set the response content type type.
            Response.ContentType = "image/bmp";
            // Stream the binary image data in the response.
            Response.BinaryWrite((byte[])dr["Photo"]);
        }
        dr.Close( );
        conn.Close( );
    }
```

Discussion

Rendering an image from a database in a Web Forms Image control is easy to do, but not straightforward. Fortunately, it is much simpler with ASP.NET than it was in ASP.

Two web pages are required: one that contains the user interface that the client sees and one that retrieves the required image from the database and serves it to the Image control on the web page that the client sees. The following steps outline the required tasks:

1. Create a web page that outputs a binary stream containing the image from the database.

2. Create a SQL statement to retrieve the required image from the database and retrieve the image using a DataReader. A DataTable or DataSet filled using a DataAdapter can also be used.

3. Set the ContentType property of the HttpResponse object to the MIME type of the image in the database. The ContentType property of the HttpResponse object gets or sets the MIME type of the output stream. The default value is *text/html*, but other types can be specified to output.

   ```
   Response.ContentType = "image/bmp";
   ```

4. Use the BinaryWrite( ) method of the HttpResponse object to output the image as a binary stream. The BinaryWrite( ) method of the HttpResponse object writes a stream of binary characters to the HTTP output stream rather than a textual stream.

   ```
   Response.BinaryWrite((byte[])dr["Photo"]);
   ```

The ImageUrl property of the Image control gets or sets the location of the image to display in the control. The location can be specified as either an absolute or relative URL. Set the ImageUrl property of the Image control in the web page that the client sees to the web page that outputs the image from the database as a binary stream.

 This example uses the modified version of Northwind, where the Photo field has been updated for all employees to remove the OLE image header. For more information, see the online sample code.

7.8 Displaying an Image from a Database in a Windows Forms Control

Problem

You need to display an image from a database in a Windows Forms control.

Solution

Read the image into a byte array and load it directly into a PictureBox control with a MemoryStream.

The sample code contains six event handlers:

Form.Load
> Sets up the sample by filling a DataTable within a DataSet with the Employees table from the Northwind sample database. The EmployeeID, LastName, and FirstName fields are bound to TextBox controls. The BindingManagerBase is obtained for the Employees table in the DataSet, a handler is attached to manage the PositionChanged event, and that handler is called to position the display on the first record.

BindingManagerBase.PositionChanged
> Updates the PictureBox with the image for the current record. This event is raised when the Position property value changes.
>
> The EmployeeID for the current record is obtained using the position information in the BindingManagerBase object. A Connection object and Command object are created and used to retrieve the Photo binary field for the employee record into a Byte array. A MemoryStream object is created from the Byte array. The static FromStream( ) method of the System.Drawing.Image class is used to load the image into the PictureBox from the MemoryStream.

Move First Button.Click
> Sets the current record of the bound controls to the first record by setting the Position property of the BindingManagerBase object to 0.

Move Previous Button.Click
> Sets the current record of the bound controls to the previous record by decrementing the Position property of the BindingManagerBase object by 1.

Move Next Button.Click
> Sets the current record of the bound controls to the next record by incrementing the Position property of the BindingManagerBase object by 1.

Move Last Button.Click
> Sets the current record of the bound controls to the last record by setting the Position property of the BindingManagerBase object to the total number of records, as returned by the Count property, minus 1.

The C# code is shown in Example 7-16.

Example 7-16. File: DisplayDatabaseImageForm.cs

```csharp
// Namespaces, variables, and constants
using System;
using System.Configuration;
using System.Drawing;
using System.Windows.Forms;
using System.IO;
using System.Data;
using System.Data.SqlClient;

private DataSet ds;
private SqlDataAdapter da;

private BindingManagerBase bm;

// ...

private void DisplayDatabaseImageForm_Load(object sender,
    System.EventArgs e)
{
    // Create the DataSet.
    ds = new DataSet();

    // Create the DataAdapter and retrieve the Employees table.
    String selectCommand =
        "SELECT EmployeeID, LastName, FirstName FROM Employees";
    da = new SqlDataAdapter(selectCommand,
        ConfigurationSettings.AppSettings["Sql_ConnectString"]);
    da.FillSchema(ds, SchemaType.Source, "Employees");
    da.Fill(ds, "Employees");

    // Bind several table fields to controls.
    employeeIdTextBox.DataBindings.Add("Text", ds,
        "Employees.EmployeeID");
    lastNameTextBox.DataBindings.Add("Text", ds, "Employees.LastName");
    firstNameTextBox.DataBindings.Add("Text", ds, "Employees.FirstName");

    // Get the binding manager base for the Employees table.
    bm = BindingContext[ds, "Employees"];
    // Update the image in response to each record reposition.
    bm.PositionChanged += new EventHandler(bm_PositionChanged);
    // Update the display for the first record.
    bm_PositionChanged(null, null);
}

private void bm_PositionChanged(Object sender, EventArgs e)
{
    // Refresh the photo displayed when the current record changes.

    // Get the new EmployeeID using the BindingManager.
    int employeeId =
        (int)ds.Tables["Employees"].Rows[bm.Position]["EmployeeID"];
```

Example 7-16. File: DisplayDatabaseImageForm.cs (continued)

```
    // Create a connection.
    SqlConnection conn = new SqlConnection(
        ConfigurationSettings.AppSettings["Sql_ConnectString"]);
    // Create a command to retrieve the employee photo.
    String sqlText = "SELECT Photo FROM Employees WHERE EmployeeID=" +
        employeeId;
    SqlCommand cmd = new SqlCommand(sqlText, conn);

    // Retrieve the employee photo to a stream.
    conn.Open( );
    Byte[] image = (Byte[])cmd.ExecuteScalar( );;
    MemoryStream ms = new MemoryStream(image);
    conn.Close( );

    // Load the image into the PictureBox from the stream.
    photoPictureBox.Image = Image.FromStream(ms);
    ms.Close( );
}

private void moveFirstButton_Click(object sender, System.EventArgs e)
{
    bm.Position = 0;
}

private void movePreviousButton_Click(object sender, System.EventArgs e)
{
    bm.Position -= 1;
}

private void moveNextButton_Click(object sender, System.EventArgs e)
{
    bm.Position += 1;
}

private void moveLastButton_Click(object sender, System.EventArgs e)
{
    bm.Position = bm.Count - 1;
}
```

Discussion

The Windows Forms PictureBox control displays bitmap, JPEG, metafile, or icon images.

In the solution, the image stored as a BLOB in the database is retrieved into a Byte array, which is in turn copied into a System.IO.MemoryStream object. The static FromStream( ) method of the Image class creates an Image object that is loaded into the PictureBox.

This example uses the modified version of Northwind, where the Photo field has been updated for all employees to remove the OLE image header. For more information, see the online sample code.

Binding Windows Forms Controls

The abstract `BindingManagerBase` class synchronizes all Windows Forms controls (i.e., `Binding` objects) that are bound to the same data source so that they display information from the object within the data source, such as a row in a `DataTable`.

The `BindingContext` class is used to instantiate a `BindingManagerBase` object and either a `CurrencyManager` or `PropertyManager` object is returned depending on the type of data source:

- The `CurrencyManager` class inherits from the `BindingManagerBase` class and maintains a pointer for the current item in a data source that implements `IList`, `IListSource`, or `IBindingList`. Data sources do not necessarily support a current-item pointer. The `CurrencyManager` notifies all data-bound controls if the current item changes so that they can refresh their data.

- The `PropertyManager` class inherits from the `BindingManagerBase` class and maintains the current property of an object, rather than an object in a list.

The `Position` property is a zero-based index that gets or sets the current position in the underlying data source list. The `Count` property returns the number of items in the list. The `Current` property returns the current object in the list, which must be cast to the type of object in the underlying data source before it can be used.

7.9 Binding a Group of Radio Buttons in a Windows Form

Problem

You need to bind a field in a database to a radio button and update the database with the radio button selected.

Solution

Use a hidden `TextBox` to retrieve and update the field value that corresponds to the radio button group. You can use the `Tag` property of each `RadioButton` control to hold its corresponding data field value.

The schema of table TBL0709 used in this solution is shown in Table 7-9.

Table 7-9. TBL0709 schema

Column name	Data type	Length	Allow nulls?
Id	int	4	No
RadioButtonItemId	int	4	No
Field1	nvarchar	50	Yes

The sample code contains seven event handlers:

Form.Load

Sets up the sample by creating a DataAdapter with the logic to select all records from table TBL0709 in the sample database and to update changes made back to the database. The DataAdapter is used to fill a DataTable in a new DataSet with the schema and data from TBL0709.

The text boxes displaying the data for the fields in the record are bound to the three columns in the table: Id, RadioButtonItemId, and Field1. The RadioButtonItemId TextBox is hidden. The BindingManagerBase is obtained for the TBL0709 table in the DataSet, a handler is attached to manage the PositionChanged event, and that handler is called to position the display on the first record.

Update Button.Click

Iterates over the group of radio buttons to identify the one selected. The Tag property for the selected radio button is transferred to the hidden bound TextBox for update back to the database.

BindingManagerBase.PositionChanged

Selects the radio button corresponding to the data field. The code iterates over the group of radio buttons. When the Tag property of a radio button matches the value in the TextBox that is bound to the data field, the radio button is selected.

Move First Button.Click

Sets the current record of the bound controls to the first record by setting the Position property of the BindingManagerBase object to 0.

Move Previous Button.Click

Sets the current record of the bound controls to the previous record by decrementing the Position property of the BindingManagerBase object by 1.

Move Next Button.Click

Sets the current record of the bound controls to the next record by incrementing the Position property of the BindingManagerBase object by 1.

Move Last Button.Click

Sets the current record of the bound controls to the last record by setting the Position property of the BindingManagerBase object to the total number of records, as returned by the Count property, minus 1.

The C# code is shown in Example 7-17.

Example 7-17. File: RadioButtonForm.cs

```csharp
// Namespaces, variables, and constants
using System;
using System.Windows.Forms;
using System.Data;
using System.Data.SqlClient;

private const String TABLENAME = "TBL0709";

private DataSet ds;
private SqlDataAdapter da;

private BindingManagerBase bm;

// ...

private void RadioButtonForm_Load(object sender, System.EventArgs e)
{
    // Create the DataSet.
    ds = new DataSet();

    // Create the select and update commands for the DataAdapter.
    String selectCommand = "SELECT Id, RadioButtonItemId, Field1 FROM " +
        TABLENAME;
    String updateCommand = "UPDATE " + TABLENAME + " " +
        "SET RadioButtonItemId=@RadioButtonItemId, Field1=@Field1 " +
        "WHERE Id=@Id";

    // Create the DataAdapter.
    da = new SqlDataAdapter(selectCommand,
        ConfigurationSettings.AppSettings["Sql_ConnectString"]);
    da.UpdateCommand = new SqlCommand(updateCommand,
        da.SelectCommand.Connection);
    da.UpdateCommand.CommandType = CommandType.Text;
    da.UpdateCommand.Parameters.Add("@Id", SqlDbType.Int, 0, "Id");
    da.UpdateCommand.Parameters.Add("@RadioButtonItemId", SqlDbType.Int, 0,
        "RadioButtonItemId");
    da.UpdateCommand.Parameters.Add("@Field1", SqlDbType.NVarChar, 50,
        "Field1");

    // Retrieve the data and schema for the table.
    da.FillSchema(ds, SchemaType.Source, TABLENAME);
    da.Fill(ds, TABLENAME);

    // Bind all of the controls, including hidden text box, to the DataSet.
    idTextBox.DataBindings.Add("Text", ds, TABLENAME + ".Id");
    radioButtonItemIdTextBox.DataBindings.Add("Text", ds, TABLENAME +
        ".RadioButtonItemId");
    radioButtonItemIdTextBox.Visible = false;
    field1TextBox.DataBindings.Add("Text", ds, TABLENAME +  ".Field1");

    // Get the binding manager base for the table.
    bm = BindingContext[ds, TABLENAME];
```

Example 7-17. File: RadioButtonForm.cs (continued)

```
        // Update the correct radio button in response to each record
        // reposition.
        bm.PositionChanged += new EventHandler(bm_PositionChanged);
        // Update the display for the first record.
        bm_PositionChanged(null, null);

}

private void updateButton_Click(object sender, System.EventArgs e)
{
        // Retrieve the selected radio button based on the value in the
        // tag field to the hidden text box.
        foreach(RadioButton rb in radioButtonGroupBox.Controls)
        {
            if (rb.Checked)
            {
                radioButtonItemIdTextBox.Text = rb.Tag.ToString( );
                break;
            }
        }

        // End the current update and update the record using the DataAdapter.
        bm.EndCurrentEdit( );
        da.Update(ds.Tables[TABLENAME]);
}

private void bm_PositionChanged(Object sender, EventArgs e)
{
        // Refresh the checked radio button when the current record changes.
        foreach(RadioButton rb in radioButtonGroupBox.Controls)
        {
            if (rb.Tag.ToString( ) == radioButtonItemIdTextBox.Text)
            {
                rb.Checked = true;
                break;
            }
        }
}

private void moveFirstButton_Click(object sender, System.EventArgs e)
{
        bm.Position = 0;
}

private void movePreviousButton_Click(object sender, System.EventArgs e)
{
        bm.Position -= 1;
}

private void moveNextButton_Click(object sender, System.EventArgs e)
{
        bm.Position += 1;
}
```

Example 7-17. File: RadioButtonForm.cs (continued)

```
private void moveLastButton_Click(object sender, System.EventArgs e)
{
    bm.Position = bm.Count - 1;
}
```

Discussion

While a RadioButton control can be set to simple-bind to data, there is no way to bind a group of RadioButton controls to a data source. Binding a single radio button to a data source isn't a particularly common requirement—nor is it particularly useful—since radio buttons are normally used in groups to allow an option to be selected from a group of mutually exclusive options.

Web Forms provides a RadioButtonList control that works as a parent control to a collection of radio button list items. It inherits from the ListControl class and as a result works similarly to the ListBox and DropDownList controls. There is no RadioButtonList control available for Windows Forms applications. For more information about the RadioButtonList class, see the MSDN Library.

Radio button data binding can be simulated in a Windows Form application by following these steps:

1. Add the RadioButton controls to the form. For each radio button, set its Tag property to the data value that corresponds to the selection of the radio button.

2. Create a hidden TextBox control to take the value of the selected RadioButton from the group.

3. Bind the Text property of the TextBox to the data source:

   ```
   radioButtonItemIdTextBox.DataBindings.Add("Text", ds, TABLENAME +
       ".RadioButtonItemId");
   ```

4. Get the BindingManagerBase for the DataTable using the indexer (Item property in VB.NET) of the BindingContext class.

   ```
   bm = BindingContext[ds, TABLENAME];
   ```

   The overload used in the sample takes two arguments, the data source and the data member, because the data source is a DataSet. For a DataTable, an overload of the BindingContext indexer is used that takes only the data source argument.

5. Attach an event handler for the PositionChanged event of the BindingManagerBase. This event indicates that the selected row in the DataTable has changed.

   ```
   bm.PositionChanged += new EventHandler(bm_PositionChanged);
   ```

6. Create the event handler for the PositionChanged event. In the handler, iterate over the collection of radio buttons. Check the radio button that has a Tag matching the hidden TextBox that is bound to the data. This will select the radio button corresponding to the column value for the current row in the DataTable.

This event handler must be called for the first record, as done in the Form.Load event of the sample:

```
bm_PositionChanged(null, null);
```

7. If the application permits modifying the data using the radio buttons, add code in the update method to iterate over the collection of radio buttons, transferring the Tag value of the checked radio button to the hidden data bound TextBox before the updating logic.

7.10 Creating Custom Columns in a Windows Forms DataGrid

Problem

You need to create a DataGrid having columns with custom formatting and attributes.

Solution

Use the DataGridTableStyle class.

The sample code contains two event handlers:

Form.Load
 Sets up the sample by creating a DataAdapter and using it to fill a DataTable with data from the ProductID, ProductName, and Discontinued columns of the Products table in the Northwind database. The DataGridTableStyle class is used to define a data grid containing three custom columns—two text boxes and one check box—corresponding to the ProductID, ProductName, and Discontinued columns. Finally, the default view of the Products DataTable is bound to the data grid on the form.

Update Button.Click
 Uses the DataAdapter created in the Form.Load event handler to update changes made to the Products DataTable back to the database.

The C# code is shown in Example 7-18.

Example 7-18. File: CustomColumnsInDataGridForm.cs

```
// Namespaces, variables, and constants
using System;
using System.Configuration;
using System.Windows.Forms;
using System.Data;
using System.Data.SqlClient;

private SqlDataAdapter da;
private DataTable dt;
```

Example 7-18. File: CustomColumnsInDataGridForm.cs (continued)

```csharp
// ...

private void CustomColumnsInDataGridForm_Load(object sender,
    System.EventArgs e)
{
    // Create the DataAdapter.
    String selectCommand = "SELECT ProductID, ProductName, Discontinued " +
        "FROM Products";
    da = new SqlDataAdapter(selectCommand,
        ConfigurationSettings.AppSettings["Sql_ConnectString"]);
    // Use CommandBuilder to handle updates back to the data source.
    SqlCommandBuilder cb = new SqlCommandBuilder(da);

    // Retrieve the table schema.
    dt = new DataTable("Products");
    da.FillSchema(dt, SchemaType.Source);
    // Default the check box column to false.
    dt.Columns["Discontinued"].DefaultValue = false;
    // Fill the table.
    da.Fill(dt);

    // Define the table for the grid.
    DataGridTableStyle ts = new DataGridTableStyle();
    ts.MappingName = "Products";

    // Define and add the columns to the grid.
    DataGridTextBoxColumn productIDCol = new DataGridTextBoxColumn();
    productIDCol.MappingName = "ProductID";
    productIDCol.HeaderText = "Product ID";
    productIDCol.ReadOnly = true;
    ts.GridColumnStyles.Add(productIDCol);

    DataGridTextBoxColumn productNameCol = new DataGridTextBoxColumn();
    productNameCol.MappingName = "ProductName";
    productNameCol.HeaderText = "Name";
    productNameCol.Width = 200;
    productNameCol.Alignment = HorizontalAlignment.Center;
    ts.GridColumnStyles.Add(productNameCol);

    DataGridBoolColumn discontinuedCol = new DataGridBoolColumn();
    discontinuedCol.MappingName = "Discontinued";
    discontinuedCol.HeaderText = "Discontinued";
    discontinuedCol.AllowNull = false;
    ts.GridColumnStyles.Add(discontinuedCol);

    dataGrid.TableStyles.Add(ts);

    // Bind the default view of the table to the grid.
    dataGrid.DataSource = dt.DefaultView;
}
```

Example 7-18. File: CustomColumnsInDataGridForm.cs (continued)

```
private void updateButton_Click(object sender, System.EventArgs e)
{
    // Update the data using the DataAdapter.
    da.Update(dt);
}
```

Discussion

The `TableStyles` property of the `DataGrid` exposes a collection of `DataGridTableStyle` objects. The `GridColumnStyles` property of the `DataGridTableStyle` object exposes a `GridColumnStylesCollection` containing all `DataGridColumnStyle` objects for the table. This property allows a custom set of column styles to be created for the `DataGrid`. Once defined, the `Add( )` method of the `DataGridTableStyles` object is used to add the custom column styles to the `DataGrid`.

The `MappingName` property of the `DataGridTableStyle` is set to the `DataSource`. The `MappingName` of each `DataGridColumnStyle` object must be associated with the name of a `DataColumn` to synchronize the `DataGrid` display column with the data column. An exception will be thrown if duplicate mapping names are used.

The `DataGridTextBoxColumn` class inherits from the abstract `DataGridColumnStyle` class. It defines the attributes, display format, and behavior of cells in a `DataGrid` column. At runtime, each cell in the column hosts a `DataGridTextBox` control.

The `DataGridBoolColumn` inherits from the abstract `DataGridColumnStyle` class. It defines the attributes, display format, and behavior of cells in a `DataGrid` column representing a Boolean value. At runtime, each cell in the column hosts a `CheckBox` control that can have one of three states: checked (`true`), unchecked (`false`), or unchecked (`DBNull.Value`). The allowable states of the check box are controlled by the properties described in Table 7-10.

Table 7-10. DataGridBoolColumn properties related to the underlying value

Property	Description
AllowNull	Gets or sets a Boolean value indicating whether `null` values are allowed
FalseValue	Gets or sets the value pushed to the data source when the column value is set to `false`
NullValue	Gets or sets the value pushed to the data source when the column value is `null`
TrueValue	Gets or sets the value pushed to the data source when the column value is set to `true`

A new column class can be created to meet special requirements by inheriting from `DataGridColumnStyle`, where the `Abort( )`, `Commit( )`, `Edit( )`, and `Paint( )` methods must be overridden.

By default, a collection of `DataGridColumnStyle` objects is created behind the scenes when the `DataSource` property of the `DataGrid` is set. The class used for each column depends on the DataType of the DataColumn associated with the DataGridColumnStyle object. A column with a Boolean data type will be represented by a DataGridBoolColumn object while other columns will be represented by a DataGridTextBoxColumn object. You can use the GetType( ) method of the DataGridColumnStyle object to determine the column's data type.

7.11   Populating a Windows Forms ComboBox

Problem

You need to populate a ComboBox from a database, bind a field in a database to the ComboBox so that the correct value is selected from the list, and use the value selected in the ComboBox to update the database.

Solution

You must:

- Fill a ComboBox from a database (pay attention to the difference between the SelectedIndex and SelectedValue).
- Bind a ComboBox to a field in a result set so that the value is selected in the ComboBox corresponding to the value in a field for the record displayed.
- Use the selection events returned by the ComboBox.
- Update the database with the value selected in the ComboBox.

The schema of table TBL0711 used in this solution is shown in Table 7-11.

Table 7-11. TBL0711 schema

Column name	Data type	Length	Allow nulls?
Id	int	4	No
ComboBoxItemId	int	4	No
Field1	nvarchar	50	Yes

The schema of table TBL0711_ComboBoxSource used in this solution is shown in Table 7-12.

Table 7-12. TBL0711_ComboBoxSource schema

Column name	Data type	Length	Allow nulls?
ComboBoxItemId	int	4	No
Description	nvarchar	50	No

The sample code contains seven event handlers:

`Form.Load`
> Sets up the sample by creating a `DataAdapter` with the logic to select all records from table TBL0709 in the sample database and to update changes made back to the database. The `DataAdapter` is used to fill a `DataTable` in a new `DataSet` with the schema and data from TBL0709. A `DataTable` is filled from table TBL0709_ComboBoxSource and added to the `DataSet`. A `DataRelation` is created between the two tables in the `DataSet`.
>
> The `ComboBox` control is filled by linking its properties to table TBL0709_ComboBoxSource in the `DataSet`. The text boxes displaying the data for the *ID* and Field1 columns and the `ComboBox` displaying data for the `ComboBoxItemId` column are bound to the `DataTable` TBL0709. Finally, the `BindingManagerBase` is obtained for the TBL0709 table in the `DataSet`.

Update `Button.Click`
> Ends the current edit and uses the `DataAdapter` created in the `Form.Load` event handler to update the database.

`ComboBox.SelectionChangeCommitted`
> Displays the values for the `SelectedIndex`, `SelectedValue`, and `SelectedText` properties of the `ComboBox` after its selected item has changed.

Move First `Button.Click`
> Sets the current record of the bound controls to the first record by setting the `Position` property of the `BindingManagerBase` object to 0.

Move Previous `Button.Click`
> Sets the current record of the bound controls to the previous record by decrementing the `Position` property of the `BindingManagerBase` object by 1.

Move Next `Button.Click`
> Sets the current record of the bound controls to the next record by incrementing the `Position` property of the `BindingManagerBase` object by 1.

Move Last `Button.Click`
> Sets the current record of the bound controls to the last record by setting the `Position` property of the `BindingManagerBase` object to the total number of records, as returned by the `Count` property, minus 1.

The C# code is shown in Example 7-19.

Example 7-19. File: ComboBoxForm.cs

```
// Namespaces, variables, and constants
using System;
using System.Configuration;
using System.Windows.Forms;
using System.Data;
using System.Data.SqlClient;
```

Example 7-19. File: ComboBoxForm.cs (continued)

```csharp
private const String TABLENAME                   = "TBL0711";
private const String TABLENAME_COMBOBOXSOURCE = "TBL0709_ComboBoxSource";
private const String RELATIONNAME                = "REL0711";

private DataSet ds;
private SqlDataAdapter da;

private BindingManagerBase bm;

// ...

private void ComboBoxForm_Load(object sender, System.EventArgs e)
{
    // Create the DataSet.
    ds = new DataSet( );

    // Create the select and update commands for the DataAdapter.
    String selectCommand = "SELECT Id, ComboBoxItemId, Field1 FROM " +
        TABLENAME;
    String updateCommand = "UPDATE " + TABLENAME + " " +
        "SET ComboBoxItemId = @ComboBoxItemId, Field1 = @Field1 " +
        "WHERE Id = @Id";

    // Create the DataAdapter.
    da = new SqlDataAdapter(selectCommand,
        ConfigurationSettings.AppSettings["Sql_ConnectString"]);
    da.UpdateCommand = new SqlCommand(updateCommand,
        da.SelectCommand.Connection);
    da.UpdateCommand.CommandType = CommandType.Text;
    da.UpdateCommand.Parameters.Add("@Id", SqlDbType.Int, 0, "Id");
    da.UpdateCommand.Parameters.Add("@ComboBoxItemId", SqlDbType.Int, 0,
        "ComboBoxItemId");
    da.UpdateCommand.Parameters.Add("@Field1", SqlDbType.NVarChar, 50,
        "Field1");

    // Retrieve the data and schema for the table.
    da.FillSchema(ds, SchemaType.Source, TABLENAME);
    da.Fill(ds, TABLENAME);

    // Create and fill the schema for the ComboBox table.
    String sqlText = "SELECT ComboBoxItemId, Description FROM " +
        TABLENAME_COMBOBOXSOURCE;
    SqlDataAdapter daCB = new SqlDataAdapter(sqlText,
        da.SelectCommand.Connection);
    DataTable comboBoxSourceTable =
        new DataTable(TABLENAME_COMBOBOXSOURCE);
    daCB.FillSchema(comboBoxSourceTable, SchemaType.Source);
    // Sdd the instructions for the user as the first element.
    comboBoxSourceTable.Rows.Add(new object[] {-1, "<Select>"});
    // Fill the rest of the data for the ComboBox.
    daCB.Fill(comboBoxSourceTable);
```

Example 7-19. File: ComboBoxForm.cs (continued)

```
    // Add the ComboBox source table to the DataSet.
    ds.Tables.Add(comboBoxSourceTable);

    // Relate the parent and ComboBox tables.
    ds.Relations.Add(new DataRelation(RELATIONNAME,
        ds.Tables[TABLENAME_COMBOBOXSOURCE].Columns["ComboBoxItemId"],
        ds.Tables[TABLENAME].Columns["ComboBoxItemId"],
        true));

    // Set up the ComboBox with the DataSet.
    comboBox.DataSource = ds.Tables[TABLENAME_COMBOBOXSOURCE];
    comboBox.ValueMember = "ComboBoxItemId";
    comboBox.DisplayMember = "Description";

    // Bind all of the controls to the DataSet.
    idTextBox.DataBindings.Add("Text", ds, TABLENAME + ".Id");
    comboBox.DataBindings.Add("SelectedValue", ds,
        TABLENAME + ".ComboBoxItemId");
    field1TextBox.DataBindings.Add("Text", ds, TABLENAME +  ".Field1");

    // Get the binding manager base for the parent table.
    bm = BindingContext[ds, TABLENAME];
}

private void updateButton_Click(object sender, System.EventArgs e)
{
    // End the current update and update the record using the DataAdapter.
    bm.EndCurrentEdit( );
    da.Update(ds.Tables[TABLENAME]);
}

private void comboBox_SelectionChangeCommitted(object sender, System.EventArgs e)
{
    resultTextBox.Text="SelectedIndex = " + comboBox.SelectedIndex +
        Environment.NewLine +
        "SelectedValue = " + comboBox.SelectedValue +
        Environment.NewLine +
        "SelectedText = " +
        ((DataRowView)comboBox.Items[comboBox.SelectedIndex])
        ["Description"];
}

private void moveFirstButton_Click(object sender, System.EventArgs e)
{
    bm.Position = 0;
}

private void movePreviousButton_Click(object sender, System.EventArgs e)
{
    bm.Position -= 1;
}
```

Example 7-19. File: ComboBoxForm.cs (continued)

```
private void moveNextButton_Click(object sender, System.EventArgs e)
{
    bm.Position += 1;
}

private void moveLastButton_Click(object sender, System.EventArgs e)
{
    bm.Position = bm.Count - 1;
}
```

Discussion

Combo boxes are most commonly used to browse data, enter new data, or edit existing data in a data source.

There are two ways to fill a ComboBox: either use the Add( ) method or bind the ComboBox to a data source. The Windows Forms ComboBox control has three properties that are used to control data binding to an ADO.NET data source. These are described in Table 7-13.

Table 7-13. ComboBox properties for data binding

Property	Description
DataSource	Gets or sets the data source for the control. This can be a DataTable, DataView, or any class that implements the IList interface.
DisplayMember	Gets or sets the property of the data source that is displayed in the control. In a DataTable or DataView, this is the name of a column.
ValueMember	Gets or sets the property of the data source that supplies the value for the control. In a DataTable or DataView, this is the name of a column. The default is an empty string.

The DataBindings property of a control exposes the ControlBindingsCollection object for the control. The Add( ) method of this collection adds a Binding to the collection. The overload of the Add( ) method used in the solution takes three arguments:

PropertyName
> The name of the control property to bind

DataSource
> The name of the data source to bind

DataMember
> The name of the property of the data source to bind

In the solution, as shown in this excerpt, the SelectedValue property of the ComboBox is bound to the ComboBoxItemId field in the destination table TBL0709 in the DataSet *ds*:

```
comboBox.DataBindings.Add("SelectedValue", ds,
    TABLENAME + ".ComboBoxItemId");
```

The SelectionChangeCommitted event raised by the ComboBox occurs when the item selected is changed and the change is committed. The event handler receives an EventArgs argument. You can use the handler for the event to get the new value of the ComboBox once it has been changed.

7.12 Binding a Windows DataGrid to Master-Detail Data

Problem

You need to bind both a parent table and child table within a DataSet to a DataGrid so that the child data is displayed when the parent is expanded, and update the database with edits made to data in both tables.

Solution

Use the approach demonstrated in the sample code.

The sample uses eight stored procedures, which are shown in Examples 7-20 through 7-27:

GetOrders
    Used to retrieve a single record from the Orders table if the optional *@OrderId* parameter is specified or all Orders records if it is not

DeleteOrders
    Used to delete the record specified by the *@OrderId* parameter from the Orders table

InsertOrders
    Used to insert a record into the Orders table and return the OrderID identity value for the new record

UpdateOrders
    Used to update all field values for the record in the Orders table specified by the *@OrderId* input parameter

GetOrderDetails
    Used to retrieve a single record from the Order Details table if the optional *@OrderId* and *@ProductID* parameters are specified, or all Order Details records if it is not

DeleteOrderDetails
    Used to delete the record specified by the *@OrderId* and *@ProductID* parameters from the Order Details table

InsertOrderDetails

Used to insert a record into the Order Details table

UpdateOrderDetails

Used to update all field values for the record in the Order Details table specified by the *@OrderId* and *@ProductID* input parameters

Example 7-20. Stored procedure: GetOrders

```
CREATE PROCEDURE GetOrders
    @OrderID int=null
AS
    SET NOCOUNT ON

    if @OrderID is not null
    begin
        select
            OrderID,
            CustomerID,
            EmployeeID,
            OrderDate,
            RequiredDate,
            ShippedDate,
            ShipVia,
            Freight,
            ShipName,
            ShipAddress,
            ShipCity,
            ShipRegion,
            ShipPostalCode,
            ShipCountry
        from
            Orders
        where
            OrderID=@OrderID

        return 0
    end

    select
        OrderID,
        CustomerID,
        EmployeeID,
        OrderDate,
        RequiredDate,
        ShippedDate,
        ShipVia,
        Freight,
        ShipName,
        ShipAddress,
        ShipCity,
        ShipRegion,
        ShipPostalCode,
```

Example 7-20. Stored procedure: GetOrders (continued)

```
        ShipCountry
    from
        Orders

    return 0
```

Example 7-21. Stored procedure: DeleteOrders

```
CREATE PROCEDURE DeleteOrders
    @OrderID int
AS
    SET NOCOUNT ON

    delete
    from
        Orders
    where
        OrderID=@OrderID

    return 0
```

Example 7-22. Stored procedure: InsertOrders

```
CREATE PROCEDURE InsertOrders
    @OrderID int output,
    @CustomerID nchar(5),
    @EmployeeID int,
    @OrderDate datetime,
    @RequiredDate datetime,
    @ShippedDate datetime,
    @ShipVia int,
    @Freight money,
    @ShipName nvarchar(40),
    @ShipAddress nvarchar(60),
    @ShipCity nvarchar(15),
    @ShipRegion nvarchar(15),
    @ShipPostalCode nvarchar(10),
    @ShipCountry nvarchar(15)
AS
    SET NOCOUNT ON

    insert Orders(
        CustomerID,
        EmployeeID,
        OrderDate,
        RequiredDate,
        ShippedDate,
        ShipVia,
        Freight,
        ShipName,
        ShipAddress,
```

Example 7-22. Stored procedure: InsertOrders (continued)

```
            ShipCity,
            ShipRegion,
            ShipPostalCode,
            ShipCountry)
    values (
            @CustomerID,
            @EmployeeID,
            @OrderDate,
            @RequiredDate,
            @ShippedDate,
            @ShipVia,
            @Freight,
            @ShipName,
            @ShipAddress,
            @ShipCity,
            @ShipRegion,
            @ShipPostalCode,
            @ShipCountry)

    if @@rowcount=0
        return 1

    set @OrderID=Scope_Identity( )

    select @OrderId OrderId

    return 0
```

Example 7-23. Stored procedure: UpdateOrders

```
CREATE PROCEDURE UpdateOrders
    @OrderID int,
    @CustomerID nchar(5),
    @EmployeeID int,
    @OrderDate datetime,
    @RequiredDate datetime,
    @ShippedDate datetime,
    @ShipVia int,
    @Freight money,
    @ShipName nvarchar(40),
    @ShipAddress nvarchar(60),
    @ShipCity nvarchar(15),
    @ShipRegion nvarchar(15),
    @ShipPostalCode nvarchar(10),
    @ShipCountry nvarchar(15)
AS
    SET NOCOUNT ON

    update
        Orders
    set
```

Example 7-23. Stored procedure: UpdateOrders (continued)

```
        CustomerID=@CustomerID,
        EmployeeID=@EmployeeID,
        OrderDate=@OrderDate,
        RequiredDate=@RequiredDate,
        ShippedDate=@ShippedDate,
        ShipVia=@ShipVia,
        Freight=@Freight,
        ShipName=@ShipName,
        ShipAddress=@ShipAddress,
        ShipCity=@ShipCity,
        ShipRegion=@ShipRegion,
        ShipPostalCode=@ShipPostalCode,
        ShipCountry=@ShipCountry
    where
        OrderID=@OrderID

    if @@rowcount=0
        return 1

    return 0
```

Example 7-24. Stored procedure: GetOrderDetails

```
CREATE PROCEDURE GetOrderDetails
    @OrderID int=null,
    @ProductID int=null
AS
    SET NOCOUNT ON

    if @OrderID is not null and @ProductID is not null
    begin
        select
            OrderID,
            ProductID,
            UnitPrice,
            Quantity,
            Discount
        from
            [Order Details]
        where
            OrderID=@OrderID and
            ProductID=@ProductID

        return 0
    end

    select
        OrderID,
        ProductID,
        UnitPrice,
        Quantity,
```

Example 7-24. Stored procedure: GetOrderDetails (continued)

```
        Discount
    from
        [Order Details]

    return 0
```

Example 7-25. Stored procedure: DeleteOrderDetails

```
CREATE PROCEDURE DeleteOrderDetails
    @OrderID int,
    @ProductID int
AS
    SET NOCOUNT ON

    delete
    from
        [Order Details]
    where
        OrderID=@OrderID and
        ProductID=@ProductID

    return 0
```

Example 7-26. Stored procedure: InsertOrderDetails

```
CREATE PROCEDURE InsertOrderDetails
    @OrderID int,
    @ProductID int,
    @UnitPrice money,
    @Quantity smallint,
    @Discount real
AS
    SET NOCOUNT ON

    insert [Order Details](
        OrderID,
        ProductID,
        UnitPrice,
        Quantity,
        Discount)
    values (
        @OrderID,
        @ProductID,
        @UnitPrice,
        @Quantity,
        @Discount)

    if @@rowcount=0
        return 1

    return 0
```

Example 7-27. Stored procedure: UpdateOrderDetails

```
CREATE PROCEDURE UpdateOrderDetails
    @OrderID int,
    @ProductID int,
    @UnitPrice money,
    @Quantity smallint,
    @Discount real
AS
    SET NOCOUNT ON

    update
        [Order Details]
    set
        UnitPrice=@UnitPrice,
        Quantity=@Quantity,
        Discount=@Discount
    where
        OrderID=@OrderID and
        ProductID=@ProductID

    if @@rowcount=0
        return 1

    return 0
```

The sample code contains two event handlers:

Form.Load

Sets up the sample by creating a DataSet containing the Orders and Order Details DataTable objects. A DataRelation object is created relating the tables. DataAdapter objects are created for each DataTable; the select, delete, insert, and update Command objects are specified for each using the custom logic in the eight stored procedures used by this solution. The DataAdapter objects are used to fill both tables in the DataSet. Finally, the default view of the Orders table is bound to the data grid on the form.

Update Button.Click

Uses the DataAdapter for the Orders and Order Details DataTable objects to update offline changes back to the database.

The C# code is shown in Example 7-28.

Example 7-28. File: HierarchicalDataGridForm.cs

```
// Namespaces, variables, and constants
using System;
using System.Configuration;
using System.Data;
using System.Data.SqlClient;

private DataSet ds;
// Private SqlDataAdapter daParent, daChild
private SqlDataAdapter daOrder, daOrderDetail;
```

Example 7-28. File: HierarchicalDataGridForm.cs (continued)

```
// Table name constants
private const String ORDERS_TABLE        = "Orders";
private const String ORDERDETAILS_TABLE  = "OrderDetails";

// Relation name constants
private const String ORDERS_ORDERDETAILS_RELATION =
    "Orders_OrderDetails_Relation";

// Field name constants for Orders table
public const String ORDERID_FIELD        = "OrderID";
public const String CUSTOMERID_FIELD     = "CustomerID";
public const String EMPLOYEEID_FIELD     = "EmployeeID";
public const String ORDERDATE_FIELD      = "OrderDate";
public const String REQUIREDDATE_FIELD   = "RequiredDate";
public const String SHIPPEDDDATE_FIELD   = "ShippedDate";
public const String SHIPVIA_FIELD        = "ShipVia";
public const String FREIGHT_FIELD        = "Freight";
public const String SHIPNAME_FIELD       = "ShipName";
public const String SHIPADDRESS_FIELD    = "ShipAddress";
public const String SHIPCITY_FIELD       = "ShipCity";
public const String SHIPREGION_FIELD     = "ShipRegion";
public const String SHIPPOSTALCODE_FIELD = "ShipPostalCode";
public const String SHIPCOUNTRY_FIELD    = "ShipCountry";

// Stored procedure name constants
public const String DELETEORDERS_SP      = "DeleteOrders";
public const String GETORDERS_SP         = "GetOrders";
public const String INSERTORDERS_SP      = "InsertOrders";
public const String UPDATEORDERS_SP      = "UpdateOrders";

// Stored procedure parameter name constants for Orders table
public const String ORDERID_PARM         = "@OrderID";
public const String CUSTOMERID_PARM      = "@CustomerID";
public const String EMPLOYEEID_PARM      = "@EmployeeID";
public const String ORDERDATE_PARM       = "@OrderDate";
public const String REQUIREDDATE_PARM    = "@RequiredDate";
public const String SHIPPEDDDATE_PARM    = "@ShippedDate";
public const String SHIPVIA_PARM         = "@ShipVia";
public const String FREIGHT_PARM         = "@Freight";
public const String SHIPNAME_PARM        = "@ShipName";
public const String SHIPADDRESS_PARM     = "@ShipAddress";
public const String SHIPCITY_PARM        = "@ShipCity";
public const String SHIPREGION_PARM      = "@ShipRegion";
public const String SHIPPOSTALCODE_PARM  = "@ShipPostalCode";
public const String SHIPCOUNTRY_PARM     = "@ShipCountry";

// Field name constants for OrderDetails table
public const String ORDERID_FIELD        = "OrderID";
public const String PRODUCTID_FIELD      = "ProductID";
public const String UNITPRICE_FIELD      = "UnitPrice";
public const String QUANTITY_FIELD       = "Quantity";
public const String DISCOUNT_FIELD       = "Discount";
```

Example 7-28. File: HierarchicalDataGridForm.cs (continued)

```csharp
// Stored procedure name constants
public const String DELETEORDERDETAILS_SP = "DeleteOrderDetails";
public const String GETORDERDETAILS_SP    = "GetOrderDetails";
public const String INSERTORDERDETAILS_SP = "InsertOrderDetails";
public const String UPDATEORDERDETAILS_SP = "UpdateOrderDetails";

// Stored procedure parameter name constants for OrderDetails table
public const String ORDERID_PARM          = "@OrderID";
public const String PRODUCTID_PARM        = "@ProductID";
public const String UNITPRICE_PARM        = "@UnitPrice";
public const String QUANTITY_PARM         = "@Quantity";
public const String DISCOUNT_PARM         = "@Discount";

// ...

private void HierarchicalDataGridForm_Load(object sender,
    System.EventArgs e)
{
    ds = new DataSet();

    // Fill the Order table and add it to the DataSet.
    daOrder = new SqlDataAdapter(GETORDERS_SP,
        ConfigurationSettings.AppSettings["Sql_ConnectString"]);
    daOrder.SelectCommand.CommandType = CommandType.StoredProcedure;
    DataTable dtOrder = new DataTable(ORDERS_TABLE);
    daOrder.FillSchema(dtOrder, SchemaType.Source);
    daOrder.Fill(dtOrder);
    ds.Tables.Add(dtOrder);

    // Fill the OrderDetails table with schema and add it to the DataSet.
    daOrderDetail = new SqlDataAdapter(GETORDERDETAILS_SP,
        ConfigurationSettings.AppSettings["Sql_ConnectString"]);
    daOrderDetail.SelectCommand.CommandType = CommandType.StoredProcedure;
    DataTable dtOrderDetail = new DataTable(ORDERDETAILS_TABLE);
    daOrderDetail.FillSchema(dtOrderDetail, SchemaType.Source);
    daOrderDetail.Fill(dtOrderDetail);
    ds.Tables.Add(dtOrderDetail);

    // Create a relation between the tables.
    ds.Relations.Add(ORDERS_ORDERDETAILS_RELATION,
        ds.Tables[ORDERS_TABLE].Columns[ORDERID_FIELD],
        ds.Tables[ORDERDETAILS_TABLE].Columns[ORDERID_FIELD],
        true);

    // Build the orders delete command.
    SqlCommand deleteCommand = new SqlCommand(DELETEORDERS_SP,
        daOrder.SelectCommand.Connection);
    deleteCommand.CommandType = CommandType.StoredProcedure;
    SqlParameterCollection sqlParams = deleteCommand.Parameters;
    sqlParams.Add(ORDERID_PARM, SqlDbType.Int, 0, ORDERID_FIELD);
    daOrder.DeleteCommand = deleteCommand;
```

Example 7-28. File: HierarchicalDataGridForm.cs (continued)

```csharp
// Build the orders insert command.
SqlCommand insertCommand = new SqlCommand(INSERTORDERS_SP,
    daOrder.SelectCommand.Connection);
insertCommand.CommandType = CommandType.StoredProcedure;
sqlParams = insertCommand.Parameters;
sqlParams.Add(ORDERID_PARM, SqlDbType.Int, 0,
    ORDERID_FIELD).Direction = ParameterDirection.Output;
sqlParams.Add(CUSTOMERID_PARM, SqlDbType.NChar, 5, CUSTOMERID_FIELD);
sqlParams.Add(EMPLOYEEID_PARM, SqlDbType.Int, 0, EMPLOYEEID_FIELD);
sqlParams.Add(ORDERDATE_PARM, SqlDbType.DateTime, 0, ORDERDATE_FIELD);
sqlParams.Add(REQUIREDDATE_PARM, SqlDbType.DateTime, 0,
    REQUIREDDATE_FIELD);
sqlParams.Add(SHIPPEDDDATE_PARM, SqlDbType.DateTime, 0,
    SHIPPEDDDATE_FIELD);
sqlParams.Add(SHIPVIA_PARM, SqlDbType.Int, 0, SHIPVIA_FIELD);
sqlParams.Add(FREIGHT_PARM, SqlDbType.Money, 0, FREIGHT_FIELD);
sqlParams.Add(SHIPNAME_PARM, SqlDbType.NVarChar, 40, SHIPNAME_FIELD);
sqlParams.Add(SHIPADDRESS_PARM, SqlDbType.NVarChar, 60,
    SHIPADDRESS_FIELD);
sqlParams.Add(SHIPCITY_PARM, SqlDbType.NVarChar, 15, SHIPCITY_FIELD);
sqlParams.Add(SHIPREGION_PARM, SqlDbType.NVarChar, 15,
    SHIPREGION_FIELD);
sqlParams.Add(SHIPPOSTALCODE_PARM, SqlDbType.NVarChar, 10,
    SHIPPOSTALCODE_FIELD);
sqlParams.Add(SHIPCOUNTRY_PARM, SqlDbType.NVarChar, 15,
    SHIPCOUNTRY_FIELD);
daOrder.InsertCommand = insertCommand;

// Build the orders update command.
SqlCommand updateCommand = new SqlCommand(UPDATEORDERS_SP,
    daOrder.SelectCommand.Connection);
updateCommand.CommandType = CommandType.StoredProcedure;
sqlParams = updateCommand.Parameters;
sqlParams.Add(ORDERID_PARM, SqlDbType.Int, 0, ORDERID_FIELD);
sqlParams.Add(CUSTOMERID_PARM, SqlDbType.NChar, 5, CUSTOMERID_FIELD);
sqlParams.Add(EMPLOYEEID_PARM, SqlDbType.Int, 0, EMPLOYEEID_FIELD);
sqlParams.Add(ORDERDATE_PARM, SqlDbType.DateTime, 0, ORDERDATE_FIELD);
sqlParams.Add(REQUIREDDATE_PARM, SqlDbType.DateTime, 0,
    REQUIREDDATE_FIELD);
sqlParams.Add(SHIPPEDDDATE_PARM, SqlDbType.DateTime, 0,
    SHIPPEDDDATE_FIELD);
sqlParams.Add(SHIPVIA_PARM, SqlDbType.Int, 0, SHIPVIA_FIELD);
sqlParams.Add(FREIGHT_PARM, SqlDbType.Money, 0, FREIGHT_FIELD);
sqlParams.Add(SHIPNAME_PARM, SqlDbType.NVarChar, 40, SHIPNAME_FIELD);
sqlParams.Add(SHIPADDRESS_PARM, SqlDbType.NVarChar, 60,
    SHIPADDRESS_FIELD);
sqlParams.Add(SHIPCITY_PARM, SqlDbType.NVarChar, 15, SHIPCITY_FIELD);
sqlParams.Add(SHIPREGION_PARM, SqlDbType.NVarChar, 15,
    SHIPREGION_FIELD);
sqlParams.Add(SHIPPOSTALCODE_PARM, SqlDbType.NVarChar, 10,
    SHIPPOSTALCODE_FIELD);
```

Example 7-28. File: HierarchicalDataGridForm.cs (continued)

```csharp
    sqlParams.Add(SHIPCOUNTRY_PARM, SqlDbType.NVarChar, 15,
        SHIPCOUNTRY_FIELD);
    daOrder.UpdateCommand = updateCommand;

    // Build the order details delete command.
    deleteCommand = new SqlCommand(DELETEORDERDETAILS_SP,
        daOrderDetail.SelectCommand.Connection);
    deleteCommand.CommandType = CommandType.StoredProcedure;
    sqlParams = deleteCommand.Parameters;
    sqlParams.Add(ORDERID_PARM, SqlDbType.Int, 0, ORDERID_FIELD);
    sqlParams.Add(PRODUCTID_PARM, SqlDbType.Int, 0, PRODUCTID_FIELD);
    daOrderDetail.DeleteCommand = deleteCommand;

    // Build the order details insert command.
    insertCommand = new SqlCommand(INSERTORDERDETAILS_SP,
        daOrderDetail.SelectCommand.Connection);
    insertCommand.CommandType = CommandType.StoredProcedure;
    sqlParams = insertCommand.Parameters;
    sqlParams.Add(ORDERID_PARM, SqlDbType.Int, 0, ORDERID_FIELD);
    sqlParams.Add(PRODUCTID_PARM, SqlDbType.Int, 0, PRODUCTID_FIELD);
    sqlParams.Add(UNITPRICE_PARM, SqlDbType.Money, 0, UNITPRICE_FIELD);
    sqlParams.Add(QUANTITY_PARM, SqlDbType.SmallInt, 0, QUANTITY_FIELD);
    sqlParams.Add(DISCOUNT_PARM, SqlDbType.Real, 0, DISCOUNT_FIELD);
    daOrderDetail.InsertCommand = insertCommand;

    // Build the order details update command.
    updateCommand = new SqlCommand(UPDATEORDERDETAILS_SP,
        daOrderDetail.SelectCommand.Connection);
    updateCommand.CommandType = CommandType.StoredProcedure;
    sqlParams = updateCommand.Parameters;
    sqlParams.Add(ORDERID_PARM, SqlDbType.Int, 0, ORDERID_FIELD);
    sqlParams.Add(PRODUCTID_PARM, SqlDbType.Int, 0, PRODUCTID_FIELD);
    sqlParams.Add(UNITPRICE_PARM, SqlDbType.Money, 0, UNITPRICE_FIELD);
    sqlParams.Add(QUANTITY_PARM, SqlDbType.SmallInt, 0, QUANTITY_FIELD);
    sqlParams.Add(DISCOUNT_PARM, SqlDbType.Real, 0, DISCOUNT_FIELD);
    daOrderDetail.UpdateCommand = updateCommand;

    // Fill the parent and child table.
    daOrder.Fill(dtOrder);
    daOrderDetail.Fill(dtOrderDetail);

    // Bind the default view of the order table to the grid.
    dataGrid.DataSource = dtOrder.DefaultView;
}

private void updateButton_Click(object sender, System.EventArgs e)
{
    // Update order and order details tables.
    daOrderDetail.Update(ds.Tables[ORDERDETAILS_TABLE].Select(null, null,
        DataViewRowState.Deleted));
    daOrder.Update(ds.Tables[ORDERS_TABLE].Select(null, null,
        DataViewRowState.Deleted));
```

Example 7-28. File: HierarchicalDataGridForm.cs (continued)

```
    daOrder.Update(ds.Tables[ORDERS_TABLE].Select(null, null,
        DataViewRowState.ModifiedCurrent));
    daOrder.Update(ds.Tables[ORDERS_TABLE].Select(null, null,
        DataViewRowState.Added));
    daOrderDetail.Update(ds.Tables[ORDERDETAILS_TABLE].Select(null, null,
        DataViewRowState.ModifiedCurrent));
    daOrderDetail.Update(ds.Tables[ORDERDETAILS_TABLE].Select(null, null,
        DataViewRowState.Added));
}
```

Discussion

The DataGrid control can display a single DataTable or a DataSet containing a set of DataTable objects with a hierarchical relationship between them. The DataGrid provides a user interface for the data, navigation between related tables as well as formatting and editing capabilities. If a DataGrid is bound to a DataSet containing related tables, and navigation is enabled for the DataGrid, expanders will be displayed for each row that has a child relationship.

The DataGrid must be bound to a data source using its DataSource and DataMember properties at design time, or by using the DataSource property or SetBindingMethod( ) at runtime. Valid data sources for the DataGrid include DataTable, DataSet, DataView, and DataViewManager objects.

The DataGrid control dynamically reflects any changes made to the data source. If the ReadOnly property of the DataGrid is set to false, the data source is updated when changes are made to data in the DataGrid. This automatic update happens when the field being edited changes or when the EndEdit( ) method is called on the data source for the DataGrid. The data object that is bound to the DataGrid is responsible for updating the underlying data source.

7.13 Loading a Windows PictureBox with Images Stored by Access as OLE Objects

Problem

You need to display images from a Microsoft Access database in a PictureBox control.

Solution

Strip the OLE image header that Microsoft Access adds to the image.

The sample code contains six event handlers:

Form.Load

Sets up the sample by filling a DataTable within a DataSet with the Categories table from the Microsoft Access Northwind sample database. The CategoryID, CategoryName, and Description fields are bound to TextBox controls. The BindingManagerBase is obtained for the Categories table in the DataSet, a handler is attached to manage the PositionChanged event, and that handler is called to position the display on the first record.

BindingManagerBase.PositionChanged

Updates the PictureBox with the image for the current record. This event is raised when the Position property value changes.

The CategoryID for the current record is obtained using the position information in the BindingManagerBase object. A Connection object and Command object are created and used to retrieve the Picture binary field for the category record into a Byte array. A MemoryStream object is created and the image written into it from the Byte array using an offset to strip the OLE image header. The static FromStream( ) method of the System.Drawing.Image class is used to load the image into the PictureBox from the MemoryStream.

Move First Button.Click

Sets the current record of the bound controls to the first record by setting the Position property of the BindingManagerBase object to 0.

Move Previous Button.Click

Sets the current record of the bound controls to the previous record by decrementing the Position property of the BindingManagerBase object by 1.

Move Next Button.Click

Sets the current record of the bound controls to the next record by incrementing the Position property of the BindingManagerBase object by 1.

Move Last Button.Click

Sets the current record of the bound controls to the last record by setting the Position property of the BindingManagerBase object to the total number of records, as returned by the Count property, minus 1.

The C# code is shown in Example 7-29.

Example 7-29. File: DisplayMsAccessImageForm.cs

```
using System;
using System.Configuration;
using System.Drawing;
using System.Windows.Forms;
using System.IO;
using System.Data;
using System.Data.OleDb;
```

Example 7-29. File: DisplayMsAccessImageForm.cs (continued)

```
private const int MSACCESSIMAGEOFFSET = 78;

private DataSet ds;
private OleDbDataAdapter da;

private BindingManagerBase bm;

// ...

private void DisplayMsAccessImageForm_Load(object sender,
    System.EventArgs e)
{
    // Create the DataSet.
    ds = new DataSet( );

    // Create the DataAdapter and retrieve the Categories table.
    String selectCommand =
        "SELECT CategoryID, CategoryName, Description FROM Categories";
    da = new OleDbDataAdapter(selectCommand,
        ConfigurationSettings.AppSettings["MsAccess_ConnectString"]);
    da.FillSchema(ds, SchemaType.Source, "Categories");
    da.Fill(ds, "Categories");

    // Bind table fields to controls.
    categoryIdTextBox.DataBindings.Add("Text", ds,
        "Categories.CategoryID");
    categoryNameTextBox.DataBindings.Add("Text", ds,
        "Categories.CategoryName");
    descriptionTextBox.DataBindings.Add("Text", ds,
        "Categories.Description");

    // Get the binding manager base for the parent table.
    bm = BindingContext[ds, "Categories"];
    // Update the image in response to each record reposition.
    bm.PositionChanged += new EventHandler(bm_PositionChanged);
    // Update the display for the first record.
    bm_PositionChanged(null, null);
}

private void bm_PositionChanged(Object sender, EventArgs e)
{
    // Refresh the photo displayed when the current record changes.

    // Get the new CategoryID using the BindingManager.
    int categoryId =
        (int)ds.Tables["Categories"].Rows[bm.Position]["CategoryID"];

    // Create a connection.
    OleDbConnection conn = new OleDbConnection(
        ConfigurationSettings.AppSettings["MsAccess_ConnectString"]);
```

Example 7-29. File: DisplayMsAccessImageForm.cs (continued)

```
    // Create a command to retrieve the category photo.
    String sqlText = "SELECT Picture FROM Categories WHERE CategoryID=" +
        categoryId;
    OleDbCommand cmd = new OleDbCommand(sqlText, conn);

    // Retrieve the image from the database.
    conn.Open( );
    Byte[] image = (Byte[])cmd.ExecuteScalar( );
    // Write to a stream removing the image header.
    MemoryStream ms = new MemoryStream( );
    ms.Write(image, MSACCESSIMAGEOFFSET,
        image.Length - MSACCESSIMAGEOFFSET);
    conn.Close( );

    // Load the image into the PictureBox from the stream.
    picturePictureBox.Image = Image.FromStream(ms);
    ms.Close( );
}

private void moveFirstButton_Click(object sender, System.EventArgs e)
{
    bm.Position = 0;
}

private void movePreviousButton_Click(object sender, System.EventArgs e)
{
    bm.Position -= 1;
}

private void moveNextButton_Click(object sender, System.EventArgs e)
{
    bm.Position += 1;
}

private void moveLastButton_Click(object sender, System.EventArgs e)
{
    bm.Position = bm.Count - 1;
}
```

Discussion

The Windows Forms PictureBox control displays bitmap, JPEG, metafile, or icon images.

Microsoft Access stores an image as an OLE object that wraps the actual image. This means that the image is prefixed with a variable-length header that must be stripped off to retrieve the image. The length of this header for bitmap images stored in the Northwind sample database is 78 bytes.

In the solution, the image stored as a BLOB in the database is retrieved into a Byte array. The Byte array is copied into a MemoryStream object using an overload of the

Write( ) method that allows the 78 byte offset to be specified. The static FromStream( ) method of the Image class creates an Image object from the MemoryStream that is loaded into the PictureBox.

7.14   Using a DataView to Control Edits, Deletions, or Additions in Windows Forms

Problem

You need to selectively prevent users from editing, deleting, or adding data in a Windows Forms application.

Solution

Bind a DataView to Windows Forms controls.

The sample code contains four event handlers:

Form.Load
> Sets up the sample by filling a DataTable with the Orders table from the Northwind sample database. A DataView is created from the table and bound to the data grid on the form.

Allow Delete Button.Click
> Sets whether the DataView allows records to be deleted based on the value in a check box.

Allow Edit Button.Click
> Sets whether the DataView allows records to be edited based on the value in a check box.

Allow Insert Button.Click
> Sets whether the DataView allows records to be inserted based on the value in a check box.

The C# code is shown in Example 7-30.

Example 7-30. File: ControlDataEditWithDataViewForm.cs

```
// Namespaces, variables, and constants
using System;
using System.Configuration;
using System.Data;
using System.Data.SqlClient;

private DataView dv;

// ...
```

Example 7-30. File: ControlDataEditWithDataViewForm.cs (continued)

```csharp
private void ControlDataEditWithDataViewForm_Load(object sender,
    System.EventArgs e)
{
    // Fill the Order table.
    SqlDataAdapter da = new SqlDataAdapter("SELECT * FROM Orders",
        ConfigurationSettings.AppSettings["Sql_ConnectString"]);
    DataTable dtOrders = new DataTable("Orders");
    da.FillSchema(dtOrders, SchemaType.Source);
    da.Fill(dtOrders);

    // Create a view and bind it to the grid.
    dv = new DataView(dtOrders);
    dataGrid.DataSource = dv;
}

private void allowDeleteCheckBox_CheckedChanged(object sender,
    System.EventArgs e)
{
    dv.AllowDelete = allowDeleteCheckBox.Checked;
}

private void allowEditCheckBox_CheckedChanged(object sender,
    System.EventArgs e)
{
    dv.AllowEdit = allowEditCheckBox.Checked;
}

private void allowInsertCheckBox_CheckedChanged(object sender,
    System.EventArgs e)
{
    dv.AllowNew = allowInsertCheckBox.Checked;
}
```

Discussion

The DataGrid control does not have properties that control the adding, editing, or deleting the data in the control. Binding a DataGrid to a DataTable binds to the default view of the underlying DataTable.

The DataView class represents a view of the DataTable that can be data bound on both Windows Forms and Web Forms. The DataView can be customized for editing, filtering, searching, and sorting.

The DataView class can be used to add, edit, or delete records in the underlying DataTable. The properties described in Table 7-14 control the data modification permitted in a DataView.

Table 7-14. DataView properties

Property	Description
AllowDelete	Gets or sets a Boolean value indicating whether deletes are allowed
AllowEdit	Gets or sets a Boolean value indicating whether edits are allowed
AllowNew	Gets or sets a Boolean value indicating whether new rows can be added

If AllowNew is true, the record is not added until the EndEdit( ) method is called either explicitly or implicitly. The CancelEdit( ) method of the DataRowView can be called to discard the row before it is added.

If AllowEdit is true, the changes to the row are not committed until the EndEdit( ) method is called either explicitly or implicitly. Only one row can be edited at a time. The CancelEdit( ) method of the DataRowView can be called to discard the row before it is added.

If the AddNew( ) or BeginEdit( ) method of the DataRowView is called, EndEdit( ) is called implicitly on the pending row; this applies the changes to the row in the underlying DataTable. In data controls that allow editing multiple records, EndEdit( ) is called implicitly when the current row is changed.

7.15   Adding Search Capabilities to Windows Forms

Problem

You need to use a search criteria specified by a user to locate a record displayed in a DataGrid without executing a query against the database.

Solution

Use the Find( ) method of the DataView with a sort key value to locate a record displayed in a DataGrid and reposition the row in the DataGrid.

The sample code contains two event handlers:

Form.Load
> Sets up the sample by creating a DataTable and filling it with the Customers table from the Northwind sample database. A DataView is created based on the default view of the Customers DataTable, its sort key is set to the CustomerID column, and it is bound to the data grid on the form. Finally, a CurrencyManager is created from the DataView.

Go Button.Click
> Uses the Find( ) method of the DataView to locate a record with the CustomerID specified by the user. If the CustomerID is found, the CurrencyManager created in

the Form.Load event handler is used to select the matching record in the data grid.

The C# code is shown in Example 7-31.

Example 7-31. File: SearchDataGridForm.cs

```
// Namespaces, variables, and constants
using System;
using System.Configuration;
using System.Windows.Forms;
using System.Data;
using System.Data.SqlClient;

private DataView dv;
private CurrencyManager cm;

// ...

private void SearchDataGridForm_Load(object sender, System.EventArgs e)
{
    // Create the DataAdapter and load the Customers data in a table.
    String sqlText = "SELECT * FROM Customers";
    SqlDataAdapter da = new SqlDataAdapter(sqlText,
        ConfigurationSettings.AppSettings["Sql_ConnectString"]);
    DataTable dt = new DataTable( );
    da.Fill(dt);

    // Create a view from the default view for the table.
    dv = dt.DefaultView;
    dv.Sort = "CustomerID";

    // Bind the view to the grid.
    findDataGrid.DataSource = dv;

    // Get the CurrencyManager for the DataView.
    cm = (CurrencyManager)findDataGrid.BindingContext[dv];
}

private void findButton_Click(object sender, System.EventArgs e)
{
    if(findTextBox.Text != "")
    {
        // Find the customer.
        int i = dv.Find(findTextBox.Text);
        if(i < 0)
            // A match was not found.
            MessageBox.Show("No matching records found.", "Find",
                MessageBoxButtons.OK,
                MessageBoxIcon.Information);
        else
            // Reposition the grid record using the CurrencyManager.
            cm.Position = i;
    }
```

Example 7-31. File: SearchDataGridForm.cs (continued)

```
    else
    {
        MessageBox.Show("Enter find criteria.", "Find",
            MessageBoxButtons.OK, MessageBoxIcon.Question);
        findTextBox.Focus( );
    }
}
```

Discussion

The Find( ) method of the DataView locates a row matching a specified sort key value. The Sort property gets or sets the column or columns that the DataView is sorted on. The Sort property is a string that contains the column name, or multiple column names separated by commas, followed by an optional ASC or DESC clause specifying sort direction.

There are two methods that you can use to locate records in a DataView:

Find( )

This method of the DataView returns the index of the first row matching the specified sort key value or and array of sort key values, for sort keys based on multiple columns. If no records match, it returns –1.

FindRows( )

This method of the DataView returns an array of rows matching the specified sort key value or array of sort key values. It returns an empty array if the sort key value does not exist.

The Find( ) and FindRows( ) methods use the current index of the DataView without requiring the index to be rebuilt.

Both methods take an argument that is an object array of values whose length matches the number of columns in the sort order of the DataView. The order of columns in the array must match the order of columns specified in the Sort property. A single value can be passed instead of an array if the sort is based on a single column. The sort key value must match exactly in order to return a result. The RowFilter property can be used to locate records matching an expression. For an example, see Recipe 3.1.

The sort order must be specified either by setting the ApplyDefaultSort property of the DataView to true or by setting the Sort property explicitly; otherwise, an exception is thrown. The case sensitivity of the search is controlled by the CaseSensitive property of the underlying DataTable.

7.16   Dynamically Creating Crystal Reports

Problem

You need to define a DataTable at runtime and bind it to a Crystal Report.

Solution

Create a DataAdapter and use it to fill a DataTable with a subset of records (specified by a range of OrderID values, from the Orders table joined to Order Details records from the Northwinds sample database demonstrated in the following example). Create a new report document and set its data source to the DataTable. To display the report, set the source of the report view to the report document.

The C# code is shown in Example 7-32.

Example 7-32. File: CrystalReportsForm.cs

```
// Namespaces, variables, and constants
using System;
using System.Configuration;
using System.Windows.Forms;
using CrystalDecisions.CrystalReports.Engine;
using CrystalDecisions.Shared;
using System.Data;
using System.Data.SqlClient;

private CrystalDecisions.Windows.Forms.CrystalReportViewer crv;

// ...

// Get the user entered OrderID range.
int orderIdFrom, orderIdTo;
try
{
    orderIdFrom = Convert.ToInt32(orderIdFromTextBox.Text);
    orderIdTo = Convert.ToInt32(orderIdToTextBox.Text);
}
catch (Exception ex)
{
    MessageBox.Show(ex.Message, "Dynamic Crystal Reports",
        MessageBoxButtons.OK, MessageBoxIcon.Error);
    return;
}

Cursor.Current = Cursors.WaitCursor;

// Create a DataAdapter and fill the table.
String sqlText = "SELECT * FROM Orders " +
    "JOIN [Order Details] Order_Details ON Orders.OrderID = " +
    "Order_Details.OrderID " +
    "WHERE Orders.OrderID BETWEEN " + orderIdFrom + " AND " + orderIdTo;
```

Example 7-32. File: CrystalReportsForm.cs (continued)

```
SqlDataAdapter da = new SqlDataAdapter(sqlText,
    ConfigurationSettings.AppSettings["Sql_ConnectString"]);
DataTable dt = new DataTable( );
da.Fill(dt);

// Create a new ReportDocument.
ReportDocument cr = new ReportDocument( );
// Load the report.
cr.Load(ConfigurationSettings.AppSettings["Project_Directory"] +
    @"Chapter 07\OrderWithDetailsCrystalReport.rpt");
// Set the data source for the report.
cr.SetDataSource(dt);

// Set the report document for the report view.
crv.ReportSource = cr;

Cursor.Current = Cursors.Default;
```

Discussion

Follow these steps to use a DataTable created at runtime as the data source for a Crystal Report:

1. Using the Crystal Report Designer in Visual Studio.NET, design and create the Crystal Report *.RPT* file. Link the report to the database in the designer to get the fields for the report as would normally be done. For more information about using the Crystal Report Designer, see the MSDN Library (you might have to change the filter in MSDN to "(no filter)" from ".NET Framework").

2. In the application, use a DataAdapter to fill a DataTable with the data required by the report.

3. Create a new ReportDocument object:

   ```
   ReportDocument cr = new ReportDocument( );
   ```

   The ReportDocument class represents a report and contains methods and properties including those used define, format, and load the report.

4. Use the Load( ) method of the ReportDocument to load the report defined in step 1:

   ```
   cr.Load(ConfigurationSettings.AppSettings["Project_Directory"] +
       @"Chapter 07\OrderWithDetailsCrystalReport.rpt");
   ```

5. Use the SetDataSource( ) method of the ReportDocument to pass the data source to the report engine:

   ```
   cr.SetDataSource(dt);
   ```

6. Set the ReportSource property of the CrystalReportViewer to the ReportDocument to display the report in the viewer:

   ```
   crv.ReportSource = cr;
   ```

The CrystalReportViewer class provides methods, properties, and events that allow control of viewer appearance and functionality.

7.17   Using ADO.NET Design-Time Features in Classes Without a GUI

Problem

The design-time environment provides controls and wizards to facilitate creation of and management of properties of ADO.NET objects. You want to use that design-time functionality when creating classes that do not have a GUI.

Solution

Create a component and use its design-time functionality.

The solution contains two parts: the component and the test container for the component. To create the component *Component0717.cs*, add two controls to its design surface:

- Drop a SqlDataAdapter onto the design surface and use the Data Adapter Configuration Wizard to connect to the Northwind sample database on the local SQL Server. Accept all wizard defaults; supply the following SQL statement when prompted to generate the SQL statements:

```
SELECT
    OrderID,
    CustomerID,
    EmployeeID,
    OrderDate,
    RequiredDate,
    ShippedDate,
    ShipVia,
    Freight,
    ShipName,
    ShipAddress,
    ShipCity,
    ShipRegion,
    ShipPostalCode,
    ShipCountry
FROM
    Orders
```

After the wizard completes, rename the SqlDataAdapter control to *da*.

- A SqlConnection control is automatically added to the design surface when the SqlDataAdapter wizard is completed; rename it to *conn*.

The sample code for the component exposes one property and one method:

MyDataTable

A read-only property that returns a DataTable filled using the SqlDataAdapter control.

Update( )

This method takes a DataTable object argument that uses the SqlDataAdapter control to update changes to the DataTable (retrieved using the MyDataTable property of the component) back to the database.

The C# code for the component is shown in Example 7-33.

Example 7-33. File: Component0717.cs

```
// Namespaces, variables, and constants
using System;
using System.Data;
using System.Data.SqlClient;

// ...

public DataTable MyDataTable
{
    get
    {
        // Fill a table using the DataAdapter control.
        DataTable dt = new DataTable( );
        da.Fill(dt);

        return dt;
    }
}

public void Update(DataTable dt)
{
    // Update the table back to the data source.
    da.Update(dt);
}
```

The test container sample code contains two event handlers:

Form.Load

Instantiates the component *Component0717* and binds the default view of the DataTable that it exposes (through the MyDataTable property) to the DataGrid on the form.

Update Button.Click

Instantiates the component *Component0717* and calls the Update( ) method of the component to update changes made in the DataGrid to the DataTable retrieved in the Form.Load event handler.

The C# code for the test container is shown in Example 7-34.

Example 7-34. File: UsingDesignTimeFeauresWithComponentsForm.cs

```
// Namespaces, variables, and constants
using System;
using System.Data;

// ...

private void UsingDesignTimeFeauresWithComponentsForm_Load(object sender,
    System.EventArgs e)
{
    // Bind the default of the table from the component to the grid.
    Component0717 c = new Component0717();
    dataGrid.DataSource = c.MyDataTable.DefaultView;
}

private void updateButton_Click(object sender, System.EventArgs e)
{
    // Update the table to the data source using the component.
    Component0717 c = new Component0717();
    c.Update(((DataView)dataGrid.DataSource).Table);
}
```

Discussion

The component and control are special-purpose classes in the .NET Framework:

- A *component* is a class that implements the IComponent interface or inherits from a class that implements that interface, such as System.ComponentModel.Component. A component has no user interface; it supports a visual design surface similar to the component tray on controls with a visual design surface that you can use to add or arrange components used by the component. The arrangement of components on the design surface is not important because there is no user interface for a component.

- A *control* is a component that provides user interface functionality and inherits from the System.Windows.Forms.Control class, which in turn derives from the Component. A control is a component, but a component is not necessarily a control.

To create a component, simply right-click on a project or folder in the Solution Explorer window and select Add → Add Component. The View Designer button in the Solution Explorer window accesses the design surface of the component.

CHAPTER 8

Working with XML

8.0   Introduction

ADO.NET and XML classes are tightly integrated in the .NET Framework. The DataSet can be filled with data or a schema from an XML stream or document. The DataSet can persist or serialize its data or schema to an XML stream or document. ADO synchronizes the DataSet with an XmlDataDocument. Data can be modified simultaneously using either class as needed; all changes made in one class are immediately reflected in the other class. This chapter focuses on XML support in ADO.NET and in SQL Server 2000.

The XML support in .NET is provided by integrated classes in five namespaces:

System.Xml
    Contains classes that provide standards-based support for processing XML

System.Xml.Schema
    Contains classes that provide standards-based support for XML Schema Definition (XSD) language schemas

System.Xml.Serialization
    Contains classes that serialize objects into XML documents or streams

System.Xml.XPath
    Contains classes that parse and evaluate XPath

System.Xml.Xsl
    Contains classes that support Extensible Stylesheet Language (XSL) transformations

The DiffGram is an XML format that identifies current and original versions of data allowing the contents of a DataSet to be recreated accurately. The DiffGram allows you to identify the changes made to a DataSet since it was filled. The DataSet uses the DiffGram format to persist and to serialize its contents for transport across a network. Recipe 8.8 shows how to create a DiffGram of changes made to a DataSet.

SQL Server 2000 introduced support for retrieving the results of queries in XML format using the FOR XML clause. The XmlReader provides direct forward-only, read-only access to the XML result set stream from the SQL Server. Recipe 8.5 shows how to use the FOR XML clause to retrieve XML-format data from a SQL Server using an XmlReader.

The SQLXML managed classes expose SQLXML functionality that allows .NET applications to access XML data from SQL Server 2000, process the XML data, and update the SQL Server using an XML DiffGram representation of the data. SQLXML classes support template queries, an XML document containing one or more SQL queries or stored procedures, to execute. Recipe 8.10 shows how to use template queries.

OpenXML allows an XML document to be used in a SQL statement in the same way a table or view is used. Recipe 8.11 shows how to use OpenXML from ADO.NET.

8.1   Using XSD Schema Files to Load and Save a DataSet Structure

Problem

You need to create an XSD schema from a DataSet and define the schema of a DataSet from an XSD schema.

Solution

Use the XmlTextWriter and XmlTextReader classes.

The sample code contains three event handlers:

Write Button.Click
> Creates a DataSet containing the Orders table and Order Details table from Northwind and a relation between the two. The XSD schema for the DataSet is written both to a file and to a text box on the form.

Read Button.Click
> Creates a DataSet and reads in the schema from a file containing a previously serialized XSD schema. The XSD schema is written from the DataSet to a stream and displayed.

Clear Button.Click
> Clears the DataGrid and the result text box.

The C# code is shown in Example 8-1.

Example 8-1. File: XsdSchemaFileForm.cs

```
// Namespaces, variables, and constants
using System;
using System.Configuration;
using System.Windows.Forms;
using System.Text;
using System.IO;
using System.Xml;
using System.Xml.Schema;
using System.Data;
using System.Data.SqlClient;

// Table name constants
private const String ORDERS_TABLE       = "Orders";
private const String ORDERDETAILS_TABLE = "OrderDetails";

// Relation name constants
private const String ORDERS_ORDERDETAILS_RELATION =
    "Orders_OrderDetails_Relation";

// Field name constants
private const String ORDERID_FIELD      = "OrderID";

// ...

private void writeSchemaButton_Click(object sender, System.EventArgs e)
{
    DataSet ds = new DataSet( );

    SqlDataAdapter da;

    // Fill the Order table and add it to the DataSet.
    da = new SqlDataAdapter("SELECT * FROM Orders",
        ConfigurationSettings.AppSettings["Sql_ConnectString"]);
    DataTable orderTable = new DataTable(ORDERS_TABLE);
    da.FillSchema(orderTable, SchemaType.Source);
    da.Fill(orderTable);
    ds.Tables.Add(orderTable);

    // Fill the OrderDetails table and add it to the DataSet.
    da = new SqlDataAdapter("SELECT * FROM [Order Details]",
        ConfigurationSettings.AppSettings["Sql_ConnectString"]);
    DataTable orderDetailTable = new DataTable(ORDERDETAILS_TABLE);
    da.FillSchema(orderDetailTable, SchemaType.Source);
    da.Fill(orderDetailTable);
    ds.Tables.Add(orderDetailTable);

    // Create a relation between the tables.
    ds.Relations.Add(ORDERS_ORDERDETAILS_RELATION,
        ds.Tables[ORDERS_TABLE].Columns[ORDERID_FIELD],
        ds.Tables[ORDERDETAILS_TABLE].Columns[ORDERID_FIELD],
        true);
```

Example 8-1. File: XsdSchemaFileForm.cs (continued)

```csharp
        // Bind the default view of the Orders table to the grid.
        resultDataGrid.DataSource = ds.Tables[ORDERS_TABLE].DefaultView;

        // Write the XSD schema to a file.
        // Display file dialog to select XSD file to write.
        SaveFileDialog sfd = new SaveFileDialog( );
        sfd.InitialDirectory = System.IO.Path.GetTempPath( );
        sfd.Filter = "XSD Files (*.xsd)|*.xsd|All files (*.*)|*.*";
        sfd.FilterIndex = 1;

        if (sfd.ShowDialog( ) == DialogResult.OK)
        {
            FileStream fs = new FileStream(sfd.FileName, FileMode.Create,
                FileAccess.Write);
            // Create an XmlTextWriter using the file stream.
            XmlTextWriter xtw = new XmlTextWriter(fs, Encoding.Unicode);

            try
            {
                // Write the XSD schema to the file.
                ds.WriteXmlSchema(xtw);

                resultTextBox.Text="XSD file written.";
            }
            catch(Exception ex)
            {
                MessageBox.Show(ex.Message);
            }
            finally
            {
                xtw.Close( );
            }
        }
    }

    private void readSchemaButton_Click(object sender, System.EventArgs e)
    {
        // Write the XSD schema from a file.
        // Display file dialog to select XSD file to read.
        OpenFileDialog ofd = new OpenFileDialog( );
        ofd.InitialDirectory = System.IO.Path.GetTempPath( );
        ofd.Filter = "XSD Files (*.xsd)|*.xsd|All files (*.*)|*.*";
        ofd.FilterIndex = 1;

        if (ofd.ShowDialog( ) == DialogResult.OK)
        {
            FileStream fs = new FileStream(ofd.FileName, FileMode.Open,
                FileAccess.Read);
            // Create an XmlTextReader using the file stream.
            XmlTextReader xtr = new XmlTextReader(fs);
```

Example 8-1. File: XsdSchemaFileForm.cs (continued)

```
        try
        {
            // Read the schema into the DataSet.
            DataSet ds = new DataSet( );
            ds.ReadXmlSchema(xtr);

            // Bind the default view of the Orders table to the grid.
            resultDataGrid.DataSource =
                ds.Tables[ORDERS_TABLE].DefaultView;

            // Write the XSD schema to a memory stream and
            // display the XSD schema.
            MemoryStream ms = new MemoryStream( );
            ds.WriteXmlSchema(ms);
            byte[] result = ms.ToArray( );
            ms.Close( );

            resultTextBox.Text =
                Encoding.UTF8.GetString(result, 0, result.Length);
        }
        catch(Exception ex)
        {
            MessageBox.Show(ex.Message);
        }
        finally
        {
            xtr.Close( );
        }
    }
}

private void clearButton_Click(object sender, System.EventArgs e)
{
    // Clear the data grid and the result text box.
    resultDataGrid.DataSource = null;
    resultTextBox.Clear( );
}
```

Discussion

The solution uses the XmlTextWriter and XmlTextReader classes to write and read the XSD schema information. The XmlTextWriter is a writer that provides a fast, non-cached, forward-only way to generate streams or files of XML data. The encoding generated is specified using one of the static property values from System.Text.Encoding described in Table 8-1.

Table 8-1. Character encoding members of the System.Text.Encoding class

Encoding	Description
ASCII	ASCII (7 bit) character set
BigEndianUnicode	Unicode format in big-endian byte order
Default	Encoding for system's current ANSI code page
Unicode	Unicode format in little-endian byte order
UTF7	UTF-7 format
UTF8	UTF-8 format. This is the default

The XmlTextReader provides fast, non-cached, forward-only access to XML data. The XmlTextReader does not validate the XML. For validation, use the XmlValidatingReader class.

The XmlTextWriter and XmlTextReader classes conform to the W3C XML 1.0 and the Namespaces in XML recommendations.

For more information about the XmlTextWriter and XmlTextReader classes, see the MSDN Library.

The WriteXmlSchema( ) and ReadXmlSchema( ) methods of the DataSet class are used to write and read the XSD schema for the XML data. The schema is written using the XSD standard and includes tables, relations, and constraint definitions. Example 8-2 shows the XSD schema written by this solution.

Example 8-2. Orders with order details XSD schema

```
<?xml version="1.0" encoding="utf-16"?>
  <xs:schema id="NewDataSet" xmlns=""
    xmlns:xs="http://www.w3.org/2001/XMLSchema"
    xmlns:msdata="urn:schemas-microsoft-com:xml-msdata">
    <xs:element name="NewDataSet"
      msdata:IsDataSet="true">
    <xs:complexType>
      <xs:choice maxOccurs="unbounded">
        <xs:element name="Orders">
          <xs:complexType>
            <xs:sequence>
              <xs:element name="OrderID" msdata:ReadOnly="true"
              msdata:AutoIncrement="true" type="xs:int" />
              <xs:element name="CustomerID" minOccurs="0">
                <xs:simpleType>
                  <xs:restriction base="xs:string">
                    <xs:maxLength value="5" />
                  </xs:restriction>
                </xs:simpleType>
              </xs:element>
              <xs:element name="EmployeeID" type="xs:int"
```

Example 8-2. Orders with order details XSD schema (continued)

```
          minOccurs="0" />
        <xs:element name="OrderDate" type="xs:dateTime"
          minOccurs="0" />
        <xs:element name="RequiredDate" type="xs:dateTime"
          minOccurs="0" />
        <xs:element name="ShippedDate" type="xs:dateTime"
          minOccurs="0" />
        <xs:element name="ShipVia" type="xs:int"
          minOccurs="0" />
        <xs:element name="Freight" type="xs:decimal"
          minOccurs="0" />
        <xs:element name="ShipName" minOccurs="0">
          <xs:simpleType>
            <xs:restriction base="xs:string">
              <xs:maxLength value="40" />
            </xs:restriction>
          </xs:simpleType>
        </xs:element>
        <xs:element name="ShipAddress" minOccurs="0">
          <xs:simpleType>
            <xs:restriction base="xs:string">
              <xs:maxLength value="60" />
            </xs:restriction>
          </xs:simpleType>
        </xs:element>
        <xs:element name="ShipCity" minOccurs="0">
          <xs:simpleType>
            <xs:restriction base="xs:string">
              <xs:maxLength value="15" />
            </xs:restriction>
          </xs:simpleType>
        </xs:element>
        <xs:element name="ShipRegion" minOccurs="0">
          <xs:simpleType>
            <xs:restriction base="xs:string">
              <xs:maxLength value="15" />
            </xs:restriction>
          </xs:simpleType>
        </xs:element>
        <xs:element name="ShipPostalCode" minOccurs="0">
          <xs:simpleType>
            <xs:restriction base="xs:string">
              <xs:maxLength value="10" />
            </xs:restriction>
          </xs:simpleType>
        </xs:element>
        <xs:element name="ShipCountry" minOccurs="0">
          <xs:simpleType>
            <xs:restriction base="xs:string">
              <xs:maxLength value="15" />
```

Example 8-2. Orders with order details XSD schema (continued)

```
                </xs:restriction>
              </xs:simpleType>
            </xs:element>
          </xs:sequence>
        </xs:complexType>
      </xs:element>
      <xs:element name="OrderDetails">
        <xs:complexType>
          <xs:sequence>
            <xs:element name="OrderID" type="xs:int" />
            <xs:element name="ProductID" type="xs:int" />
            <xs:element name="UnitPrice" type="xs:decimal" />
            <xs:element name="Quantity" type="xs:short" />
            <xs:element name="Discount" type="xs:float" />
          </xs:sequence>
        </xs:complexType>
      </xs:element>
    </xs:choice>
  </xs:complexType>
  <xs:unique name="Constraint1" msdata:PrimaryKey="true">
    <xs:selector xpath=".//Orders" />
    <xs:field xpath="OrderID" />
  </xs:unique>
  <xs:unique name="OrderDetails_Constraint1"
    msdata:ConstraintName="Constraint1" msdata:PrimaryKey="true">
    <xs:selector xpath=".//OrderDetails" />
    <xs:field xpath="OrderID" />
    <xs:field xpath="ProductID" />
  </xs:unique>
  <xs:keyref name="Orders_OrderDetails_Relation" refer="Constraint1">
    <xs:selector xpath=".//OrderDetails" />
    <xs:field xpath="OrderID" />
  </xs:keyref>
  </xs:element>
</xs:schema>
```

Use the `WriteXml( )` and `ReadXml( )` methods of the `DataSet` to write and read the XML data in addition to the schema information.

8.2   Saving and Loading a DataSet from XML

Problem

You need to save a `DataSet` as an XML file and create a `DataSet` from an XML file.

Solution

Use the `XmlTextWriter` and `XmlTextReader` classes.

The sample code contains three event handlers:

Write Button.Click

> Creates a DataSet containing the Orders and Order Details tables from Northwind and a relation between the two tables. The XML schema and data for the DataSet is written both to a file and to a text box on the form.

Read Button.Click

> Creates a DataSet and reads in schema and data from a file containing a previously serialized XML. The XML is written from the DataSet to a stream and displayed.

Clear Button.Click

> Clears the data grid and the result text box.

The C# code is shown in Example 8-3.

Example 8-3. File: XmlFileForm.cs

```
// Namespaces, variables, and constants
using System;
using System.Configuration;
using System.Windows.Forms;
using System.Text;
using System.IO;
using System.Xml;
using System.Xml.Schema;
using System.Data;
using System.Data.SqlClient;

// Table name constants
private const String ORDERS_TABLE        = "Orders";
private const String ORDERDETAILS_TABLE  = "OrderDetails";

// Relation name constants
private const String ORDERS_ORDERDETAILS_RELATION =
    "Orders_OrderDetails_Relation";

// Field name constants
private const String ORDERID_FIELD       = "OrderID";

// ...

private void writeXmlButton_Click(object sender, System.EventArgs e)
{
    DataSet ds = new DataSet();

    SqlDataAdapter da;

    // Fill the Order table and add it to the DataSet.
    da = new SqlDataAdapter("SELECT * FROM Orders",
        ConfigurationSettings.AppSettings["Sql_ConnectString"]);
    DataTable orderTable = new DataTable(ORDERS_TABLE);
    da.FillSchema(orderTable, SchemaType.Source);
```

Example 8-3. File: XmlFileForm.cs (continued)

```
    da.Fill(orderTable);
    ds.Tables.Add(orderTable);

    // Fill the OrderDetails table and add it to the DataSet.
    da = new SqlDataAdapter("SELECT * FROM [Order Details]",
        ConfigurationSettings.AppSettings["Sql_ConnectString"]);
    DataTable orderDetailTable = new DataTable(ORDERDETAILS_TABLE);
    da.FillSchema(orderDetailTable, SchemaType.Source);
    da.Fill(orderDetailTable);
    ds.Tables.Add(orderDetailTable);

    // Create a relation between the tables.
    ds.Relations.Add(ORDERS_ORDERDETAILS_RELATION,
        ds.Tables[ORDERS_TABLE].Columns[ORDERID_FIELD],
        ds.Tables[ORDERDETAILS_TABLE].Columns[ORDERID_FIELD],
        true);

    // Bind the default view of the Orders table to the grid.
    resultDataGrid.DataSource = ds.Tables[ORDERS_TABLE].DefaultView;

    // Write the XSD schema and data to a file.
    // Display file dialog to select XML file to write.
    SaveFileDialog sfd = new SaveFileDialog();
    sfd.InitialDirectory = System.IO.Path.GetTempPath();
    sfd.Filter = "XML Files (*.xml)|*.xml|All files (*.*)|*.*";
    sfd.FilterIndex = 1;

    if (sfd.ShowDialog() == DialogResult.OK)
    {
        FileStream fs = new FileStream(sfd.FileName, FileMode.Create,
            FileAccess.Write);
        // Create an XmlTextWriter using the file stream.
        XmlTextWriter xtw = new XmlTextWriter(fs, Encoding.Unicode);

        try
        {
            // Write the XML to the file.
            ds.WriteXml(xtw, XmlWriteMode.WriteSchema);

            resultTextBox.Text = "XML file written.";
        }
        catch(Exception ex)
        {
            MessageBox.Show(ex.Message);
        }
        finally
        {
            xtw.Close();
        }
    }
}
```

Example 8-3. File: XmlFileForm.cs (continued)

```csharp
private void readXmlButton_Click(object sender, System.EventArgs e)
{
    // Write the XML schema from a file.
    // Display file dialog to select XML file to read.
    OpenFileDialog ofd = new OpenFileDialog( );
    ofd.InitialDirectory = System.IO.Path.GetTempPath( );
    ofd.Filter = "XML Files (*.xml)|*.xml|All files (*.*)|*.*";
    ofd.FilterIndex = 1;

    if (ofd.ShowDialog( ) == DialogResult.OK)
    {
        FileStream fs = new FileStream(ofd.FileName, FileMode.Open,
            FileAccess.Read);
        // Create an XmlTextReader using the file stream.
        XmlTextReader xtr = new XmlTextReader(fs);

        try
        {
            // Read the schema into the DataSet.
            DataSet ds = new DataSet( );
            ds.ReadXml(xtr, XmlReadMode.ReadSchema);

            // Bind the default view of the Orders table to the grid.
            resultDataGrid.DataSource =
                ds.Tables[ORDERS_TABLE].DefaultView;

            // Write the XML to a memory stream and display it.
            MemoryStream ms = new MemoryStream( );
            ds.WriteXml(ms, XmlWriteMode.WriteSchema);
            byte[] result = ms.ToArray( );
            ms.Close( );

            resultTextBox.Text = Encoding.UTF8.GetString(result, 0,
                result.Length);
        }
        catch(Exception ex)
        {
            MessageBox.Show(ex.Message);
        }
        finally
        {
            xtr.Close( );
        }
    }
}

private void clearButton_Click(object sender, System.EventArgs e)
{
    // Clear the data grid and the result text box.
    resultDataGrid.DataSource = null;
    resultTextBox.Clear( );
}
```

Discussion

The solution uses the XmlTextWriter and XmlTextReader classes to write and read the XML data for the DataSet. For more information about these classes, see the Discussion for Recipe 8.1 and the MSDN Library.

The WriteXml( ) and ReadXml( ) methods of the DataSet are used to write and read the XML for the DataSet. The WriteXml( ) method takes an optional argument that specifies a value from the XmlWriteMode enumeration described in Table 8-2.

Table 8-2. XmlWriteMode enumeration

Value	Description
DiffGram	The DataSet is written as a DiffGram, which is an XML format used by .NET to persist and serialize a DataSet. A DiffGram includes all information required to recreate the DataSet including original and current values, row errors, and row order. A DiffGram does not include information about the DataSet schema.
IgnoreSchema	The DataSet is written without inline schema information. This is the default.
WriteSchema	The DataSet is written with an inline XSD schema for the relational structure of the DataSet.

If an in-line schema is not written, the ReadXml( ) method can still be used to read the data into a DataSet, but the method will not be able to completely recreate the schema for the DataSet.

The XmlRead( ) method takes an optional argument that specifies a value from the XmlReadMode enumeration described in Table 8-3.

Table 8-3. XmlReadMode enumeration

Value	Description
Auto	Uses the most appropriate of the following settings: • DiffGram if the data is a DiffGram • ReadSchema if the DataSet already has a schema or the XML document contains an inline schema • InferSchema if the DataSet does not already have a schema and the XML document does not contain an inline schema Auto is the default.
DiffGram	Reads a DiffGram applying the changes to the DataSet. The target DataSet must have the same schema as the DataSet from which the WriteXml( ) method created the DiffGram. Otherwise, an exception is raised.
Fragment	Reads an XML document such as one generated by queries with the FOR XML clause.
IgnoreSchema	Ignores any inline schema and reads data from the XML document into the existing DataSet schema. Data not matching the existing schema is discarded.
InferSchema	Ignores any inline schema, infers the schema from the data, and loads the data into the DataSet. The DataSet schema is extended by adding new tables and columns as required.
ReadSchema	Reads any inline schema and loads the data into the DataSet. If the DataSet already contains tables, new tables will be added but an exception will be raised if any tables defined by the inline schema already exist in the DataSet.

Example 8-4 shows the XML file with inline schema written by this solution.

Example 8-4. Orders with order details XML file, with schema

```
<NewDataSet>
  <xs:schema id="NewDataSet" xmlns=""
    xmlns:xs="http://www.w3.org/2001/XMLSchema"
    xmlns:msdata="urn:schemas-microsoft-com:xml-msdata"><
    <xs:element name="NewDataSet" msdata:IsDataSet="true">
      <xs:complexType>
        <xs:choice maxOccurs="unbounded">
          <xs:element name="Orders">
            <xs:complexType>
              <xs:sequence>
                <xs:element name="OrderID" msdata:ReadOnly="true"
                msdata:AutoIncrement="true" type="xs:int" />
                <xs:element name="CustomerID" minOccurs="0">
                  <xs:simpleType>
                    <xs:restriction base="xs:string">
                      <xs:maxLength value="5" />
                    </xs:restriction>
                  </xs:simpleType>
                </xs:element>
                <xs:element name="EmployeeID" type="xs:int"
          minOccurs="0" />
                <xs:element name="OrderDate" type="xs:dateTime"
          minOccurs="0" />
                <xs:element name="RequiredDate" type="xs:dateTime"
          minOccurs="0" />
                <xs:element name="ShippedDate" type="xs:dateTime"
          minOccurs="0" />
                <xs:element name="ShipVia" type="xs:int"
          minOccurs="0" />
                <xs:element name="Freight" type="xs:decimal"
          minOccurs="0" />
                <xs:element name="ShipName" minOccurs="0">
                  <xs:simpleType>
                    <xs:restriction base="xs:string">
                      <xs:maxLength value="40" />
                    </xs:restriction>
                  </xs:simpleType>
                </xs:element>
                <xs:element name="ShipAddress" minOccurs="0">
                  <xs:simpleType>
                    <xs:restriction base="xs:string">
                      <xs:maxLength value="60" />
                    </xs:restriction>
                  </xs:simpleType>
                </xs:element>
                <xs:element name="ShipCity" minOccurs="0">
                  <xs:simpleType>
                    <xs:restriction base="xs:string">
                      <xs:maxLength value="15" />
                    </xs:restriction>
```

Example 8-4. Orders with order details XML file, with schema (continued)

```
              </xs:simpleType>
            </xs:element>
            <xs:element name="ShipRegion" minOccurs="0">
              <xs:simpleType>
                <xs:restriction base="xs:string">
                  <xs:maxLength value="15" />
                </xs:restriction>
              </xs:simpleType>
            </xs:element>
            <xs:element name="ShipPostalCode" minOccurs="0">
              <xs:simpleType>
                <xs:restriction base="xs:string">
                  <xs:maxLength value="10" />
                </xs:restriction>
              </xs:simpleType>
            </xs:element>
            <xs:element name="ShipCountry" minOccurs="0">
              <xs:simpleType>
                <xs:restriction base="xs:string">
                  <xs:maxLength value="15" />
                </xs:restriction>
              </xs:simpleType>
            </xs:element>
          </xs:sequence>
        </xs:complexType>
      </xs:element>
      <xs:element name="OrderDetails">
        <xs:complexType>
          <xs:sequence>
            <xs:element name="OrderID" type="xs:int" />
            <xs:element name="ProductID" type="xs:int" />
            <xs:element name="UnitPrice" type="xs:decimal" />
            <xs:element name="Quantity" type="xs:short" />
            <xs:element name="Discount" type="xs:float" />
          </xs:sequence>
        </xs:complexType>
      </xs:element>
    </xs:choice>
  </xs:complexType>
  <xs:unique name="Constraint1" msdata:PrimaryKey="true">
    <xs:selector xpath=".//Orders" />
    <xs:field xpath="OrderID" />
  </xs:unique>
  <xs:unique name="OrderDetails_Constraint1"
    msdata:ConstraintName="Constraint1" msdata:PrimaryKey="true">
    <xs:selector xpath=".//OrderDetails" />
    <xs:field xpath="OrderID" />
    <xs:field xpath="ProductID" />
  </xs:unique>
  <xs:keyref name="Orders_OrderDetails_Relation" refer="Constraint1">
    <xs:selector xpath=".//OrderDetails" />
    <xs:field xpath="OrderID" />
```

Example 8-4. Orders with order details XML file, with schema (continued)

```
        </xs:keyref>
      </xs:element>
    </xs:schema>
    <Orders>
      <OrderID>10248</OrderID>
      <CustomerID>VINET</CustomerID>
      <EmployeeID>5</EmployeeID>
      <OrderDate>1996-07-04T00:00:00.0000000-04:00</OrderDate>
      <RequiredDate>1996-08-01T00:00:00.0000000-04:00</RequiredDate>
      <ShippedDate>1996-07-16T00:00:00.0000000-04:00</ShippedDate>
      <ShipVia>3</ShipVia>
      <Freight>32.38</Freight>
      <ShipName>Vins et alcools Chevalier</ShipName>
      <ShipAddress>59 rue de l'Abbaye</ShipAddress>
      <ShipCity>Reims</ShipCity>
      <ShipPostalCode>51100</ShipPostalCode>
      <ShipCountry>France</ShipCountry>
    </Orders>
    <Orders>
      <OrderID>10249</OrderID>
      <CustomerID>TOMSP</CustomerID>
      <EmployeeID>6</EmployeeID>
      <OrderDate>1996-07-05T00:00:00.0000000-04:00</OrderDate>
      <RequiredDate>1996-08-16T00:00:00.0000000-04:00</RequiredDate>
      <ShippedDate>1996-07-10T00:00:00.0000000-04:00</ShippedDate>
      <ShipVia>1</ShipVia>
      <Freight>11.61</Freight>
      <ShipName>Toms Spezialitäten</ShipName>
      <ShipAddress>Luisenstr. 48</ShipAddress>
      <ShipCity>Münster</ShipCity>
      <ShipPostalCode>44087</ShipPostalCode>
      <ShipCountry>Germany</ShipCountry>
    </Orders>

<!-- ... -->

    <Orders>
      <OrderID>11076</OrderID>
      <CustomerID>BONAP</CustomerID>
      <EmployeeID>4</EmployeeID>
      <OrderDate>1998-05-06T00:00:00.0000000-04:00</OrderDate>
      <RequiredDate>1998-06-03T00:00:00.0000000-04:00</RequiredDate>
      <ShipVia>2</ShipVia>
      <Freight>38.28</Freight>
      <ShipName>Bon app'</ShipName>
      <ShipAddress>12, rue des Bouchers</ShipAddress>
      <ShipCity>Marseille</ShipCity>
      <ShipPostalCode>13008</ShipPostalCode>
      <ShipCountry>France</ShipCountry>
    </Orders>
    <Orders>
      <OrderID>11077</OrderID>
```

Example 8-4. Orders with order details XML file, with schema (continued)

```
      <CustomerID>RATTC</CustomerID>
      <EmployeeID>1</EmployeeID>
      <OrderDate>1998-05-06T00:00:00.0000000-04:00</OrderDate>
      <RequiredDate>1998-06-03T00:00:00.0000000-04:00</RequiredDate>
      <ShipVia>2</ShipVia>
      <Freight>8.53</Freight>
      <ShipName>Rattlesnake Canyon Grocery</ShipName>
      <ShipAddress>2817 Milton Dr.</ShipAddress>
      <ShipCity>Albuquerque</ShipCity>
      <ShipRegion>NM</ShipRegion>
      <ShipPostalCode>87110</ShipPostalCode>
      <ShipCountry>USA</ShipCountry>
    </Orders>
    <OrderDetails>
      <OrderID>10248</OrderID>
      <ProductID>11</ProductID>
      <UnitPrice>14</UnitPrice>
      <Quantity>12</Quantity>
      <Discount>0</Discount>
    </OrderDetails>
    <OrderDetails>
      <OrderID>10248</OrderID>
      <ProductID>42</ProductID>
      <UnitPrice>9.8</UnitPrice>
      <Quantity>10</Quantity>
      <Discount>0</Discount>
    </OrderDetails>

<!-- ... -->

    <OrderDetails>
      <OrderID>11077</OrderID>
      <ProductID>75</ProductID>
      <UnitPrice>7.75</UnitPrice>
      <Quantity>4</Quantity>
      <Discount>0</Discount>
    </OrderDetails>
    <OrderDetails>
      <OrderID>11077</OrderID>
      <ProductID>77</ProductID>
      <UnitPrice>13</UnitPrice>
      <Quantity>2</Quantity>
      <Discount>0</Discount>
    </OrderDetails>
</NewDataSet>
```

Use the `WriteXmlSchema( )` and `ReadXmlSchema( )` methods of the `DataSet` to write and read just the XSD schema information.

8.3   Synchronizing a DataSet with an XML Document

Problem

You need to work with both a DataSet and its XML representation.

Solution

Use a synchronized DataSet and XmlDataDocument.

The sample code contains two event handlers and one method:

Go Button.Click

> Synchronizes a DataSet and an XmlDataDocument using one of three methods specified by the user. The default view for the Orders table of the DataSet is bound to the data grid on the form and the contents of the XmlDataDocument are displayed in the text box.

Clear Button.Click

> Clears the contents of the data grid displaying the DataSet and the text box displaying the contents of the XmlDataDocument.

FillDataSet( )

> This method loads the DataSet with a subset of the Orders and Order Details data from Northwind and creates a relation between the tables.

The C# code is shown in Example 8-5.

Example 8-5. File: SyncDataSetWithXmlDocForm.cs

```
// Namespaces, variables, and constants
using System;
using System.Configuration;
using System.Windows.Forms;
using System.Xml;
using System.Data;
using System.Data.SqlClient;

// Table name constants
private const String ORDERS_TABLE        = "Orders";
private const String ORDERDETAILS_TABLE = "OrderDetails";

// Relation name constants
private const String ORDERS_ORDERDETAILS_RELATION =
    "Orders_OrderDetails_Relation";

// Field name constants
private const String ORDERID_FIELD       = "OrderID";
```

Example 8-5. File: SyncDataSetWithXmlDocForm.cs (continued)

```csharp
private const String XMLFILENAME =
    ConfigurationSettings.AppSettings["Project_Directory"] +
    @"Chapter 08\Orders_OrderDetails.xml";

// ...

private void goButton_Click(object sender, System.EventArgs e)
{
    Cursor.Current = Cursors.WaitCursor;

    DataSet ds = null;
    XmlDataDocument xmlDoc = null;

    if (method1RadioButton.Checked)
    {
        // Load DataSet with schema and data.
        ds = FillDataSet(true);

        // Get the XML document for the DataSet.
        xmlDoc = new XmlDataDocument(ds);
    }
    else if(method2RadioButton.Checked)
    {
        // Create DataSet with schema, but no data.
        ds = FillDataSet(false);

        // Get the XML document for the DataSet.
        xmlDoc = new XmlDataDocument(ds);

        // Load the data into the XML document from the XML file.
        xmlDoc.Load(XMLFILENAME);
    }
    else if(method3RadioButton.Checked)
    {
        // Create an XML document.
        xmlDoc = new XmlDataDocument( );
        // Get the DataSet for the XML document.
        ds = xmlDoc.DataSet;
        // Get schema for the DataSet from the XSD inline schema.
        ds.ReadXmlSchema(XMLFILENAME);
        // Load the data into the XML document from the XML file.
        xmlDoc.Load(XMLFILENAME);
    }

    // Display the XML data.
    resultTextBox.Text = xmlDoc.OuterXml;
    // Bind the DataSet to the grid.
    dataGrid.DataSource = ds.Tables[ORDERS_TABLE].DefaultView;

    Cursor.Current = Cursors.Default;
}
```

Example 8-5. File: SyncDataSetWithXmlDocForm.cs (continued)

```
private DataSet FillDataSet(bool includeData)
{
    DataSet ds = new DataSet("Orders_OrderDetails");

    SqlDataAdapter da;

    // Fill the Order table and add it to the DataSet.
    da = new SqlDataAdapter("SELECT * FROM Orders",
        ConfigurationSettings.AppSettings["Sql_ConnectString"]);
    DataTable orderTable = new DataTable(ORDERS_TABLE);
    da.FillSchema(orderTable, SchemaType.Source);
    if (includeData)
        da.Fill(orderTable);
    ds.Tables.Add(orderTable);

    // Fill the OrderDetails table with schema and add it to the DataSet.
    da = new SqlDataAdapter("SELECT * FROM [Order Details]",
        ConfigurationSettings.AppSettings["Sql_ConnectString"]);
    DataTable orderDetailTable = new DataTable(ORDERDETAILS_TABLE);
    da.FillSchema(orderDetailTable, SchemaType.Source);
    if (includeData)
        da.Fill(orderDetailTable);
    ds.Tables.Add(orderDetailTable);

    // Create a relation between the tables.
    ds.Relations.Add(ORDERS_ORDERDETAILS_RELATION,
        ds.Tables[ORDERS_TABLE].Columns[ORDERID_FIELD],
        ds.Tables[ORDERDETAILS_TABLE].Columns[ORDERID_FIELD],
        true);

    return ds;
}
```

Discussion

The .NET Framework allows real-time, synchronous access to both a DataSet and its XML representation in an XmlDataDocument object. The synchronized DataSet and XmlDataDocument work with a single set of data.

The solution shows three ways to synchronize a DataSet with an XmlDataDocument:

Method 1

Populate a DataSet with both schema and data. Synchronize it with a new XmlDataDocument, initializing it with the DataSet in the constructor.

Method 2

Populate a DataSet with a schema but no data. Synchronize it with a new XmlDataDocument, initializing it with the DataSet in the constructor. Load an XML document into the XmlDataDocument. The table and column names in the DataSet schema to be synchronized must match those in the XmlDataDocument.

Method 3

Create a new XmlDataDocument and access its DataSet through the DataSet property. Populate the schema for the DataSet. In the example, the schema is read from the XSD inline schema in the XML document. If the XML document does not have an inline schema, it might be possible to infer the schema using the InferSchema( ) method. Otherwise, the entire DataSet schema must be defined programmatically. Next, load the XML document into the synchronized XmlDataDocument. The table and column names in the DataSet schema to be synchronized must match those in the XmlDataDocument.

Example 8-6 shows the XML file used in this solution.

Example 8-6. Orders with Order Details XML file, with schema

```
<Orders_OrderDetails>
  <xs:schema id="Orders_OrderDetails" xmlns=""
    xmlns:xs="http://www.w3.org/2001/XMLSchema"
    xmlns:msdata="urn:schemas-microsoft-com:xml-msdata">
    <xs:element name="Orders_OrderDetails" msdata:IsDataSet="true">
      <xs:complexType>
        <xs:choice maxOccurs="unbounded">
          <xs:element name="Orders">
            <xs:complexType>
              <xs:sequence>
                <xs:element name="OrderID" msdata:ReadOnly="true"
                  msdata:AutoIncrement="true" type="xs:int" />
                <xs:element name="CustomerID" minOccurs="0">
                  <xs:simpleType>
                    <xs:restriction base="xs:string">
                      <xs:maxLength value="5" />
                    </xs:restriction>
                  </xs:simpleType>
                </xs:element>
                <xs:element name="EmployeeID" type="xs:int"
                  minOccurs="0" />
                <xs:element name="OrderDate" type="xs:dateTime"
                  minOccurs="0" />
                <xs:element name="RequiredDate" type="xs:dateTime"
                  minOccurs="0" />
                <xs:element name="ShippedDate" type="xs:dateTime"
                  minOccurs="0" />
                <xs:element name="ShipVia" type="xs:int" minOccurs="0" />
                <xs:element name="Freight" type="xs:decimal"
                  minOccurs="0" />
                <xs:element name="ShipName" minOccurs="0">
                  <xs:simpleType>
                    <xs:restriction base="xs:string">
                      <xs:maxLength value="40" />
                    </xs:restriction>
                  </xs:simpleType>
                </xs:element>
                <xs:element name="ShipAddress" minOccurs="0">
```

Example 8-6. Orders with Order Details XML file, with schema (continued)

```xml
            <xs:simpleType>
              <xs:restriction base="xs:string">
                <xs:maxLength value="60" />
              </xs:restriction>
            </xs:simpleType>
          </xs:element>
          <xs:element name="ShipCity" minOccurs="0">
            <xs:simpleType>
              <xs:restriction base="xs:string">
                <xs:maxLength value="15" />
              </xs:restriction>
            </xs:simpleType>
          </xs:element>
          <xs:element name="ShipRegion" minOccurs="0">
            <xs:simpleType>
              <xs:restriction base="xs:string">
                <xs:maxLength value="15" />
              </xs:restriction>
            </xs:simpleType>
          </xs:element>
          <xs:element name="ShipPostalCode" minOccurs="0">
            <xs:simpleType>
              <xs:restriction base="xs:string">
                <xs:maxLength value="10" />
              </xs:restriction>
            </xs:simpleType>
          </xs:element>
          <xs:element name="ShipCountry" minOccurs="0">
            <xs:simpleType>
              <xs:restriction base="xs:string">
                <xs:maxLength value="15" />
              </xs:restriction>
            </xs:simpleType>
          </xs:element>
        </xs:sequence>
      </xs:complexType>
    </xs:element>
    <xs:element name="OrderDetails">
      <xs:complexType>
        <xs:sequence>
          <xs:element name="OrderID" type="xs:int" />
          <xs:element name="ProductID" type="xs:int" />
          <xs:element name="UnitPrice" type="xs:decimal" />
          <xs:element name="Quantity" type="xs:short" />
          <xs:element name="Discount" type="xs:float" />
        </xs:sequence>
      </xs:complexType>
    </xs:element>
  </xs:choice>
</xs:complexType>
<xs:unique name="Constraint1" msdata:PrimaryKey="true">
  <xs:selector xpath=".//Orders" />
```

Example 8-6. Orders with Order Details XML file, with schema (continued)

```
          <xs:field xpath="OrderID" />
      </xs:unique>
      <xs:unique name="OrderDetails_Constraint1"
        msdata:ConstraintName="Constraint1" msdata:PrimaryKey="true">
        <xs:selector xpath=".//OrderDetails" />
        <xs:field xpath="OrderID" />
        <xs:field xpath="ProductID" />
      </xs:unique>
      <xs:keyref name="Orders_OrderDetails_Relation" refer="Constraint1">
        <xs:selector xpath=".//OrderDetails" />
        <xs:field xpath="OrderID" />
      </xs:keyref>
    </xs:element>
  </xs:schema>
  <Orders>
    <OrderID>10248</OrderID>
    <CustomerID>VINET</CustomerID>
    <EmployeeID>5</EmployeeID>
    <OrderDate>1996-07-04T00:00:00.0000000-04:00</OrderDate>
    <RequiredDate>1996-08-01T00:00:00.0000000-04:00</RequiredDate>
    <ShippedDate>1996-07-16T00:00:00.0000000-04:00</ShippedDate>
    <ShipVia>3</ShipVia>
    <Freight>32.38</Freight>
    <ShipName>Vins et alcools Chevalier</ShipName>
    <ShipAddress>59 rue de l'Abbaye</ShipAddress>
    <ShipCity>Reims</ShipCity>
    <ShipPostalCode>51100</ShipPostalCode>
    <ShipCountry>France</ShipCountry>
  </Orders>
  <Orders>
    <OrderID>10249</OrderID>
    <CustomerID>TOMSP</CustomerID>
    <EmployeeID>6</EmployeeID>
    <OrderDate>1996-07-05T00:00:00.0000000-04:00</OrderDate>
    <RequiredDate>1996-08-16T00:00:00.0000000-04:00</RequiredDate>
    <ShippedDate>1996-07-10T00:00:00.0000000-04:00</ShippedDate>
    <ShipVia>1</ShipVia>
    <Freight>11.61</Freight>
    <ShipName>Toms Spezialitäten</ShipName>
    <ShipAddress>Luisenstr. 48</ShipAddress>
    <ShipCity>Münster</ShipCity>
    <ShipPostalCode>44087</ShipPostalCode>
    <ShipCountry>Germany</ShipCountry>
  </Orders>
  <Orders>
    <OrderID>10250</OrderID>
    <CustomerID>HANAR</CustomerID>
    <EmployeeID>4</EmployeeID>
    <OrderDate>1996-07-08T00:00:00.0000000-04:00</OrderDate>
    <RequiredDate>1996-08-05T00:00:00.0000000-04:00</RequiredDate>
    <ShippedDate>1996-07-12T00:00:00.0000000-04:00</ShippedDate>
    <ShipVia>2</ShipVia>
```

Example 8-6. Orders with Order Details XML file, with schema (continued)

```
    <Freight>65.83</Freight>
    <ShipName>Hanari Carnes</ShipName>
    <ShipAddress>Rua do Paço, 67</ShipAddress>
    <ShipCity>Rio de Janeiro</ShipCity>
    <ShipRegion>RJ</ShipRegion>
    <ShipPostalCode>05454-876</ShipPostalCode>
    <ShipCountry>Brazil</ShipCountry>
  </Orders>
  <OrderDetails>
    <OrderID>10248</OrderID>
    <ProductID>11</ProductID>
    <UnitPrice>14</UnitPrice>
    <Quantity>12</Quantity>
    <Discount>0</Discount>
  </OrderDetails>
  <OrderDetails>
    <OrderID>10248</OrderID>
    <ProductID>42</ProductID>
    <UnitPrice>9.8</UnitPrice>
    <Quantity>10</Quantity>
    <Discount>0</Discount>
  </OrderDetails>
  <OrderDetails>
    <OrderID>10248</OrderID>
    <ProductID>72</ProductID>
    <UnitPrice>34.8</UnitPrice>
    <Quantity>5</Quantity>
    <Discount>0</Discount>
  </OrderDetails>
  <OrderDetails>
    <OrderID>10249</OrderID>
    <ProductID>14</ProductID>
    <UnitPrice>18.6</UnitPrice>
    <Quantity>9</Quantity>
    <Discount>0</Discount>
  </OrderDetails>
  <OrderDetails>
    <OrderID>10249</OrderID>
    <ProductID>51</ProductID>
    <UnitPrice>42.4</UnitPrice>
    <Quantity>40</Quantity>
    <Discount>0</Discount>
  </OrderDetails>
  <OrderDetails>
    <OrderID>10250</OrderID>
    <ProductID>41</ProductID>
    <UnitPrice>7.7</UnitPrice>
    <Quantity>10</Quantity>
    <Discount>0</Discount>
  </OrderDetails>
  <OrderDetails>
    <OrderID>10250</OrderID>
```

Example 8-6. Orders with Order Details XML file, with schema (continued)

```
      <ProductID>51</ProductID>
      <UnitPrice>42.4</UnitPrice>
      <Quantity>35</Quantity>
      <Discount>0.15</Discount>
    </OrderDetails>
    <OrderDetails>
      <OrderID>10250</OrderID>
      <ProductID>65</ProductID>
      <UnitPrice>16.8</UnitPrice>
      <Quantity>15</Quantity>
      <Discount>0.15</Discount>
    </OrderDetails>
</Orders_OrderDetails>
```

8.4   Storing XML to a Database Field

Problem

You need to store XML to a field in a database.

Solution

Store the contents of the InnerXml of the XmlDocument to the database. You can later load this into an empty XmlDocument with LoadXml( ).

The schema of table TBL0804 used in this solution is shown in Table 8-4.

Table 8-4. TBL0804 schema

Column name	Data type	Length	Allow nulls?
Id	int	4	No
XmlField	nvarchar	4000	Yes

The sample code contains five event handlers:

Form.Load
> Sets up the DataTable that contains the text field, XmlField, containing the XML and the DataAdapter for the table.

Write Button.Click
> Adds or updates a record in the table with the Id and XmlField entered by the user.

Read Button.Click
> Loads the XML for the specified Id into an XmlDocument and displays it on the form in the XmlField text box.

Sample Button.Click

Generates sample XML data from the Orders table in Northwind and displays it on the form in the XmlField text box.

Clear Button.Click

Clears the contents of the Id and XmlField text boxes on the form.

The C# code is shown in Example 8-7.

Example 8-7. File: StoreXmlFieldForm.cs

```csharp
// Namespaces, variables, and constants
using System;
using System.Configuration;
using System.Windows.Forms;
using System.IO;
using System.Xml;
using System.Data;
using System.Data.SqlClient;

private DataTable dt;
private SqlDataAdapter da;

private const String TABLENAME = "TBL0804";

// ...

private void StoreXmlFieldForm_Load(object sender, System.EventArgs e)
{
    String selectText = "SELECT Id, XmlField FROM " + TABLENAME;
    String insertText = "INSERT " + TABLENAME + " (Id, XmlField) " +
        "VALUES (@Id, @XmlField)";
    String updateText = "UPDATE " + TABLENAME + " " +
        "SET XmlField = @XmlField " +
        "WHERE Id = @Id";

    // Create the data adapter.
    da = new SqlDataAdapter(selectText,
        ConfigurationSettings.AppSettings["Sql_ConnectString"]);

    da.UpdateCommand = new SqlCommand(updateText,
        da.SelectCommand.Connection);
    da.UpdateCommand.CommandType = CommandType.Text;
    da.UpdateCommand.Parameters.Add("@Id", SqlDbType.Int, 0, "Id");
    da.UpdateCommand.Parameters.Add("@XmlField", SqlDbType.NText, 0,
        "XmlField");

    da.InsertCommand = new SqlCommand(insertText,
        da.SelectCommand.Connection);
    da.InsertCommand.CommandType = CommandType.Text;
    da.InsertCommand.Parameters.Add("@Id", SqlDbType.Int, 0, "Id");
    da.InsertCommand.Parameters.Add("@XmlField", SqlDbType.NText, 0,
        "XmlField");
```

Example 8-7. File: StoreXmlFieldForm.cs (continued)

```csharp
    dt = new DataTable( );
    da.FillSchema(dt, SchemaType.Source);
    da.Fill(dt);
}

private void writeButton_Click(object sender, System.EventArgs e)
{
    // Load the ID into variable and text box into XmlDoc.
    int id = 0;
    XmlDocument xmlDoc = new XmlDocument( );
    try
    {
        id = Int32.Parse(idTextBox.Text);
        xmlDoc.LoadXml(xmlTextBox.Text);
    }
    catch(Exception ex)
    {
        MessageBox.Show("ERROR: " + ex.Message);
        return;
    }

    // Find the row with the ID entered.
    DataRow row = dt.Rows.Find(new object[] {id});
    if(row != null)
        // For an existing row, update the XmlField.
        row["XmlField"] = xmlDoc.InnerXml;
    else
        // For a new row, add the row with the ID and XmlField.
        dt.Rows.Add(new object[] {id, xmlDoc.InnerXml});

    // Update the database using the DataAdapter.
    da.Update(dt);
}

private void readButton_Click(object sender, System.EventArgs e)
{
    // Load the ID into variable from text box.
    int id = 0;
    try
    {
        id = Int32.Parse(idTextBox.Text);
    }
    catch(Exception ex)
    {
        MessageBox.Show("ERROR: " + ex.Message);
        return;
    }

    // Find the row with the ID entered.
    DataRow row = dt.Rows.Find(new object[] {id});
    if(row != null)
    {
```

Example 8-7. File: StoreXmlFieldForm.cs (continued)

```
        // If found, load the XML column value from the row.
        XmlDocument xmlDoc = new XmlDocument( );
        xmlDoc.LoadXml(row["XmlField"].ToString( ));

        // Display the XML.
        xmlTextBox.Text = xmlDoc.InnerXml;
    }
    else
        xmlTextBox.Text = "Record not found for Id = " + id;

}

private void sampleXmlButton_Click(object sender, System.EventArgs e)
{
    DataSet ds = new DataSet( );

    // Fill the Categories table and add it to the DataSet.
    SqlDataAdapter da = new SqlDataAdapter("SELECT TOP 3 * FROM Orders",
        ConfigurationSettings.AppSettings["Sql_ConnectString"]);
    da.FillSchema(ds, SchemaType.Source, "Orders");
    da.Fill(ds, "Orders");

    // Write the XML for the DataSet to a StringWriter, and output.
    StringWriter sw = new StringWriter( );
    ds.WriteXml(sw, XmlWriteMode.WriteSchema);
    xmlTextBox.Text = sw.ToString( );
    ds.Dispose( );

    idTextBox.Clear( );
}

private void clearButton_Click(object sender, System.EventArgs e)
{
    idTextBox.Clear( );
    xmlTextBox.Clear( );
}
```

Discussion

The solution demonstrates how to store XML data in a text field of a database table and subsequently read it into an XmlDocument using the LoadXml( ) method. Standard database access techniques using a DataAdapter and DataTable are used.

8.5   Reading XML Data Directly from SQL Server

Problem

You need to read XML data directly from the SQL Server.

Solution

Use the FOR XML clause in the stored procedure or SQL statement.

The C# code is shown in Example 8-8.

Example 8-8. File: ReadXmlDirectForm.cs

```
// Namespaces, variables, and constants
using System;
using System.Configuration;
using System.Xml;
using System.Data;
using System.Data.SqlClient;

// ...

// Select statement to read XML directly.
String sqlText = "SELECT * FROM Orders FOR XML AUTO, XMLDATA";

// Create the connection.
SqlConnection conn = new SqlConnection(
    ConfigurationSettings.AppSettings["Sql_ConnectString"]);
conn.Open( );
// Create the command.
SqlCommand cmd = new SqlCommand(sqlText, conn);

// Read the XML data into a XML reader.
XmlReader xr = cmd.ExecuteXmlReader( );

// Read the data from the XML reader into the DataSet.
DataSet ds = new DataSet( );
ds.ReadXml(xr, XmlReadMode.Fragment);
xr.Close( );
conn.Close( );

xmlTextBox.Text = ds.GetXml( );
```

Discussion

SQL Server 2000 introduced support for retrieving data in XML format using the FOR XML clause. The .NET SQL Server data provider SqlCommand object has an ExecuteXmlReader( ) that allows you to retrieve an XML stream directly from SQL Server, where it returns an XmlReader that contains the results of the SQL query. The ExecuteXmlReader( ) method can only be used with SQL statements that return XML data, such as those with a FOR XML clause. The ExecuteXmlReader( ) method can also be used to return ntext data containing valid XML.

For more information about the FOR XML clause, see Microsoft SQL Server Books Online.

8.6 Using XPath to Query Data in a DataSet

Problem

You need to use an XPath expression to extract certain rows from a DataSet.

Solution

Use SelectSingleNode( ) or SelectNodes( ).

The sample code contains two event handlers:

Form.Load

Sets up the sample by creating a DataSet containing the Orders table and Order Details table from Northwind and a nested relation between the two tables.

Go Button.Click

Executes an XPath query to retrieve the Orders and Order Details data for an OrderID specified by the user to an XmlNode. The results are displayed by iterating over the XmlNode to retrieve the Orders and the XmlNodeList containing the Order Details.

The C# code is shown in Example 8-9.

Example 8-9. File: XPathQueryForm.cs

```
// Namespaces, variables, and constants
using System;
using System.Configuration;
using System.Windows.Forms;
using System.Text;
using System.Xml;
using System.Data;
using System.Data.SqlClient;

// Table name constants
private const String ORDERS_TABLE        = "Orders";
private const String ORDERDETAILS_TABLE  = "OrderDetails";

// Relation name constants
private const String ORDERS_ORDERDETAILS_RELATION =
    "Orders_OrderDetails_Relation";

// Field name constants
private const String ORDERID_FIELD       = "OrderID";

private DataSet ds;

// ...

private void XPathQueryForm_Load(object sender, System.EventArgs e)
{
```

Example 8-9. File: XPathQueryForm.cs (continued)

```
    ds = new DataSet("Orders_OrderDetails");
    SqlDataAdapter da;

    // Fill the Order table and add it to the DataSet.
    da = new SqlDataAdapter("SELECT * FROM Orders",
        ConfigurationSettings.AppSettings["Sql_ConnectString"]);
    DataTable orderTable = new DataTable(ORDERS_TABLE);
    da.Fill(orderTable);
    ds.Tables.Add(orderTable);

    // Fill the OrderDetails table and add it to the DataSet.
    da = new SqlDataAdapter("SELECT * FROM [Order Details]",
        ConfigurationSettings.AppSettings["Sql_ConnectString"]);
    DataTable orderDetailTable = new DataTable(ORDERDETAILS_TABLE);
    da.Fill(orderDetailTable);
    ds.Tables.Add(orderDetailTable);

    // Create a relation between the tables.
    ds.Relations.Add(ORDERS_ORDERDETAILS_RELATION,
        ds.Tables[ORDERS_TABLE].Columns[ORDERID_FIELD],
        ds.Tables[ORDERDETAILS_TABLE].Columns[ORDERID_FIELD],
        true);

    ds.Relations[ORDERS_ORDERDETAILS_RELATION].Nested = true;
}

private void goButton_Click(object sender, System.EventArgs e)
{
    int orderId = 0;
    // Get the user-entered Order ID.
    try
    {
        orderId = Int32.Parse(orderIdTextBox.Text);
    }
    catch(Exception ex)
    {
        MessageBox.Show(ex.Message);
        return;
    }

    // Use an XPath query to select the order.
    String xPathQuery =
        "/Orders_OrderDetails/Orders[OrderID = " + orderId + "]";
    XmlNode xmlNode =
        (new XmlDataDocument(ds)).SelectSingleNode(xPathQuery);

    StringBuilder result = new StringBuilder();

    if (xmlNode != null)
    {
        // Retrieve the query results for the Order.
        result.Append("OrderID = " +
```

Example 8-9. File: XPathQueryForm.cs (continued)

```
                  xmlNode.ChildNodes[0].InnerText + Environment.NewLine);
            result.Append("CustomerID = " +
                  xmlNode.ChildNodes[1].InnerText + Environment.NewLine);
            result.Append("OrderDate = " +
                  xmlNode.ChildNodes[3].InnerText + Environment.NewLine);
            result.Append("Line Items:" + Environment.NewLine);

            // Retrieve the query results for the Order Details.
            XmlNodeList xmlNodeList = xmlNode.SelectNodes("OrderDetails");
            for (int i = 0; i < xmlNodeList.Count; i++)
            {
                result.Append("\tProductID = " +
                    xmlNodeList[i].ChildNodes[1].InnerText +
                    Environment.NewLine);
                result.Append("\tQuantity = " +
                    xmlNodeList[i].ChildNodes[2].InnerText +
                    Environment.NewLine);
                result.Append("\tUnitPrice = " +
                    xmlNodeList[i].ChildNodes[3].InnerText +
                    Environment.NewLine + Environment.NewLine);
            }
        }
        else
        {
            result.Append("No data found for Order ID = " + orderId);
        }

        xPathQueryResultTextBox.Text = result.ToString( );
}
```

Discussion

The W3C XML Path Language (XPath) is a navigation language used to select nodes from an XML Document. It is defined by W3 as a standard navigation language. The specification can be found at *http://www.w3.org/TR/xpath*. Microsoft SQL Server 2000 implements a subset of the language as described in SQL Server Books Online under the topics "Guidelines for Using XPath Queries" and "Using XPath Queries."

In .NET, the DataSet is synchronized with the XmlDataDocument. As a result, in some cases XML services can be used to access the XmlDataDocument to perform certain functionality more conveniently than could be accomplished using the DataSet directly. To execute an XPath query against the contents of a DataSet, call the SelectSingleNode( ) method of the XmlDataDocument for the DataSet, passing the XPath query as an argument as shown in the example:

```
    XmlNode xmlNode = (new XmlDataDocument(ds)).SelectSingleNode(xPathQuery);
```

The example iterates over the Order Details for the Orders by accessing the XmlNodeList containing that data within the XmlNode retrieved by the XPath query:

```
    XmlNodeList xmlNodeList = xmlNode.SelectNodes("OrderDetails");
```

This works because the Nested property is set to true for the DataRelation relating the tables containing the Orders and Order Details data. If the Nested property were false, you'd have to use a second XPath query to retrieve the Order Details data from the XMLDataDocument for the DataSet.

8.7   Transforming a DataSet Using XSLT

Problem

You need to use an XSLT stylesheet to transform the contents of a DataSet.

Solution

Create an XslTransform object and call the Transform( ) method.

You'll need to add the Microsoft Web Browser control to the Toolbox from the COM tab in the Customize Toolbox Dialog. You'll also need a reference to the Microsoft HTML Object Library from the COM tab in Visual Studio .NET's Add Reference Dialog.

Example 8-10 uses one XML file:

Category.xslt

> The XSLT stylesheet used to transform the XML for the Categories table in the DataSet into HTML displaying the Categories data in an HTML table. The contents of this XML file are shown in Example 8-10.

The sample code contains three event handlers:

Form.Load

> Sets up the sample by filling a DataSet with the Categories table from Northwind.

Transform Button.Click

> Initializes a WebBrowser control. Once the control is initialized, the DocumentComplete event is raised. The handler for the DocumentComplete event completes the XSLT transformation.

DocumentComplete

> Gets the XmlDataDocument for the DataSet, creates an XSLTransform class, and transforms the XML document using the XSLT stylesheet. The results are displayed both in the WebBrowser control and as XML.

Example 8-10. File: Category.xslt

```
<?xml version="1.0" encoding="UTF-8" ?>
<xsl:stylesheet xmlns:xsl=http://www.w3.org/1999/XSL/Transform
    version="1.0">
<xsl:template match="/">
```

Example 8-10. File: Category.xslt (continued)

```html
<html>
<body>
    <table>
        <tr bgcolor="#AAAAAA">
            <td>Category ID</td>
            <td>Name</td>
            <td>Description</td>
        </tr>

        <xsl:for-each select="/CategoriesDS/Categories">
            <tr>
                <td>
                    <xsl:value-of select="CategoryID" />
                </td>
                <td>
                    <xsl:value-of select="CategoryName" />
                </td>
                <td>
                    <xsl:value-of select="Description" />
                </td>
            </tr>
        </xsl:for-each>
    </table>
</body>
</html>
</xsl:template>
</xsl:stylesheet>
```

The C# code is shown in Example 8-11.

Example 8-11. File: XslTransformForm.cs

```csharp
// Namespaces, variables, and constants
using System;
using System.Configuration;
using System.IO;
using System.Xml;
using System.Xml.Xsl;
using System.Data;
using System.Data.SqlClient;

// Table name constants
private const String CATEGORIES_TABLE = "Categories";

private const String XSLTFILENAME =
    ConfigurationSettings.AppSettings["Project_Directory"] +
    @"Chapter 08\Category.xslt";

private DataSet ds;

// ...
```

Example 8-11. File: XslTransformForm.cs (continued)

```csharp
private void XslTransformForm_Load(object sender, System.EventArgs e)
{
    // Fill the Categories within a DataSet.
    SqlDataAdapter da = new SqlDataAdapter("SELECT * FROM Categories",
        ConfigurationSettings.AppSettings["Sql_ConnectString"]);
    ds = new DataSet("CategoriesDS");
    da.Fill(ds, CATEGORIES_TABLE);
}

private void transformButton_Click(object sender, System.EventArgs e)
{
    // Create parameters to create web browser.
    String url = "about:blank";
    object flags = 0;
    object targetFrameName = String.Empty;
    object postData = String.Empty;
    object headers = String.Empty;

    // Must wait for the navigation to complete so use the
    // DocumentComplete event for the rest of the processing
    webBrowser.Navigate(url, ref flags, ref targetFrameName, ref postData,
        ref headers);
}

private void webBrowser_DocumentComplete(object sender,
    AxSHDocVw.DWebBrowserEvents2_DocumentCompleteEvent e)
{
    // Apply the XML transformation storing results to StringWriter.
    XslTransform xslt = new XslTransform( );
    xslt.Load(XSLTFILENAME);
    StringWriter sw = new StringWriter( );
    xslt.Transform(new XmlDataDocument(ds), null, sw, (XmlResolver)null);

    // Load the results of the transformation into the web browser.
    mshtml.IHTMLDocument2 htmlDoc =
        (mshtml.IHTMLDocument2)webBrowser.Document;
    htmlDoc.body.innerHTML = sw.ToString( );

    // Display the results of the transformation.
    resultTextBox.Text = sw.ToString( );
}
```

Discussion

Extensible Stylesheet Transformations (XSLT) evolved from the Extensible Stylesheet Language (XSL). XSLT defines a standard for XML data transformation—parsing an input XML document and converting it into a result XML document. One common use for XSLT is to transform XML data returned from a middle tier component into one or more result documents (often HTML) to support different user interface or device requirements. For more information about XSLT, see Microsoft's MSDN Library.

In .NET, the DataSet is synchronized with the XmlDataDocument. As a result, in some cases XML services can be used to access the XmlDataDocument to perform certain functionality more conveniently than could be accomplished using the DataSet directly. To use XSLT to transform the contents of a DataSet, create an XslTransform object and call the Transform( ) method on that object, as shown in this example:

```
XslTransform xslt = new XslTransform( );
xslt.Load(XSLTFILENAME);
StringWriter sw = new StringWriter( );
xslt.Transform(new XmlDataDocument(ds), null, sw, (XmlResolver)null);
```

The results of the transformation can be sent to a variety of output formats using overloaded versions of the Transform( ) method.

8.8   Creating an XML File That Shows Changes Made to a DataSet

Problem

When you use the GetXML( ) method of the DataSet, you may see only the current values in the DataSet. You want to get the original values and see which rows were added, edited, or deleted.

Solution

Create an XML DiffGram, which is a document that details the modifications made to a DataSet.

The sample code contains two event handlers and a single method:

Form.Load
> Sets up the sample by loading the Categories table from Northwind into a DataSet and displays the DiffGram for the DataSet before modification.

Make Changes Button.Click
> Deletes the first row, modifies the second row, inserts a row before the first row, and adds a row to the end of the Categories DataTable

DisplayDiffGram( )
> This method outputs the DiffGram for the DataSet to both a file and to a textbox on the form.

The C# code is shown in Example 8-12.

Example 8-12. File: XmlDiffgramForm.cs

```csharp
// Namespaces, variables, and constants
using System;
using System.Configuration;
using System.Text;
using System.IO;
using System.Xml;
using System.Xml.Schema;
using System.Data;
using System.Data.SqlClient;

// Table name constants
private const String CATEGORIES_TABLE    = "Categories";

// Field name constants
private const String CATEGORYNAME_FIELD  = "CategoryName";

private const String XMLDIFFGRAMFILENAME =
    ConfigurationSettings.AppSettings["Temp_Directory"] +
    "CategoriesDiffgram.xml";

private DataSet ds;

// ...

private void XmlDiffgramForm_Load(object sender, System.EventArgs e)
{
    // Select fields from Categories table without the Picture BLOB.
    String sqlText = "SELECT CategoryID, CategoryName, Description " +
        "FROM Categories";

    // Load the Categories table into the DataSet.
    SqlDataAdapter da = new SqlDataAdapter(sqlText,
        ConfigurationSettings.AppSettings["Sql_ConnectString"]);
    ds = new DataSet( );
    da.Fill(ds, "Categories");

    DisplayDiffGram( );
}

private void makeChangesButton_Click(object sender, System.EventArgs e)
{
    // Disable the make changes button.
    makeChangesButton.Enabled = false;

    DataTable dt = ds.Tables["Categories"];

    // Delete the first row.
    dt.Rows[0].Delete( );

    // Modify the second row.
    dt.Rows[1][CATEGORYNAME_FIELD] += "New ";
```

Example 8-12. File: XmlDiffgramForm.cs (continued)

```
    // Insert a row.
    DataRow row = dt.NewRow( );
    row.ItemArray = new object[] {0, "New Category0",
        "New Category0 Description"};
    dt.Rows.InsertAt(row, 0);

    // Add a row.
    dt.Rows.Add(new object[] {9, "New Category9",
        "New Category9 Description"});

    DisplayDiffGram( );
}

private void DisplayDiffGram( )
{
    // Write the XML diffgram to a memory stream.
    MemoryStream ms = new MemoryStream( );
    ds.WriteXml(ms, XmlWriteMode.DiffGram);

    // Write the memory stream to a file.
    FileStream fs = new FileStream(XMLDIFFGRAMFILENAME, FileMode.Create,
        FileAccess.Write);
    ms.WriteTo(fs);
    fs.Close( );

    // Display the XML DiffGram.
    byte[] result = ms.ToArray( );
    ms.Close( );
    resultTextBox.Text = Encoding.UTF8.GetString(result,0,result.Length);
}
```

Discussion

A DiffGram is an XML format used to specify both the original and current values for the contents of a DataSet. It does not include any schema information. The DiffGram is also the primary serialization format used by the .NET Framework to persist and serialize a DataSet. The DiffGram format is XML-based, making it platform and application independent. It is not, however, widely used or understood outside of Microsoft .NET applications.

The DiffGram format is divided into three sections—current, original, and errors—as shown in the following example:

```
<?xml version="1.0"?>
<diffgr:diffgram
    xmlns:msdata="urn:schemas-microsoft-com:xml-msdata"
    xmlns:diffgr="urn:schemas-microsoft-com:xml-diffgram-v1">

    <DataInstanceName>
        ...
    </DataInstanceName>
```

```
    <diffgr:before>
        ...
    </diffgr:before>

    <diffgr:errors>
        ...
    </diffgr:errors>
</diffgr:diffgram>
```

Here are descriptions of the three `DiffGram` sections:

<DataInstanceName>

> The *DataInstanceName* is the name of the `DataSet` or `DataTable`. This block contains the current version of the data containing all modifications. Modified elements are identified with the `diffgr:hasChanges="modified"` annotation while new elements are identified with the `diffgr:hasChanges="inserted"` annotation. Deleted elements are not annotated, rather, they appear only in the *<diffgr:before>* section.

<diffgr:before>

> This section contains the original version of the elements that have been modified or deleted. Elements in this section are matched to elements in the *<DataInstanceName>* section using the `diffgr:id` annotation with matching values.

<diffgr:errors>

> This section contains error information for an element in the *<DataInstanceName>* section. Elements in this section are matched to elements in the *<DataInstanceName>* section using the `diffgr:id` annotation with matching values.

The example loads all Categories from Northwind into a `DataTable` called Categories in a `DataSet`. The first row is deleted, the second is modified, a row is inserted before the first row, and a row is added to the end of the `DataTable`. After these modifications, the `DiffGram` for the `DataSet` is:

```
<diffgr:diffgram xmlns:msdata="urn:schemas-microsoft-com:xml-msdata"
    xmlns:diffgr="urn:schemas-microsoft-com:xml-diffgram-v1">
  <NewDataSet>
    <Categories diffgr:id="Categories9" msdata:rowOrder="0"
        diffgr:hasChanges="inserted">
     <CategoryID>0</CategoryID>
     <CategoryName>New Category0</CategoryName>
     <Description>New Category0 Description</Description>
    </Categories>
    <Categories diffgr:id="Categories2" msdata:rowOrder="2"
        diffgr:hasChanges="modified">
     <CategoryID>2</CategoryID>
     <CategoryName>CondimentsNew </CategoryName>
     <Description>Sweet and savory sauces, relishes, spreads, and
       seasonings</Description>
    </Categories>
    <Categories diffgr:id="Categories3" msdata:rowOrder="3">
      <CategoryID>3</CategoryID>
      <CategoryName>Confections</CategoryName>
```

```
            <Description>Desserts, candies, and sweet breads</Description>
          </Categories>

     <!-- ... -->

          <Categories diffgr:id="Categories8" msdata:rowOrder="8">
            <CategoryID>8</CategoryID>
            <CategoryName>Seafood</CategoryName>
            <Description>Seaweed and fish</Description>
          </Categories>
          <Categories diffgr:id="Categories10" msdata:rowOrder="9"
              diffgr:hasChanges="inserted">
            <CategoryID>9</CategoryID>
            <CategoryName>New Category9</CategoryName>
            <Description>New Category9 Description</Description>
          </Categories>
        </NewDataSet>
        <diffgr:before>
          <Categories diffgr:id="Categories1" msdata:rowOrder="1">
            <CategoryID>1</CategoryID>
            <CategoryName>Beverages</CategoryName>
            <Description>Soft drinks, coffees, teas, beers, and ales</Description>
          </Categories>
          <Categories diffgr:id="Categories2" msdata:rowOrder="2">
            <CategoryID>2</CategoryID>
            <CategoryName>Condiments</CategoryName>
            <Description>Sweet and savory sauces, relishes, spreads,
            and seasonings</Description>
          </Categories>
        </diffgr:before>
      </diffgr:diffgram>
```

As expected, the DiffGram contains both the annotation indicating inserted and modified records. The <diffgr:before> section contains the original record for the deleted records with *CategoryID*=1 and the modified record with *CategoryID*=2.

As shown in the example, a DiffGram is written for the DataSet by specifying an XmlWriteMode of DiffGram when calling the WriteXml( ) method of the DataSet. The GetXml( ) method cannot be used to generate a DiffGram. A DataSet can be loaded from an XML DiffGram by specifying an XmlWriteMode of DiffGram when calling the ReadXml( ) method.

8.9   Formatting Column Values When Outputting Data as XML

Problem

You need to save some of the columns in a DataTable as attributes instead of elements when you write out the data as XML.

Solution

Use the `ColumnMapping` property.

The sample code contains two event handlers:

`Form.Load`
> Sets up the sample by creating a `DataSet` containing the first two records of the Customers table from Northwind.

Refresh `Button.Click`
> Iterates over all of the columns in all of the Customers tables and sets the `ColumnMapping` property to the specified value. The `ColumnMapping` for the `ContactName` column is then set to the specified value. The XML output for the `DataSet` is displayed.

The C# code is shown in Example 8-13.

Example 8-13. File: XmlElementsOrAttributesForm.cs

```
// Namespaces, variables, and constants
using System;
using System.Configuration;
using System.Data;
using System.Data.SqlClient;

private DataSet ds;

// ...

private void XmlElementsOrAttributesForm_Load(object sender,
    System.EventArgs e)
{
    ds = new DataSet("CustomersDataSet");

    // Get the top two rows from the Customers table.
    SqlDataAdapter da = new SqlDataAdapter(
        "SELECT TOP 2 * FROM Customers",
        ConfigurationSettings.AppSettings["Sql_ConnectString"]);
    da.Fill(ds, "Customers");
}

private void refreshButton_Click(object sender, System.EventArgs e)
{
    // Set the mapping type for each column in the table.
    foreach(DataTable table in ds.Tables)
        foreach(DataColumn column in table.Columns)
        {
            if(tableAttributeRadioButton.Checked)
                column.ColumnMapping = MappingType.Attribute;
            else if(tableElementRadioButton.Checked)
                column.ColumnMapping = MappingType.Element;
```

Example 8-13. File: XmlElementsOrAttributesForm.cs (continued)

```
            else if(tableHiddenRadioButton.Checked)
                column.ColumnMapping = MappingType.Hidden;
    }

    // Set the mapping type for the ContactName column.
    DataColumn dc = ds.Tables["Customers"].Columns["ContactName"];
    if(columnAttributeRadioButton.Checked)
        dc.ColumnMapping = MappingType.Attribute;
    else if(columnElementRadioButton.Checked)
        dc.ColumnMapping = MappingType.Element;
    else if(columnHiddenRadioButton.Checked)
        dc.ColumnMapping = MappingType.Hidden;
    else if(columnSimpleContentRadioButton.Checked)
        dc.ColumnMapping = MappingType.SimpleContent;

    // Display the XML.
    xmlTextBox.Text = ds.GetXml();
}
```

Discussion

The ColumnMapping property of the DataColumn specifies how the value of a column will be written when the DataSet is output as an XML document with the GetXml( ) method or WriteXml( ) method. The property value is one of the MappingType enumeration values described in Table 8-5.

Table 8-5. MappingType enumeration

Value	Description

Attribute	The value is written as an XML attribute. For example:
	
	`<MyRow>`
	`    <MyColumn>my column value</MyColumn>`
	`</MyRow>`

Element	The value is written as an XML element. For example: `<MyRow MyColumn="my column value" />` This is the default.
Hidden	The value is not written in the XML output.
SimpleContent	The value is written as text in the XML element for its row. For example: `<MyRow>my column value</MyRow>` This value can only be used if the table has neither Element columns nor nested relations.

There is no way to set the ColumnMapping property for all columns in a DataTable or DataSet at once. Each column must be set individually.

8.10   Filling a DataSet Using an XML Template Query

Problem

You have an XML template query that you need to use from ADO.NET. You need to fill a DataSet using an XML template query.

Solution

Use an XML template query to fill a DataSet using the SQLXML Managed Classes.

The sample uses one XML file as shown in Example 8-14:

OrdersForCustomerQuery.xml
> Contains the XML template query

The sample code contains two event handlers and one method:

Form.Load
> Loads all Customers from Northwind into a DataTable. The default view of the DataTable is bound to the top data grid on the form. The DataGrid. CurrentCellChanged event handler is called to refresh the bottom data grid.

DataGrid.CurrentCellChanged
> Gets the CustomerID for the selected row in the top data grid and calls the LoadOrderGrid( ) method to refresh the bottom grid.

LoadOrderGrid( )
> This method creates a SqlXmlCommand template query and its single SqlXmlParameter object. The parameter is set to the user-specified value. A SqlXmlDataAdapter object is created and executed to fill a new DataSet based on the template query. The default view of the Orders table in the result DataSet is bound to the lower data grid on the form displaying the orders for the selected customer.

Example 8-14. File: OrdersForCustomerQuery.xml

```
<?xml version="1.0" encoding="utf-8" ?>
<ROOT xmlns:sql='urn:schemas-microsoft-com:xml-sql'>
    <sql:header>
        <sql:param name="CustomerID" />
    </sql:header>
    <sql:query>
        select
            Orders.OrderID,
            Orders.CustomerID,
            Orders.EmployeeID,
            Orders.OrderDate,
            Orders.RequiredDate,
```

Example 8-14. File: OrdersForCustomerQuery.xml (continued)

```
            Orders.ShippedDate,
            Orders.ShipVia,
            Orders.Freight,
            Orders.ShipName,
            Orders.ShipAddress,
            Orders.ShipCity,
            Orders.ShipRegion,
            Orders.ShipPostalCode,
            Orders.ShipCountry,
            [Order Details].ProductID,
            [Order Details].UnitPrice,
            [Order Details].Quantity,
            [Order Details].Discount
        from
            Orders inner join [Order Details] on
            Orders.OrderID=[Order Details].OrderID
        where
            Orders.CustomerID=@CustomerID
        for xml auto
    </sql:query>
</ROOT>
```

The C# code is shown in Example 8-15.

Example 8-15. File: UsingXmlTemplateQueriesForm.cs

```
// Namespaces, variables, and constants
using System;
using System.Configuration;
using System.Windows.Forms;
using Microsoft.Data.SqlXml;
using System.Data;
using System.Data.SqlClient;

private const String XMLQUERYFILENAME =
    ConfigurationSettings.AppSettings["Project_Directory"] +
    @"Chapter 08\OrdersForCustomerQuery.xml";

// ...

private void UsingXmlTemplateQueriesForm_Load(object sender,
    System.EventArgs e)
{
    String sqlText = "SELECT * FROM Customers";

    // Load the list of customers into a table.
    SqlDataAdapter da = new SqlDataAdapter(sqlText,
        ConfigurationSettings.AppSettings["Sql_ConnectString"]);
    DataTable table = new DataTable("Customers");
    da.Fill(table);

    // Bind the default view of the table to the customer grid.
    customerDataGrid.DataSource = table.DefaultView;
```

Example 8-15. File: UsingXmlTemplateQueriesForm.cs (continued)

```csharp
        // Update orders grid based on the default row selected.
        customerDataGrid_CurrentCellChanged(null, null);
    }

    private void customerDataGrid_CurrentCellChanged(object sender,
        System.EventArgs e)
    {
        // Retrieve the selected row from the customer grid.
        int row = customerDataGrid.CurrentRowIndex;
        // Get the customer ID.
        String customerId =
            ((DataView)customerDataGrid.DataSource).Table.
            Rows[row][0].ToString();
        // Call method to load orders for selected customer.
        LoadOrderGrid(customerId);
    }

    private void LoadOrderGrid(String customerId)
    {
        // Create the SQL XML command.
        SqlXmlCommand cmd = new SqlXmlCommand(
            ConfigurationSettings.AppSettings["OleDb_SqlAuth_ConnectString"]);
        cmd.CommandType = SqlXmlCommandType.TemplateFile;
        cmd.CommandText = XMLQUERYFILENAME;
        cmd.SchemaPath = XMLSCHEMAFILENAME;

        // Set the customer ID parameter for the command.
        SqlXmlParameter param = cmd.CreateParameter();
        param.Name = "@CustomerID";
        param.Value = customerId;

        // Create the DataSet.
        DataSet ds = new DataSet();

        // Create the SQL XML DataAdapter.
        SqlXmlAdapter da = new SqlXmlAdapter(cmd);

        // Fill the DataSet.
        try
        {
            da.Fill(ds);
        }
        catch(Exception ex)
        {
            MessageBox.Show(ex.Message);
        }

        // Bind the default view of the orders table to the orders grid.
        orderDataGrid.DataSource = ds.Tables["Orders"].DefaultView;
        orderDataGrid.CaptionText = "Orders [CustomerID: " + customerId + "]";
    }
```

Discussion

SQLXML Managed Classes

The SQLXML Managed Classes expose SQLXML functionality from the Microsoft .NET Framework. They allow access to XML data from instance of Microsoft SQL Server 2000 or later. SQLXML Managed Classes consist of three classes:

SqlXmlCommand

> Represents a command to execute against the SQL Server database.

SqlXmlParameter

> Stores parameters used by the SqlXmlCommand object. The parameter is created using the CreateParameter( ) method of the SqlXmlCommand class.

SqlXmlAdapter

> Links the SQLXML managed classes to the disconnected ADO.NET DataSet class.

A description of the methods and properties of these classes are shown in Tables 8-6 through 8-8.

Table 8-6 describes the methods of the SqlXmlCommand class.

Table 8-6. SqlXmlCommand methods

Method	Description
ExecuteNonQuery( )	Executes a command that does not return a result or result set—for example, an update-gram or DiffGram update
ExecuteStream( )	Returns a query result set as a stream
ExecuteToStream( )	Writes query result set to an existing stream
ExecuteXmlReader( )	Returns the result set of the query as an XmlReader object
CreateParameter( )	Creates a SqlXmlParameter object used to pass parameters to a command using the Name and Value properties
ClearParameters( )	Clears SqlXmlParameter objects for a command

Table 8-7 describes the properties of the SqlXmlCommand class.

Table 8-7. SqlXmlCommand properties

Property	Description
BasePath	The directory path used when specifying a relative path for an XSL file.
ClientSideXml	Whether the conversion of the result set occurs on the client (true) or server (false). The default is false.
CommandText	The text of the command to execute.

Table 8-7. SqlXmlCommand properties (continued)

Property	Description
CommandType	The type of command to execute. Takes one of the following values from the SqlXmlCommandType enumeration:
	DiffGram
	Executes a DiffGram
	XmlTemplate
	Executes an XML template
	TemplateFile
	Executes an XML template file consisting of one or more SQL or XPath queries
	Sql
	Executes a SQL command
	UpdateGram
	Executes an updategram
	XPath
	Executes an XPath command
CommandStream	The stream to execute the command from.
Namespaces	The namespace for XPath queries.
OutputEncoding	The encoding for the stream returned by the command.
RootTag	The single root-level tag for XML output returned by the command.
SchemaPath	The name of the mapping schema file and its directory path, either absolute or relative.
XslPath	The name of the XSL file and its directory path, either absolute or relative.

The SqlXmlParameter class has no methods. Table 8-8 describes the properties of the SqlXmlParameter class.

Table 8-8. SqlXmlParameter properties

Property	Description
Name	The name of the parameter for an SqlXmlCommand object
Value	The value of the parameter

The SqlXmlAdapter class has no properties. Table 8-9 describes the methods of the SqlXmlAdapter class.

Table 8-9. SqlXmlAdapter methods

Method	Description
Fill	Fills a DataSet with the XML data retrieved from the SQL Server database
Update	Updates the SQL Server database with the changes made to the DataSet

For more information about the SQLXML Managed Classes, see the Microsoft SQLXML release documentation.

Template queries

A template query is an XML document containing one or more SQL queries or stored procedures to execute. Template queries, like stored procedures, promote code reuse, facilitate security, and encourage good design by encapsulating database-specific functionality.

Parameters for the query are identified by the `<sql:param>` tag with the name attribute used to specify the parameter name and the parameter default value optionally specified between the `<sql:param>` and `<sql:param>` tags. Parameter tags are enclosed within the `<sql:header>` tags. The example shows one parameter named CustomerID without a default value:

```
<sql:header>
    <sql:param name="CustomerID" />
</sql:header>
```

If the CustomerID parameter had a default value of ALFKI, the parameter would be defined as follows:

```
<sql:param name="CustomerID">ALFKI</sql:param>
```

The SQL command text must be enclosed within `<sql:query>` tags. This is shown in the example:

```
<sql:query>
    select
        Orders.OrderID,
        Orders.CustomerID,

    ...

        [Order Details].Quantity,
        [Order Details].Discount
    from
        Orders inner join [Order Details] on
        Orders.OrderID=[Order Details].OrderID
    where
        Orders.CustomerID=@CustomerID
    for xml auto
</sql:query>
```

The query is a standard SQL command with the required FOR XML clause to return the result set as XML. The query could also execute a stored procedure with the EXEC or EXECUTE command followed by the name of the stored procedure and a list of parameter values as required.

The query in the previous example has a single parameter, CustomerID, which is prepended with an @ when referred to in the query:

```
where Orders.CustomerID=@CustomerID
```

8.11 Using a Single Stored Procedure to Update Multiple Changes to a SQL Server Database

Problem

You need to update a SQL Server 2000 database with changes to multiple rows in a DataSet by executing a single stored procedure.

Solution

Use OpenXML with an XMLdocument representing a DataSet of the changes made.

The schema of table TBL0811 used in this solution is shown in Table 8-10.

Table 8-10. TBL0811 schema

Column name	Data type	Length	Allow nulls?
Id	int	4	No
Field1	nvarchar	50	Yes
Field2	nvarchar	50	Yes

Example 8-16 uses a single stored procedure:

SP0811_Update
> Used to update the table TBL0811 with the changes made to the DataSet passed in as an NText input parameter @data. The parameters @data and @datadeleted contain an XML representation of a DataSet containing all updated and added records and all deleted records, respectively. These parameters are parsed using the system stored procedure sp_xml_preparedocument that returns a handle that is subsequently used to access the parsed XML document. OpenXML is used to update, insert, and delete the DataSet changes made to TBL0811. Finally, the system stored procedure sp_xml_removedocument is used to free the memory used by the parsed XML documents.

The sample code contains two event handlers:

Form.Load
> Sets up the sample by creating a DataSet containing the contents of the table TBL0811. The ColumnMapping for each column is set to MappingType.Attribute. The default view of the table is bound to the data grid on the form.

Update Button.Click
> Writes the XML representation of the added and changed records in the DataSet to the stored procedure NText parameter @data and the XML representation of deleted records in the DataSet to the stored procedure NText parameter @datadelete. The stored procedure *SP0811_Update* is called to update the database with the batched changes.

Example 8-16. Stored procedure: SP0811_Update

```
ALTER PROC SP0811_Update
    @data ntext = null,
    @datadelete ntext = null
AS

DECLARE @hDoc int

-- updated and inserted records
if @data is not null
begin
    EXEC sp_xml_preparedocument @hDoc OUTPUT, @data

    UPDATE TBL0811
    SET
        TBL0811.Field1 = XmlTBL0811.Field1,
        TBL0811.Field2 = XmlTBL0811.Field2
    FROM
        OPENXML(@hDoc, 'NewDataSet/TBL0811')
    WITH (
        Id Integer,
        Field1 nvarchar(50),
        Field2 nvarchar(50)
    ) XmlTBL0811
    WHERE
        TBL0811.Id = XmlTBL0811.Id

    INSERT INTO TBL0811
    SELECT
        Id,
        Field1,
        Field2
    FROM
        OPENXML(@hdoc, 'NewDataSet/TBL0811')
    WITH (
        Id Integer,
        Field1 nvarchar(50),
        Field2 nvarchar(50)
    ) XmlTBL0811
    WHERE
        XmlTBL0811.Id NOT IN (SELECT Id from TBL0811)

    EXEC sp_xml_removedocument @hDoc
end

-- deleted records
if @datadelete is not null
begin
    EXEC sp_xml_preparedocument @hDoc OUTPUT, @datadelete
```

Example 8-16. Stored procedure: SP0811_Update (continued)

```
    DELETE TBLO811
    FROM
        TBLO811 INNER JOIN
    OPENXML(@hDoc, 'NewDataSet/TBLO811')
    WITH (
        Id Integer,
        Field1 nvarchar(50),
        Field2 nvarchar(50)
    ) XmlTBLO811
        ON TBLO811.Id = XmlTBLO811.Id

    EXEC sp_xml_removedocument @hDoc
end
```

The C# code is shown in Example 8-17.

Example 8-17. File: StoredProcedureMultipleRowsForm.cs

```csharp
// Namespaces, variables, and constants
using System;
using System.Configuration;
using System.Windows.Forms;
using System.Text;
using System.IO;
using System.Data;
using System.Data.SqlClient;

private DataSet ds;

private const String TABLENAME              = "TBLO811";
private const String STOREDPROCEDURE_NAME   = "SP0811_Update";

// ...

private void StoredProcedureMultipleRowsForm_Load(object sender,
    System.EventArgs e)
{
    ds = new DataSet( );

    // Create the DataAdapter.
    SqlDataAdapter da = new SqlDataAdapter("SELECT * FROM " + TABLENAME,
        ConfigurationSettings.AppSettings["Sql_ConnectString"]);
    // Load the schema and data for the table.
    da.FillSchema(ds, SchemaType.Source, TABLENAME);
    da.Fill(ds, TABLENAME);

    // Columns in XML representation of data as attributes
    foreach(DataColumn col in ds.Tables[TABLENAME].Columns)
        col.ColumnMapping = MappingType.Attribute;

    // This technique supports only update and insert; turn off delete
    // records in the default view.
    ds.Tables[TABLENAME].DefaultView.AllowDelete = false;
```

Example 8-17. File: StoredProcedureMultipleRowsForm.cs (continued)

```
    // Bind the default view of the table to the grid.
    dataGrid.DataSource = ds.Tables[TABLENAME].DefaultView;
}

private void updateButton_Click(object sender, System.EventArgs e)
{
    StringBuilder sb;
    StringWriter sw;

    // Create a connection and command for the update stored procedure.
    SqlConnection conn = new SqlConnection(
        ConfigurationSettings.AppSettings["Sql_ConnectString"]);
    SqlCommand cmd = new SqlCommand( );
    cmd.Connection = conn;
    cmd.CommandText = STOREDPROCEDURE_NAME;
    cmd.CommandType = CommandType.StoredProcedure;

    // Inserted and updated records
    if (ds.HasChanges(DataRowState.Added | DataRowState.Modified))
    {
        sb = new StringBuilder( );
        sw = new StringWriter(sb);

        ds.GetChanges(
            DataRowState.Added | DataRowState.Modified).WriteXml(sw,
            XmlWriteMode.WriteSchema);
        cmd.Parameters.Add("@data", SqlDbType.NText);
        cmd.Parameters["@data"].Value = sb.ToString( );

        sw.Close( );
    }

    // Deleted records
    if (ds.HasChanges(DataRowState.Deleted))
    {
        sb = new StringBuilder( );
        sw = new StringWriter(sb);

        // Get the DataSet containing the records deleted and call
        // RejectChanges( ) so that the original version of those rows
        // are available so that WriteXml( ) works.
        DataSet dsChange = ds.GetChanges(DataRowState.Deleted);
        dsChange.RejectChanges( );
        dsChange.WriteXml(sw, XmlWriteMode.WriteSchema);

        cmd.Parameters.Add("@datadelete", SqlDbType.NText);
        cmd.Parameters["@datadelete"].Value = sb.ToString( );

        sw.Close( );
    }
```

Example 8-17. File: StoredProcedureMultipleRowsForm.cs (continued)

```
    // Execute the stored procedure.
    conn.Open( );
    cmd.ExecuteNonQuery( );
    conn.Close( );

    ds.AcceptChanges( );

    MessageBox.Show("Update completed.",
        "Multiple Row Update/Insert Stored Procedure",
        MessageBoxButtons.OK, MessageBoxIcon.Information);
}
```

Discussion

OpenXML provides a result set view of an XML document allowing you to use the XML document in a T-SQL statement in the same way a result set provider such as a table or view is used.

The simple form of the OpenXML command is:

```
    OPENXML(int iDoc, nvarchar rowPattern)
    WITH (SchemaDeclaration)
```

The two input arguments are:

iDoc

> The document handle of the internal representation of an XML document created by using the system stored procedure sp_xml_preparedocument

rowPattern

> The XPath query used to select the nodes in the XML document to be processed

The argument for the WITH clause is:

SchemaDeclaration

> The format of the result set. If not supplied, the results are returned in an *edge table* format representing the XML document structure in a single table.

The system stored procedure sp_xml_preparedocument reads XML as input text using the MSXML parser and returns a handle that you can use to access the internal representation of the XML document. The handle is valid for the duration of the connection to the SQL Server or until it is reset. The handle can be invalidated and the associated memory freed by calling the system stored procedure sp_xml_removedocument. The syntax of the stored procedure is:

```
    sp_xml_preparedocument hDoc OUTPUT, [xmlText], [xpathNamespaces]
```

The arguments are:

hDoc

> An integer parameter that returns a handle to the internal representation of the XML document.

xmlText

> A text parameter that specifies the original XML document. The default value is null which results in the return of a handle to an internal representation to an empty XML document.

xpathNamespaces

> A text parameter that specifies the namespace declarations used in row and column XPath expressions in OpenXML. The default value is:
>
> ```
> <root xmlns:mp="urn:schemas-microsoft-com:xml-metaprop">
> ```

The system stored procedure sp_xml_removedocument removes the internal representation of an XML document specified by a document handle obtained from the system stored procedure sp_xml_preparedocument and invalidates the handle. The syntax of the stored procedure is:

```
sp_xml_removedocument hDoc
```

The argument is:

hDoc

> An integer parameter that returns a handle to the internal representation of the XML document.

For more information about the OpenXML command and the system stored procedures sp_xml_preparedocument and sp_xml_removedocuemnt, see Microsoft SQL Server Books Online.

Optimizing .NET Data Access

9.0 Introduction

This chapter examines asynchronous processing, caching, paging, batching, and class-specific methods and techniques to improve application performance. Before optimizing any application, profile it to ensure that you have a good understanding of where the real bottlenecks are.

A query can run asynchronously on background threads to improve application responsiveness and perceived performance by not blocking processing. This can also be used to give the user an opportunity to cancel a request that is taking too long. Recipe 9.1 shows how to use a background thread to run a query. Recipe 9.2 shows how to let the user cancel a query running on a background thread.

Caching data allows data to be retrieved once and saved in order to service subsequent requests for the same data. The load on the database server is reduced, potentially improving application performance. On the downside, cached data becomes less current (and less accurate) over time. The .NET Framework provides classes to allow both client- and server-side caching of data. On the client-side, caching requires few server-side resources, but increases network bandwidth required to move data back and forth with each round trip. Caching on the server-side consumes more network resources; however, it is less expensive in terms of bandwidth required. In either case, applications should be designed to retrieve the minimum data necessary to optimize performance and scalability. Recipe 9.3 shows how to use caching in an ASP.NET application.

Even if data is not cached, it can still get out of date. A timer can track the time that data was retrieved from the database in order to periodically refresh the data and thus present the data with a current view. Recipe 9.14 shows how to use the extended properties of a DataSet to automatically refresh the data a user sees.

This chapter also covers the following:

Paging

Paging is common in applications where a subset of a result set—a page—is displayed to the user. The way that paging is implemented affects both scalability and performance. .NET provides automatic paging in many Windows Forms and Web Forms controls; however, manual paging offers the best performance. This allows paging requirements to be met exactly, rather than automatically, which is the default. Recipe 9.4 shows a high-performance custom paging solution.

Moving large amounts of data

Storing binary large objects (BLOBs) in a database is becoming an increasingly viable option as vendors enhance database capabilities in response to demands that ubiquitous high-bandwidth has created for storing digital assets. Storing BLOBs in a database is simpler than other approaches because there is no need to synchronize database fields acting as pointers to an external repository such as the file system. BLOBs are easier to administer and are automatically backed up with the database. Built-in database functionality, such as full-text searching, can be used on BLOB fields, and it leverages tools already in the database rather than requiring external tools. Recipe 9.11 shows how to store and retrieve BLOBs in a SQL Server and Recipe 9.12 shows how to store and retrieve BLOBs in an Oracle database.

The DataSet is an in-memory database containing both relation and constraint objects to maintain the integrity of the data. These objects, can, however, slow performance when filling a DataSet with large amounts of data that has complex interdependencies and constraints. Turning off the constraints temporarily can sometimes improve performance in these situations, which Recipe 9.9 discusses.

Large amounts of data sometimes need to be loaded into a SQL Server database quickly. SQL XML Bulk Load objects allow XML data to be loaded into SQL Server tables providing high performance when large amounts of data need to be inserted. All that is required is an XML schema and an XML document or fragment containing the data. Recipe 9.5 shows how to do this.

Minimizing roundtrips and conversions

A DataAdapter makes a roundtrip to update the data source for every row that has been changed. In some situations, this can cause performance problems. You can batch these DataAdapter updates by handling DataAdapter events. Roundtrips are reduced and performance is improved. Recipe 9.13 shows how this is done.

DataReader typed accessor methods improve performance by eliminating type conversions when retrieving data from a DataReader. You can dynamically retrieve column ordinals at runtime and use them instead of column names to further improve performance when accessing data with a DataReader. Recipes 9.6 and 9.7 show how to use these techniques with a DataReader.

Simplifying your code

There are several ways to get a single data value from a result set without incurring the overhead of using a DataSet. The ExecuteScalar( ) method returns the first value of the first row in the result set. A stored procedure output parameter can be used similarly to getting a single row of data. A DataReader can also be used. If the DataReader might return multiple rows, remember to call the Cancel( ) method before calling Close( ) so that the remaining rows are not transmitted unnecessarily back to the client who needs only one value. The ExecuteScalar( ) and stored procedure output parameter approaches offer better performance than using a DataReader. Recipe 9.10 shows how to retrieve a single value efficiently.

Debugging

Visual Studio .NET supports debugging SQL Server stored procedures both in standalone mode and from managed code when called using the .NET provider for SQL server. This can help to optimize and troubleshoot stored procedures. Recipe 9.8 shows how to debug stored procedures from Visual Studio .NET.

9.1   Filling a DataSet Asynchronously

Problem

Given some database queries that return large result sets and cause the calling application to be unresponsive, you need to make the application more responsive during the fill.

Solution

Create a background thread and use it to run a query to fill a DataSet. You can also fill a DataGrid object from a background thread.

The sample code contains one event handler and two methods:

Go Button.Click

Checks whether there is an existing background thread loading the DataSet. If the DataSet is not being loaded, a new thread is created invoking the AsyncFillDataSet( ) method to fill a DataSet. Otherwise, a message is displayed stating that the DataSet is currently being filled.

AsyncFillDataSet( )

This method loads a DataSet with the Orders and Order Details tables from the Northwind database. The BindDataSetToDataGrid( ) method is called asynchronously on the form's thread to display the results. Finally, messages are displayed to indicate that the `AsyncFillDataSet( )` method has started and when it has completed.

`BindDataSetToDataGrid( )`

This method binds the default view of the Orders table in the `DataSet` to the data grid on the form.

The C# code is shown in Example 9-1.

Example 9-1. File: AsynchronousFillForm.cs

```csharp
// Namespaces, variables, and constants
using System;
using System.Configuration;
using System.Threading;
using System.Runtime.Remoting.Messaging;
using System.Data;
using System.Data.SqlClient;

private delegate void BindDataSetToDataGridDelegate(DataSet ds);

// Table name constants
private const String ORDERS_TABLE        = "Orders";
private const String ORDERDETAILS_TABLE = "OrderDetails";

// Relation name constants
private const String ORDERS_ORDERDETAILS_RELATION =
    "Orders_OrderDetails_Relation";

// Field name constants
private const String ORDERID_FIELD      = "OrderID";
private const String ORDERDATE_FIELD    = "OrderDate";

private bool isWorking = false;

// ...

private delegate void BindDataSetToDataGridDelegate(DataSet ds);

private void goButton_Click(object sender, System.EventArgs e)
{
    // Check if the DataSet is already being filled.
    if (!isWorking)
    {
        isWorking = true;

        // Clear the data grid.
        resultDataGrid.DataSource = null;

        // Create and start a new thread to fill the DataSet.
        Thread thread = new Thread(new ThreadStart(AsyncFillDataSet));
        thread.Start( );
    }
    else
```

Example 9-1. File: AsynchronousFillForm.cs (continued)

```
    {
        // DataSet already being filled. Display a message.
        statusTextBox.Text += "DataSet still filling ..." +
            Environment.NewLine;
    }
}

private void AsyncFillDataSet( )
{
    statusTextBox.Text = "Filling DataSet ..." + Environment.NewLine;

    DataSet ds = new DataSet("Source");

    SqlDataAdapter da;

    // Fill the Order table and add it to the DataSet.
    da = new SqlDataAdapter("SELECT * FROM Orders",
        ConfigurationSettings.AppSettings["Sql_ConnectString"]);
    DataTable orderTable = new DataTable(ORDERS_TABLE);
    da.FillSchema(orderTable, SchemaType.Source);
    da.Fill(orderTable);
    ds.Tables.Add(orderTable);

    // Fill the OrderDetails table and add it to the DataSet.
    da = new SqlDataAdapter("SELECT * FROM [Order Details]",
        ConfigurationSettings.AppSettings["Sql_ConnectString"]);
    DataTable orderDetailTable = new DataTable(ORDERDETAILS_TABLE);
    da.FillSchema(orderDetailTable, SchemaType.Source);
    da.Fill(orderDetailTable);
    ds.Tables.Add(orderDetailTable);

    // Create a relation between the tables.
    ds.Relations.Add(ORDERS_ORDERDETAILS_RELATION,
        ds.Tables[ORDERS_TABLE].Columns[ORDERID_FIELD],
        ds.Tables[ORDERDETAILS_TABLE].Columns[ORDERID_FIELD],
        true);

    statusTextBox.Text += "DataSet Fill complete." + Environment.NewLine;

    // Call the BindDataSetToDataGrid method asynchronously
    // on the Form's thread.
    this.BeginInvoke(
        new BindDataSetToDataGridDelegate(BindDataSetToDataGrid),
        new object[] {ds});

    // Set flag indicating that the async fill is complete.
    isWorking = false;
}

private void BindDataSetToDataGrid(DataSet ds)
{
```

Example 9-1. File: AsynchronousFillForm.cs (continued)

```
    // Bind the default view of the Orders table to the data grid.
    resultDataGrid.DataSource = ds.Tables[ORDERS_TABLE].DefaultView;
}
```

Discussion

When a synchronous call is made, the caller thread is blocked until the call completes. An asynchronous call returns immediately, freeing the calling thread to continue with its work while a new thread is created to run the method in parallel.

A new instance of a Thread is initialized using a constructor that takes a ThreadStart delegate argument, which references the method to be executed when the Thread starts executing. The Start( ) method of the Thread changes the state of the Thread to ThreadState.Running allowing the operating system to schedule it for execution. Once it begins executing, the ThreadStart delegate supplied in the Thread constructor invokes its method.

Windows Form or control methods, such as a DataGrid, cannot be called on any thread other than the one that created the form or control because they are based on a single-threaded apartment (STA) model. Method calls from other threads must be marshaled to the creation thread. This can be done asynchronously by calling the BeginInvoke( ) method of the form, forcing the method to be executed on the thread that created the form or control.

9.2   Canceling an Asynchronous Query

Problem

Given a query running that runs asynchronously on a background thread, you want to give the user the option to cancel the query if it is taking too long.

Solution

Abort the background thread and clean up in an exception handler.

The sample code contains two event handlers and a single method:

Start Button.Click
> Checks whether there is an existing background thread loading the DataSet. If the DataSet is not being loaded, a new thread is created invoking the AsyncFillDataSet( ) method to fill a DataSet. Otherwise, a message is displayed stating that the DataSet is currently being filled.

Cancel Button.Click
> Aborts the background thread filling the DataSet.

AsyncFillDataSet( )

This method loads a DataSet with the Orders and Order Details tables from the Northwind database. The method displays a message when the method has started and when it has completed. The method also traps the ThreadAbortException to handle the situation where the fill on the background thread is canceled.

The C# code is shown in Example 9-2.

Example 9-2. File: AsynchronousFillCancelForm.cs

```csharp
// Namespaces, variables, and constants
using System;
using System.Configuration;
using System.Threading;
using System.Data;
using System.Data.SqlClient;

// Table name constants
private const String ORDERS_TABLE        = "Orders";
private const String ORDERDETAILS_TABLE = "OrderDetails";

// Relation name constants
private const String ORDERS_ORDERDETAILS_RELATION =
    "Orders_OrderDetails_Relation";

// Field name constants
private const String ORDERID_FIELD       = "OrderID";
private const String ORDERDATE_FIELD     = "OrderDate";

private Thread thread;

// ...

private void startButton_Click(object sender, System.EventArgs e)
{
    // Check if a new thread can be created.
    if (thread == null ||
        (thread.ThreadState & (ThreadState.Unstarted |
        ThreadState.Background)) == 0)
    {
        // Create and start a new thread to fill the DataSet.
        thread = new Thread(new ThreadStart(AsyncFillDataSet));
        thread.IsBackground = true;
        thread.Start( );
    }
    else
    {
        // DataSet already being filled. Display a message.
        statusTextBox.Text += "DataSet still filling ..." +
            Environment.NewLine;
        statusTextBox.Refresh( );
    }
}
```

Example 9-2. File: AsynchronousFillCancelForm.cs (continued)

```csharp
private void cancelButton_Click(object sender, System.EventArgs e)
{
    // Check if the thread is running and an abort has not been requested.
    if (thread != null &&
        (thread.ThreadState &
        (ThreadState.Stopped | ThreadState.Aborted |
        ThreadState.Unstarted | ThreadState.AbortRequested)) == 0)
    {
        try
        {
            // Abort the thread.
            statusTextBox.Text += "Stopping thread ..." +
                Environment.NewLine;
            statusTextBox.Refresh();
            thread.Abort();
            thread.Join();
            statusTextBox.Text += "Thread stopped." +
                Environment.NewLine;
        }
        catch (Exception ex)
        {
            statusTextBox.Text += ex.Message + Environment.NewLine;
        }
    }
    else
    {
        statusTextBox.Text += "Nothing to stop." + Environment.NewLine;
    }
}

private void AsyncFillDataSet()
{
    try
    {
        statusTextBox.Text = "Filling DataSet ..." +
            Environment.NewLine;
        statusTextBox.Refresh();

        DataSet ds = new DataSet("Source");

        SqlDataAdapter da;

        // Fill the Order table and add it to the DataSet.
        da = new SqlDataAdapter("SELECT * FROM Orders",
            ConfigurationSettings.AppSettings["Sql_ConnectString"]);
        DataTable orderTable = new DataTable(ORDERS_TABLE);
            da.FillSchema(orderTable, SchemaType.Source);
        da.Fill(orderTable);
        ds.Tables.Add(orderTable);

        // Fill the OrderDetails table and add it to the DataSet.
        da = new SqlDataAdapter("SELECT * FROM [Order Details]",
            ConfigurationSettings.AppSettings["Sql_ConnectString"]);
```

Example 9-2. File: AsynchronousFillCancelForm.cs (continued)

```
        DataTable orderDetailTable = new DataTable(ORDERDETAILS_TABLE);
        da.FillSchema(orderDetailTable, SchemaType.Source);
        da.Fill(orderDetailTable);
        ds.Tables.Add(orderDetailTable);

        // Create a relation between the tables.
        ds.Relations.Add(ORDERS_ORDERDETAILS_RELATION,
            ds.Tables[ORDERS_TABLE].Columns[ORDERID_FIELD],
            ds.Tables[ORDERDETAILS_TABLE].Columns[ORDERID_FIELD],
            true);

        statusTextBox.Text += "DataSet fill complete." +
            Environment.NewLine;
    }
    catch (ThreadAbortException ex)
    {
        // Exception indicating that thread has been aborted
        statusTextBox.Text += "AsyncFillDataSet(): " + ex.Message +
            Environment.NewLine;
    }
}
```

Discussion

Recipe 9.1 discusses using a background thread to fill a DataSet to improve application performance.

The ThreadState of a thread specifies its execution state. This value is a bitwise combination of ThreadState enumeration described in Table 9-1.

Table 9-1. ThreadState enumeration

Value	Description
Aborted	The thread is stopped.
AbortRequested	The Abort( ) method of the thread has been called but the thread has not yet received the ThreadAbortException that will terminate it.
Background	The thread is being executed on a background thread rather than a foreground thread. This is specified by the IsBackground property of the thread.
Running	The thread has been started, is not blocked, and there is no pending ThreadAbortException.
Stopped	The thread is stopped.
StopRequested	The thread is being requested to stop. This value is for internal use only.
Suspended	The thread is suspended.
SuspendRequested	The thread is being requested to suspend.
Unstarted	The thread is not started and the Start( ) method has not been called on the thread.
WaitSleepJoin	The thread is blocked by a Wait( ), Sleep( ), or Join( ) method.

In the solution, a background thread is used to fill the DataSet. The ThreadState of the thread object is used to determine whether it can be started or whether it can be aborted, as follows:

- A thread can be started only if it does not have a ThreadState of Unstarted or Background.
- A thread can be aborted only if its ThreadState is not Stopped, Aborted, Unstarted, or AbortRequested.

The Abort( ) method of the Thread raises a ThreadAbortException in the thread on which it is invoked and begins the process of terminating the thread. ThreadAbortException is a special exception, although it can be caught, it is automatically raised again at the end of a catch block. All finally blocks are executed before killing the thread. Because the thread can do an unbounded computation in the finally blocks, the Join( ) method of the thread—a blocking call that does not return until the thread actually stops executing—is used to guarantee that the thread has terminated. Once the thread is stopped, it cannot be restarted.

9.3   Caching Data

Problem

Given a Web Forms application that is performing poorly because it is repeatedly reading data that doesn't change very often, you need to cache the data to eliminate unnecessary queries and improve the performance.

Solution

Use the ASP.NET Cache class.

The Web Forms page defines the data grid used to display the contents of a DataSet, a button to clear the cache, and a label that displays whether the data was retrieved from the cache or from the database. The code for the Web Forms page is shown in Example 9-3.

Example 9-3. File: ADOCookbookCS0903.aspx

```
<form id="ADOCookbookCS0903" method="post" runat="server">
    <asp:HyperLink id="HyperLink1"
        style="Z-INDEX: 101; LEFT: 16px; POSITION: absolute; TOP: 24px"
        runat="server" NavigateUrl="default.aspx">Main Menu
    </asp:HyperLink>
    <asp:DataGrid id="customersDataGrid"
        style="Z-INDEX: 102; LEFT: 16px; POSITION: absolute; TOP: 128px"
        runat="server" AllowPaging="True">
        <HeaderStyle Font-Bold="True"></HeaderStyle>
    </asp:DataGrid>
```

Example 9-3. File: ADOCookbookCS0903.aspx (continued)

```
    <asp:Label id="cacheStatusLabel"
        style="Z-INDEX: 103; LEFT: 16px; POSITION: absolute; TOP: 96px"
        runat="server" ForeColor="Green"></asp:Label>
    <asp:Button id="clearCacheButton"
        style="Z-INDEX: 104; LEFT: 16px; POSITION: absolute; TOP: 56px"
        runat="server" Text="Clear Cache">
    </asp:Button>
</form>
```

The code-behind contains three event handlers and two methods:

Page.Load

> Checks the cache for an object with the key CustomerDataSet. If an entry is not found, the DataSet is loaded by calling the LoadDataSet( ) method. If an entry is found, the cached object is retrieved and cast to a DataSet. In either case, the source of the data is displayed to the user. If the page is being loaded for the first time, the CurrentPageIndex of the data grid on the page is set to 0 (the first page) and the BindDataGrid( ) method is called to bind the default view of the Customers table to the data grid on the form.

LoadDataSet( )

> This method loads a DataSet with the Customers table from the Northwind database. The DataSet is added to the cache with the key CustomerDataSet and an expiration time of 15 seconds into the future.

BindDataGrid( )

> This method binds the default view of the Customers table in the DataSet to the DataGrid on the page. The key for the DataGrid is set to the CustomerID field.

DataGrid.PageIndexChange

> Sets the current page index of the DataGrid to the new value of the page index. The BindDataGrid( ) method is called.

Clear Button.Click

> Removes the DataSet containing the Customers data from the cache.

The C# code for the code-behind is shown in Example 9-4.

Example 9-4. File: ADOCookbookCS0903.aspx.cs

```
// Namespaces, variables, and constants
using System;
using System.Configuration;
using System.Data;
using System.Data.SqlClient;

// ...

private void Page_Load(object sender, System.EventArgs e)
{
```

Example 9-4. File: ADOCookbookCS0903.aspx.cs (continued)

```
        // Load the data from database or cache and
        // display where the data came from.
        if(Cache["CustomersDataSet"] == null)
        {
            LoadDataSet( );
            cacheStatusLabel.Text = "DataSet retrieved from database.";
        }
        else
        {
            ds = (DataSet)Cache["CustomersDataSet"];
            cacheStatusLabel.Text = "DataSet retrieved from cache.";
        }

        if(!Page.IsPostBack)
        {
            // When page is first opened, position to first grid page.
            customersDataGrid.CurrentPageIndex = 0;
            BindDataGrid( );
        }
    }

    private void LoadDataSet( )
    {
        // Create a DataAdapter.
        String sqlText = "SELECT * FROM Customers";
        SqlDataAdapter da =
            new SqlDataAdapter(sqlText,
            ConfigurationSettings.AppSettings["DataConnectString"]);
        ds = new DataSet( );
        // Fill the a customers table in the DataSet with all customers.
        da.Fill(ds, "Customers");

        // Save the DataSet to the cache expiring in 15 seconds.
        Cache.Insert("CustomersDataSet", ds, null,
            DateTime.Now.AddSeconds(15), System.TimeSpan.Zero);
    }

    private void BindDataGrid( )
    {
        // Bind the default view of the customers table to the grid.
        customersDataGrid.DataSource = ds.Tables["Customers"].DefaultView;
        customersDataGrid.DataKeyField = "CustomerID";
        customersDataGrid.DataBind( );
    }

    private void customersDataGrid_PageIndexChanged(object source,
        System.Web.UI.WebControls.DataGridPageChangedEventArgs e)
    {
        // Change the current page of the grid and rebind.
        customersDataGrid.CurrentPageIndex = e.NewPageIndex;
        BindDataGrid( );
    }
```

Example 9-4. File: ADOCookbookCS0903.aspx.cs (continued)

```
private void clearCacheButton_Click(object sender, System.EventArgs e)
{
    // Remove the cache when user presses "clear" button.
    Cache.Remove("CustomersDataSet");
    cacheStatusLabel.Text = "Cache cleared.";
}
```

Discussion

Data used by an application can be recreated in each roundtrip to the server or it can be cached and retrieved from the cache in subsequent page processing. Recreating data tends to improve its accuracy; however, this can require significant additional processing. Caching data, on the other hand, uses more system resources to store the data, which can become a problem if many users are caching data.

Data can be cached on the client—in the page using the view state—or on the server in a session state or application state variable or using a cache. Client-side caching uses no server resources for the cache, but requires network bandwidth to transmit the cached information back and forth with each roundtrip to the server. Server-side caching uses server-side resources but little bandwidth for caching. In either case, the amount of data cached should be minimized to optimize application performance and scalability.

ASP.NET implements a System.Web.Caching.Cache class to store objects that require a lot of server resources to create so that they do not have to be recreated each time they are needed. Instances of the Cache class are created for each application domain and remain active as long as the application domain remains active. When an application is restarted, its instance of the Cache class is recreated. You can programmatically access information about an instance of the Cache class through the Cache property of either the HttpContext object or the Page object.

Data is placed in a Cache object using key-and-value pairs. The Add( ) method is used to create an entry for a new key value that will fail if the key already exists, while the Insert( ) method will create either a new entry or overwrite an existing entry. The Remove( ) method is used to remove a key-and-value pair from the Cache object.

The Cache class allows an expiration policy to be established for items in the cache. Items can be set to expire at a specific time, called *absolute expiration*, or after not being accessed for a specific period of time, called *sliding expiration*. Items that have expired return a null value. Generally, the expiration policy is set so that data is cached only as long as it remains current.

Caching data can improve performance by reducing the number of trips between the server and the data source. Drawbacks of caching include server memory that is consumed by the cache and the data in the cache being out of sync with the data source.

9.4   Improving Paging Performance

Problem

Given an application that allows the user to page through a large result set in a data grid, you need to improve the performance of the paging.

Solution

Build a custom paging solution that overcomes the performance limitations of the overloaded Fill( ) method of the DataAdapter.

The sample uses a single stored procedure, which is shown in Example 9-5:

SP0904_PageOrders

Used to return 10 records from the Orders table of the Northwind database that correspond the first, last, next, or previous page, or a specific page. The procedure has the following arguments:

@PageCommand

An input parameter that accepts one of the following values: FIRST, LAST, PREVIOUS, NEXT, or GOTO. This specifies the page of results to return to the client.

@FirstOrderId

An input parameter that contains the OrderID of the first record of the client's current page of Orders data.

@LastOrderId

An input parameter that contains the OrderID of the last record of the client's current page of Orders data.

@PageCount

An output parameter that returns the number of pages, each of which contains 10 records, in the result set.

@CurrentPage

An output parameter that returns the page number of the result set returned.

Example 9-5. Stored procedure: SP0904_PageOrders

```
ALTER PROCEDURE SP0904_PageOrders
    @PageCommand nvarchar(10),
    @FirstOrderId int = null,
    @LastOrderId int = null,
    @PageCount int output,
    @CurrentPage int output
AS
    SET NOCOUNT ON

    select @PageCount = CEILING(COUNT(*)/10) from Orders
```

Example 9-5. Stored procedure: SP0904_PageOrders (continued)

```
-- first page is requested or previous page when the current
-- page is already the first
if @PageCommand = 'FIRST' or (@PageCommand = 'PREVIOUS' and
    @CurrentPage <= 1)
begin
    select top 10 *
    from Orders
    order by OrderID

    set @CurrentPage = 1

    return 0
end

-- last page is requested or next page when the current
-- page is already the last
if @PageCommand = 'LAST' or (@PageCommand = 'NEXT' and
    @CurrentPage >= @PageCount)
begin
    select a.*
    from
        (select TOP 10 *
        from orders
        order by OrderID desc) a
    order by OrderID

    set @CurrentPage = @PageCount

    return 0
end

if @PageCommand = 'NEXT'
begin
    select TOP 10 *
    from Orders
    where OrderID > @LastOrderId
    order by OrderID

    set @CurrentPage = @CurrentPage+1

    return 0
end

if @PageCommand = 'PREVIOUS'
begin
    select a.*
    from (
        select TOP 10 *
        from Orders
        where OrderId < @FirstOrderId
        order by OrderID desc) a
    order by OrderID
```

Example 9-5. Stored procedure: SP0904_PageOrders (continued)

```
        set @CurrentPage = @CurrentPage-1

        return 0
    end

    if @PageCommand = 'GOTO'
    begin
        if @CurrentPage < 1
            set @CurrentPage = 1
        else if @CurrentPage > @PageCount
            set @CurrentPage = @PageCount

        declare @RowCount int
        set @RowCount = (@CurrentPage * 10)

        exec ('select * from
        (select top 10 a.* from
        (select top ' + @RowCount + ' * from Orders order by OrderID) a
        order by OrderID desc) b
        order by OrderID')

        return 0
    end

    return 1
```

The sample code contains six event handlers and a single method:

Form.Load

> Sets up the sample by loading the schema for the Orders table from the North-wind database into a DataTable. Next, a DataAdapter is created to select records using the stored procedure to perform the paging through the DataTable. The GetData( ) method is called to load the first page of Orders data.

GetData( )

> This method accepts a page navigation argument. The parameters for the stored procedure created in the Form.Load event are set. The Fill( ) method of the DataAdapter is called to execute the stored procedure to retrieve the specified page of records and the output parameters of the stored procedure—@PageCount and @CurrentPage—are retrieved.

Previous Button.Click

> Calls the GetData( ) method with the argument PREVIOUS to retrieve the previous page of data from the Orders table.

Next Button.Click

> Calls the GetData( ) method with the argument NEXT to retrieve the next page of data from the Orders table.

First Button.Click

Calls the GetData( ) method with the argument FIRST to retrieve the first page of data from the Orders table.

Last Button.Click

Calls the GetData( ) method with the argument LAST to retrieve the last page of data from the Orders table.

Goto Button.Click

Sets the value of the current page to the specified page value and calls the GetData( ) method with the argument GOTO to retrieve that page of data from the Orders table.

The C# code is shown in Example 9-6.

Example 9-6. File: ImprovePagingPerformanceForm.cs

```csharp
// Namespaces, variables, and constants
using System;
using System.Configuration;
using System.Windows.Forms;
using System.Data;
using System.Data.SqlClient;

private SqlDataAdapter da;
private DataTable table;

// Stored procedure name constants
public const String PAGING_SP      = "SP0904_PageOrders";

// Field name constants
private const String ORDERID_FIELD = "OrderID";

private int currentPage;
private int firstOrderId;
private int lastOrderId;

// ...

private void ImprovePagingPerformanceForm_Load(object sender,
    System.EventArgs e)
{
    // Get the schema for the Orders table.
    da = new SqlDataAdapter("SELECT * FROM Orders",
        ConfigurationSettings.AppSettings["Sql_ConnectString"]);
    table = new DataTable("Orders");
    da.FillSchema(table, SchemaType.Source);

    // Set up the paging stored procedure.
    SqlCommand cmd = new SqlCommand();
    cmd.CommandText = PAGING_SP;
    cmd.Connection = new SqlConnection(
        ConfigurationSettings.AppSettings["Sql_ConnectString"]);
```

Example 9-6. File: ImprovePagingPerformanceForm.cs (continued)

```
        cmd.CommandType = CommandType.StoredProcedure;
        cmd.Parameters.Add("@PageCommand", SqlDbType.NVarChar, 10);
        cmd.Parameters.Add("@FirstOrderId", SqlDbType.Int);
        cmd.Parameters.Add("@LastOrderId", SqlDbType.Int);
        cmd.Parameters.Add("@PageCount", SqlDbType.Int).Direction =
            ParameterDirection.Output;
        cmd.Parameters.Add("@CurrentPage", SqlDbType.Int).Direction =
            ParameterDirection.InputOutput;
        da = new SqlDataAdapter(cmd);

        // Get the first page of records.
        GetData("FIRST");
        dataGrid.DataSource = table.DefaultView;
    }

    public void GetData(string pageCommand)
    {
        da.SelectCommand.Parameters["@PageCommand"].Value = pageCommand;
        da.SelectCommand.Parameters["@FirstOrderId"].Value = firstOrderId;
        da.SelectCommand.Parameters["@LastOrderId"].Value = lastOrderId;
        da.SelectCommand.Parameters["@CurrentPage"].Value = currentPage;

        table.Clear();
        da.Fill(table);

        if(table.Rows.Count > 0)
        {
            firstOrderId = (int)table.Rows[0][ORDERID_FIELD];
            lastOrderId =
                (int)table.Rows[table.Rows.Count - 1][ORDERID_FIELD];
        }
        else
            firstOrderId = lastOrderId = -1;

        int pageCount = (int)da.SelectCommand.Parameters["@PageCount"].Value;
        currentPage = (int)da.SelectCommand.Parameters["@CurrentPage"].Value;

        dataGrid.CaptionText =
            "Orders: Page " + currentPage + " of " + pageCount;
    }

    private void previousButton_Click(object sender, EventArgs args)
    {
        GetData("PREVIOUS");
    }

    private void nextButton_Click(object sender, EventArgs args)
    {
        GetData("NEXT");
    }
```

Example 9-6. File: ImprovePagingPerformanceForm.cs (continued)

```
private void firstButton_Click(object sender, System.EventArgs e)
{
    GetData("FIRST");
}

private void lastButton_Click(object sender, System.EventArgs e)
{
    GetData("LAST");
}

private void gotoPageButton_Click(object sender, System.EventArgs e)
{
    try
    {
        currentPage = Convert.ToInt32(gotoPageTextBox.Text);
    }
    catch(Exception ex)
    {
        MessageBox.Show(ex.Message, "Improving Paging Performance",
            MessageBoxButtons.OK, MessageBoxIcon.Warning);
        return;
    }

    GetData("GOTO");
}
```

Discussion

Overloads of the Fill( ) method of the DataAdapter allow a subset of data to be returned from a query by specifying the starting record and the number of records to return as arguments. This method should be avoided for paging through result sets—especially large ones—because it retrieves the entire result set for the query and subsequently discards the records outside of the specified range. Resources are used to process the entire result set instead of just the subset of required records.

The solution shows how to create a stored procedure that will return a result set corresponding to a page of data from a larger result set. The TOP and WHERE clauses are used together with the primary key (any unique identifier would do) and the sort order. This allows first, last, next, and previous paging. The goto paging is done by nesting SELECT TOP *n* statements with alternate ascending and descending sorts to get the subset of the records for the page specified. The goto select statement uses a dynamic SQL statement executed using the T-SQL EXEC command. This allows a variable number of TOP *n* records to be selected within the statement. The EXEC command could also be used to dynamically calculate the top records for all statements so that the number of records per page could be supplied as an input parameter to the stored procedure rather than hardcoded.

9.5   Performing a Bulk Insert with SQL Server

Problem

Given many records in an XML file that you need to add to a SQL Server 2000 database, you need to perform a bulk insert with optimal performance.

Solution

Perform a fast bulk insert and update using the XML bulk load functionality in Microsoft SQL Server 2000.

You'll need a reference to the Microsoft SQLXML BulkLoad 3.0 Type Library from the COM tab in Visual Studio .NET's Add Reference Dialog.

The sample uses a single XSD file:

Customers.xsd
> The schema for the data that is bulk loaded into the Customers table

The sample uses a single XML file:

Customers.xml
> Contains the data that is bulk loaded into the Customers table

The sample code creates a bulk load object SQLXMLBulkLoad and sets the connection string and error log file for the object. The Execute( ) method of the SQLXMLBulkLoad object is used to bulk load the Customers data in the XML file into the Customers table in the Northwind database. The Customers table must be empty prior to running this sample, otherwise, a primary key constraint error will be raised and written to the error log.

The Customers XSD file is shown in Example 9-7, and the XML file is shown in Example 9-8.

Example 9-7. File: Customers.xsd

```
<xsd:schema xmlns:xsd="http://www.w3.org/2001/XMLSchema"
    xmlns:sql="urn:schemas-microsoft-com:mapping-schema">
    <xsd:element name="ROOT" sql:is-constant="true">
        <xsd:complexType>
            <xsd:sequence>
                <xsd:element ref="Customers" />
            </xsd:sequence>
        </xsd:complexType>
    </xsd:element>
    <xsd:element name="Customers" sql:relation="Customers">
        <xsd:complexType>
            <xsd:sequence>
                <xsd:element name="CustomerID" type="xsd:string"
                    sql:datatype="nvarchar(5)" />
```

Example 9-7. File: Customers.xsd (continued)

```
                <xsd:element name="CompanyName" type="xsd:string"
                    sql:datatype="nvarchar(40)" />
                <xsd:element name="ContactName" type="xsd:string"
                    sql:datatype="nvarchar(30)" />
                <xsd:element name="ContactTitle"
                    type="xsd:string"
                    sql:datatype="nvarchar(30)" />
                <xsd:element name="Address" type="xsd:string"
                    sql:datatype="nvarchar(60)" />
                <xsd:element name="City" type="xsd:string"
                    sql:datatype="nvarchar(15)" />
                <xsd:element name="Region" type="xsd:string"
                    sql:datatype="nvarchar(15)" />
                <xsd:element name="PostalCode" type="xsd:string"
                    sql:datatype="nvarchar(10)" />
                <xsd:element name="Country" type="xsd:string"
                    sql:datatype="nvarchar(15)" />
                <xsd:element name="Phone" type="xsd:string"
                    sql:datatype="nvarchar(24)" />
                <xsd:element name="Fax" type="xsd:string"
                    sql:datatype="nvarchar(24)" />
            </xsd:sequence>
        </xsd:complexType>
    </xsd:element>
</xsd:schema>
```

Example 9-8. File: Customers.xml

```
<ROOT>
    <Customers>
        <CustomerID>ALFKI</CustomerID>
        <CompanyName>Alfreds Futterkiste</CompanyName>
        <ContactName>Maria Anders</ContactName>
        <ContactTitle>Sales Representative</ContactTitle>
        <Address>Obere Str. 57</Address>
        <City>Berlin</City>
        <PostalCode>12209</PostalCode>
        <Country>Germany</Country>
        <Phone>030-0074321</Phone>
        <Fax>030-0076545</Fax>
    </Customers>

<!-- ... -->

    <Customers>
        <CustomerID>WOLZA</CustomerID>
        <CompanyName>Wolski  Zajazd</CompanyName>
        <ContactName>Zbyszek Piestrzeniewicz</ContactName>
        <ContactTitle>Owner</ContactTitle>
        <Address>ul. Filtrowa 68</Address>
        <City>Warszawa</City>
```

Example 9-8. File: Customers.xml (continued)

```
        <PostalCode>01-012</PostalCode>
        <Country>Poland</Country>
        <Phone>(26) 642-7012</Phone>
        <Fax>(26) 642-7012</Fax>
    </Customers>
</ROOT>
```

The C# code is shown in Example 9-9.

Example 9-9. File: BulkInsertForm.cs

```
// Namespaces, variables, and constants
using System;
using System.Configuration;
using System.Windows.Forms;
using SQLXMLBULKLOADLib;
using System.Data;
using System.Data.SqlClient;

private const String DATAFILENAME =
    ConfigurationSettings.AppSettings["Project_Directory"] +
    @"Chapter 09\Customers.xml";
private const String SCHEMAFILENAME =
    ConfigurationSettings.AppSettings["Project_Directory"] +
    @"Chapter 09\Customers.xsd";
private const String ERRORLOGFILENAME =
    ConfigurationSettings.AppSettings["Temp_Directory"] +
    "BulkLoadError.log";

// ...

// Create the bulk load object, defining connection, and error log.
SQLXMLBulkLoad bl = new SQLXMLBulkLoad();
bl.ConnectionString =
    ConfigurationSettings.AppSettings["OleDb_Msde_ConnectString"];
bl.ErrorLogFile = ERRORLOGFILENAME;

// Execute the bulk load.
try
{
    bl.Execute(SCHEMAFILENAME, DATAFILENAME);
    MessageBox.Show("Bulk load completed successfully.", "Bulk Load",
        MessageBoxButtons.OK, MessageBoxIcon.Information);
}
catch (Exception)
{
    MessageBox.Show("ERROR. See " + ERRORLOGFILENAME + " for details.",
        "Bulk Load Error", MessageBoxButtons.OK, MessageBoxIcon.Error);
}
finally
{
    bl = null;
}
```

Discussion

The SQL Server XML Bulk Load component is used through COM interop to bulk insert data contained in a XML document into a SQL Server database. This component controls the execution of a XML bulk load operation. The example defines an optional error log file, where the default is an empty string meaning that no error log is created.

You can bulk load data into multiple parent-child tables at the same time, a feature that is not available in the OpenXML Transact-SQL extension.

For information about the XML Bulk Load component and its methods and properties, see the topic "XML Bulk Load" in the MSDN Library.

9.6   Improving DataReader Performance with Typed Accessors

Problem

You need to improve performance when accessing data from a DataReader.

Solution

Use DataReader typed accessors to improve performance by eliminating repeated boxing and unboxing of object data to and from .NET Framework data types.

The sample code measures the time to access data in a DataReader using three techniques: typed accessor, column ordinal, and column name. The user specifies the technique by selecting a radio button. To ensure accuracy in each case, the routine reads all data from the DataReader 100 times and measures the total time in ticks, which are 100-nanosecond intervals.

The C# code is shown in Example 9-10.

Example 9-10. File: DataReaderPerformanceForm.cs

```
// Namespaces, variables, and constants
using System;
using System.Configuration;
using System.Windows.Forms;
using System.Data;
using System.Data.SqlClient;

// ...

Cursor.Current = Cursors.WaitCursor;

int orderId;
String customerId;
```

Example 9-10. File: DataReaderPerformanceForm.cs (continued)

```
int employeeId;
DateTime orderDate;
DateTime requiredDate;
DateTime shippedDate;
int shipVia;
Decimal freight;
String shipName;
String shipAddress;
String shipCity;
String shipRegion;
String shipPostalCode;
String shipCountry;

String sqlText = "SELECT OrderID, CustomerID, EmployeeID, " +
    "OrderDate, RequiredDate, ShippedDate, " +
    "ShipVia, Freight, ShipName, ShipAddress, ShipCity, " +
    "ShipRegion, ShipPostalCode, ShipCountry " +
    "FROM Orders";

// Create the connection and the command.
SqlConnection conn = new SqlConnection(
    ConfigurationSettings.AppSettings["Sql_ConnectString"]);
SqlCommand cmd = new SqlCommand(sqlText, conn);

String accessMethod = typedAccessorRadioButton.Checked ? "Typed accessor":
    ordinalRadioButton.Checked ? "Ordinal":"Column name";
int startTick = 0;
int elapsedTick = 0;

conn.Open( );
for(int i = 1; i < 100; i++)
{
    // Create the DataReader and retrieve all fields for each
    // record in the DataReader according to user request.
    SqlDataReader dr = cmd.ExecuteReader( );

    if (typedAccessorRadioButton.Checked)
    {
        startTick = Environment.TickCount;
        while (dr.Read( ))
        {
            orderId = dr.GetInt32(0);
            if(!dr.IsDBNull(1))
                customerId = dr.GetString(1);
            if(!dr.IsDBNull(2))
                employeeId = dr.GetInt32(2);
            if(!dr.IsDBNull(3))
                orderDate = dr.GetDateTime(3);
            if(!dr.IsDBNull(4))
                requiredDate = dr.GetDateTime(4);
            if(!dr.IsDBNull(5))
                shippedDate = dr.GetDateTime(5);
```

Example 9-10. File: DataReaderPerformanceForm.cs (continued)

```
            if(!dr.IsDBNull(6))
                shipVia = dr.GetInt32(6);
            if(!dr.IsDBNull(7))
                freight = dr.GetDecimal(7);
            if(!dr.IsDBNull(8))
                shipName = dr.GetString(8);
            if(!dr.IsDBNull(9))
                shipAddress = dr.GetString(9);
            if(!dr.IsDBNull(10))
                shipCity = dr.GetString(10);
            if(!dr.IsDBNull(11))
                shipRegion = dr.GetString(11);
            if(!dr.IsDBNull(12))
                shipPostalCode = dr.GetString(12);
            if(!dr.IsDBNull(13))
                shipCountry = dr.GetString(13);
        }
        elapsedTick += Environment.TickCount-startTick;
    }

    if (ordinalRadioButton.Checked)
    {
        startTick = Environment.TickCount;
        while (dr.Read( ))
        {
            if (!dr.IsDBNull(0))
                orderId = Convert.ToInt32(dr[0]);
            if (!dr.IsDBNull(1))
                customerId = Convert.ToString(dr[1]);
            if (!dr.IsDBNull(2))
                employeeId = Convert.ToInt32(dr[2]);
            if (!dr.IsDBNull(3))
                orderDate = Convert.ToDateTime(dr[3]);
            if (!dr.IsDBNull(4))
                requiredDate = Convert.ToDateTime(dr[4]);
            if (!dr.IsDBNull(5))
                shippedDate = Convert.ToDateTime(dr[5]);
            if (!dr.IsDBNull(6))
                shipVia = Convert.ToInt32(dr[6]);
            if (!dr.IsDBNull(7))
                freight = Convert.ToDecimal(dr[7]);
            if (!dr.IsDBNull(8))
                shipName = Convert.ToString(dr[8]);
            if (!dr.IsDBNull(9))
                shipAddress = Convert.ToString(dr[9]);
            if (!dr.IsDBNull(10))
                shipCity = Convert.ToString(dr[10]);
            if (!dr.IsDBNull(11))
                shipRegion = Convert.ToString(dr[11]);
            if (!dr.IsDBNull(12))
                shipPostalCode = Convert.ToString(dr[12]);
```

Example 9-10. File: DataReaderPerformanceForm.cs (continued)

```
                if (!dr.IsDBNull(13))
                    shipCountry = Convert.ToString(dr[13]);
            }
            elapsedTick += Environment.TickCount-startTick;
        }


        if (columnNameRadioButton.Checked)
        {
            startTick = Environment.TickCount;
            while (dr.Read())
            {
                if (dr["OrderID"] != DBNull.Value)
                    orderId = Convert.ToInt32(dr["OrderID"]);
                if (dr["CustomerID"] != DBNull.Value)
                    customerId = Convert.ToString(dr["CustomerID"]);
                if (dr["EmployeeID"] != DBNull.Value)
                    employeeId = Convert.ToInt32(dr["EmployeeID"]);
                if (dr["OrderDate"] != DBNull.Value)
                    orderDate = Convert.ToDateTime(dr["OrderDate"]);
                if (dr["RequiredDate"] != DBNull.Value)
                    requiredDate =
                        Convert.ToDateTime(dr["RequiredDate"]);
                if (dr["ShippedDate"] != DBNull.Value)
                    shippedDate =
                        Convert.ToDateTime(dr["ShippedDate"]);
                if (dr["ShipVia"] != DBNull.Value)
                    shipVia = Convert.ToInt32(dr["ShipVia"]);
                if (dr["Freight"] != DBNull.Value)
                    freight = Convert.ToDecimal(dr["Freight"]);
                if (dr["ShipName"] != DBNull.Value)
                    shipName = Convert.ToString(dr["ShipName"]);
                if (dr["ShipAddress"] != DBNull.Value)
                    shipAddress = Convert.ToString(dr["ShipAddress"]);
                if (dr["ShipCity"] != DBNull.Value)
                    shipCity = Convert.ToString(dr["ShipCity"]);
                if (dr["ShipRegion"] != DBNull.Value)
                    shipRegion = Convert.ToString(dr["ShipRegion"]);
                if (dr["ShipPostalCode"] != DBNull.Value)
                    shipPostalCode =
                        Convert.ToString(dr["ShipPostalCode"]);
                if (dr["ShipCountry"] != DBNull.Value)
                    shipCountry = Convert.ToString(dr["ShipCountry"]);
            }
            elapsedTick += Environment.TickCount-startTick;
        }

        dr.Close();
    }

    resultTextBox.Text += "Access method: " + accessMethod +
        "; Elapsed time: " + elapsedTick + " ticks." + Environment.NewLine;
```

Example 9-10. File: DataReaderPerformanceForm.cs (continued)

```
conn.Close( );

Cursor.Current = Cursors.Default;
```

Discussion

You can access the data in a DataReader row using a column name, a column ordinal, or a typed accessor method such as GetInt32( ) and GetString( ). The typed accessor allows a column value to be accessed in its native data type reducing the amount of type conversion required when retrieving a column value. When the underlying type is known, this reduces the type conversion effort required when retrieving the column value and thereby improves performance. For a list of typed accessor methods for SQL Server and OLE DB data providers, see Recipe 2.8.

Each typed accessor takes a single argument: the zero-based column ordinal of the column for which to retrieve the value. An IndexOutOfRangeException is raised if the ordinal value is not valid. An InvalidCastException is raised if the accessor method specifies an invalid cast. If the column might contain a nonexistent or missing value, call the IsDBNull( ) method prior to calling the typed accessor method to avoid raising an exception in case the column value is equivalent to DBNull.

Executing the solution shows the following relative performance when accessing DataReader column values using the different methods:

- A column ordinal is about 30% faster than a column name
- A typed accessor method is about 15% faster than a column ordinal and 40% faster than a column name.

9.7   Improving DataReader Performance with Column Ordinals

Problem

You want to use column ordinals rather than column names to retrieve data from a DataReader to improve application performance and without hard-coding the ordinal values.

Solution

Enumerate the column ordinals using the GetOrdinal( ) method and use those values to retrieve data from the DataReader.

The sample code contains two event handlers:

Form.Load
> Sets up the sample by using a DataReader to retrieve the ordinals for all columns in the Orders table of the Northwind database.

Go Button.Click
> Builds a new DataReader containing the TOP 5 records from the Orders table in the Northwind database. The code iterates over the records in the DataReader and demonstrates techniques to retrieve data from the OrderID, CustomerID, OrderDate, and ShipRegion using accessors that are index-based, nonspecific, provider-specific, nonspecific with null check, and provider-specific with null check.

The C# code is shown in Example 9-11.

Example 9-11. File: DataReaderColumnOrdinalForm.cs

```
// Namespaces, variables, and constants
using System;
using System.Configuration;
using System.Text;
using System.Data;
using System.Data.SqlClient;

private int co_OrderId;
private int co_CustomerId;
private int co_EmployeeId;
private int co_OrderDate;
private int co_RequiredDate;
private int co_ShippedDate;
private int co_ShipVia;
private int co_Freight;
private int co_ShipName;
private int co_ShipAddress;
private int co_ShipCity;
private int co_ShipRegion;
private int co_ShipPostalCode;
private int co_ShipCountry;

// ...

private void OptimizingDataRetrievalDataReaderForm_Load(object sender,
    System.EventArgs e)
{
    String sqlText = "SELECT * FROM Orders";

    // Create the connection and command.
    SqlConnection conn = new SqlConnection(
        ConfigurationSettings.AppSettings["Sql_ConnectString"]);
    SqlCommand cmd = new SqlCommand(sqlText, conn);
    conn.Open();
```

Example 9-11. File: DataReaderColumnOrdinalForm.cs (continued)

```
    // Create the DataReader to retrieve ordinals.
    SqlDataReader dr = cmd.ExecuteReader(CommandBehavior.SchemaOnly);

    // Retrieve the column ordinals for each field.
    co_OrderId = dr.GetOrdinal("OrderID");
    co_CustomerId = dr.GetOrdinal("CustomerID");
    co_EmployeeId = dr.GetOrdinal("EmployeeID");
    co_OrderDate = dr.GetOrdinal("OrderDate");
    co_RequiredDate = dr.GetOrdinal("RequiredDate");
    co_ShippedDate = dr.GetOrdinal("ShippedDate");
    co_ShipVia = dr.GetOrdinal("ShipVia");
    co_Freight = dr.GetOrdinal("Freight");
    co_ShipName = dr.GetOrdinal("ShipName");
    co_ShipAddress = dr.GetOrdinal("ShipAddress");
    co_ShipCity = dr.GetOrdinal("ShipCity");
    co_ShipRegion = dr.GetOrdinal("ShipRegion");
    co_ShipPostalCode = dr.GetOrdinal("ShipPostalCode");
    co_ShipCountry = dr.GetOrdinal("ShipCountry");

    // Close the DataReader and connection.
    dr.Close( );
    conn.Close( );
}

private void goButton_Click(object sender, System.EventArgs e)
{
    StringBuilder sb = new StringBuilder( );

    String sqlText = "SELECT TOP 5 * FROM Orders";

    // Create the connection and command.
    SqlConnection conn = new SqlConnection(
        ConfigurationSettings.AppSettings["Sql_ConnectString"]);
    SqlCommand cmd = new SqlCommand(sqlText, conn);
    conn.Open( );

    // Create the DataReader to retrieve data.
    SqlDataReader dr = cmd.ExecuteReader( );

    // Iterate over the records in the DataReader.
    while(dr.Read( ))
    {
        // Access the fields based on their column ordinals.
        sb.Append(
            // Index-based access
            "OrderID: " + dr[co_OrderId] + Environment.NewLine +
            // Nonspecific accessor
            "CustomerID: " + dr.GetString(co_CustomerId) +
            Environment.NewLine +
            // Provider-specific accessor
            "OrderDate: " + dr.GetSqlDateTime(co_OrderDate) +
            Environment.NewLine +
```

Example 9-11. File: DataReaderColumnOrdinalForm.cs (continued)

```
            // Nonspecific accessor with NULL
            "ShipRegion (non-specific): " +
            (dr.IsDBNull(co_ShipRegion) ? "null" :
            dr.GetString(co_ShipRegion)).ToString() +
            Environment.NewLine +
            // Provider-specific accessor with NULL
            "ShipRegion (Sql-specific): " +
            (dr.GetSqlString(co_ShipRegion).IsNull ? "null" :
            dr.GetSqlString(co_ShipRegion)).ToString() +
            Environment.NewLine + Environment.NewLine);
    }

    // Close the DataReader and connection.
    dr.Close();
    conn.Close();

    resultTextBox.Text = sb.ToString();
}
```

Discussion

The GetOrdinal( ) method of the DataReader object gets the column ordinal for a specified column name. As discussed in Recipe 9.6, reading data from a DataReader is significantly faster using column ordinals instead of column names. The GetOrdinal( ) method can be used in the constructor to retrieve all column ordinals based on the column names. Column ordinals can then be used to read data from the DataReader to improve performance without having to code absolute column ordinal values.

The GetName( ) method of the DataReader takes a column ordinal and returns the column name.

9.8 Debugging a SQL Server Stored Procedure

Problem

Given an application that uses a SQL Server stored procedure that is causing errors, you need to debug the stored procedure.

Solution

Use Visual Studio .NET to debug SQL Server stored procedures (in both standalone mode and from managed code).

Discussion

Debugging a stored procedure in standalone mode

You can debug a stored procedure in standalone mode from Visual Studio .NET Server Explorer by following these steps:

1. Open the Server Explorer window in Visual Studio .NET by selecting it from the View menu.
2. Create a connection to the database or select an existing connection.
3. Select and expand the node for the database that contains the stored procedure.
4. Expand the Stored Procedures node.
5. Right-click on the stored procedure to be debugged and select Step Into Stored Procedure from the popup menu.
6. If requested, supply the parameter values on the Run Stored Procedure dialog.

Alternatively, if the stored procedure is already open in a source window in Visual Studio .NET:

1. Right-click on the stored procedure to be debugged and select Step Into Stored Procedure from the popup menu.
2. If requested, supply the parameter values on the Run Stored Procedure dialog.

Debugging a stored procedure from managed code

To debug a stored procedure from managed code, SQL debugging must be enabled for the project. Follow these steps:

1. Open the solution.
2. In the Solution Explorer window, select the project and right-click. Select Properties from the popup menu.
3. In the Property Pages dialog, select Debug from the Configuration drop-down list box.
4. Select the Configuration Properties folder in the left pane and choose Debugging.
5. In the Debuggers section of the right pane, set Enable SQL Debugging to true.
6. Click OK to close the dialog.

Table 9-2 lists the components that must be installed for SQL Server debugging.

Table 9-2. SQL Server debugging components

Component	Installation location
SQLLE.DLL	Client
SQLDBG.DLL	Client and server

Table 9-2. SQL Server debugging components (continued)

Component	Installation location
MSSDBI98.DLL	Server in the *binn* directory of the SQL Server instance
SQLDBREG2.EXE	Client

There are some other significant limitations to SQL Server Debugging:

- It is not possible to debug SQL statements that are outside of a stored procedure.
- It is not possible to step into a stored procedure from managed or unmanaged code, or into managed or unmanaged code from a stored procedure. Set a breakpoint at entry point in the stored procedure or in the reentry point in the code as required. Alternatively, open the code or stored procedure and right-click on the line to break on. Select Run to Cursor from the shortcut menu to reach the desired line without setting a breakpoint.
- The database connection from your application must be established with the .NET data provider for SQL Server before debugging a mixed-language application. After that, you can open stored procedures and set breakpoints in the same way as for other applications.
- When connection pooling is enabled, debugging a stored procedure called from native or managed code might not work after the first time. When a connection is obtained from the pool rather than created, SQL debugging is not reestablished.
- Changes to locals or parameter variables that are cached by the SQL interpreter are not automatically modified and there is no way to force the cache to refresh. SQL Server caches variables when the execution plan determines that they will not be dynamically loaded for each statement execution or reference.

For more information about debugging SQL stored procedures, see the topic "Debugging SQL" in the MSDN Library.

9.9   Improving Performance While Filling a DataSet

Problem

Given a DataSet containing many related tables that takes a long time to fill, you need to improve the performance.

Solution

Use the EnforceConstraints property of the DataSet and the BeginLoadData() and EndLoadData() methods of the contained DataTable objects to improve performance while filling a complex DataSet.

The sample code contains one event handler and one method:

Go `Button.Click`

> Times the filling of the `DataSet` created by the `CreateDataSet( )` method (described next). The `EnforceConstraints` property of the `DataSet` is set as specified and the `BeginLoadData( )` and `EndLoadData( )` methods of the contained `DataTable` objects are used, if specified. A `DataAdapter` is used to fill a specified `DataSet` with data from the Orders and Order Details tables in the Northwind database. Ten iterations are performed, and the total fill time is returned in ticks, which are 100-nanosecond intervals.

`CreateDataSet( )`

> This method builds a `DataSet` containing the table schema for the Orders and Order Details tables from the Northwind database and creates a data relation between the tables. The `DataSet` is returned by the method.

The C# code is shown in Example 9-12.

Example 9-12. File: DataSetFillPerformanceForm.cs

```
// Namespaces, variables, and constants
using System;
using System.Configuration;
using System.Windows.Forms;
using System.Data;
using System.Data.SqlClient;

// Table name constants
public const String ORDERS_TABLE            = "Orders";
public const String ORDERDETAILS_TABLE      = "OrderDetails";

// Field name constants for Orders table
public const String ORDERID_FIELD           = "OrderID";
public const String CUSTOMERID_FIELD        = "CustomerID";
public const String EMPLOYEEID_FIELD        = "EmployeeID";
public const String ORDERDATE_FIELD         = "OrderDate";
public const String REQUIREDDATE_FIELD      = "RequiredDate";
public const String SHIPPEDDDATE_FIELD      = "ShippedDate";
public const String SHIPVIA_FIELD           = "ShipVia";
public const String FREIGHT_FIELD           = "Freight";
public const String SHIPNAME_FIELD          = "ShipName";
public const String SHIPADDRESS_FIELD       = "ShipAddress";
public const String SHIPCITY_FIELD          = "ShipCity";
public const String SHIPREGION_FIELD        = "ShipRegion";
public const String SHIPPOSTALCODE_FIELD    = "ShipPostalCode";
public const String SHIPCOUNTRY_FIELD       = "ShipCountry";

// Field name constants for OrderDetails table
public const String PRODUCTID_FIELD         = "ProductID";
public const String UNITPRICE_FIELD         = "UnitPrice";
public const String QUANTITY_FIELD          = "Quantity";
public const String DISCOUNT_FIELD          = "Discount";
```

Example 9-12. File: DataSetFillPerformanceForm.cs (continued)

```csharp
// Relation name constants
private const String ORDERS_ORDERDETAILS_RELATION =
    Orders_OrderDetails_Relation";

// ...

private void buttonGo_Click(object sender, System.EventArgs e)
{
    Cursor.Current = Cursors.WaitCursor;

    int startTick = 0;
    int totalTick = 0;

    for(int i = 0; i <= 10; i++)
    {
        // Create and fill the DataSet counting elapsed ticks.
        DataSet ds = CreateDataSet();

        if (enforceConstraintsOffCheckBox.Checked)
            ds.EnforceConstraints = false;

        SqlDataAdapter da;

        // Fill the Order table in the DataSet.
        da = new SqlDataAdapter("SELECT * FROM Orders",
            ConfigurationSettings.AppSettings["Sql_ConnectString"]);
        if (loadDataCheckBox.Checked)
            ds.Tables[ORDERS_TABLE].BeginLoadData();

        startTick = Environment.TickCount;
        da.Fill(ds, ORDERS_TABLE);
        totalTick += Environment.TickCount - startTick;

        if (loadDataCheckBox.Checked)
            ds.Tables[ORDERS_TABLE].EndLoadData();

        // Fill the OrderDetails table in the DataSet.
        da = new SqlDataAdapter("SELECT * FROM [Order Details]",
            ConfigurationSettings.AppSettings["Sql_ConnectString"]);
        if (loadDataCheckBox.Checked)
            ds.Tables[ORDERDETAILS_TABLE].BeginLoadData();

        startTick = Environment.TickCount;
        da.Fill(ds, ORDERDETAILS_TABLE);
        totalTick += Environment.TickCount - startTick;

        if (loadDataCheckBox.Checked)
            ds.Tables[ORDERDETAILS_TABLE].EndLoadData();

        if (enforceConstraintsOffCheckBox.Checked)
            ds.EnforceConstraints = true;
    }
```

Example 9-12. File: DataSetFillPerformanceForm.cs (continued)

```
    resultTextBox.Text +=
        "Ticks = " + totalTick + "; " +
        "Enforce constraints = " +
        !enforceConstraintsOffCheckBox.Checked + "; " +
        "BeginLoadData/EndLoadData = " + loadDataCheckBox.Checked +
        Environment.NewLine;

    Cursor.Current = Cursors.Default;
}

private DataSet CreateDataSet( )
{
    DataSet ds = new DataSet( );

    // Create the Orders table.
    DataTable dtOrders = new DataTable(ORDERS_TABLE);
    DataColumnCollection cols = dtOrders.Columns;

    // Add the identity field.
    DataColumn col = cols.Add(ORDERID_FIELD, typeof(System.Int32));
    col.AllowDBNull = false;
    col.AutoIncrement = true;
    col.AutoIncrementSeed = -1;
    col.AutoIncrementStep = -1;
    // Add the other fields.
    cols.Add(CUSTOMERID_FIELD, typeof(System.String)).MaxLength=5;
    cols.Add(EMPLOYEEID_FIELD, typeof(System.Int32));
    cols.Add(ORDERDATE_FIELD, typeof(System.DateTime));
    cols.Add(REQUIREDDATE_FIELD, typeof(System.DateTime));
    cols.Add(SHIPPEDDDATE_FIELD, typeof(System.DateTime));
    cols.Add(SHIPVIA_FIELD, typeof(System.Int32));
    cols.Add(FREIGHT_FIELD, typeof(System.Decimal));
    cols.Add(SHIPNAME_FIELD, typeof(System.String)).MaxLength = 40;
    cols.Add(SHIPADDRESS_FIELD, typeof(System.String)).MaxLength = 60;
    cols.Add(SHIPCITY_FIELD, typeof(System.String)).MaxLength = 15;
    cols.Add(SHIPREGION_FIELD, typeof(System.String)).MaxLength = 15;
    cols.Add(SHIPPOSTALCODE_FIELD, typeof(System.String)).MaxLength = 10;
    cols.Add(SHIPCOUNTRY_FIELD, typeof(System.String)).MaxLength = 15;
    // Set the primary key.
    dtOrders.PrimaryKey = new DataColumn[] {cols[ORDERID_FIELD]};
    // Add the Orders table to the DataSet.
    ds.Tables.Add(dtOrders);

    // Create the OrderDetails table.
    DataTable dtOrderDetails = new DataTable(ORDERDETAILS_TABLE);
    cols = dtOrderDetails.Columns;

    // Add the PK fields.
    cols.Add(ORDERID_FIELD, typeof(System.Int32)).AllowDBNull = false;
    cols.Add(PRODUCTID_FIELD, typeof(System.Int32)).AllowDBNull = false;
    // Add the other fields.
    cols.Add(UNITPRICE_FIELD, typeof(System.Decimal)).AllowDBNull = false;
```

Example 9-12. File: DataSetFillPerformanceForm.cs (continued)

```
    cols.Add(QUANTITY_FIELD, typeof(System.Int16)).AllowDBNull = false;
    cols.Add(DISCOUNT_FIELD, typeof(System.Single)).AllowDBNull = false;
    // Set the primary key.
    dtOrderDetails.PrimaryKey = new DataColumn[]
        {
            cols[ORDERID_FIELD],
            cols[PRODUCTID_FIELD]
        };
    // Add the OrderDetails table to the DataSet.
    ds.Tables.Add(dtOrderDetails);

    // Create a relation between the tables.
    ds.Relations.Add(ORDERS_ORDERDETAILS_RELATION,
        dtOrders.Columns[ORDERID_FIELD],
        dtOrderDetails.Columns[ORDERID_FIELD],
        true);

    return ds;
}
```

Discussion

Filling a DataSet is slowed by the time that the DataSet spends maintaining indexes and validating integrity constraints. Performance can be improved by turning off this functionality while filling a DataSet and turning it back on once the DataSet is filled.

The EnforceConstraints property of the DataSet indicates whether constraint rules—unique and foreign key constraints—are verified when updating data in the DataSet.

Setting EnforceConstraints to false prior to loading data into a DataSet prevents the constraints on the DataSet from being validated when each row is added. Instead, when EnforceConstraints is set to true an attempt is made to enable the constraints. A ConstraintException is raised if the DataSet contains constraint violations.

The BeginLoadData( ) and EndLoadData( ) methods of the DataTable turn off notifications, index maintenance, and constraints while loading data using the LoadDataRow( ) method. These two methods must be called as each DataTable in the DataSet is loaded with data.

9.10   Retrieving a Single Value from a Query

Problem

Given a stored procedure that returns a single value, you need the fastest way to get this data.

SQL Server Debugging and Connection Pooling

If you are running your application from the Visual Studio .NET IDE and SQL debugging is enabled, connections are not reused from the pool as quickly as usual. This can cause your application to unexpectedly run out of connections.

To control SQL debugging for a project:

1. Right-click the Project in the Solution Explorer window and click the Properties item in the submenu to open the Property Pages dialog.
2. Select Configuration Properties → Debugging in the left pane of the Project Pages dialog.
3. The Enable SQL Debugging option in the right pane controls whether debugging of SQL commands is enabled.

For more information about debugging SQL Server stored procedures, see Recipe 9.8.

Solution

Use the ExecuteScalar( ) method to return a single value from a stored procedure.

The sample code uses the ExecuteScalar( ) method to get the number of records in the Orders table of the Northwind database.

The C# code is shown in Example 9-13.

Example 9-13. File: ExecuteScalarForm.cs

```
// Namespaces, variables, and constants
using System;
using System.Configuration;
using System.Data.SqlClient;

// ...

String sqlText = "SELECT COUNT(*) FROM Orders";

// Create the connection and the command.
SqlConnection conn = new SqlConnection(
    ConfigurationSettings.AppSettings["Sql_ConnectString"]);
SqlCommand cmd = new SqlCommand(sqlText, conn);
conn.Open( );
// Execute the scalar SQL statement and store results.
int count = Convert.ToInt32(cmd.ExecuteScalar( ));

conn.Close( );

resultTextBox.Text="Count of Orders records: " + count;
```

Discussion

The ExecuteScalar( ) method of the Command object returns a single value from the data source rather than a table or data stream. While the ExecuteScalar( ) method does not result in a performance improvement when compared to retrieving a single value using an output parameter or using a DataReader, it allows a single value to be returned with the least code and may therefore improve readability and maintainability.

If the result set returns more than one result, the first column of the first row is returned as a scalar value. A null reference is returned if the result set is empty or if the result set is a Ref Cursor when using the Oracle .NET data provider.

9.11   Reading and Writing Binary Data with SQL Server

Problem

You need to read and write binary data from and to a SQL Server 2000 database.

Solution

Use the techniques from the following example.

The schema of table TBL0911 used in this solution is shown in Table 9-3.

Table 9-3. TBL0911 schema

Column name	Data type	Length	Allow nulls?
Id	int	4	No
Description	nvarchar	50	Yes
BlobData	image	16	Yes

The sample code contains nine event handlers:

Form.Load

Creates a DataAdapter to read and update the Id and Description fields from table TBL0911. A TextBox is bound to the Id column and another TextBox is bound to the Description field. A DataSet is filled with all records from TBL0911. The BindingManager is retrieved for the table in the DataSet. A handler is attached to the BindingManager.PositionChanged event. Finally, the display is updated for the current record in the table.

BindingManagerBase.PositionChanged

Clears the image displayed in the PictureBox on the form. The ID of the current record is retrieved. A connection is created to select the field BlobData—an image—from TBL0911 corresponding to the current record. The image is retrieved using a DataReader. A MemoryStream is created from the image retrieved and the MemoryStream is loaded into the PictureBox using the Image.FromStream( ) method passing the image in the MemoryStream as an argument.

Select Image Button.Click

Opens a file dialog to allow an image to be selected by the user. The image is retrieved using a FileStream and loaded into the PictureBox using the Image.FromStream( ) method.

Clear Image Button.Click

Clears the selected image from the PictureBox on the form.

Update Button.Click

Gets the ID of the current record from the BindingManager and builds a SQL statement to update the image in the field BlobData. A connection is created and a stored procedure command is created to update the image. A parameter for the image is added to the stored procedure command. The ExecuteNonquery( ) method of the Command object is used to update the image in the database. The DataAdapter is used to update the other data—the Description field in this sample.

<< (move first) Button.Click

Moves to the first record by setting the Position property of the BindingManager to 0.

< (move previous) Button.Click

Moves to the previous record by setting the Position property of the BindingManager to one less than the current value.

> (move next) Button.Click

Moves to the next record by setting the Position property of the BindingManager to one more than the current value.

>> (move last) Button.Click

Moves to the last record by setting the Position property of the BindingManager to one less than the number of records.

The C# code is shown in Example 9-14.

Example 9-14. File: BinaryDataForm.cs

```
// Namespaces, variables, and constants
using System;
using System.Configuration;
using System.Drawing;
using System.Windows.Forms;
using System.IO;

using System.Data;
using System.Data.SqlClient;

private const String TABLENAME = "TBL0911";
```

Example 9-14. File: BinaryDataForm.cs (continued)

```csharp
private DataSet ds;
private SqlDataAdapter da;

private BindingManagerBase bm;
private Byte[] image;

// ...

private void BinaryDataForm_Load(object sender, System.EventArgs e)
{
    // Create the DataSet.
    ds = new DataSet();

    // Define select and update commands for the DataAdapter.
    String selectCommand = "SELECT Id, Description FROM " + TABLENAME;
    String updateCommand = "UPDATE " + TABLENAME + " " +
        "SET Description = @Description " +
        "WHERE Id = @Id";

    // Create the DataAdapter.
    da = new SqlDataAdapter(selectCommand,
        ConfigurationSettings.AppSettings["Sql_ConnectString"]);
    da.UpdateCommand = new SqlCommand(updateCommand,
        da.SelectCommand.Connection);
    da.UpdateCommand.CommandType = CommandType.Text;
    da.UpdateCommand.Parameters.Add("@Id", SqlDbType.Int, 0, "Id");
    da.UpdateCommand.Parameters.Add("@Description", SqlDbType.NVarChar,
        50, "Description");
    // Fill the schema and the data from the table.
    da.FillSchema(ds, SchemaType.Source, TABLENAME);
    da.Fill(ds, TABLENAME);

    // Bind all of the controls to the DataSet.
    idTextBox.DataBindings.Add("Text", ds, TABLENAME + ".Id");
    descriptionTextBox.DataBindings.Add("Text", ds,
        TABLENAME + ".Description");

    // Get the binding manager base for the parent table.
    bm = BindingContext[ds, TABLENAME];
    // Handler to update the correct image in response to
    // each record reposition
    bm.PositionChanged += new EventHandler(bm_PositionChanged);
    // Update the display for the first record.
    bm_PositionChanged(null, null);
}

private void bm_PositionChanged(Object sender, EventArgs e)
{
    // Handler for the binding manager record change

    // Clear the image and picture box.
    image = null;
    imagePictureBox.Image = null;
```

Example 9-14. File: BinaryDataForm.cs (continued)

```csharp
// Get the ID for the record from the binding manager.
int Id = (int)ds.Tables[TABLENAME].Rows[bm.Position]["ID"];

// Create the connection.
SqlConnection conn = new SqlConnection(
    ConfigurationSettings.AppSettings["Sql_ConnectString"]);
// Create the command to retrieve the image from the database.
String sqlText = "SELECT BlobData FROM " + TABLENAME +
    " WHERE Id = " + Id;
SqlCommand cmd = new SqlCommand(sqlText, conn);

// Retrieve the image to a stream.
conn.Open();
try
{
    int bufferSize = 100;
    byte[] outbyte = new byte[bufferSize];
    long retVal = 0;
    long startIndex = 0;

    SqlDataReader
        dr = cmd.ExecuteReader(CommandBehavior.SequentialAccess);
    dr.Read();

    // Check to see if the field is DBNull.
    if (!dr.IsDBNull(0))
    {
        // Create the memory stream to hold the output.
        MemoryStream ms = new MemoryStream();

        // Read the bytes into outbyte.
        retVal = dr.GetBytes(0, startIndex, outbyte, 0,
            bufferSize);

        // Keep reading while there are more bytes
        // beyond the buffer.
        while (retVal == bufferSize)
        {
            // Write the bytes to the memory stream.
            ms.Write(outbyte, 0, outbyte.Length);

            // Update the start index and
            // fill the buffer again.
            startIndex += bufferSize;
            retVal = dr.GetBytes(0, startIndex, outbyte, 0,
                bufferSize);
        }

        // Write the bytes remaining in the buffer.
        ms.Write(outbyte, 0, (int)retVal - 1);
        // Transfer the memory stream to the image.
        image = ms.ToArray();
```

Example 9-14. File: BinaryDataForm.cs (continued)

```
        }
    }
    catch (System.InvalidCastException)
    {
        // Image is null or invalid in the database. Ignore.
    }
    finally
    {
        conn.Close( );
    }

    if (image != null)
    {
        // Load the image into a stream.
        MemoryStream ms = new MemoryStream(image);
        try
        {
            // Set the PictureBox image to the value of the stream.
            imagePictureBox.Image = Image.FromStream(ms);
        }
        catch(Exception ex)
        {
            MessageBox.Show(ex.Message);
        }

        // Close the stream.
        ms.Close( );
    }
}

private void selectImageButton_Click(object sender, System.EventArgs e)
{
    // Create the file dialog to select image.
    OpenFileDialog ofd = new OpenFileDialog( );
    ofd.InitialDirectory = System.IO.Path.GetTempPath( );
    ofd.Filter = "Bitmap Files (*.bmp)|*.bmp|JPEG files (*.jpg)|*.jpg|" +
        "All files (*.*)|*.*";
    ofd.FilterIndex = 2;

    if (ofd.ShowDialog( ) == DialogResult.OK)
    {
        // Read image into file stream, and from there into Byte array.
        FileStream fs =  new FileStream(ofd.FileName, FileMode.Open,
            FileAccess.Read);
        image = new Byte[fs.Length];
        fs.Read(image, 0, image.Length);
        try
        {
            // Set the PictureBox image from the stream.
            imagePictureBox.Image = Image.FromStream(fs);
        }
        catch (Exception ex)
```

Example 9-14. File: BinaryDataForm.cs (continued)

```
        {
            MessageBox.Show(ex.Message);
            image = null;
        }
        fs.Close( );
    }
}

private void clearImageButton_Click(object sender, System.EventArgs e)
{
    // Clear the image and picture box.
    image = null;
    imagePictureBox.Image = null;
}

private void updateButton_Click(object sender, System.EventArgs e)
{
    // Update the data and image to the database.

    // Get the ID for the record from the binding manager.
    int Id = (int)ds.Tables[TABLENAME].Rows[bm.Position]["ID"];
    String sqlWrite = "UPDATE " + TABLENAME +
        " SET BlobData = @BlobData WHERE ID = " + Id;

    // Create the connection and command.
    SqlConnection conn = new SqlConnection(
        ConfigurationSettings.AppSettings["Sql_ConnectString"]);
    SqlCommand cmdWrite = new SqlCommand(sqlWrite, conn);

    // Create parameter for insert command.
    SqlParameter prm;
    if(image != null)
    {
        // Add a parameter for the image binary data.
        prm = new  SqlParameter("@BlobData", SqlDbType.VarBinary,
            image.Length, ParameterDirection.Input, false,
            0, 0, null, DataRowVersion.Current, image);
    }
    else
    {
        // Add a parameter for a null image.
        prm = new  SqlParameter("@BlobData", SqlDbType.VarBinary, 0,
            ParameterDirection.Input, false,
            0, 0, null, DataRowVersion.Current,
            System.DBNull.Value);
    }

    // Add the parameter to the command.
    cmdWrite.Parameters.Add(prm);

    // Execute the command to update the image in the database.
    conn.Open( );
```

Example 9-14. File: BinaryDataForm.cs (continued)

```
        cmdWrite.ExecuteNonQuery( );
        conn.Close( );

        // End the binding manager edit.
        bm.EndCurrentEdit( );
        // Use the DataAdapter to update the table data.
        da.Update(ds.Tables[TABLENAME]);
    }

    private void moveFirstButton_Click(object sender, System.EventArgs e)
    {
        bm.Position = 0;
    }

    private void movePreviousButton_Click(object sender, System.EventArgs e)
    {
        bm.Position -= 1;
    }

    private void moveNextButton_Click(object sender, System.EventArgs e)
    {
        bm.Position += 1;
    }

    private void moveLastButton_Click(object sender, System.EventArgs e)
    {
        bm.Position = bm.Count - 1;
    }
```

Discussion

You can write a BLOB to a data source using several techniques:

- Issue a SQL INSERT or UPDATE statement and pass in the BLOB value as an input parameter as shown in the solution code. With SQL Server, if the BLOB contains character data, use a SqlDbType.Text or SqlDbType.NText parameter and pass in the BLOB as a String; if the BLOB contains binary data, use a SqlDbType. Image parameter and pass in the BLOB as a Byte array.

- Create a DataRow and define its schema for the binary types as described previously or retrieve the schema from the data source using the FillSchema( ) method of the DataAdapter. Add the row to a DataTable and use the Update( ) method of the DataAdapter to update the data source. Recipe 9.13 shows an example of this technique.

You can read a BLOB from a data source using several techniques:

- Use a DataReader as shown in the solution code. While this approach is more complicated than using the ExecuteScalar( ) solution, it is more flexible and capable of dealing with very large BLOB data. Large BLOB data needs to be treated differently than other data when reading with a DataReader since the data cannot be contained in a single row. The ExecuteReader( ) method of the Command object that is used to create the DataReader has an overload that takes an argument from the CommandBehavior enumeration.

Passing the value CommandBehavior.SequentialAccess causes the DataReader to load the data sequentially as it is received rather than the default behavior of loading one row of data at a time. Some data sources do not behave in this way—for example, Microsoft Access reads the entire BLOB into memory rather than loading it sequentially as it is received. The default behavior of the DataReader allows data to be read from fields in the row in any order. When using SequentialAccess, the fields must be read in the order that they are retrieved and once a field is read, the previous fields in that row are no longer available.

- Use the GetBytes( ) typed accessor method to read the binary data from the BLOB into a Byte array. This method allows you to read the data as a sequence of smaller pieces of a defined number of bytes (chunks) to reduce system resources required when with dealing with large files. The solution demonstrates this using a buffer with an arbitrary size of 100 bytes.

- Use the GetChars( ) typed accessor method to read character BLOB data into a Char array or the GetString( ) typed accessor method to read the data into a String variable. Check for null values when using typed accessor methods, if necessary.

- Use the ExecuteScalar( ) method of the Command object with a SQL SELECT statement that returns the BLOB. Cast the result of the ExecuteScalar( ) method to a Byte array if it contains binary data or to a String if it contains character data. The following code demonstrates this technique:

```
image = (Byte[])cmd.ExecuteScalar( );
```

A BLOB can be quite large and may require a lot of system memory to be written to a data source as a single value. In addition to reading BLOBs in chunks, some data sources allow you to write a BLOB to the data source in chunks. For more information consult the MSDN Library and the documentation for your .NET data provider.

9.12 Reading and Writing Binary Data with Oracle

Problem

You need to read and write binary data from and to an Oracle database.

Solution

Use the techniques shown in the following example.

The sample code contains two event handlers:

Read Button.Click

Clears the controls on the form and builds a SQL statement to get the record for the specified ID from the Oracle table TBL0912. A connection is created and a command is built using the SQL statement and executed to build a DataReader. The BLOB is retrieved from the DataReader and displayed in the PictureBox on the form. The CLOB and NCLOB values are retrieved from the DataReader and displayed in text boxes on the form.

Write Button.Click

Gets the ID from the TextBox on the form. A BLOB is retrieved from a user-specified file and loaded into a Byte array. An Oracle DataAdapter is created and a new table is created using the FillSchema( ) command. A CommandBuilder is created from the DataAdapter. A new row is created where the BLOB value is set from the file specified by the user and the CLOB, and NCLOB values are set from the text boxes on the form. The new row is added to the table and the data updated back to the source.

The C# code is shown in Example 9-15.

Example 9-15. File: ReadWriteBinaryDataFromOracleForm.cs

```csharp
// Namespaces, variables, and constants
using System;
using System.Configuration;
using System.Drawing;
using System.Windows.Forms;
using System.Text;
using System.IO;

using System.Data;
using System.Data.OracleClient;

private OpenFileDialog ofd;

private const String TABLENAME        = "TBL0912";

private const String ID_FIELD         = "ID";
private const String BLOBFIELD_FIELD  = "BLOBFIELD";
private const String CLOBFIELD_FIELD  = "CLOBFIELD";
private const String NCLOBFIELD_FIELD = "NCLOBFIELD";

// ...

private void readButton_Click(object sender, System.EventArgs e)
{
```

Example 9-15. File: ReadWriteBinaryDataFromOracleForm.cs (continued)

```
    // Clear the controls.
    blobPictureBox.Image = null;
    clobTextBox.Clear( );
    nclobTextBox.Clear( );

    String sqlText = "SELECT * FROM " + TABLENAME + " WHERE ID = " +
        idTextBox.Text;

    // Create the connection and command.
    OracleConnection conn = new OracleConnection(
        ConfigurationSettings.AppSettings["Oracle_ConnectString"]);
    OracleCommand cmd = new OracleCommand(sqlText, conn);
    conn.Open( );

    // Create the DataReader.
    OracleDataReader dr = cmd.ExecuteReader( );
    // Iterate over the collection of rows in the DataReader.
    if(dr.Read( ))
    {
        // Retrieve the BLOB into a stream.
        Byte[] blob = null;
        if(!dr.IsDBNull(1))
            blob = (Byte[])dr.GetOracleLob(1).Value;
        MemoryStream ms = new MemoryStream(blob);
        // Display the BLOB in the PictureBox.
        blobPictureBox.Image = Image.FromStream(ms);
        ms.Close( );

        // Get the CLOB.
        if(!dr.IsDBNull(2))
            clobTextBox.Text = dr.GetOracleLob(2).Value.ToString( );

        // Get the NCLOB.
        if(!dr.IsDBNull(3))
            nclobTextBox.Text = dr.GetOracleLob(3).Value.ToString( );
    }
    else
    {
        MessageBox.Show("No record found.", "Access Oracle LOB Data",
            MessageBoxButtons.OK, MessageBoxIcon.Exclamation);
    }

    dr.Close( );
    conn.Close( );
}

private void writeButton_Click(object sender, System.EventArgs e)
{
    // Get the user-supplied ID.
    int id;
    try
    {
```

Example 9-15. File: ReadWriteBinaryDataFromOracleForm.cs (continued)

```csharp
        id = Convert.ToInt32(idTextBox.Text);
}
catch(System.Exception ex)
{
    MessageBox.Show(ex.Message, "Access Oracle LOB Data",
        MessageBoxButtons.OK, MessageBoxIcon.Exclamation);
    return;
}

// Save the BLOB, CLOB, and NCLOB.
if (ofd.ShowDialog( ) == DialogResult.OK)
{
    // Get a BLOB from a user-specified file.
    FileStream fs = new FileStream(ofd.FileName,
        FileMode.OpenOrCreate, FileAccess.Read);
    Byte[] blob = new Byte[fs.Length];
    fs.Read(blob, 0, blob.Length);
    fs.Close( );

    // Create a DataAdapter and table.
    OracleDataAdapter da = new OracleDataAdapter("SELECT * FROM " +
        TABLENAME,
        ConfigurationSettings.AppSettings["Oracle_ConnectString"]);
    DataTable table = new DataTable( );
    // Just get the schema.
    da.FillSchema(table, SchemaType.Source);
    OracleCommandBuilder cb = new OracleCommandBuilder(da);

    // Create a row containing the new BLOB, CLOB, and NCLOB data.
    DataRow row = table.NewRow( );
    row[ID_FIELD] = id;
    row[BLOBFIELD_FIELD] = blob;
    if(clobTextBox.TextLength > 0)
        row[CLOBFIELD_FIELD] = clobTextBox.Text;
    if(nclobTextBox.TextLength > 0)
        row[NCLOBFIELD_FIELD] = nclobTextBox.Text;
    // Add the row to the table.
    table.Rows.Add(row);

    // Update the Oracle database using the DataAdapter.
    try
    {
        da.Update(table);
    }
    catch(System.Exception ex)
    {
        MessageBox.Show(ex.Message, "Access Oracle LOB Data",
            MessageBoxButtons.OK,
            MessageBoxIcon.Exclamation);
        return;
    }
```

Example 9-15. File: ReadWriteBinaryDataFromOracleForm.cs (continued)

```
    MessageBox.Show("Record successfully created.",
        "Access Oracle LOB Data", MessageBoxButtons.OK,
        MessageBoxIcon.Information);
    }
}
```

Discussion

The GetOracleLob( ) typed accessor method of the OracleDataReader gets the value of the specified column as an OracleLob object representing a Large Object Binary (LOB) data type stored on an Oracle server. An Oracle LOB can be one of three types as described in Table 9-4.

Table 9-4. Oracle LOB data type

Data Type	Description
Blob	Oracle data type containing binary data with a maximum size of 4 GB. This data type maps to a Byte array.
Clob	Oracle data type containing character data based on the default character set of the server with a maximum size of 4 GB. This data type maps to a String.
NClob	Oracle data type containing character data based on the national character set of the server with a maximum size of 4 GB. This data type maps to a String.

The Oracle .NET data provider handles CLOB and NCLOB data as Unicode. Each character is therefore two bytes long.

See Recipe 9.12 for a general discussion about reading and writing BLOB data from and to a data source.

9.13 Performing Batch Updates with a DataAdapter

Problem

When you use a DataAdapter to perform updates, it makes a separate round trip to the server for each row. You want to batch all of the updates into a single call to the server to improve performance.

Solution

Use the RowUpdating event raised by the DataAdapter to build a single batched SQL statement that gets executed using the ExecuteNonQuery( ) method.

The sample code contains three event handlers:

Form.Load

Sets up the sample by creating a DataAdapter based on a SELECT statement of CategoryID, CategoryName, and Description fields of the Categories table in the Northwind database. A CommandBuilder is created to supply updating logic. A method is attached to the RowUpdating event of the DataAdapter. A new table is created and filled with the schema and data from the Categories table from the Northwind database. The properties of the AutoIncrement *CategoryID* field are set up. Finally, the default view of the table is bound to the data grid on the form.

Update Button.Click

Calls the Update( ) method of the DataAdapter. The DataAdapter.RowUpdating handler (described next) builds a batch SQL update string, which is executed using the ExecuteScalar( ) method after Update( ) is called.

DataAdapter.RowUpdating

Is called before each row is updated by the DataAdapter. The SQL command to be used to update the row by the DataAdapter is retrieved from the CommandText property of the Command object. The parameters for the Command are iterated over and each parameter variable in the update statement is replaced with the value for that parameter. Single quote delimiters are added around the string values. Finally, the statement is added to a StringBuilder object and the Status property of the Command is set to UpdateStatus.SkipCurrent row so that the data source is not updated by the DataAdapter. Instead, the update is performed by executing the batch SQL statement created by this event handler.

The C# code is shown in Example 9-16.

Example 9-16. File: CustomAdapterBatchUpdateForm.cs

```csharp
// Namespaces, variables, and constants
using System;
using System.Configuration;
using System.Text;
using System.Data;
using System.Data.SqlClient;

private const String CATEGORIES_TABLE    = "Categories";
private const String CATEGORYID_FIELD    = "CategoryID";

private DataTable dt;
private SqlDataAdapter da;
private SqlCommandBuilder cb;
private StringBuilder sb;

// ...
```

Example 9-16. File: CustomAdapterBatchUpdateForm.cs (continued)

```csharp
private void CustomAdapterBatchUpdateForm_Load(object sender,
    System.EventArgs e)
{
    String sqlText = "SELECT CategoryID, CategoryName, Description " +
        "FROM Categories";

    // Fill the categories table for editing.
    da = new SqlDataAdapter(sqlText,
        ConfigurationSettings.AppSettings["Sql_ConnectString"]);
    // CommandBuilder supplies updating logic.
    cb = new SqlCommandBuilder(da);
    // Handle the RowUpdating event to batch the update.
    da.RowUpdating += new SqlRowUpdatingEventHandler(da_RowUpdating);
    // Create table and fill with orders schema and data.
    dt = new DataTable(CATEGORIES_TABLE);
    da.FillSchema(dt, SchemaType.Source);
    // Set up the autoincrement column.
    dt.Columns[CATEGORYID_FIELD].AutoIncrementSeed = -1;
    dt.Columns[CATEGORYID_FIELD].AutoIncrementStep = -1;
    // Fill the DataSet.
    da.Fill(dt);

    // Bind the default view of the table to the grid.
    dataGrid.DataSource = dt.DefaultView;
}

private void updateButton_Click(object sender, System.EventArgs e)
{
    // Create a new SQL statement for all updates.
    sb = new StringBuilder();

    // Update the data source.
    da.Update(dt);

    if(sb.Length > 0)
    {
        // Create a connection command with the aggregate update command.
        SqlConnection conn = new SqlConnection(
            ConfigurationSettings.AppSettings["Sql_ConnectString"]);
        SqlCommand cmd = new SqlCommand(sb.ToString(), conn);
        // Execute the update command.
        conn.Open();
        cmd.ExecuteScalar();
        conn.Close();

        // Refresh the DataTable.
        dt.Clear();
        da.Fill(dt);
    }
}
```

Example 9-16. File: CustomAdapterBatchUpdateForm.cs (continued)

```
private void da_RowUpdating(object sender, SqlRowUpdatingEventArgs e)
{
    // Get the command for the current row update.
    StringBuilder sqlText =
        new StringBuilder(e.Command.CommandText.ToString());
    // Replace the parameters with values.
    for(int i = e.Command.Parameters.Count - 1; i >= 0; i--)
    {
        SqlParameter parm = e.Command.Parameters[i];
        if(parm.SqlDbType == SqlDbType.NVarChar ||
            parm.SqlDbType == SqlDbType.NText)
            // Quotes around the CategoryName and Description fields
            sqlText.Replace(parm.ParameterName,
                "'" + parm.Value.ToString() + "'");
        else
            sqlText.Replace(parm.ParameterName,
                parm.Value.ToString());
    }
    // Add the row command to the aggregate update command.
    sb.Append(sqlText.ToString() + ";");

    // Skip the DataAdapter update of the row.
    e.Status = UpdateStatus.SkipCurrentRow;
}
```

Discussion

When a DataAdapter is used to update the data source with changes made to disconnected data in a DataSet or DataTable, a RowUpdating event is raised before the command to update each changed row executes. The event handler receives the SqlRowUpdatingEventArgs argument containing information about the event. Table 9-5 lists the properties of SqlRowUpdatingEventArgs used to access information specific to the event.

Table 9-5. SqlRowUpdatingEventArgs properties

Property	Description
Command	Gets or sets the Command executed to perform the row update.
Errors	Gets errors raised by the .NET Framework data provider when the Command executes.
Row	Gets the DataRow that is being updated.
StatementType	Gets the type of SQL statement to execute to update the row. This is one of the following values: Select, Insert, Update, or Delete.
Status	Gets the UpdateStatus of the Command. This is one of the UpdateStatus enumeration values described in Table 9-6.
TableMapping	Gets the DataTableMapping object to use when updating.

The UpdateStatus is set to ErrorsOccurred when an error occurs while updating a row; otherwise it is set to Continue. UpdateStatus can be used to specify what to do with the current and remaining rows during an update. Table 9-6 describes the UpdateStatus enumeration values.

Table 9-6. UpdateStatus enumeration values

Value	Description
Continue	Continue processing rows.
ErrorsOccurred	Raise an error.
SkipAllRemainingRows	Do not update the current row and do not update the rows that have not yet been processed.
SkipCurrentRow	Do not update the current row. Continue processing with the next row.

To batch the update commands generated by the DataAdapter, the solution does the following in the RowUpdating event handler for each row updated:

- Gets the CommandText that will be used to update the row in the data source.
- Replaces the parameters in the CommandText with the parameter values applying required delimiters to each value. Appends the result to the batch command text.
- Sets the UpdateStatus of the Command to SkipCurrentRow so that the update for the row is not performed.

Once all of the rows have been processed, execute the assembled batch command text against the data source using the ExecuteScalar( ) method of a Command object.

The solution delimits the string values for the CategoryName and Description fields in the Categories table from the Northwind database used in this example. Ensure that strings, dates, and any other fields are properly delimited when values are substituted for parameter names in the DataAdapter.RowUpdating event handler. Delimit column and table names as well, if necessary.

Although this solution uses the CommandBuilder to generate the updating logic for the DataAdapter, the solution remains fundamentally the same if you use your own custom updating logic. One thing to keep in mind: the solution code iterates in reverse order through the parameters collection so that parameters are replaced correctly if there are more than nine parameters; if they were processed in forward order, parameter @p1 would cause the replacement for parameter @p10, @p11, and so on. When using custom updating logic, consider the potential problems that might occur if one parameter name is the start of another parameter name when replacing the parameters with the values in the DataRow.RowUpdating event handler.

Ensure that you set the AutoIncrementSeed and AutoIncrementStep properties prior to filling the DataSet; otherwise, the seed will be incorrect starting at one less than the largest AutoIncrement field value retrieved from the database.

9.14 Refreshing a DataSet Automatically Using Extended Properties

Problem

You need to automatically refresh a DataSet periodically.

Solution

Use extended properties and a timer.

The sample code contains two event handlers and one method:

Form.Load

> Sets up the sample by creating a DataTable containing the Categories table from the Northwind database. The default view of the table is bound to a data grid on the form. A second DataTable with the auto-refreshing functionality is created that also contains the Categories table from the Northwind database. The default view of the auto-refreshing table is bound to a second data grid on the form. An extended property RefreshTime is added to the auto-refreshing table and set to 15 seconds—the value of the constant DATAREFRESH_SECONDS in the sample—into the future. Finally, a thread timer is created with a TimerClassback delegate CheckRefreshDataSet, with a due time of one second, and a period of one second.

Update Button.Click

> Uses a DataAdapter to update changes made to the first DataTable back to the data source.

CheckRefreshDataSet( )

> This method is called periodically by the thread timer. The method checks whether the current time is later than the time in the RefreshTime extended property of the auto-refreshing table. If it is, a DataAdapter is used to fill the table with the latest data from the data source and the RefreshTime extended property is once again set to 15 seconds into the future.

The C# code is shown in Example 9-17.

Example 9-17. File: AutomaticRefreshDataSetForm.cs

```
// Namespaces, variables, and constants
using System;
using System.Configuration;
using System.Threading;
using System.Data;
using System.Data.SqlClient;

private const String CATEGORIES_TABLE          = "Categories";
```

Example 9-17. File: AutomaticRefreshDataSetForm.cs (continued)

```
private const int DATAREFRESH_SECONDS            = 15;
private const int DATASETCHECKREFRESHINTERVAL_MS = 1000;

private DataTable dt, dtRefresh;
private SqlDataAdapter da, daRefresh;

private System.Threading.Timer timer;

// ..

private void AutomaticRefreshDataSetForm_Load(object sender,
    System.EventArgs e)
{
    String sqlText =
        "SELECT CategoryID, CategoryName, Description FROM Categories";

    // Fill the categories table for editing.
    da = new SqlDataAdapter(sqlText,
        ConfigurationSettings.AppSettings["Sql_ConnectString"]);
    SqlCommandBuilder cd = new SqlCommandBuilder(da);
    dt = new DataTable(CATEGORIES_TABLE);
    da.FillSchema(dt, SchemaType.Source);
    da.Fill(dt);

    // Bind the default view of the table to the grid.
    dataGrid.DataSource = dt.DefaultView;

    // Fill the autorefresh categories table.
    daRefresh = new SqlDataAdapter(sqlText,
        ConfigurationSettings.AppSettings["Sql_ConnectString"]);
    dtRefresh = new DataTable(CATEGORIES_TABLE);
    daRefresh.FillSchema(dtRefresh, SchemaType.Source);
    daRefresh.Fill(dtRefresh);

    // Bind the default view of the table to the grid.
    refreshDataGrid.DataSource = dtRefresh.DefaultView;

    // Set the refresh time for the data.
    dtRefresh.ExtendedProperties["RefreshTime"] =
        DateTime.Now.AddSeconds(DATAREFRESH_SECONDS).ToString();
    // Start the timer.
    timer = new System.Threading.Timer(
        new TimerCallback(CheckRefreshDatabase), null,
        DATASETCHECKREFRESHINTERVAL_MS, DATASETCHECKREFRESHINTERVAL_MS);
}

private void updateButton_Click(object sender, System.EventArgs e)
{
    // Update the categories edited to the data source.
    da.Update(dt);
}
```

Example 9-17. File: AutomaticRefreshDataSetForm.cs (continued)

```csharp
private void CheckRefreshDatabase(Object state)
{
    DateTime now = DateTime.Now;
    // Check if the specified number of seconds have elapsed.
    if (Convert.ToDateTime(dtRefresh.ExtendedProperties
        ["RefreshTime"].ToString()) < now)
    {
        // Refresh the table.
        daRefresh.Fill(dtRefresh);
        // Update the next refresh time.
        dtRefresh.ExtendedProperties["RefreshTime"] =
            now.AddSeconds(DATAREFRESH_SECONDS).ToString();

        resultTextBox.Text = "Table refreshed (" + now.ToString("T") +
            ")" + Environment.NewLine + resultTextBox.Text;
    }
}
```

Discussion

The `ExtendedProperties` property accesses a `PropertyCollection` of custom information for a `DataSet`, `DataTable`, `DataColumn`, `DataRelation`, or `Constraint` object. The `PropertyCollection` extends the `Hashtable` class to store information as a collection of key-and-value pairs. The extended property data must be stored as strings; otherwise, it will not be persisted when the data is written as XML. Add items to the collection using the `Add( )` method, remove them with the `Remove( )` method, and access them using the indexer in C# or the `Item( )` property in VB.NET. For more information about members of the `PropertyCollection` class, see the MSDN Library.

There are three timers in the Visual Studio .NET and the .NET Framework:

- The Windows-based timer `System.Windows.Form.Timer` (available on the Windows Form tab of the Toolbox) is designed for a single-threaded environment where UI threads are used for processing. This is the simplest timer to use but also the least accurate with an accuracy limited to 55ms.

- The thread timer `System.Threading.Timer` is a simple, lightweight timer that uses callback methods to periodically run a task on a separate thread. This timer can only be used programmatically. This timer is more accurate than the Windows-based timer since the time interval between callbacks is specified in milliseconds.

- The server-based timer `System.Timers.Timer` (available on the Components tab of the Toolbox) is designed for use with worker threads in a multi-threaded environment. This timer uses server ticks generated out-of-process and is the most accurate of the three since the time interval between timer event firings is specified in milliseconds.

The thread timer uses a ThreadCallback delegate to specify the method to execute. This delegate is specified when the Timer is constructed and cannot be changed. The method executes in a thread pool supplied by the system rather than in the thread that created the timer.

When the thread timer is created, the *due time* (the time to wait before first execution of the method) and the *period* (the amount of time to wait between subsequent executions) are specified in the constructor. A due time of 0 results in the callback being invoked immediately; a due time of Timeout.Infinite results in the callback method never being invoked. A period value of 0 or Timeout.Infinite results in the callback invoked only once as long as the due time is not infinite. You can change the behavior of the timer at any time by using the Change( ) method. When the timer is no longer needed, call the Dispose( ) method to free its resources.

CHAPTER 10

Enumerating and Maintaining Database Objects

10.0 Introduction

This chapter describes techniques to get schema information and metadata from databases, manage database objects, and enumerate installed database providers and drivers.

There are many ways to get schema information and other information from a SQL Server database. Some of these techniques are:

- SQL Server Distributed Management Objects (SQL-DMO) is a collection of objects that encapsulate SQL Server database and replication management. You can use SQL-DMO to automate SQL Server tasks, create and administer SQL Server objects, and install and configure replication. You can use SQL-DMO from a .NET application through COM interop. Recipe 10.1 shows how to use SQL-DMO to get a list of SQL Servers on your network.

- SQL Server 2000 introduced *information schema views* that provide system-table independent access to SQL Server metadata. They provide an alternative to system stored procedures and conform to the SQL-92 Standard and are less tightly bound to the underlying database. Recipe 10.2 shows how to use information schema views to retrieve database schema information. Recipe 10.11 uses information schema views to create relationships in a DataSet at runtime based on the relationships defined in the SQL server.

- System stored procedures can be used to get database schema information. Recipe 10.3 shows how to use the sp_helpconstraint system stored procedure to get default values for columns. Recipe 10.4 shows how to use the sp_help system stored procedure to get the length of non-string columns.

The Connection object in the OLE DB .NET data provider has a GetOleDbSchemaTable( ) method that returns schema information from an OLE DB data source. Recipe 10.2 shows how to use this method to return SQL server database schema information. Recipe 10.12 shows how to list the tables in a Microsoft Access database using this method.

Recipe 10.5 shows how to use the ExecuteScalar( ) method of the Command object to efficiently determine how many records are in a result set matching specified criteria.

Data Definition Language (DDL) statements are used to manage objects in a SQL Server database—for example, adding or modifying objects such as databases, tables, indices, and views. You can execute a DDL statement through a .NET data provider to manipulate the database or catalog schema. Since DDL commands do not return a result set as a query does, these statements are executed using the ExecuteNonQuery( ) method of the Command object. Recipe 10.7 shows how to execute a DDL statement to create a new SQL Server database. Recipe 10.8 shows how to create a new table in a SQL Server database. Recipe 10.15 creates a method CreateTableFromSchema( ) that dynamically constructs a DLL statement from a DataTable schema and executes that DDL to create a table in a SQL Server database.

ADO Extensions for DDL and Security (ADOX) extend the ADO objects and programming model with objects for schema creation and maintenance and for security. Recipe 10.6 shows how to use ADOX programmatically from .NET though COM interop to create a new Microsoft Access database. Recipe 10.14 shows how to use ADOX to list the tables in a Microsoft Access database.

The Jet OLE DB Provider and Replication Objects (JRO) library was created to isolate Jet-specific functionality from the generic ADO library. Recipe 10.10 shows how to use JRO to compact a Microsoft Access database.

The SQL SET statements alter session handling of current information. Recipe 10.9 shows how to retrieve the execution plan for a query. Recipe 10.12 shows how to retrieve only column metadata when a query is executed.

Every Windows system has ODBC drivers and OLE DB providers installed on it. You can examine the registry to get a list of which are installed. Recipe 10.16 does this for ODBC drivers while Recipe 10.13 does it for OLE DB Providers. Recipe 10.16 also uses a SQL Server extended stored procedure to enumerate the OLE DB providers.

10.1 Listing SQL Servers

Problem

You need to obtain a list of SQL Servers available on the network.

Solution

Use SQL Server Distributed Management Objects (SQL-DMO) to retrieve a list of available SQL Servers.

You'll need a reference to the Microsoft SQLDMO Object Library from the COM tab in Visual Studio .NET's Add Reference Dialog.

The sample code retrieves and displays a list of all SQL Servers running on a local network segment by using SQL-DMO through COM interop.

The C# code is shown in Example 10-1.

Example 10-1. File: ServerListForm.cs

```
// Namespaces, variables, and constants
using System;

// ...

serverListListBox.Items.Clear( );

// Create a SQL Distributed Management Objects (SQL-DMO)
// application object.
SQLDMO.Application dmo = new SQLDMO.Application( );
// Retrieve the available servers.
SQLDMO.NameList serverNameList = dmo.ListAvailableSQLServers( );

// Iterate over the collection of available servers.
for(int i = 0; i < serverNameList.Count; i++)
{
    if (serverNameList.Item(i) != null)
        serverListListBox.Items.Add(serverNameList.Item(i));
}
serverListListBox.Items.Add("End of list.");
```

Discussion

SQL Server Distributed Management Objects (SQL-DMO) is a collection of objects that encapsulate SQL Server database and replication management. SQL-DMO is used to automate SQL Server tasks, create and administer SQL Server objects, and install and configure replication. You can use SQL-DMO from a .NET application through COM interop. For more information about SQL-DMO, see Microsoft SQL Server Books Online.

The ListAvailableSQLServers( ) method of the SQL-DMO Application object returns a NameList object that enumerates all running servers that listen on named pipes and are located in the same domain. Any servers running on Windows 9*x* will not be reported because they do not listen on named pipes. The discovery is based on a network broadcast, so if you are disconnected from a network, local servers will not be enumerated.

This procedure does not return desktop (MSDE) instances.

10.2 Retrieving Database Schema Information from SQL Server

Problem

You need to retrieve database schema information from a SQL Server database.

Solution

Retrieve table schema information using either information schema views or the OLE DB .NET data provider `Connection` object.

The sample code retrieves a list of tables in the Northwind sample database.

The C# code is shown in Example 10-2.

Example 10-2. File: DatabaseSchemaForm.cs

```
// Namespaces, variables, and constants
using System;
using System.Configuration;
using System.Data;
using System.Data.SqlClient;
using System.Data.OleDb;

// ...

DataTable schemaTable;

if(sqlServerRadioButton.Checked)
{
    String getSchemaTableText = "SELECT * " +
        "FROM INFORMATION_SCHEMA.TABLES " +
        "WHERE TABLE_TYPE = 'BASE TABLE' ORDER BY TABLE_TYPE";

    // Retrieve the schema table contents.
    SqlDataAdapter da = new SqlDataAdapter(getSchemaTableText,
        ConfigurationSettings.AppSettings["Sql_ConnectString"]);
    schemaTable = new DataTable( );
    da.Fill(schemaTable);

    schemaDataGrid.CaptionText = "SQL Server .NET Provider";
}
else
{
    OleDbConnection conn = new OleDbConnection(
        ConfigurationSettings.AppSettings["OleDb_ConnectString"]);
    conn.Open( );
    // Get the schema table.
    schemaTable = conn.GetOleDbSchemaTable(OleDbSchemaGuid.Tables,
        new object[] {null, null, null, "TABLE"});
    conn.Close( );
```

Example 10-2. File: DatabaseSchemaForm.cs (continued)

```
        schemaDataGrid.CaptionText = "OLE DB .NET Provider";
}

// Bind the default view of schema table to the grid.
schemaDataGrid.DataSource = schemaTable.DefaultView;
```

Discussion

The first solution uses information schema views that are available in SQL Server 7.0 and later. These views provide system-table independent access to SQL Server metadata. Although based on the sysobjects and syscomments system tables, the views allow applications to continue to work properly even if the system tables change. They provide an alternative to the system stored procedures that were previously used and are still available. The INFORMATION_SCHEMA views conform to the SQL-92 Standard.

The views are defined within each database in a schema named INFORMATION_SCHEMA. To access them, specify the fully qualified view name. In the solution, the view for the tables is accessed through the following syntax:

```
INFORMATION_SCHEMA.TABLES
```

Table 10-1 lists the information schema views available in SQL Server 2000.

Table 10-1. Information schema views

Name	Description
CHECK_CONSTRAINTS	CHECK constraints
COLUMN_DOMAIN_USAGE	Columns that have a user-defined data type
COLUMN_PRIVILEGES	Columns with a privilege granted to or by the current user
COLUMNS	All columns
CONSTRAINT_COLUMN_USAGE	Columns that have a constraint defined on them
CONSTRAINT_TABLE_USAGE	Tables that have a constraint defined on them
DOMAIN_CONSTRAINTS	User-defined data types with a rule bound to them
DOMAINS	All user-defined data types
KEY_COLUMN_USAGE	Columns constrained as a key
PARAMETERS	All parameters for user-defined functions and stored procedures
REFERENTIAL_CONSTRAINTS	All foreign constraints
ROUTINE_COLUMNS	Columns returned by table-valued functions
ROUTINES	All user-defined functions and stored procedures
SCHEMATA	All databases
TABLE_CONSTRAINTS	All table constraints
TABLE_PRIVILEGES	Tables with a privilege granted to or by the current user

Table 10-1. Information schema views (continued)

Name	Description
TABLES	All tables
VIEW_COLUMN_USAGE	Columns used in a view definition
VIEW_TABLE_USAGE	Tables used in a view
VIEWS	All views

The metadata returned will be limited to that which the user has permission to view. Like any other views, information schema views can also be joined in queries or participate in complex queries to extract specific information. For detailed information about the different views available, refer to SQL Server Books Online.

The solution shows how to retrieve table metadata using the INFORMATION_SCHEMA. TABLES view. It returns data as shown in Table 10-2.

Table 10-2. INFORMATION_SCHEMA.TABLES metadata

Column name	Data type	Description
TABLE_CATALOG	nvarchar(128)	Database name
TABLE_SCHEMA	nvarchar(128)	Table owner
TABLE_NAME	sysname	Table name
TABLE_TYPE	varchar(10)	Table type (either BASE_TABLE or VIEW)

The TABLES view is queried for all columns where the table type is BASE_TABLE in order to return only information about tables and not views.

The second solution uses the GetOleDbSchemaTable( ) method of the OleDbConnection object. This method returns schema information from a database as indicated by a GUID enumerated in the OleDbSchemaGuid class and detailed in Table 10-3.

Table 10-3. OleDbSchemaGuid public fields

Field	Description
Assertions	Assertions
Catalogs	Physical attributes and assertions for catalogs accessible from the data source
Character_Sets	Character sets
Check_Constraints	Check constraints
Check_Constraints_By_Table	Check constraints defined for a catalog
Collations	Character collations
Columns	Columns in tables and view
Column_Domain_Usage	Columns that are dependant on a domain defined in the catalog
Column_Privileges	Privileges on columns

Table 10-3. OleDbSchemaGuid public fields (continued)

Field	Description
Constraint_Column_Usage	Columns used by referential constraints, unique constraints, check constraints, and assertions
Constraint_Table_Usage	Tables used by referential constraints, unique constraints, check constraints, and assertions
DbInfoLiterals	Provider-specific literals used in text commands
Foreign_Keys	Foreign key columns
Indexes	Indexes
Key_Column_Usage	Columns constrained as keys
Primary_Keys	Columns that comprise primary keys
Procedures	Procedures
Procedure_Columns	Columns of row sets returned by procedures
Procedure_Parameters	Parameters and return codes of procedures
Provider_Types	Base data types supported by the .NET data provider for OLE DB
Referential_Constraints	Referential constraints
Schemata	Schema objects
Sql_Languages	Conformance levels, options, and dialects supported by the SQL implementation processing data
Statistics	Statistics
Tables	Tables and views
Tables_Info	Tables and views
Table_Constraints	Table constraints
Table_Privileges	Table privileges
Table_Statistics	Available statistics on tables
Translations	Defined character translations
Trustee	Trustee defined in the data source
Usage_Privileges	USAGE privileges on objects
Views	Views
View_Column_Usage	Columns in views
View_Table_Usage	Tables in views

As for information schema views, the metadata returned is limited to that which the user has permission to view. In addition to taking the Guid schema argument, you can further restrict the results of the GetOleDbSchemaTable( ) through the second argument, which is an object array specifying column restrictions applied to the result columns in the order in which they are returned. In this example, the schema argument is Tables, which returns a four-column result set containing all tables and views in the database. The fourth column describes the table type; specifying TABLE as the fourth object in the restrictions object array limits the result set to user tables.

10.3 Retrieving Column Default Values from SQL Server

Problem

The DataColumn object exposes a Default property. While the FillSchema( ) method of the DataAdapter returns schema information, it does not include the default values for columns. You want to retrieve the default values of columns in a SQL Server table.

Solution

Use system stored procedures.

The sample code executes the system stored procedure sp_helpconstraint to get constraint information for the columns in the Orders table in the Northwind sample database. Column default values are identified and retrieved from the result set.

The C# code is shown in Example 10-3.

Example 10-3. File: ColumnDefaultsForm.cs

```
// Namespaces, variables, and constants
using System;
using System.Configuration;
using System.Text;
using System.Data;
using System.Data.SqlClient;

// ...

StringBuilder result = new StringBuilder( );

// Fill the Orders table with schema and data.
SqlDataAdapter da = new SqlDataAdapter("SELECT * FROM Orders",
    ConfigurationSettings.AppSettings["Sql_ConnectString"]);
DataTable ordersTable = new DataTable(ORDERS_TABLE);
da.FillSchema(ordersTable, SchemaType.Source);
da.Fill(ordersTable);

SqlConnection conn = new SqlConnection(
    ConfigurationSettings.AppSettings["Sql_ConnectString"]);

// Command for system stored procedure returning constraints
SqlCommand cmd = new SqlCommand("sp_helpconstraint", conn);
cmd.CommandType = CommandType.StoredProcedure;
cmd.Parameters.Add("@objname",SqlDbType.NVarChar,776);
cmd.Parameters[0].Value = "Orders";
cmd.Parameters.Add("@nomsg",SqlDbType.VarChar,5);
cmd.Parameters[1].Value = "nomsg";
```

Example 10-3. File: ColumnDefaultsForm.cs (continued)

```
// Create a DataReader from the stored procedure.
conn.Open( );
SqlDataReader dr = cmd.ExecuteReader( );

// Iterate over the constraints records in the DataReader.
while(dr.Read( ))
{
    // Select the default value constraints only.
    String constraintType = dr["constraint_type"].ToString( );
    if (constraintType.StartsWith("DEFAULT"))
    {
        String constraintKeys = dr["constraint_keys"].ToString( );
        // Only strips single quotes for numeric default types
        // add necessary handling as required for nonnumeric defaults
        String defaultValue =
            constraintKeys.Substring(1, constraintKeys.Length - 2);

        String colName = constraintType.Substring(
            (constraintType.LastIndexOf("column") + 7));

        ordersTable.Columns[colName].DefaultValue = defaultValue;

        result.Append("Column: " + colName + "   Default: " +
            defaultValue + Environment.NewLine);
    }
}
dr.Close( );
conn.Close( );

resultTextBox.Text = result.ToString( );
```

Discussion

The default value for a column in SQL Server is stored as a DEFAULT constraint. The system stored procedure sp_helpconstraint returns information about all constraints on a table. The procedure takes one mandatory parameter that specifies the table for which to return the constraint information.

The first column that the stored procedure returns is called constraint_type. As its name suggests, it specifies the type of constraint using the following pattern {constraint_type} [on column {column_name}]. For example, the default constraint on the Freight column in the Orders table in the Northwind sample database has a constraint type of DEFAULT on column *Freight*.

In the solution, a result set is created from the system stored procedure sp_helpconstraint specifying the Orders table. The constraint_type column is examined for each row to determine whether it begins with the word DEFAULT indicating a default constraint. For default constraints, the column name is the string following the word column in the constraint_type column.

Once the default constraints have been identified, the overloaded `constraint_keys` column contains the default value for the column. The default value is surrounded by parentheses as well as delimiters for nonnumeric fields—for example, single quotes by default in SQL Server for dates and strings, and an additional prefix N in the case of Unicode strings. These delimiters need to be stripped from the value before it can be assigned to the `DefaultValue` property for the column.

For more information about the `sp_helpconstraint` system stored procedure, see Microsoft SQL Server Books Online.

10.4   Determining the Length of Columns in a SQL Server Table

Problem

The `FillSchema( )` method of the `DataAdapter` returns the correct length in the `MaxLength` property for string columns in a SQL Server database, but it returns −1 for the length of all other fields. You need to get the length of columns other than string type columns.

Solution

Use the system stored procedure `sp_help`.

The sample code executes a batch query to return all rows from both the Orders and Order Details tables in the Northwind sample database. The extended stored procedure `sp_help` is used to get the length, precision, and scale of all columns in both tables.

The C# code is shown in Example 10-4.

Example 10-4. File: ColumnSchemaForm.cs

```
// Namespaces, variables, and constants
using System;
using System.Configuration;
using System.Collections;
using System.Text;
using System.Data;
using System.Data.SqlClient;

// ...

StringBuilder schemaInfo = new StringBuilder();

// Create a batch query to retrieve order and details.
String sqlText = "select OrderID, CustomerID, EmployeeID, OrderDate, " +
    "RequiredDate, ShippedDate, ShipVia, Freight, ShipName, " +
```

Example 10-4. File: ColumnSchemaForm.cs (continued)

```
    " ShipAddress, ShipCity, ShipRegion, ShipPostalCode, ShipCountry " +
    "FROM Orders;" +
    "SELECT OrderID, ProductID, UnitPrice, Quantity, Discount " +
    "FROM [Order Details];";

// Create the connection.
SqlConnection conn = new SqlConnection(
    ConfigurationSettings.AppSettings["Sql_ConnectString"]);

// Create DataAdapter.
SqlDataAdapter da = new SqlDataAdapter(sqlText, conn);

// Add table mappings.
da.TableMappings.Add("Table", "Orders");
da.TableMappings.Add("Table1", "Order Details");

// Create the DataSet.
DataSet ds = new DataSet( );
// Fill the schema and data.
da.FillSchema(ds, SchemaType.Mapped);
da.Fill(ds);

// Iterate over the table collection in the DataSet.
foreach(DataTable dt in ds.Tables)
{
    schemaInfo.Append("TABLE: " + dt.TableName + Environment.NewLine);

    // Create the command to retrieve column information.
    cmd = new SqlCommand("sp_help", conn);
    cmd.CommandType = CommandType.StoredProcedure;
    cmd.Parameters.Add("@objname", SqlDbType.NVarChar, 776);
    cmd.Parameters[0].Value = dt.TableName;

    conn.Open( );
    // Create the DataReader from the command.
    SqlDataReader dr = cmd.ExecuteReader( );
    // Get the second result set containing column information.
    dr.NextResult( );

    Hashtable colInfo = new Hashtable( );
    // Iterate over the second result to retrieve column information.
    while(dr.Read( ))
    {
        colInfo.Add(dr["Column_name"].ToString( ),
            "Length = " + dr["Length"] +
            "; Precision = " + dr["Prec"] +
            "; Scale = " + dr["Scale"]);
    }
    dr.Close( );
    conn.Close( );
```

Example 10-4. File: ColumnSchemaForm.cs (continued)

```csharp
// Iterate over the column collection in the table.
foreach(DataColumn col in dt.Columns)
{
    // Get column information.
    schemaInfo.Append("\tCOLUMN: " + col.ColumnName +
        Environment.NewLine);
    schemaInfo.Append("\tAllowDBNull: " + col.AllowDBNull +
        Environment.NewLine);
    schemaInfo.Append("\tAutoIncrement: " + col.AutoIncrement +
        Environment.NewLine);
    schemaInfo.Append("\tDataType: " + col.DataType +
        Environment.N      
                                                  .MaxLength +

                                                  ique +

                                                  [col.ColumnName] +
```

, in addition to the length of all fields, iate.

one optional parameter. When this result set returns data including the in columns named Length, Prec, and

in bytes, meaning that Unicode data le the value of the MaxLength property pCountry column of the Orders table 15 characters long) and Length = 30 (requires 30 characters to store the 15 Unicode characters).

For both the Orders and Order Details tables, the solution adds column length, precision, and scale data for each row in the sp_help result set to a Hashtable keyed on the column name. The code then iterates over the collection of columns in the table and displays the length, precision, and scale for each from the Hashtable. Information from the FillSchema( ) method of the DataAdapter is also included. The data type and nullable properties are available using both sp_help and FillSchema( ).

For more information about the sp_help system stored procedure, refer to Microsoft SQL Server Books Online.

The GetSchemaTable( ) method of the DataReader also returns all column lengths. The method returns a DataTable containing column metadata for a DataReader, where the ColumnSize column contains the lengths. For more information about the GetSchemaTable( ) method, see the discussion for Recipe 5.3.

10.5   Counting Records

Problem

You want to determine how many rows that meet certain criteria are in a table.

Solution

Use the ExecuteScalar( ) method of the Command object to determine the number of records in the table.

The sample code executes the COUNT function on the results of a query returning rows from the Orders table in the Northwind sample database, where the rows match a user-specified CustomerID.

The C# code is shown in Example 10-5.

Example 10-5. File: CountRecordForm.cs

```
// Namespaces, variables, and constants
using System;
using System.Configuration;
using System.Data;
using System.Data.SqlClient;

//...

// Create the connection.
SqlConnection conn = new SqlConnection(
    ConfigurationSettings.AppSettings["Sql_ConnectString"]);

// Build the query to count, including CustomerID criteria if specified.
String selectText = "SELECT COUNT(*) FROM Orders";
if(customerIdTextBox.Text.Trim( ) != "")
    selectText += " WHERE CustomerId='" + customerIdTextBox.Text + "'";

// Create the command to count the records.
SqlCommand cmd = new SqlCommand(selectText, conn);
// Execute the command, storing the results.
conn.Open( );
int recordCount = (int)cmd.ExecuteScalar( );
conn.Close( );
```

Discussion

The ExecuteScalar( ) method of the Command object returns a single value from a query rather than a table or a data stream. If the query returns a result set, this method returns the value of the first column of the first row.

The number of records matching certain criteria can be determined by executing a SQL statement that returns the COUNT(*) aggregate function and including a WHERE clause that specifies the criteria. Use the ExecuteScalar( ) method to execute the statement and return the count. Cast the result to an integer data type.

This technique can also be used with other aggregate functions to determine values such as averages or sums. For more information about aggregate functions, see Microsoft SQL Server Books Online.

10.6 Creating a New Access Database

Problem

You need to create a new Microsoft Access database.

Solution

Use ActiveX Database Objects Extensions (ADOX) from .NET through COM interop.

You'll need a reference to Microsoft ADO Ext. 2.7 for DDL and Security from the COM tab in Visual Studio .NET's Add Reference Dialog.

The sample code contains an event handler and a single method:

Button.Click
>   Allows the user to specify the filename for the new Access database and then calls the CreateAccessDatabase( ) method in the sample to create the database.

CreateAccessDatabase( )
>   This method uses ADOX through COM interop to create the new Access database having the specified filename.

The C# code is shown in Example 10-6.

Example 10-6. File: CreateAccessDatabaseForm.cs

```
// Namespaces, variables, and constants
using System;
using System.Windows.Forms;

// ...
```

Example 10-6. File: CreateAccessDatabaseForm.cs (continued)

```csharp
private void createButton_Click(object sender, System.EventArgs e)
{
    // Create the save file dialog object.
    SaveFileDialog sfd = new SaveFileDialog();
    sfd.InitialDirectory = System.IO.Path.GetTempPath();
    // Set the filter for Access databases.
    sfd.Filter = "Microsoft Access (*.mdb)|*.mdb";

    // Open the dialog.
    if (sfd.ShowDialog() == DialogResult.OK)
    {
        // Of OK selected, create the Access database.
        String fileName = sfd.FileName;

        try
        {
            CreateAccessDatabase(fileName);

            MessageBox.Show("Microsoft Access database " +
                fileName + " created.", "Create Access Database",
                MessageBoxButtons.OK,
                MessageBoxIcon.Information);
        }
        catch (System.Exception ex)
        {
            MessageBox.Show("Could not create database " +
                fileName + ". " + ex.Message,
                "Create Access Database",
                MessageBoxButtons.OK, MessageBoxIcon.Error);
        }
    }
}

private void CreateAccessDatabase(String fileName)
{
    String connectString =
        @"Provider=Microsoft.Jet.OLEDB.4.0;Data Source=" +
        fileName + ";";

    // Use ADOX to create the Access database.
    ADOX.Catalog cat = new ADOX.Catalog();
    try
    {
        cat.Create(connectString);
    }
    finally
    {
        cat = null;
    }
}
```

Discussion

ADO Extensions for DDL and Security (ADOX) extends the ADO objects and programming model with objects for schema creation and modification, and for security. ADOX is used to programmatically access and manipulate the objects in a database.

You can use ADOX from .NET through COM interop to create a new Microsoft Access database. Use the Create( ) method of the ADOX.Catalog object, passing a connection string for the new Access database as the argument.

10.7 Creating a New SQL Server Database

Problem

You need to create a new database in your SQL Server.

Solution

Use the CREATE DATABASE statement.

The sample code executes the DDL statement—using the ExecuteNonQuery( ) method of the Command object—to create a new database named *MyDatabase* in SQL Server.

The C# code is shown in Example 10-7.

Example 10-7. File: CreateServerDatabaseForm.cs

```
// Namespaces, variables, and constants
using System;
using System.Configuration;
using System.Text;
using System.Data;
using System.Data.SqlClient;

// ...

StringBuilder sb = new StringBuilder( );

// SQL DDL command text to create database.
String sqlText = "CREATE DATABASE MyDatabase ON PRIMARY " +
        "(NAME = MyDatabase_Data, " +
        "FILENAME = '" + DATAFILENAME + "', " +
        "SIZE = 2MB, MAXSIZE = 10MB, FILEGROWTH = 10%) " +
        "LOG ON (NAME = MyDatabase_Log, " +
        "FILENAME = '" + LOGFILENAME + "', " +
        "SIZE = 1MB, " +
        "MAXSIZE = 5MB, " +
        "FILEGROWTH = 10%)";
```

Example 10-7. File: CreateServerDatabaseForm.cs (continued)

```
sb.Append(sqlText + Environment.NewLine + Environment.NewLine);

// Create a connection.
SqlConnection conn = new SqlConnection(
    ConfigurationSettings.AppSettings["Sql_Master_ConnectString"]);

// Create the command to create the database.
SqlCommand cmd = new SqlCommand(sqlText, conn);
// Create the new database.
try
{
    conn.Open();
    cmd.ExecuteNonQuery();
    sb.Append("DataBase created successfully.");
}
catch (System.Exception ex)
{
    sb.Append(ex.ToString());
}
finally
{
    if (conn.State == ConnectionState.Open)
        conn.Close();
    conn.Close();
}

resultTextBox.Text = sb.ToString();
```

Discussion

There are two categories of SQL statements:

Database Definition Language (DDL)

> Used to manage all objects in the database, generally with CREATE, ALTER, and DROP statements to create, modify, and delete objects, respectively. These statements generally require DBA permissions to execute.

Database Management Language (DML)

> Used to manipulate—select, insert, update, and delete—data in the database objects. Database objects are defined using DDL.

The solution executes a DDL CREATE DATABASE statement to create a new database on a SQL Server.

You can programmatically drop the database by using the DROP DATABASE statement in a similar way. To drop the database created in the previous example, use the following code:

```
DROP DATABASE MyDatabase
```

The DROP DATABASE statement will fail if the database is in use; therefore, it might be necessary to restart the SQL Server in order to drop the database. System databases—master, model, msdb, and tempdb—cannot be dropped.

For more information about the CREATE DATABASE statement, the DROP DATABASE statement, or DDL, see Microsoft SQL Server Books Online.

The solution for Oracle databases and other databases is similar to that shown for SQL Server although the DDL syntax for each database varies slightly because of differences in database server capabilities and architecture. For more information about Oracle SQL syntax, see *Oracle in a Nutshell* (O'Reilly).

10.8   Adding Tables to a Database

Problem

You need to add a table to an existing database.

Solution

Use the CREATE TABLE statement.

The sample code executes the DDL statement—using the ExecuteNonQuery( ) method of the Command object—to add a table to an existing SQL Server database.

The C# code is shown in Example 10-8.

Example 10-8. File: AddTableToDatabaseForm.cs

```
// Namespaces, variables, and constants
using System;
using System.Configuration;
using System.Data;
using System.Data.SqlClient;

// ...

SqlConnection conn = new SqlConnection(
    ConfigurationSettings.AppSettings["Sql_ConnectString"]);

String createSql = "CREATE TABLE MyTable " +
    "(MyTableId int IDENTITY(1,1) PRIMARY KEY CLUSTERED)";

SqlCommand cmd = new SqlCommand(createSql, conn);
// Create the table in the database.
try
{
    conn.Open( );
    cmd.ExecuteNonQuery( );
    resultTextBox.Text = "Table created successfully";
```

Example 10-8. File: AddTableToDatabaseForm.cs (continued)

```
}
catch (System.Exception ex)
{
    resultTextBox.Text = ex.ToString( );
}
finally
{
    if (conn.State == ConnectionState.Open)
        conn.Close( );
}
```

Discussion

There are two categories of SQL statements:

Database Definition Language (DDL)
> Used to manage all objects in the database, generally with CREATE, ALTER, and DROP statements to create, modify, and delete objects, respectively. These statements generally require DBA permissions to execute.

Database Management Language (DML)
> Used to manipulate—select, insert, update, and delete—data in the database objects. Database objects are defined using DDL.

The solution executes a DDL CREATE TABLE statement to create a table in the database and a primary key on the new table in a SQL Server database.

You can programmatically drop a table using the DROP TABLE statement in a similar way. To drop the table created in this example, use the following code:

```
DROP TABLE MyTable
```

The DROP TABLE statement will fail if the table is in use; therefore, it might be necessary to restart the SQL Server.

For more information about the CREATE TABLE statement or the DROP TABLE statement, see Microsoft SQL Server Books Online.

The solution for Oracle databases and other databases is similar to that shown for SQL Server. However, the DDL syntax for each database varies slightly because of differences in database server capabilities and architecture. For example, the CREATE TABLE statement for Oracle is different because Oracle does not support identity columns and uses *sequences* instead (see Recipe 4.4 for more information about Oracle sequences). For more information about Oracle SQL syntax, see *Oracle in a Nutshell* by Rick Greenwald and David C. Kreines (O'Reilly).

10.9   Getting a SQL Server Query Plan

Problem

You need to retrieve information about how query statements are executed by the SQL Server.

Solution

Use the SET SHOWPLAN_TEXT statement.

The sample code executes the SET SHOWPLAN_TEXT statement, using the ExecuteNonQuery( ) method of the Command object, to retrieve how query statements are executed by the SQL Server.

The C# code is shown in Example 10-9.

Example 10-9. File: ShowPlanForm.cs

```
// Namespaces, variables, and constants
using System;
using System.Configuration;
using System.Text;
using System.Data;
using System.Data.SqlClient;

// ...

StringBuilder sb = new StringBuilder( );

// Open a new connection.
SqlConnection conn = new SqlConnection(
    ConfigurationSettings.AppSettings["Sql_ConnectString"]);

// Create and execute the command to retrieve the plan.
SqlCommand cmd = new SqlCommand("SET SHOWPLAN_TEXT ON", conn);
conn.Open( );
cmd.ExecuteNonQuery( );

// Create the command to get the plan for.
cmd.CommandText = "SELECT * FROM Customers WHERE Country='USA' " +
    "ORDER BY CompanyName";

// Retrieve the plan into DataReader.
SqlDataReader dr = cmd.ExecuteReader( );

// Iterate over all result sets and all rows to get plan.
do
{
    while (dr.Read( ))
        sb.Append(dr.GetString(0) + Environment.NewLine);
    sb.Append(Environment.NewLine);
```

Example 10-9. File: ShowPlanForm.cs (continued)

```
} while(dr.NextResult());
dr.Close();

// Create and execute the command to retrieve query results.
cmd = new SqlCommand("SET SHOWPLAN_TEXT OFF", conn);
cmd.ExecuteNonQuery();

conn.Close();

resultTextBox.Text = sb.ToString();
```

Discussion

The SQL SET statement alters current session handling of specific information. Table 10-4 describes the categories of SET statements.

Table 10-4. SET statement categories

Category	Description
Date and Time	Alters current session settings for handling of date and time data
Locking	Alters current session settings for handling SQL Server locking
Miscellaneous	Alters current session settings for miscellaneous SQL Server functionality
Query Execution	Alters current session settings for query execution and processing
SQL-92 Settings	Alters current session settings for using SQL-92 default settings
Statistics	Alters current session settings for displaying statistics
Transactions	Alters current session settings for handling SQL Server Transactions

When SHOWPLAN_TEXT (from the Query Execution category) is ON, SQL Server returns a result set containing detailed information about how the SQL statements are going to be executed rather than actually executing the statements. Two result sets are returned for each statement, both containing a single column StmtText. The first result set contains the SQL statement while the second contains rows detailing the plan. For batch SQL statements, the result sets alternate between statement and plan for each statement in the batch.

SHOWPLAN_TEXT does not need to be explicitly set to OFF. It only affects the command issued subsequent to the statement in which it is SET ON, not all of the commands executed while the connection object is open.

SHOWPLAN_ALL returns more information about the plan than just the StmtText column but is turned on and off in the same way.

For more information about the SET statement, SHOWPLAN_TEXT, or SHOWPLAN_ALL, see the topic "SET" in Microsoft SQL Server Books Online.

10.10 Compacting an Access Database

Problem

You need to compact or repair an Access database.

Solution

Use COM interop to the compact the Access database using JRO, or the `Process.Start( )` method to compact the database using a command line switch.

You'll need a reference to the Microsoft Jet and Replication Objects 2.6 Library from the COM tab in Visual Studio .NET's Add Reference Dialog.

The sample code contains one event handler and a single method:

Compact `Button.Click`
> Allows the user to specify the Access database to compact and the filename for the compacted Access database. It then calls the `CompactAccessDatabase( )` method in the sample to compact the database.

`CompactAccessDatabase( )`
> This method uses ADOX through COM interop to compact the specified Access database to the specified location.

The C# code is shown in Example 10-10.

Example 10-10. File: CompactAccessForm.cs

```
// Namespaces, variables, and constants
using System;
using System.Windows.Forms;

// ...

private void compactButton_Click(object sender, System.EventArgs e)
{

    // Create the open file dialog object to get
    // the Access database to compact.
    OpenFileDialog ofd = new OpenFileDialog();
    ofd.InitialDirectory = System.IO.Path.GetTempPath();
    // Set the filter for Access databases.
    ofd.Filter = "Microsoft Access (*.mdb)|*.mdb";

    // Open the dialog.
    if (ofd.ShowDialog() != DialogResult.OK)
        // Return, if not user is not OK.
        return;

    String sourceFileName = ofd.FileName;
```

Example 10-10. File: CompactAccessForm.cs (continued)

```
        // Create the save file dialog object to get
        // the filename for the compacted database.
        SaveFileDialog sfd = new SaveFileDialog();
        sfd.InitialDirectory = System.IO.Path.GetTempPath();
        // Set the filter for Access databases.
        sfd.Filter = "Microsoft Access (*.mdb)|*.mdb";

        // Open the dialog.
        if (sfd.ShowDialog() == DialogResult.OK)
        {
            // If OK selected, compact the Access database.
            resultTextBox.Text = "Beginning compact." +
                Environment.NewLine;
            resultTextBox.Refresh();

            String destFileName = sfd.FileName;

            // Compact the database.
            try
            {
                CompactAccessDatabase(sourceFileName, destFileName);

                resultTextBox.Text += "Finished compact.";
            }
            catch (System.Exception ex)
            {
                resultTextBox.Text += "ERROR: " + ex.Message;
            }
        }
    }

    private void CompactAccessDatabase(String sourceFileName,
        String destFileName)
    {
        // Define connection string for original and compacted database.
        String sourceConnection =
            @"Provider=Microsoft.Jet.OLEDB.4.0;Data Source=" +
            sourceFileName + ";";
        String destConnection =
            @"Provider=Microsoft.Jet.OLEDB.4.0;Data Source=" +
            destFileName + ";";

        // Create new Jet and Replication Objects (JRO) JetEngine object.
        JRO.JetEngine je = new JRO.JetEngine();

        // Compact the database.
        try
        {
            je.CompactDatabase(sourceConnection, destConnection);
        }
```

Example 10-10. File: CompactAccessForm.cs (continued)

```
    finally
    {
        je = null;
    }
}
```

Discussion

Neither ADO.NET nor ADO provides a way to compact or repair an Access database. To isolate functionality specific to JET from the more generic ADO library, the Jet OLE DB Provider and Replication Objects (JRO) library was created. JRO can be used from .NET through COM interop to compact, repair, or create a replica from an Access database. The CompactDatabase( ) method of the JRO JetEngine object compacts an Access database. It takes two arguments: the connection strings to both the source and destination databases. In both cases, the connection string needs the path and filename of the Access database as well as any additional connection properties for security or encryption information.

An alternative to JRO is available. The .NET framework provides a Process class in the System.Diagnostics namespace to allow access to local and remote processes and to allow you to start and stop local processes. The Start( ) method starts a process and has three overloads. The one that you need to compact an Access database takes two arguments: the filename of the application to run and the command-line arguments to pass when starting the process. So, to compact an Access database located in c:\ named *MyDB.mdb* into the database *MyDBCompact.mdb* in the same directory, the following statement could be used:

```
    System.Diagnostics.Process.Start(
        @"C:\Program Files\Microsoft Office\Office10\msaccess.exe",
        @"C:\MyDB.mdb /compact C:\MyDBCompact.mdb");
```

With either technique, the JET Engine requires exclusive access to the database file to compact it. Otherwise, an exception will be raised.

10.11 Creating DataSet Relationships from SQL Server Relationships

Problem

You need to create relationships between DataTable objects within your DataSet at runtime based on the relationships that are defined in your SQL Server database.

Solution

Use INFORMATION_SCHEMA views and system tables to create relationships automatically at runtime.

The schema of table TBL1011a used in this solution is shown in Table 10-5.

Table 10-5. TBL1011a schema

Column name	Data type	Length	Allow nulls?
a	int	4	No
b	int	4	No
c	int	4	No

The schema of table TBL1011b used in this solution is shown in Table 10-6.

Table 10-6. TBL1011b schema

Column name	Data type	Length	Allow nulls?
d	int	4	No
e	int	4	No
a2	int	4	No
b2	int	4	No

The sample code creates a DataSet containing the Orders table and Order Details table from the Northwind sample database. The tables TBL1011a and TBL1011b—related through a multicolumn key—are also added to the DataSet. Next, the result set of a query of the INFORMATION_SCHEMA views are examined to determine the relationships specified in the data source between the tables in the DataSet. DataRelation objects are created in the DataSet for the identified relationships.

The C# code is shown in Example 10-11.

Example 10-11. File: AutoDataRelationForm.cs

```
// Namespaces, variables, and constants
using System;
using System.Configuration;
using System.Collections;
using System.Text;
using System.Data;
using System.Data.SqlClient;

// ...

DataSet ds = new DataSet( );

SqlDataAdapter da;
```

Example 10-11. File: AutoDataRelationForm.cs (continued)

```
// Add the Orders and Order Details tables to the DataSet.
da = new SqlDataAdapter("SELECT * FROM Orders",
    ConfigurationSettings.AppSettings["Sql_ConnectString"]);
da.Fill(ds, ORDERS_TABLE);
da = new SqlDataAdapter("SELECT * FROM [Order Details]",
    ConfigurationSettings.AppSettings["Sql_ConnectString"]);
da.Fill(ds, ORDERDETAILS_TABLE);

// Add the TBL1011a and TBL1101b tables to the DataSet.
da = new SqlDataAdapter("SELECT * FROM TBL1011a",
    ConfigurationSettings.AppSettings["Sql_ConnectString"]);
da.Fill(ds, PARENTMULTICOLKEYTABLE);
da = new SqlDataAdapter("SELECT * FROM TBL1011b",
    ConfigurationSettings.AppSettings["Sql_ConnectString"]);
da.Fill(ds, CHILDMULTICOLKEYTABLE);

StringBuilder result = new StringBuilder();

String sqlText = "SELECT rc.CONSTRAINT_NAME, rc.UPDATE_RULE, " +
    "rc.DELETE_RULE, " +
    "kcuP.TABLE_NAME ParentTable, kcuC.TABLE_NAME ChildTable, " +
    "kcuP.COLUMN_NAME ParentColumn, kcuC.COLUMN_NAME ChildColumn " +
    "FROM INFORMATION_SCHEMA.REFERENTIAL_CONSTRAINTS rc " +
    "LEFT JOIN INFORMATION_SCHEMA.KEY_COLUMN_USAGE kcuP ON " +
    "rc.UNIQUE_CONSTRAINT_NAME = kcuP.CONSTRAINT_NAME " +
    "LEFT JOIN INFORMATION_SCHEMA.KEY_COLUMN_USAGE kcuC ON " +
    "rc.CONSTRAINT_NAME = kcuC.CONSTRAINT_NAME AND " +
    "kcuP.ORDINAL_POSITION = kcuC.ORDINAL_POSITION " +
    "ORDER BY rc.CONSTRAINT_NAME, kcuP.ORDINAL_POSITION";

// Create the connection and command to retrieve constraint information.
SqlConnection conn = new SqlConnection(
    ConfigurationSettings.AppSettings["Sql_ConnectString"]);
SqlCommand cmd = new SqlCommand(sqlText, conn);

// Fill the DataReader with constraint information.
conn.Open();
SqlDataReader reader = cmd.ExecuteReader();

String prevConstraintName = "";
String constraintName = "";
String parentTableName = "";
String childTableName = "";
bool updateCascade = false;
bool deleteCascade = false;
String relationName = "";

// Arrays to store related columns from constraints in DataReader
ArrayList parentColsAL = new ArrayList();
ArrayList childColsAL = new ArrayList();
DataColumn[] parentCols;
DataColumn[] childCols;
```

Example 10-11. File: AutoDataRelationForm.cs (continued)

```csharp
DataRelation dr;

bool isRecord = false;
// Iterate over the constraint collection for the database.
do
{
    // Read the next record from the DataReader.
    isRecord = reader.Read( );

    // Store the current constraint as the previous constraint name
    // to handle multicolumn-based relations.
    prevConstraintName = constraintName;

    // Get the current constraint name.
    constraintName = isRecord ? reader["CONSTRAINT_NAME"].ToString( ) : "";

    // If the constraint name has changed and both tables exist,
    // create a relation based on the previous constraint column(s).
    if (prevConstraintName != "" &&
        constraintName != prevConstraintName &&
        ds.Tables.Contains(parentTableName) &&
        ds.Tables.Contains(childTableName))
    {
        // Create the parent and child column arrays.
        parentCols = new DataColumn[parentColsAL.Count];
        parentColsAL.CopyTo(parentCols);
        childCols = new DataColumn[childColsAL.Count];
        childColsAL.CopyTo(childCols);

        // Create the relation name based on the constraint name.
        relationName = prevConstraintName.Replace("FK_","RELATION_");

        // Create the relation and add it to the DataSet.
        dr = new DataRelation(relationName, parentCols, childCols,
            true);
        ds.Relations.Add(dr);
        // Set the cascade update and delete rules.
        dr.ChildKeyConstraint.UpdateRule =
            updateCascade ? Rule.Cascade : Rule.None;
        dr.ChildKeyConstraint.DeleteRule =
            deleteCascade ? Rule.Cascade : Rule.None;

        // Clear the parent and child column arrays for the previous
        // constraint.
        parentColsAL.Clear( );
        childColsAL.Clear( );

        result.Append("Added relationship " + relationName +
            " to DataSet." + Environment.NewLine);
    }
```

Example 10-11. File: AutoDataRelationForm.cs (continued)

```
    if (isRecord)
    {
        // Store the current parent and child table names.
        parentTableName = reader["ParentTable"].ToString();
        childTableName = reader["ChildTable"].ToString();
        // Store the cascade update and delete for the current
        // constraint.
        updateCascade = (reader["UPDATE_RULE"].ToString() ==
            "CASCADE");
        deleteCascade = (reader["DELETE_RULE"].ToString() ==
            "CASCADE");

        // Add the parent and child column for the current constraint
        // to the ArrayLists, if both parent and child are in DataSet.
        if (ds.Tables.Contains(parentTableName) &&
            ds.Tables.Contains(childTableName))
        {
            parentColsAL.Add(ds.Tables[parentTableName].Columns[
                reader["ParentColumn"].ToString()]);
            childColsAL.Add(ds.Tables[childTableName].Columns[
                reader["ChildColumn"].ToString()]);
        }
    }
} while(isRecord);

// Close the DataReader and connection.
reader.Close();
conn.Close();

resultTextBox.Text = result.ToString();
```

Discussion

There is no ADO.NET data provider method that automatically returns information about table relationships that are defined in a database. To get the relation information, information views in SQL Server must be queried.

The information required to reconstruct relationships between tables requires a query that pulls together information from two different information views, INFORMATION_SCHEMA.REFERENTIAL_CONSTRAINTS and INFORMATION_SCHEMA.KEY_COLUMN_USAGE, and requires two joins into the latter table to obtain required information for both unique and foreign key constraints. The REFERENTIAL_CONSTRAINTS table contains a row for each foreign key constraint in the database. The KEY_COLUMN_USAGE table contains one row for each row constrained as a key in the database.

The solution starts by loading a DataSet with two sets of tables. These tables are the Orders and Order Details tables from Northwind and a pair of sample tables—TBL0011a and TBL0011b—which demonstrate retrieving relation information for tables related on more than one column.

Next, the query to retrieve the data relationship information is constructed. The SQL statement used is:

```
SELECT
    rc.CONSTRAINT_NAME, rc.UPDATE_RULE, rc.DELETE_RULE,
    kcuP.TABLE_NAME ParentTable, kcuC.TABLE_NAME ChildTable,
    kcuP.COLUMN_NAME ParentColumn, kcuC.COLUMN_NAME ChildColumn
FROM INFORMATION_SCHEMA.REFERENTIAL_CONSTRAINTS rc
LEFT JOIN INFORMATION_SCHEMA.KEY_COLUMN_USAGE kcuP ON
    rc.UNIQUE_CONSTRAINT_NAME = kcuP.CONSTRAINT_NAME
LEFT JOIN INFORMATION_SCHEMA.KEY_COLUMN_USAGE kcuC ON
    rc.CONSTRAINT_NAME = kcuC.CONSTRAINT_NAME AND
    kcuP.ORDINAL_POSITION = kcuC.ORDINAL_POSITION
ORDER BY rc.CONSTRAINT_NAME, kcuP.ORDINAL_POSITION
```

This statement retrieves the constraint information needed to create the relations in the DataSet based on the schema information in the database. Specifically, the columns returned are shown in Table 10-7.

Table 10-7. Relation query columns

Column	Description
CONSTRAINT_NAME	Name of the constraint
UPDATE_RULE	NO ACTION or CASCADE
DELETE_RULE	NO ACTION or CASCADE
ParentTable	Name of the parent table in the relationship
ChildTable	Name of the child table in the relationship
ParentColumn	Name of the column in the parent table
ChildColumn	Name of the column in the child table

For relationships that are based on more than one column, there will be more than one row in the result set that must be combined to create the DataRelation object in the DataSet. Notice that the statement groups the results that are returned by the constraint name, grouping all records related to a single relation. The result set is ordered by the ORDINAL_POSITION field that defines the order of the columns in the relation. When iterating over the query results, if both the parent and child names are contained in the result set, a relationship has been identified and processing continues. For those relationships, the column names for the parent and child tables are loaded into arrays allowing relations based on multiple columns to be created.

Once all of the columns for a relation have been loaded (this is determined by a change in the constraint name and the names of the parent and child tables), the DataRelation is created in the DataSet based on the parent and child column names in the arrays. The update and delete cascade rules are set for the relation. Although not necessary, the sample names the relation based on the name of the constraint without the *FK_* prefix. Once the DataRelation is created, processing of the result set resumes to determine the remaining relations.

10.12 Getting SQL Server Column Metadata Without Returning Data

Problem

You need to retrieve the column metadata from a SQL Server command or stored procedure without returning any data.

Solution

Use the SET FMTONLY ON statement.

The sample code creates and executes a query statement to retrieve only column metadata from the Orders table in the Northwind sample database. A new DataTable is created from this information.

The C# code is shown in Example 10-12.

Example 10-12. File: ColumnSchemaSPForm.cs

```
// Namespaces, variables, and constants
using System;
using System.Configuration;
using System.Data;
using System.Data.SqlClient;

// ...

// Create the SQL statement to retrieve only the column schema.
String cmdText = "SET FMTONLY ON;" +
    "SELECT * FROM Orders;" +
    "SET FMTONLY OFF;";

// Use a DataAdapter to fill the DataTable.
SqlConnection conn = new SqlConnection(
    ConfigurationSettings.AppSettings["Sql_ConnectString"]);
SqlCommand cmd = new SqlCommand(cmdText, conn);
SqlDataAdapter da = new SqlDataAdapter(cmd);
DataTable dt = new DataTable( );
da.Fill(dt);

// Bind the default view of the table to the grid.
dataGrid.DataSource = dt.DefaultView;
```

Discussion

Recipe 10.9 discusses the SQL SET statement.

When SET FMTONLY is ON, no rows are processed or sent to a client when a SQL statement or stored procedure is executed; only metadata is returned to the client. The

DataTable created is identical to one that would have been created if the SQL command used a WHERE clause that returned an empty result set.

For more information about the SET FMTONLY statement, see the topic "SET" in Microsoft SQL Server Books Online.

10.13 Listing Installed OLE DB Providers

Problem

You need a list of the OLE DB providers installed on the machine running your code.

Solution

Use a SQL Server extended stored procedure or search the registry.

In the first case, the sample code executes the extended stored procedure xp_enum_oledb_providers. The result set containing the installed OLE DB providers is displayed.

In the second case, the sample code uses the Microsoft.Win32.Registry class to examine the registry, identify OLE DB provider subkeys, and retrieve and display the OLE DB provider names from these subkeys.

The C# code is shown in Example 10-13.

Example 10-13. File: OleDbProvidersForm.cs

```
// Namespaces, variables, and constants
using System;
using System.Configuration;
using System.Text;
using Microsoft.Win32;
using System.Data;
using System.Data.SqlClient;

// ...

// SQL Server extended stored procedure
StringBuilder result =
    new StringBuilder("Using SQL Server xp_enum_oledb_providers." +
    Environment.NewLine);
int count = 0;

SqlConnection conn = new SqlConnection(
    ConfigurationSettings.AppSettings["Sql_Master_ConnectString"]);

// Create a command to execute the extended stored procedure to
// retrieve OLE DB providers.
SqlCommand cmd = new SqlCommand("xp_enum_oledb_providers", conn);
cmd.CommandType = CommandType.StoredProcedure;
```

Example 10-13. File: OleDbProvidersForm.cs (continued)

```
// Create the DataReader.
conn.Open( );
SqlDataReader rdr = cmd.ExecuteReader( );
// Iterate through the OLE DB providers in the DataReader.
while(rdr.Read( ))
{
    result.Append(++count + ": " + rdr["Provider Description"].ToString( )
        + Environment.NewLine);
}
conn.Close( );

resultTextBox.Text = result.ToString( );

// Registry Scan
StringBuilder result = new StringBuilder("Using Registry scan." +
    Environment.NewLine);
int count = 0;

// Get the HKEY_CLASSES_ROOT/CLSID key.
RegistryKey keyCLSID = Registry.ClassesRoot.OpenSubKey("CLSID", false);
// Iterate through the collection of subkeys.
String[] keys = keyCLSID.GetSubKeyNames( );
for(int i = 0; i < keys.Length; i++)
{
    // Look for the OLE DB Provider subkey and retrieve the value if found.
    RegistryKey key = keyCLSID.OpenSubKey(keys[i], false);
    RegistryKey subKey = key.OpenSubKey("OLE DB Provider", false);
    if(subKey != null)
    {
        result.Append(++count + ": " +
            subKey.GetValue(subKey.GetValueNames( )[0]) +
            Environment.NewLine);
    }
}

resultTextBox.Text = result.ToString( );
```

Discussion

The solution shows two ways to get a list of OLE DB providers installed on a computer.

The first technique uses an extended stored procedure xp_enum_oledb_providers available in SQL Server 7.0, or later. Executing the stored procedure against the master database returns a result set of all OLE DB providers installed on the SQL Server. The result set contains the information described in Table 10-8.

Table 10-8. xp_enum_oledb_providers result set

Column Name	Description
Provider Name	Default value of the class ID (CLSID) key
Parse Name	Class ID (CLSID)
Provider Description	Name of the OLE DB provider

The SQL Server extended stored procedure xp_enum_oledb_providers does not list all installed OLE DB providers. Providers such as MSDataShape are excluded because they do not work as linked servers. Other providers, such as Microsoft Jet 3.51 OLE DB, are excluded because a later version of the provider is installed, for example Microsoft Jet 4.0 OLE DB.

The second technique uses a registry scan and is necessary if SQL Server 7.0, or later, is not installed on the computer, although it can be used with later versions as well.

The .NET Framework classes that manipulate the registry are found in the Microsoft.Win32 namespace. The class IDs that represent OLE DB providers can be identified by the presence of a subkey OLE DB Provider in a class ID. So, to enumerate the OLE DB providers on a computer, iterate over all of the subkeys of the HKEY_CLASSES_ROOT\CLSID key and check for the presence of the OLE DB Provider subkey. The provider name returned by the SQL Server extended stored procedure is the default value for the ProgID subkey while the OLE DB provider name is the default value for the OLE DB Provider subkey.

10.14 Listing Tables in an Access Database

Problem

You need a list of all tables in your Access database.

Solution

Use the GetOLEDBSchemaTable( ) method of the OleDbConnection class or use ADOX through COM interop.

The first technique uses the GetOLEDBSchemaTable( ) method to return schema information about user tables. These results are then displayed.

For the second technique, you'll need a reference to the Primary Interop Assembly (PIA) for ADO provided in the file *ADODB.DLL*; select *adodb* from the .NET tab in Visual Studio .NET's Add Reference Dialog. You'll also need a reference to Microsoft ADO Ext. 2.7 for DDL and Security from the COM tab in Visual Studio .NET's Add Reference Dialog.

The second technique creates an ADOX Catalog object through COM interop. The Tables property of this object accesses the collection of tables from which the name and other information are displayed.

The C# code is shown in Example 10-14.

Example 10-14. File: ListAccessTablesForm.cs

```
// Namespaces, variables, and constants
using System;
using System.Configuration;
using System.Text;
using System.Data;
using System.Data.OleDb;

// ...

// OLE DB
StringBuilder result = new StringBuilder( );

// Open the OLE DB connection.
OleDbConnection conn = new OleDbConnection(
    ConfigurationSettings.AppSettings["MsAccess_ConnectString"]);
conn.Open( );

// Retrieve schema information for all tables.
DataTable schemaTable = conn.GetOleDbSchemaTable(OleDbSchemaGuid.Tables,
    new object[] {null, null, null, "TABLE"});

result.Append("TABLE" + Environment.NewLine);
// Iterate over the collection of table records.
foreach(DataRow row in schemaTable.Rows)
{
    result.Append(row["TABLE_NAME"] + Environment.NewLine);
}

conn.Close( );

resultTextBox.Text = result.ToString( );

// ADOX
StringBuilder result = new StringBuilder( );

// Open the connection.
ADODB.Connection conn = new ADODB.ConnectionClass( );
conn.Open(ConfigurationSettings.AppSettings["MsAccess_ConnectString"],
    "", "", 0);

// Create an ADOX catalog object for the connecton.
ADOX.Catalog cat = new ADOX.Catalog( );
cat.ActiveConnection = conn;
```

Example 10-14. File: ListAccessTablesForm.cs (continued)

```
result.Append("TABLE\tKEY" + Environment.NewLine);
// Iterate over the collection of tables.
foreach(ADOX.Table table in cat.Tables)
{
    if(table.Type == "TABLE")
    {
        result.Append(table.Name + Environment.NewLine);
        // Iterate over the collection of keys for the table.
        foreach(ADOX.Key key in table.Keys)
        {
            result.Append("\t" + key.Name + " (");
            // Iterate over the collection of columns for the key.
            foreach(ADOX.Column col in key.Columns)
            {
                result.Append(col.Name + ", ");
            }
            result.Remove(result.Length - 2, 2).Append(")" +
                Environment.NewLine);
        }
        result.Append(Environment.NewLine);
    }
}

cat = null;
conn.Close();

resultTextBox.Text = result.ToString();
```

Discussion

The solution shows two techniques that you can use to get a list of tables in an Access database.

The first technique uses the GetOleDbSchemaTable( ) method of the OLE DB connection object. This technique is discussed in Recipe 10.2.

The second technique uses ActiveX Database Objects Extensions (ADOX) from COM interop. ADOX has a Tables property that exposes a collection of Table objects in the database. The user tables are determined by iterating over the collection of tables and selecting only those where Type property of the Table is TABLE.

The Table object also exposes collections of Columns, Indexes, Keys, and Properties that can be used to further investigate the database. As an example, the sample code iterates over the collection of Keys in each table to get the list of both primary and foreign keys.

10.15 Creating a Table in the Database from a DataTable Schema

Problem

You need to create a table in a database from an existing DataTable schema.

Solution

Use the CreateTableFromSchema( ) method shown in this solution.

The sample code contains one event handler and two methods:

Button.Click

Creates a DataTable containing the schema from the Orders table in the Northwind sample database. The method CreateTableFromSchema( ) in the sample code is called to create a table in the database from this schema.

CreateTableFromSchema( )

This method creates a schema in the database for the schema of the DataTable argument. The method builds a DDL statement from the schema information and executes it against the data source specified by the connection string argument to create the table.

NetType2SqlType( )

This method is called by the CreateTableFromSchemaMethod( ) to map .NET data types to SQL Server types when building the DDL statement.

The C# code is shown in Example 10-15.

Example 10-15. File: CreateDatabaseTableFromDataTableSchemaForm.cs

```
// Namespaces, variables, and constants
using System;
using System.Configuration;
using System.Windows.Forms;
using System.Text;
using System.Data;
using System.Data.SqlClient;

// ...

private void goButton_Click(object sender, System.EventArgs e)
{
    // Fill a table with the Orders table schema.
    String sqlText = "SELECT * FROM [Orders]";
    SqlDataAdapter da = new SqlDataAdapter(sqlText,
        ConfigurationSettings.AppSettings["Sql_ConnectString"]);
    DataTable dt = new DataTable("Orders");
    da.FillSchema(dt, SchemaType.Source);
```

```
    CreateTableFromSchema(dt,
        ConfigurationSettings.AppSettings["Sql_ConnectString"]);

    MessageBox.Show("Table " + TABLENAME + " created.",
        "Create DataTable from schema.",
        MessageBoxButtons.OK, MessageBoxIcon.Information);
}

private void CreateTableFromSchema(DataTable dt, String connectionString)
{
    // Drop the new table if it is already there.
    StringBuilder sqlCmd = new StringBuilder(
        "if exists (SELECT * FROM dbo.sysobjects WHERE id  = " +
        "object_id('[" + TABLENAME + "]') " +
        "AND OBJECTPROPERTY(id, 'IsUserTable')  =  1)" +
        Environment.NewLine +
        "DROP TABLE " + TABLENAME + ";" + Environment.NewLine +
        Environment.NewLine);

    // Start building a command string to create the table.
    sqlCmd.Append("CREATE TABLE [" + TABLENAME + "] (" +
        Environment.NewLine);
    // Iterate over the column collection in the source table.
    foreach(DataColumn col in dt.Columns)
    {
        // Add the column.
        sqlCmd.Append("[" + col.ColumnName + "] ");
        // Map the source column type to a SQL Server type.
        sqlCmd.Append(NetType2SqlType(col.DataType.ToString(),
            col.MaxLength) + " ");
        // Add identity information.
        if(col.AutoIncrement)
            sqlCmd.Append("IDENTITY ");
        // Add AllowNull information.
        sqlCmd.Append((col.AllowDBNull ? "" : "NOT ") + "NULL," +
            Environment.NewLine);
    }
    sqlCmd.Remove(sqlCmd.Length - (Environment.NewLine.Length + 1), 1);
    sqlCmd.Append(") ON [PRIMARY];" + Environment.NewLine +
        Environment.NewLine);

    // Add the primary key to the table, if it exists.
    if(dt.PrimaryKey != null)
    {
        sqlCmd.Append("ALTER TABLE " + TABLENAME +
            " WITH NOCHECK ADD " + Environment.NewLine);
        sqlCmd.Append("CONSTRAINT [PK_" + TABLENAME +
            "] PRIMARY KEY CLUSTERED (" + Environment.NewLine);
        // Add the columns to the primary key.
        foreach(DataColumn col in dt.PrimaryKey)
        {
            sqlCmd.Append("[" + col.ColumnName + "]," +
                Environment.NewLine);
```

```csharp
        }
        sqlCmd.Remove(sqlCmd.Length -
            (Environment.NewLine.Length + 1), 1);
        sqlCmd.Append(") ON [PRIMARY];" + Environment.NewLine +
            Environment.NewLine);
    }

    sqlTextBox.Text = sqlCmd.ToString( );

    // Create and execute the command to create the new table.
    SqlConnection conn = new SqlConnection(connectionString);
    SqlCommand cmd = new SqlCommand(sqlCmd.ToString( ), conn);
    conn.Open( );
    cmd.ExecuteNonQuery( );
    conn.Close( );
}

private String NetType2SqlType(String netType, int maxLength)
{
    String sqlType = "";

    // Map the .NET type to the data source type.
    // This is not perfect because mappings are not always one-to-one.
    switch(netType)
    {
        case "System.Boolean":
            sqlType = "[bit]";
            break;
        case "System.Byte":
            sqlType = "[tinyint]";
            break;
        case "System.Int16":
            sqlType = "[smallint]";
            break;
        case "System.Int32":
            sqlType = "[int]";
            break;
        case "System.Int64":
            sqlType = "[bigint]";
            break;
        case "System.Byte[]":
            sqlType = "[binary]";
            break;
        case "System.Char[]":
            sqlType = "[nchar] (" + maxLength + ")";
            break;
        case "System.String":
            if(maxLength == 0x3FFFFFFF)
                sqlType = "[ntext]";
            else
                sqlType =  "[nvarchar] (" + maxLength + ")";
            break;
```

```
        case "System.Single":
            sqlType = "[real]";
            break;
        case "System.Double":
            sqlType = "[float]";
            break;
        case "System.Decimal":
            sqlType = "[decimal]";
            break;
        case "System.DateTime":
            sqlType = "[datetime]";
            break;
        case "System.Guid":
            sqlType = "[uniqueidentifier]";
            break;
        case "System.Object":
            sqlType = "[sql_variant]";
            break;
    }

    return sqlType;
}
```

Discussion

The solution dynamically constructs a Data Definition Language (DDL) statement to create a table in a SQL Server database from the schema of a DataTable. The complete statement that is generated is shown in Example 10-16.

Example 10-16. DDL generated to create database table from DataTable schema

```
if exists
  (SELECT * FROM dbo.sysobjects WHERE id = object_id('[TBL1015]') AND
  OBJECTPROPERTY(id, 'IsUserTable') = 1)
    DROP TABLE TBL1015;

CREATE TABLE [TBL1015] (
  [OrderID] [int] IDENTITY NOT NULL,
  [CustomerID] [nvarchar] (5) NULL,
  [EmployeeID] [int] NULL,
  [OrderDate] [datetime] NULL,
  [RequiredDate] [datetime] NULL,
  [ShippedDate] [datetime] NULL,
  [ShipVia] [int] NULL,
  [Freight] [decimal] NULL,
  [ShipName] [nvarchar] (40) NULL,
  [ShipAddress] [nvarchar] (60) NULL,
  [ShipCity] [nvarchar] (15) NULL,
  [ShipRegion] [nvarchar] (15) NULL,
  [ShipPostalCode] [nvarchar] (10) NULL,
  [ShipCountry] [nvarchar] (15) NULL
```

```
) ON [PRIMARY];

ALTER TABLE TBL1015 WITH NOCHECK ADD
  CONSTRAINT [PK_TBL1015] PRIMARY KEY CLUSTERED (
    [OrderID]
  ) ON [PRIMARY];
```

The first command—the DROP statement—is not strictly required and is included here so that the example does not crash if it has been run previously. It might be more appropriate in your situation to check if the table already exists in the database and if it does, abort execution since your table might contain important data. If that is the case, return the results of the EXISTS query to the calling application and use that to control whether the new table is created.

The second DDL command uses the CREATE TABLE statement to create the table in the database. The code iterates over the collection of the columns in the DataTable schema to retrieve the name and the maximum length of the column and whether the column is an identity column or allows null values. A method is called to map the .NET data types of the DataTable to SQL Server data types. This method does not work perfectly because there is not a one-to-one mapping between .NET data types and SQL Server data types. Make the mapping decisions based on the requirements of your application. The mapping method also adds the field length for the DDL column description for string-type columns. For more information about mapping SQL Server data types to .NET Framework data types, see Recipe 2.8.

The third DDL command creates the primary key constraint on the newly constructed table. While single-column primary keys can easily be added to the CREATE TABLE command, the easiest way to handle compound keys is by using an ALTER TABLE statement with an ADD CONSTRAINT statement and PRIMARY KEY argument. Iterate over the collection of columns exposed by the PrimaryKey property of the table to add the columns to the command.

If you have a number of tables in a DataSet that you want to create in a database, you can iterate through the collection of DataRelation objects for the DataSet and use the ALTER TABLE statement with the ADD CONSTRAINT command and a FOREIGN KEY argument to add the table relations to the database.

For more information about DDL syntax, see Microsoft SQL Server Books Online.

10.16 Listing Installed ODBC Drivers

Problem

You need a list of the ODBC drivers installed on the computer running your code.

Solution

Consult the registry.

The sample code uses the `Microsoft.Win32.Registry` class to display a list of all installed ODBC drivers.

The C# code is shown in Example 10-17.

Example 10-17. File: OdbcDriversForm.cs

```csharp
// Namespaces, variables, and constants
using System;
using System.Text;
using Microsoft.Win32;

// ...

StringBuilder result = new StringBuilder( );

// Get the HKEY_LOCAL_MACHINE\SOFTWARE\ODBC\ODBCINST.INI\ODBC Drivers key.
RegistryKey keyLocalMachine =
    Registry.LocalMachine.OpenSubKey(@"SOFTWARE\ODBC\ODBCINST.INI\ODBC Drivers", false);
string[] valueNames = keyLocalMachine.GetValueNames( );
for(int i = 0; i < valueNames.Length; i++)
    result.Append(valueNames[i] + Environment.NewLine);

resultTextBox.Text = result.ToString( );
```

Discussion

The .NET Framework classes that manipulate the registry are found in the `Microsoft.Win32` namespace. The registry key `HKEY_LOCAL_MACHINE\SOFTWARE\ODBC\ODBCINST.INI\ODBC Drivers` contains a value name for each installed ODBC driver.

Converting from C# to VB Syntax

Although all of the examples in this book are shown using C# syntax, it is easy to mentally convert to Visual Basic syntax. This appendix will provide the information you need to convert the documentation for each type into the syntax used by Visual Basic.

 This appendix doesn't try to completely cover the syntax for each language element it discusses. Instead, it focuses on direct translation of the syntax of the types used in ADO.NET programming from C# to VB.

General Considerations

The most evident difference between C# and Visual Basic (VB) syntax is that C# uses the semicolon (;) as a statement terminator, whereas VB uses a line break. As a result, a statement in C# can occupy multiple lines as long as it is terminated with a semicolon. A VB statement must occupy only a single line. Multiline statements in VB must appear with the VB line continuation character (a space followed by an underscore) on all but the last line.

A second, and not quite so evident, difference is that C# is case sensitive, whereas VB isn't. (Uniform case use for VB code is enforced by the Visual Studio environment, but it is by no means required.)

Finally, all types and their members have access modifiers that determine the type or member's accessibility. The keywords for these access modifiers are nearly identical in VB and C#, as Table A-1 shows.

Table A-1. Access modifiers in C# and VB

C# keyword	VB keyword
public	Public
private	Private

C# keyword	VB keyword
protected	Protected
internal	Friend
protected internal	Protected Friend

Classes

C# uses the class statement along with opening and closing braces, {}, to indicate the beginning and end of a class definition. For example:

```
public class DataException : SystemException {
    // Member definitions
}
```

In VB, a class definition is indicated by the Class... End Class construct:

```
Public Class DataException
    Inherits SystemException
    ' member definitions
End Class
```

In addition, C# classes can be marked as abstract or sealed; these correspond to the VB MustInherit and NonInheritable keywords, as shown in Table A-2.

Table A-2. C# and equivalent VB class modifiers

C# keyword	VB keyword
abstract	MustInherit
sealed	NonInheritable

C# uses the colon to indicate either inheritance or interface implementation. Both the base class and the implemented interfaces are part of the class statement. For example:

```
public class DataSet : MarshalByValueComponent, IListSource,
    ISupportInitialize, ISerializable
```

In VB, the base class and any implemented interfaces are specified on separate lines immediately following the Class statement. A class's base class is indicated by preceding its name with the Inherits keyword; any implemented interfaces are indicated by the Implements keyword. Hence, the previous definition of the DataSet class in C# would appear as follows in VB:

```
Public Class DataSet
    Inherits MarshalByValueComponent
    Implements IListSource, ISupportInitalize, ISerializable
```

Structures

C# uses the struct statement along with opening and closing braces to indicate the beginning and end of a structure definition. For example, System.Windows.Forms.DataGridCell is defined in C# as follows:

```
public struct DataGridCell {
    // Member definitions
}
```

In VB, a structure definition is indicated by the Structure... End Structure construct:

```
Public Structure DataGridCell
    ' member definitions
End Structure
```

C# uses the colon with structures to indicate interface implementation. Any implemented interfaces are part of the class statement. In VB, any implemented interfaces are specified by an Implements statement on the line immediately following the Structure statement.

Interfaces

C# uses the interface statement along with opening and closing braces to indicate the beginning and end of an interface definition. For example:

```
public interface IDataAdapter {
    // Member definitions
}
```

In VB, an interface definition is indicated by the Interface... End Interface construct:

```
Public Interface IDataAdapter
    ' member definitions
End Interface
```

C# uses the colon with interfaces to specify any implemented interfaces. For example:

```
public interface IDataReader : IDisposable, IDataRecord
```

In VB, any implemented interfaces are specified by an Implements statement on the line immediately following the Interface statement. The previous definition of IDataReader in C# would appear as follows in VB:

```
Public Interface IDataReader
    Implements IDisposable, IDataRecord
```

Class, Structure, and Interface Members

Classes, structures, and interfaces can contain one or more fields, methods, properties, and events. This section discusses converting the C# syntax for each of these constructs to Visual Basic.

Note that .NET supports both static (or shared) members (which apply to the type as a whole, and typically don't require that an object of that type be instantiated) and instance members (which apply only to an instance of that type). Shared or static members are indicated by using the `static` keyword in C#. For example:

```
public static string ToString(long value);
```

The corresponding VB keyword is `Shared`, so the `ToString` method, when converted to VB, has the following syntax:

```
Public Shared Function ToString(value As Long) As String
```

Fields

A field is simply a constant or a variable that is exposed as a publicly accessible member of a type. In C#, for example, the `Value` field of the `System.DBNull` class has the syntax:

```
public static readonly DBNull Value;
```

Note that C# indicates the data type of a field before the name of the field. (For C# data types and their VB equivalents, see Table A-3.) Also note that fields are frequently read-only. Constant fields, in fact, are always read-only. As a result, the use of the C# `readonly` keyword and the VB `ReadOnly` keyword with fields is quite common.

The syntax for the `Value` field in Visual Basic then becomes:

```
Public Shared ReadOnly Value As DBNull
```

Methods

In C#, all methods have a return value, which appears before the name of the function; in contrast, VB differentiates between function and subprocedures. C# functions without an explicit return value return void. For example, one of the overloads of the `DataSet` class's `AcceptChanges` method has the following syntax in C#:

```
public void AcceptChanges();
```

C# methods that return void are expressed as subprocedures in VB. Here's the corresponding syntax of the `AcceptChanges` method:

```
Public Sub AcceptChanges()
```

All C# methods other than those returning void are functions in VB. The function's return value appears in an `As` clause at the end of the function declaration. C# data types and their VB equivalents are shown in Table A-3. Methods that return arrays are indicated by adding brackets ([ ]), to the return data type in C# and parentheses, ( ), to the return data type in VB.

Table A-3. C# data types and their VB equivalents

C# data type	VB data type
bool	Boolean
byte	Byte
char	Char
decimal	Decimal
double	Double
float	Single
int	Integer
long	Long
object	Object
sbyte	System.SByte
short	Short
string	String
System.Currency	Currency
System.DateTime	Date
uint	System.UInt32
ulong	System.UInt64
ushort	System.UInt16
<class_name>	<class_name>
<delegate_name>	<delegate_name>
<interface_name>	<interface_name>
<structure_name>	<structure_name>

For example, a method that returns an array would look like this in C#:

```
public int[] ReturnsArray();
```

The VB equivalent is:

```
Public Function ReturnsArray() as Integer()
```

Method parameters in C# take the general form:

```
<data_type> <parameter_name>
```

In VB, method parameters take the form:

```
<parameter_name> As <data_type>
```

where the <data_type> will be any of the data types listed in Table A-3. If a parameter is an array, its data type is followed by brackets in C#, such as string[] Name, while in VB the parameter name is followed by parentheses in VB, such as Name() As String.

For example, one of the versions of the DataTable class's Select method has the following syntax in C#:

```
public DataRow[] Select(string filterExpression, string sort,
    DataViewRowState recordStates);
```

The VB equivalent is:

```
Overloads Public Function Select(ByVal filterExpression As String, _
    ByVal sort As String, ByVal recordStates As DataViewRowState _
    ) As DataRow( )
```

 VB allows methods to be called using either named and positional parameters. If named parameters are used, the parameter name must correspond to that shown in the documentation. For instance, DataTable.Select can be called as follows using named parameters:

```
dr = DataTable.Select(filterexpression:=flt, _
    sort:=sd, _
    recordstates:=DataViewRowState.CurrentRows)
```

C# also uses a number of object-oriented qualifiers with methods. These, and their VB equivalents, are shown in Table A-4.

Table A-4. C# keywords used with methods and their VB equivalents

C# keyword	VB keyword
abstract	MustOverride
override	Overrides
sealed	NotOverridable
virtual	Overridable

In both C# and VB, constructors have a special syntax. In C#, constructors have the same name as the classes whose objects they instantiate and they don't indicate a return value. For example, the default constructor for the SqlCommand class is:

```
public SqlCommand( );
```

In VB, the constructor is represented by a call to a class's New subprocedure. The equivalent call to the SqlCommand class constructor in VB is:

```
Public Sub New( )
```

Properties

The SqlCommand.CommandText property provides a typical example of a property definition using C# syntax:

```
public string CommandText {get; set;}
```

Like all C# type definitions, the property's data type precedes the property name. The get; and set; property accessors indicate that this is a read-write property.

Read-only properties are indicated with only a get; while write-only properties are indicated with only a set.

The equivalent VB property definition is:

```
Public Property CommandText As String
```

Note that read-write properties aren't decorated with additional keywords in VB. Read-only properties, on the other hand, are indicated with the ReadOnly keyword in front of the Property keyword, while write-only properties have the WriteOnly keyword before the Property keyword.

Note that properties, like methods, can use the object-oriented modifiers listed in Table A-4.

Events

Events are declared in C# using the event keyword, which is followed by the delegate type returned by the event and the name of the event. For example, the RowUpdated event of the SqlDataAdapter class has the following syntax:

```
public event SqlRowUpdatedEventHandler RowUpdated;
```

The equivalent VB syntax is:

```
Public Event RowUpdated As SqlRowUpdatedEventHandler
```

In addition, the C# event keyword and the VB Event keyword can be preceded by the object modifiers listed in Table A-4.

Delegates

The syntax for a delegate in C# closely follows the syntax for a method. The delegate statement is followed by the delegate's return type (or void, if there is none) and the delegate name. This in turn is followed by the delegate's parameter list, in which each parameter takes the form:

```
<parameter_type> <parameter_name>
```

For example:

```
public delegate void StateChangeEventHandler(object sender,
    StateChangeEventArgs e);
```

In a VB Delegate statement, the Delegate keyword is followed by the Sub keyword (if the delegate returns a void in C#) or the Function keyword (if the delegate returns some other value). For example, in VB, the StateChangeEventHandler delegate has the following syntax:

```
Public Delegate Sub StateChangeEventHandler( _
    ByVal sender As Object, ByVal e As StateChangeEventArgs)
```

Enumerations

C# uses the enum statement along with opening and closing braces, {}, to indicate the beginning and end of an enumeration definition. For example:

```
public enum CommandType {
    // Enumeration members
}
```

In VB, an enumeration is defined by the Enum... End Enum construct. For example, the VB version of the CommandType enum declaration is:

```
Public Enum CommandType
    ' enumeration members
End Enum
```

In both C# and VB, the member listing consists of the name of the enumerated member and its value. These are identical in C# and VB, except that C# adds a comma to separate one member of the enumeration from another, whereas VB requires that they be on separate lines. For example, the full declaration of the CommandType enumeration in C# is:

```
public enum CommandType {
    Text = 1,
    StoredProcedure = 4,
    TableDirect = 512
}
```

The VB equivalent is:

```
Public Enum CommandType
    Text = 1
    StoredProcedure = 4
    TableDirect = 512
End Enum
```

Index

A

AcceptChanges( ) method, 72
Access
    AutoNumber values, 168–171
    compacting, 565–567
    connecting, 9–10
        ASP.NET, 13–14
        user-level security, 11–12
    creating, 557–559
    images, 420–424
    servers, configuring, 14
    tables, listing, 576–578
    workgroup files, connecting, 11–12
access
    deleted rows, 70–73
    ODBC, 4
    output parameters, 82–84
    stored procedures, returning values, 89–92
    text files, 47–50
    (see also connections)
access modifiers, 585
adding
    columns, 102–104
    expression columns, 126–129
    images, 420
    parameters to SQL statements, 115–117
    parent/child rows, 175–177
    records, 177–180
    tables, 561–562
ad-hoc connector names, SQL statements, 139
ADO Extensions for DDL and Security
        (ADOX), 545
ADO Recordset schema, converting, 261
ADO.NET
    overview of, 1–3
    (see also databases)
ADOX (ADO Extensions for DDL and
        Security), 545
algorithms, encryption, 254

annotations, 107
    null value, 107, 109
AppleTalk ADSP network library, 15
application configuration files, 31
applications
    connection pooling, 37–40
    hardcoding, 31
    .NET, connecting ODBC data sources, 4–5
    servers, 30
applying
    XPath, 462–465
    XSLT, 465–468
arrays, exporting queries from, 275–279
ASP.NET
    Access, connecting, 13–14
    authentication, 13
    Cache class, 496–499
    images, 390–392
    multiple columns, 365–367
assigning names, 104–108
associating transactions, 295
asymmetric key algorithms, 254
asynchronous queries, canceling, 492–496
attributes
    AutoComplete, 284
    Extended Properties, 7
    Network Address, 14
    Network Library, 14
    Persist Security Info connection string, 29
authentication
    ASP.NET, 13
    SQL Server, 19
    (see also security)
AutoComplete attribute, 284
AutoIncrement columns,
        troubleshooting, 160–162
auto-incrementing keys, adding parent/child
        rows, 175–177
AutoIncrementSeed property, 175

We'd like to hear your suggestions for improving our indexes. Send email to *index@oreilly.com*.

About the Author

Bill Hamilton is a software architect who specializes in designing, developing, and implementing distributed applications using .NET and J2EE technologies. Over the last 10 years, he has provided consulting services in B2B, B2C, B2E, data integration, and portal initiatives for banking, retail, accounting, manufacturing, and financial services. An early technology adopter, he frequently evaluates, recommends, and helps his clients use new technologies effectively. Bill has designed and helped build several award-winning software packages.

Colophon

Our look is the result of reader comments, our own experimentation, and feedback from distribution channels. Distinctive covers complement our distinctive approach to technical topics, breathing personality and life into potentially dry subjects.

The animal on the cover of *ADO.NET Cookbook* is a white spoonbill (*Platelea leucorodia*), also called the common or Eurasian white spoonbill, named for its large, spatulate bill. Spoonbills feed by wading through the shallow waters of their marshy habitats, moving their partly opened bills from side to side to filter out mud and water. When the sensitive nerve endings inside their bills detect an edible morsel, they snap them shut. A spoonbill's typical diet includes insects, larvae, small crustaceans, and tiny fish.

Mature white spoonbills are about 85 centimeters long from the tips of their tails to the tips of their bills, and their wingspans average 125 centimeters. As the name suggests, white spoonbill feathers are a creamy white. During breeding season, however, adults develop yellow patches on their breasts, faces, and bills.

White spoonbills are found in northeast Africa and much of Europe and Asia. They nest in trees and reed beds, typically in large colonies and sometimes with other bird species in the Threskiornithidae family, such as herons and storks. Males gather nesting materials, and females weave these sticks and reeds into shallow, bowl-shaped nests. Females generally lay a clutch of 3 to 4 eggs per year and share incubation duties with their mates.

Although the white spoonbill is an endangered species, conservation efforts have led to a slow increase in population in some areas, particularly in northwestern Europe. Loss of breeding sites due to land clearance and pesticide use are the main threats to the white spoonbill's survival.

Matt Hutchinson was the production editor for *ADO.NET Cookbook*. Argosy Publishing, Inc. provided production services. Mary Brady, Sarah Sherman, and Claire Cloutier provided quality control.

Emma Colby designed the cover of this book, based on a series design by Edie Freedman. The cover image is from *Bewick's British Birds*. Emma Colby produced the cover layout with QuarkXPress 4.1 using Adobe's ITC Garamond font.

David Futato designed the interior layout. This book was converted by Julie Hawks to FrameMaker 5.5.6 with a format conversion tool created by Erik Ray, Jason McIntosh, Neil Walls, and Mike Sierra that uses Perl and XML technologies. The text font is Linotype Birka; the heading font is Adobe Myriad Condensed; and the code font is LucasFont's TheSans Mono Condensed. The tip and warning icons were drawn by Christopher Bing. This colophon was written by Genevieve d'Entremont.